CAPOTE: A BIOGRAPHY

"To read *Capote* is to have the sense that someone has put together all the important pieces of this consumate artist's life, has given everything its due emphasis, and comprehended its ultimate meaning. In short, Mr. Clarke makes one feel at last as if one really understands Mr. Capote—and he helps one to recognize anew that, for all Mr. Capote's frivolousness, absurdity and latter-day degeneration, he was a man and an artist well worth understanding."

Bruce Bawer
The Wall Street Journal

"This is literary biography the way it should be written, as rich and densely textured as a novel. It has an elaborate plot (sex,suicide, betrayal); picturesque locales (Venice, Rome, Paris); and memorable characters (Humphrey Bogart, Cecil Beaton, the aristocracy of talent). . . .*Capote* is engrossing, vivid, beautifully written, a large-scale portrait of the rich and famous. . . ."

James Atlas
Vogue

"Thoroughly researched, intelligent, and stylishly written. It is also—how could it be otherwise?—a slap-and-tickle biography of the first order, naming names, stirring up old feuds and scandals, chronicling every empty pill or vodka bottle from those last, tired years. What *Edie* did for the Warhol gang, *Capote* does for Truman's. . . ."

Gail Caldwell
The Boston Globe

"Extensively researched, perceptively written biography. . . . Clarke carries it off with considerable finesse."

John Blades
Chicago Tribune

CAPOTE

A Biography

Gerald Clarke

Ballantine Books • New York

Library of Congress Card Number: 88-92221

ISBN: 0-345-36078-8

This edition published by arrangement with Simon & Schuster Inc.

Cover design by Richard Aquan

Cover photo by Nancy Crampton

Photo editor: Vincent Virga

Manufactured in the United States of America

First Ballantine Books Edition: May 1989

10 9 8 7 6 5 4 3 2 1

GRATEFUL ACKNOWLEDGEMENT IS MADE TO RANDOM HOUSE, INC.,
FOR PERMISSION TO QUOTE FROM THE COPYRIGHTED WORKS OF
TRUMAN CAPOTE, AND FROM THE LETTERS OF ROBERT LINSCOTT AND
BENNETT CERF TO TRUMAN CAPOTE.

"ISCHIA," COPYRIGHT 1950 BY W.H. AUDEN; FROM *W.H. AUDEN: COLLECTED
POEMS*, EDITED BY EDWARD MENDELSON; QUOTED BY PERMISSION
OF RANDOM HOUSE, INC.

To L.A.S.

FOR FAITH AND FORTITUDE

De la Bibliothèque
Duhau de Bérenx

"There's the one and only T.C. There was nobody like me before, and there ain't gonna be anybody like me after I'm gone."—T R U M A N CAPOTE, IN CONVERSATION, JUNE, 1984.

"And I only wrote half of what I saw . . ."—A Q U O T A T I O N F R O M MARCO POLO, TORN FROM A MAGAZINE AND FOUND IN THE PAPERS OF TRUMAN CAPOTE.

ONE

1

IN those days people moved more slowly down there, and Arch, who did just the opposite, might almost have been taken for a Yankee. Strutting down the street on that April afternoon, pausing only long enough to raise his hat to ladies he knew, he seemed to walk faster, talk faster and think faster than anybody else in Troy, or anybody else in all of Alabama for that matter. But then Arch was a young man on his way, and the day he met Lillie Mae, like most other days, he was working on a deal that would set him on the road to riches.

They passed each other on East Three Notch Street, right in front of the Folmar Building, and Arch, who thought he knew every attractive girl in town, was stopped by the prettiest young woman he had ever seen: small, just an inch or two above five feet, with dark blond hair and eyes the color of fine bourbon whiskey. "She like to have knocked me dead," he later remembered, and without hesitating a second, he turned around and followed her. When she walked into McLeod's Pharmacy, he waited nervously outside, wanting to strike up a conversation but not sure, probably for the first time in his life, what to say or how to say it. He was still deliberating when she came out and solved the problem for him.

"Hello there, Arch Persons," she said. "How's Bill McCorvey getting along?" Now, Bill McCorvey was an old friend of Arch's from Monroeville, a little farm town to the west, and Lillie Mae, who came from there, was using his name to tell Arch that she knew who he was even if he did not know who she was.

"Honey, I know you," he lied. "But I've forgotten your name."

"I'm Lillie Mae Faulk," she answered.

After that Arch had no trouble finding things to say. He walked her back to her dormitory—she was in her first year at the teachers college on Normal Avenue—and returned after dinner to talk some more in the parlor. What they discussed has long been forgotten, but Arch, who, with his bottle-thick glasses and thinning blond hair, was not really a handsome man, must have wound his charms around her, as he did around nearly everyone else, because when he left for Colorado on one of his money-making expeditions the next day, she promised she would write.

She was as good as her word. They corresponded nearly every day, and when he came back to Alabama at the end of the summer, that road to riches still waiting to be discovered, he headed straight for Monroeville and Lillie Mae. They resumed their courtship where their letters had left off, and after a stop at the courthouse to get a license from Judge Fountain, they were married a short time later, on August 23, 1923. Arch was less than two weeks away from his twenty-sixth birthday; Lillie Mae was seventeen.

Her widowed mother had died four years before, leaving a comfortable estate for her five children, and since then all but one of them had been living with their Faulk cousins, three old maids and a bachelor brother. It was in their home on Alabama Avenue that the wedding took place. Giant ferns lined the front hallway, Mrs. Lee from next door played the piano, and a Baptist minister read the vows. The day was typical of that tropical month, so hot and steamy that men tugged at their collars, women wilted inside their heavy corsets, and everyone crowded into the dining room after the ceremony to cool off with lemonade before tasting the wedding cake. When the time came for the happy couple to leave, Mr. Wiggins, the local odd-job man, drove them forty miles to Atmore, which was the nearest stop of the Louisville and Nashville Railroad. There, in high spirits and high hopes, they boarded a train for their honeymoon on the Gulf Coast.

For Lillie Mae, however, disappointment was as near as the end of the ride. Short of funds, as was usually the case, Arch passed up the grand, white-shingled hotels that dotted the Gulf and took her instead to a rooming house near Gulfport, Mississippi, whose owner, an old business acquaintance, offered him a discount. They spent a week or so there and then moved on to New Orleans, where they had a few more days before there was an even greater disappointment: Arch ran out of money and their honeymoon skidded to a halt.

While he stayed behind to try to raise some cash, he put Lillie Mae back aboard a train and sent her home to Monroeville, calling ahead to her guardian, her cousin Jennie Faulk, to pick her up in Atmore. He did not let on to Jennie, who was famous for her fierce temper, that he was broke. His story was that he was working on a big deal that required him to travel and he did not want to leave an unsophisticated girl like Lillie Mae alone in a strange city. If Jennie, who was as shrewd as she was suspicious, did not guess the truth then, she soon learned it from Lillie Mae, and when Arch came to reclaim his bride, four or five weeks later, Jennie informed him that he was no longer welcome in her house. "Get out and don't ever darken my door again!" she screamed. "Don't even put your foot in my yard!" Only after he had spent the night in the Purafore Hotel did she relent and allow him to join his wife in her old back bedroom.

Mortified by the abrupt conclusion of her honeymoon, Lillie Mae was even more chagrined when Arch eventually did show up. One of the reasons she had married him was to get away from her quarrelsome, meddlesome cousins. But here she was, married, yet still living with them, as if there had been no wedding at all. He seemed to assume that it was only right and natural that Jennie take care of him too.

He was obviously not the man he had led Lillie Mae to believe he was, and many people in town who had seen him come and go over the years, breezing into town in an expensive LaSalle or Packard Phaeton when he had money, sponging off his friends when he was strapped, knew it and secretly delighted in her misfortune. Everyone conceded that she was a fine-looking young woman, perhaps the most fetching girl Monroe County had produced in a generation. What people objected to was the fact that she made no secret that she shared their high opinion. She had thrown over one perfectly nice local boy to marry Arch, and she had made it abundantly clear that she did not plan to spend the rest of her days in Monroeville, baking cakes for the Baptist missionary circle. Her eyes were fixed on distant horizons, on New Orleans, St. Louis, even New York City. Yet the sweet but cruel fact was that with all of her airs, here she was, back in town almost before her bridal bouquet had had time to wither. Her fall from pride had come more swiftly than anyone had dared to hope, and her misjudgment was much talked about that fall and winter. "People in Monroeville thought that Arch was a slick operator and that it was a sad, sad day that my sister married him," said her brother Seabon. "They felt that she should have known better."

No one believed that more firmly than Lillie Mae herself. She was too young and too resilient, with far too much spirit, to mope around the house for very long, however. Since Arch could not take care of her, she made plans to take care of herself. Rather than go back to college, she chose a more practical course, enrolling in a business school in Selma. It was there, during an exercise class in the winter of 1924, that she fainted and in that rude way learned that she was pregnant. It was not a happy discovery, given the apparent hopelessness of her marriage, and the prospect of bearing Arch's child must have seemed like a sentence to prison, something that would make her mistake in marrying him permanent and irrevocable. Although Arch by this time had found a job with a steamship company in New Orleans, Lillie Mae was not convinced that he had reformed, and without telling him her news, she abandoned her classes and returned once again to Monroeville, determined to have an abortion. That was not easy thing to do in 1924, and she very likely asked Jennie for help. And Jennie almost certainly said no, commanding the prospective father to come and retrieve his pregnant wife.

Lillie Mae's resolve to have an abortion was as strong as ever, and she now addressed her demand to Arch, pleading, cajoling, and arguing with him all through the spring of 1924. "Of course I kept stalling and excusing," he explained, "because I wanted a little son more than anything else in the world. Finally, when June came around, I arranged for her to go with some friends of mine to Colorado, which had a wonderful climate for her to be in." When Lillie Mae returned to Monroeville in July, her pregnancy had advanced too far for an abortion to be considered; like it or not, she was going to have Arch's child.

Arch was content to let Jennie and her sisters preside over the birth of his baby, but when Lillie Mae's time came near, Jennie sent her down to New Orleans, where Arch rented a suite in the Monteleone Hotel, on the edge of the French Quarter, and arranged for the services of Dr. E. R. King, one of the city's best gynecologists and obstetricians. Finally, on the morning of Tuesday, September

30, Lillie Mae began having labor pains. After summoning her brother Seabon, Arch carried her to a cab and took her to the Touro Infirmary. While the father and the uncle paced the hallway together, the baby—the boy Arch had wanted so much—was delivered about three o'clock that afternoon. Arch named him Truman after Truman Moore, an old friend from military school, and Streckfus after the New Orleans family that employed him: Truman Streckfus Persons.

2

A<small>T</small> the beginning, anyway, Lillie Mae put aside her earlier misgivings and acted like any other happy new mother, trying, in an almost comical way, to teach Truman to talk and recognize things around him even before he could lift his head off the pillow. Arch surprised her by making a great success of his new job, which was to book clubs and churches aboard the Streckfus Company's fleet of Mississippi excursion boats. Fall and winter he worked out of New Orleans; spring and summer, out of St. Louis.

Rarely is anyone so well suited for a job as Arch was to his, and probably no one since Mark Twain has made a cruise on the Mississippi sound more exciting. Whatever the group, he had the pitch that would bring it aboard. "If you could be sold, Arch could sell you," said his boss, Captain Verne Streckfus. "He was the best." After years of searching, Arch had found his calling. Just as some men are natural athletes, or musicians, or leaders of troops in battle, he was a born salesman. In the time it would take a prospective customer to drink a cup of coffee, he could cast a spell that would turn the cream pitcher into Aladdin's Lamp, the sugar bowl into a chest full of treasure.

Arch was not an ordinary charmer, however, and his ability to persuade did not rest on flattery, backslapping, or the telling of funny stories—though he could do all of those things with practiced ease. His charm had a firmer foundation: after a few minutes of conversation, he could divine a person's secret dreams, much as a fortune-teller can reconstruct one's past from a few clues unwittingly volunteered, and he could make those hidden dreams seem as close and attainable as tomorrow's newspaper. He was mesmerizing; he was tantalizing; he was, in his own way, a magician, Svengali in a white linen suit. His magnetic appeal became so celebrated that *The Circle*, the company magazine, officially declared him "the Streckfus Line's Prince Charming."

His was a dazzling talent, too large to be confined to his job with the Streckfuses. During March and August, his two free months, and in whatever other spare time he had, he continued to hunt for that gold mine, as he called it, that was waiting just over the hill. During the years when Truman was a baby, he tried any number of schemes, each one of which he expected to be the mother lode. One year he managed a prizefighter who went by the name of Joe Littleton. Arch wanted to stage a match in Monroeville, right on the courthouse square, and, to get publicity, he sent the main attraction jogging around town in his boxing shorts. "All the ladies were scandalized," remembered Lillie Mae's sister Mary Ida Carter. "They had never seen a man's legs before." But the city council, alarmed by the uproar, passed an ordinance banning boxing within the town limits, and Joe Littleton put his trousers back on and returned home to New Orleans.

Another time, Arch spied that elusive gold mine in the Great Pasha, otherwise known as Sam Goldberg from the Bronx. Goldberg, who wore a turban and a robe, made his living putting on a kind of grotesque variety act. His best trick, the gimmick that excited Arch so much, was his ability to survive burial. With the help of what was advertised as a secret Egyptian drug, he could retard his heartbeat to such an abnormally slow rate that he hardly needed to breathe; he could remain alive in an airtight coffin for up to five hours. Calling him the "World's Foremost Man of Mystery," Arch staged his Pasha show—"Burial Alive, Blindfold Drive, Nailed to Cross, Torture Act and 100 others"—in half a dozen places. In Monroeville, people came to see it from a hundred miles around; even the banks closed for the day. Despite their success, Arch and the Pasha eventually quarreled and parted. For Arch it may have been just as well. Not long after their breakup, Goldberg's Egyptian drug failed him, and one day when his coffin was dug up, the Great Pasha was as still as the Pharaohs.

Arch had other projects: a plan to syndicate shorthand lessons in newspapers, a magazine for sororities and fraternities, a series of popularity contests for high school girls. There was, in fact, no end to his schemes. His mind shot off ideas like a Fourth of July sparkler, and he thought of little else but new ways to make his fortune. "Money is the sixth sense, without which the other five are of no avail," he liked to say, and he believed that it was his destiny to be rich. If he had had some extra quality—perhaps nothing more extraordinary than patience—he might have fulfilled that destiny and become as famous a promoter as Billy Rose, Mike Todd, or the man he resembled most of all, P. T. Barnum. But whatever that quality was, he did not possess it. His emotional barometer was subject to too many fluctuations—ebullience one day, depression the next—and he did not have the temperament to stick to any single thing for very long. He was, moreover, not always scrupulous about how he acquired his money. As he rushed toward fortune, he sometimes stooped very low to pick up a dollar and looked less and less like a visionary promoter and more and more like an ordinary con man. The image that remains from those years is that of the local sheriff automatically fingering the keys to the lockup every time Arch came to town. Even his mother, who was convinced that God meant for him to do something grand and important, complained that he did not know the difference between right and wrong.

3

LOOKING back years later, Lillie Mae often said that she had married Arch only to get away from home. Sometimes, however, when she was in a mellow mood, she admitted that she had once loved him—and that is doubtless the truth of the matter. "Arch was so romantic," said Mary Ida. "He would always bring her a bouquet of flowers—even if he had to go to the side of the yard to pick them." But their romance scarcely outlasted their courtship: Arch was an easy man to like, but he was not an easy man to love; the very thing that made him so charming—all those promises he passed out so freely—invariably led to disenchantment. Instead of forgiving him his feckless ways, as she might have done if he had not raised her hopes so high, Lillie Mae held them against him, convinced that he had deceived her. "She thought that she had been hooked into marrying him," said Seabon. "She had thought she was marrying a man who would give her some security and a home life." Arch could give her neither, and if she had not become pregnant, it is doubtful that they would have stayed together more than a year.

As it was, their marriage did not so much end as it dissolved, slowly at first and then faster and faster, like a cube of sugar dropped into an iced drink. Lillie Mae appears to have made an effort to preserve it for a few months after Truman was born, but she soon gave up and other men entered her life. "She'd take a notion to a fellow and she just couldn't wait to get into bed with him," said Arch. "She wanted a thrill and she would get it. Then in three or four weeks she'd be through with it and ready to go on to something else." In the seven years they were man and wife, Arch claimed to have counted twenty-nine such affairs. His brother John, who also had been tricked and lied to by Arch, was willing to forgive Lillie Mae her adulteries; what he could not forgive her was her poor choice in men. "Invariably," he complained in one letter, "they are either Greeks, Spaniards, college sheiks, foolish young city upstarts, or just as immature small-town habitants."

The first on the list may have been a Central American who appeared in the summer of 1925. Matching all the stereotypes of the hot-blooded Latin lover, he was passionate, he lavished presents on her, and he threatened to kill her if he ever saw her with another man, excluding her husband, of course. Arch did not like her seeing him—or so he later said—but he did not make an issue of it. "What could I do?" he asked plaintively. "She'd slip around and see him when I was working. It was just something I didn't talk about."

To avoid embarrassing confrontations, Lillie Mae would usually see her Latin in the afternoon. But sometimes at night, after she had told him where she and Arch were going, he would also follow them into a movie theater. She would help Arch find a seat in the front row—he was so shortsighted that he could barely see the screen if he was farther back—and she would then join her lover in a secluded corner in the rear. When the film was over, she would return to Arch and the other man would go home to his own wife. Nearsighted as he was, Arch was usually aware of what was happening.

Several times she carried out her trysts in front of Truman, believing, no doubt, that he was too young to notice. In that she was mistaken. "She once went to bed with a man in St. Louis," Truman recalled. "I was only two or so, but I remember it clearly, right down to what he looked like—he had brown hair. We were in his apartment, and I was sleeping on a couch. Suddenly they had a big fight. He went over to a closet, pulled out a necktie, and started to strangle her with it. He only stopped when I became hysterical. A couple of years after that, she took me to Jacksonville to leave me with my grandmother. She and my father were more or less separated by that time, and she went out with several young men while she was there. One night I could hear them doing whatever they were doing in the rumble seat of a car. Another night she brought a man right into the house. She must have been drinking, because I could hear her giggling and her voice sounded funny. Suddenly all the lights came on and she and my grandmother were yelling at each other. She then started packing and every few minutes she would come on to the porch where I was sleeping. She would cry, put her arms around me and tell me she would never leave me. Once again I became hysterical, and at that point my memory stops cold."

Not all of her lovers were Greeks, Spaniards, or college sheiks. One, Jack Dempsey, the ex–heavyweight champion of the world, satisfied even John Persons' exacting standards. Lillie Mae met him when she was traveling with Truman on a train from Memphis to St. Louis. "We were sitting in the coach section when a man walked up and down the aisle and looked at my mother—I was used to men looking at my mother. Then he asked us to have a drink in Dempsey's compartment. I knew even then who Dempsey was, or at least I knew that he was somebody famous. So we went to his compartment and my mother talked to him. After a while Dempsey suggested to the man, who must have been his manager, that he take me to the observation car for a Coke, and he and I went back there and sat watching the rails for most of the afternoon. I remember saying, 'Where's my mother?' But I knew where she was. Things like that happened a lot."

One reason Arch remained so quiet all those years, methodically counting his wife's lovers as if he were keeping score in a card game, was that he was not above using them to help him turn a dollar. When they were first married, for example, he persuaded her to cash bad checks for him, employing her good looks as a come-on. In Dempsey, for example, he saw one of his gold mines—bigger even than the Great Pasha—and with Lillie Mae as his go-between, he persuaded the ex-champ, who was still an enormously popular figure, like Charles Lindbergh or Will Rogers, to referee a wrestling match in Columbus, Mississippi. He sent out thousands of promotional fliers, had letterheads printed with both his picture and Dempsey's, and erected wooden stands to seat 11,500. "There wasn't a big enough place in the state to hold the people we expected!" he exclaimed. But luck eluded him yet again. A terrible storm pelted Columbus on "Jack Dempsey Day," November 10, 1930, and even Dempsey was not popular enough to persuade more than 3,000 people to sit in the wind and rain. Arch failed to meet his expenses.

Though she was not faithful, Lillie Mae stuck by Arch in most other ways, long after most women would have dismissed him. She overlooked his failures, defended him during his increasingly frequent troubles with the law, and helped him when she could.

Though their times together grew progressively shorter, neither mentioned divorce; both of them seemed content with their civilized arrangement.

The only one hurt was Truman, and if it is true, as psychologists say, that a child's greatest anxiety—the original fear—is that he will be deserted by his parents, then he had good reason to be anxious. Between Arch's schemes and Lillie Mae's affairs, there was little time for him. When he was with them, they would sometimes lock him in their hotel room at night, instructing the staff not to let him out even if he screamed, which, in his fright, he would often do. "Eventually," he recalled, "I would become so exhausted that I would just throw myself on the bed or on the floor until they came back. Every day was a nightmare, because I was afraid that they would leave me when it turned dark. I had an intense fear of being abandoned, and I remember practically all of my childhood as being lived in a state of constant tension and fear." An early memory, undoubtedly the recollection of a dream rather than an actual event, is symbolic of those lonely years: as he was walking through the St. Louis Zoo with a black nurse, he heard screams—a lion was loose. The nurse ran away and he was left all by himself, with no place to hide and no safety anywhere.

Lillie Mae made sporadic attempts to keep him with her. In the winter of 1929 she even took him to Kentucky, where, still hoping to find a career for herself, she spent a few weeks in a business college. Arch also professed endless love. But neither one was willing to be a full-time parent or make any permanent sacrifice. They loved him, in short, only when they were not otherwise engaged. Sometimes they left him with Arch's widowed mother, who had married a Presbyterian minister in Jacksonville. More often they deposited him with Lillie Mae's relations in Monroeville. Finally, in the summer of 1930, a few months before his sixth birthday, they left him there for good—or for as long as anyone could then foresee. Arch busied himself with his projects; Lillie Mae went off to visit friends in Colorado. Truman's fear that they would abandon him had finally come true.

4

─────

I T was a strange household he entered in Monroeville, unique to the South, peculiar to the time: three quarrelsome sisters in late middle age, their reclusive older brother, and an atmosphere heavy with small secrets and ancient resentments. Jennie, Callie, Sook, and Bud, united by blood and the boundaries of the rambling old house on Alabama Avenue, divided by jealousy and the accumulated hurts of half a century.

Jennie, a handsome but slightly masculine-looking woman with red hair, was the boss, the final and absolute authority on all matters of consequence. As a young woman, she had realized that she was the only one capable of supporting the family, and she had gone off to learn the hat trade in St. Louis and Pensacola, Florida, returning to open her own shop on the courthouse square. At that time women would not step out the door without some extravagant display on their heads, and Jennie prospered, turning their vague and unarticulated fantasies into fireworks of frills and feathers. Eventually she expanded her shop until it carried everything a woman could want but the shoes on her feet. She would not stoop to fit smelly feet, Jennie declared. "She was the strongest woman I've ever seen," said Seabon, "and one of the finest businesswomen who ever lived. She was one of the first stockholders of both the Monroe County Bank and the First National Bank of Monroeville. She had her hand into everything." Jennie was also known for her violent temper. She once whipped a lazy yardman with a dog chain; another time, spotting someone who she thought had cheated her, she jumped out of her car and attacked him on his own front porch, in front of his wife and children. People walked on tiptoes when Jennie was around.

Callie, the youngest and at one time the prettiest of the sisters, with curly black hair, had started out as a schoolteacher. When Jennie's hat shop began to make money, Jennie ordered her to quit and help with accounts, and like everyone else in that house, Callie did as she was told, keeping the books and pecking out business letters on an old typewriter. But Callie, like many weak people, retaliated by constantly nagging and complaining, her head held high in a permanent position of moral superiority. When Jennie decided to skip church, for example, as she sometimes did, Callie would become indignant. "Oh, Jennie, that's so sinful!" she would say. "I'm goin'!" And so she would, steaming out the door in her Sunday best like a liner leaving harbor, pennants flying and horns tooting. Knowing that both Jennie and Sook, the third sister, were secret tipplers—good Baptists, particularly good Baptist ladies, were not supposed to indulge—she also made it one of her tasks in life to ferret out and empty the bottles of bourbon they had stashed away. Jennie, for one, was unrepentant and always managed to keep a safe supply; weekend mornings she often could be found on the porch sipping what she discreetly called iced tea. If a neighbor, like Mrs. Lee from next door, happened by, she would invite her in for a glass—and then go into the kitchen to brew a pot of real tea.

Jennie put up with Callie's sniping, but it was not in her nature to remain silent, and the two of them bickered endlessly. Indeed, there was almost nothing they did not quarrel about: whether they should have company for dinner, serve steak or chicken, set the table this way or that. According to a script they had followed a thousand times, Callie was invariably victorious in those small battles; but Jennie would win all the big ones, and when she did, Callie would run to her room in tears.

Two years older than Jennie and four years older than Callie, Sook was nonetheless the youngest in mind and spirit. Somewhat stout, with white hair cropped close to her head, she was so childlike that she was thought to be retarded by many people; in fact she was merely so shy and unworldly as sometimes to appear simpleminded. She had rarely left Monroe County; she had never read anything but the Bible and Grimm's fairy tales in all of her adult years; and she had never been to a movie, never had seen Rudolph Valentino, Mary Pickford, Douglas Fairbanks, or any of the other stars everyone was talking about, never even noticed when the silents learned to talk. Her job was to stay home and take care of the house, and she knew little of the world outside its gates.

Only occasionally did she make longer excursions. One was on that day each fall when she went into the woods to find ingredients for her dropsy cure, whose recipe had come down to her from the Indians, or the gypsies—no one knew for sure. When she returned, she would boil all her gleanings, chiefly herbs and sourwood, in a giant washpot in the backyard, and neighbors would know from the red glow that night that Sook was making her medicine. Whatever it was, it seemed to work, and several victims of the disease praised her as they would a saint.

A second excursion also took place in the fall when she searched the woods for pecans to put into her Christmas fruitcakes. She would make a dozen or so and give them away to relatives and people she admired, such as the man who peddled tinware from a wagon or President and Mrs. Roosevelt; the Roosevelts' thank-you note, which bore both signatures on White House stationery, was one of her most treasured possessions. Yet even the gentle, innocent Sook had a dark side, an addiction to morphine, which had been prescribed as a painkiller after a mastectomy, and her habit sometimes made her moody and irritable. "If she ran out of her medicine, she'd act wild and wouldn't be fit to talk to," recalled Seabon. " 'Oh! Oh!' she would moan, and call to me: 'Seabon! Run down to Dr. Coxwell's and get my medicine. I gotta have my medicine!' "

Surrounded by contentious, difficult women and half-invalided by asthma, Bud, who was as tall as he was thin, kept to himself. Though he was the putative head of the clan, by both gender and age, he long since had deferred to Jennie, and much of the time he would remain in his room, breathing the acrid fumes of a cough-suppressor called Green Mountain, which he burned in a saucer turned upside down on the fireplace mantel. The rest of the time he spent either supervising the farm he owned outside of town or rocking in a chair on the front porch. Jennie and Callie had had their share of beaux, but Bud had never taken out a woman, or shown an interest in sex of any kind; no one presumed to ask why. He never spoke harshly about anyone, and the only person in the world he seemed to dislike was his younger brother, Howard, who lived with his wife on a farm nearby. Long ago they had argued over land they had inherited from their father, and they had not spoken since. When Howard and his wife came to dinner, as they did every Sunday afternoon, the two brothers would sit across the table from each other and exchange not so much as a syllable.

Yet beneath the emotional storms, the fights, tearful exits, and oddities of manners and behavior, there was a foundation of calm, order and a now-vanished simplicity to life on Alabama Avenue, and it is easy to understand why Lillie Mae, who had wanted so desperately to leave, was drawn back so often. For all their intrigues and harsh words, the Faulks were a family. They knew that whatever was said, in the end they could always count on one another. They took care of their own.

In 1930, when Truman went there to live, Monroeville was a small country town, scarcely more than a furrow between fields of corn and cotton. That year's census listed 1,355 people, but even that tiny figure probably was exaggerated by local officials, who wanted a number big enough to qualify for a post office. There was not one paved street, and a row of oak trees grew right down the middle of Alabama Avenue. On hot summer days cars and horses kicked up red dust every time they passed by; when it rained that dust turned to mud. Without a map it was hard to know where the town began and the surrounding farmland ended. Yards were big, with two or three outbuildings, and most people kept chickens, some pigs, and at least one cow. The Faulks did not have a cow—Sook would not milk one—but they did raise chickens, and turkeys too, and every winter Bud would bring in from his farm a couple of hogs, which were soon sent to the smokehouse.

Everyone followed farmers' hours, up by dawn, in bed by eight or nine. In the Faulk household, Sook and old Aunt Liza—all elderly blacks were called "aunt" or "uncle" by the white people they worked for—would start cooking breakfast, the big meal of the day, at five: ham, eggs, and pancakes, of course; but also, in an almost excessive display of the land's bounty, fried chicken, pork chops, catfish, and squirrel, according to the season. Along with all that, there would be grits and gravy, black-eyed peas, collards (with corn bread to sop up the collard liquor), biscuits and homemade jams and preserves, pound cake, sweet milk, buttermilk, and coffee flavored with chicory. After that cockcrow banquet Jennie and Callie would walk down to their store, Bud would retire to his bedroom, and Sook would go on to her other domestic chores, which included keeping an eye on Aunt Liza and overseeing Anna Stabler, the old black retainer who lived in a little shack in the backyard. Anna was almost part of the family, and so cantankerous that she made Jennie and Callie sound almost sweet-tempered. "Fuss! You could hear her fussing two miles away!" said Mary Ida. "A Negro didn't sass a white person then, but Anna said anything she pleased to any white person she wanted to. Sook would cuss her out for not cleaning in places you couldn't see, like the bottom of the piano, and Anna would just stand up and blister her back. Then they would both laugh and go on with what they were doing." Part Indian, Anna denied that she had any black blood at all, plastering her cheeks with rouge to prove that she had red skin. Weekends she sat on her porch and played her accordion, proudly wearing her best dress and stuffing her jaws with cotton in a vain effort to disguise the fact that she had no teeth.

Jennie and Callie came home for lunch, which was usually leftovers from breakfast, then came back again for an early supper, much of which had also been part of that early-morning feast. When dinner was over, everyone wandered out to the porch, which was the center of activity most of the year; winters are short in southern Alabama and some years so mild that they are scarcely noticed at all, fall merging into spring with only the briefest punctuation in between. After a while neighbors dropped by to gossip: talk was the chief form of entertainment, and everybody knew all there was to know about everybody else. Once a week Sook and Callie invited in some friends, usually Dr. Logan and Dr. Bear, to play a card game called rook. Sook, who was the best player on the street, would mix up a batch of divinity candy for the occasion and dance around in a fever of excitement all day. Jennie was the only one who remained aloof; card games, she said, were a damned-fool business. Her only passion was her garden. Her japonica bushes were a neighborhood landmark, and she guarded them as if they were precious jewels, which to her way of thinking they were.

Even the Depression, which hit the South first and hardest, did not alter that placid routine. There were more people for Sook to distribute hand-me-downs to, and "Hoover cars," horse-drawn wagons with rubber tires stripped off scrapped Model-T's, were beginning to make their appearance. But money had never been as plentiful or as important in small towns like Monroeville as it had been in the cities, and its sudden disappearance mattered comparatively less. The Faulks were hurt by the hard times, but they never suffered real deprivation. There was, as always, an around-the-clock banquet in Sook's kitchen.

For Truman, who had stayed in that house so many times before, often for weeks on end, there was nothing to get used to, there were no adjustments to be made. All that summer of 1930 he swam every day at Hatter's Mill, which was the place, out Drewry Road, where most of Monroeville went to picnic, swim, and applaud the daring young men who dived from a window on the third story of the old millhouse. He slept in a bedroom next to Sook's, and when he was not swimming at the pond, he was usually with her, in the kitchen, the yard, or the fields beyond. After he entered first grade in September, they had less time together. But they still had afternoons and weekends, and as the air began to stir again after the close days of summer, she taught him how to fly a kite. He, in turn, accompanied her on her autumnal forays into the woods, helping her gather the ingredients for her dropsy medicine and the pecans for her Christmas cakes. She did her best to be both mother and friend, and to a large extent she succeeded.

Truman had only one other real companion, and that was Harper Lee, the youngest daughter of the family next door. By local standards, the Lees were considered bookish. Mr. Lee, who was a lawyer, had once been part owner and editor of the Monroe *Journal*, and he had also spent some time in Montgomery, the capital of Alabama, as a state senator. His wife, the same Mrs. Lee who had played the piano at Arch and Lillie Mae's wedding, was a crossword-puzzle whiz, a woman of gigantic proportions who sat for hours on her front porch, intently matching words and boxes. Her mind was not altogether right, however. She wandered up and down the street saying strange things to neighbors and passersby, and twice she tried to drown Harper—or Nelle, as she was then called—in the bathtub. "Both times Nelle was saved by one of her older sisters," said Truman. "When they talk about Southern grotesque, they're not kidding!"

Harper survived the dunkings to become the tomboy on the block, a girl who, as Mary Ida phrased it, could beat the steam out of most boys her age, or even a year or so older, as Truman was. Indeed, he was one of her favorite targets. But that did not stop them from becoming constant companions, and a treehouse in the Lees' china-berry tree became their fortress against the world, a leafy refuge where they read and acted out scenes from their favorite books, which chronicled the exploits of Tarzan, Tom Swift, and the Rover Boys.

The bond that united them was stronger than friendship—it was a common anguish. They both bore the bruises of parental rejection, and they both were shattered by loneliness. Neither had many other real friends. Nelle was too rough for most other girls, and Truman was too soft for most other boys. He was small for his age, to begin with, and he did not enjoy fighting and rolling in the dirt, as most boys around there did. Without meaning to do so, Lillie Mae, who sent him his clothes by mail, dressed him too well, and his freshly laundered shirt and crisp linen shorts made him as conspicuous as Little Lord Fauntleroy. People often remarked that with his white-blond hair and sky-blue eyes, he was pretty enough to be a girl. He was, in short, regarded as a sissy.

There are photographs of Truman at that age—a tiny towhead with a huge grin—but Harper provided the best picture thirty years later. She modeled one of the characters in her novel *To Kill a Mockingbird* after him, and described him as a true curiosity: "He wore blue linen shorts that buttoned to his shirt, his hair was snow white and stuck to his head like duckfluff; he was a year my senior but I towered over him. As he told us [an] old tale his blue eyes would lighten and darken; his laugh was sudden and happy; he habitually pulled at a cowlick in the center of his forehead. . . . We came to know [him] as a pocket Merlin, whose head teemed with eccentric plans, strange longings, and quaint fancies."

Although he was not much appreciated by most of his contempo-raries, he was an affectionate and beguiling child, this pocket Merlin, and if they did not take to him immediately, as Sook had done, Jennie and Callie soon did so. "I fear if there is such a thing, we all love him too much," Callie confessed in one of her reports to Arch's mother. "He is a darling sweet boy," she added later. "We do enjoy having him. He is the sunshine of our home." He was uncommonly bright, and Callie, the old schoolteacher, took pride in his budding mind, remarking that she and Sook read to him every night—and he to them. "I just love to see his little mind developing and taking in things," she said.

As the self-appointed guardian of morals on Alabama Avenue, Callie also assured his grandmother that he was doing well in Sunday school—had, in fact, been promoted with honors—and that he was receiving proper spiritual guidance at home as well. "We give him every pleasure that we can," she wrote, "but of course we do try to teach him that there is a right way to have pleasure. I tried to get him interested in memorizing the 23rd. Psalm, also the Ten Commandments. So I told him (he almost knew it anyway) that it was a low standard of teaching, but if he would memorize the 23rd. Psalm perfectly, I would give him 25 cents—but not to do it just for the 25 cents, but for the love of God and the love he had for God. So he readily agreed that he would memorize it because it was right for him to do so. He did perfectly and I gave him the 25 cents and Sook added a bit to it. Now, he has commenced on the Ten Commandments. I told him just to take one each day and it wouldn't seem so hard."

Despite Callie's assurances, Truman was not happy. His own descriptions of his life in Monroeville are almost grim, and Callie might have been surprised at how unfavorably she was remembered. Compared with Sook, both Callie and Jennie were viewed as cold and unloving, as purse-mouthed and pinchpenny spinsters. He probably expected too much from them, or he may have been misled by Jennie's gruff manner and wearied by Callie's righteousness; his own memory of his religious instruction saw him constantly being marched off to church, with no more choice than the prisoners who worked in chain gangs on the roads outside town. Still, it is hard to imagine what more the Faulk sisters could have done for him. Although Lillie Mae and—on rare occasions—Arch paid most of his expenses, it was that peculiar family that actually took care of him.

Truman's complaint was not that Jennie was short-tempered, that Callie was a nag, or that there was not enough money for all the tantalizing things he saw in store windows in Mobile. It was that none of the Faulk sisters, even the beloved Sook, could take the place of his real parents. Lillie Mae, it is true, would appear occasionally from some distant place, her stylish, expensive clothes exciting envious glances from her friends. But she soon disappeared in a fragrant cloud of Evening in Paris, her favorite perfume. Truman was always desolate when she drove off; once, finding a perfume bottle she had forgotten, he drank it to the bottom, as if he could bring back the woman with her scent. On one visit he convinced himself that she was going to take him away with her. "But after three or four days she left," he said, "and I stood in the road, watching her drive away in a black Buick, which got smaller and smaller and smaller. Imagine a dog, watching and waiting and hoping to be taken away. That is the picture of me then."

Arch created a stir of his own in Monroeville. When one of his schemes was going well, he would pull into town in a fancy convertible, announcing his arrival by honking the glittering, trumpetlike horns that preened themselves on the hood. Caesar himself could not have asked for a louder or more triumphal fanfare. When his plans were not working, on the other hand, which was increasingly the case in those dark Depression years, he would slink in and quietly make his way to the Faulks' so that no one, particularly his creditors, would know that he was there. Even in that effort he was usually unsuccessful. One night at eleven o'clock, long after everyone had gone to bed, a marshal knocked on the door to serve him with a warrant; fortunately for Arch, he had left after dinner. Whether he was noisy or silent, however, he was not able to impress many people in Monroeville: they knew a con man when they saw one. "People made fun of him," said Mary Ida. "He was always after that million dollars just beyond his reach, something too big to grasp. And that caused what I reckon you would call psychological problems for Truman. Even when he was a little boy he felt there was something wrong with his daddy."

As he had everyone else in his life, Arch dazzled Truman with promises, and when he felt that he was not being properly treated on Alabama Avenue, Truman would defiantly mention his daddy, who he said would come to rescue him from his woe. Arch said he would buy him a dog and books, both of which Truman desperately wanted. But neither the dog nor the books ever arrived. More than once Arch swore that he would take him down to one of the beaches on the Gulf Coast. "Truman would be so excited that he would skip," said Mary Ida. "He would jump up into the air he would be so happy, and he would get a new swimsuit and be all ready to go. But Arch wouldn't come through. He never took him down there once."

Eventually even Truman saw through his father and realized how empty all those promises were. The day of revelation came when Arch, bestowing smiles and How-do-you-do's on everyone in sight, drove into town in one of his big cars and offered to take Truman and a couple of his friends to lunch in Mobile. Truman gathered his friends, Sook gave him two dollars—a fairly substantial sum at that time—to buy some books, and Arch, as good as his word, piled everybody into the car and set off for Mobile. Disappointment was delayed until they were in the restaurant, where Arch, whispering into Truman's ear, asked him for the two dollars Sook had given him. "I never trusted him again after that," Truman said.

6

As rarely as they saw Truman, his parents saw each other even less, and by the fall of 1930 the story of Arch and Lillie Mae was rapidly approaching its conclusion: after six years of their strange, twilight marriage Lillie Mae wanted out. She had many reasons, but the deciding incident, the one that convinced her, seems to have been the discovery that he had tricked her into driving a carload of bootleg liquor into Monroeville.

She had, in fact, probably done the same thing many times before without knowing it; because he was night-blind as well as near-sighted, Arch often asked her, or anybody else who was around, to sit behind the wheel when he wanted to go anywhere after dark. But he did not tell her what was in the trunk, and when she found out that she was engaged in such a common, low, and even hazard-ous pursuit as carrying illegal hootch, she was furious and unforgiv-ing. "That was the final straw for her," said Mary Ida. "She couldn't stand for him to disgrace her like that in Monroeville. A bootlegger was beneath anybody's nose."

He had finally gone too far, but Lillie Mae's problem was what it had always been: a lack of money. She had never earned her own living, and Arch's income, unsteady and increasingly irregular as it was, was all that separated her from total reliance on Jennie's char-ity. Twice before, first in Selma, then in Bowling Green, she had attended business schools in hopes of preparing herself for a career, and both times she had dropped out. Now she tried once again. The Elizabeth Arden School of Beauty in New York had offered her a scholarship, and in a moment of uncharacteristic generosity, Arch, who had recently come into some money—compensation for injuries he had suffered after falling into a ditch in St. Louis—promised to send her forty dollars a week for expenses. "The only reason I consented was because my brother Sam was living in New York," he later explained, "and I figured he'd more or less keep an eye on her. The course was only supposed to take three months, at which time she was supposed to come back to Monroeville." With that understanding, Lillie Mae left for New York on January 15, 1931. Sam, the third of the three Persons brothers, had no use at all for Arch, and not much more for Lillie Mae. "Seems to me she is always studying something or taking some kind of course, but not actually going to work," he wrote John. He nonetheless played the good brother and met her when she arrived the next morning.

It is certain, in the light of what followed, that Lillie Mae had not been candid with Arch and, one way or another, hoped to stay on past her allotted three months. New York had always been her eventual destination, and once there, she was in no hurry to rush back to Monroeville. And she did in fact remain. Indeed, she had little choice. As he had on their honeymoon, Arch ran out of money, this time leaving her stranded far from home. In difficulty with the law in Alabama, he began sending her bad checks or persuaded his mother to wire the forty-dollar allowance. It was at that point that John, who saw himself as his mother's defender, stepped in. He explained the situation to Lillie Mae—"Arch is headed for immediate serious trouble"—and pointedly suggested that she look for support from some other source than the Persons family. "I can well understand why you are so desirous of finishing your course there —now more than ever," he wrote her. "But apparently Arch can't be depended upon for the regular expenses, and Mother hasn't the money for any more telegrams, even if it were right for her to send it." A few days later, on March 16, John telegraphed the sequel: Arch was in jail in Birmingham, charged with writing bad checks and extortion.

Lillie Mae had guessed that something was wrong when his checks began to bounce, and in early March, even before she had received John's warning letter, she had taken a job in a restaurant on lower Broadway. Still, she was shaken when John wired her that Arch was actually behind bars, and on a tiny dime-store notepad, the only stationery at hand, she breathlessly replied: "Please excuse this paper, etc. Your wire just received and I'm too nervous & upset to write. Your letter more or less prepared me for your wire—there's just nothing to say. Why—Why—Why? Do you know anything? I just can't write you I'm so nervous. As soon as [he] started letting checks come back on me I knew something was wrong. I haven't heard from him in 2 wks. I only make enough to *exist* on but I believe I will try it for awhile as there is nothing I could do if I came back as I have no money. What would you advise? Please write me fully."

The panic was soon over. Arch was still in trouble, but for the moment he was out on bail. As she had done so many times before, his mother had come to his rescue, pledging a month's salary to pay his hundred-and-fifty-dollar bond. "When he gets in trouble, she would mortgage her life, if necessary, to get him out," explained the exasperated John to Lillie Mae. "This has been done, as you well know, for many, many years. It isn't fair, and it is most inconsiderate of Arch to force these situations on her, but inasmuch as she always gets him out, I suppose he feels she will so continue, and goes right ahead to his next difficulty." Indeed, far from feeling shamefaced, Arch complained that the authorities in Alabama had something against him, and in hurt, petulant tones he threatened to leave the state, perhaps even the country.

When they are forced to, people who have depended on others are often able not only to manage but to thrive. Such was the case with Lillie Mae, who was belatedly learning that she could take care of herself. She was well regarded by her employers, and by the middle of June she had been promoted to branch manager, at a salary of thirty-two dollars a week. Though much of that was sent home to Monroeville to cover Truman's expenses, she still was able to scrape by in New York. She was clever, as well as attractive, and if she had steadfastly pursued a career, she might well have succeeded. But her basic goal was what it had always been: home, security, and a place in society. Sometime that winter or spring, not long after she had arrived, she discovered—or rediscovered—the man who was to give her all three.

His name was Joseph Garcia Capote, and he was another of the Latins she favored. His father, a colonel in the Spanish army, had arrived in Cuba in 1894, when it was a Spanish colony, and had fought against Theodore Roosevelt's Rough Riders at the Battle of San Juan Hill. He became a landowner, returned to Barcelona to

marry, and then came back to Cuba to raise three boys, of whom
Joe was the oldest, in solid middle-class comfort. Educated at the
University of Havana, Joe left for New Orleans in 1924, when he
was twenty-four, to look for a job in the United States. It was in
New Orleans, during the summer of 1925, that he met Lillie Mae in
the lobby of the Monteleone hotel.

Captivated by her vivacity and beauty, he instantly fell in love
with her, just as Arch had done. She liked him because his accent
reminded her of her absent lover, the jealous Central American.
They had dinner together and they may even have made love; but if
they did have an affair, it did not last long. She already had one
lover, not to mention a husband and a baby, and Joe was not in a
financial position to stay around. Unable to find work in New Orleans, he transferred his job hunt to New York, where he soon
married a secretary in one of the offices he visited. He corresponded
with Lillie Mae even so, and it is possible that he encouraged her,
and perhaps even gave her money, to come North. However it was
arranged, they did meet in New York, picking up their romance
where they had left it in New Orleans.

They had both matured in the five intervening years. When they
had first met, she was just twenty, still a wild and unsettled girl,
and he was a youth himself, uncertain what he wanted to do and
where he wanted to go. When they saw each other the second time,
she was twenty-six and somewhat chastened by experience; he was
an aspiring young executive with a promising future on Wall Street.
For four years, while he was working as a shipping clerk during the
day, he had spent his nights studying accounting and business administration at New York University, and by 1931 he was earning a
comfortable income as the office manager of an old and respected
textile-brokerage firm, Taylor, Clapp and Beall.

Lillie Mae could not have fallen in love with a drudge, and Joe
was a lively man with a sense of humor and fun, who enjoyed
spending money even more than making it. He liked having a good
time; he appreciated fine food and wine; he dressed well, in the
conservative way of Wall Street; and he was fastidious in his personal habits. "I never saw a man who was any cleaner than Joe
Capote," said Lillie Mae's brother Seabon. "He would take a bath in
the morning before he went to his office, then take another one and
put on clean underwear and a clean shirt before he would have his
dinner." Short, round, and bespectacled, with dark, slicked-back

hair, he was not handsome in any conventional sense. But Lillie Mae was not the only woman who found him attractive, and bigger men soon learned not to provoke him. Underneath his dark suit was the build of a boxer: strong, muscular arms, a thick neck, and a big, powerful chest.

Arch had not met him, or even heard about him, as he had some of the other men in Lillie Mae's life, when Joe was in New Orleans in 1925. Not long after she had taken up residence in New York, however, by April, 1931, at the latest, he had guessed that there was someone new in her life: she was no longer writing to him, he complained to John. By that summer she had confirmed his suspicion, and frantic that she would leave him, he begged her to quit her job and return home immediately. Finally, she agreed to meet him July Fourth—or so he believed—in Jacksonville, where he was putting on a show with the Great Pasha. When she failed to appear, John, who lived in Jacksonville, wired Sam in New York, asking him to plead Arch's case to her. "His mental state concerning her desperate otherwise okay," John telegraphed Sam, adding, without any evidence whatsoever, that Arch had done a complete about-face and was now able to support her.

That was too much for the hardheaded Sam, who was now almost as irritated with his younger brother for speaking in Arch's favor as he was with Arch for asking him to do so. "The enclosed wire came last night after I had gone to bed," he replied. "John's name is signed to it but it is hard to believe he could have sent such a foolish message. Let me analyze it briefly:

"1. 'Arch's mental state desperate otherwise okay.' Why should his mental state be desperate because Lillie Mae has too much sense to quit a job and go back to a husband who has failed to support her, and who has humiliated her on countless occasions?

"2. 'She promised him come fourth, etc. etc.' She shouldn't have done that, but Arch's letters were worded so pitifully (his old trick when he is desperate of appealing to sympathy) that she thought she would promise him anything which might temporarily relieve his feelings.

"3. 'Strongly recommend that she come immediately.' How utterly ridiculous. Why should she come? Arch hasn't a nickel to his name, no job, hunted by the police, owes everybody under the sun, and you recommend that she return to that. Have you lost your mind, John?

"4. 'No further question about A's complete about-face and ability support her now.' This is even more absurd than No. 3. There is *every* question about his complete about-face. He has been giving trouble continuously for about twenty years—serious and endless trouble—and it will be a miracle indeed if the day should ever dawn when he acts like a normal person."

Lillie Mae could not have stated her case better, and when she finally did travel south to meet Arch, her purpose was not to discuss their marriage, but to end it. With Joe paying her way, she left New York in mid-July, 1931, and, picking up Truman in Monroeville on her way, met Arch in Pensacola, Florida, on July 24. There was no discussion. Within fifteen minutes she had told him that she wanted a divorce so that she could marry another man. "She wouldn't tell me who he was," Arch remembered. "She just said his initials were J.C. and that he was a big executive with a textile firm in New York. She didn't tell me he was a Spaniard or spic or nothin' like that." Joe's name was not secret very long, but months later Arch still pretended not to know it. In letters to his family, Capote was misspelled as Capotey or Catobey or dropped altogether in favor of "the foreigner," "the Spaniard," "the N.Y. dago," "that lousy cheap Cuban," or, finally, "a Cuban, the lowest type of white person imaginable."

In her divorce complaint, Lillie Mae alleged cruelty, and Jennie swore in an affidavit that she had seen Arch strike her. Arch denied it—although he later said that she sometimes deserved it; but he seemed happy—delighted, even—to play the part of the innocent and righteously angry husband. In letters to his family and friends, he wallowed in self-pity, splashing in his own tears as he bewailed the terrible injury that had been done him. Trying to find money to please Lillie Mae was what had led to his problems with the law, he said; it was her "greed and unprincipled actions" that had led him astray. "I am the deserted boy," he concluded, complaining that she had been both disloyal and ungrateful. In everything that had transpired he believed himself to be blameless. The supreme salesman, he was his own best customer, and his capacity for self-delusion verged on the pathological.

Lillie Mae's lawyer formally filed for divorce August 2, and at the end of August, three weeks after she had returned to New York, Arch was presented with legal papers. In a letter to John he once again bemoaned his unlucky fate. Lillie Mae, he reported, had phoned to tell him "that she wanted to marry Joe at once, and that she loved him, and that I had never meant anything to her. So that's that. She was just as cruel and heartless about it as possible. Girls are sure a pain." There was a short delay in the proceedings when, out of pique and spite, he spent a couple of days dodging a sheriff who was trying to serve him with papers. But by November 9, 1931, the divorce was final and that really was that. Arch and Lillie Mae were no longer man and wife.

UNDER the terms of the divorce settlement, Lillie Mae was to have custody of Truman nine months of the year, Arch the other three, from June 1 through August 31. But for the time being, and for some time to come, that was merely a paper agreement, with neither one assuming the duties of a full-time parent. As far as Truman was concerned, the divorce scarcely mattered; he remained in Monroeville and his parents saw him only occasionally, as they had before.

If she had wanted to do so, Lillie Mae could have taken him with her to New York at the end of the year, when she and Joe moved into their own apartment. She did not do so, however, and the bedroom he might have had was given to her sister Marie—Tiny was her nickname—who came north to become Joe's personal secretary. Finally, Joe's own divorce came through on March 18, 1932, and less than a week later, on Thursday, March 24, he and Lillie Mae were married. Yet even then, secure in her new home and assured of the support of a doting, hardworking husband, Lillie Mae did not send for Truman.

Arch, for his part, often spoke about his "little angel," but the time he actually spent with him could be counted in hours, rather than days. At the end of February, he did treat him to a long weekend in New Orleans, and in April he grandly talked about spending the summer with him in Colorado. But when the first of June, the day he was supposed to assume custody, came around, he was, as usual, busy elsewhere. During the entire three months he had charge of him, Arch spent exactly two days with his little angel.

That did not prevent him from being outraged when Lillie Mae brought Joe down to Monroeville in July. His feelings toward her, which had warmed considerably after the divorce, had turned frigid again after she remarried. When she sent him a conciliatory letter, he scrawled on it "not interested" and mailed it back. When she accused him of failing to provide the required forty dollars a month in child support, he dispatched a letter of such vituperation that both John and his mother warned him that he might be violating postal regulations.

He soon had other, more pressing matters to occupy his thoughts. In early August he was in jail once again, confined to New Orleans Parish Prison for writing eighteen hundred dollars' worth of bad checks. This time John put up bail, wryly remarking to his mother that what Arch really needed was a guardian to keep him away from fountain pens and checkbooks. To no one's great surprise, he was uncontrite when he was released, blaming all his troubles on his good nature in trying to do a favor for a larcenous hotel clerk. "I am as innocent of wrongdoing as a baby," he maintained.

In the first week of September, 1932, what he feared most finally happened: belatedly asserting her rights and duties as a mother, Lillie Mae sent for her son. Accompanied by Lucy Brown, a black woman who was going north to be the Capotes' cook, Truman boarded a train for New York. Arch drove down from Birmingham to say goodbye, but he was too late and in a letter to John three weeks later expressed his bitterness and frustration: "Today is Truman's birthday. I did not have money to send him a present, or even a wire. I never hear from him or about him as of course the Spaniard forbids any communication with me. Isn't that a hell of a position to be in? Next summer, it will be a different story. I will take possession June 1st, and then somebody else will be up against a wall of silence. In fact, when I get on my feet, I am going to ask the Court for a new deal on the custodianship as her marriage changes the situation entirely, and I have good reason to think Truman's welfare is not best served by being in daily association with a man who must dislike him and what he stands for—especially a person of that type."

The truth about Joe was just the opposite. Far from disliking Truman, Joe was an indulgent stepfather, more likely than Lillie Mae to spoil him or forgive him when he was bad. To demonstrate to Arch how well they were all doing in New York—or, more likely, just to show off—Lillie Mae took Truman and Joe to visit Sam in October. The car was new, and Lillie Mae was "dressed to kill," Sam reported, "full of bull and brag" as usual. Yet Truman, he grudgingly acknowledged, was being well taken care of.

Lillie Mae's sudden affluence must have been galling, in fact, to everyone in the Persons family; even Sam and John, steady and industrious as they were, had been gravely hurt by the Depression. But to Arch her obvious prosperity must have been a particular wound. He not only was destitute, but also stood a good chance of being sent to Alabama's Angola State Prison—the toughest in the world, he observed, with customary hyperbole. At Christmas all he could afford was fifty cents to send Truman a telegram; that was enough to break even Sam's heart, and he sent the boy a pair of skates, with a card indicating that it came from his father rather than his uncle. More bad news still came Arch's way in the first week of 1933, when he received a subpoena from Monroeville, telling him that Lillie Mae, who had not received child support since the previous May, was petitioning the court for full custody. For once he had a good reason to feel sorry for himself; he was a man fighting off a pack of lions with his bare hands, he said.

He was not about to give Truman up without a struggle, however, and when Truman returned to Monroeville for the summer, Arch was determined that he stay there. The court hearing was scheduled for August, and while Lillie Mae was enjoying a belated honeymoon in Europe, he was preparing a surprise for her return. He would give up his three months of custody if she would give up her nine. Truman, the prize in that give-and-take, would be left with Jennie and Callie and would be allowed to leave Alabama only to attend the Gulf Coast Military Academy, Arch's own alma mater, in neighboring Mississippi. He was working hard, Arch wrote John, to save Truman from that "she-devil."

Everything he could do Arch did do. He hired Jennings Ratcliffe, a well-known local lawyer, to represent him, and he prevailed upon his old friend Bill McCorvey to talk to the judge, who had been the law partner of Bill's father. Arch persuaded his mother, Truman's grandmother, to write as well, and he sent a letter to the judge himself, reminding him that he had been a friend of his own father. "Little Truman," he told him, "is every inch a Persons—the image of my late father—and we do not propose to have him forced to adopt this Cuban as his father—in fact." As the day of the hearing approached, he radiated confidence. The judge was reported to be on his side, and lawyer Ratcliffe guaranteed victory. He was further heartened by Lillie Mae's general unpopularity thereabouts. After Truman had described the "fast life" she was leading in New York, her reputation, which had never been high, had sunk still further, he triumphantly reported to John. Lillie Mae, he predicted, would be in for a bad day.

That day was Thursday, August 24. Lillie Mae and her relatives testified in the morning, Arch and his friends in the afternoon. He tried to sell the judge as he had everyone else in his life. As he warmed to his subject, all of his disputes with Jennie were forgotten, and that house of ill and aging eccentrics was portrayed as the ideal place for a young boy to grow into adolescence. "I have never appreciated any home as much as theirs and probably never will," Arch said. "And I feel that his best interest would be served to keep him here among his kind of people. If the court were to award me the custody, the full custody, to have him to do with as I saw fit, I would take the child and place him in the same hands that I am asking that he be placed. I would not accept full custody."

He must have suffered a few uneasy moments when Lillie Mae's lawyer pressed him to admit that he had not contributed to Truman's support for sixteen months. He must have experienced a few more such moments when he was forced to own up to his collisions with the law. He had been arrested "five or six times," he said, but "just for foolishness every time." Nonetheless, when he walked out of the courtroom, Arch was convinced that he had won, and believed Lillie Mae thought so too. He accepted her invitation to dinner at the house that night as her graceful bow to defeat. The day was marred for him by only one thing: Truman's mail, he noticed, was addressed "Truman Capote."

Once again, however, he had succeeded in selling only himself. He did not want his son, but he did not want Lillie Mae to have him either, and the judge saw through him completely. The decision, which was handed down the following Monday, gave Lillie Mae absolute custody; Arch was given nothing. "I think it would be a calamity for the child to be placed in boarding school for months on end with not even a weekend at home," the judge declared. "No lonelier, more forlorn situation can be pictured. There is nothing in the record indicating unfitness on the part of the mother. Her present husband appears to be a man of means and responsibility, and willing to spend his means on his stepson. The best interest of the child lies with the mother." Almost immediately after hearing that, Lillie Mae and Truman left for New York.

Angry and bitter, complaining that he had been done in by small-town politics, Arch blamed everyone but himself. "I didn't know a man could be robbed of his child in a civilized country," was his despairing comment to John. Yet even Arch's mother, who had no more liking for Lillie Mae than anybody else in the Persons family, privately applauded the decision, telling John that she would not want to see a boy as young as Truman locked away in a boarding school. Lillie Mae would take care of him, she said, adding something Arch had either forgotten or considered too unimportant to take into account: Truman loved his mother.

Still, Arch persisted, more eager, it seemed, to get back at Lillie Mae than he was to have Truman. When he heard that Truman would be spending the summer of 1934 in Monroeville, he began plotting a second time to keep him there, convincing himself that Lillie Mae would give Truman up voluntarily if he threatened to expose her supposedly lurid past to Joe. "We have the goods on her in black and white," he told John, "and she will want to save her present soft bed." He never carried out his threat, however, and in April he walked into a federal court in Mobile to plead guilty to the forgery of a postal money order. His sentence, three years in the federal penitentiary in Atlanta, was suspended, but the close-up vision of cell bars apparently chastened him: he meekly agreed to let Joe adopt Truman as his legal son. He made only one condition: that Truman retain the Persons name.

Now in command, Lillie Mae was unwilling to give in even on that, and on July 11, 1934, she filed formal adoption papers in Manhattan's Surrogate's Court. Trying to prove Arch's unfitness as a father, she declared that she could not even find him to ask for child support. "My former husband makes it a practice to travel from place to place on the slightest occasion and in pursuits best known to him," she said with some venom. A helpful friend had sent her news of his conviction in federal court, and she added to her evidence the clipping from a Mobile newspaper. "SENTENCE IS SUSPENDED," read the headline; "MAN ENTERS PLEA OF GUILTY TO FORGING POST OFFICE MONEY ORDER."

Feeling himself cornered, Arch once again talked of blackmail. "Can you imagine anything so terrible as that—giving that gorgeous kid a legal spic name, and naming him for the man who stole my wife?" he asked John. "It beats storybooks." But when the adoption hearing began in Manhattan's Hall of Records on the morning of September 28, 1934, there was never any real doubt as to the outcome, and four and a half months later, on February 14, 1935, Lillie Mae's petition was granted: Joe became a father, and at the age of ten Truman Streckfus Persons was renamed Truman Garcia Capote. Arch alone clung to the old name, as if by doing so he could preserve his place as the rightful father. Finally, Truman himself asked him to stop addressing him the old way. "As you know my name was changed from Person's to Capote," he scrawled on a piece of school notebook paper, inserting, probably as a deliberate insult, an incorrect apostrophe in the family name. "And I would appreciate it if in the future you would address me as Truman Capote, as everyone knows me by that name."

8

WHEN he was in Alabama, Truman had longed to be in the North with his mother. Now that his wish had been granted, he looked back, with sharp and unexpected nostalgia, to his life in Monroeville. For several years before he joined her, he had known Lillie Mae only as a visitor, an adored relation who would suddenly appear, awing him with her beauty and glamour, and then disappear just as abruptly, leaving behind, like a whisper on the air, the promise that someday she would take him with her. From those tantalizing glimpses his busy mind had constructed a woman more of fiction than of fact. Much as he had done with Arch, he had turned Lillie Mae into a character out of one of his storybooks, someone who would transport him to a more romantic and exciting world, a place where he would be loved, protected, and ceaselessly admired.

Living with her in New York, he discovered that neither that world nor that woman existed in fact. The city was exciting, certainly, but big and alarming as well; even Brooklyn, where the Capotes had rented a house, seemed too fast and too impersonal to a boy who was accustomed to the amiable shuffle of Monroeville. If Lillie Mae had given him the love that Sook had poured on him as freely as bathwater, in time he probably would have become used to his new life. But the Lillie Mae who had smothered him with kisses in Alabama was stingy with her affection in New York. She had taken him with her, as he had prayed so many times, but the rest of the story was not following the plot he had imagined. His disappointment was complete, and he felt that she had betrayed him, as Arch had done so many times before. The difference was that Arch had promised only books and toys and trips to the Gulf Coast. Lillie Mae had promised herself, and that, it seemed, was the one thing she would not give him.

Her new husband commanded most of her attention, in any event, and there was little room in her life for Truman or anyone else but Joe. They were consumed by each other: instead of taming their romance, turning it toward the ordinary and the domestic, as is usually the case, marriage had made it more ardent and impassioned than it had been before, and all the affection they had been unable to give their former spouses they now rained upon each other. "They were madly in love," said Lyn White, one of Lillie Mae's closest friends. "They didn't want to do anything but be together."

To outsiders, their life together seemed charmed, almost enchanted. Living at the top of Joe's salary, and above, they appeared to have the best of everything: weekends at the racetrack, evenings at the theater or in fashionable nightclubs, vacations in East Hampton, Cuba, Bermuda, or even Europe, which they toured twice during the thirties. They were rarely still, and for them the Depression brought not hard times, but one long, boisterous party. All of Lillie Mae's ambitions had been realized. She was exactly where she wanted to be, doing precisely what she wanted to do, in the company of the only man she wanted to do it with. Like a lovely plant that had been stunted by lack of light, she blossomed under the sunshine of a happy, prosperous marriage, and before the decade was over, she had transformed herself from an unsophisticated country girl into a woman of worldly tastes and glamorous occupations.

The metamorphosis even included a change in her first name. Along with most of her Southern accent, she discarded the hillbilly name of Lillie Mae in favor of one that was more cosmopolitan, more in keeping with her new life—Nina—and to everyone but her friends and family in Alabama, Nina was what she was called henceforth.

The new Nina Capote had only one serious regret, and that was, having had a child with a man she did not love, she could not, several years into her new marriage, have one with a man she so fervently did love. But she had only herself to blame. Jennie and Arch had prevented her from having an abortion when she was pregnant with

Truman, but Joe was not able to stop her from terminating the two pregnancies that followed after she came to New York. "I will not have another child like Truman," she told him, "and if I do have another child, it will be like Truman." Something went wrong on the operating table during the course of one of those abortions, however, and she very nearly lost her life. The doctor, in a panic, called Joe in his office, demanding that he come and take her home. Although she soon recovered, she had suffered permanent damage to the reproductive organs, and a few years later, when she had changed her mind and finally did want to have a baby, she was no longer capable of doing so. She conceived two, perhaps three times; but each time she had a tubal pregnancy that ended in a miscarriage. "I think it did something to her head, because she was never the same afterward," Truman said. "She really wanted to have a child with him."

"If a man has been his mother's undisputed darling," Freud wrote, "he retains throughout life the triumphant feeling, the confidence in success, which not seldom brings success with it." The reverse might also be said, and a man who has been denied maternal esteem has also been denied that easy confidence, that wonderful feeling of triumph, with which the mother's darling automatically greets every morning. If he does manage to achieve success, he often views it not as a gift, not as a birthright, but as a loan, and for the rest of his life he worries that it may be snatched away and given to someone more deserving. The emotional cost, the tension and the anxiety, may be considerable. Such was to be the case with Truman, at any rate, and it is impossible to dispute his bleak and chilling judgment of his own mother: "she was the single worst person in my life."

She did not hate him; if she had, he could at least have hated her in return, simply and unconditionally. Nor, though she continued to dump him in the laps of other people, did she really ignore him; if she had, he perhaps could have ignored her too. What she did was worse. She let him know that after all the years, and after all her battles to gain custody from Arch, she still regarded him with ambivalence: she loved him and she did not love him; she wanted him and she did not want him; she was proud to be his mother and she was ashamed of him. Her feelings toward him oscillated between polar extremes, in other words, and from one day to another, sometimes from one hour to another, he could not predict how she would greet him.

The loving mother, the one he had known in Monroeville, remained warm and full of concern. The unloving mother looked on him suspiciously, as if he were not her child, but the son of the father he so much resembled—and only a poor substitute for the boy she really wanted to have and at last felt she should have had with Joe. This mother could be cold and cruelly critical, eager to find and eradicate fault.

She often accused him of lying, and she worried that he might have inherited Arch's inability to distinguish truth from falsehood. Joe tried to calm her, assuring her that all boys tell fibs, but she was not persuaded. Jealous of the monopoly Joe seemed to have on his mother's affections, Truman was not grateful for his help either. Joe did his best to be a good stepfather, but Truman went out of his way to antagonize him, making fun of his Cuban accent, for instance, by repeating, like a parrot, every word he spoke. Joe took such affronts patiently; Nina did not. Both his lying and his rudeness to her new husband were mere irritations, however, normal annoyances she could live with. What truly bothered her about Truman, what she found embarrassing and intolerable, and what she could not accept, was something he could do nothing about: his effeminate, girlish behavior.

People in Monroeville had already marked him down as a sissy, and for almost as far back as his memory carried him, he had been aware that he was the subject of talk, someone both his parents and his Faulk relations thought they had to defend and make excuses for. According to his Aunt Tiny, Nina's sisters refused even to let their children play with him because of his "sissyish traits." As the years passed, the differences between him and other boys became even more pronounced: he remained small and pretty as a china doll, and his mannerisms, little things like the way he walked or held himself, started to look odd, unlike those of other boys. Even his voice began to sound strange, peculiarly babylike and artificial, as if he had unconsciously decided that that part of him, the only part he could stop from maturing, would remain fixed in boyhood forever, reminding him of happier and less confusing times. His face and body belatedly matured, but his way of speaking never did. "His voice today is identical to what it was when he was in the fourth grade," observed one of his teachers many years later, when Truman was well into middle age. "I hear him on television or the radio and I recall him as a young boy."

Yet no one was more aware that something was wrong than Truman himself. For much of his childhood, until he was nine or so, he found being a boy so demanding and burdensome that he actually wanted to be a girl. "I didn't feel as if I were imprisoned in the wrong body. I wasn't transsexual. I just felt things would be easier for me if I were a girl." Any parent would have been concerned about such a boy. Nina, who had always been hypersensitive to the opinions of other people, was more than concerned; she was obsessed. When her New York friends made comments, she angrily stopped them—no one except his mother was allowed to criticize her son—but their remarks wounded nonetheless. Her problem with Truman was never far from her mind, and she made certain that it was never far from his mind either. She nagged him, bullied him, and belittled him.

When nothing she said or did helped, she took him to two different psychiatrists in hopes of finding a cure, a drug or therapy that would turn him into a real boy. One psychiatrist suggested that she not worry, promising her that the traits she disliked would disappear as he grew older. Whatever it was the other said to her, it annoyed her so much that she refused to tell even Joe what it was, leading him to suspect that the psychiatrist had blamed no one but her for Truman's odd behavior. She gave up on psychiatry after that, but she did not give up her search for a remedy. "She was always very worried about him," Joe said. "She wanted him to be an ordinary fellow, straight in every way. But Truman was reluctant to be an ordinary fellow. He had to be himself."

The Capotes did not remain in Brooklyn very long. When Truman returned from his Alabama vacation in the fall of 1933, they had already moved to an apartment on Riverside Drive in Manhattan, and at the end of September he began fourth grade at the Trinity School, one of New York's oldest and best private schools for boys.

Trinity, then a High Episcopal school, held morning prayers four days a week, required the boys to kneel for the litany on Friday, and celebrated Communion on holy days. It was a hard-marking institution whose primary goal was to send its students to Ivy League colleges. Although he was the butt of a few jokes, Truman was for the most part accepted, regarded by many of his classmates as the class mascot. He refused to join in team sports—which, fortunately for him, Trinity did not require—but when he was on his own, he was a surprisingly good athlete, an excellent swimmer and an accomplished figure skater who spent much of the winter practicing at the Gay Blades, a skating rink on the West Side. He enjoyed school theatricals, and not long after he arrived, he took the part of a blond-braided Little Eva in *Uncle Tom's Cabin*.

The first year he was at Trinity his grades averaged 83, which was considered good; but his average dropped to 78 in the fifth grade, then went down still further, to 73, which was considered only fair, in the sixth grade. The reason for the decline was clear to both his teachers and the school's administrators: he was a very disturbed child. "I always felt sorry for Truman," said one of them. "I had the feeling that he was somewhat of an unwanted child. There were problems at home, and his mother would call to talk about his temper tantrums, which I gather were not uncommon. She was completely at a loss to know what to do. The year he entered I witnessed one such incident myself. He was lying on his back in the hallway, kicking his feet like a child of two. He was obviously on the verge of hysteria." Like many disturbed children, he was a sleepwalker; on more than one occasion he suddenly woke up to find himself in pajamas in the lobby of his apartment building.

The people Nina called at Trinity were not very helpful, or, indeed, very sympathetic, and one of them, a teacher now long dead, probably compounded his problems. The teacher would sometimes walk him home, Truman said, stopping on the way at a movie theater, the Olympia, on upper Broadway. They would sit in the privacy of the back row, and while the teacher fondled him, Truman would masturbate the teacher. What effect that tawdry little scene had on a boy like Truman is impossible to say, but it was, at the very least, a sorry initiation into the mysteries of sex.

Nina did not know about those trips to the movies, but it was plain, even so, that Truman was not becoming the ordinary, masculine boy she wanted him to be. Coming from the South, she had known many boys, her brother Seabon included, who had proudly worn the uniform of a military-school cadet, and she reasoned that where she and the psychiatrists had failed, tough drill instructors and the company of other, more virile boys might succeed. Thus it was that after Truman had spent three years at Trinity, she decided to send him to military school. Joe argued with her, and so may have some of the teachers at Trinity. "How could she have been so insane as to send that boy to a military school?" asked one of them long after. "It was cruel, the last place in the world he should have been sent. I couldn't believe it." Where Truman was concerned, Nina always prevailed, and in the fall of 1936, shortly before his twelfth birthday, she registered him at St. John's Military Academy, a now-defunct Episcopal school in Ossining, New York, about thirty miles up the Hudson River from Manhattan. Arch's dream that his son should wear a cadet's uniform was to be fulfilled, albeit three years later and in a different climate altogether.

Truman himself was excited, thinking more, no doubt, about the pleasures rather than the pains of such a place, about the opportunity he would have to ride horses rather than about the martial discipline. In a rare burst of enthusiasm, he wrote Arch that he would soon be attending a "wonderful Military school." Once he was there, however, he quickly changed his mind, and it is impossible to imagine a boy who was less suited to a military education than Truman. He disliked wearing a uniform, and he was uncomfortable living in a dormitory. Although he made some friends, his fellow cadets were not so tolerant of him as the boys at Trinity had been, and they found a dozen ways to make his life miserable, including mocking his Southern accent and ridiculing his mannerisms. He was able to alter his accent; but his mannerisms neither he nor St. John's could change.

If Nina had deliberately wanted to encourage his manifest homosexual tendencies, she could not, in fact, have chosen a better place than a military school. St. John's did the exact opposite of what she thought it would do. The smallest and prettiest boy in his class, Truman was looked upon as sexual prey by several cadets—the tough, manly types he was supposed to emulate—and when the lights went out, he was occasionally forced into some stronger boy's bed. As he recalled it, none of what took place beneath those sheets went beyond adolescent sex play—kissing, fondling, and "belly rubbing," with him providing the belly and some bigger boy doing the rubbing. Still, the threat of coercion turned those relatively innocent sexual experiences into something ugly and unpleasant. "I was afraid of most of the boys at St. John's," he said. "They took sex very seriously. Instead of making me happy and secure, being chased after like that had the opposite effect. It was as if I were in prison. I've talked to a lot of prisoners and I know what it's like. There is always some young pretty convict everybody is after."

The end of the school year was the only escape from St. John's, and Nina was not about to take him out before then. During the months he was there, she seems to have pushed him out of her mind, as well as her life. She was pregnant when he left home—probably another reason for her sending him away—and she had the shock and pain of another miscarriage while he was gone. Even so, she was inexcusably negligent. St. John's was only an hour away from Manhattan, an easy journey by either car or train, but if Truman's count was correct, she visited him only twice during the school year.

Once again he felt rejected by his mother, but this time he did not have Sook to turn to. He was isolated and intensely lonely in his expensive jail cell on the Hudson. The Alabama judge who had rejected Arch's proposal to send him to military school was proved correct, and looking back, Truman's chief memory was of the hours he spent crying. "I would have been much happier if my mother had just left me in Alabama," he said. And very probably he was right. Even Nina must have realized that his year there had been a disaster, and in the fall of 1937 she sent him back to Trinity.

9

TRUMAN had been buffeted around so much, sent from place to place and pushed and pulled by so many different people, that until the first year of his teens, his own character was somewhat unfocused. The various pieces were there, but they did not form a pattern. Rather than allowing his own nature to take form, he had, until then, been reacting to what those around him, most particularly his mother, thought he should be. After that dreadful year at St. John's, he seemed to have hardened himself and to have begun, perhaps unconsciously, to come to terms with himself. He had attempted to become what his mother had wanted, and he had failed. Now, at the age of thirteen, he seemed to have given up trying, and his personality began to take the shape it was to keep through all the years thereafter.

He was no less anxious to be liked than he had been, but he was now old enough and experienced enough to seek favor on his own terms, deliberately and with design. The pocket Merlin who had enthralled Harper Lee with his fantastical tales was becoming a polished storyteller who promised entertainment every time he opened his mouth. The ordinary accomplishments of ordinary boys were beyond his reach, but he had an ability few of them could ever hope to match: if he wanted, he could charm almost anyone.

"It was fascinating to watch him," said Howard Weber, Jr., who was his closest friend at the time. "There would be very social pre-deb dances during the Christmas holidays. My aunt would give dinners beforehand for my cousin Louise, who was our age, and I would take Truman and three or four other friends along in tuxedos.

My aunt never forgot Truman, because when he walked in the door, all the boys would go over and sit around him in a circle, knowing that he would tell stories and entertain them. The girls would become wallflowers, all by themselves on the other side of the room. My aunt was fascinated to see the way it happened, but it did happen, it absolutely did! The explanation was that, unlike the girls at that age, Truman read everything and could talk about everything; he had a wonderful wit, and he had a biting sarcasm, which all of his friends thought was very funny."

Many adults were beguiled by him as well, and, overlooking his miserable grades, several of his teachers at Trinity made him a special favorite. "Mr. Putney, who taught dramatics, had a spot for Truman in every play we did," said Weber. "Since both Truman and I were rather good-looking, we were always girls, and in one play we joined with another boy to be three princesses sitting on a wall. Truman would get everybody into costume, and then he would tell Mr. Putney who should wear the red wig, who should wear the black wig, and so on. He was in his glory!"

At home he was still a disturbed child, however, and once again Nina was calling the school for advice. Although he was fourteen and in the eighth grade, he was still lying on the floor and kicking his legs in the air when he did not get his way. What should she do? No one at Trinity knew, or had ever before encountered such behavior in a boy his age. His teachers saw only a hint of his obstreperousness. "The biology teacher nearly went frantic over Truman, because he would sit in class and comb his hair all the time," Weber recalled. " 'Please put that comb away!' he would say. Truman couldn't have cared less. He would just go right on combing his hair." His grades reflected his cavalier attitude; he did poorly in all of his courses during his second stay at Trinity, barely passing several, including biology, and failing one, algebra, by a very wide margin. None of his courses, he had concluded, would help prepare him for his life's role. He had already decided what he wanted to do: he was going to be a writer.

He had arrived at that decision several years before. "For some reason I began to read in Alabama and discovered I loved it," he said. "Then one day, when I was nine or ten, I was walking along the road, kicking stones, and I realized that I wanted to be a writer, an artist. How did it happen? That's what I ask myself. My relatives were nothin', dirt-poor farmers. I don't believe in possession, but something took over inside me, some little demon that made me a writer. How else can it be explained?"

The same question might be asked, of course, about most writers who do not grow up amidst books or in the company of those who love them, and the answer is never satisfactory. Although the Faulks were neither poor, as Truman claimed, nor illiterate, as he implied, it is true that they were not readers. Except for the Bible, there was little to read in the house on Alabama Avenue.

To drop the question there would be misleading, however. Truman's background was not literary in a conventional sense, but more than he liked to acknowledge, it did provide a literary viewpoint, a way of looking at people as characters in a drama and a way of viewing life itself as a tale to be unfolded. His relatives did not read stories; they told them or listened to their neighbors telling them in the normal course of conversation. Plots, centering on family feuds, were close at hand, and on a hot summer night dozens of tales would be recounted on the front porches of Monroeville. Truman could not find many books in the Faulk house, but he heard the equivalent of hundreds in the soft, dusky hours between dinner and bed.

His father's side of the family was not bookish either, but in their own way the Persons clan were extremely literary. For years not a week passed without an exchange of letters between Arch's mother, Mabel, and her three boys, and a further exchange among the sons themselves. Mother and sons felt compelled to lay out their lives on paper, and taken together, their letters, which number in the hundreds, paint a multihued picture of both their family and the South itself during the Depression. Almost all are well written; many bear the imprint of true writers: they are vivid, uninhibited, and pungently phrased, with sudden and surprising flashes of insight. Truman inherited both their compulsion and their talent. He could read before he set foot inside a schoolroom, and when he was still in short pants, no more than five or six years old, he was carrying a tiny dictionary wherever he went, along with a pencil and paper on which he could scribble notes. He later set up a little office in a corner of his room on Alabama Avenue, and there he sat for hours tapping out stories on his own typewriter. By the time he entered Trinity, his choice of career was fixed and unshakable. "He's the only one I ever knew who at age twelve knew exactly what he wanted to do and discarded everything else," said his friend Howard. "He did not care about anything but writing."

There are few surviving examples of his early expeditions into the craft, and those few—sixteen themes, stories, and poems—were saved by one of his English teachers at Trinity, John E. Langford. Twelve were written in the sixth grade and four in the eighth, after he returned from St. John's. The sixth-grade efforts seem unremarkable for the most part, about what could be expected from a boy of that age, with many obvious grammatical errors and many more misspellings. The four later pieces, those from the eighth grade, are still the work of a boy, but now a boy with talent. Truman is self-consciously reaching for literary effects—a woman does not say something, she ejaculates; a man does not smile, he smirks in delight —but they move swiftly, with a small measure of grace, and so far as can be judged on such slim evidence, he is trying to give his work shape as well as size.

The most interesting story from those Trinity years, however, is one that exists only in memory. His ninth-grade English teacher, John Lasher, handed it one day to a colleague, C. Bruner-Smith, without saying who had written it. The story described, in a dream-like way, the sensation of rolling down a hill and tumbling into unconsciousness. "It was a rather lengthy manuscript," recalled Bruner-Smith, "and I was struck and impressed by it. It had to do with children, and it had a feeling that I found very remarkable. Very few writers, even great writers, are able to get inside the mind of a child. Mark Twain could do it, and so could Booth Tarkington. But Shakespeare couldn't. The story that Lasher handed me showed that facility. The spelling was bad, but I still couldn't believe that a boy of thirteen or fourteen could have produced it. 'Who wrote this?' I asked Lasher, and he answered, 'Truman Capote said he did.' And so he had."

Not long after that, Truman's life once again abruptly changed course, and in June, 1939, the Capotes left New York for Greenwich, Connecticut. They rented a house on Orchard Drive in the Millbrook section, a small upper-middle-class enclave that maintained a careful, if friendly, distance from the rest of the town. Stone columns marked its entrance from the main road, a private policeman patrolled its pretty, winding streets, and its ninety or so houses were, like the Capotes', all built in traditional Tudor styles. To give it a rural appearance, the people who laid it out in the twenties had left reminders of the country: hills, trees, streams, and two large lakes, which were used for boating in the summer and skating in the winter. Small as it was, the community had its own country club, to which only residents could belong. Millbrook was not the richest part of Greenwich, nor was it the most prestigious, but those who lived there usually stayed there; people from Millbrook tended to spend their time with other people from Millbrook.

Joe and Nina, gregarious both, soon felt at home. They brought with them their maid and her husband, whom they employed as chauffeur, and Nina was free to spend her afternoons shopping, playing bridge, or gossiping with other wives at the country club. Then, nearly every night, shortly after the commuting husbands returned from Manhattan, there would be a larger gathering. Liquor flowed freely in Greenwich, and the Capotes' new acquaintances enjoyed a good time as much as they did. For Joe and Nina, who had been enjoying themselves in such ways and with such friends for the better part of a decade, the party had merely changed addresses.

Surprisingly, considering the pain previous disruptions had caused him, the move to Greenwich was just as easy for Truman, who entered Greenwich High School as a tenth-grader in September. A few hostile remarks were directed his way, of course. By the standards of the time, he did not look right, sound right, or dress right; while the other boys wore slacks and shoes, he came to class, a generation too early, in sloppy-looking blue jeans and sneakers. But it was mild disapproval, all in all, and if Truman cared what was said about him, he did not show it. "Those who knew him accepted him as an equal," said one of his classmates, Crawford Hart, Jr. "He looked down his nose at the others."

Indeed, he probably welcomed the attention. At Trinity he had learned how to set himself apart from everyone else; at Greenwich he went a step further: he discovered how to turn the spotlight on himself and himself alone. "Truman was vividly nonconventional," said Thomas Flanagan, a classmate who later became a historical novelist of considerable renown. "He was full of energy and self-confidence, and quite flamboyant, a show-off. He had a sense of himself as a special person, a fact he was under no impulse to conceal from other people. For Truman to like you you had to have something special, like wit or social status. That was not a characteristic that was likely to win friends, and those who didn't like him—and they were a sizable group—would have described him as affected and precious. But he was not crushed by the harsh opinions of others."

What did crush him was to be ignored. Even to receive second billing in something as unimportant as a school play was hurtful to his ego, and he was keenly disappointed, Flanagan recalled, when he was assigned a bit part in an historical epic, *If I Were King*. While the rest of the cast swept across the stage in colorful costumes, he and Flanagan, who played executioners, were little more than props. It was obviously not a large enough role for a fourteen-year-old show-off, and Truman was determined to make it bigger. If he could not play François Villon, the man who saved France, he could at least be the most loquacious hangman in the history of the theater, and on opening night he used the script merely as a starting point for his own soliloquy on hanging: "Not every day of a hanging is like this. Do you remember four years ago when we hanged . . ." It was as if one of the spear carriers in *Hamlet* had pushed the lead aside to recite "To be or not to be," and even before the curtain was down, the furious drama teacher was chasing him across the stage— a scene that was doubtless more interesting, and certainly more amusing, than any that had preceded it. "At the end of the play Villon is almost hanged," said Flanagan, "and I thought to myself: 'If Truman really wants to star, next time he'll hang the son-of-a-bitch for real.' "

Such a display of ego did not make him popular, but Truman's real problem at Greenwich was not his fellow students; it was the school administration, which did not view kindly his poor attendance record, his refusal to work at anything that bored him, and his loud and adamant boycott of gym classes. "His attendance was very irregular, and he demonstrated his creativity with his excuses for his tardiness and absentee record," recalled Andrew Bella, the school principal. "His downfall was Physical Education. He was the despair of the coaches, and I remember one of his numerous visits to my office. Standing at the tall office counter, he spread his elbows like wings, his chin barely above the top, and announced defiantly: 'I will not take gym.' Our explanation that gym was required by state laws and that a doctor's excuse was necessary to get him out of it was of no avail. He thought it was not necessary for him."

. . .

Bad marks and failures—he flunked algebra, French, and Spanish —did not deter him from concentrating, doggedly and single-mindedly, on the only thing that mattered to him: his writing. Given his fierce determination, he doubtless would have persisted despite every discouragement, but every young writer, however confident, needs encouragement, someone older to assure him that his scribblings are not just adolescent doodles. Truman was no exception, and he had the extreme good fortune to come under the wing of an English teacher, Catherine Wood, who not only shared his faith in himself, but believed that it was her duty, her mission and sacred obligation, to help bring his talents to blossom.

He came to her attention as aggressively as he could manage. She was taking her students on a tour of the school library and had just picked out a book by Sigrid Undset to give to one of the girls. "Suddenly," she said, "this little fellow, who was not in my group, turned around from where he was sitting and interrupted me. 'Must be wonderful to read her in the original,' he said. 'Oh, I wouldn't think of anything else!' I replied, although of course I didn't know a word of Norwegian. From that time on I saw Truman, and when he came into my class the next year, in the eleventh grade, I saw him all the time."

A tall, gray-haired spinster who shared a house with another English teacher off the Post Road, Miss Wood invited him often to dinner, read his stories, catered to him in class, and encouraged her colleagues to do the same. "I made out a schedule for him," she said, "and tried to make the other teachers understand him, so that they would not expect a great deal from him. Some people objected to my doing that, and the principal, who did not appreciate him, wouldn't make any exception for him. So I told him: 'I know that the time will come when you would like to say that Truman Capote graduated from Greenwich High School!' " Even Nina could not escape the empassioned advocacy of this resolute woman with the long, sheeplike face. "His mother couldn't understand this boy who liked such different things," she said. "I remember sitting in my little dining room and saying to her that it was hard for me to tell his own mother this, but that in years to come the other, regular boys, who do the usual things in the usual way, would still be doing those things while Truman would be famous."

Truman himself was convinced of it, and the hours he spent

practicing his craft at last started to show results. At Trinity the best evidence of his ability had been his persistence; with a few exceptions, like his stream-of-consciousness description of rolling down a hill, his writing itself had not been unusual. At Greenwich his talent began to bud, if not flower, and it was soon displayed in the pages of the school literary magazine, which published several pieces of prose that were, considering his age, remarkably good.

Written when he was sixteen, the best of the lot is "Lucy," a beautifully painted portrait of Lucy Brown, the black maid who brought him north from Monroeville in 1932: her thrill at coming north, her eventual homesickness, and finally, her return South. "New York was just vast loneliness," Truman wrote. "The Hudson River kept whispering 'Alabama River,' yes, Alabama River, with its red, muddy water flowing high to the bank and with all its swampy little tributaries." The other pieces are equally proficient in terms of style, but are marred by contrived plotting and an obvious and self-conscious literary tone. Yet all his Greenwich works are highly polished, products of a surprisingly sure and confident hand. More important than technical competence, which many diligent students can acquire, they show a genuine and unmistakable gift for the creation of real and vital characters, which is, after all, the primary duty of any writer of fiction.

10

I F many of his contemporaries in Greenwich disliked Truman, those he wanted to be his friends, those he went after, he usually got. Few could resist the unrelenting onslaught of his affection. "He had a great, and immense, capacity for friendship," said Phoebe Pierce, one of the first to succumb. Others soon followed, and before long he was the leader of a sprightly and spirited Millbrook band, a group of a dozen or so that included, most prominently, the pretty little Jaeger sisters, Marion and Lucia, handsome Ted Walworth, wild Joan Ackerman, and Phoebe herself, whose ambition to be a poet was as strong as Truman's was to be a writer. Bright and lively, with the shining smiles, radiant confidence, and all-American good looks of models in a toothpaste ad, they were normality itself in that pre-war world of the jitterbug and the jalopy. Yet invariably, when they could not think what to do, they turned to the distinctly abnormal newcomer from New York. "Truman brought happiness into our lives," said Marion Jaeger. "He said, 'Let's do it! Don't be afraid!' He created the fun, and if we got bored, he would come up with an idea of how we could get unbored."

After school they would often rendezvous at his house, and his bedroom became a hangout where they could smoke Joe's long, dark Cuban cigarettes; drink liquor, mostly sweet fruit brandies they had filched from their parents; and dance to jazz records. On weekends they would move their boisterous convention to the cavernous old Pickwick Theater on the Boston Post Road. Emboldened by the omnipresent sweet brandy, which they would sneak in in paper bags, they would laugh when they were expected to cry, pretend to cry when they were supposed to laugh, and vie with one another in embellishing Hollywood's love scenes with a more amusing dialogue of their own invention. Eventually the actors themselves could not be heard above their din, and the weary ushers yet again would chase them out into the evening twilight. "We were out to shock and we did," said Phoebe. "We were just awful. We couldn't buy an ice cream cone without causing a riot. We were rude and intolerant, and we had perfected to the point of magnificence what the British army calls 'dumb insolence.' We did things partly to please ourselves and partly to set everybody else on edge. We were creative trouble-makers."

Friday or Saturday night, they might drive to nightclubs in nearby towns, like the Glen Island Casino in New Rochelle or Aladdin's Cave in Stamford, to dance to the music of the big bands. Truman, who was almost always short of cash, would depend on the dutiful Jaeger sisters to help pay his share of the bill; but there was one memorable occasion on which he made up for past omissions. All that day he walked the halls of Greenwich High, asking everyone he met for a penny to buy a stamp, and when they set out for Aladdin's Cave that night, his pants were sagging from the weight. "I've got a surprise," he explained mysteriously. Later, when the two sisters automatically reached for their purses, he stopped them. "This is my treat," he announced proudly. Emptying his bulging pockets, he covered the table with a coppery mound, hundreds of his hard-earned pennies. To the sputtering waiter he said: "Just because of your rudeness we don't care to come here again. We don't like the people who come here, anyway."

It was a privileged and, to all appearances, a carefree, idyllic life Truman and his company enjoyed in those months before Pearl Harbor. Spring and summer they would swim and play tennis at the country club. Winter they would skate on the upper lake, and Mrs. Jaeger would greet them with steaming mugs of hot cocoa when they returned, cold but exhilarated, to shore. Autumn they would attend a never-ending round of parties.

Nina herself organized one such party, a scavenger hunt, setting the example, with her usual flair in such matters, for many happy evenings to follow. "It was the Halloween of 1939," said Howard Weber, Truman's friend from Trinity days, who was visiting that weekend. "There was a full moon and it was a clear, crystal night, with a smell of burning leaves in the air. You had to draw a name out of a hat, and when I drew mine, Truman's mother said, 'Ah, you've got the cream of the crop!' She was right—the name I had drawn was Phoebe's—and off we went, shuffling through the un-raked leaves to people's doors, asking them to loan us statues of the Venus de Milo or whatever else was on our list. When we had found what we needed, we rushed back to the Capotes', where everybody danced, including the parents. The boys all wore coats and ties, and the girls looked sensational in their sweaters and skirts, saddle shoes, and camel's-hair coats. We had a great time. Truman had some wonderful friends, and I was so envious I could hardly see straight to watch them having as much fun as they were."

They were all good friends, but Truman's closest companion in those Greenwich years, the partner of his secret thoughts, was the girl Nina had exclaimed so over, the witty and amusing Phoebe. Truman met her at a party shortly after he arrived from New York, and once they started to talk, they found it hard to stop. "For the first time in my life I thought I could really speak to someone and share what I was feeling," said Phoebe, "and that person was Tru-man. We cared tremendously, deeply and passionately, about writ-ing and poetry. We loved *The New Yorker*, we loved Oscar Wilde, we loved Saki." They talked about everything in the weeks that followed, but no matter how far they let their imaginations wander, they always ended up on their fondest, most enduring dream: to move to Manhattan and become part of the smart literary life they were certain awaited them there. "Our dream was to get out of Greenwich and to go to New York," she said. "Manhattan was Oz to us, a place where we could let loose and enjoy ourselves."

Tall and attractive, with huge brown eyes and lustrous dark hair, Phoebe was a unique combination of several usually irreconcilable qualities. She was sophisticated far beyond her years, and as much as a girl in her early teens can be glamorous, she was glamorous, with a sure knowledge of how to dress and act and a never-failing ability to enliven any conversation. Even in her early teens she had the figure of a young woman; while the other girls went to parties in dresses that carefully covered the fact that they did not yet have much bosom to cover, she wore gowns that revealed that she most decidedly did. "My parents gave me a party," said Marion Jaeger, recalling one such time, "and my father, who was very German and very strict, said, 'Your mother will choose your dress.' She did and it was pink, with lace up to my neck. Then Phoebe came in in a strapless gown and took over the whole party. I was never so disappointed in my entire life. Truman pulled me into a corner and said, 'You look like a little old maid!' "

They were not yet old enough to move there, but in their midteens, Truman and Phoebe would sometimes visit Oz on a Saturday night. Not telling anyone else what they were up to, they would spend weeks collecting their money and putting their clothes together; by the time they were ready, the forty-five-minute train ride into Manhattan had taken on the colors of a daring, illicit adventure. They would first stop at a couple of the jazz joints that lined West Fifty-second Street, where they would listen to Billie Holiday, Dinah Washington, or Lionel Hampton; then, as midnight approached, they would walk a block or so east and fast-talk their way into those glittering seats of Café Society, El Morocco and the Stork Club. Truman had been to both places with Joe and Nina, but even his bravado wilted under the stares of headwaiters the first time he went alone with Phoebe. She looked as if she were going to a high school prom and wore white gloves and a white, full-length silk gown covered with sparklers. He looked like her little brother and was terrified that despite all their efforts, they had not scraped together enough money to pay the bill. "Don't order anything expensive!" he whispered as they sat down on one of El Morocco's zebra-striped banquettes.

They were not thrown out, however, and after that first nervous night they breezed through the door, those two brassy teenagers, as if they were the Duke and Duchess of Windsor. "We were such a wild-looking pair that the maître d's never knew what to say to us," said Phoebe, who thereafter left her gloves in their drawer and exchanged her sparkler-covered white gown for the black cocktail dresses the other women were wearing. "They always thought that Truman was too young to drink. But since I looked older, they would take a bet on us. We really got in because we were interesting to watch. We were both wonderful dancers—there was never anyone on the floor who could dance those Latin rhythms the way Truman could—and when we got onto the floor, we were forgiven everything else. We were an unusual couple, and we must have been figures of fun. So we danced for our supper."

They talked for it as well, making up for their perennial shortage of cash by mastering the knack of cadging drinks and dinners from charitable older couples at the bar. "We're on the hockey team at Princeton," Truman would joke, while Phoebe would display her expansive eyes and charm their barside benefactors with her effervescent chatter. After a night of such strenuous activity, they would rush out the door, like Cinderella leaving the ball, and race down to Grand Central Station, arriving just in time to catch the last train to Greenwich.

They climbed only rarely to such dizzying altitudes, however, and when they descended, they had to confront an unpleasant reality. All their friends knew that Phoebe was unhappy at home. Her mother was an alcoholic with a history of mental illness, and her father, whom she adored, died when she was sixteen. What their friends did not know was that Truman was equally miserable. Beyond New York and the nightclubs, beyond even their shared devotion to writing, Truman and Phoebe had in common a similar sadness. Their secret excursions to New York were not only trips to Oz; they were also escapes from the ugly scenes they found inside their doors. "What an odd and lonely pair of children we were!" marveled Phoebe. "We were like a brother and sister, and we helped each other through the dark, because really, life was terribly lonely for both of us."

Loneliness was nothing new to Truman, of course. From earliest childhood he had felt isolated and unwanted. Even during the happy times with Sook, even while he was enjoying the exuberance of the Millbrook gang, he lived with the knowledge, sometimes distant, sometimes close, that things were not right at home. His mother's ambivalence toward him had neither died nor lessened in the years since she had brought him North. It had instead become more pronounced, and when she had been drinking, as she did more and more in Greenwich, the loving, good Nina could change into the bad and unloving Nina with terrifying speed.

The good Nina was the one most of his friends saw, the woman who made the Capote house on Orchard Drive an inviting and congenial place for them to meet. Gregarious and fun, she treated his friends as her friends, laughing with them at risqué jokes, dancing with them, and winking indulgently at their infractions of ordinary rules. Few other mothers would have put up with their noise, looked the other way when they smuggled in their stolen bottles of liquor, or pretended not to see them carry out the empties. "We were all just smitten with her," said Howard Weber. "She seemed very young, and we thought of her as being more of our generation than that of our parents."

This public Nina was also a devoted mother whose concern for her son was shown in little things as well as big. Howard Weber, who visited often, noticed, for example, that she would stop whatever she was doing to give Truman a fond but careful scrutiny before he went out at night, wetting her finger with her tongue to slick back his straying cowlick and unruly eyebrows. And, added Weber, "when she and Joe went out, she never failed to come into his room when they returned. Truman and I made a pretense of being alseep, but we were usually wide awake, having made a mad dash for the beds after polishing off a bottle of apricot brandy. She would tuck him in, kiss him good night, and check to see that the windows were closed. She always seemed very fond of him in front of me."

Yet even those who liked her best noticed something unusual about her relationship with Truman. She did not seem comfortable playing the role of his mother, and if she treated his friends as equals, she also treated him as an equal—like a brother or perhaps a lover, but rarely like a son. It was the old story updated. She could be protective and loving, and she could also be cruel and degrading. "Sometimes I thought she hated him because of the way he behaved," Joe said. Truman returned her ambivalence with an ambivalence of his own. Just as she loved him, he loved her, and just as she hated him, he hated her. "No one made him as happy as she could," said Phoebe, "and no one got under his skin the way she could. It was the kind of relationship that would make teams of psychiatrists happy for years."

More and more, the bad Nina was released by a bottle of Scotch, and within months after she arrived in Greenwich, Nina—chic, sophisticated, fastidious Nina—had turned from being a woman who likes to drink into a woman who likes to drink too much. Joe claimed that she started to drink heavily because she was ashamed of Truman and worried that he was becoming homosexual. "She wasn't realistic about him," he said. "She didn't want to face facts." Her brother Seabon, who worked in New York, thought, on the other hand, that she drank because of her problems with Joe. Their remarkable passion had not cooled over the years—"I loved my wife and she loved me," Joe said—and each reacted strongly to the smallest hint of a flirtation by the other. Marion Jaeger recalled a time when Joe, who was teaching her the steps to a Latin rhythm, was brusquely pushed aside by Nina. "I'll teach Marion," she said. On the other side, Joe himself recalled another incident, similar to the one at the Stork Club a few years earlier, when he caught another man putting his arm around Nina at a party. "I grabbed his hand," he said, "jerked it away, and pushed him so hard that he fell down. Oh, I was so goddamned mad!" Both were still attractive, with an appeal that photographs cannot convey. "Nina had a sexual allure that just oozed," said Lucia Jaeger. "My mother was a pretty woman, but if she and Nina were together, men would look at Nina and not at my mother." Joe, at the same time, had a Latin charm that many women found almost irresistible.

That Latin charm carried with it a Latin attitude toward marriage, and he could not resist amusing himself with other women—"a shot here, a shot there," as he later said. Occasionally he would spend a Saturday with a girlfriend in New York, asking young Carl Jaeger to drive him to the train station in Port Chester, so that no one in Greenwich would wonder why he was traveling into Manhattan on a weekend; then, at his request, Carl would call Nina to tell her that he had gone into the city. "I know," would be her leaden reply. But his infidelities gnawed at her. In retaliation, she engaged in one or two affairs of her own. She lavished so much attention on some of Truman's good-looking friends that Truman later suspected, with some reason, that she had gone to bed with one of them as well.

Her life was not perfect, but still, from all outward appearances, she had achieved as much as she could have dreamed of when she was Lillie Mae Faulk, wistfully looking at the roads leading away from Monroeville. She had achieved as much even as Arch, that purveyor of promises, had offered her on that long-ago April in Troy. All that she had was in the end not enough, and she harbored a terrible disappointment—exactly what it was no one could say— that she did not have the will or the strength to confront. In a place where there was little for an intelligent woman to do and where everyone else drank so much, it was easy to find relief in alcohol. Before long, she would start filling her glass with Scotch in the afternoon, and she would continue filling it through the evening and into the night. She was not a reeling, messy drunk, and few of her friends in that boozy town would not have called her an alcoholic at all. But she was, and Truman suffered because of it.

"The clue that she had been drinking too much was a kind of ominous, razor-edge gaiety," said Phoebe, who had learned the symptoms from her own mother. "She could turn in a moment from almost being unpleasant to being very unpleasant indeed. She could be very nasty to Truman." During one drunken rage she tore up one of his manuscripts in front of him; another time she accused him of stealing the idea for a story from a novel she had read. Both actions seemed designed to destroy the one thing he had confidence in, his knowledge that he could write. Her usual target, however, her main source of anger toward him, was what it had always been: his inability to look, act, or be like other boys. Miss Wood and all her pleas for tolerance had had no effect whatsoever. "You're a pansy!" Nina would scream at him. "You're a fairy! You're going to wind up in jail. You're going to wind up on the streets."

Truman reacted the way any child of an alcoholic parent does— with confusion, embarrassment, and rage of his own. "I was furious with her practically all the time because of her drinking," he said. "She kept me in a constant state of anxiety." Fueled by his anger, his own behavior was still often that of a disturbed child. He no longer kicked and screamed on the floor, but he could be equally, and impossibly, immature. Once, one of his friends saw Joe give him a reprimand for some supposed misdeed. Truman answered by spitting in Joe's face, an insult that Joe, as usual, stoically ignored. Propelled by his talent and ambition, Truman had leaped far beyond his age in some ways; emotionally he was still a small boy.

Nina had been right in one of her drunken accusations, and that which she had long been frightened would happen had happened: Truman was now, clearly and unambiguously, a homosexual. Looking as he did and acting as he did was at this point, ironically, something of a blessing. He could not hide what he was—not even from himself—and he never was afflicted with the paralyzing doubt and guilt that ruin the lives of many young homosexuals, who do not find out for years, or sometimes ever, who they are. By his mid-teens Truman knew who he was; indeed, he probably had known, unconsciously at least, since he was a child. "I always had a marked homosexual preference," he said, "and I never had any guilt about it at all. As time goes on, you finally settle down on one side or another, homosexual or heterosexual. And I was homosexual."

Just as she had years before, when she unsuccessfully took him to psychiatrists, Nina tried once again to change him, packing him into the car one afternoon for a mysterious trip to New York. Truman bitterly recalled the day: "When we were on our way, she said to me, 'I'm taking you to Dr. Murphy. I think you're homosexual, and I want him to give you some male-hormone shots.' In effect, she was saying, 'I think you're homosexual, you little monster!' I said, 'Stop the car this minute!' and she pulled off the road. 'You're an idiot,' I said. 'I've got news for you. I am homosexual, and you're not taking me to Dr. Murphy, whom you were going to bed with up until two years ago.' She leaned over and slapped my face as hard as she could, and I just looked at her. 'If you ever do that again,' I said, 'I'll break your nose. I'll do just what I want to do.' After that she didn't bother me about it, though she complained that I was homosexual to everyone who came within earshot."

And so she did. "Well, my boy's a fairy," she would say to a group of his friends, who, frozen with embarrassment, would try to laugh, pretending that she was making a joke. In fact, some of them may not have known what she meant. Not many people talked openly about homosexuality at that time, and though they knew he was different, of course, few of his friends, even sophisticated ones like Tom Flanagan, who had read Oscar Wilde and knew about such things, guessed his sexual inclination. "He was very affectionate," said Marion Jaeger, one of the many who remained in the dark, "and he would hug and kiss like all the other boys." Their parents usually knew what Nina was talking about, though a friend of the Webers was the only one rude enough, or drunk enough, to say so. "How can you let your son have contact with this obviously raging fairy?" she asked Howard's mother and father.

By his mid-teens, Truman had formed some romantic attachments. He had a long-standing relationship with a boy he had known in New York, and he later developed a passionate crush on another boy in Greenwich, a tall, handsome, athletic classmate— someone, in short, who was the exact image of the son Nina wanted. Although he was, in his own way, good-looking, Truman did not feel attractive, and he used all his considerable cunning to seduce his idol, flattering him, smothering him with attention, and opening a bottle of bourbon every time he entered the door. Eventually his efforts succeeded.

"He was the handsomest boy I've ever seen, and the most popular boy in school," he said, sounding like a fisherman who will carry with him forever the moment of triumph and elation when he hooked the biggest trout in the lake. "Everyone, boys and girls, was crazy about him. And the funny thing was—he chose me! We used to go off in his car and neck, and we had an active mutual-masturbation scene. Finally, one day I decided that this had gone on too long, and I reached down and gave him a blow job. For some reason that bothered him, and he felt very guilty about it. But not guilty enough to stop. Then on my sixteenth birthday he gave me a book of poems by Edgar Allan Poe, in which he had inscribed, 'Like ivy on the wall, love must fall.' That tore me apart, and I cried, because I really did love him. We had sex after that, but emotionally it was never the same. Some connection had been broken."

As he grew older, Truman's connection with Phoebe also became strained. He knew that there was no hope of romance between them, but irrational as it was, he nonetheless felt angry and rejected when he saw her dating other boys. His jealousy was as virulent as his mother's. He did not want Phoebe for himself, but he did not want anyone else to have her either. In his anger he even attempted to keep potential boyfriends away, spreading rumors that she was not interested in the opposite sex at all, a tactic that fooled no one. For a time, frustration and rage consumed him: a visitor saw him throw her picture into the fireplace, then spit on it every time he walked by. "As much as Truman could be in love with a woman, he was in love with Phoebe," said one of their friends. It was, however, only a partial and, to her, an unfulfilling love. "He loved me for the person I was, not the woman I was," she said. "Several times he asked me to marry him. 'You could live your life,' he said, 'and I'll live mine.' I told him, 'Truman, I couldn't bear it.' " Nor could he have. His road led in a different direction, and now, with no qualms or second thoughts, he began to follow it.

TWO

Six months after Pearl Harbor, in June, 1942, the Capotes abandoned Connecticut and, with a collective sigh of relief, moved back to New York. They had had good times as well as bad in Greenwich, but all in all, their three years there had not been a success for any of them—and for Nina they had been calamitous. "Goodbye, girls, I'm going back to the city," a jubilant Truman yelled to the Jaeger sisters as his train began to pull out of the Greenwich station. Then, in his excitement, he accidentally pulled the emergency cord, bringing his departure to a lurching halt. "Let's go before anybody sees us," Lucia said to Marion. "How many times can Truman embarrass us?" He eventually reached Grand Central Station nonetheless, and the Capotes quickly established themselves in an apartment at Park Avenue and Eighty-seventh Street, on Manhattan's Upper East Side.

The happy part of Truman's Greenwich life had ended that month, in any event, when high school graduation ceremonies sent his little Millbrook band scattering off to college or into the armed forces. Truman, whose bad grades prevented him from receiving a diploma with the rest of the class of '42, did neither. After a trip south to see Arch, who had finally found his gold mine—marriage to a woman of means in Louisiana—at Nina's insistence he began his senior year all over again at the Franklin School, a private school on the West Side. Catering mainly to students who could not get into better places, Franklin gave him a light schedule, allowed him to come and go as he pleased, and indulged him by looking the other way when he skipped classes, which he did frequently, without guilt or regret.

He had never paid more than passing attention to school or grades, of course, but even if he had, how could he study when everything he wanted, all that he and Phoebe had talked about and dreamed about in their Greenwich exile, was at his doorstep? "In New York," said Phoebe, who was in Manhattan herself, attending Barnard College, "Truman was happy and free for the first time in his life." The little boy from Monroeville who had been terrified of sidewalks and tall buildings when he arrived ten years before had grown into a young man who had a romantic attachment to the city, "this island, floating in river water like a diamond iceberg," as he was soon to write.

He had an immense capacity for friendship, Phoebe had said, and he demonstrated it soon enough. He met a girl, Eleanor Marcus, who introduced him to her sister Carol. Carol, a "licensed screwball," in Phoebe's words, was enchanted by him and introduced him to her own best friends, Oona O'Neill and Gloria Vanderbilt. For the next several months, through the end of 1942 and well into 1943, they were a foursome: Carol, the blond madcap; Gloria, the most famous heiress of the era; Oona, the daughter of the country's greatest playwright; and Truman, the amusing newcomer from the suburbs. Truman had lost Phoebe, but he had gained three substitutes, each unusual and each remarkably attractive in her own, quite distinctive way.

Now he was at El Morocco or the Stork Club all the time. Sherman Billingsley, the Stork Club's owner, was delighted to welcome three girls who were so often in the columns and offered them—and Truman too—free lunch. In the afternoons they would go to a favorite bar on East Fifty-third Street, where they would ask the piano player to play Cole Porter's least popular songs. At night they might return to the Stork Club or El Morocco. "We thought we were being terrific," said Carol, "and we thought that the Stork Club was a terrific place for us to be." Truman finally felt at home, just where he wanted to be. New York was fun, exciting, and glamorous, and he now loved the very things that once had made him hate it—its crowds, its frenzied movement, its intensity. But the nightclubs and amusing people were only part of its appeal. Most of all, he had learned to appreciate the opportunity waiting for him on that glittering but dangerously slippery chunk of ice.

Armed with an almost religious vision of his career as a writer—
no martyr to the Cross had ever been more certain in his faith—he
could almost touch his brilliant future as he walked down Fifth
Avenue. It was all but within his grasp, that idealized future, casting
its spell on him, leading him onward as surely as the promise of
riches had once led Arch on. But Truman would not deceive himself
with crazy schemes, as his father had done, or sit back and wait for
fortune to smile. He would ruthlessly seize his glorious future the
way a condor does its prey, and in a poem, "Sand for the Hour
Glass," that he wrote for the Franklin literary magazine, he boldly
said so. Constructed out of metaphors of violence—he compared
himself to that condor searching for its dinner—the poem is a young
man's manifesto, a declaration of war against a world not so much
hostile as indifferent, which was, in Truman's eyes, almost worse.
He planned to be famous:

> Like the mighty Condor,
>   Its vulture wings
>   Against a copper sky,
>   I have waited and watched,
>   For my prey!
>   My victim is immortality—
>   To be somebody and be remembered—
>   Is that not, too, your idle dream?
>   For in remembrance we hold life itself
>   Cupped tenderly in aged hands.
>   You say—"He's a fool and a dreamer."
>   I laugh and let my laughter,
>   Like a bright and terrible knife,
>   Go tearing through your hearts!
>   For you know and I know,
>   No matter how young, how old,
>   We are only waiting,
>   Waiting to see our names in Scriptures of Stone.
>   So it is today and so it will be tomorrow!

How could the world resist a will so determined, an ambition so
pointed?

Even a young condor does not find its prey the day it leaves the
nest, and Truman's first step into New York's literary world was

also that of a fledgling. Sometime toward the end of 1942, or perhaps the beginning of 1943, while he was still attending Franklin, he found a part-time job as copyboy on *The New Yorker*, a magazine he and Phoebe only months before had been talking about in the hushed tones of worshipers at a shrine. Reading it every week in Greenwich, they thought it the ultimate in wit and sophistication, and to Truman, as well as many other young writers, its dingy offices on West Forty-third Street seemed like the best possible place, perhaps the only possible place, for a sensitive writer to find congenial employment. At last one of his dreams was coming true.

Working in that strange and eccentric place was not as enjoyable as he had envisioned, however, and there was none of the conviviality of a newspaper city room along those chilly and unfriendly corridors. Many writers never came into the office at all, and those who did seldom spoke. Introductions were rarely made, it was considered a grave breach of etiquette even to speak in the elevator, and people could see one another every day without exchanging so much as a nod. For years Edmund Wilson, the magazine's literary critic, mistook the art editor for the fiction editor, for example, and one of the female staffers believed that a middle-aged messenger to the printer, who wore a black derby and carried an air of shabby gentility about him, was Wilson himself. When Truman arrived, much of the staff had gone or was going off to battle, and the atmosphere in those nineteenth-floor offices was even more rarefied and peculiar than it had been in peacetime. "*The New Yorker* is a worse madhouse than ever now," complained E. B. White, "on account of the departure of everybody for the wars, leaving only the senile, the psychoneurotic, the maimed, the halt, and the goofy to get out the magazine. There is hardly a hormone left in the place. . . ."

Although Truman probably did not know it when he walked in that first morning, aglow with excitement, *New Yorker* copyboys had never been looked upon as potential writers or reporters, as they often were at other publications, and with the war, they were held in even lower regard than before. They tended to be either old and decrepit, thieves, or whistlers—Harold Ross, the magazine's editor, could not stand whistlers—and for one reason or another, many were hired and fired in the same week. Those who stayed were supposed to be silent and, if at all possible, invisible. Hiring Truman, then, was a sign of wartime desperation: by any measure, he was the most visible, least silent copyboy the magazine had ever had in its employ—or probably has had since. Indeed, those supposedly sophisticated people he and Phoebe had admired from a distance might just as well have been farmers from Iowa the way they gawked at him as he sharpened pencils and carried manuscripts. They were accustomed to odd-looking writers—the halt and the goofy, as White had called them; but they were not accustomed to odd-looking copyboys, particularly one who, in the words of William Shawn, then the nonfiction editor, seemed "like a small boy, almost like a child."

Shawn's description was not an exaggeration; at eighteen, Truman could have passed for a boy of twelve. He had no visible trace of a beard; he was still unusually short, perhaps not even as tall as his adult height of five feet, three inches; and he remained unnaturally pretty, with wide, arresting blue eyes and blond bangs tumbling over his forehead like a thatch of straw. If his appearance did not shock, his childlike voice did—it was so high, went one unfriendly joke, that only a dog could hear it. Truman may have thought of himself as a bird of prey, but to his new colleagues he seemed like an exotic breed of canary. "For God's sake! What's that?" Ross himself demanded when he peered out of his office and saw him drifting down the hall.

Before his first week was out, he was one of the chief topics of hallway conversation. Two of the elevator men were so confused that they bet a dollar on his gender. "You're going to lose your money," Ebba Jonsson, the librarian, told the loser. "It is definitely a boy." One of the women was so vividly impressed by him that she dreamed that his veins were filled with milk—whole or skimmed, she did not say. Truman added to the chatter, no doubt deliberately, by having his lunch delivered not from delicatessens, as everyone else did, but from expensive midtown restaurants, like "21" and Le Ruban Bleu. A rumor circulated that he was rich, and when someone saw him at a nightclub with one of his celebrated girlfriends, the rumor became established fact. Much of the reaction might have been predicted by anybody who knew him and his many ways of gaining attention. What could not have been foreseen, however, and what really caused heads to turn, was something that was in fact remarkable: Truman, almost alone on the staff, had managed to make a friend of Daise Terry, the terrible-tempered office manager.

A short, elderly woman of notoriously mean and cantankerous disposition, Terry frightened everyone, editors and copyboys alike.

Very few on the magazine liked her, and she liked very few of them. "She was a wicked, wicked woman," said Andy Logan, who had just begun her long career as a reporter for the magazine when Truman arrived. "I once saw a copyboy weeping bitterly after one of her tongue-lashings, and I know a man now who was once an office boy here and who will still, in late middle age, wake up in a cold sweat remembering that awful woman."

How Truman tamed her no one knew, but he had always had a knack, like that of a stray dog, for finding and making himself agreeable to those, like his high school teacher Miss Wood, who could help him. "It's in his stars, or his destiny, or his health line, or whatever you want to call it, that he travel in the right direction," said one friend at the time. "His instinct leads him to the people who are on his side." But opportunism was only half of the equation; he also genuinely liked the people who were on his side. He did not pretend to be Terry's friend because she could help him; she could help him and that made him her friend. It was a perfect marriage of affection and opportunism.

"She was a very feisty little woman and quite lonely," he said. "Everybody hated her but me. Even Ross was afraid of her. But she was totally devoted to the magazine, and there wasn't a thing that went on there that she didn't know. She thought of me as some sort of child, which I was in a way, and she always used to cover up for me when I did things that were kind of sloppy." Soon, despite the nearly half-century separating them, that incongruous couple would be seen leaving the office together for lunch, going off to dinner and the theater after work, even meeting on Saturdays, when the office was closed. His friendship was rewarded, and as the other copyboys watched enviously, she became his protector. When it rained, someone else would run errands outside the building; when there was late duty, someone else would be stuck with it. Finally, after only a few weeks, she gave him the best job of all, copyboy for the art department.

In a very minor way, the art department's copyboy performed an editorial function, sorting through the dozens of unsolicited cartoons and cartoon ideas that were submitted every week and separating the possibles from the impossibles. The art director would select from the gleanings, then show his own choices to Ross, Gus Lobrano, the fiction editor, Rea Irvin, who had drawn *The New Yorker*'s first cover, and Terry, all of whom would attach their comments to each drawing. That Tuesday-afternoon conference was always a loud, lively session, and when Ross did not like or understand a cartoon, which frequently was the case, his voice could be heard "baying the moon of despair," as James Thurber phrased it. "Do women wear hats like that today?" was a question he might ask; or he would complain that a figure that was supposed to represent an army major looked like "a goddamn doorman."

"The copyboy's job was to clean the place, put all the chairs in order, and make sure that Ross's knitting needle was there," said Albert Hubbell, who was the art director during much of Truman's tenure. "Ross would sometimes get very excited and jab at the drawings to point things out. When he used a pencil he would leave marks, and someone thought to provide him with a dull knitting needle, which was harmless. When the copyboy had prepared everything, he gathered all the drawings—there were usually thirty or forty—and held them up on an easel for the editors to look at. Until then the art boys had always been automatons. Not Truman. He would make faces when he didn't like something, laugh when he did, and react to what the editors said. That was unheard of, and Ross asked me: 'Who is that boy? Where did he come from?' Then he said: 'Tell him not to do that. We don't need another opinion.' I told Truman, and he pretty well shut up after that. But he couldn't resist little asides once in a while."

Dozens, even hundreds of drawings had to be kept in order, and occasionally Truman would be drowned in the deluge. "Sometimes I would get the cartoons all messed up and confused. Then I would just throw them into one of those holes and say to myself, 'Well, I'll straighten that out later.' I managed somehow to lose about seven hundred of them that way. I didn't deliberately destroy them, and I don't know how I lost track of them. But I did. Understandably, a lot of people were very annoyed. That was one of those times Daise Terry covered up for me."

After the editors had made their decisions, Truman would pass them along to the artists, commiserate with those whose drawings had been rejected, and generally hold their hands. For Thurber, who was almost blind, he had to do a good bit more. It was his onerous duty to lead Thurber around, convey him to his assignations with one of the magazine's secretaries, and even wait in her living room while the two of them consummated their loud passion in the bedroom. Their lovemaking, he later complained, sounded as romantic as the squeals of hogs being butchered. When the noise had stopped, he would help Thurber on with his clothes. Once he put Thurber's socks on wrong side out, and a sharp-eyed Mrs. Thurber, who had put them on correctly that morning, noticed the difference. The next morning the artist accused him of having made the mistake on purpose. "Thurber was the rudest, meanest man I've ever seen," Truman said. "He was terrifically hostile—maybe because he was blind—and everybody hated him but that one secretary he was going to bed with. She was the ugliest thing you've ever seen, but he didn't care because he couldn't see her."

For a humor magazine, *The New Yorker* was a serious, somber place to work, and Truman, who could not suppress his high spirits, betrayed a noticeably cavalier attitude as he went about his humble duties. In a playful parody of his job, he found a big feather duster and made a great show of dusting desks. "Everybody was being drafted at that time," said Hubbell, "and one night he came to me and said, 'I've got my greetings. I've got to go to Grand Central Station tomorrow for my examination, and they may ship me out right after that.' So we gave him a little party just in case they did. But when I walked in the next morning, there he was, with a cloth around his waist and the feather duster in his hand. 'I've been turned down for everything,' he told me, 'including the WACs.' " Truman later explained why he was not sent off to war: "They thought I was quite neurotic. I wasn't at the examination center even fifteen minutes before they said, 'We will postpone this.' And I never heard from them again."

Everybody at the magazine seemed to recognize that the art department's copyboy was more than just unusual-looking, and he made no secret of his intention to be a writer. "He used to stand behind my desk," said Barbara Lawrence, who had a second-level editorial job, "and one day he said, 'You know, I write stories.' " He showed her some, and for the next few years she read them, giving support and suggestions, much as Miss Wood had done in Greenwich. "Most of Barbara's ideas were about cutting things," he said. "She was a very, very good cutter. At that time I had a tendency to not block my paragraphs properly, to let them run on too long. She was very helpful about breaking them up and that sort of thing."

She was the only one who was helpful, or offered encouragement, and in the inexplicable ways of magazines, he was not even allowed a tryout as a writer. "There was a tendency—*New Yorker* snobbery —not to take office boys seriously," said E. J. Kahn, a staff writer for many years. "And they thought that Truman was an effeminate, silly little boy." One of his side duties, after sorting cartoons, was to scour the newspapers for ideas for "The Talk of the Town," the section of anecdotal items about comings and goings in New York. But when he asked to report and write a few "Talk" pieces himself, he was refused. "Even though we thought that he could probably do it," said Shawn, "we didn't see how we could send anybody that young to report for us." Truman also submitted some of his short stories to the fiction department, which gave them mild praise, but turned them down as well. "Very good. But romantic in a way this magazine is not" was Truman's memory of one such remark. "It is a scandal that we didn't publish any of Truman's short stories," said Brendan Gill, *The New Yorker*'s unofficial historian. "But it's also a scandal that we didn't publish anything by Hemingway or Faulkner and only one story by Fitzgerald."

Scandal or not, Truman doubtless was hurt by such persistent rejection from a magazine he had once revered. Although he was always to retain an admiration for *The New Yorker*, he was no longer awed by it, or the people who worked for it. "Nobody cared what happened outside that office. They were very strange, secretive people, like bears that hide themselves away in caves at the zoo. Shawn never came out of his cave, and E. B. White wouldn't come out even when the keeper rapped on his door. Everyone—literally everyone —was scared to death of Ross. He looked ferocious, and he was ferocious. Even I was frightened, and I don't scare easily. There has never been such a collection of bitchy people. They were all obsessive gossips, and they were absolutely consumed with one another. I was never gangy or very chummy with any of them. I guess one of the real reasons was that I knew they were going to stay there, and I wasn't. It was like being in a school where you knew certain people were going to graduate and certain people weren't. But I'm glad I was there. At that time it was probably the best magazine in the world, and working there was a hell of a lot better than going to college."

He thought that he was ready to graduate from *The New Yorker* in the fall of 1943, when he quit so that he could write full time. Manhattan was not the place to do that, however, and the Capote apartment provided neither peace nor privacy. Nina, who was still drinking, was disruptive and often hostile, moreover, and objected, even when she was sober, to the noise his little portable made when he typed on the kitchen table. Inevitably, his eyes looked south, and he returned to the home in which he had spent most of his childhood, to Monroeville and Jennie's house on Alabama Avenue. But he could not write there either. The comfortable old house he had known had burned down in 1937, and the new one was as inhospitable as the Capote apartment. "This is *certainly* not the place," he wrote Arch on December 2, in one of his rare letters to his father. "I have a cold and feel rotten, it's so damned uncomfortable here. I think I will be going back to New York soon as Alabama is definitely not a writer's haven."

Within weeks he was back in Manhattan, sorting cartoons at *The New Yorker*. His final exit from the magazine, in the summer of 1944, was both more sudden and more unpleasant than he could have wanted. Despite the lack of encouragement, he had been writing all along, and in August he used his vacation to attend Vermont's Bread Loaf Writers' Conference. Mentioning his connection to *The New Yorker* when he arrived, he probably gave the impression that he wrote copy rather than delivered it. That was what Robert Frost, who had reached the craggy peak of his eminence, believed, anyway, and when Truman walked out of one of his readings, the old poet took it as a deliberate insult from both Truman and the magazine that employed him.

The insult, if insult it was, was not intentional. "It just so happened," Truman said, "that I was recovering from the flu and still had a very stiff neck. I was sitting in the front row. I bent down to rub my ankle and found I couldn't straighten up again because of my neck. There I was, bent away over, with my hand on my ankle. It must have looked as though I had fallen asleep. And there he was up there on the platform, reading. Being unable to straighten up, I worked my way out of my seat and began to hobble as quietly as I could up the aisle—still bent away over. That was when he decided I was sneaking out. I heard him slam the book. Then he said: 'Well, if that's what the representative of *The New Yorker* thinks of my reading, I shall stop.' Then he threw the book."

Word of the incident flew to New York and to *The New Yorker*. Some of the women who had attended the reading, and probably Frost himself, wrote angry letters to Ross, and Ross, who apparently

believed, perhaps correctly, that Truman had misrepresented himself as a *New Yorker* writer, demanded an accounting. That Truman
refused to provide, giving the editor of *The New Yorker* the same
stubborn no he used to give the principal of Greenwich High
School. "I told him that I wouldn't give an explanation, that I hadn't
done anything wrong, and that I hadn't been there on *New Yorker*
business anyway." Whether he quit before he was fired even he
could not remember. Whichever it was, he left that day, and Ross
gave orders that he not be allowed back on the nineteenth floor.
"Truman came home crying," Joe Capote recalled. "He was so disappointed. But I told him not to let it bother him, there was nothing
to worry about. Then he said, 'I want to finish the book I'm working
on. Will you take care of me while I write it?' I said I would."

ALTHOUGH Truman could not have known it that day, Ross had done him a favor, an unintentional kindness, in firing him. Indeed, if the reverse had happened, if by some bureaucratic aberration he had been made a writer at *The New Yorker*, the result might well have been disastrous for both his writing and his career. He was only just beginning to find his true voice, his distinctive style as a writer, and if he had stayed and moved up, he might have been tempted, perhaps without even knowing it, to trim his increasingly luxuriant prose to the more muted, understated pattern favored by the magazine. Such a mutation, a kind of protective coloration, has been the fate of other spirited young talents, certainly, at *The New Yorker* and elsewhere; an embrace, if it comes with strings and conditions, can be more damaging than a rejection, and at that age even Truman might have been flattered into *The New Yorker*'s genteel conformity. As it was, Ross gave him no choice: he had to be himself, and as he turned twenty that fall of 1944, he at last began the life of a full-time writer, whose only concern, from morning to night, was to put words onto a page.

Once again, and for the same reasons—his mother's drinking and the need for solitude in which to work—he looked south. There was little inducement to stay in New York anyway; he had lost not only his job, but for the moment, most of his friends as well. Phoebe had transferred from Barnard to Bennington College in Vermont, and Carol Marcus and Oona O'Neill had gone to California and married famous men—Carol had married William Saroyan; Oona, the great Charlie Chaplin. Alabama may not have been a writer's haven, but it was at least quiet and, as long as he stayed with his relatives, cheap.

This time, fortunately, he was happier and more comfortable than he had been the previous year. "It was early winter when I arrived there," he later wrote, "and the atmosphere of the roomy farmhouse, entirely heated by stoves and fireplaces, was well suited to a fledgling novelist wanting quiet isolation. The household rose at four-thirty, breakfasted by electric light, and was off about its business as the sun ascended." That house belonged to his Aunt Lucille, but dividing his time, he also stayed with Jennie and with his other Monroeville aunt, Mary Ida. "He seemed happy-happy," recalled Mary Ida. "He would sit down and talk just as fast as he could, just as I did. I wasn't listening to him, and he wasn't listening to me. But when he worked, he really worked."

The uncompleted book he had brought down from New York, the one he had asked Joe's help to let him finish, was called *Summer Crossing*. It was a social comedy, revolving around a Fifth Avenue debutante and the parties she gave one summer while her parents were in Europe—the summer crossing of the title. In Alabama, however, that subject seemed less compelling than it had in New York. Seeing the stretched-out branches of the chinaberry tree, where he and Harper Lee had traded secrets in their tree house, walking the dusty-red streets of Monroeville, through which Arch had once paraded the Great Pasha, and tramping through the swampy woods around town, where he and Sook had hunted for the ingredients of her dropsy medicine, he found that Fifth Avenue was very far away and his own childhood very close, everywhere he looked, everywhere he walked, in the air itself. "More and more," he wrote, "*Summer Crossing* seemed to me thin, clever, unfelt. Another language, a secret spiritual geography, was burgeoning inside me, taking hold of my nightdream hours as well as my wakeful daydreams."

The accumulations of the past suddenly overwhelmed him, he said, one frosty December afternoon when he wandered out to Hatter's Mill, where he had learned to swim and where, one terrible day, he had been bitten by a cottonmouth moccasin. Deserted and forlorn under the thin and milky winter sun, the still waters of the pond seemed like his own subconscious, holding within their gloomy depths all the days and weeks of his boyhood. Gazing beneath the surface of that moody pond, he saw the outlines of an entirely new book, a book not about the sleek and smooth world of Fifth Avenue society, which he scarcely knew at all, but about a boy growing up, lost, lonely, starving for love, in a backwoods town in Alabama. Memory crowded upon memory, and "excitement—a variety of creative coma—overcame me. Walking home, I lost my way and moved in circles round the woods, for my mind was reeling with the whole book.

"It was dark when I got home, and cold, but I didn't feel the cold because of the fire inside me. My Aunt Lucille said she had been worried about me, and was disappointed because I didn't want any supper. She wanted to know if I was sick; I said no. She said, 'Well, you *look* sick. You're white as a ghost.' I said good night, locked myself in my room, tossed the manuscript of *Summer Crossing* into a bottom bureau drawer, collected several sharp pencils and a fresh pad of yellow lined paper, got into bed fully clothed, and with pathetic optimism, wrote: '*Other Voices*, *Other Rooms*—a novel by Truman Capote.' "

Very likely, that description is a shorthand version of what took place over a period of days or weeks. No matter. The result was the same. *Summer Crossing* was put aside, and the new novel with its evocative and haunting title, *Other Voices, Other Rooms*, was begun. "It is unusual, but occasionally it happens to almost every writer that the writing of some particular story seems outer-willed and effortless," Truman said. "It is as though one were a secretary transcribing the words of a voice from a cloud. The difficulty is maintaining contact with this spectral dictator. Eventually it developed that communication ran highest at night, as fevers are known to do after dusk. So I took to working all night and sleeping all day, a routine that distressed the household and caused constant disapproving comment: 'But you've got everything turned upside down. You're ruining your health.' That is why I thanked my exasperated relatives for their generosity, their burdened patience, and bought a ticket on a Greyhound bus to New Orleans."

There, probably in January, 1945, he rented a room—"noisy as a steel mill," he said—at 711 Royal Street, in the heart of the French Quarter. Streetcars clattered and tourists chattered outside during the day; at night soldiers and sailors turned the street into a raucous party. Still, maintaining the same nocturnal schedule that had worried his relatives, he worked steadily, finishing several short stories as well as the first part of his new novel. Joe Capote apparently sent him some money, but it was not enough to live on, and in an attempt to earn more, Truman turned out some quick paintings, which he, like many others, tried to sell to the tourists in Jackson Square. "He couldn't paint worth a damn," said Patsy Streckfus, one of his New Orleans friends. "He brought a couple of his paintings out to the house, and even he agreed that they were terrible." Despite the hardships, he looked back on his months in the French Quarter as "the freest time of my life. I had no commitments to anyone or anybody."

That time did not last long. With his suitcase full of work completed or well under way, he longed once again for that diamond iceberg floating between the Hudson and the East River. Throwing away his paintbrushes, he headed north once again for the place he now realized was home, New York City.

Several times Truman had tried to get his prose into *The New Yorker*, thinking it the only home for a gifted young writer, and several times he had been politely rebuffed. What he did not know was that he was knocking on the wrong door. The place he was looking for, the place where new writers were not only accepted but welcomed, was not Harold Ross's sometimes stuffy establishment on West Forty-third Street, but a less famous, less likely address altogether: that of the women's fashion magazines, particularly *Harper's Bazaar* and *Mademoiselle*, which for upwards of two decades, from the mid-thirties through the mid-fifties, published the most interesting and original short fiction in the United States.

That remarkable, but little-remembered, moment in American literary history, when fine fiction found a nest in a forest of lingerie ads, was largely the work of a man who is also little remembered, a fat, lazy, but always brilliant editor by the name of George Davis. At one time a talented young writer himself, Davis developed a terminal case of writer's block. But the words he could not coerce from his own head he teased, cajoled, and yanked from the heads of others, as fiction editor first, from 1936 to 1941, of *Harper's Bazaar*, then, for the following eight years, of *Mademoiselle*.

Though the business offices of those magazines grumbled about the highbrow and often startling stories he chose, such as a Ray Bradbury fantasy about a vampires' Thanksgiving, his top editors, two extremely formidable women, Carmel Snow at *Harper's Bazaar* and Betsy Talbot Blackwell at *Mademoiselle*, were resolute in their support. The publishers, who looked upon fiction and poetry as nothing more than padding for the pictures and ads in any event, shrugged their shoulders and gave in, assuming, perhaps correctly, that their readers were wise enough to avoid large and offensive blocks of type. As a result, Davis had far more freedom working for the fashion glossies than he would have had at *The New Yorker*, *The Atlantic*, or any other magazine whose primary concern was words. He was allowed to publish pieces by Virginia Woolf, the Sitwells, and Colette, to commission Christopher Isherwood and W. H. Auden to report on their trip to China at war, and to devote much of two issues to Carson McCullers' stark and, at that time, shocking novella *Reflections in a Golden Eye*.

When Truman started to write for them, at the end of World War II, the fashion magazines, and *Harper's Bazaar* most particularly, were among the liveliest publications in America. During the thirteen years of her tenure, the remarkable Mrs. Snow, Dublin-born and endowed with an Irishwoman's tenacity, had transformed the *Bazaar* from a simple fashion magazine into a haven for the new and daring, in photography and design as well as fiction. Diana Vreeland, who brought the conviction of a John Calvin to questions of hemlines and hairstyles, was her fashion editor; Alexey Brodovitch, who had designed sets for Diaghilev and the Ballet Russe, was her art director; and Mary Louise Aswell, who combined a warm manner with cold and rigorous standards, was her fiction editor, as good in her way as Davis had been in his. "There were extraordinary people editing *Harper's Bazaar*," said Richard Avedon, who was just starting his career as a photographer. "There was no question in my mind that that was the magazine I wanted to work for. It stood for the things I cared about, and those editors got the best out of everybody. You would do anything for them! And because Hearst, which owned the *Bazaar*, was such a chintzy operation, you not only did anything for them, but you paid for it as well."

In some ways, Carmel Snow depended on Aswell the most. Although she knew everything about fashion and photography, Mrs. Snow knew very little about words and relied on her fiction editor to provide the best. Even so, as a devout Catholic, she was always worried about the propriety of the works she published, and she was mortified when the Post Office, complaining about a racy poem, threatened not to deliver the offending issue. "This is too dreadful," she said to one of her editors. "I can't hold my head up walking down Fifth Avenue." Then, selecting the most innocuous passage from the poem—"he kissed her on the nape"—she said, "Now tell me. Just what is the nape?" After that brush with the law, whenever she was puzzled by a story that was about to appear in print, she would nervously approach Aswell. "Now, Mary Louise, I know you are a lady to your fingertips and have beautiful judgment," she would say. "But are you sure this story is all right?" "Yes, Carmel," Mary Louise would reply, and Mrs. Snow would be satisfied.

For all their faults, their silliness and frivolity, the fashion magazines were lively places to work, and the contrast with Truman's former employer was striking. If the writers and editors at *The New Yorker* were bears who scurried into their caves whenever anyone approached, their counterparts at *Harper's Bazaar* and *Mademoiselle* were energetic cubs, often egotistical, frequently vain, but also intensely curious and, above all, open to new ideas and new people. "We were always complaining," said Avedon. "But we knew that those were the golden years."

It was that vibrant and expansive world Truman entered when he came back to New York from New Orleans. Sometime in the spring of 1945, he walked into the offices of *Mademoiselle* on East Forty-second Street and told the receptionist that he had a short story he wanted to submit. "That's fine, little boy," she said. "Have you got your name and address on it?" His answer, delivered with serene self-assurance, was a reply she had probably never heard before— "I'll wait while they read it"—and she immediately called George Davis, who dispatched his assistant, Rita Smith, to "see what sort of nut is outside." Smith, who was only two years older than Truman, shyly peeked into the waiting room and tiptoed back to report that there was in fact no one there but a little boy. Davis sent her back again, and she finally approached that precocious boy and was handed his manuscript, which was most likely "The Walls Are Cold," a short, bitter story about a spoiled rich girl who gets her comeuppance from an ignorant sailor. Smith liked it and wanted to buy it, but Davis, quite rightly, overruled her: the story was imitation *New Yorker* fiction without any distinctive voice, something that could have been produced by any good writer.

To someone who had become accustomed to hearing the word no from *The New Yorker*, Smith's enthusiasm was encouraging all the same, and Truman soon went back to show her a far better, wildly comic tale called "My Side of the Matter." In that story, a teenage bridegroom from Mobile returns with his pregnant wife to her hometown in backwoods Alabama, deposits her like a bag of groceries, then, uninvited and unwelcome, moves in with her and her two aunts. There is a hint of Arch in that freeloading bridegroom, a trace of Lillie Mae in the young bride, and bits of Jennie and Callie in the two quarrelsome old-maid aunts; Truman had obviously absorbed much of his family's history during those hot, gossipy nights on the front porch in Monroeville. Although the manner in which the story is told, as a whining monologue by the bridegroom, was almost certainly influenced by Eudora Welty's "Why I Live at the P.O.," the style—loose, hyperbolic, and extremely funny—can fairly be labeled Truman's. Smith, who came from Georgia—she was, in fact, Carson McCullers' younger sister—was delighted with the piece. Although Truman had already sold it to *Story* magazine, she asked to see more of what he had written.

The more was "Miriam," an altogether different kind of tale, an eye-catching and arresting psychological mystery, which, once read, is hard to forget: Miriam is a sinister little girl with silver-white hair and unblinking adult eyes who attaches herself to a middle-aged widow, Mrs. Miller. At first Mrs. Miller, who lives by herself in a small apartment near the East River, is charmed by her pretty clothes and the coincidence that they both bear the same first name. Gradually, however, her tidy but solitary little world begins to disintegrate with each visit the girl makes; Miriam takes over her life and, as the story ends, moves in with her, to assume her identity as well. Truman skillfully maintains a tone of suspenseful ambiguity, and at the conclusion the reader is left with a tantalizing question: is Miriam real? is she supernatural? or is she—Truman's own interpretation—a part of Mrs. Miller herself, the terrifying creation of a woman drifting into schizophrenia?

One is dark, one is sunny, but "Miriam" and "My Side of the Matter" have this in common: they are both far superior to anything that Truman had written before, so insightful about character and psychology, so rich in image and metaphor, that they might almost have been written by a different person. In a sense, they had been. Those hard and lonely months in the South had enabled him to throw off the yoke of what he thought was the acceptable way to write a story and to discard the graven image of *The New Yorker*. In what seemed like a moment, he had made a breakthrough, leaping from conventional subjects and conventional prose into a stylistic and fictional world of his own creation. He had not only found the idea for *Other Voices, Other Rooms* in those generous waters at Hatter's Pond; he had discovered his authentic voice as a writer.

Prodded by Rita Smith, Davis was quick to respond to that voice, and shortly after Truman showed it to them, *Mademoiselle* published "Miriam" in its June, 1945, issue. Short stories attracted more attention in those days than they do now—people talked about them the way they might discuss a hit movie or a best-selling novel today—and the reaction was almost instantaneous, more satisfying than even Truman could have wished. That one story put him where he had always wanted to be: in the center of the literary spotlight, admired, appreciated, and sought after. "I saw 'Miriam' in *Mademoiselle*, and I said, 'This is somebody we've got to get for *Harper's Bazaar*,' " recalled Mary Louise Aswell. "When this little thing, this little sprite turned up, I told him, 'I want to see anything you've got.' "

He gave her "A Tree of Night," which is a story as chilling as "Miriam," and in many ways better. A college girl, traveling late at night on a crowded train, finds a seat across from two grotesques, a zombielike man, deaf and dumb, and a freakish-looking little woman with an oversized head and a rouge-smeared face. The two travel from one Southern town to another and perform a kind of carnival show, in which the man, who goes by the name Lazarus, is buried alive and then resurrected. For the girl, traveling with this sinister pair becomes a journey into her subconscious, and it brings back "a childish memory of terrors that once, long ago, had hovered above her like haunted limbs on a tree of night. Aunts, cooks, strangers—each eager to spin a tale or teach a rhyme of spooks and death, omens, spirits, demons. And always there had been the unfailing threat of the wizard man: stay close to the house, child, else a wizard man'll snatch you and eat you alive! He lived everywhere, the wizard man, and everywhere was danger." More subtle in its use of symbolism than "Miriam," "A Tree of Night" treats the same theme in a different way, as a supposedly rational woman succumbs to the terrors that lie hidden within her soul. For Truman, the story was also a visit to the past, a return to his childhood; the model for Lazarus is of course Arch's trickster, the Great Pasha.

Harper's Bazaar published that eerie story in October, 1945, and in December *Mademoiselle* came out with "Jug of Silver," a warm, charming tale of a wish fulfilled. The juxtaposition of two such dissimilar works followed a pattern set earlier by "Miriam" and "My Side of the Matter," and throughout the forties Truman's short fiction alternated between the dark and the sunny, the terrifying and the amusing. The two magazines continued their tug-of-war over him for the rest of the decade. "*Harper's* and *Mademoiselle* turned into temples which the cultist[s] entered every month with the seldom fulfilled hope that the little god would have published a new story there," was the way one critic, Alfred Chester, described the interest he aroused.

In January, 1945, Truman was an ex–*New Yorker* copyboy, with a bleak and uncertain future. A few months later he was already being mentioned as a potential star of the postwar generation of writers. In the spring of 1946, Herschel Brickell, editor of the annual *O. Henry Memorial Award Prize Stories*, assessed the year just past and ventured a prophecy: "The most remarkable new talent of the year was, in the opinion of the editor, that of Truman Capote, the *e* being accented, a young man from New Orleans just past his majority. It is safe to predict that Mr. Capote will take his place among the best short-story writers of the rising generation." That sharp-eyed and tireless little condor had finally grabbed his prey, and as he turned twenty-one, he was on his way to becoming famous.

13

MIRIAM, that evil little girl, opened doors for him all over New York, and Truman, like many before, and many after, discovered that once one is inside the circle, the big city is a small town and that the most significant difference between Manhattan and Monroeville is that one is in the North, the other in the South. The recognition he had wanted so desperately the year before now came his way easily, casually, almost as a matter of course; what had looked like a climb up Everest in 1944 was, only twelve months later, a stroll through a garden of summer flowers. One person introduced him to another, and that person to someone else, who led him to another still. And so it went until—it all seemed to happen in an instant—he had met everyone he wanted or needed to know.

Admission to the circle was not just a matter of meeting the right people, of course. Many other talented writers were given the same opportunity, allowed to step inside, then booted out and lost to sight as if they had never existed. But Truman was not to be forgotten; nor, once he was inside that invisible boundary, was he to be dislodged. All the things that had shocked his colleagues at *The New Yorker*—his manner, his appearance, and his baby voice—guaranteed that he would be remembered; his seductive personality guaranteed that he would be accepted. When it came to charm, even Arch, who could talk a snake out of its rattles, had to stand aside for Truman.

One of those most intrigued by him was George Davis, who recognized something of himself, or the self he had been twenty years before, behind that smooth little-boy face. "George had pipit monstrosities in his head," said Leo Lerman, who also worked as a writer, a kind of odd-job man, for the fashion magazines. "They were absolute perfection, George's monstrosities. He took one look at Truman and recognized the monster that lurked in there to produce things that were really quite beautiful."

For a time Davis' relationship with Truman was almost that of a master and his apprentice. George liked to tease, banter, and instruct, and Truman was properly respectful, careful, like everyone else, not to cross him. "George had the nastiest tongue I've ever encountered," said another young writer, Pearl Kazin, who discerned deep-rooted malice behind his slightly hooded eyes and exaggerated, stereotyped homosexual mannerisms. "He had that look of a rotten peach. You had the feeling that if you pressed your finger into his skin, the dent would stay."

It was not a bad comparison, and there was something overripe about George, a satiety with the usual pleasures, perhaps with life itself, that led him to seek the decadent and the unwholesome. Like one of those misshapen sea creatures that diving bells photograph thousands of feet below the ocean's surface, he was at home in the dark and shied away from the light, which is to say the ordinary, that satisfied most other people. He had a fascination with the low life; he frequented seedy dives and was attracted to tough sailors and hustlers, one of whom was to beat him so badly a few years later that he nearly died. His delight in the malformed drew him to sideshow freaks, and he made frequent visits to a colony of pinheads at Coney Island, stopping only when someone was rude enough to ask him what relationship he had to the family.

There was that side to him certainly, the dark and unpleasant side, but there was also another. Although his tongue could leave lasting scars, it could also be extremely funny. He had an epigrammatic turn of phrase that would have pleased Oscar Wilde, and his friend W. H. Auden called him the wittiest person he had ever known. George could sometimes be cruel, but he could also be as charitable as Santa Claus; many writers owed their careers, and more, to his generosity. To someone like Carson McCullers, who needed more than the usual amount of support and encouragement, he offered a plenitude of both. Typically, however, he broadcast his nasty deeds and kept his good ones hidden, as if he were afraid to be accused of something so common as sentimentality. "Knowing

George was a career in itself," said Phoebe Pierce, who worked for him at the end of the forties. "It was not that he was malicious. He was just incapable of saying anything good about anyone. Yet even while he was being bitchy, he could be doing something very nice. His mean facade concealed kindness and good judgment."

Truman did not make a career of it, but, fascinated by George's odd balance of brilliance and triviality, good and bad, he did make a hobby of knowing him. Just as George saw something of himself in Truman, Truman doubtless detected a hint of what he might become in George, the monster in middle age. Evil has its attraction, and George showed him subterranean vistas that he had not known existed. When the two of them were together, Truman even took on some of his teacher's mannerisms, in the same way that a man with a mynah-bird ear unconsciously imitates the accent of the person he is with. Gossiping about mutual friends, for instance, he would become uncharacteristically mean-spirited, much as George was, and even slow his normal torrent of excited words to the trickle of a drawl, which is how George talked. "George brought out the worst in Truman," said Pearl Kazin, "and I didn't enjoy seeing them together."

One trick Truman learned from George is that the surest way to find out a secret is to tell one—your own, if no one else's. It seems impolite, even churlish, to keep secrets yourself when the person across the table has just discarded the last veil and left himself naked; self-revelation, or, better still, self-mortification can be used as a kind of bait to forge a bond of instant intimacy. That was a ploy that George had turned into an art. Though he told scandalous stories about nearly everyone he knew, the most scandalous, most revealing, and sometimes most humiliating ones were always about himself. Nearly everyone, for example, had heard his favorite: when he was young, good-looking, and living in Paris, he was picked up by a handsome black man who invited him to a seedy hotel for an evening of sex. Only at the end did George hear a titter from the next room and realize that he had been an unwitting actor in a sex show—an audience in the adjoining room had watched the entire performance through a false mirror.

On the day he met Truman, he established just such a bond by spending most of a lunch giving an account of his sexual history. "He claimed that there wasn't a single man he hadn't been to bed with in his hometown in Michigan," said Truman, "and he told me all about the affair he was then having with a French sea captain. George made up so many stories—but perhaps they were all true." After that lunch, George occasionally invited him to parties in his shabby brownstone on East Eighty-sixth Street. Stuffed, basement to rafters, with Victoriana, the house could not have been called attractive. Yet there, seated on a hard and lumpy couch or standing beside a hideous statue, could be found some of the most interesting people alive, everyone from Auden and Jean Cocteau, to Dorothy Parker and Gypsy Rose Lee, who was, so they both said, George's fiancée. "The people George knew were a legion," said the poet Howard Moss. "You wouldn't have been surprised if Shakespeare suddenly appeared out of another room."

They were one of a kind, Truman and George, but although they saw each other frequently in the next several years, they were never comfortable friends. George made it plain that Truman was Rita Smith's discovery, not his, and that he did not share her enthusiasm for his work. With uncharacteristic obtuseness—at the time he said it, Truman was only twenty-two—he even declared that Truman's "slender talent" had already been completely realized. Beyond his habitual sarcasm, there was a hint of envy in his comments, as if Truman were gaining the acclaim George himself would have received had he not suffered from writer's block. In fact, George had, or was to gain, more respect for Truman's writing than he let on. A decade later, when he was living in Europe, he asked a friend to airmail only two articles from the United States; both were by Truman.

Truman's feelings about George were equally ambivalent. He acknowledged his brilliance, but it was not in Truman's nature to forgive his slights. If revenge were needed, however, he finally achieved his in 1976 when he used George, who by then had been dead for nearly twenty years, as the model for an extraordinarily unpleasant character, Turner Boatwright, in his stories "Unspoiled Monsters" and "Kate McCloud."

A much closer friend was Leo Lerman, who, on the surface, was so much like George that George's friends called him the "fake George Davis." Truman met him in the fall of 1945 at Mary Louise's, sat quietly through dinner, and then, hiding on the stairs as Lerman was leaving, jumped onto his shoulders. "It was spectacular in a truly Truman way," said Lerman, "and it should have warned me about him for the rest of my life. It didn't." Despite that bruising introduction, they became warm friends. Since Leo lived only a block from the Capote apartment, they saw each other almost daily. When Leo was sick, Truman went over in the morning, lit his gas stove—Leo had a morbid fear of lighting fires—and made his coffee. In exchange, Leo offered Truman refuge from Nina, who was drinking even more than she had in Greenwich. "Nina sometimes became rather violent when she was drinking," Leo said. "One time she threw an enormous quantity of Truman's letters out the window onto Park Avenue. Another time he suddenly appeared in the middle of the night and said, 'She's breaking the china!' When he just couldn't stand it any longer, he would fly around the corner, climb up all my stairs, and sleep on my couch."

Ten years older than Truman, tall, with a bald head and a long beard that already gave him the look of a middle-aged rabbi, Leo had started out as an actor, turning to writing only after a car accident destroyed his looks. After that his life did indeed parallel Davis' in many ways. He also did most of his work for the fashion magazines, he also loved to gossip, and he also stuffed his apartment with Victoriana. Finally, perhaps the most persuasive parallel of all, he also gave parties that attracted the celebrated.

The similarities were all on the surface, however; the differences, profound. Leo had very little of Davis' talent, but he also had very little of his malice. Whereas George was surrounded by a halo of boredom, as if he thought life an overrated play that did not deserve its good reviews, Leo was a gusher of praise and enthusiasm, a magpie of a man who was fascinated, at least briefly, by nearly everything. His real gift was neither writing nor editing, but his ability to spot what was in vogue and whose star was rising—or setting. "He knew without a doubt the precise moment when the James 'revival' went into decline," was the way Pearl Kazin described a fictional character many people assumed was modeled on Leo, "that Stendhal was old hat, Cocteau a bore, and Genet the newest freshest genius of them all. Never less than fully informed, he was always more than certain when what would happen, and where next."

Much of that information Leo gathered at his Sunday-night parties, which were a New York institution throughout the forties. Taking a perverse pride in being able to attract people despite the lack of the usual amenities, he served nothing but the kind of cheese usually found in mousetraps and offered nothing to drink but jug wine, so bad, he liked to brag, that wise people refused to touch it. Still they came: playwrights, poets, and novelists, Broadway stars and movie stars, ballerinas and chorus boys—almost anyone, in fact, who could survive the alpine climb up four flights of stairs. One man, who was thought to live in a cave in Central Park, always came early, gobbled a mound of the mouse cheese, spilled some red wine down his throat, and hastily departed. Another regular, a woman whose identity was equally mysterious, always wore the same Chinese dress and coolie hat, giving birth to jokes that when she was not at Leo's, she was pulling a rickshaw along Fifth Avenue.

At George's parties, no one would have been surprised to see Shakespeare come staggering through the doorway; at Leo's, no one would have noticed, so many people were jammed in so little space. The host himself, wearing a colorful costume, such as a red robe topped by a fez, often greeted his guests from his bed. But whether he was standing, sitting, or lying down, he would spread a happy glow over the festivities, and despite the confusion and the haphazard, thrown-together atmosphere, his parties were as carefully choreographed as a hit musical. He made sure that the people he wanted showed up, that those he did not want stayed away, and that everybody who came was happy to be present. "You knew exactly what you were going to get there," said Mary Louise. "He was a wonderful host, genuinely welcoming and funny, and you could be certain that Sunday night at Leo's would be very jolly."

Shakespeare, said Truman's friend Marguerite Young, must have known someone very much like Truman when he created Ariel and Puck. One moment he was an ethereal wisp of cloud and sky, Ariel in all but name; the next moment he was a mischievous earthbound sprite, Puck making merry in the concrete forest of Manhattan. And half one, half the other is what he was then and for many years to come. As Ariel, he was warm and sympathetic, generous with time and with money too, when he had it. As Puck, he enjoyed playing tricks and telling tales on his friends; more naughty than bad, he liked to stir up trouble and create the dramas that he loved to see swirling around him. "Little T can be absolutely adorable or such a pain in the neck that you want to take a swift kick at him" was how Mary Louise described him to a reporter at the time.

"We love him up here," she added, however—the "here" being

the offices of *Harper's Bazaar* and its sister magazine, *Junior Bazaar*. "He is in and out all the time." In fact, he spent so much time there with Mary Louise and Barbara Lawrence, who had left *The New Yorker* to become features editor of *Junior Bazaar*, that Carmel Snow assumed he was Barbara's little brother and offered him a glass of milk the first time someone brought him to one of her cocktail parties. When Mary Louise told her that that innocent-looking boy was the author of those nightmare visions, "Miriam" and "A Tree of Night," Mrs. Snow quickly put a martini into his hand instead.

It was the first of many she was to share with him during the next few years, and she became yet another in the succession of middle-aged women who clasped him to their bosoms and caused heads to turn wherever they went with him. She was the famous editor, a perfectionist who was seen only in Balenciaga; he was the stripling writer, more than thirty-five years her junior, whose only distinction in dress was the long Bronzini scarf that fluttered after him like a ship's pennant in a stiff breeze. A more curious and singular pair could scarcely be pictured; yet there they were, having lunch or drinks together and gossiping like ancient friends, and there he was, the sought-after extra man who added the spice to her dinner parties, entertaining her guests as much as he did her. "Carmel and Diana Vreeland were both fascinated by him and adored him," said Mary Louise. "They both had an eye for the unusual and the extraordinarily gifted. I had nothing at all to do with those glamorous, beautifully dressed women in the fashion department—the literary department was the absolute stepchild of the Hearst organization—but one day Diana came up to me and said, 'I like you because you're a friend of Truman Capote's!' "

With those empresses of fashion he was like an amusing godson, who appeared on command for a few hours of happy chatter but minded his manners, as godsons usually do. Real intimacy was reserved for several other women he met at that time, to whom he was more of a pal, a playmate, a younger brother. He had and was to have many male friends, heterosexual as well as homosexual, with whom he felt a bond of confidence. But he had a special rapport with women, an easygoing relationship that few men ever enjoy, whatever their sexual preference. Women liked being with him, he with them, and he often found his closest companions among members of the opposite sex. "It's too bad I don't like going to bed with women," he lamented years later, with what sounded like genuine regret. "I could have had any woman in the world, from Garbo to Dietrich. Women always love me, and I love attractive and beautiful women, but as friends, not lovers. I can't understand why anyone would want to go to bed with a woman. It's boring, boring, boring!"

Two of those with whom he felt most relaxed were Barbara Lawrence and Mary Louise. Not only did he spend hours encamped in their offices, he also went to exercise classes with them, had dinner with them, and dared them, as he had the Jaeger sisters in Greenwich, to join him in some amusing devilment. "Oh, those were funny days!" said Mary Louise. "Truman was never embarrassed about speaking his mind, and we got thrown out of practically every Schrafft's in New York because we laughed so much." Even his silliness made them laugh. Once they invited him to a concert, only to be turned down when he found out they would be sitting in the balcony: he could not afford to be seen in such cheap seats, he informed them; it would ruin his image. "He was mighty airy in those days," said Mary Louise, "and Barbara and I used to tease him an awful lot about his delusions of grandeur."

Playing the part of the helpful older sister, as she had at *The New Yorker*, Barbara continued to read drafts of his stories; at her suggestion he had changed the ending of "Miriam," dropping the last two paragraphs before submitting it to *Mademoiselle*. Mary Louise was more like a mother; not since Sook had he met a woman who was so warm and unstinting in her affection. One of those rare beings who receive universal devotion, she seemed to make good people want to be better and encouraged mediocre writers to put music into their prose. She was, in short, an ideal editor as well as companion. "She was perfect for Truman, someone Truman could go to and talk," said his friend Andrew Lyndon. "She admired him as an artist and found him lovable too. And I don't think many people up to that time had found Truman as lovable as she did."

Inspired to assume the unaccustomed role of the good son, Truman was also a great comfort to Mary Louise, who bore more than the usual burdens of sadness. Not long before, troubled by some emotional disturbance, she had been persuaded by an incompetent therapist to enter a mental hospital; when she emerged, she made the devastating discovery that her ex-husband had gained custody of their two children. "She was in a very shaky state," said Pearl Kazin. "Yet, young as he was, Truman was a great support and gave her the reassurance she needed. I was astounded by that. There was no one else I knew at that age, or any other age for that matter, who was able to be as intuitive, affectionate, and helpful to her as he was. His friendship mattered a very great deal to her."

His letters confirm that assessment. For the next several years, whenever Mary Louise was feeling low, he was there to raise her up. "As an editor it seems to me as though you quite persistently refuse to acknowledge your role as one of the two or three people serious artists, particularly the young, can look to with any hope of commercial recognition," he wrote when she was considering leaving *Harper's Bazaar*. "That is a responsibility, Marylou, a role I do not know that I could forgive you for quitting . . . if ever, in some strange moment, you did. Isn't it true you choose and publish and encourage the best short fiction in this country? And that is no accident, darling. It all, I suppose, depends on what one considers important; if you think art important, as you do and I do, then you are one of the most important people in the world.

"All human life has its seasons, and no one's personal chaos can be permanent: winter, after all, does not last forever, does it? There is summer, too, and spring, and though sometimes when branches stay dark and the earth cracks with ice, one thinks they will never come, that spring, that summer, but they do, and always."

If Barbara was the dutiful but sometimes boring older sister, Doris Lilly was her glamorous, fun-loving twin. Tall and pretty, with long legs and streaked blond hair, she belonged to a species that was soon to become extinct: the good-time party girl whose only goal, openly and honestly stated, was to make a rich catch. It was a pursuit for which she was admirably equipped. A one-time starlet, whose movie career can only be called fleeting—she had one line in one picture, *The Story of Dr. Wassell*—she was bouncy and buoyant, not subject to moods or given to silences of more than thirty seconds. She reminded some of her literary friends of Rosie Driffield, the embodiment of the life force in W. Somerset Maugham's novel *Cakes and Ale*.

When Truman met her, not long after she had arrived from California, she had not yet found either a millionaire or a job, and she had time to take long walks with him, have dinner with him in her East Seventy-eighth Street walk-up—ordering in, of course—and talk to him for hours on the phone. Once she failed to pay her rent, and her landlord turned off the heat and lights. "Who thought about those things?" she later explained. "I was so busy going out every night. I mentioned the problem to some man I was seeing, but instead of sending a check, he sent two dozen candles. Finally it was so cold that Truman and I took the shelves out of the kitchen closet and burned them in the fireplace." Scatterbrained in most matters, Doris was capable of perfect concentration when she was trying to please a man, and even a sourhead like Evelyn Waugh, who was then at the apex of his fame, temporarily put aside his ingrained dislike of Americans to pay court. "Do you know anything about a writer named Waugh?" she asked Andrew Lyndon. "Do you mean Evelyn Waugh?" he replied. "No, dear," she said patiently. "This is a man."

Her madcap sense of fun and adventure appealed to Truman as much as it did to most other men, and she was to be one of the models for Holly Golightly in *Breakfast at Tiffany's*. She helped to provide him with a character, and he returned the favor, suggesting both the subject and the title for her first book. "Write about what you know," he told her. "You know about millionaires, so write about them, and call it *How to Meet a Millionaire*. After all, every girl in the world wants to know how to do it. I'll help you write it." And he did.

"The first time I saw her—a tall slender wand of a girl, slightly stooped and with a fascinating face that was simultaneously merry and melancholy—I remember thinking how beautiful her eyes were: the color of good clear coffee, or of a dark ale held to the firelight to warm. Her voice had the same quality, the same gentle heat, like a blissful summer afternoon that is slow but not sleepy." So Truman described Carson McCullers, who was the most extraordinary of all the women who came into his life in that year of first success. Rita Smith thought that he should meet her famous older sister, and sometime in the spring or summer of 1945, not long after Rita herself had met him, she invited him to Nyack, where the two sisters and their widowed mother shared a large old house overlooking the Hudson.

Rita had judged them perfectly, and Carson and Truman took to each other immediately, as well they should have: they were alike in everything but sex and body, and when they looked closely at each other, they saw someone very familiar. When her first novel, *The Heart Is a Lonely Hunter*, was published in 1940, Carson too had been a *Wunderkind*, the darling of the fashion magazines. George Davis doted on her, and they would sit for hours, studying his photo collection of freaks, like fond parents browsing through the family album.

Precocious success was only one of the things she and Truman had in common, however. She had also grown up in the South. She was also thought to be odd-looking—too tall and skinny, in her case, rather than too short—and to have quirky mannerisms. Although she was married to Reeves McCullers, she was primarily attracted to members of her own sex. Even their writing was similar in substance, though not in style, dwelling on loneliness and the perverse nature of love. Small wonder, then, that Truman instantly became devoted to her. "I was very, very fond of Carson," he said. "She was a devil, but I respected her." Small wonder, too, that, as her cousin Jordan Massee reported, "she was enchanted with him and regarded him as her own private little protégé."

He became a regular visitor to Nyack, and learned what it meant to be her friend, what it meant to be barraged by her questions, enveloped by her concern, manacled by her demands. She was a toucher, a hugger, a kisser, and her friends were overwhelmed by her embrace even on the telephone. Still in her twenties when Truman met her, she had already suffered several serious illnesses, and like many people who are chronically sick, she felt that she had an almost imperial right to the time and attention of those around her. Many, like Truman, were caught in her spell and granted her that privilege; others stayed well away. "An hour with a dentist without Novocain was like a minute with Carson McCullers" was Gore Vidal's acid memory.

Her house in Nyack looked out on the Hudson, but those fast-flowing Yankee waters might just as well have belonged to some languid stream in Georgia, with alligators lazily sunning themselves in the shallows, so deep-fried Southern was the atmosphere inside the door. For Phoebe visiting there with Truman was a journey into bayou country. "Carson's family was wildly Southern," she said, "and when they were all together—her brother had come up from the South with his wife when I was there—it was quite a scene. Carson had taken to her bed, but the rest of us sat in the living room and listened to Brother-Man play the piano. I have never heard anything so execrable in my life. 'Play it again, Brother-Man!' everybody would cry, and he would. This had been going on for some time, and I asked to use the bathroom, thinking I could go upstairs. Not at all! Carson's mother pointed to the one at the side of the living room. The house was being remodeled, and the bathroom was complete, commode and all, except for the one thing—it had no walls. 'Close your eyes now, everybody, so Phoebe can use the bathroom,' she said, and they all closed their eyes while I went into the bathroom without walls. But it was all right: Brother-Man kept on playing the piano.''

As strange as that household seemed to her, it was as normal as grits and butter beans to Truman, a nostalgic reminder of summer evenings on Jennie's front porch. More than one of his friends remarked that when they were together, he became more Southern than Carson, who had spent more of her life in the South and had a greater claim to the acreage. His Southern accent, which he had long since dropped, awoke from its slumber, and his whole manner changed, in perceptible, if undefinable, ways. "Somehow Northerners have the vague idea that Southerners are just like them, except for their funny way of talking," said Phoebe. "I know I thought that. Seeing Truman with Carson, however, I realized that there is a whole shared experience in being Southern, and that he and Carson had that together."

She demanded a great deal from her friends, but Carson gave as much as she received, and she helped no other young writer as enthusiastically as she did Truman. Together with Rita, she found him an agent, Marion Ives, and she wrote a warm letter of recommendation to Robert Linscott, a senior editor with Random House. A tall, tweedy New Englander who had begun his publishing career as an office boy in 1904, Linscott was as impressed by "Miriam" as most other people, and on October 22, 1945, he signed Truman to a contract for *Other Voices, Other Rooms*, with a small advance, twelve hundred dollars, to be doled out in installments of a hundred dollars a month beginning December 1. "Now you're going to be a writer and an artist," Linscott told him. "We're going to support you, take care of you. You're like a racehorse." Linscott's boss, Bennett Cerf, described what happened next: "Well, *that* was a day when Truman arrived at Random House! He had bangs, and nobody could believe it when this young prodigy waltzed in. He looked about eighteen. He was bright and happy and absolutely self-assured. Everybody knew that somebody important had arrived upon the scene—particularly Truman!"

14

Throughout those hectic months of baby renown, all through the fall of 1945 and the winter of 1946, the literary world's newest lion cub pressed on with his novel. Maintaining the same upside-down schedule that had dismayed his early-to-bed, early-to-rise relatives in Alabama the year before, he began writing about ten at night, lying on his bed with a notebook perched on his upraised knees, went to sleep about four the next morning, and woke up at noon, just in time for lunch. "Night after night I would see him working in there," said Joe Capote. And so it might have continued if it had not been for his mother. Writers can work standing up, sitting down, or lying on their backs; they can put their words on paper in heat or in cold, in the morning or at night. Very few can create anything as large as a novel, however, without some degree of tranquility, some measure of repose in which they can concentrate and construct. But tranquility was the one thing in short supply in Nina's house. No matter what hours Truman kept, he had to contend with her agitated movements and lightning rages. There is no such thing as peace and quiet around an alcoholic.

His dilemma was that he could not afford to leave, but it was impossible to stay, and once again Carson came to his aid, suggesting that he join her in the spring at Yaddo, the writers' and artists' colony near Saratoga Springs, where she herself had often found a restful haven. There would be no expenses, she told him—Yaddo provided everything but transportation—and to be accepted he had only to ask: she would pull the necessary strings; Newton Arvin, one of the trustees, was one of her best friends, and Elizabeth Ames, the matriarchal director, would do almost anything for her. Truman did agree, of course, and on May 1, 1946, he and Leo Lerman, another prospective inmate, traveled by train to Saratoga Springs in upstate New York, about four hours from Manhattan.

Surrounded by gentle hills, shady woods, and inviting lakes, Yaddo did indeed provide him the quiet Carson had said it would—and a great deal more. The guest list was small, never more than fifteen or twenty, and the spaces were large. Some guests were housed in cottages and studios on the grounds; others lived in the stone mansion, which was the center of social activity. Tranquility was not only promised; it was enforced, and any violation of the rules resulted in a sternly worded note from the vigilant Mrs. Ames. "She was a strange, creepy sort of woman," said Truman, "silent and sinister like Mrs. Danvers in *Rebecca*. She was always going around spying, seeing who was working and not working and what everybody was up to." Yaddo was a working community, the rules emphasized, and from nine to four guests were expected to be by themselves, doing whatever they had come there to do; the kitchen even provided box lunches so that they would not be interrupted by a formal midday meal. So much labor brought its reward, however, and after four, the silence was broken. Doors banged open, invitations were issued, and most years the visitors played as hard as they worked. Each summer ended with stories of drinking and dancing, games on the lawn, romances begun and ended under the northern stars.

Carson had already been in residence more than a month when Truman arrived, and during the eleven weeks he was there—he left July 17—a score of others came or went, including several who became his particular favorites: Marguerite Young and John Malcolm Brinnin represented the younger generation of writers and poets; Newton Arvin and another of Carson's friends, Howard Doughty, were the middle-aged academics; and Katherine Anne Porter, still beautiful at fifty-six, was the glamorous and much-admired older writer.

Adhering to Yaddo's schedule with as much determination as everyone else, Truman worked on *Other Voices, Other Rooms*, wrote a short story, "The Headless Hawk," and prepared to return, when his stay was up, to New Orleans for *Harper's Bazaar*, which wanted him to do an impressionistic travel article. During the other hours, playtime, he was, as might have been expected, the center of attention. With the tail of his shirt flapping outside his trousers, "he always seemed to be stepping right out of a cloud," said Marguerite Young. "He walked as if every step were choreographed to some music that he alone heard. You would see him—or just the tail of that white shirt—for an instant and then he would be gone. I remember him as being absolutely enthralling that summer, high-spirited, generous, loving. We all thought he was a genius."

That was the Ariel side, but there was also Puck, who was the instigator of most of the amusements that year. "Spontaneous when others are cautious, he has a child's directness, a child's indifference to propriety," Brinnin wrote in his diary, "and so gets to the heart of matters with an audacity strangers find outrageous, then delightful. Yet nothing he says or does accounts for the magnet somewhere in his makeup that exerts itself like a force beyond logic; he's responsible for turning the summer into a dance of bees. His slightest movements throughout the mansion, about the grounds, or on the side streets of Saratoga are charted and signaled by sentries visible only to one another. Schemes to share his table at dinner are laid at breakfast, sometimes by single plotters, sometimes by teams united in shamelessness. There's always laughter at his table, echoing across the moat of silence in which the tables around it are sunk."

Although Carson, an accomplished attention-getter herself, remained only through May, they behaved like brother and sister while she was there. Whatever he had she wanted; she wore his clothes, even his shoes, and snatched his long-tailed white shirts whenever she could. Rummaging through his chest of drawers one day, she discovered a paper that carried his original name and threatened to inform everyone that he was an impostor, not Truman Capote at all but someone with the leaden name of Truman Streckfus Persons. "You just go right ahead, honey chile," he coolly told her, "and I'll tell them your real name is Lula Smith." Even Porter was fascinated by the surprising spectacle they made dancing together in the huge kitchen: the tall partner, Carson, awkwardly jiggling up and down while the short one, Truman, was doing graceful little pirouettes of his own devising. In all her wanderings she had probably never seen anyone like Truman before, and turning to Mrs. Ames, who was hard of hearing, she asked, in a voice so loud that her Southern accent could be heard across the room, "From where did he come, dear?" "From *Harper's Bazaar*," was Mrs. Ames's unperturbed if nonsensical reply.

Katherine Anne, who danced with him too, later averred that he was a career climber who had latched on to her because of her literary fame, but in a letter to Mary Louise he seemed notably unimpressed and, indeed, rather cheeky in his description of her. "She must be about sixty," he said, "but oh how she can do the hootchy-cootchy. She tries to act like a Southern belle of sixteen or so. She is so unserious it is hard to believe she can write at all. She thinks I am a wonderful dancer, and makes me dance with her all the time: it is simply awful, because she hasn't the faintest notion of how to do the simplest steps."

Something similar could have been said about poor Leo, who, out in the country, away from the friendly pavements he was used to, exhibited a whole new array of curious frights and phobias. Assigned to a studio away from the mansion, as Truman was, he kept a light burning all night to ward off ghosts, and once begged Truman to let him stay the night in his studio, where he then huddled in an old wicker chair until the sun came up. Sending a dispatch from the front to Mary Louise, Truman bravely reported that he himself was not afraid—except, of course, when bats flew into his room. "I simply can't stand that cheap cheap crying as they circle in the dark," he told her.

The existence of spirits was a matter of speculation; the presence of snakes was not and led, indirectly but very quickly, to Truman's receiving a severe reprimand from the ever-watchful Mrs. Ames. In another letter to Mary Louise—at the top of which he commanded "*Destroy!!!*"—he explained what had happened. "Well, I knew it was too good to last: I'm in trouble, and it's all Leo's fault. According to Mrs. Ames, Howard Doughty and I are 'insistently persecuting' him. See, Leo has a real aberration about snakes: he makes me escort him every day from the mansion to his studio; but he has dramatized the whole thing to such a ridiculous extent that everybody here thought he was half-way joking. So yesterday Howard came to my studio for lunch. When he left he stepped on a snake in my yard, and picked it up. Leo, who was standing in his doorway across the road, saw it, and began to scream: 'You're mean, you're cruel!' then slammed his door, pulled down all his shades, and curled up under his desk, and stayed there the whole afternoon, in a real fit of terror: no one, of course, had any intention of frightening him. But two workmen who were putting firewood in our studios saw the whole thing and reported it to Mrs. A., who promptly sent a little 'blue note' (all communication is carried on through these blue notes) saying that Mr. Lerman had been made ill by our (Howard's and mine) insistent persecution. I suppose it will blow over, but it's all too absurd for words. Leo, of course, feels very badly that he got us in so much trouble. Howard wrote a wonderful reply explaining everything (we felt like little naughty schoolboys, which annoyed Howard, for he is a professor at Harvard, and 42 years old)."

In one of his letters to Mary Louise, Truman listed the friends he had made at Yaddo, then added, "Of all the people here I like Howard Doughty best." He neglected only to give the reason: he and Howard had become the latest chapter in Yaddo's long history of summer romances, and it was to their affair Truman was probably alluding when he wrote Mary Louise that "the strangest thing is going on, I'm dying to tell you, but am so afraid of putting it in a letter." To the consternation of Howard, who maintained a public facade of heterosexuality, Truman told nearly everyone else, however. "The little one has been talking again," Howard would grimly inform a friend who was in on his secret. Years later Truman succinctly summarized their relationship. "Howard and I just got together for sex," he said. "He was very attractive, but I wasn't in love with him."

Both statements seem to have been true. By all accounts Doughty *was* an attractive man, lean and lanky, about six feet tall, with dark hair, a craggy face and the aristocratic manners befitting a descendant of Cotton Mather. "He had a marvelous voice," recalled Brinnin, "with all those echoes that take ten generations to produce." Much of his adult life, upwards of twenty years, was devoted to a biography of Francis Parkman, the great nineteenth-century historian. Finally published in 1962, too late in his life to be of much help to him in the academic job market, his book, beyond its other merits, showed his spiritual affinity with Parkman. "Howard was prone to very depressed spells," said his wife, Frances, who was aware of his homosexuality even before they married. "He had some breakdowns, and he had many spells of just wanting to turn his head to the wall. Ours was not an easy marriage, and I contemplated getting a divorce. But we liked so many of the same things, and for the most part we had a very good life together, except sexually."

If Howard had been born a generation later, he probably would not have married at all, but would have become instead, insofar as either of them was capable of such involvement, the lifelong companion of Newton Arvin, a professor of literature at Smith College and almost certainly the strongest influence on his adult life. Even without a formal relationship, the bond between them was indissoluble. They saw each other frequently for thirty years or more and, according to Arvin's diaries, made love almost every time they met. Though each had separate affairs, in their hearts they were never far apart. "You know how much I love you," Arvin wrote Howard on May 14, even as Howard may have been making love to Truman. "It is a luxury only to allow oneself to *say* it from time to time. I am still, after all these years, incredulous that I should have come upon you. Is a completer mutual sympathy conceivable between fallible human beings? I should certainly not expect it."

It was at that point that Truman, without hint or warning, entered their lives, hurtling toward them like a shooting star, stunning them, dazing them, dazzling them altogether. "Have you happened to run across any of Truman Capote's stories?" Howard wrote Newton on June 2. "The child really has an uncanny talent—almost frightening. He seems to have had practically no education except the back-files of the little magazines and is almost entirely unencumbered with ideas except on the practice of his art, but a mediumistic voice speaks through him in the most impeccable of accents. It's a long time since I've read anybody with such a specific gift for writing —like a musician's for music."

Arvin himself arrived on June 12 for his annual summer visit. Within hours that shooting star had struck him, and he professed himself instantly smitten, encircled by what he called the "magic ring" of love. Howard immediately decamped for Boston—whether by prearrangement or sudden inspiration, it is hard to say—and as he departed, he took with him the singular picture of his past and present lovers walking hand in hand into nirvana.

The date that magic ring closed, which probably meant the first time Truman and Newton made love, was Friday, June 14. "I can't down the desire to tell you, and only you," Newton wrote Howard a few days later, "how magically the powers of nature, beginning last Friday (June 14, 1946, as I am not likely to forget), and outward circumstances generally connived to furnish the kind of medium or ambiente for this Thing that one can surely expect but once or twice in a lifetime. The weather was supernatural on Friday, and then again on Sunday, and on Tuesday too; and maybe some time I can tell you what the cool blue air, and the green light, and then a certain wash of moonlight falling into this room of mine as the twilight fused imperceptibly into it—what things of this sort did to my eyes and my command of speech and my senses, and my whole nature."

For Truman, June 14 was also a supernatural day. In a moment he had forgotten Howard's aristocratic voice and his Jimmy Stewart looks and had fallen in love with Newton, the least likely candidate for his affections: forty-five, bald, bespectacled, slight, shy, anemic, a victim of depression, vertigo, and a score of other psychological ailments—almost a parody, in short, of the popular image of the mousy college professor. "Newton looked like a clerk, and his attraction was a puzzle to me," said Brinnin, who was expressing a common opinion. Truman viewed him with different eyes, and saw virtues that probably even Howard had missed. "Newton was a charming person," he said, "cultivated in every way, with the most wonderfully subtle mind. He was like a lozenge that you could keep turning to the light, one way or another, and the most beautiful colors would come out."

Given such feelings on both sides, there was no need for courtship, and during the next month the new lovers enjoyed the equivalent of a honeymoon, a honeymoon made more delicious still because of its surprise: it was as if they had walked from Yaddo's broad, sunlit public lawns into the woods beyond and discovered a hidden glade carpeted with bluebonnets and perfumed by wild wisteria. They had lunch and dinner together, alone or with others, went into town to the movies, and at the end of the evening took long walks around the grounds.

Although they talked constantly, Newton, a man of the pen, also felt compelled to put his tender feelings on paper. "But you know, dearest T.C.," he said in one note, "that if I ever really began a 'letter' to you it could have no imaginable end—or even beginning —for it would just have to circle forever and ever, like a great wheel, about the one central fact, and you know what that fact is, and there are either millions of ways of telling it or only one way. I love you dearly, and if you wish, I will write that over and over again until this page is filled up, and many more pages, like a bad boy kept in after school, whose teacher (in some perverse way) wishes to make him happy instead of wretched. Only I'm not a bad boy, and neither are you; we are very good indeed, and we shall be better and better as time wears on—for we are at the source of good, and we are drinking the water of truth, and what we are making between us is purely beautiful. Is it possible to be better than that?"

Newton had not read any of Truman's stories—to answer the question Howard had asked in his letter of June 2—but he quickly did his homework at Yaddo and left him a note of praise, touchingly worded and elegantly phrased: "I have read three of your stories, dearest T.C., 'A Tree of Night,' 'Miriam,' and 'Jug of Silver.' They are very lovely and frightening and pure and tender, and they have given me a strange, beautiful experience. I respect you so much for having written them. They will gleam out in my mind from time to time for many days, and indeed much longer, like something seen suddenly and magically by snowfall or in some watery light: I have not found the right way of saying how real and yet how fantastically poetic they seem to me. A famous man once said (quotes) that there is no true beauty but has some mark of strangeness on it, and he was very right, and all good writers have always known it: *you* know it too, dear Truman, and no one can take the knowledge from you. It will deepen and enrich and amplify itself with every day you live, and there *need* be no end to what you can express for all of us of what it is to be human and afraid and in love and intensely happy. So many things! It's all before you, and *you* won't make the mistake of not boarding the train that is drawing out to your destination.

"It would not be possible, it seems to me, for me to cherish you more tenderly, with more of myself, than I already do, but if it were possible, the reading of your stories would have that effect. Where did you come from, Truman? and how did I find myself moving toward the point where you were? It's the agency of some beneficent geniuses, I can only imagine."

Newton had only one worry while he was imbibing the water of truth, and that was that in falling in love with Truman he had injured Howard. "As for T.C. I can hardly broach that subject in this letter," he nervously wrote Howard on June 17, beginning several days of what was to be a flurry of charming, richly brocaded letters between them. "My head is still whirling with quite a differ-ent kind of vertigo from that I complained of to you, and I am too deeply moved to talk about it easily. The important thing for the moment is that this should not in some clumsy way be made still another source of anxiety and confusion to *you*."

Whatever he felt, Howard could scarcely have answered more graciously than he did two days later: "You dope—how can you think for a moment that a *rapprochement* (to use a very feeble word for what I surmise to be the circumstances) between you and T.C. would cause me the least iota of anxiety or confusion—would be the source to me of any emotion but the warmest delight? I have never in my life known in anyone, man, woman, or child, such delicacy and purity of feeling as is the native *habitus* of T.C.'s psyche, nor can I think of anyone on the wide earth except you, my dear, more capable of responding to these feelings as they should be responded to or with a more abundant store of wisdom and experience to enrich and deepen them. God's benison on you both."

Thus assured, Newton felt emboldened to describe the heavenly rapture he was experiencing inside what he called a magic ring. "You are very understanding and imaginative, as I secretly knew you would be about T.C. and me," he answered, with obvious relief. "I only dislike so intensely the thought of giving you a moment's pain that I ran out ahead of the unreal danger as if that would avert it! Now that I both intuit and 'know' how unreal it is, nothing is left—absolutely nothing, as it seems to me—to jar or discolor the unbe-lievable perfectness of this experience. I am hopelessly contradictory about it: at one moment I feel that I must tell everyone within hearing distance how preternaturally happy I am, and why; at an-other moment, I feel that I cannot and will not say one word about it to any mortal soul, *even you*. And for the time perhaps this latter is the wiser impulse."

To which Howard replied on June 21 with more extravagant words and a bouquet of seventeenth-century poetry: "I can't tell you, my dear, how glad I am all this has come about. It seems to me a miracle. Don't you feel that every minute of your life is justified, all the scrupulous 'cultivation' of one's sensibilities and perceptions, the keeping in trim of one's psyche, the discipline of spirit that sometimes seems so hard until it is triumphantly vindicated by what it can bring to moments like these? And the false trails you have been up, the people who wouldn't or couldn't see what was good for them—and now the miracle of time that has brought forth T.C. Really, it gives me the *frisson* of an historic moment—a new marriage of Faustus and Helena.

"Do you remember a poem of Marvell's called 'The Picture of Little T.C. in a Prospect of Flowers'? The title snapped into my mind one night when we were walking by the tennis court and T.C. with that incomparable elegance and grace of movement which is sometimes his ran to the violet bed there and sitting down cross-legged began to plait violets into the buttonholes of his shirt. I couldn't find the poem at Yaddo and just looked it up. It has some charming lines:

> Who can foretell for what high cause
> This darling of the gods was born? . . .
> Meantime, whilst every verdant thing
> Itself does at thy beauty charm,
> Reform the errors of the spring;
> Make that—the tulips may have share
> Of sweetness, seeing they are fair;
> And roses of their thorns disarm;
> 　　But most procure
> That violets may a longer age endure.
>
> But O, young beauty of the woods,
> Whom Nature courts with fruit and flowers,
> Gather the flowers, but spare the buds,
> Lest Flora, angry at thy crime
> To kill her infants in their prime,
> Do quickly make the example yours;
> 　　And ere we see
> Nip in the blossom, all our hopes and thee.

Returning to Yaddo July 8, Howard was able to give his benediction in person. He looked like "a million dollars," Newton wrote his friend Granville Hicks. But the next day Howard's million dollars had shrunk to a few lackluster pennies, and he took to his bed. Whether it was actually seeing the two lovers together that did him in or some other emotional upset it is impossible to say; but it seems likely that despite all his generous remarks to Newton, he was more troubled by their liaison than he himself knew. How, indeed, could he not have been? "Howard was endlessly bemused by the affair between Newton and Truman," said Brinnin, "and perhaps a little hurt." On close inspection, even some of his gushing words of blessing reveal his ambivalent emotions. "A new marriage of Faustus and Helena" Howard had labeled their romance, ostensibly implying, in a high-flown literary way, that Truman's youth would rub off on Newton and make him feel young too. But Newton, whose life had been spent probing beneath the surface of words, must have been a little jarred at hearing himself compared to Faustus and Truman to Helena: Helena, according to the legend, was one of the devil's gifts to Faustus; in return, Faustus gave his soul.

Howard did not really recover until Truman left on July 17 for his *Harper's Bazaar* assignment in New Orleans. "Much of the day spent with Howard," Newton wrote in his diary on July 18, "early in the morning at his studio, lunch there, and then the evening here in my studio. Much converse about little T.C. naturally." They had much to discuss. Newton's honeymoon with little T.C. was over, but his romance had just begun, and they already had arranged to meet in August at Newton's home in Massachusetts.

Truman's departure had changed the atmosphere at Yaddo, and Howard and Newton were not the only ones to notice it: the catalyst for so much of the evening's amusement had disappeared, life was duller, and those who remained behind had to search out their own fun. It was as if autumn had arrived two months early, and the leaves had prematurely turned to a melancholy gold. "Suddenly the tower room was empty, the cabals of the breakfast table dispersed," said Brinnin. "Adrift, those of us left at Yaddo began to look for partners at Ping-Pong, Chinese checkers, croquet. Relieved of the nightly jostle for position, old friends met in an atmosphere of affectionate contempt. Truman was everywhere. To speak of him would have certified his absence. No one did."

15

Was Newton an important critic? Truman had asked Brinnin. An important critic like Edmund Wilson? Brinnin, who taught at Vassar College and was supposed to know about such things, answered yes on both counts—and he was right. Newton was not nearly so well known as Wilson, and he did not have Wilson's enormous range, but in his own field, American literature of the nineteenth century, he ranked at the top of the list. He wrote biographies of Hawthorne, Longfellow, Whitman, and Melville, the last of which won the National Book Award in 1951. His judgment was shrewd and sound, and he probably knew more about the Golden Age of American letters than any critic other than his old friend and mentor, Van Wyck Brooks.

He was immensely, almost impossibly learned in other literatures too—he read French, German, Italian, Spanish, Latin, and a little Greek—and one of the distinguishing marks of his criticism was his ability to place American literature in a broad historical perspective. Alfred Kazin, also a critic of considerable reputation, appraised his Melville biography as "the wisest and most balanced single piece of writing on Melville I have ever seen," and wisdom and balance, rather than advocacy or innovation, characterized most of Newton's writing. If he was passionate about anything, it was good writing; bad writing, he said, is a kind of immorality. His own style, as can be seen in his letters to Howard and Truman, is both lively and precise. Wilson himself praised him for his "charm of style," adding that "among the writers who have really devoted their lives to the study of our literature, I can think of only two who can themselves be called first-rate writers: Van Wyck Brooks and Newton Arvin."

When he said Newton had devoted his life to a study of "our literature," Wilson meant it in the conventional career sense; but Newton really had devoted his life to literature—so much so, indeed, that it can almost be said that he had no life outside of books. Born in Valparaiso, Indiana, in 1900, he found the world most congenial on the printed page: his father, a successful businessman, spent most of his time in Chicago or Indianapolis; on those rare weekends when he returned home, he fought with his wife and made fun of Newton for being a sissy, which, by ordinary standards, he was. "Misbegotten"—which is to say contemptible—is the label Newton later applied to his younger self. He escaped East to Harvard, but once again buried himself in books, giving not a moment, as he regretfully recalled, to anything that might be considered fun. He was, in his own eyes and probably everybody else's as well, a grind, a drudge. Although he graduated summa cum laude, his father, implacable still, refused to allow Newton's admiring mother to attend the graduation ceremonies.

After Harvard, he went to Smith, where he remained, except for a few brief excursions into the wider world, for the rest of his life. One of the Seven Sisters, the female equivalent in those days of the male Ivy League, Smith was one of the few places in which a man like Newton could have existed. Located in Northampton, in the hills of western Massachusetts, several hours away from both Boston and New York, the college offered a feeling of isolation and protection, which in Newton's mind were almost synonymous. He rarely left, and even weekend trips to New York would often be cut short as he raced, in a seeming panic, for the first available train from Grand Central. "He was a fearful, timorous man," said Daniel Aaron, who was one of his best friends on the Smith faculty. "He really could not tear himself away from Northampton; that was a bastion of safety for him."

Deeply ashamed of being homosexual, he made the mistake of marrying one of his students, Mary Garrison, in 1932. A large, vibrant, strikingly handsome blonde, she was his opposite in almost every way, blessed with what he called "high animal spirits." She was outgoing where he was shy, vivacious where he was dispirited, resilient where he was depressed. Her temperament was, in fact,

very much like Truman's, and Newton was probably drawn to both
for much the same reason—they gave him contact with life. Wanting to be honest with her, yet embarrassed to come right out and
say he was homosexual, he tried to tell her by showing her a poem
by another homosexual, Walt Whitman, which he thought would
explain everything.

> Primeval my love for the woman I love,
> O bride! O wife! more resistless, more enduring than I
>   can tell, the thought of you!
> Then separate, as disembodied, the purest born,
> The ethereal, the last athletic reality, my consolation,
> I ascend—I float in the regions of your love, O man,
> O sharer of my roving life.

Did she understand it? he asked anxiously, in what must have
been a moment of high intellectual comedy. She said she did, and
he was so relieved that he inquired no further. Her interpretation of
those extremely ambiguous lines was, in fact, as different from his
as his may have been from Whitman's. She thought the poet was
talking about a conflict between a man and a woman and that Newton, in his oblique and indirect fashion, was warning her that their
marriage might be difficult. His real message escaped her, and the
result of such confusion was eight years of misery for both of them:
Newton's bride, unlike Howard's, did not know then or for several
years thereafter that her husband was homosexual.

"He was extremely generous and very sweet to me," she remembered long after. "But everybody said he treated me like a child.
When we got home from our honeymoon, he pointed to the telephone and said, 'When that thing rings, no matter what anybody
wants, the answer is no!' My job was to keep people away from him
and not interrupt his work. I never even knocked on his door. If I
wanted to say something to him, I put a note under it." After they
divorced in 1940, both his depression and his isolation intensified.
"Saw no one all day. A bath of solitude" was one typical entry in
his diary. Analyzing himself with the same dispassion he might have
brought to a poem by Longfellow, he explained the nature of his
emotional defects to Howard: "There is such a thing as a sort of
affectional impotence. I don't mean now what is called psychic impotence or certainly literal impotence (though both or either may be

involved), but, in the sphere of the emotions, a great and poignant need of love combined with an incapacity, at the last moment, either to possess or to be possessed—and again I mean something intangible. Every capacity for tenderness is present—except the one power of penetrating or being penetrated with the last intimacy." Even in his fantasies he was by himself. Instead of counting sheep or silently reciting lines of poetry when he had trouble falling asleep, he would imagine that he was on an alien planet, and that his task was to name all the trees and creatures he discovered there. But from horizon to horizon he was the only human being to be seen. He had the entire planet to himself.

Aside from his books, happiness eluded him, and he tried to commit suicide at least three times. One of those attempts was stamped with a particular, telling pathos. It was winter, and he walked to a pond near his apartment to watch a group of skaters, ruby-cheeked in the frigid air and glowing with the undimmed vitality of youth. It must have been a scene—and so Newton, whose mind always turned to literary analogies, may have thought too—very much like one in Thomas Mann's *Tonio Kröger:* Tonio, the writer, the observer, the eternal outsider, witnesses a similar group of carefree young people dancing—"you blond, you living, you happy ones!" They evoke memories of his boyhood, and, overcome by the thought of what could have been, he retreats to his bed and sobs with "nostalgia and remorse."

So it was with Newton, who at that moment probably would have traded everything he had done and all he had written if he could have exchanged places with one of those robust young athletes skating effortlessly across the ice. After gazing at them for some time, he trudged home to his apartment, opened a bottle of liquor, and played, over and over, a recording of John McCormack singing Hugo Wolf's *Ganymede.* As McCormack's rich and expressive tenor poured out, in words and music, what Newton had just seen, the glories of youth and beauty, Newton swallowed sixteen Nembutals. Luck alone brought a friend into his apartment the next morning, before they had finished their terrible work.

This was the anguished and tormented man who came to Yaddo in the summer of 1946. "Woke again just after five," he wrote in his diary a few months earlier. "Thoughts of death and self-destruction. 'Morning tears.' " In May he described himself as feeling "rather blue," and that is probably how he still felt when he met Truman, who doubtless seemed, that naughty, amusing Ganymede, to belong to the blissful race of the blond, the living, and the happy ones.

When he was around Truman, or merely even thinking about him, Newton was a man transformed, a different person altogether from the gloom-shrouded depressive who had been muttering about suicide a few months before. He described his unfamiliar feeling of "psychological euphoria" to Granville Hicks and added proudly: "I was never more chipper in my life." His only complaint in those waning days of July was the bittersweet one familiar to any ardent lover who is deprived of the one he loves. Although Truman was sending him as many as three letters a day from New Orleans, they were no substitute for Truman himself. Just a few weeks short of his forty-sixth birthday, Newton had apparently conquered his "affectional impotence" and with great excitement was exploring emotions he previously had encountered only in fiction. For probably the first time in his adult life he needed not just the occasional, but the constant company of another human being.

"All would be fair indeed, on the personal plane, if it were not for this apartness from little T.C.," he told Howard a few days after Truman had left Yaddo. "It came too soon and is lasting too long. At this stage we really should be inseparable." He was also afraid, he added, that the *Harper's Bazaar* assignment might bring illness or breakdown to his young lover, who was reporting that he and Henri Cartier-Bresson, the *Bazaar*'s photographer, were marching miles every day in New Orleans' tropical heat. "However, as you say, he is young, blessedly young, God be praised, and buoyant, and tough too in his way, and I am not really fretting like an old woman. But I love him so tenderly that I can't be wholly indifferent to these possibilities."

Their separation only seemed long, however, and on July 28, just twelve days after they had said goodbye at Yaddo, Truman flew back to New York, raced from the airport to Grand Central, and caught the first train to Northampton. "Look where I am!" he exultantly wrote Howard that night, alone for a moment while his host was off shopping for their dinner. "Arrived today and needless to say, am delighted: with Northampton (of which I've seen nothing), Newton's apartment, and Newton." He remained delighted during the four days he was there, and on his return to New York, he gave a final accounting to Mary Louise, who was vacationing in Maine. "I had a wonderful time in Northampton with Newton. I love him most tenderly, more really than I can tell you, for he is the sweetest, gentlest person, next to yourself, that I ever met."

August was a busy and difficult month for both of them: Newton was unhappily teaching summer classes at Wesleyan, an all-male college in Middletown, Connecticut; accustomed to instructing women, he was finding it unnerving to lecture to men, whose faces, viewed from his podium, looked distressingly unresponsive and in-scrutable. Truman's days were equally trying: after more than a year of being treated like *Harper's Bazaar*'s crown prince, he was jarred by an unpleasant dispute with the editors. In Mary Louise's absence, they were balking at paying the full expenses for his trip South, which had turned out to be far more costly than he had anticipated, and talking also about postponing publication of the story he had written at Yaddo, "The Headless Hawk," which had been scheduled for the October issue. The prospect of actually los-ing rather than making money on the New Orleans article was an-noying enough, but the possibility that "The Headless Hawk" might be locked away and forgotten in some editor's file cabinet was more than annoying; it sent him into a panic. His name had not been attached to any new fiction since "A Jug of Silver" came out in *Mademoiselle* at the end of 1945, and his precociously shrewd sense of how a writer should manage his career warned him that he would have to appear with a story soon or stand in danger of forfeiting the reputation he had so suddenly acquired with "Miriam."

Those problems were in fact resolved to his satisfaction. His fi-nances were straightened out; "The Headless Hawk" was scheduled for the November issue, a month after "Notes on N.O."; and he was free to concentrate his emotional energies on Newton. They faithfully wrote each other at least once a day, and for both of them the arrival of the mailman was the brightest, most impatiently awaited moment of the day. "Your letters make a music like Mozart in my ears," Newton said. In early August, Truman sent him a picture of himself as a boy and a pair of silver cuff links engraved with his initials. "Dearest," Truman said. "The cuff links were given to me by someone else who loved me too, dear, darling Sooky, on my 12th birthday—wear them, darling, if you can. I love you. T." They were small treasures to Truman—Sook had died just a few months before—and Newton responded with as much gratitude as if they had been a rare first edition of Hawthorne or Longfellow. "I am still looking at the cuff links and at the little picture, my angel, with tears just *behind* my eyes; was ever anyone's feller so prodigal to him as mine is? I despair of telling even you what a strange tender feeling they have given me. Could I not now, please, have one of your eyes or one of your hands by return mail? Oh, my dearest, dearest, how terribly much you signify to me. I love you."

A few days later, on August 14, exactly two months after that magic ring had closed around him, Newton reminded his angel how important the fourteenth day of any month now was to him. "Today *is* an anniversary, and I have been thinking of it for days now. I have never remembered a date like *this* in my life—remembered it so intensely, I mean, for of course there never *was* a date like June 14, before, not in this life, and I shouldn't suppose in any." Crowding into a few months the love letters he had not written in all the years before, he wrote again and again in the same impassioned spirit. "I woke up in the night last night," he said, "plagued not by a night-ingale but by a mosquito—and as I lay going back to sleep again, I longed unspeakably to have you there in my arms and to float off into sleep with *you*. Not having you was an ache of loneliness and loss." His neat and tidy world had been turned upside-down by such unruly and unfamiliar emotions, and he half-jokingly added: "You little monster! I never planned or designed to fall hopelessly in love this way, at this time; it is extremely distracting and against efficiency; and I can ill afford the constant thought and time it entails."

Some who knew Newton, astonished and made jealous perhaps by his unprecedented outpouring of emotion, worried that he had allowed his passion to overrule his reason. Carson, who only a few months before had informed him that he was her most precious friend, suspected that Truman might toy with him for a while, then, when he was bored, leave him, inflicting some mortal wound in the process. Howard, who had decided that Truman was not, after all, the darling of the gods, feared just the opposite. In a letter to John Malcolm Brinnin, he likened Truman to Truman's own creation, the evil, manipulating Miriam; he was afraid, Howard said, that Truman might now try to play Newton's Miriam, attaching himself so tightly that Newton would be crushed by his embrace, as Mrs. Miller was in the story.

Truman inadvertently fed that suspicion by letting it be known that Newton might leave both Smith and Northampton so that they could be together in New York. "I hear all sorts of interesting rumors *a ton sujet*," Howard boldly reported to Newton. "I hope you aren't doing anything too drastic in the Way of the World Well Lost —though, come to think of it, you are about Antony's age and T.C. is what A. never had, Cleopatra in her prime!" Newton, who must have been tired of Howard's once again bracketing him with a doomed and tragic character, rather coolly replied: "What interesting rumors you must hear! I wish I knew what some of them were. But I'm afraid there isn't a very solid basis for them."

In fact, it was Truman who regularly made the four-hour journey to Northampton, taking with him some of his own jazz records so that he could listen to something besides what he called "that gloomy old funeral music" that Newton enjoyed—that gloomy old funeral music being symphonies and concertos by Mozart, Beethoven, and the like. Newton occasionally, if nervously, ventured down to New York, dragging Truman, who had hitherto avoided such elevated pursuits, to the opera and the art museums. He acted, recalled Daniel Aaron, like a euphoric bridegroom with his new bride, and like bride and bridegroom, Truman and he played the usual newlywed games. Reversing the spelling of their names, they had affectionate code words for each other; Newton was Notwen Nivra, Truman, Namurt Etopac. In one letter Notwen so forgot himself that he even made a sexual joke, tepid though it may have been: "LOST Probably in Manhattan. One peppermint-stick, beautifully pink and white, wonderfully straight, deliciously sweet. About a hand's length. Of great intrinsic and also sentimental value to owner."

Newton had had other romances with younger men, but none had affected him like this one, and Truman made him feel youthful —younger, no doubt, than he had felt when he actually was young —and even giddy, bestowing on him a portion of his own remarkable zest and enthusiasm. "It was like a draught of some exquisite liqueur to hear your actual voice—and to laugh so gaily with you— as *I* can't do, and never could, with any other human being," he wrote Truman after one phone conversation. At the end of a Saturday in September, Newton allowed his diary a brief but rather touching glimpse into one of their happy days in Northampton. They had had lunch at a restaurant in town, he said, but then they had spent the rest of the day alone in his apartment. In the late afternoon they drank their ritual Manhattans. After that, he noted: "No third meal at all. No time for it. Rather violent or at least intense amour, followed by sudden and profound sleep together."

Truman was equally entranced. "I miss [Newton] most dreadfully," he told Howard, "and, though I see people constantly, am very lonely. It is very curious, isn't it, how everything worked out? I appreciate your generosity, dear Howard, in giving N. to me; I'm afraid I could never be so generous."

Once again, however, his affection could not be separated from his need, and he also recognized how useful Newton could be to a young man who, for all practical purposes, had received no formal education. Truman's reading had been wide, certainly, but so scattered and haphazard that he had missed entirely many of the standard works of literature familiar to any graduate of a good liberal-arts college. Many of his friends, who had that advantage, were often amazed, as well as amused, by how open and naive he was in expressing his ignorance. Andrew Lyndon recalled going with him to Radio City Music Hall to see the movie version of *Great Expectations*. "Truman was still writing *Other Voices, Other Rooms*, whose hero was raised by strangers, as Pip, the boy in Dickens, was. There we were in that vast theater, and Truman was squirming in his seat, becoming more and more nervous. All of a sudden he put both hands on my arms and said, 'Oh, my God, darling! They've stolen my plot!' He really was an insane combination of sophistication and naïveté. I remember telling Newton about it, and he said, 'Just wait until he discovers Shakespeare. That's going to be interesting.' "

A quick learner, Truman lacked only a good college English teacher, someone who could point out what was important to know, what was less important, and what he could safely skip. There was no better guide through the literary jungles than Newton, who had read everything and skipped nothing: Truman's infallible divining rod had directed him yet again to the one person who could help him most at the moment when he most needed help. "I always thought Truman picked Newton because he believed he would be good for him," said Andrew. "That was the idea he gave me, at any rate. Bragging about Newton, he once said: 'He reads Greek at the breakfast table!' " Truman was not joking when he himself proclaimed: "Newton was my Harvard."

He often sat in the back of Newton's classes that fall of 1946, and, in what amounted to a crash course in the essentials of literature, also enrolled in a private, after-hours seminar at Newton's Prospect Street apartment. "It was Newton who got me to read Proust and the Nineteenth Century American classics, Hawthorne and Melville, for example—though *Moby Dick* bored me to death. I had already read all the early Henry James novels and found them easy going, but I had trouble with the later things like *The Golden Bowl*. I would never have finished them without Newton. Not that I admire them; they're too figured for my taste. I had read poetry before I met Newton, but I read a lot more afterwards. He made poetry accessible to me, whereas it had not been entirely so before. I remember one period of two months when I read dozens of American poets, from Walt Whitman to Wallace Stevens. We would talk about whatever I was reading, and he would open things up for me, showing me that what I thought was obvious was not necessarily so. He had a very original and curious mind, and he gave me a perspective on my reading."

For his part, Newton was proud, even excited, to be his guide. Teaching was his life's work, and far from feeling used or manipulated, he was eager to impart as much of his learning as he could. Indeed, he seemed to need to play Pygmalion, not only with Truman, but also with the other young men he was involved with over the years, as if by doing so he could legitimize his relationship with them and raise it above the purely sensual. "Newton was only interested in young men who had some kind of literary connection," said Daniel Aaron, "and he liked to think that his solicitude was something more than sexual appetite, that he was actually being of help to them. It was not unlike the vaguely homoerotic feelings that Henry James had for his young protégés. If Newton liked somebody, he was almost angry if he didn't write well. I remember his talking about Truman even before I met him: this marvelous boy, this genius, this incredible figure who was wildly uneducated and yet had this gift."

Lover, teacher, editor, and admirer, Newton was also something else, the father Arch had never been. He was, in fact, only three years younger than Arch, and the role seemed to come naturally to him. His letters often began, "Dearest child," "Darling child," or

"Darling boy." Writing to Mary Louise, he worried that the life his "poor boy" was leading in New York was not right for his work and spiritual calm. "I wish I knew what his truest needs are in this respect and all others," he said fretfully. "I am too fond of him to want to interfere at the wrong points or to fail him at the right ones." The happiest picture of that paternal devotion dates from the following summer. Staying with them in a rented house on Nantucket, Mary Louise walked into the living room one day to find them sitting side-by-side on the couch, reading a book. "They looked like a father and his little boy," she said, and they were so absorbed in the words in front of them that they were unaware of anything else, including her, the house, and the sea outside.

1

Even as a baby in the rural South, Truman instinctively caught the camera's eye, and he never let it go in all the years that followed.

Truman's mother, Lillie Mae (left below), was desperate to make her way in the world. In the winter of 1929 she traveled to an unfamiliar land of ice and snow—Kentucky— to attend a business school, taking her four-year-old son along with her.

His father called him his "little angel," but Arch was happy to let others provide food, shelter and love while he went off looking for that elusive road to riches. This 1932 picture shows father and son in one of their few moments together.

2

3

"He is the sunshine of our home," said his middle-aged cousin Callie. But Truman's own memory of his lonely childhood in Monroeville was bittersweet. Here he is shown at watermelon picking time; with his beloved cousin Sook; and with his uncle, Seabon Faulk.

7

8

He graduated from Manhattan's Franklin School in 1943, but Truman, who liked to think of himself as a "mighty Condor" searching for fame, rarely attended. Both mind and body were usually elsewhere, at The New Yorker, *where he was the most visible copyboy in the magazine's history, or at jazz joints and nightclubs with girls like Phoebe Pierce (left), his friend from Greenwich High School days, and that "licensed screwball," Carol Marcus.*

9

10

11

*An uncanny but unerring instinct
led Truman to the right person
(clockwise) at the right time.
Daise Terry,* The New Yorker's
*terrible-tempered office manager,
took him under her protective
wing. George Davis (shown with
Lotte Lenya) published his early
fiction in* Mademoiselle.
*And Mary Louise Aswell, the
fiction editor of* Harper's Bazaar,
became both mentor and mother.

12

13

At first Carson McCullers thought of him as her little brother, found him an agent and an editor and arranged for his admission to Yaddo, the writers' and artists' colony in Saratoga Springs. But she soon became envious of his success and turned into one of his most bitter enemies. Truman did not return the compliment. "She was a devil," he said, "but I respected her."

14

In 1946 Truman had a brief romance with tall and handsome Howard Doughty (right) at Yaddo, but quickly abandoned him for Doughty's exact physical opposite, the bald and bespectacled literary critic Newton Arvin (left). Arvin is shown here in a Nantucket whaling museum, where he was doing research for his biography of Herman Melville, which won the National Book Award in 1951.

15

16

17

Hard work and fun at Yaddo: during the morning and afternoon guests were expected to work by themselves, but at four o'clock doors banged open and invitations were issued. Leo Lerman tests his skill at croquet, while Truman, with Newton at his right, commands the dinner table. "There's always laughter at his table," said a fellow guest, "echoing across the moat of silence in which the tables around it are sunk."

18

19

ESOTERIC, NEW ORLEANS-BORN TRUMAN CAPOTE, 22, WRITES HAUNTING SHORT STORIES. HIS NOVEL, "OTHER VOICES, OTHER ROOMS," WILL BE OUT THIS FALL

YOUNG U.S. WRITERS

A REFRESHING GROUP OF NEWCOMERS ON THE LITERARY SCENE IS READY TO TACKLE ALMOST ANYTHING

Just as soon as the end of war promised an end to paper rationing, U.S. book publishers started shopping around for new talent. They found, ready and waiting with manuscript in hand, a brand-new batch of writers who had grown up during the depression. Some had also fought through World War II. All of them seemed more studious, more sober and less pessimistic than "the lost generation" which followed World War I.

These young writers of the 1940s, of whom LIFE presents on these pages a representative selection,

are bringing a new freshness to the American literary scene. One of them, 30-year-old Robert Lowell, has just won the Pulitzer Prize for poetry (LIFE, May 19). A young team wrote the novel, *Mrs. Mike,* the March Literary Guild selection. Other young writers have produced four best-sellers and a half-dozen major and minor critical successes. As a group these new writers, many of whom are in their early 20s, do not suffer in comparison with the early fiction produced by the writers of the 1920s and 1940s. They are busily tackling, in every con-

ceivable style and manner of fiction, almost every subject under the American sun—schooldays, family life, county fairs, mountain lions, Freudian symbolism, roadside drive-ins, Pacific cargo boats, Northwest nunneries, Southern poor whites, lack of communication between human beings, and kleptomania.

On pages 81 and 82 LIFE's John Chamberlain, who, as New York Times's and Harper's famous critic, watched the last literary generation grow up, gives his estimate of these new young writers.

In 1947 Life *magazine spotlighted the young American writers who had emerged after World War II. All except Truman had published one or more novels, but "esoteric, New Orleans–born" Truman was the one who was given star treatment. A rival publisher demanded to know how he had pulled off such a coup, but the answer was simple: Truman knew how to seduce the camera.*

When Truman met him, Tennessee Williams was already considered one of America's greatest playwrights. Sometimes friends, sometimes enemies, he and Truman traded compliments and insults for more than thirty years.

"Well, how does it feel to be an enfant terrible?*" Truman asked fellow writer Gore Vidal when they were introduced in 1945. But they both knew that there could be only one* enfant terrible *at a time, and thus began one of the longest-lasting and most famous rivalries in American literary history. "You would think they were running neck-and-neck for some fabulous gold prize," complained Tennessee.*

23

*Bennett Cerf, one of the
founders of Random House,
was a self-admitted ham with a
weakness for bad puns. But he
recognized and encouraged
talent, and he and his wife
Phyllis favored Truman over
almost all of their other
writers.*

24

*He would take care of his author the way a
trainer takes care of a racehorse, said Truman's
Random House editor Robert Linscott, and
Linscott did, praising Truman when he was good
and prodding him when he was bad.*

25

*Truman and Newton Arvin spent the summer
of 1947 in Nantucket, together with
Truman's friend Andrew Lyndon, Leo
Lerman, and Christopher Isherwood, that
"appreciative merry little bird," as Virginia
Woolf had once called him.*

26

*Denham Fouts succeeded in his
ambition to become the Best-Kept
Boy in the World and thereby
inspired several writers,
including Truman, to model
characters after him. Truman
met him in Paris in 1948, but
was frightened off by Denny's
addiction to drugs.*

The famous photograph: Harold Halma's picture on the dustjacket of Other Voices, Other Rooms *(1948) caused as much comment and controversy as the prose inside. Truman claimed that the camera had caught him off guard, but in fact he had posed himself and was responsible for both the picture and the publicity.*

"A darling of the gods," one of his friends had called him, and when he was a young man, Truman was indeed blessed with good fortune and good spirits. Clowning for Cecil Beaton's camera in Tangier in the summer of 1949, he was captured as many remembered him—ebullient, uninhibited, irrepressible.

29

Photographers found Truman irresistible. Beaton shot him against a backdrop of roses on his first trip to England in 1948, causing Tennessee Williams to sarcastically observe that his little face had a "look of prenatal sorrow, as if he were still in the womb and already suspected how cold the world is beyond the vaginal portals." Henri Cartier-Bresson recorded a more seductive expression in New Orleans in 1946, while Karl Bissinger caught him in a more pensive and reflective mood.

30

31

She wanted to put things right with Truman, said Nina Capote, and in 1950 she and Joe Capote traveled to Sicily, where Truman was then living, so that she could try to undo the wrongs of the previous twenty-six years. Here, on a visit to Venice, the three Capotes are shown with Truman's friend Donald Windham.

Stagestruck, Truman turned his short novel The Grass Harp into a play. But even with the help of such experienced hands as (clockwise) composer Virgil Thomson, director Robert Lewis, producer Saint Subber, and designer Cecil Beaton, he was not able to gain success on Broadway. Part of the problem may have been Beaton's enormous tree, which overshadowed Truman's delicate and evocative drama.

34

Two more mismatched souls could not have come together, yet Truman and Jack Dunphy fitted together like pieces in a picture puzzle. "We amused each other all the time," explained Jack. "That's a very rare thing."

After spending several weeks with them in Tangier in 1949, Truman admired Paul Bowles and worshiped his wife Jane, whom he placed near the top of his list of favorite American women writers, behind Willa Cather and Edith Wharton.

35

36

Beat the Devil *was supposed to be a mystery in an offbeat key, like* The Maltese Falcon, *but then Truman came along and concocted a plot of wild skids and nutty dialogue. Filming it, said its director John Huston (the passenger in the sedan chair) was "a hell of a lark," not only for the cast, which included Humphrey Bogart, Gina Lollobrigida and Peter Lorre, but also for such eminent visitors as Carmel Snow.*

38

39

No one was more at home in the age of nightclubs than Truman, who is seen here raising glasses at the Blue Angel in 1955 with Gloria Vanderbilt and Pearl Bailey, the star of his second Broadway show, the charming but ill-fated House of Flowers.

40

Arriving in the Soviet Union with the Porgy and Bess *troupe in 1955, Truman was all bundled up "like a little bunny," in the words of one member of the company. The Russians, who had never seen anyone quite like him, stared and tittered. "Laugh, you dreary people," he said. "But what will you do for laughs next week, when I'm gone from here?"*

41

42

Three famous friends: Truman saw Montgomery Clift and Elizabeth Taylor, shown here in 1950 on the set of A Place in the Sun, *through good times and bad. Marilyn Monroe, his dance partner at El Morocco in 1954, was, in his words, "a beautiful child."*

43

16

"Iт is beautiful here, the weather, crystal" was Truman's rhapsodic report from Northampton in October, 1946, to which,
in a letter to Mary Louise, he added: "The mountains rim-
ming the town are burning green and blue and there is the cold
brown touch of Autumn everywhere. An enormous apple tree, very
heavy with fruit, grows under the window; aside from burning
leaves, is there anything more nostalgic than the odor of ripening
October apples? I am working hard, and *thinking clearly*, and am so
very happy here with Newton: he is so good to me, and for me." To
Howard he wistfully observed: "I love October so much I wish it
could always be." Most of his problems had disappeared with the
hot weather, his career was back on schedule with the publication
of his two pieces in *Bazaar*, and, most important, he was in love. All
would have been as idyllic as that scene he pictured for Mary Lou if
it had not been for one seemingly insoluble concern: Nina.

Her drinking had grown steadily worse in the previous months,
and the ugly scenes that forced him to fly around the corner for
refuge at Leo Lerman's were becoming increasingly common. Most
of her alcoholic rage was directed at Joe, whose infidelity was a
constant and unslackening torment. They still loved each other—
that much was obvious—but that did not prevent him from making
a habit of stopping off to visit other women on his way home from
Wall Street, or prevent her from inspecting his underwear for semen
stains while he was taking his evening shower. "He's so stupid,
Lyn!" she would say to her friend Lyn White. "There were pecker
tracks all over his shorts!"

To some outsiders, the resulting battles, which usually ended in embraces and kisses, seemed to be a part of their marriage, a necessary Elizabeth Taylor–Richard Burton kind of ritual that demonstrated the depth of their passion. "I thought that they had a wild and romantic relationship," said Nina's friend Eleanor Friede. "She always used to threaten him. 'I'll take a butcher knife to you!' she would say. 'Don't you ever do that again!' But that was just their way. I thought they were a glamorous, flamboyant, marvelous couple." More and more, however, particularly when the Scotch bottle was nearing empty, their fights were becoming squalid brawls. She slapped his face during a dinner party; in retaliation, he pushed her out of her chair, causing her to cut her lip so badly that a doctor had to be called. Another time, while they were fighting in their bedroom, she grabbed his testicles so hard that they bled, sending him to the hospital in his bathrobe. The months after that marked the lowest point in their marriage: he moved out and embarked on a romance with another woman, and she engaged in affairs of her own —her only way of revenging herself against his philandering, she said.

Joe's infidelity was perhaps even more wounding to her than it would have been to many other women, who did not take such almost insolent pride in their ability to attract men. Now in her early forties, Nina was still vivacious and attractive, still slim, chic, and stylish. Carefully dressed and meticulously groomed, with frequent visits to a beauty parlor that kept her hair a continuous blond, she seemed, to a younger woman like Friede, to be the embodiment of sophistication. But now for the first time she appeared a little lost, like one of the women in a Tennessee Williams play who nurses some vague hurt or disappointment from the past. "There was a tragic aura about Nina," said Michael Brown, a songwriter who observed her at many late-night parties. "There was something almost hysterical in her fluttering, in her incessant flow of words, in her Southernness."

She was more destructive to herself than she was to Truman or Joe, and sometime during that troubled period she tried to commit suicide by taking an overdose of sleeping pills; but like Newton, she was saved when a friend summoned help. "A day or so after she did it, Truman called me and asked me to come over," said Andrew. "We knew by then that she was all right, but through some mixup he had just received the note she had left him. She had written the usual farewells, then added: 'I am putting my jewelry in a box under the radiator in the dining room. I don't want that woman to have my things. They're for you. Love, Mother.' It was a very dignified letter except for the P.S., which went something like this: 'On second thought, you had better rent a safety deposit box for my jewelry at the Chase Manhattan Bank. You're rather careless sometimes, and I will want to know where my things are when I need them.' I think she really intended to kill herself, though; she was still a Southern belle, and she didn't like her man doing anything wrong."

Her alcoholic anger was not directed at Joe alone, and when Joe was away, Truman was her target—for all the old reasons. Truman had not wound up on the streets or in jail, as she had predicted, but she rarely hid from him the fact that despite everything he had accomplished, he had let her down: he had not been the boy she had hoped for, and he was not now the man she wanted her son to be either. "She was a wonderful person when she was not drinking, impossible when she was," he said. "She was a Jekyll and Hyde, much more neurotic and difficult than anybody realized."

She might have overlooked his behavior herself—she became very chummy with some of his homosexual friends—but she could not ignore the judgments of others. No one hears so many whispers, real or imagined, as someone who has been brought up in a small town, and talk about Arch's embarrassing escapades and scrapes with the law, along perhaps with questions about her own fast life, may have left her unusually sensitive. She was worried to a morbid degree about what people would say about her and hers, and she was always watching for a sign of disapproval, straining to hear derogatory remarks in conversations across a room. "She was the most uptight person I've ever met," said Harper Lee, "pulled taut just like a violin string."

When she discussed Truman's homosexuality with Lyn White, she clenched her hands so tightly in anger and frustration that her knuckles blanched. "Nina, would you rather have a football player or a genius for a son?" asked White, an ebullient, free-spirited young Texan. "Oh, Lyn," she would reply. "You just don't know what it's like!" What it was like for her was almost unceasing humiliation, and she almost certainly would have wished her son to be a linebacker rather than a genius, or, more particularly, a homosexual genius. She could have looked at Truman in many ways, but sadly for her, as well as for him, she most often saw him not as an almost spectacularly successful young writer, but as an oddity who generated looks and snickers and prompted a delivery boy to scrawl on the wall outside her own apartment: *"CAPOTE THE FAG."*

She was a woman of stark contradictions—still the good Nina and the bad Nina—and she seemed destined to carry her ambivalence about him to her grave. She was too intelligent, drunk or sober, not to appreciate his achievements, and there were moments when she even seemed resigned, however reluctantly and with however much exasperation, to who and what he was. Both the resignation and the exasperation were evident in an amusing exchange that Truman and his friends quickly turned into legend. Cheryl Crawford, who was an important Broadway producer, telephoned one day, and not finding Truman at home, asked Nina to tell him that "Miss Crawford" had called. Confused by Crawford's voice, which was unusually low for a woman, closer to bass than that of many men, Nina answered: "You know, whatever you boys do is perfectly all right with me. But I do think it's going a little far when you start calling yourself *Miss!*" And she hung up the phone.

There were periods, too, when, like one of Williams' self-deceiving, aging Southern belles, she would simply brush away the disagreeable truth and pretend, even with close friends like White and Friede, that Truman was just an ordinary young man with ordinary inclinations. She was puzzled, she said, why he could not meet a nice girl and settle down. "Lyn, would you marry my son?" she asked White. "Nina," answered White, who did not want to play her game of make-believe, "I don't think your son would be any more interested than I am." To Friede her display of feigned ignorance was almost embarrassing. "We were so intimate that she would even tell me what she and Joe did in bed," said Friede. "But here she was indulging in this fantasy about Truman. Of course she knew about him, but she *wouldn't* know about him. He was her brilliant son who one of these days was going to knock off playing around with the boys and raise a family. What was I going to say to that? I didn't say anything. I just looked the other way."

There were few hours of peace at 1060 Park Avenue during the fall of 1946, and the never-ending turmoil was exacting its price on Truman. "T.C.—pale and tired-looking, poor child, after a horrible scene with Nina," Newton noted in his diary early in September.

Recurring tonsillitis forced him to have his tonsils removed at the end of October, but there was another horrible scene even while he was in bed recuperating. That night Newton outlined in his diary what had happened: "Two calls from T.C.—one from 1060 Park Avenue in the morning (when he seemed well) and one early in the evening from Leo's—whither, it appeared, he had been driven from a sick-bed by his mother's insane behavior. The poor poor child." What led to his flight into the chilly night, a reason that the poor child probably kept to himself, was his discovery that she had been reading the dozens of letters Newton had written him since June. "I had put them into a drawer," he said. "One day they weren't there, and when I found her reading them, I went into a rage! A fury!" He had forgiven much, but she had finally done something unforgivable, and he decided at long last to move as far away from her as he could get—to Brooklyn.

He made the decision after a visit to Andrew Lyndon, who was living there in a rooming house owned by two elderly ladies who ran a telephone-answering service in the basement. Spying his salvation, Truman soon joined him. "I have changed addresses, have moved to a little lost mews in darkest Brooklyn," he told Brinnin, making the mud towers of Timbuktu sound less distant and mysterious than the borough across the Bridge. "I wanted most to get away from hectic, nerve-racking influences, to escape and get on with my work. I had reached a point where I was so nervous I could hardly hold a cigarette, and my work was not going too well." For the sum of ten dollars a week, an astonishingly low figure even in 1946, he was able to rent two sunny rooms. Filled with enough Victoriana to make even George Davis envious, the house, at 17 Clifton Place, in the Clinton Hill section, was clean, well heated, and as quiet as a church. Aside from the owners, who only occasionally ascended for air, he and Andrew were the only occupants.

Sometimes he did not leave his new neighborhood for three or four days in a row, traveling into Manhattan only for lunches or parties or to catch the train to Northampton. Invariably, he would try to persuade Andrew, who was attending the New School in Manhattan, to skip his classes and keep him company. Andrew, who was also attempting to become a writer, would often oblige. For a few weeks Truman enjoyed believing he had found a secret haven, and he would not give Nina, or many others, his telephone number. "Under no circumstances are you to tell it to anyone, neither family nor friends," he sternly admonished Brinnin. It did not take long for him to miss Manhattan, however, and the forty-minute subway journey into midtown came to seem like a journey of a thousand miles. "Truman regards the trip to Brooklyn about as Livingstone must have his trip to Africa" was the wry comment of one of his friends. The location of his Brooklyn hideout was a short-lived secret; soon he was begging people to visit him.

By December he and his mother had reconciled. He took her to the theater as part of a peace settlement, and although he kept his rooms at Clifton Place for most of the winter, he also spent many nights at 1060 Park, where a measure of quiet had returned. Mother and son still walked warily around each other, but they seemed to have come to an understanding, a modus vivendi that satisfied, if it did not entirely please, both of them. Their tacit truce was illustrated by a scene Friede witnessed. On his way to a dinner party, Truman emerged from his room in his most stylish dinner clothes: a black velvet suit, a red velvet vest, a ruffled white shirt, and shiny patent leather pumps. "It was a bizarre outfit then," said Friede, "and he looked a little bit as if he were going to a costume ball. Nina took one glance and said, 'Truman, you come over here! What are you wearing? You go right back in there and put on your gray flannel suit from Brooks Brothers. I don't want you going out dressed like that.' He kind of pouted, but he went back into his room anyway. When he came out again, he had on his gray Brooks Brothers suit. He hadn't given in entirely, however. He was still wearing his red velvet vest and his patent leather pumps."

For months after they met, Newton continued his highbrow gushing. "As Thoreau would say, we live not in harmony, but in melody also; and it was an exquisite melody this weekend," he told Truman in October. "You *aren't* a human being; not a mere human being, I mean," he later added. "I've been sure of that all along. You only have all the conceivable *charm* of a human being, but in fact you are a Supernatural Helper, as the folklorists say, and if I'm not as good as I'm supposed to be, you'll just vanish on me someday, in a puff of fragrant colored vapor—and where will *I* be?" His comments in his diary were briefer than those in his letters, without all that intellectual filigree, but they sounded no less heartfelt. "Wonderful to see him," he said at the beginning of one of their weekends in Northampton. "T.C. leaves again for New York—painful as always to have him go," he said at the end of another.

Wonderful as it was for him to see him, Newton did not want to see him very often, however. He could enjoy that exquisite melody for only short periods before being afflicted by a feeling of claustrophobia and a need to be quiet and alone. More than once he said that he was truly alive only when they were together; but the fact remained, towering over both of them, as stubborn and irrefutable as Gibraltar, that he wanted to be truly alive in that way only once or twice a month. The rest of the time he preferred the less demanding companionship of the authors on his bookshelves. "Sweetened my mouth with a little Montaigne" was how he described his bedtime reading in his diary; he would not have written about the act of sex with greater or more sensual pleasure.

Truman, by contrast, could engage only in intimate relationships. He did not know how to be cool or standoffish, and he retained his boyhood habit of hugging, kissing, and opening his arms even to comparative strangers. That puppylike warmth was basic to his personality. He could not switch it on and off, and if he loved someone, as he did Newton, he assumed that he would be with that person as much as possible. Newton's friends made the same assumption. Hearing him babble about his T.C., Howard and Brinnin had feared that he had fallen so completely under Truman's spell that he would throw away his life for him. The truth was the opposite: Newton only talked like a man obsessed; his feet were as firmly planted in Northampton as the ancient maples that shaded the Smith campus, and he did not plan to have his life disrupted. When he did not want to see Truman, he told him so, causing Truman no end of pain and confusion.

More than once, as he was preparing to leave for Northampton, Truman would receive a last-minute call from Newton, asking if he would mind not coming that weekend. "One time, when we were living in Brooklyn, Truman was all ready to go," recalled Andrew. "At the last second Newton rang up and said, in that rather cautious way of his: 'You perhaps best not come up this weekend, Truman, because I believe that some friends are motoring in the vicinity, and it might be embarrassing if they chanced to stop by.' When he hung up, Truman started to cry, and he asked me to get into bed with him and cuddle—nothing sexual ever went on between us; he just wanted to be held and told that everything would be all right. After a few minutes, he got up and shrugged his shoulders, as if he were shaking off something physical. Then he returned to his room and went back to writing his book. Later in the day he came to my door and said, 'Take my advice. Never be without a novel. There are moments when you need one.' "

All that fall Newton tried to explain away what seemed like inexcusable callousness, attempting to make comprehensible a state of mind that even he admitted was incomprehensible. "It distresses me unspeakably that things should be such hell for you there in the city, and that you should be so far from well, in the midst of everything else," he wrote in late October, when Nina's drunken rages were reaching their crescendo. "The impulse is almost overwhelming to call you on the phone or wire you, and insist on your coming back to Northampton and staying with me indefinitely. I have just barely courage enough to tell myself No—courage enough and perhaps cruelty enough. But, dearest Truman, for the time being I cannot conceal from myself that this might be a terrible disappointment to both of us, and if it were, might do something to our happiness in each other that I cannot bear to have done. I have never felt such grief over my own limitations as I do this fall. But self-knowledge can be flouted only at deadly peril, and though I cannot explain it even to myself, still less to you (and therefore not at all to anyone else), I know too well what this primordial, unanswerable hunger for a certain number of hours or days of solitude means, or is—I know it too well to be willing to lie to you. It is as if something physical like blood were ebbing out of me—not always, but much of the time—when I am not alone; and the point comes when my identity begins to slip away from me, and I cease to be a whole person even for someone I love. . . ."

That was as clear and comprehensive a statement of his feelings as he was to give, his *apologia pro vita sua,* and it was honest enough, as far as it went: his needs for privacy were enormous, yet he did love Truman all the same. What he did not say was that his guilt about being homosexual was the central fact of his life—and that Truman often embarrassed him around other people. "I feel as if I were, indeed I am, going about in disguise, though luckily it is a disguise I have worn so long that no doubt it looks as if it fitted me," he had written Truman not long after they met. "I am an impostor.

Won't I some time be caught and exposed? . . . But you know, my dear, I *seriously* believe that we must learn to live part of our lives in enemy country: the penalty for doing the other is even more terrible." Given such fears, it was more than a little ironic, then, that he fell in love with someone who had never tried to disguise himself, who had no such fears, and who, holding his hand as they strolled around campus, gave him away every time they were together. "When I first met him, Truman kissed me!" said Newton's colleague Daniel Aaron. "It was the only time that a man had ever kissed me. I was absolutely mortified! I was stunned! It was as if he had given me a blow in the face. It seemed to me as if he were camping rather dreadfully, with a certain kind of malice, that first time. I think he sensed that Newton was ashamed and ought not to be—that he ought to be much more open than he was. And he wanted to get back at him a little bit."

Still, hard as it may have been for him, Newton now took off his disguise with a few of his friends at least, and over the next year or so he introduced his young lover to several of those who resided in the highest reaches of the literary establishment: Lionel and Diana Trilling, that intimidating pair from Columbia; Harvard's Harry Levin and F. O. Matthiessen; Granville Hicks, the radical critic and writer; Louis Kronenberger, the drama critic of *Time* magazine; and Edmund Wilson himself. The reaction, however, was not what Newton had hoped for. Indeed, when he said he wanted to take Truman to a dinner at the Trillings', the hostess, a formidable woman by any measure, gave him a firm no. "When I want anybody to come to my house to dinner, I invite them," she indignantly answered. "You were invited to dinner; you were not asked to bring your friends." Newton angrily showed her reply to Truman, who tore it up. "Of course you have to go anyway," Truman told him, and Newton did. "The academic community was very chilly to me, and it must have been very hard for him," Truman said. "As I think back on it, I must have looked like a male Lolita to those people."

Most of the time he and Newton were happiest alone, and that is how they ended 1946. "A rather quiet, solitary day for the two of us" was the way Newton described their New Year's celebration in his diary. "Champagne. Records. The slow movement of the Mozart clarinet concerto. To bed rather early, but we woke at midnight (on hearing the chimes) & welcomed in the New Year in each other's arms."

WHEN I was young, wrote Swift, I felt that I could leap over the moon. So Truman must have felt as that new year, 1947, began. His most serious problems with his mother were behind him, he and Newton had arrived at a tolerable understanding, and his fame as a writer, like Jack's wonderful beanstalk, seemed to grow by itself, ascending heavenward from a very small seed, a handful of short stories and only the promise of a novel. Yet that tiny output, coupled with curiosity about Truman himself, was enough to excite intense interest in publishing offices all over Manhattan and to raise a few murmurs of enthusiasm even in Hollywood. On the bare chance that there might be a movie in those unseen pages, Twentieth Century–Fox paid $1,500 for an option on *Other Voices* and the second novel that would presumably follow.

"After the war everybody was waiting for the next Hemingway-Fitzgerald generation to appear," said Gore Vidal, in partial explanation. "That's why so much attention was devoted to novelists and poets, and that's why a new novel by one of us was considered an interesting event." Reporting on the postwar American scene for the British magazine *Horizon*, Cyril Connolly, the English critic, exaggerated only slightly when he described the hubbub in New York literary circles: "The hunt for young authors who, while maintaining a prestige value . . . may yet somehow win the coveted jackpot is feverish and incessant. Last year's authors are pushed aside and this year's—the novelist Jean Stafford, her poet husband Robert Lowell or the dark horse, Truman Capote—are invariably mentioned. They may be quite unread, but their names, like a new issue on the market, are constantly on the lips of those in the know. 'Get Capote'—at this minute the words are resounding on many a sixtieth floor."

Life, which could bestow instant celebrity with a flick of a camera shutter, much as television talk shows do today, selected its own group of up-and-coming writers. Except for Truman, all had at least one novel between hard covers; but it was that small dark horse, the pony of the herd, whose picture, blown up to nearly a full page, the editors chose to lead their article. And it was "esoteric, New Orleans–born Truman Capote," as he was described in the caption, whom most readers doubtless remembered. The day the issue appeared, Bennett Cerf received a call from his friend and competitor Richard Simon, the Simon of Simon and Schuster. "How the hell do you get a full-page picture of an author in *Life* magazine before his first book even comes out?" Simon demanded. "Do you think I'm going to tell you? Does Macy's tell Gimbels?" answered Cerf. "Come on. How did you wangle that?" Simon insisted. "Dick, I have no intention of telling you" was Cerf's stubborn reply. "He hung up in a huff," Cerf later wrote, "and I hung up too, and cried, 'For God's sake, get me a copy of *Life*.' That was the first I knew about the whole affair! Truman had managed to promote that full-page picture for himself, and how he did it, I don't know to this day."

In fact, he had not promoted it, and the reason for such prominent display was too obvious for Simon, Cerf, or perhaps even Truman himself to guess. *Life*'s editors had focused on him for the same reason they had printed two pictures of him in a spread they had done on Yaddo the year before: he looked unusual, which is to say, newsworthy. Giving the appearance of a jaded and world-weary child as he sat pouting amid Leo Lerman's Victorian bric-a-brac, he was the only one in the group who would make a reader stop before turning the page. Most of the other young novelists, a selection that included Thomas Heggen, Jean Stafford, Calder Willingham, and Vidal, could just as easily have illustrated a story about young advertising executives—or junior editors at *Life* itself. Like a movie star, or a very clever child, Truman instinctively knew how to seduce the camera, when to stand and when to sit, when to smile and when to frown, and the editors of *Life*, like many other editors in years to come, could scarcely avoid giving him the spotlight he craved.

. . .

It is impossible to conceive of so much excitement being aroused today by such a young writer with such a slim output. The New York that resounded with his name in those years just after the war has now vanished, and a new city, different in spirit as well as body, has taken its place. That Manhattan was the unchallenged center of the planet, "the supreme metropolis of the present," as Connolly told his English readers; it was what London had once been and what Rome had been so long before that. The great capitals of Europe lay prostrate and impoverished from the battles that had raged around them; European intellectuals, who had sought refuge in seedy but congenial West Side caravansaries, lingered on; and the cities of the Sunbelt—there was no such word then—basked in sleepy obscurity, unaware that soon they would seek to become rival centers themselves. Political decisions were made in Washington, but most of the other decisions that counted in the United States— those involving the disposition of money and fame and the recognition of literary and artistic achievement—were made on that rocky island, that diamond iceberg between the rivers. No wonder successful New Yorkers felt proud, and perhaps a little smug, about being who they were and where they were: they had all climbed to the top of what Disraeli had called the "greasy pole." And no wonder that Truman, who had arrived at that dizzying height before he was old enough to vote, found the view so exhilarating.

The El still rumbled along a dingy Third Avenue, coal dust had turned the limestone and brick of Park Avenue to a sooty gray, and summers, in that era before universal air conditioning, meant hot and sleepless nights listening to the sound of a whirring fan. But it was also a time, as John Cheever observed long after, "when the city of New York was still filled with a river light, when you heard the Benny Goodman quartet from a radio in the corner stationery store, and when almost everybody wore a hat." For those who dwelt along those streets and avenues, there was a feeling of romance and wonder about their city that is now hard to reconstruct, even in imagination. Green-and-yellow double-decker buses, so elegant and imposing that they were called Queen Marys, after the Cunard steamer, cruised serenely down Fifth Avenue; incoming ocean liners preened themselves as they passed the Statue of Liberty; and a regal red carpet was rolled out at Grand Central Terminal each night when the *Twentieth Century Limited* arrived from the West with its pampered freight of Hollywood stars. The skyline itself was romantic: the first flat-roofed glass skyscraper had yet to be erected, and Manhattan was still an island of grand and ebullient architectural fantasies—minarets, ziggurats, domes, pyramids, and spires. Banks resembled cathedrals, office buildings masqueraded as palaces, and spike-topped towers unabashedly vied for a place in the clouds.

Except for a few seamy areas, people walked wherever they wanted, whenever they wanted: street crime was rare. Hustling for news, eight major papers made everything that happened in the five boroughs, no matter how trivial, sound grave and consequential, while a battalion of gossip columnists, like nosy telephone operators in a small town, made the city seem smaller than it was with their breathless chatter about the famous, and those who would like to be famous. Broadway was a never-ending feast; theatergoers, sated with the variety before them, probably expected every year to be as bountiful as 1947, which not only saw the openings of *A Streetcar Named Desire*, *Brigadoon*, and *Finian's Rainbow*, but enjoyed also the continuing runs of *Oklahoma!*, *Annie Get Your Gun*, *Harvey*, and *Born Yesterday*.

To Connolly, and many others, so much exuberance and vitality painted "an unforgettable picture of what a city ought to be: that is, continuously insolent and alive, a place where one can buy a book or meet a friend at any hour of the day or night, where every language is spoken and xenophobia almost unknown, where every purse and appetite is catered for, where every street with every quarter and the people who inhabit them are fulfilling their function, not slipping back into apathy, indifference, decay. If Paris is the setting for a romance, New York is the perfect city in which to get over one, to get over anything. Here the lost *douceur de vivre* is forgotten and the intoxication of living takes its place."

The darling of the gods, as Howard had called Truman, was becoming the darling of half of Manhattan as well. The members of New York's smart set were as fascinated as nearly everyone else by "this extraordinary boy," as Phyllis Cerf called him. In a scene that was repeated, with only slight variations, many times during that period, she described how easily, how seemingly effortlessly, he captivated one of her celebrity-crowded gatherings. "We were having a black-tie dinner party, and since I was short of men, I told Bennett to invite some of his Random House authors. He did, and as the guests were arriving, the butler suddenly came up to me. 'Are you expecting a child?' he asked. I said no, I wasn't. Bennett said, 'That's Truman Capote!' and rushed to greet him. Truman then came up the stairs, looking very thin, very waifish, very childlike, with his blondish hair and bangs, and walked into the room rather blindly—he wasn't wearing his glasses. The first guest to arrive had been Edna Ferber. She had come when our son, Chris, who was then six or seven years old, came down in his pajamas to say good night. I introduced him to Miss Ferber and sent him off to bed. But throughout the evening she pointed Truman out to people and whispered: 'Really! Things couldn't have been so bad that Phyllis had to bring her own child to the table in a dinner jacket! When I arrived, that young man was in his pajamas.' "

The combination of that little-boy facade with an acute adult intelligence only made him more intriguing to the Cerfs' high-octane guests. The women in their jewels and gowns instantly surrounded him after dinner—"really instantly," insisted Phyllis—and listened intently as he told his well-polished stories about fortune-tellers and bragged about his hitherto undisclosed ability to foresee the future. "They were absolutely enchanted by him," said Phyllis, "and from then on people of that group began inviting him to parties themselves."

No one invited him more often than the Cerfs, and he was often a guest at that brownstone on East Sixty-second Street or at the Columns, their estate in Mount Kisco. Phyllis adored him, and Bennett may well have recognized a kindred spirit behind those deceptively innocent blue eyes: like a teddy bear, which exists only to be hugged. Bennett too was desperate for the spotlight, which he finally received a few years later as one of the panelists on the popular television quiz show *What's My Line?* "Everybody always said, 'Oh, Bennett Cerf, he's kind of a joke. He just wants to be on television and make those dreary puns,' " said Truman. "And there was that side of him, to be sure. But he was also an extremely sensitive and sound person—you could really talk to him. His advice was always excellent; he had very, very good taste; and he knew the difference between good and bad. People thought he didn't, but he knew the difference better than anyone else."

Along with Bob Linscott, Bennett advised Truman, sometimes becoming so fatherly in his attentions that Truman liked to embarrass him with affectionate embraces and cries of "Big Daddy." Bennett later admitted, "I do things for Truman that I wouldn't do for any other writer. I love him." For fear of hurting Truman's feelings, Bennett would deputize his wife to issue his scoldings. Intelligent and sympathetic but also extremely tough and even pugnacious— Bennett himself called her "the General"—she would usually convey his advice over lunch. Truman did not always follow it, but since it was delivered by Phyllis, he accepted it in good humor. "I loved her," he said. "Very few people did. But she was a really feisty, good-hearted, loyal person who would do anything for you if she really liked you—and anything against you if she didn't. If she didn't like you, it was best to get a passport and leave the country."

Rarely has a young novelist, particularly an unpublished young novelist, been as praised and petted by a publisher as Truman was by Random House. In those more luxurious days, the company maintained its office in one of those commercial buildings masquerading as palaces, a mock Italian palazzo on Madison Avenue. No other publisher in New York could boast such an impressive suite of offices, and Truman seemed to believe that if he did not own it, he had, at the minimum, a long-term lease. William Goyen, a novelist who was signed by Linscott after Truman, had a similar impression: "He was considered a kind of naughty but very talented little kid at Random House, like somebody from an *Our Gang* comedy. 'Look out,' everybody seemed to say, 'or the little devil will trip you up on a banana peel!' I have a vivid memory of coming in those great doors one time and finding him sitting on a bench by the reception desk, a baseball cap on his head and his feet not touching the floor. It was as if he were saying: 'This is my place. It's a wonderful place, and I'm going to take you all through it and introduce you to everybody.' And he did take me to people, give me hints about what to do, and make me feel more at home there."

It was his place, that magnificent Renaissance building, the first home Truman had felt himself welcome in since Jennie's house on Alabama Avenue. The Cerfs had all but adopted him, and true to his word, Linscott took special care of him, wrapping him in a blanket of satiny solicitude. As he had done with Carson McCullers and a few others, Linscott, who was a widower, gave him a key to his apartment on East Sixty-third Street so that he could have a quiet place to work during the day; he told Truman to bring Newton along for weekends at Linscott's farm, which was only twenty miles from Northampton; and he constantly lauded him to everyone within hailing distance. "Bob believed Truman led a madly glamorous life," said Linscott's assistant, Naomi Bliven, "that he knew everybody there was to know and that he could give him tips to all the best places. My husband and I often had dinner with Bob, and we always went to restaurants that Truman had suggested. We finally wound up going only to the Plaza Hotel because Truman had recommended their chicken hash."

Many writers eventually felt let down by Linscott, whose enthusiasm, which was so invigorating when he was happy with a manuscript, could turn to gelid disdain when he was disappointed. During the twelve years they worked together—Linscott retired in 1957—he was never seriously disappointed by Truman, however. From Truman's standpoint, he was an ideal editor, one who was perceptive enough to occasionally make helpful suggestions but shrewd enough to realize that his real job was not to pencil copy but to hold hands. "As an artist, a craftsman, [Truman] is completely sure of himself," Linscott told an interviewer in 1948. "As a human being, he has a great need to be loved and to be reassured of that love. Like other sensitive people he finds the world hostile and frightening. Truman has all the stigmata of genius. I am convinced that genius must have stigmata. It must be wounded."

N<small>EW</small> York is like a city made out of modeling clay," Truman once said. "You can make it whatever you want. It's the only city in the world in which you can have totally separate lives, groups of friends that don't know one another or anything about one another." What he made it in those postwar years was a never-ending party, with clusters of people scattered around a vast room that extended all the way from Ninety-sixth Street down to Greenwich Village. The Cerfs and the high-powered people he met through them were in one corner, the Leo Lerman set was in another, Mary Louise Aswell and all those who looked to her for warmth and advice were in a third, his close homosexual friends were over by the windows, and the nonaligned singles, a varied list that included Tallulah Bankhead, Dorothy Parker, and Tennessee Williams, were conveniently close to the bar. During the course of a month, he saw nearly all of them at least once, darting from one to another like a hummingbird on a long summer's day, determined to extract nectar from every flower in the garden before dusk turns to dark. When he said that Truman had a great need to be loved, Linscott did not realize just how great—how boundless and insatiable—that need actually was.

A few times when Joe and Nina were away, and a couple of times when they were not, he brought his separate lives together at 1060 Park. "Truman had really begun to move in New York," said Phyllis Cerf, recalling what was probably his first big party, which brought out everybody from Marlene Dietrich to Walter Winchell. "It was staggering to see who was there; an extraordinary group. But Truman didn't have any concept about how to give a party, and his mother was absolutely horrified at the number of people he had invited. It was a madhouse, hilarious, as if somebody had said, 'Come and get a thousand dollars!' There was no room to get in, get a drink, or get out the door again."

In addition to his trips to Northampton, he occasionally traveled outside the city to visit the Cerfs or the composers Gian-Carlo Menotti and Samuel Barber, who shared a house in Mount Kisco—Capricorn it was called—with Robert Horan, a talented young poet. Many people passed through Capricorn, and Bill Goyen, who was Barber's lover for a while, described Truman's arrival at the Mount Kisco station. "We all went to meet his train, and he appeared with a flourish. He was all in velvet—he liked lots of velvet—and his descent was so measured that it seemed to take him at least five minutes to get down the steps. He seemed to think the press was waiting for him, but it was just us guys."

When it came to grand flourishes, however, even Truman had to give way to Tallulah. "She drank a lot, and she used to call me up at two o'clock in the morning," Truman said. "She talked about every romance she had ever had, every person she had ever been to bed with, and all the fights she had ever had. She had done everything, including going to bed with women, although I don't think that was much of a thing with her." She came by Capricorn once when he was there and shocked the neighborhood with her flamboyance. Wilted by the heat, the whole party moved to a cooler house nearby, where the hostess, offering them bathing suits, invited them for a swim in her pool. "I never wear a suit," declared Tallulah, who, good as her word, was soon standing on the diving board dressed in nothing but her pearls. "Everybody, particularly the teenage boys, looked on with open mouths," said Horan. "But it was a typical Tallulah scene, down to the fact that her chauffeur had to go back later and fish the pearls out of the water. When I asked her why she had done it, she said, 'I just wanted to prove that I was a natural ash blonde.' She had the bravura, the grand theatricality, which carried those things off. I never felt that way about Truman. His performances were rather small-scale, defensive and extremely human. I understood them. They were acts of defiance, as if he were saying: 'I'm really quite vulnerable, and so before you wound me in some way, I'm going to assert myself.' "

Perhaps being able to drop so many names was part of his armor, and he seemed to derive an almost palpable sense of power out of knowing such a wide variety of people: he liked to think that he alone knew all of them and was privy to their secrets. In his fondest fantasy, he was like a tourist in the Sahara, sneaking through the darkness from tent to tent, campfire to campfire, to spy on the natives. "He was everywhere, and on the phone all the time," said Goyen. "My God, he was a busy little boy! He really wanted to think he was discovering love affairs and making matches."

Of all the friendships he made during those years, no other was quite so unusual as the one with Gore Vidal. Younger than he was by almost exactly a year, Vidal had worked even more furiously for early success and had already finished two novels when they met in December, 1945, at the apartment of Anaïs Nin, who was to become famous for her diaries. "When the bell rang I went to the door," she wrote, describing Truman's entrance. "I saw a small, slender young man, with hair over his eyes, extending the softest and most boneless hand I had ever held, like a baby's nestling in mine." A few minutes later that baby's hand was also extended to Vidal for the first time. "Well, how does it feel to be an *enfant terrible*?" Truman asked him, giving that French phrase a mangled pronunciation all his own. However he pronounced it, he was aware what it meant and that there could be but one *enfant terrible* at a time. Even as he shook that little hand, Vidal knew the same, and from the beginning theirs was more a rivalry, a bloodthirsty match of wits, than an alliance of affection.

Aside from youth and promise, they appeared totally dissimilar. Vidal was tall, fair, and good-looking, with a pencil-sharp profile that was appropriate for his pugnacious personality; unlike Truman, he was masculine in appearance, dress and manner. Unlike Truman too, he had enjoyed a conventional, if highly privileged, boyhood. His grandfather was a senator from Oklahoma; his father had held a sub-Cabinet office in the Roosevelt Administration. His mother, after their divorce, had married an Auchincloss and provided Gore with an entrée into society; before entering the Army in 1943, he had graduated from one of the country's best and oldest prep schools, Phillips Exeter Academy in New Hampshire.

In other, perhaps more profound ways, they were surprisingly alike, however: both felt that they had been emotionally abandoned by their mothers, both were attracted to members of their own sex, and both were possessed by the desire to achieve immortality through the written word. Gore later declared that he wanted to be remembered "as the person who wrote the best sentences in his time," and that was Truman's wish too. If Truman thought of himself as a condor waiting to pounce on literary fame, Gore believed that he was a golden eagle who, if he could not find fame first, would quickly snatch it away. "Gore was terribly anxious to be the number one young American writer," said Truman, "and he was afraid that maybe I was going to do him out of it." For a year or more, they were content nonetheless to soar together in relative harmony over the fields and canyons of Manhattan. Gore took Truman to the Everard Baths, a well-known homosexual bathhouse. Truman took Gore to Phil Black's Celebrity Club, a vast, mostly homosexual dance hall in Harlem. Almost every week they met for lunch in the Oak Room of the Plaza, where they nibbled at their friends during the first course, devoured their enemies during the second, and savored their own glorious futures over coffee and dessert. "It was deadly to get caught in the crossfire of their conversation," recalled someone who once joined them. "They were a pair of gilded youths on top of the world."

"I rather liked Gore," Truman said. "He was amusing, bright, and always very vinegary, and we had a lot of things in common. His mother was an alcoholic, and my mother was an alcoholic. His mother's name was Nina, and my mother's name was Nina. Those things sound superficial, but they're not. And we were both terribly young and at the same time very knowledgeable about what we were doing. We used to sit at those little lunches at the Plaza, and he would explain to me exactly, in the greatest detail—he was very methodical about it—how he was going to manage his life. He planned to become the grand old man of American letters, the American Somerset Maugham. He wanted to write popular books, make lots of money, and have a house on the Riviera, just as Maugham did. He always used to say, 'Longevity's the answer. If you live long enough, everything will turn your way.' I would say, 'Gore, you will do it all if you really want to.' And he did, too. He got it all except for one thing: he will never be as popular as Maugham was, and none of his books will ever be as good or readable as the best of Maugham. He has no talent, except for writing essays. He has no interior sensitivity—he can't put himself into someone else's place—and except for *Myra Breckinridge*, he never really found his voice. Anybody could have written *Julian* or *Burr*."

An eventual collision was all but ordained, and it finally came, perhaps as early as 1948, in the apartment of Tennessee Williams. "They began to criticize each other's work," said Williams. "Gore told Truman he got all of his plots out of Carson McCullers and Eudora Welty. Truman said: 'Well, maybe you get all of yours from the *Daily News*.' And so the fight was on. They never got over it." Truman himself could not recall the origin of the dispute, but did remember that "it was very, very, very unpleasant, whatever it was about, and after that Gore and I were never friends. Tennessee just sat back and giggled."

From then on it was open war, and their friends were soon entertaining one another with the latest reports from the battlefield. When one of them was praised for having achieved so much so early, the other (his identity varies according to who is telling the story) angrily exploded: "Why, he's twenty-two if he's a day!"—a comment so delightfully daffy that it soon acquired a small fame of its own. "The first time I ever saw Gore, I remarked how extremely talented Truman was," said Glenway Wescott, an older writer who claimed neutrality. "Gore, who was lunatic competitive, blew up and said, 'How can you call anybody talented who's written only one book at twenty-three? I've written three books, and I'm only twenty-two!' " In like manner, Truman became furious whenever Gore's name was mentioned, stamping his feet like Rumpelstiltskin. "He has no talent!" he would exclaim. "None, none, none!"

Much as he carried on about it—"Have you heard what Gore's done now?" he would indignantly ask Phoebe Pierce—their feud was more of a game than a real war for Truman, and it seemed clear to those who knew them both that Truman was less concerned about Gore than Gore was about him. The reason was obvious to everyone but Gore: Truman had won; the title of reigning literary prodigy was his. Young as he was, he was a mature writer with a distinct and confident voice. Prolific as he was, Gore was still floundering for both a style and a subject, and few took his work very seriously. Williams privately complained that Gore's third novel, *The City and the Pillar*, which gained a certain notoriety because of its homosexual theme, contained not one "really distinguished line," and Anaïs Nin, to whom Gore was closely attached, found his work lifeless. "Action, no feeling," she wrote in her diary. Truman's stories, on the other hand, "entranced" her, and she admired "his power to dream, his subtlety of style, his imagination. Above all, his sensitivity." Such sentiments, echoed nearly everywhere he went, were bitterly galling to Gore, who could not accept the image of that tiny figure standing on a pedestal he believed to be rightfully his. Traveling through Europe with Tennessee in 1948, he spent much of his time talking about Truman. "He's infected with that awful competitive spirit and seems to be continually haunted over the successes or achievements of other writers, such as Truman Capote," Tennessee wrote a friend. "He is positively obsessed with poor little Truman Capote. You would think they were running neck-and-neck for some fabulous gold prize."

WHEN he was not jousting with Gore or adding new names to his address book, Truman continued in much the accustomed pattern. He still labored over *Other Voices*, still worried about Nina, who had finally turned to Alcoholics Anonymous for help with her drinking. After giving up his rooms in Brooklyn for a small flat on Second Avenue, he saw even more of such old friends as Mary Louise Aswell, Leo Lerman, Phoebe Pierce and Andrew Lyndon, who had moved to Manhattan to be with his new lover, a rising young photographer named Harold Halma. None of them had much money, and rather than go out, they frequently ate dinner at one or another's apartment—at Andrew's most often, in grateful deference to Harold's culinary skills. "Well, is he taking all of his meals over there?" an exasperated Nina finally asked Andrew, after Truman had skipped several dinners at 1060. Truman had accepted, however reluctantly, Newton's singular need for solitude, and approximately twice a month they joined each other for long and happy weekends. Come summer, they planned to spend several unbroken weeks together, as they had at Yaddo, and in March Truman signed a two-month lease on a house in Nantucket. "It sounds charming, and I can think of no more attractive scene or circumstance for our summer together," wrote Newton. "How I long for June to come!"

Taking Andrew with him, Truman arrived on the island first, on Tuesday, June 10, and telephoned Newton with an enthusiastic description of the house, which was comfortable but otherwise nondescript, filled with the dilapidated wicker furniture peculiar to rented summer cottages. Newton came a week later, and almost a year to the day after they had met, they attempted once again to close that magic ring around them.

Mornings they all worked: Truman on *Other Voices*, which was nearing completion, Newton on his Melville biography, and Andrew on a short story. Afternoons, depending on the weather, Truman and Andrew sunbathed and swam; Newton sometimes joined them, but more often he stayed in the house and relaxed with what he considered light hammock reading: Thomas Browne's *Religio Medici*, *Don Quixote*, Pascal, Schopenhauer, and Shakespeare. Evenings they drank Manhattans or martinis before going off to dinner in Siasconset, the nearby town. After dinner they returned home, talked for an hour or two, then headed early to bed. Occasionally they went to the movies or exchanged visits with another group congregating around Leo, who had rented a converted Coast Guard station at Quidnet, a forty-five-minute walk down the beach. Over the Fourth of July holiday they entertained Barbara Lawrence and Mary Louise, who was preparing to return with her two children at the end of the month. Aside from those small diversions, nothing interrupted their placid routine, and their first few weeks on the island were both peaceful and productive. "We are keeping a regular schedule of work, and I am getting a tremendous lot done," Truman told Mary Louise. "A few weeks more, and the book will be finished. Can you believe it?"

Living at 1060 had inured him to noise, and, unlike many writers who need a still, quiet place in which to work, or a special desk or particular chair, Truman could write almost anywhere, under almost any circumstances. On Nantucket he wrote in bed, which was his usual custom, allowing nothing to distract him during those sacred hours before noon. " 'To watch Truman concentrate is one of the most frightening sights of the twentieth century,' Tennessee once remarked, and I could see what he meant," said Andrew. "He would clench his hands, grit his teeth, and squint his eyes so hard that he would cause a muscle to flick on his cheekbone. He could concentrate through anything. A bomb going off in the next room wouldn't have caused him to blink an eyelid." Andrew and Newton received daily, sometimes hourly, reports on his book's progress; eager for a response, he would often stop at the completion of a paragraph and read it aloud. Three days after Newton arrived, Truman finished his next-to-last chapter and read it to them; then, without pausing for a moment's breath, he began his run to the finish line, starting the final chapter the following morning.

He knew how his book would end: indeed, one of his compulsions as a writer was his need to know how a book or a story would end before he could begin. Having a conclusion in mind was not the same as having it on paper, however, and the final chapter of *Other Voices* proved unexpectedly obstinate. The book that had leaped from a "creative coma" on a frosty December afternoon in Alabama two and a half years earlier slowed to a crawl during those warm summer mornings at 'Sconset. "These last few pages! Every word takes blood," Truman wrote Linscott. "I don't know why this should be, especially since I know exactly what I'm doing."

As he was agonizing over those last few pages—twenty-nine pages, ultimately—Newton, who had read the rest of the novel bit by bit over the preceding year, went back to the beginning and started all over again, so that he could view it as a whole, with the eye of a critic rather than a lover. He made "some small corrections," he told his diary, probably in spelling and grammar, and methodically jotted down his observations. He apparently did not suggest major changes, but it is probable, given his acute literary intelligence, that he was helpful nonetheless, if only in pointing out the weak spots that bedevil almost any long piece of prose. Yet on July 30, the day Newton left and Mary Louise and her children arrived, Truman was still wrestling with that final obdurate chapter. Mary Louise was upstairs when he wrote the last words on August 11. "Truman's little voice came floating up," she recalled, "and he said, 'I've finished!'" They danced a celebratory jig, and that night Newton was pleased to note: "T.C. called me just after lunch to tell me the great news that he had just finished his book."

The magic ring closed only briefly around them that summer. Deprived of his baths of solitude and made nervous by unfamiliar faces, Newton suffered bouts of anxiety and depression. Andrew moved over to Leo's establishment when Harold Halma came to the island July 9, but four days later Newton's tranquility was shattered again when he and Truman welcomed two new and lively guests, Christopher Isherwood and his lover, Bill Caskey. Soon Newton was complaining to his diary: "A difficult day owing to my jitters— guest trouble."

The blame belonged to Truman, who, without consulting him,

had impulsively issued the invitation in May. An expatriate English-man who lived in California, Isherwood was visiting Random House when his friends there, invoking the hallowed name of Proust, bragged about "this remarkable young writer" they wanted him to meet. "I thought, 'Ha! Just another young writer,' " said Isherwood, "when this extraordinary little figure came into the room with his hand raised rather high, possibly indicating that one should kiss it. My first reaction was 'My God! He's not kidding!' But then I real-ized that though he was putting on an act, it was an act that repre-sented something very deliberate and quite genuine. Something happened which one wishes occurred far more often in life: I loved him immediately. We hadn't been talking for more than a few min-utes when he invited me to spend some weeks on Nantucket. I went back to Bill Caskey and said: 'The most astounding thing has hap-pened. I've done something I never, never have done before. I've accepted an invitation from a complete stranger for both of us to stay with him. When you see him, I think you'll know why.' Bill met him and had exactly the same reaction. We were both delighted with him. He was perfectly cool-headed, but at the same time he was a sort of cuddly little koala bear."

Truman was no less delighted with Isherwood, the author of *Goodbye to Berlin*, the creator of the irrepressible Sally Bowles, and the storyteller who, in Somerset Maugham's opinion, held "the fu-ture of the English novel in his hands." His company was much sought after by younger writers, who hoped that he might confide in them some of the secrets of their craft, and who breathlessly quizzed him, as Truman did, about the English literary world and the famous writers he had known. Truman was undoubtedly thrilled at the prospect of having such a literary celebrity as his guest, but knowing Newton, he must also have known that he would cause him pain and anxiety when he issued the invitation that brought Isherwood and his friend to 'Sconset on July 13.

Although the mornings were still dedicated to work, the after-noons and evenings were suddenly alive with the activity Truman thrived on—and Newton so profoundly detested. Looking much younger than forty-two, Isherwood was still the "appreciative merry little bird" that Virginia Woolf had called him ten years earlier. Caskey, a good-looking American in his mid-twenties, was just as merry, with an uninhibited, loose-tongued sense of humor that often shocked staider folk. When the three happy spirits of the Capote household combined with those in Leo's house, the adult world was banished, and Nantucket became a boys' camp from which all the counselors had mysteriously disappeared. As always, Truman was the ringleader, the one who decided what they should do, and at his direction they made daily trips to the beach, took bicycle tours around the island, and played hide-and-seek and various other child-hood games.

Nearly everything they did was too silly for Newton, certainly, who remained "very much in the background, rather like a tutor," said Caskey. He never accompanied them to the beach, and he hid in the house more and more, sometimes scrambling eggs for himself so that he did not have to take part in their long, laugh-filled dinners. Yet, ironically, he too reverted to childhood, which for him had meant only misery and humiliation: locking himself inside the house with his books while everyone else was outside having fun was exactly what he had done as that misbegotten boy in Indiana. "I stay here & mope," he disconsolately told his diary on July 15. Even after Isherwood and Caskey had gone, he was jumpy, counting the hours until he would be once again safely encased behind his book-cases at Smith. "I am uncontrollably eager to get back to Hamp this week and dig my way in at the office for a long, steady, uninter-rupted spell of work on the [Melville] book, such as I can only do there at home, and must do, if the goblins are not to get me," he wrote Mary Louise just before he departed the island. "It's been a wonderful outing down here," he added politely, "but I don't want to spend ages in Purgatory on the ledge of Sloth."

Truman returned to New York four days after completing *Other Voices*, and a few days later he also traveled to Northampton, where he helped Newton celebrate his forty-seventh birthday. "Very happy owing to T.C.'s being here" was how Newton recorded the date. "Supper here—with cake and candles." A month later another candle-studded cake was placed on that table for Truman's birthday, his twenty-third. So went the autumn, with the two of them quietly resuming their New York–Northampton shuttle after their long and, for Newton anyway, not altogether successful summer on Nantucket.

The only real excitement that fall was an impromptu evening of farce in late November, when Truman took a small party, including Andrew, Newton, and Phoebe, up to Harlem for the Celebrity

Club's annual drag dance. It was always one of the best shows of the year, and things proceeded in their usual amusing fashion— "The queens all flamed like Marie Antoinette," said Andrew—when another uniformed contingent, dressed in policeman's blue, burst through the doors. "A raid! A raid!" screamed the drag queens, lifting their gowns as they sprinted toward the exits. "Oh, my reputation, my reputation," moaned Newton, who imagined his name spelled out in the next morning's headlines. "Your reputation isn't worth a damn if you're caught up here, honey," Phoebe said to herself as Truman's band of revelers fought their way to the door. Only when they were safely outside did they learn that it had not been a raid at all and that the police were merely checking for violations of the fire code. But when they regrouped to head back downtown, they could not find Newton, who had disappeared in the panic—some suspected that his fright had already driven him halfway to Northampton. Going back inside to search for him, Truman discovered him hiding in a telephone booth. "Do you think it's all right to come out?" he fearfully asked as Truman pulled him out. Even by his standards, Newton's account of the night was a masterpiece of understatement. "To Blackie's (the Celebrity Club) in Harlem, which we have to leave in a hurry at midnight," he wrote in his diary.

Relieved of the burden of working on his book, Truman accepted an assignment that fulfilled at least one of the ambitions he had harbored in Greenwich: *Vogue* asked him to fly to California to take a fresh look at an old subject, Hollywood, and write the same kind of nonfactual, impressionistic piece he had written about New Orleans for *Harper's Bazaar*. He made his pilgrimage to the Hollywood shrine in early December and was pleased to discover that at least in some ways it was just as he had imagined. "I'm the only person of any sex whatever who's not being kept in this place," he breezily wrote Andrew. "And you wouldn't believe what they think worth keeping in Southern California!"

Oona O'Neill, who was now Mrs. Charlie Chaplin, gave a party for him, and Joan Crawford, "the fabled Miss C.," as he discreetly disguised her in print, invited him to lunch. Dressed in a housecoat, with no makeup and her hairpins dangling loosely, Crawford "skipped like a schoolgirl across the room," apologizing for keeping him waiting—she had been upstairs making the beds. Katherine

Anne Porter, who was moonlighting as a screenwriter, cooked dinner for him at her apartment in Santa Monica. "Still on the prowl for celebrities, he couldn't have been in a more promising ambience," Porter sourly recalled, forgetting all their good times at Yaddo. "He was surrounded by famous people he had always wanted to know. And he was determined to meet them." Meet them he did during his two busy weeks, and Porter offered an equally acerb, but probably accurate account of one of their conversations:

"Guess who I had lunch with yesterday?" Truman asked. "In the star's dining room, I'll have you know."

"I can't possibly imagine, Truman, but I'm sure you're going to tell me."

"Well, it was Greta Garbo herself, and she was perfectly delightful."

"How wonderful. But how did you manage this magnificent coup?"

"Well, I've got my ways, Katherine Anne. I've got my ways."

That encounter with the great Garbo had magically lengthened into seven full days when it came time to describe it to his New York friends. "I spent the first week with Greta Garbo and the second week with Charlie Chaplin," he informed Cerf, who, starstruck himself, believed every word.

Nineteen forty-seven ended for him, as it began, in Northampton, and on Christmas Eve, just two days after his return from Hollywood, he yet again made that familiar journey north from Grand Central. Unlike the previous New Year's, the beginning of 1948 truly marked a turning in his life. Random House had begun shipping *Other Voices* to the stores while he was in California, and reviewers were at last able to read and judge the first book of the most famous unpublished novelist in America. "[Truman's] novel comes out in mid-January," Newton wrote Granville Hicks. "Something of an Event, inevitably, and one hopes that the publishers and others have not Built it Up to a dangerous hubristic extent. All those New York gents (and ladies) will destroy him if they can—destroy him as a writer, I mean—but my impression is that they will have real difficulty in doing so. He has a kind of toughness they may not suspect."

"*Other Voices, Other Rooms* was an attempt to exorcise demons," Truman wrote a quarter of a century later, "an unconscious, altogether intuitive attempt, for I was not aware, except for a few incidents and descriptions, of its being in any serious degree autobiographical. Rereading it now, I find such self-deception unpardonable." Self-deception perhaps, unpardonable no, and the middle-aged man who pronounced that judgment was too severe on the young author who produced a work of such extraordinary power and intensity. Indeed, it was his good fortune that he was blind, at least on the conscious level, to what he was doing. Self-consciousness would have stilled his hand helplessly above the page if he had realized that he was in fact writing not just a novel, but his psychological autobiography: charting, under the guise of fiction, the anguished journey that ended in his discovery of his identity as a man, as a homosexual, and as an artist.

His self-deception is understandable, because on the surface there are only a few similarities between the course of his own life and the gothic plot of his book. His hero is thirteen-year-old Joel Harrison Knox, who, after his mother dies, is sent from New Orleans, where he has grown up, to live in an isolated plantation house with his father, whom he has never seen and whose last name, Sansom, he does not even bear. As the book begins, he makes his way to Noon City, the town nearest the plantation. There he is met by an ancient black retainer, Jesus Fever, whose mule-drawn wagon carries him, as if in a dream, along dark and lonely country roads to Skully's Landing, the house in which his father resides.

The remnant of what once was a great mansion, Skully's Landing is a place outside time, ruled by decadence and decay. There is neither electricity nor running water, and five white columns, the only reminders of a burned-down wing, give the garden "the primitive, haunted look of a lost ruin." The only occupants are Joel's sharp-tongued stepmother, Miss Amy; her effeminate, narcissistic cousin, Randolph; and Joel's father, who, despite Joel's inquiries, remains mysteriously out of sight. All those who live in and near the Landing are in some way abnormal and even grotesque: the twins from a neighboring farm, feminine but prissy Florabel and her wild tomboy sister, Idabel; dwarfish Jesus Fever, who has a touch of the wizard in his century-old eyes; his granddaughter, Zoo, whose giraffelike neck displays the knife scar her bridegroom gave her on their wedding night; and Little Sunshine, a black hermit who makes his home in the swamp-shrouded remains of a once fashionable resort, the Cloud Hotel. Most disturbing of all to Joel is the apparition of a spectral face he sees peering at him from a top-floor window, a "queer lady" wearing a towering white wig with "fat dribbling curls," like a countess at the court of Louis XVI.

Randolph, who is in his mid-thirties, puzzles Joel with his odd behavior, his peculiar appearance—he dresses in silk pajamas and kimonos—and his ironic, Oscar Wilde–like way of speaking. "All children are morbid; it's their one saving grace" is one of his epigrams. Joel is flattered by his attention, however, and as Randolph tells the story of his thwarted passion for a Mexican boxer, Pepe Alvarez, Joel begins to understand and sympathize with him. "The brain may take advice, but not the heart, and love, having no geography, knows no boundaries," Randolph explains. "Weight and sink it deep, no matter, it will rise and find the surface: and why not? any love is natural and beautiful that lies within a person's nature; only hypocrites would hold a man responsible for what he loves, emotional illiterates and those of righteous envy, who, in their agitated concern, mistake so frequently the arrow pointing to heaven for the one that leads to hell." In this and other passages, Randolph becomes the spokesman for the novel's major themes—and the themes that dominate all of Truman's writing: the loneliness that afflicts all but the stupid or insensitive; the sacredness of love, whatever its form; the disappointment that invariably follows high expectation; and the perversion of innocence.

When Joel is finally allowed to see his father, he finds not the handsome, dashing man around whom he has built his fantasies, but an almost speechless paralytic who demands help by bouncing red tennis balls onto the floor from his bed. It was not his father's, but Randolph's spidery handwriting, in red ink on water-green paper, that had been on the letter bringing him to the Landing. Feeling both cheated and trapped, Joel runs away with Idabel, only to catch pneumonia from the rain and to be returned to the Landing. He is nursed back to health by Randolph, and in the end he realizes that there is no running away: the Landing is now his home, the place where he belongs. The queer lady with fat dribbling curls was Randolph, nostalgically dressed in the costume that had once attracted Pepe Alvarez at a Mardi Gras ball. When her ghostly face beckons from the window a second time, Joel obeys, pausing only, in the book's last words, to look back at "the boy he had left behind."

Although Truman had never lived at any place as bizarre as Skully's Landing and had never known a silver-tongued transvestite like Randolph, he had borrowed traits from real people for some of his characters. He could be examining a picture of himself at thirteen, for instance, when he describes Joel, who is "too pretty, too delicate and fair-skinned" to be a real boy; he could also be referring to himself when he gives Joel his mother's last name, Knox, rather than his father's, Sansom. Harper Lee was a partial model for the rough and boyish Idabel—"sissy-britches," she calls Joel—and poor Callie Faulk was the stand-in for the ever-complaining Miss Amy.

Such surface similarities are insignificant compared with the hidden resemblances. On that subterranean level Truman has written, in symbol and allegory, the story of his boyhood. Joel is his alter ego, his emotional and spiritual *Doppelgänger*. Joel's mother rejects him by dying; Nina rejected Truman by leaving him so often in the care of Sook and her other Faulk relations. The invalid at Skully's Landing is Joel's father in name only; so was Arch little more than a name to Truman. Joel is desperate for love—"God, let me be loved," he prays—and so too, of course, was Truman. Joel makes several attempts to be a normal, heterosexual boy: he kisses Idabel, but is violently rebuffed; he tries to kill a dangerous swamp snake, but is petrified with fear. So too, in various ways, had a younger Truman tried and failed to be the normal boy his mother and everyone else wanted him to be. Finally, when he goes to join the queer lady in the window, Joel accepts his destiny, which is to be homosexual, to always hear other voices and live in other rooms. Yet acceptance is not a surrender: it is a liberation. "I am me," he whoops. "I am Joel, we are the same people." So, in a sense, had Truman rejoiced when he made peace with his own identity. Not for him were the guilt, disguises and endless remorse of a Newton.

Almost nothing in Truman's fictional world represents merely what it appears to be: it has another, deeper meaning as well. When a bell once used to summon slaves from the fields is uprooted from the ground, it signals Joel's summons to a new life; when Idabel's green-tinted play glasses are broken, she and Joel are forced to look at life as it is, in its true and often unpleasant colors. Symbol follows symbol in an intricate and quite deliberate pattern. Noon City, for example, was called Cherryseed City in Truman's first draft, and Skully's Landing was Minton's Landing. Neither name had the extra dimension he was seeking; only in his second draft did he bestow upon them their more appropriate, symbolic names, which underline Joel's psychological journey from day into night, from the active, aboveground world into the underground world of dreams. When he conveys Joel from the glare of Noon City through dark back roads to Skully's Landing, Truman is entering his own subconscious.

The people Joel encounters there are also meant to be understood symbolically. In its lack of realism and its reliance on symbolism, *Other Voices* is less a novel than a romance. A novel is, or should be, inhabited by realistic characters with a past and a future, as well as a present; a romance, by contrast, contains unrealistic, stylized figures who stand as psychological archetypes. "That is why the romance so often radiates a glow of subjective intensity that the novel lacks," explains the critic Northrop Frye, "and why a suggestion of allegory is constantly creeping in around the fringes." Randolph, Jesus Fever, and Joel's father are all such stylized and archetypal figures, and the allegory that is creeping in around the fringes of Truman's romance is an age-old one: the son in search of his father, the young man in quest of his identity. Although he arrives at another destination, a different concept of manhood, Joel Harrison Knox is walking in the footsteps of many a hero of myth and legend.

A fiction so dense and freighted with symbols owes as much to poetry as it does to prose. "A poetic explosion in highly suppressed emotion" was Truman's own description of *Other Voices*. With the youthful exuberance of a lyric poet, he has rearranged the dictionary, exalting ordinary words into images of permanent beauty. When Joel first visits his father, he sets in motion "a menagerie of crystal chimes [that] tinkled on the mantel like brookwater"; in the eerie gloom of the Cloud Hotel, "water-snakes slithering across the strings made night-songs on the ballroom's decaying piano." At times, in his almost ecstatic reworking of language, Truman crowds too many of those vivid word pictures into too small a space, and his style veers into what might be called Swamp Baroque. But those overladen passages are uncommon and scarcely detract from the overall work, which is the product of a mature artist in sovereign control of his very considerable powers. *Other Voices* still surprises and astounds, as dreams and nightmares do.

A month or so after he had finished writing it, Truman ran into his friend Doris Lilly on Madison Avenue. He was "bounding along like a goat in springtime," she said, and although he stopped for a few seconds to say hello, he was too excited to stand still, bouncing up and down so vigorously that his glasses slid to the end of his nose. "They're going to publish it!" he shouted. "My novel!" Then he bounded down the street again, "happy the way I have never seen a human being happy," she said, "as he made his story come true."

As fall changed to winter, however, excitement waned and worry took its place. Rarely had a writer of fiction left himself so naked in print. For a mere two dollars and seventy-five cents, anyone could follow him to the most private corners of his mind. Nor could he claim, as novelists usually do, that his hero had sprung from his imagination, because there, on the back of the dust jacket, was a photograph of an author who exactly matched the description of Joel Harrison Knox. Appearing no more than thirteen himself, Truman lay languidly on a couch and peered up at the camera with eyes so wide and an expression so provocative that he seemed to be aiming at a seduction. That, certainly, was the message Newton had received when he had seen the picture a year earlier. "There is a look in [those] eyes that I know oh, so well," he had said, "and that I decidedly hope no other human being knows in the same way. Do assure me that you were thinking of Notwen Nivra when you assumed that look!"

Truman may well have been thinking of Notwen Nivra when he stared into Harold Halma's Leica in January, 1947. But he had something else on his mind—publicity—when he showed his pictures to Bob Linscott, who chose that one for the dust jacket. Publicity was also on his mind when he said what he wanted written on the jacket's inside flap, where authors traditionally list such things as their academic credits. Truman's biography was, by contrast, more fictional than the story inside. He had, it stated, "written speeches for a third-rate politician, danced on a river boat, made a small fortune painting flowers on glass, read scripts for a film company, studied fortunetelling with the celebrated Mrs. Acey Jones, worked on *The New Yorker*, and selected anecdotes for a digest magazine. . . ."

When he wrote that in the fall, he had been, in his exhilarated mood, half in jest. Sitting in Northampton during the frigid and snowy Christmas holiday of 1947, suffering from a cold and sniffles, he had second thoughts, and normal prepublication jitters turned to panic. Most of the country—most of the world—seemed to him to be waiting for that slim volume of 231 pages. Booksellers reported that their customers had begun ordering it as early as October; Random House had scheduled an unusually large printing (for a first novel) of 10,000 copies; and unsolicited bids had already been received from eleven British and three French publishers, "an unprecedented situation for an author of a first novel that hasn't even been published as yet," declared the *New York Herald Tribune*. As Newton had predicted, publication of his book had become something of an event. Now Truman could only wonder: what would people say when they actually read it?

The first reviews, which began appearing in early January, were not calming. "Much lush writing, frequently trailing off into illusory fancies of sick brains, losing its way, yet withal picturesque," said the *Library Journal*. "Not recommended for libraries." Then came a long barrage from the popular press. "The story of Joel Knox did not need to be told, except to get it out of the author's system," said Carlos Baker in *The New York Times Book Review*, the most influential such journal in the country. "Mr. Capote has concocted a witch's brew which boils and boils to no avail," said the critic for the *Saturday Review*. "[The book] is immature and its theme is calculated to make the flesh crawl. . . . The distasteful trappings of its homosexual theme overhang it like Spanish moss," sneered *Time*; "a deep, murky well of Freudian symbols," said *Newsweek*. "A minor imitation of a very talented minor writer, Carson McCullers," adjudged Elizabeth Hardwick in *Partisan Review*.

Although the prevailing opinion of the New York critics was negative, several found so much to praise that they seemed almost to have picked up a different title. "*Other Voices, Other Rooms* abundantly justifies the critics and readers who first hailed Capote as a writer of exceptional gifts," wrote Lloyd Morris in the *New York Herald Tribune Weekly Book Review*. "It is the most exciting first novel by a young American that this reviewer has read in many years, and it leaves him with the conviction that Capote's talent is not only genuinely important but mature and resourceful." Despite a few demurrers, Orville Prescott, the critic for the daily *Times*, generally agreed: "It is impossible not to succumb to the potent magic of his writing. Here are scenes as sharp and suggestive as anything in recent fiction. . . . Many a first novel is sounder, better balanced, more reasonable than *Other Voices, Other Rooms*. But few are more artistically exciting, more positive proof of the arrival of a new writer of substantial talent."

Outside Manhattan, most reviews were admiring. Contrary to what might have been expected, the "distasteful trappings" of homosexuality that had so upset the *Time* critic and some of his supposedly sophisticated colleagues in New York caused scarcely a flutter in the hinterland. "A short novel which is as dazzling a phenomenon as has burst on the literary scene in the last ten years," proclaimed the *Chicago Tribune*. "The clashing of characters makes a story worthy of the invention of Faulkner," said the *Dallas News*. The *Indianapolis Times* announced the arrival of a masterpiece, "a book of extraordinary literary virtuosity—the kind of thing that makes most other fictional writing seem pedestrian and uninspired."

Like it or not, nearly every critic was struck by such an extravagant and dazzling display of linguistic fireworks, and many seemed compelled to make predictions about the future of its singular author. He "is gifted, dangerously gifted," said the *Times*'s Prescott, who, like a stern but kindly teacher, went on to admonish him to "ponder long on how he intends to use his exceptional talents." James Gray, a syndicated critic, appeared so stunned that he made an almost apocalyptic prophecy. Truman, he said, "seems destined to be one of our century's bright angels of destruction."

. . .

Perhaps the most interesting and in some ways the most perceptive comments were never published. One came from Newton, to whom *Other Voices* was dedicated, and it was addressed to Newton's friend Granville Hicks, who had found as much to fault as praise. "I can well understand one's having reservations about Truman's book," responded Newton. "It's not as if I didn't have any of my own. But somehow—and it's open to anyone to remark that I might be ever so slightly biased—I can't think it's terribly important to insist on the reservations just now. Whatever its limitations, the book is the work of a *writer*; the work of a boy born to be a poet and an artist, who touches with a kind of magic everything he draws near. Really, of how many young contemporary American writers can one possibly say that? And isn't it the crucial point? So many journeymen; so many *made* writers; so many hacks. And then here comes a book that, to be perhaps pretentiously Jamesian, is very evidently the real right thing. Shouldn't we simply, for the moment, thank our stars for that; and make the reservations in parentheses?"

The second such comment came from Truman's onetime mentor George Davis. Typical of the man, it was at once mean, shrewd and indelibly witty. Truman, who respected but feared the judgment of that "great literary 'fig-yur,' " as he and Andrew sarcastically referred to him, had sent George an inscribed copy, then waited in vain for the expected congratulatory call. Not long after that, they met for dinner, but George still said nothing, devoting most of his attention to a discussion of the latest opera news during a long cab ride to a restaurant far uptown in Spanish Harlem. Truman sat in silence as they drove from the Fifties through the Sixties. He may even have held his tongue through the Seventies, but somewhere around Eightieth Street he was overcome by anxiety and, swallowing his pride, said, "George, I sent you a copy of *Other Voices*."

"Yes, I know. I got it," said George, who, ignoring the hint, continued talking about the opera.

"Um . . . um . . . um . . . have you read it?"

"Oh, yes, I read it," George replied, and, obviously enjoying the exchange, turned back to opera. "Have you heard those new Rossini arias that Jennie Tourel recorded, Andrew? They're nothing like as good as Conchita Supervia's." Finally, Truman could bear the suspense no longer. "George, you said you got my copy of *Other Voices* and you said you read it," he burst in, speaking so quickly and with such agitation that the words ran together to sound like one. "What did you think of it?"

"Well," George at last drawled, pausing to purse his lips and suck in his cheeks, as he usually did when he was about to make an important pronouncement. "I suppose someone had to write the fairy *Huckleberry Finn*."

Other Voices almost immediately jumped onto the *New York Times* best-seller list, where it remained for nine weeks. It sold more than 26,000 copies, a figure which, if not sensational, was considered extremely good, particularly given the subject matter and the lack of a conventional plot. Sales, however, were only one measure of its success. Although many other novels of 1948, including Norman Mailer's *The Naked and the Dead* and Irwin Shaw's *The Young Lions*, outsold it several times over, no other was so much discussed, or became so controversial. Truman's reputation, which had been building among literary people since "Miriam," exploded in all directions. People who had never walked into a bookstore suddenly knew the name and, most certainly, the face of Truman Capote.

Indeed, his photograph on the back cover probably caused more comment than his prose. Several papers and magazines reprinted it alongside their reviews, Random House used it in ads—"This is Truman Capote"—and huge blowups were sent to the shops. One night while Truman was visiting Andrew, Harold Halma went for a walk and overheard the conversation of two middle-aged women who were studying one of the blowups in a Fifth Avenue bookstore window. "I'm telling you, he's just young," said one. "And I'm telling you, if he isn't young, he's dangerous!" replied the other. Harold sprinted back to the apartment to tell Truman, who growled and pretended to be angry, but repeated the exchange to anyone who would listen.

Some were offended and even outraged by that suggestive, insinuating pose. Merle Miller, whose own novel *That Winter* had also just come out, rose to denounce it at a publishing forum. If it was Truman's idea, he said, it was deplorable; if it was his publisher's, it was disgraceful. Someone who signed himself simply "A Critic" sent a postcard to Random House: "Sirs: Anent your newly found marvel, 'Truman Capote,' sic, it is downright foolish for you to believe this nincompoop is going anywhere, especially by his stupid poses. . . . Your ad depicts this unsuspecting fool as an inmate of the Buchenwald Camp, just released in a starving condition or a flophouse bum reclining on a Bowery chair after an all-night bout with a bottle of 'smoke.' "

Others were amused, and the book had scarcely reached the stores before columnist William Targ inserted the following bit of doggerel into his *Manhattan Letter.*

> Some like their prose a bit doughty,
> While others want fiction that's oaty.
> But only an heir
> Of Charles Baudelaire
> Would care for the work of Capote.

If Truman thought the picture would bring him publicity, humorist Max Shulman believed a funny imitation would do the same for him, and combing his dark hair over his forehead, he struck an identical pose in an identical outfit for the dust jacket of his own book, a collection titled *Max Shulman's Large Economy Size.* "Although these three books were written by Shulman at the age of eight," slyly observed the author's biography inside, "critics have pointed out that they show the insight and penetration of a man of nine."

Truman had wanted attention, not brickbats and laughter. He had not foreseen that the picture would overshadow and in some ways trivialize the work it was promoting, transforming the real right thing into something that many dismissed as the product of a brilliant publicity campaign. When he realized what damage the picture had done, he tried to disclaim responsibility for it, maintaining, first of all, that Harold had caught him unawares when he took it, and, second of all, that he had been away when Linscott had picked it for the dust jacket. Neither claim was true. He had asked Harold to take it, telling him exactly how he wanted to look. Although putting it on the back cover was in fact Linscott's idea, Truman obligingly, probably enthusiastically, went along, disregarding the wiser counsel of Mary Louise, who warned him that it was not for public consumption. Thus, in the end, he had only himself to blame for the uproar it created. Photographs had always served him well, however, and if that one made him both a target and a figure of fun, it did at least achieve its primary purpose: it gave him not only the literary, but also the public personality he had always wanted.

. . .

Book pages throughout the country, and occasionally gossip columns as well, were soon printing items about him, often repeating that spurious biography word for word. "Truman Capote has the critics in a dither, as they try to decide whether he's a genius," said a paper in as unlikely a place as Beaumont, Texas. On February 8 the *Times Book Review* said that sales of *Other Voices* were "stepping along at the rate of 700 copies a day, and already a Capote legend is in the making." During the following weeks the *Book Review* almost gave him a permanent spot in its pages, in what it called the "Capote Corner" or "this week's note on Truman Capote." When it had nothing new to say on February 29, it saved its expectant readers a fruitless search by observing: "Capote Note: Nothing new this week."

All that winter and through the spring, Truman and his book were favorite topics among noncritics as well. "You can't go to any party these days but what people will line up pro and con on the subject of Truman Capote," a young Manhattan woman told Selma Robinson, a reporter for the tabloid *PM*, who was writing a Truman profile. "Some take one side, some the other, and not necessarily those who have read his book." Random House had put a blurb from his old friend Marguerite Young on that famous dust jacket, and for a year afterward, she said, "I couldn't go to a literary cocktail party without people jumping at me, screaming and practically cursing me because I had praised 'that thing'! The book aroused absolute hysteria. Truman received suitcases of letters from people all over the United States, which he would read to me every night over the telephone."

For every attacker there was a defender. On many college campuses "that thing" was held high by student esthetes, rebelling against the more practical prose and more practical minds then prevailing. "In 1948, cruising the lunchbag-odorous Commons of Washington Square College, I used to keep an eye out for *Other Voices, Other Rooms*," wrote Cynthia Ozick. "That place and that time were turbulent with mainly dumb, mainly truculent veterans in their thirties arrived under the open enrollment of the GI Bill, and the handful of young esthetes, still dewy with high school Virgil (*O infelix Dido!*), whose doom it was to wander through that poverty-muttering postwar mob in hapless search of Beauty, found one another through Truman Capote. . . . [He] was the banner against this blight. To walk with Capote in your grasp was as distinctive, and as dissenting from the world's values, as a monk's habit."

When they look back on their careers, few writers can recall their good notices. But the bad ones are tattooed on their hearts. Truman was no exception. He forgot the good words from the *Chicago Tribune*, the *Indianapolis Times*, and all the other publications that had praised him, but the unfavorable ones he could recite almost from memory. "Except for the *Herald Tribune*, my novel got nothing but bad reviews," he said. "All the rest were terrible. I can't remember another good one."

The all but universal acclaim heaped upon his short stories had spoiled him and left him unprepared for serious disapproval. By any realistic standard, he had achieved a triumph. But his standard was not realistic, and his success was smaller than he had dreamed. "Truman thought that *Other Voices* would be the biggest thing since *Gone with the Wind*," said Andrew. "If it hadn't been a success at all, I don't think he could have survived." Partly because of the furor aroused by that languid photo, his triumph was, in his mind, tarnished. "I was so shocked and hurt that I never got any pleasure out of it at all," he said. "Everything was different than I had always thought or hoped it would be." Depressed and confused, he believed that he was the object of a conspiracy of abuse and ridicule.

Interviewing him in late January at 1060 Park, Selma Robinson of *PM* learned how little happiness it had given him to be, in her words, "the most discussed writer in New York literary circles." He was not the same person Doris Lilly had seen running down Madison Avenue a few months before. How did he feel about the reaction to his novel? she asked. "The smile left his face abruptly," she wrote, "and he looked a hurt, puzzled boy: 'I did not expect it to be the way it was. Some of the reviews seemed to be so blind. They call it a fantasy—decadent—they say I've written a book about homosexuality. I did not, nor did I intend to and I ought to know what I wanted it to be—I wrote the book.' Some of the reviews (he rose to get a handful) had a quality of personal attack that surprised him. He fingered them with an expression that was almost fear and for a swift moment his eyes were helpless, disturbed, bright, like the eyes of some small creature—a jack-rabbit, or a chipmunk, darting into a hedge."

Robinson then asked how he himself would characterize *Other*

Voices, and he replied with a kind of emotional stutter: "It's this bright moment, this ghostly moment of a completely lost child. A moment in his life, the moment when he gives up his boyhood. I can see a certain pattern to Joel's summer at Skully's Landing, though I don't know what his life will be when he grows up."

His natural resilience soon prevailed, and as the hubbub sub-
sided, Truman turned to the question that weighs on any
young novelist who has had a resounding success: what
next? A book is a major investment for a serious writer, and the
wrong choice of a theme or plot, particularly at the beginning, not
only wastes his time and dampens his enthusiasm, but also casts a
blight on his still tender reputation. It was an occupational hazard
Truman was aware of and planned to avoid; having made a name
for himself, he knew that to keep it he would not only have to work,
but to work on something that was right for him. "Publishing is the
toughest racket in the world to stay on top of," he later said. "To be
a good writer and stay on top is one of the most difficult balancing
acts ever. Talent isn't enough. You've got to have tremendous staying power. Out of all those people who began publishing when I
did, there are only three left that anybody knows about—Gore,
Norman, and me. There has to be some 'X' factor, some extra
dimension, that has kept us going. Really successful people are like
vampires: you can't kill them unless you drive a stake through their
hearts. The only one who can destroy a really strong and talented
writer is himself."

Fortunately, he had time to ponder his future. On the strength of
Other Voices, Random House was putting a collection of his short
stories on its list for the following winter, which presumably would
bring him attention through 1949. If anyone pressed him about what
would follow that, he would also talk, albeit in a vague way, about
a second novel, which he had tentatively titled *Monday's Folly*. It

would be set in Manhattan, he said, and it would be about a woman who becomes a catalytic agent for four people trying to find freedom. But he did not sound excited by it, and he appeared in no rush to sit down once again with a notebook and his favorite soft-leaded pencils, in no hurry to be possessed once more by the creative fever that had produced *Other Voices*. Like anyone else who has completed a large and taxing job, he needed a break and a change of scenery before starting off again.

The prospect of lying in a hammock on Nantucket all summer, trying to cope with Newton's almost existential pouts, did not stir him, and his search for a change of scenery took him to a different locale altogether: Europe. For the first time since the war, ordinary Americans could travel across the Atlantic, and thousands of them —perhaps as many as 100,000, according to one estimate—were booking reservations. Tennessee and Gore had sailed earlier, and several of his other friends, such as Gian-Carlo Menotti and Samuel Barber, were busy packing. By April, Truman knew that he could not face the fall in Manhattan unless he too had joined the throng that was making the Grand Tour of 1948. So it was that on the morning of Friday, May 14, after five days of saying goodbye to Newton in Northampton and several emotional phone calls to him afterward, he found himself standing in a tiny cabin on the *Queen Elizabeth*, surrounded by his new tan leather suitcases and saying farewell to a scattering of his friends. "You take good care of Newton!" he told Andrew.

His fame preceded him. Although European editions of *Other Voices* were months away, copies of the American edition, as well as of the magazines that had featured him so prominently, had made their way across the Atlantic, and many people in Britain and France were eager to meet the seductive young genius on the Victorian sofa. "Truman Capote is all the rage here," a young American living in London wrote a friend at home—a week before Truman even stepped onto the gangplank of the *Queen Elizabeth*. In Paris, the young American added, Denham Fouts, the glamorous lover of princes, lords, and millionaires, and a figure of myth and legend in international homosexual circles, was rumored to have become so infatuated with Truman's picture that he had sent him a blank check on which he had written only one word: Come. "So now," confidently predicted Waldemar Hansen, the aforementioned young American, "Capote will be turning up in Paris soon."

Truman's first stop, however, was London. Tasting one of the rewards of a best-selling author, he stayed at Claridge's, from which, following up on invitations and introductions he had received from Englishmen in New York, he sallied forth to meet a good part of the English literary and social establishment. He visited Cecil Beaton at Reddish House, Beaton's country home near Salisbury; he traveled up to Oxford for lunch with a literary don, Lord David Cecil; and he dined, or at least exchanged words, with everyone from Somerset Maugham and Evelyn Waugh to Noël Coward and Harold Nicolson, who attempted to take him to bed. Even the English, who were accustomed to eccentric characters, were surprised by him. "He looked like a child, and talked like a very sophisticated, agreeable grown-up person," recalled Lord Cecil. "He said that Evelyn Waugh's *The Loved One* was not as good as it seemed since it lacked all tenderness," Nicolson wrote in his diary. "This was said so simply that I found it attractive."

In some ways he was as naive and untutored as he seemed. A Fiji Islander who spoke only pidgin English could scarcely have landed at Southampton with such a murky idea of where he was. Someone had kindly arranged a meeting in Cambridge, for instance, with E. M. Forster, the living novelist Truman most admired. Thinking to save himself a second trip, Truman planned to amble over to Forster's rooms after his lunch with Lord Cecil. Only as he was finishing his coffee did he discover that Oxford and Cambridge were not within ambling distance, and that the only way he could make his appointment with Forster was through divine intervention, which was not forthcoming. "I had it fixed in my head that Oxford and Cambridge were the same place, sort of Oxford-and-Cambridge," he blandly confessed, without a hint of embarrassment. "It was not until I inquired the way to Mr. Forster's house—not until then did I learn that Cambridge is far more than a hundred miles in the opposite direction. Though I was very sunk indeed, I believe the incident amused Mr. Forster; at least he wrote a charming letter, regretting my error."

More such comical errors were probably prevented by Waldemar Hansen. He and Truman had been casual acquaintances in New York, and when they met in London, Waldemar volunteered to be his guide. "I was very impressed by *Other Voices*, and I took him up with open arms," said Waldemar, who was only twenty-five himself. Charming in manner and amusing in speech, with a thin, bony face surmounted by thick glasses, Waldemar was a poet who had worked as Beaton's secretary and ghostwriter; now he was the lover of Peter Watson, a millionaire patron of the arts. Through the two of them, Waldemar knew virtually everybody worth knowing in literary and artistic London; those Truman did not encounter on his own, he was introduced to by Waldemar. "Truman wasn't interested in seeing things like the Tower of London," he said, "and we didn't do the usual tourist route."

For Truman, and many others that year, two weeks in England was more than enough: in 1948 London was a depressing city, gray, dowdy and dispirited. Stringent rationing was still in effect, good food was all but impossible to find, and to conserve electricity, theaters raised their curtains at seven o'clock; by ten o'clock the streets were all but deserted. Victory over Germany had not brought the expected surcease to Britain's privations, and the whole country seemed pervaded by a mood of hopelessness and peevish exhaustion, a kind of national acedia.

Waldemar had been a great help to an innocent abroad, and now, as he prepared to leave for Paris, Truman returned the favor, instructing him how to put back together his rapidly disintegrating romance with Watson. It is easy to imagine with what delight Truman's eyes sparkled as he heard Waldemar's woeful story, which undoubtedly aroused his interest far more than anything he would have seen in the British Museum, had he cared to venture into that august institution. Pygmalion was the role he enjoyed most, and the management of other people's lives was his happiest pursuit.

He listened carefully, deliberated, then announced his conclusion: Waldemar had been too compliant; Watson, a tall, slim, attractive man of forty who had taken up temporary residence in the Pont Royal Hotel in Paris, did not feel challenged by him. "If you're going to be a grand courtesan," Truman explained, "you've got to play hard to get." But obviously, he added, Waldemar could not play hard to get at a distance—he would have to accompany Truman to Paris, telling Watson, of course, that the only reason he had come was to show the sights to someone who knew only two words of French, the "*mille tendresses*" with which, imitating Newton, Truman sometimes ended his letters. "Let's beard the lion in his den!"

Truman bravely declared. Waldemar did not require much persuasion, and, reserving two of the best seats on the boat train to Paris, they dispatched a telegram to Watson: "Changing voices, changing rooms. Two dancing daughters arriving Pont Royal Sunday evening. Perhaps they can fit you in for a tango."

The Paris that greeted the two dancing daughters might well have been on the other side of the planet, so different was its mood from London's. Although rationing-imposed shortages caused hardship and discomfort in France too, spirits were so high as to be giddy: the oppressor was gone and life was beginning again. A few weeks before, a simple command had turned on hundreds of floodlamps, and the monuments that had been dark since 1939—Notre Dame, the Arch of Triumph, the Place de la Concorde—once again decorated the night, like precious crystal that had been brought out of hiding. Another command had turned on a multitude of long-dry fountains, and their cascading waters strummed a song that had been forgotten during the decade of darkness; for months afterward their unfamiliar spray tasted like sparkling wine to light-headed Parisians, who, happy merely to be alive, could scarcely comprehend their further good fortune.

Not since the doughboys landed in 1917 had Americans, their liberators, been so welcomed by the French. University students swayed to swing music, smoked black-market Lucky Strikes, and drank Coca-Cola. At Le Boeuf sur le Toit, a gathering place for artists and writers since the twenties, Robbie Campbell, a boyish, light-skinned black from New York, put on dungarees and a straw hat to sing "Nature Boy," which was then on the *Hit Parade* back home. "Nature Boy!" or "*Jeune vagabond noir!*" passersby would shout affectionately when he walked through the streets of the Left Bank. "The French loved the world then," said Campbell. "Everybody was beautiful, everybody was bright, and everybody drank champagne." For Americans, perhaps even more than for the French, it was a memorable moment. Because of an exchange rate that was heavily tilted in their favor, they could, as in the twenties, live more cheaply, and with far more style, in France than at home. Suites at the Ritz cost about eleven dollars a day; good hotels on the Left Bank, much less. "It's very hard to describe what Paris was like then," said Vidal. "It was a glamorous, golden time for all of us. Prices were low, the food was marvelous, and there was little traffic and no pollution; the light was extraordinary. In one's memory it will always be summer, with empty streets, all that light, and just one taxicab slowly approaching in the middle distance."

For a few days, while he was feigning polite indifference to Watson, Waldemar had time to show Truman the only monuments Truman wanted to see: Le Boeuf, of course; the Café Flore, where Jean-Paul Sartre and Simone de Beauvoir sat arguing existentialism; and La Vie en Rose, an all-male club where, under a twirling ball of spangled mirrors, two middle-aged Hungarian transvestites sang and danced as Les Sisters B. Soon, however, Waldemar had no time to play tour guide. Truman's analysis of Watson had been both accurate and acute. Watson was an emotional masochist who was aroused not by affection, but by rejection. Whispering directions from behind the scenes, Truman choreographed a passionate reconciliation, the tango he and Waldemar had coyly referred to in their cable. "Truman gave me very good advice," said Waldemar, "and I think he prolonged my relationship with Peter by about a year."

Despite his ignorance of the language, Truman did not really need Waldemar to guide him around Paris, where his name and face were almost as well known as they had been in London—the *Other Voices* picture of the writer recumbent was rapidly becoming as famous as the Mona Lisa. The tabloid *France-Dimanche* sent two reporters to interview him at the Pont Royal, and even intellectuals like Jean Cocteau, the master of all arts, were curious about him. Hearing that his friend Karl Bissinger had an assignment to take photographs on the set of Cocteau's new movie, *Les Parents Terribles*, Truman insisted on tagging along, trailing behind him, despite the season, one of his long Bronzini scarves. "You don't haul your friends along to see a famous director," said Bissinger, "and if I had been more sophisticated, I wouldn't have taken Truman. But that *Other Voices* photograph had dominated the year's gossip, and, as it happened, Cocteau was fascinated by him. He called him 'the infant.' " Cocteau later introduced the infant to others, who, following the pattern set in New York and London, introduced him to still others, so that in just the month he was there, Truman again met a gallery of literary and artistic celebrities: from Colette, bedridden but still noticing everything with her catlike, kohl-encased eyes, to the designer Christian Dior, whose New Look of 1947 had forced fashionable women the world over to drop their hems almost to the ankle.

. . .

Truman had many well-positioned sponsors in Paris. "The other day at Natalie Barney's Mrs. Bradley was full of the new young Parisian hero—Truman Capote," Alice B. Toklas, who had been Gertrude Stein's companion, reported to friends in America. "Gallimard is launching his novel with immense publicity and as Mrs. Bradley is his agent she has every interest to make the most of the sensation he is causing." An elderly Frenchwoman of formidable presence—her last name came from her American husband, who had died before the war—Jenny Bradley was more than an agent. She had been on first-name, often intimate, terms with many of the century's great writers, a list that only began with Joyce, Pound and Proust. ("Ah, poor Marcel," she said. "Those sad Jewish eyes. I found him slightly ridiculous as a human being. There was no common measure between the man and his work, which is often the case.") She still represented the best American writers to French publishers and the best French writers to American publishers. Every Saturday afternoon, she served champagne to a select group in her apartment on the Ile-St.-Louis, in a house that had belonged to Louis XIII's chief minister, Cardinal Richelieu.

"I can see Truman now, sitting near the mantelpiece," she said. "He would tell his stories and meet very interesting people, whom he would sometimes charm. He reminded me a little of Ford Madox Ford in that one could not very well distinguish between what was true and what was not true. He was making up his stories as he told them. They had nothing to do with reality, and that rather charmed me. There was something naive about him, which was probably half natural and half put on. He had a kind of simplicity, which was a real gift. He was what we call *sur-doué*, an overly gifted young boy. He looked about sixteen, and at moments he could be childish. He went to the flea market one day, for example, and came back with a leather belt, which had copper locomotives running around it. Extraordinary idea! But he was so proud of it. 'Look at my belt,' he would say. 'Isn't it a beauty?' "

Through Mrs. Bradley, Truman became friendly with Natalie Barney, one of the several rich and exceptional American lesbians who had settled in Paris around the turn of the century. Miss Barney also had known many of the century's great poets, writers, and musicians, some of whom had read or performed from the steps of the small Greek temple in her garden on the Rue Jacob. Forty years previously her many love affairs had been thought a scandal. When

Truman met her, she was in her early seventies, but she was still, wonderful to say, finding new romances. Anyone who did not know her might have mistaken her for a society woman from Dayton, Ohio, which is where she and her money came from. "She was plump, pigeonlike," said Truman, and "very small, shorter even than I am. She had lovely skin, fine features, and beautiful, cool blue eyes. She always wore gray—dark gray shoes and little gray suits with a flower in the lapel; even her car was gray.

"One winter, a year or two after I met her, she said she wanted to take me to lunch and then show me something that few people had even seen. After lunch, she took me to an ordinary-looking apartment house near the Eiffel Tower, and we walked up four flights of stairs. She made me stay outside while she went into a room and turned on the lights. Finally I was let into an enormous room with perhaps a hundred pictures on the walls, each covered by a curtain: it was the studio of her lover, Romaine Brooks. We went around to each picture, and she pulled back the curtain, explaining who the woman was—only two of them were men—and what that woman's relationship was with the women in all the other pictures. It was like reading a fabulous novel. There was a portrait of Miss Barney too, but she wasn't this cozy little Miss Marple type that I knew—she was a wild thing with one hand on her hip and the other carrying a whip. I had never heard of Romaine Brooks before, but her paintings were wonderful, and we stayed up there about two hours looking at them. Miss Barney had a lot of stories to tell."

Truman claimed to have had a brief affair of his own in Paris: with Albert Camus. "He was a homely little thing," he said of the future Nobel Prize winner, "but attractive, with sensitive eyes and a compassionate face. He was my editor at Gallimard, and he took me to dinner. One thing led to another, and one afternoon he came to my room and we just went to bed. It was as simple as that. I don't think he was homosexual in any way. But that was the period when I looked my best. When he met me, he was sort of startled. I must have touched some nostalgic nerve in him, reminded him of something that happened in adolescence." That Truman knew Camus there can be no doubt; whether he went to bed with such a renowned womanizer is a question that can never be answered. It may have been one of the tales he made up; or, despite hoots of disbelief from both friends and enemies, it may have been true. In matters of sex there is only one guide: almost anything is possible.

. . .

As Waldemar had predicted, Truman wasted no time in looking up Denham Fouts, whose check he had politely returned, but whose invitation to visit he had eagerly accepted. One of those people whose only ambition was to attract other people, Denny was superb at his job, affording it no more thought or effort than a flower gives to enticing the bees that buzz before its fragrant blossoms or than a tropical fish gives to those who admire its peacock fins from the other side of the aquarium glass: he was a male whore from Jacksonville, Florida, the grand courtesan Waldemar never was, nor hoped to be. He was so fascinating a figure, as dark angels always are, that he has achieved minor immortality in several works of fiction, including Isherwood's novel *Down There on a Visit*, Vidal's short story "Pages from an Abandoned Journal," and "Unspoiled Monsters," which relates Truman's own, sometimes inaccurate version of the Fouts saga. "Denny, long before he surfaced in my cove, was a legend well-known to me," Truman wrote, "a myth entitled: Best-Kept Boy in the World."

Unlike many in his profession, Denny chose his career. When he was growing up, Jacksonville still considered itself part of the unreconstructed South. His family thought of itself as part of the Southern aristocracy; it was upright, conservative and intolerant of all those who did not accept its ossified codes—a group of outcasts that included Denny, who rebelled and shocked in every way he could. Had he lived in England, he would have been sent off to one of the colonies, some hot place in Africa, and reports of his indiscretions would occasionally have been passed around the dinner table. Not having that option, Denny's father did the next best thing: he sent him north, asking an uncle who was president of Safeway Stores to give him a job in Washington.

So it was that in 1932 or 1933, when he was only eighteen or nineteen, Denny began his wanderings, leaving Washington after a few months for Manhattan, where he found a job as a stock boy and shared a small apartment with a friend. His extraordinary good looks brought stares wherever he went: nature had "breathed upon him beauty of hair and bloom of youth," as Virgil said of Aeneas, "and kindled brilliance in his eyes, as an artist's hand gives style to ivory." Thin as a hieroglyph, he had dark hair, light brown eyes, and a cleft chin and "was about the most beautiful boy anybody had ever seen," said Jimmy Daniels, who sang at a Harlem nightclub Denny frequented. "His skin always looked as if it had just been scrubbed; it seemed to have no pores at all, it was so smooth." Adding his own distinctive colors to the portrait, Glenway Wescott observed that "he was absolutely enchanting and ridiculously good-looking—unattractively good-looking from my point of view. The only thing I liked about him was that he had the most delicious body odor; I once swiped one of his handkerchiefs."

Such attributes sometimes propelled young men to Hollywood, but Denny, whose announced intention was never to work, did not want to be famous; he wanted to be taken care of in grand style. Knowing that, his roommate asked Wescott, who often browsed in the bookstore where he worked and who seemed to know the ways of the world, to sit down and give Denny advice. Wescott happily agreed, and Denny immediately came to the point. "Now, Glenway," he said, "you know everything. I want you to tell me: how does one manage to get kept?" Wringing his hands and clicking his tongue at such a naive and blunt question, Wescott told him that such an objective must be approached indirectly, so that the prospective keeper is made to feel like a generous benefactor rather than a customer who is being billed for services rendered. "To begin with," he said, "you must never use that word—'kept.' Think of something you want to do that takes money to learn. Then ask someone for help and guidance. You'll get much more money that way than by coming at it straight on."

The first to offer such help was a German baron who took him to Europe, where Denny jumped from one titled bed to another— Prince Paul, later King of Greece, was his highest-ranking conquest —and from there he traveled the world. Writing home to his family, he said that he was engaged in secret missions for an unnamed Daddy Warbucks, some great financier with global interests. "He invented himself," said one of his friends, John B. L. Goodwin. "If people didn't know his background, he would make it up."

His last lover before the war was none other than Peter Watson, whose affections he possessed in a way that Waldemar was not able to do. Watson, it was said, could not be in the same room with Denny without getting an erection. To save that porcelain skin from being damaged by one of Hitler's blockbusters, in 1940 Watson sent him back to America. It was then that he met Isherwood in Los Angeles. "His handsome profile was bitterly sharp, like a knife edge," wrote Isherwood of his Denny character in *Down There on a*

Visit. "And goodness, underneath the looks and the charm and the drawl, how sour he was!" More than sour, Denny appeared to live at the bottom of a well of cynicism so deep that to him the sun was like a star at the ragged edge of the universe, which even the largest and most powerful telescopes must squint to see. "He thought that the world was made up of whores," said his friend Bill Harris. "To be a successful whore was all, he said. Though he didn't brag, he felt he had done pretty well at it."

His fondness for pubescent boys was doubtless what prompted him to extend an invitation to the boyish-looking author on the dust jacket of *Other Voices.* Deeply addicted to opium by the time Truman paid his respects, Denny lived in a state of near somnolence. He sometimes slept most of the day and left his apartment on the fashionable Rue du Bac only at night. A maid kept order and walked Trotsky, the huge mutt he had found in California. Though Watson, who had a horror of drugs, had given up on him as a lover, he was still fond enough to send him money and pay his rent. Aware of how powerful Denny's grasp could be, Waldemar warned Truman to keep his distance. Denny, he said, was like the feeble old man who asked Sindbad for a lift in *The Arabian Nights.* Feeling sorry for him, Sindbad took him on his back; but once he was on, the old man was on to stay and Sindbad could not get him off.

Truman nodded but did not listen. How could he pass up an opportunity to meet Denham Fouts? Fascinated by Denny, he spent hours lying beside him in Denny's darkened bedroom, talking to him, reading to him, and listening to his stories. Sex was not considered; drugs had destroyed Denny's libido. Otherwise, Denny showed no ill effects from his years of drugs and debauchery; he looked much younger than his actual age of thirty-four and retained still the well-scrubbed glow of youth. "Denny radiated a quality that was the exact opposite of what he was," said Truman, "extraordinary health, youth, and unspoiled innocence. Whatever he had done the night before, or the day before, or the week before, he always looked as if he had just awakened on the freshest and most beautiful morning in the world. To watch him walk into a room was an experience. He was beyond being good-looking: he was the single most charming-looking person I've ever seen." Oscar Wilde had written his biography before Denny was born: Denny was Dorian Gray.

Truman was scared by his addiction to drugs, however, something he had never witnessed before, and he soon tired of Denny's voracious, childlike demand for attention. "Even when he was perfectly well, Denny would often be propped up in bed, like a little boy who's sick and waiting for friends to come and visit him," said Bill Harris. "He wanted to be taken care of forever." Taking care of him was a chore Truman did not want to assume. "Denny had real magic and I adored him. But I was frightened of him and the drug scene. I was young, and I didn't plan to get involved in any of that. I wanted to get him off drugs, and he also wanted to get out of the life he had been living all those years. He loved the West and he had a fantasy about buying a gasoline station in Arizona, the sort of place that has a sign saying, 'Last Chance for Gas for Fifty Miles.' I was going to write, and he was going to run it and be cured of all the things that were wrong with him. I very foolishly let him go on about it because I knew that none of it was ever going to happen."

Even Denny could not have taken that fantasy seriously: the Best-Kept Boy in the World becoming a grizzled old gas jockey on Route 66, while his younger lover wrote best-sellers next to the Coke machine in the dusty back room. But he seemed to be sincere in his desire to be cured, and Truman helped him pack for a Swiss drug clinic. But a drug addict's or an alcoholic's zeal for salvation does not usually last long, as Truman should have known from living with his mother. "Our disturbing friend just called," he wrote Waldemar. "The Switzerland deal seems to be off. It makes me feel like a miserable heel, but what can I do now but wash my hands of the whole affair?" Wash his hands he did, soon leaving Paris for Italy.

The saga of Denham Fouts did not, in any event, have long to run. He eventually did go to the Swiss clinic, but the cure did not work. Forced out of his apartment on the Rue du Bac, he moved to a pension in Rome, where he was looked after by a devoted young Englishman, who was as captivated by him as Truman had been. "You can sit here as long as you don't start moralizing," Denny told John Goodwin, who visited him in his new quarters. "I'm sick of moralizations. Just let me go my own way." His own way was a fatal heart attack in 1949, when he was thirty-five; his body was buried in Rome's Protestant Cemetery. "I can't say what made Denny click," said Goodwin. "I can only say what his effect was on other people. He had great, great charm, and you always had the feeling that potentially he was something much more than he was."

LONDON Truman did not like, then or ever. Paris he loved that golden summer but never again. With Venice, however, which was next on his itinerary, he had a lasting romance, happily returning many times, in all seasons and all weathers. He arrived from Paris on July 4, checked into the Albergo Pilsen, and that evening, walking through St. Mark's Square, as all tourists do, encountered another young American writer, Donald Windham. They had seen each other at Leo's parties but never talked. Coming together in a strange city, they discovered that they had much in common, including friends like Tennessee. Donald, a fellow South-erner, a Georgian, had just turned twenty-eight and was trying to complete his first novel; Truman, after his six eventful weeks in London and Paris, was hoping to settle down at last and finish a short story, "Children on Their Birthdays." Their schedules thus matched exactly, and they became traveling companions; they stayed indoors during the mornings, and occasionally the afternoons as well, and met in the evening for drinks and dinner.

When he did go out to see the sights, Truman, of course, was not interested in the churches and palazzos, the Titians and Tintorettos in the Accademia. His tourist attractions tended to be places, usually restaurants and bars, where he was made to feel at home. Once he had found such a place, he could rarely be persuaded to go anywhere else. In Venice that spot was Harry's Bar, and he had dinner there nearly every night. "For him Venice was Harry's Bar," declared Donald. Once, Donald prevailed upon him to forsake Harry's for a night and try a small outdoor café near St. Mark's Square. Truman reluctantly agreed and ordered his customary martini. He sipped it and, with an I-told-you-so smile, handed it across the table. Donald tasted it and was forced to admit that it was indeed peculiar. "Ask the bartender what goes into a martini," Truman said. The answer —one-third gin, one-third vermouth, one-third cognac, and a twist of lemon peel—was convincing evidence that in Venice there was only one place to dine, and Donald never again suggested an alternative to the reliable Harry's.

Much as he enjoyed it, Truman soon realized that Venice, with its constant noise and activity, did not provide the atmosphere he needed to write, and he persuaded Donald to go with him to Sirmione, a lake resort he had heard about, midway between Venice and Milan. Their departure was delayed, however, by more noise and activity than either of them could have anticipated. On July 14, as they were preparing to leave, Palmiro Togliatti, Italy's Communist leader, was shot outside the Chamber of Deputies in Rome, and Italy's millions of Communists reacted with rage. Within hours workers were in the streets of all the major cities; the Communist labor unions ordered a general strike, and the government called out the army to preserve order. In Venice, panicky shop owners dropped iron shutters over their windows and doors, restaurants closed, and foreigners, especially Americans, were urged to remain inside their hotels. A measure of quiet returned after two days— Togliatti did not die of his wounds—and, crowding onto a bus, Truman and Donald finally made their way to a calm and peaceful Sirmione.

"An enchanted, infinitesimal village on the tip of a peninsula jutting into Lago di Garda, bluest, saddest, most silent, most beautiful of Italian lakes," Truman wrote of Sirmione. And at that time, before the tourist invasions, enchanted it was, with fewer than two dozen other outsiders sharing its charms. He and Donald chose to stay in the cheaper of the two hotels—five dollars a day, including all meals—and have dinner in the more expensive. (Expensive was not very expensive in the Italy of 1948; the excellent martinis at Harry's Bar, for instance, had cost just twenty-five cents.)

As a place to work, Sirmione was all that they had hoped it would be, and they remained until July 30, when Donald resumed his travels in Italy and Truman returned to Paris before heading back to America. "Peaches precious," he wrote Donald from the Pont Royal Hotel. "We shoulda stood in Sirmione! It is frightful hot here, and a ghost town to boot, except for millions of Americans: the worst variety, natch. And I can't begin to tell you what my trip here was like: Not only did I fail to have a wagon-lit, but I didn't even have a seat until we were in Switzerland . . . yep, stood up all the way in the worst heat ever. Anyway, Ten [Tennessee] is here, having failed to show up in London for his opening [*The Glass Menagerie*], and we went out dancing last night. The play got rather bad reviews, and he seems to be upset about it, though I can't imagine why. Good God, who cares what anyone in England thinks?"

He had ample opportunity to console Tennessee, and on Saturday, August 7, they both sailed home on the *Queen Mary*. Truman had been away only three months, but his brief exposure to Europe affected him profoundly; the extraordinary people he had met there took up permanent residence in his memory, and some of them, like Natalie Barney and Denham Fouts, eventually became characters in his fiction. "It was right that I had gone to Europe," he wrote, "if only because I could look again with wonder. Past certain ages or certain wisdoms it is very difficult to look with wonder; it is best done when one is a child; after that, and if you are lucky, you will find a bridge of childhood and walk across it. Going to Europe was like that. It was a bridge of childhood, one that led over the seas and through the forests straight into my imagination's earliest landscapes."

Truman had met Tennessee the year before at a dinner given by Andrew Lyndon and Harold Halma. "Truman went into the kitchen," Andrew recalled, "and Tennessee turned to me and said, in what he thought was a whisper, 'Baby, I think your little friend is charming! Just charming!' It was a small apartment, and Tennessee's voice tended to carry anyway. I could see Truman in the kitchen listening to every word and preening." He and Tennessee met at least a few times after that, but their first prolonged exposure to each other was during the voyage back to New York.

That Tennessee was willing to even sit with him at dinner was something of a victory for Truman, because a couple of Tennessee's closest friends, Carson most notably, had tried to recruit him into their Hate Capote Club. Believing, quite unfairly, that he had copied her work and stolen her fame, Carson had turned from friend to enemy. Even more irrationally, given the sexual equations, she resented his romance with Newton, whom she jealously regarded as her best friend, not his. The success of *Other Voices* had intensified her spiteful rage, which she had vented in her letters to Tennessee. "Aren't you allowing yourself to judge this little boy a bit too astringently?" Tennessee asked her. "I know you must have reasons which I don't know of. I see him as an opportunist and a careerist and a derivative writer whose tiny feet have attempted to fit the ten-league boots of Carson McCullers and succeeded only in tripping him up absurdly. But surely not one of the bad boys. His little face, as photographed by Cecil Beaton against a vast panorama of white roses, has a look of prenatal sorrow, as if he were still in the womb and already suspected how cold the world is beyond the vaginal portals."

Truman and Tennessee were together much of the voyage, enjoying what Tennessee described in his memoirs as "an hilariously funny" crossing: "In those days Truman was about the best companion you could want. He had not turned bitchy. Well, he had not turned *maliciously* bitchy. But he was full of fantasies and mischief. We used to go along the first-class corridors of the *Mary* and pick up the gentlemen's shoes, set outside their staterooms for shining—and we would mix them all up, set them doors away from their proper places." Scarcely had they reached deep water, he added, before an Episcopal bishop, portly and bibulous, began looking at Truman with an irreligious gleam in his eye. Everywhere they went, the unwanted bishop followed. When the lustful ecclesiastic ventured to sit down, uninvited, at their dinner table, Truman decided to send him on his way. "You know," he said, staring at the bishop's hand, "I've always wanted to have a bishop's ring."

"A bishop's ring is only available to a bishop," the bishop answered.

"Oh, I don't know," countered Truman. "It occurred to me that maybe I might find one in a pawnshop. You know, one that had been hocked by a defrocked bishop." The bishop left them alone for the rest of the trip.

When the *Queen Mary* docked on Thursday, August 12, Truman and Tennessee were reminded that in their own country they had not been forgotten. Ignoring such other passengers as Clark Gable, Spencer Tracy, and Charles Boyer, that night's television news showed the two of them disembarking and stepping back onto native soil, returning travelers with words to write and stories to tell.

· · ·

The person Truman was most eager to tell his stories to was Newton, and rushing from the dock to 1060 Park, he called to prepare him for a surprise weekend guest. Newton, who had not been expecting him for another week, was indeed surprised and instantly dispelled his buoyant excitement: he had already made plans, Newton said, to spend the weekend on Martha's Vineyard with his old friends David and Helen Lilienthal. After all his adventures and triumphs in Europe, Truman had anticipated a far more exuberant greeting, and he was, as Newton phrased it in his diary, "much distressed" that Newton would not change his plans. Probably realizing that the fault was mostly his, that he should, after all, have cabled the date of his arrival, Truman called back a few hours later in renewed spirits, and they set their joyful, if delayed, reunion for the following Wednesday, August 18.

Truman doubtless should have cabled—people who spring surprises are often unhappily surprised themselves—but his intuition, which usually served him well, had been correct, detecting a chill in Newton's voice that even Newton was probably unaware of. Newton had not given him a warmer welcome for a good reason: he was not happy to have him back, at least not so soon. Ambivalent as always, Newton had been sorry, or so he told his diary, to see him sail away in May, and he had fretted when he did not hear from him immediately. At the same time, Newton had enjoyed his newfound freedom, and he was sorry to lose it. Relying on Truman's original timetable, which would have brought him home in early September, he and Howard had planned their own joyful reunion in late August. But on August 2, after receiving word that Truman might leave Europe a week or so earlier, he warned Howard that he might have to cancel. "Of course I shall be eager to see him," Newton said, without any conviction at all, "but between you and me, and with many self-reproaches, I am dreading a little the resurgence of some of the problems I had been confronted with the last two years. Poor kid! I love him to death, but I'm terribly afraid this longish interval has proven to me beyond cavil how incapable I now am of getting my breath and filling my lungs in that rather intense and high-pitched atmosphere he so touchingly and lovably evokes around him." Four days later he added a gloomy postscript: his fears had been confirmed; Truman would be back on the weekend they hoped to meet.

Much of his sense of grievance, deprivation, and even annoyance had doubtless been conveyed over the telephone, leaving Truman with a familiar feeling of rejection. When he finally arrived in North-ampton, laden with gifts from Europe, Truman was subdued and sober. Yet Newton was warmer in person than he had been on the phone, and the next day Truman was in better temper, listening attentively as Newton read aloud the newest parts of his Melville biography. Friday, Truman's black mood returned. Why Newton did not know. But there was a reason: the minute Newton left that morning, Truman had sneaked a look at that diary Newton kept so faithfully, and he had been profoundly shocked and wounded by what he had discovered in those telltale pages.

Long ago he had learned how to unobtrusively open the locked desk drawer in which Newton kept his journal; since then it had been mandatory reading each time he visited. What he had found there had often annoyed him. On the few occasions Newton had had sex with other people there would be a bold "X" marking the date. Sometimes there would also be uncomplimentary remarks about Truman, "lots of wondering about whether my intelligence was as large as my talent," as Truman remembered. "It's a terrible thing to know that somebody has such thoughts about you as New-ton had about me and not be able to talk about it."

But that morning he received an extra jolt. As he turned the pages, he quickly apprehended an extremely unpleasant fact: Newton and Andrew had carried on a secret romance all the time he was gone— from the day after he had left, in fact, to the very day he returned. He may also have read some of the incriminating letters Newton had hidden away. "You and your Andrew," Howard said in one of them. "I am of course horribly envious." Or one from Andrew himself: "My very dearest Newton: Last weekend with you was perfect. Of course it didn't last long enough, but then quantity can hardly be a measure of perfection, can it? and perfection cannot logically be expected to endure. You are an angel and an angel to be with!" When he told Andrew to take care of Newton, Truman had not imagined that his injunction would be carried out with such maddening exactitude.

His discovery placed Truman in an awkward dilemma, however. He had learned of their deception through an unscrupulous act of his own; if he accused Newton of infidelity, he would have to ex-plain how he had found out. "I couldn't say anything without letting him know that I had read his diary—and had gone to a lot of trouble to open his desk to do it." Gritting his teeth, he realized that he could not confront him until he had returned to Manhattan and first prized a confession from Andrew. Thus, for the next several days, which included the celebration of Newton's forty-eighth birthday, Truman underwent the self-inflicted torture of anyone who has found out something infuriating by snooping where he had no right to be: he was forced to seethe in silence. "It was the most excruciating thing in the world to sit smiling, talking with him after reading that diary, knowing that everything he said was a lie," he said. When he left at last on August 25, Newton was probably as happy to see him depart as Truman was to go. "T.C. leaves in the morning, anxious, apprehensive, low-spirited. Painful to see this of course," Newton later wrote in that well-read journal.

It did not bother Truman, or bother him greatly, to know that a few others had enjoyed the pleasures of Newton's bed. How could he complain when he too occasionally had strayed from the path of fidelity? During his trip to California the year before, for instance, he had spent the night with Errol Flynn. "If he hadn't been Errol Flynn, I wouldn't remember. We were both drunk—it was the first time I ever had a hangover—and it took him the longest time to have an orgasm. I never did." He also had had a brief fling with John Garfield, who popped up from time to time at Leo's parties. "He was one of the nicest people I've ever known. My mother saw him just once and tried to get him into bed with her." The list of his sexual partners was apparently not much longer than that, and because he had not been emotionally attached, he did not feel that he had cheated on Newton. "I don't regard being with someone a week, or two weeks, or even three weeks, as an affair," he declared. "There has to be emotional involvement in an affair, and I didn't have any of that." Newton's liaison with Andrew was different from anything Truman himself had done. By Truman's definition, it was a real affair, made worse because it was conducted with his best friend. He believed that Newton had cheated on him and that Andrew had betrayed him. And so he told Andrew when he returned from Northampton on that broiling August afternoon.

"Come over, Andrew. I want to talk to you," he commanded in a strained and ominous-sounding voice. "Don't bring Harold. I want to talk to you alone." Andrew, who was the only one he had told about reading Newton's diaries, had been expecting such a call. He had been aware from the day he began seeing Newton that Truman would rush to that locked drawer on his first weekend in Northampton and would instantly know all. He had even guessed what Truman now had to say to him when, obeying his summons, he arrived at 1060.

"To think that you, my dearest friend, the one I love most, would do this to me! And the moment my back is turned! How could you?"

"Pure soap opera!" Andrew retorted, not at all abashed. "Truman, you're just looking for an excuse to get rid of Newton. You knew this would happen. You set me up for it. You arranged it all."

"Well," Truman replied, after looking at him intently for what seemed several minutes. "You're right. But you didn't need to be so damned sure!"

But Andrew was not right. Truman had not set him up—not on a conscious level, anyway—and he agreed with him now only as an expression of pride. It hurt him less if Andrew thought that he had schemed to get rid of Newton rather than that Newton had schemed to get rid of him, which was closer to the truth. He may also have paused so long because Andrew had expressed what he himself had half-realized for many months: his relationship with Newton was rapidly approaching its conclusion.

Meanwhile, with the approximately twenty thousand dollars he had made from *Other Voices*—the first real money he had ever had—Truman expanded his life in Manhattan, moving from 1060, where Nina was becoming troublesome again, to a small apartment of his own on Second Avenue and Fifty-eighth Street, which he decorated with baby pictures of himself and his friends. Success continued to come his way. "Shut a Final Door," the story *The Atlantic Monthly* had published after Mary Louise had turned it down for *Harper's Bazaar*, won first prize in the annual O. Henry Awards, and he felt vindicated, as well as gratified. Holding his three-hundred-dollar prize money tightly in his hand, he immediately went out and ordered a tailor-made, four-hundred-dollar Knize suit—"which is merely to show you how close I am to the edge of madness," he jokingly wrote Donald Windham. As far as he was concerned, it was worth every penny, however; few people gained as much pleasure as Truman did from expensive purchases, and he liked to show off the sleeves, which, unlike those on less expensive suits, could actually be unbuttoned so that they could be rolled up and down. "Honey, these cuff buttons button and unbutton!" he pointed out more than once to Phoebe Pierce.

He occasionally entertained in his new apartment, resuming where he had left off in May with old friends such as Phoebe and Andrew, whom he held largely blameless for what had gone on in Northampton. One farcical night, in fact, he and Andrew were considered partners in crime by the New York Police Department. After dinner at the Plaza, they decided to visit Tennessee, who was living nearby, in a house on East Fifty-eighth Street. But Tennessee was not at home. "How inconsiderate of him!" Truman complained. "He could have hoped we'd come." Truman had Andrew lift him up and push him through the transom, so that he could open the door from the inside. "We'll just go in and play Victrola records until he comes back," Truman said.

Unbeknownst to them, their successful housebreaking had aroused the curiosity of two plainclothesmen and a policewoman who happened to be passing by, and as if on cue, those guardians of the public order suddenly made themselves visible. "Whose house is this?" demanded one of them. "It belongs to Tennessee Williams," said Truman. "And I," he added gravely, "am Truman Capote." With one voice, they roared, "Who?" Furious, Truman sat down, and they all waited for Tennessee. There was a brief burst of activity when Andrew, reaching into a pile of suit jackets for his cigarettes, mistakenly pulled out the gun of one of the plainclothesmen instead. "They looked a bit startled at that!" Andrew recalled. "We had 'em covered. But I got the damned thing out of my hand as quickly as I could." Finally, after an hour or so, Andrew was allowed to call Tennessee's agent, Audrey Wood, who promised to send her husband over to set matters right. "Tell Audrey to send a copy of *Other Voices* too," Truman yelled as Andrew dialed her number. "I want to prove to these people that I am a writer."

Before Wood's husband could arrive, Tennessee showed up, accompanied by Gore Vidal, whose unwelcome presence provided the perfect ending to their little comedy. Tennessee and Gore found the scene highly amusing, and Tennessee decided to prolong the confusion. "They broke into your house—do you want to press charges?" asked one of the policemen. "Well, they weren't here when I left, I know that," replied Tennessee, who seemed undecided. "Listen, Tennessee," said Truman, "don't you do anything of the sort!"

There was never any real danger. Reaching into his bag of tricks, Truman had won their captors over with imitations of some of his famous friends. Andrew had mentioned that Truman was coming to dinner the next night; when they left, the policewoman, obviously impressed by the evening's entertainment, said to Truman: "I'm sorry I wasn't invited to dinner tomorrow too. I'd love to see your imitation of me."

Truman's life in Manhattan thus proceeded much as it had before his trip to Europe. He forgave Newton and continued his biweekly visits to Northampton, where, after a day's work, they took turns reading aloud Dickens' *Little Dorrit*. Yet underneath that placid routine could be heard small but disturbing sounds of distress, like those that presage an earthquake. It was a painful autumn. Although they were both groping for an exit from a no longer tenable relationship, neither was ready to admit it, even to himself. Indeed, despite everything that was pulling them apart, they still loved each other.

Truman apparently made one last, unsuccessful effort to ward off the inevitable breakup, renewing his old request for a full-time companionship. But a full-time companion Newton would never be, and he said so, noting in his diary that he was having difficult times with little T: "Our excruciating, insoluble problem." Two weeks later he recorded Truman's response to his refusal: "Talked with Truman on the telephone at noon. He seemed preoccupied and oddly unresponsive—for him." It was an almost exact replay, in reverse, of their exchange when Truman had returned from Europe, and it was now Newton's turn to receive rejection over the telephone wires—an experience he enjoyed no more than Truman had. "Insomnia & Angst," he wrote the next morning. "Intense angst," he said the day after that; "rather shaky all day," some time later. Although Truman did not say so, he had fallen in love with someone else.

It was over between them, but they continued seeing each other for several weeks, celebrating their third Christmas together in Northampton. At the beginning of February, 1949, after he had all but proclaimed the news to his friends in New York, Truman finally confessed that he had a new lover, something Newton had already guessed and accepted. "Sad but also tender and without bitterness" was his diary comment. As Truman observed, Newton even seemed

relieved. "I don't think he was up to having a very intense relationship with anybody. He was a weekend caller, one might say. He
wanted to spend the week in his own activities."

In retrospect, the end could not have been delayed much longer.
Truman was no longer the *Wunderkind* who had burst into Yaddo,
in many ways still unformed, unfinished, and uncertain. He was an
established writer with a small but growing international reputation,
and he had a much surer sense of himself, both as a man, which he
now was, and as an artist, which he also indisputably was. He was
not the "dear child" he had been during those enchanted weeks of
June, 1946, someone Newton could patronize, if ever so gently and
fondly. It is inconceivable that after having seen the wider world of
Europe, after having bitten the apple of fame, he could have continued the old routine much longer, the tedious, fortnightly train trip
to Northampton, followed by an occasional Saturday night at the
movies and listening to the NBC radio symphony on Sunday afternoon. If Newton had found it hard to breathe in the high-pitched
atmosphere that surrounded Truman, so too had Truman found it
increasingly hard to breathe in the claustrophobic, mothball-scented
atmosphere that surrounded Newton. They remained affectionate
friends nonetheless, and on June 14, 1949, three years after their
first meeting, Newton wrote: "The anniversary of a great day in
1946. Many thoughts of little T."

In 1951, Newton's biography of Melville won the National Book
Award, enhancing his already large stature as a critic. But his life
was not enlarged or made happier. Much of his sexual pleasure was
now vicarious, and he secretly began collecting and exchanging homosexual erotica—stories, nudes, and pornographic pictures. A few
years later, far more explicit photographs and movies could be ordered through the mail or purchased in adult bookshops across the
country. But in the Massachusetts of those years, posssession of
such material was illegal and dangerous, and in September, 1960,
acting on information received from a raid on a pornographic publisher, police broke into his Northampton sanctuary and discovered
more than a thousand examples of sexual stories and pictures. Newton, who abhorred profanity and vulgar language, who always spoke
and wrote with elegant precision, was arrested and charged with
being "a lewd and lascivious person in speech and behavior." His

worst fear was at last realized: he was unmasked and publicly humiliated for being homosexual. Newspapers in Boston and New York headlined his shame. "Day of the Avalanche" was all he wrote in his diary—and the rest of the year was blank. Suffering a nervous breakdown, he was allowed to enter Northampton State Hospital, or "Dippy Hall," as the Smith girls preferred to call it.

To his surprise, his friends and acquaintances, including Lillian Hellman and Van Wyck Brooks, were neither shocked nor disgusted by what he had done and rallied around him, raising money and lobbying in his behalf. "All your friends are with you, of that you can be sure," wrote Truman, who was living in Europe. "And among them please do not count me least; aside from my affection, which you already have, I will be *glad* to supply you with money should the need arise. This is a tough experience, and must be met with toughness: a calm head, a good lawyer." Though he was hard pressed himself at the time, Truman delicately, and rather disarmingly, repeated his offer of financial help a few weeks later. "When and if you need money, *please* say so; I have some, I really do, and it would not inconvenience me at all." Although Newton was never allowed to teach there again, Smith promised him a small yearly stipend and kept his name on its faculty list.

What saved him from prison, however—he received a one-year suspended sentence—was neither his friends nor the college administration. It was, alas, his own cowardice. Turning informer, he gave the police the names of at least fifteen other collectors of pornography, including two younger faculty colleagues who were sentenced to a year in jail. "He panicked and ratted, poor bastard," said Hellman. "He must have been in total terror."

Yet he survived, and a few months later he appeared happier than he had been in years, displaying a serenity he perhaps never before had known. The worst had happened; finally, at the age of sixty, he no longer had anything to hide; he had no more need for disguises. Writing to his friend Daniel Aaron, he said: "I can tell you, from a fund of experience, that one can be taken down from the rack, closer to death than to life—and then still have the most exquisite joys ahead of one." He had nearly completed another book, a biography of Longfellow, when bad fortune visited again and he was stricken with cancer. Truman talked to him on the telephone shortly before he died in March, 1963. "He knew he was dying and he said one of the most marvelous things I ever remember anybody saying: 'Never mind. At least I've grown up at last.' I knew exactly what he meant. Like most of us, all of his life he had been the victim of adolescent impulses. Contending with something formidable, he knew what it was to be an adult."

THE man who replaced Newton in Truman's affections was Newton's opposite in almost every way. His name was Jack Dunphy. He was thirty-four, vigorous and good-looking, five feet, nine inches tall, with receding red hair, a complexion as ruddy as an autumn apple, blue eyes, and the trim, athletic physique of the dancer he had been before going off to war in 1944—he had played one of the cowboys in *Oklahoma!* His ambition was to be a writer, however, and his only novel, *John Fury*, a spare, severely written tale of Philadelphia's Irish poor, had been highly praised by the reviewers. Despite those accomplishments, many people in New York thought of him chiefly as the husband, then the ex-husband, of Joan McCracken, one of Broadway's brightest young musical-comedy stars. Truman, typically, knew all about him even before they met. "I had a terrific crush on him without ever having seen him," he confessed.

Jack happened to be at Leo's when Truman telephoned one evening in the fall of 1948. Knowing Truman's interest, Leo said, "Jack Dunphy's here!" Within ten minutes Truman was walking in the door. "He was cute, adorable-looking," said Jack. "He was wearing a cap, and his skin was fresh and clear. He was trying to be his mostest and bestest. We sat on the couch together and talked about trains. I had a mad desire to go somewhere." A day or so after that, Truman invited him to a party he was planning to give at 1060 Park in mid-December. Jack accepted, but suggested that they also see each other before then. Truman gladly obliged. They had dinner in Truman's new apartment on Second Avenue, and as if adhering to a prearranged schedule, they went to bed together. "I made the advances," said Jack, "but of course Truman was leading me by the nose."

And of course, he was. "I have a theory," said Truman, "that if you want something badly enough, you'll get it, whatever it is. You've got to really want it, and concentrate on it twenty-four hours a day, but if you do, you'll get it. I have never found that to be untrue. When I finally met Jack, I thought to myself: 'That's exactly the kind of person I really, really like. Why is it that other people meet someone like that and I don't? Why can't I?' So I decided that one way or another—and I didn't know how—I was going to get him. I was absolutely dead-set and determined."

The party at 1060 was key to his campaign. Though ostensibly it was a celebration of Andrew's thirtieth birthday, its actual purpose almost certainly was to demonstrate to Jack how many famous people Truman knew. At that it succeeded. "Good Lord! Who wasn't there?" exclaimed Andrew. "Auden, George Davis, even the Marquis of Milford-Haven, who had been the best man at the wedding of Elizabeth and Prince Philip the year before. It was so crowded that you couldn't move. Beatrice Lillie had said she would sing—that was going to be her birthday present to me—but there was no room. When I met her, she was in Truman's bedroom and just said, 'Happy birthday!' " It is doubtful that Jack, who was unaccustomed to such gatherings, was favorably impressed; it is doubtful, in fact, that he was aware who all those famous people were. He buried himself in the kitchen, prompting Nina, who had never seen him before, to ask him if he were sick. Truman carefully escorted him into the dining room to show him off to a few close friends, as if he were afraid that too many curious stares would cause him to bolt for the door—which might well have happened. "Truman told me he wanted me to meet somebody," said Mary Louise. "He went through the swinging door into the kitchen and came back leading Jack, who had been lurking in there and who seemed nervous. Jack said nothing except hello, then immediately retired into the kitchen again. He looked gorgeous, and Truman was so proud and excited that you could tell that this was the real thing."

Jack was not so much shy as he was unsociable, and he had more than the usual dislike of milling throngs. "All parties are bad, as far as I'm concerned," he said. "I don't believe in social life for a reason:

it doesn't do anything for you." He was not easily intimidated, and when Truman chose him, he chose someone whose will was as strong as his own, someone who had overcome equally formidable obstacles to become a writer.

The eldest of six children, Jack had grown up in St. Monica's parish, a poor Irish neighborhood, in Philadelphia. Life there was perhaps even more inflexible and narrow than it had been in Monroeville; the residents of those drab little row houses regarded themselves as members of a clan and held in fine disdain anyone who wanted to leave for the wider world outside. They were particularly suspicious of a boy like Jack who enjoyed listening to the opera on the radio and preferred reading to baseball and football. His own relatives were shocked by his desire to write. "My God! You'd think I sold dirty pictures the way [they] acted," he complained. Unlike Truman and Newton, he was not a sissy, however: he gave back better than he received. He was twelve or thirteen when a neighbor boy taunted him for reading a book on the front porch. "Come on down and play, Mary!" the boy yelled. "Hey, Mary!" Throwing his book aside, Jack leaped over the porch railing and attacked him, smashing his head again and again against the sidewalk. "He had a terrible temper," said his sister Olive. "It was as if he were saying to the boy, 'I don't care if I kill you.' The mothers came running out when they heard the boy screaming, and there was lots of talk. But Jack was never bothered again."

His father, James Dunphy, was a newspaper Linotype operator. He fled to Baltimore when Jack was born; Jack's mother, Kate, who may not yet have had the advantage of a marriage license, tracked him down, shaming him into returning to Philadelphia by thrusting their infant child into his arms. He grudgingly did his duty, but he never forgave either mother or child. "I think Dad really did hate me," Jack said. "We were terrible enemies, blood enemies. The only time we were together was when he impregnated my ma. Truman was ambivalent about his father. I knew where I stood with mine. He read books himself—he always had something in front of his face—but he threw mine into the backyard." When they had words, which they frequently did, his father would end the argument by saying, "Please don't talk so high and mighty. Remember, you shit in your pants coming back on the train from Baltimore." Although Jack was his father's main target, the other children—two boys and three girls—did not entirely escape his ill temper. When his favorite son, Carl, was killed on the beaches of Anzio during World War II, James Dunphy turned to his son Bob and snarled, "Why wasn't it you who died instead of him?"

A swell, a spiffy dresser who had a haircut and manicure every week, he demanded much and gave little. "Now make me laugh!" he would command the radio when he sat down to listen to his favorite shows. He considered himself several steps above his wife, who could barely read, who drank her tea from the saucer in which she cooled it, and who was pregnant so often that he sarcastically nicknamed her Olan, after a Chinese peasant woman in Pearl Buck's novel *The Good Earth*. Kate did have the patience of a Chinese peasant. Though he would often stay away for weeks at a time with one woman or another, she never murmured a word of complaint. "Here comes Father!" she would gaily yell when she finally saw him walking home to Gladstone Street.

Perhaps because he was her firstborn, perhaps because his father hated him so, she worshiped Jack. When he was little, he stood behind her at night and brushed her long hair; after the other children had gone to bed, the two of them often shared a bowl of ice cream, a special treat in a poor household; his was the only name she called on her deathbed. "All the little good in me, what kindness and courtesy there is, I count from her," he wrote. "The nay-saying part of me is from him; the *Protest*ant part." As is often the case with fathers and sons, Jack became more like his hated parent than he probably knew. He almost always said exactly what he thought, without regard for the laws of tact and convention, and it was impossible to predict his sudden outbursts of anger, which arrived without warning, like tornadoes roaring across the prairie on a cloudless summer day. "You never know what Jack's reaction will be to anything," Truman was to observe. "You can say, 'I think Horn & Hardart's baked beans are better than Schrafft's,' and you will suddenly be in a fantastic quarrel with him."

"Poverty is much more than a way of life," Jack later wrote. "It goes much farther than skin-deep. It's no tattoo that fades with time. Nor a brand that can be put out of mind except when faced. Poverty, if you've known it, *is* you." So it was and so it remained for him. Quitting high school to earn his living in factories, he looked with gluttonous envy at the young men attending the University of Pennsylvania. Fired again and again—"I couldn't stand an office or a set routine"—he began attending a school for professional dancers; he had an Irish love for dance and movement and had spent many hours practicing steps next to the coal bin in the basement. To his surprise, he discovered that he could survive by shuffling his feet. "I didn't really have any talent," he admitted, "but I was good enough to do the job."

He married his classmate Joan McCracken, and they moved to New York, only to be temporarily separated when he landed a place in George Balanchine's company, which toured South America for eight months. He had always wanted to be a writer, and it was on that trip that he began *John Fury*. "I wouldn't have started it if I hadn't been so lonely. When I wrote, I wasn't lonely anymore. I cut myself off from the rest of the company. Everybody else would go out at night and screw. I would go up to my room, work, jerk off and go to sleep."

Whatever abilities he lacked as a dancer and entertainer Joan possessed in abundance. They both landed small roles in *Oklahoma!* His remained small; hers expanded—indeed, exploded. "When she came to the audition, she was very poor, wearing a coat trimmed with rabbit fur," recalled Agnes de Mille, whose innovative choreography turned that musical into a Broadway landmark. "I insisted that she be hired and created for her the part of the girl who falls down, which became a great gag. She was a memorable comedienne and an exquisite technician; she had short, dumpy legs, but she used them brilliantly. She was beautiful, with a dear little, heart-shaped face, and when she came on stage and smiled, the audience melted. You could have sopped them up with a piece of bread. She was irresistible. Her personality was that of a star."

Jack, by contrast, avoided the spotlight. When De Mille thought up something that would have focused attention on him too, he turned her down. "I'm not interested," he said. "Give it to one of the other boys." His ambition, he made clear, lay elsewhere. When he went into the Army the following year, Joan dominated his thoughts; as with many other soldiers, all he thought about was going home to his wife. "I was like a sunflower," he said, "and Joan was like the sun. I didn't have any sex at all. I didn't even masturbate." She was not so chaste, and when Jack returned from Europe in 1946, he immediately sensed that she was devoured by guilt. Guessing what had occurred, he tried to reassure her. "Don't be afraid," he said. They were on their second honeymoon in the Caribbean when she received the telegram that ended their marriage: the French composer she had had an affair with had been injured in a plane crash, and he had asked for her to come to his bedside. Forced to confess, she flew back to New York. "I would have forgiven her," Jack said. "She was like an island I had waited all my life for. But she was blackmailed in a way, made to feel guilty, by this little Jew fairy who fell out of a plane. When she left, it tore me to pieces, and a part of me died." To his family, who loved her, he said only, "She ran off with a Jew."

As devastated by the breakup as he was, Joan was unable to handle either her success or her life. She married Bob Fosse, who also became famous as a dancer and director, but she divorced a second time. She accepted the wrong roles—heavy dramatic parts —and her career foundered. "Hollywood was screaming for her, and she could have become a big star," said De Mille. "But she got lost in being arty." Although she appeared to want Jack back, he shied away. "I still liked her," he said, "but I would never have gone to bed with her again. She destroyed herself. She was hurrying toward the abyss." They remained fond friends anyway, and when she died in 1961 of a heart ailment, she left him three thousand dollars. "I looked at her face in the coffin," said De Mille, "and it was still beautiful, still seemed to give out light. I thought of some lines of John Webster: 'Cover her face; mine eyes dazzle; she died young.' "

"I would never have become homosexual if Joan had stayed with me," Jack said, and it is probably so. He had had homoerotic fantasies before, and he had moved in a dance and theatrical circle that was largely populated by homosexuals, but his sexual experience, starting in his mid-teens with a high school teacher, had been entirely with women. He was not a man who could react in a moderate or measured way, and when Joan cheated on him, he turned against the entire female sex. "Women were very distasteful to me, and I decided I wanted to go to bed with men. I had had dreamy crushes on men before, but I had never thought of doing anything about them. I knew the jars of honey were there, but I didn't know they could be opened."

Remembering the advances made to him by an Army buddy, he took a bus to Florida, where the man was living, to see if the offer was still open. It was not; his friend was now thinking civilian thoughts of marriage and children. Jack was undaunted. The jars of honey were waiting for him in New York, as they had always been, and although he fumbled and sweated, he soon learned how to open them. "When I did turn to men, it was very difficult," he explained. "I really had to work at it. Men's legs were hard." He was still working at it—he had been to bed with only two men—when Truman came through Leo's door and showed him how easy it all was.

"I've spent all my life looking for the perfect boy," Jack confessed long after, and Truman's youth and effervescence appealed to him as they did to so many others. But Jack was not in love with Truman, as Truman was with him—and Truman knew it. Truman had spent his life learning how to please, however, and now those years of training got him what he desired. Quickly picking up on what Jack wanted, he offered him a free trip to Europe. "I love to travel," said Jack, "and when he said, 'Let's go to Europe!' that was it." They waited until Truman's collection of eight short stories, *A Tree of Night*, was published at the beginning of 1949. Then, on February 26, 1949, three months after they had met at Leo's, they sailed for France on the *Queen Mary*. "I finally got him!" exulted Truman. "Completely, totally, and utterly."

THEIR scheme was to head toward the sun, meaning Sicily, where they could work for a few months. After a rough voyage that left them both with colds and raw tempers, they briefly stopped in Paris, then traveled to Venice and Rome, where they joined Tennessee and his new lover, Frank Merlo, on an excursion to the island of Ischia, offshore from Naples.

Truman and Tennessee were fated to be quarrelsome friends, and stopping in Naples, they had not one, but two disagreements. The first, which was relatively minor, came when they checked into their hotel. Truman, who was prey to any number of superstitions, looked at his room number and was horrified to discover that, added together, its digits made thirteen, which was a portent of disaster. Tennessee, who was no less superstitious, agreed to switch, but instantly demanded his key back when he learned the reason. "You're not doing that to me!" he declared. "Get back in the other room!"

The second dispute was more serious. At dinner the night before they were to leave for Ischia, Truman told what he thought was a funny story: how Margo Jones, the director of Tennessee's newest play, *Summer and Smoke*, had called the cast together during rehearsals and, in a macabre pep talk, announced. "This is the play of a dying man. We've got to give it all we've got." Tennessee, whose exaggerated hypochondria had provoked her dire pronouncement, had not heard the story and did not find it amusing. He was, in his own words, almost hysterical with hurt and anger—Vesuvius could not have exploded with greater fury. "He suddenly picked up the entire table and turned it on top of me," Truman recalled. "Then he ran out of the room and disappeared. Frankie was terribly concerned, and for some reason Jack was also annoyed that I had told the story. Well, I certainly didn't tell it out of malice. I didn't realize that I was touching the nerve nearest Tennessee's heart. He claimed he was dying every other day. It was his favorite gambit for getting sympathy. 'You don't know it, my dear,' he would say, 'but Ah'm a dyin' man!' "

While Tennessee sulked, Truman and Jack left the next day for Ischia. Frankie and Tennessee followed twenty-four hours later; but Tennessee had not forgotten. "I think you judge Truman a bit too charitably when you call him a child," he wrote Donald Windham. "He is more like a sweetly vicious old lady." He admitted, however, that part of the reason for his eruption was his jealous suspicion that Frankie preferred Truman's company to his own, which may at times have been true. "Frankie was a terrific person," Truman said, "very smart, very special. He was the best person Tennessee ever took up with." Yet Truman, ironically, also kept a close eye on Frankie, convinced that he was attracted to Jack. "Frankie had a great crush on Jack—there was a whole group of people that had a great crush on Jack. So I said to him, 'Try it on for size, Frankie, and if it fits, wear it.' At the same time I said to Jack, 'You'd better not do it!' I didn't take him away from everybody else to lose him to Frankie!" Frankie's childlike candor and unassailable integrity appealed to most people. When Jack Warner, who was entertaining Tennessee in his private dining room on the Warner Brothers lot, asked him what he did for a living, Frankie looked at him evenly and replied, "I sleep with Mr. Williams."

Once settled, in a pension in the tiny village of Forio, Truman and Jack forgot about Sicily: Ischia's eighteen square miles of volcanic rock, bathed by sea and sun, had everything they had been looking for. "What a strange, and strangely enchanted, place this is: an encantada in the Mediterranean," Truman wrote Bob Linscott. "It is an island off the coast from Naples, very primitive, populated mostly by winegrowers, goatherders, W. H. Auden and the Mussolini family." To Cecil Beaton, with whom, during his days in England, he had formed a close attachment, he observed: "It is really very beautiful and strange: we have almost a whole floor on the waterfront overlooking the sea, the sun is diamond-hard and everywhere there is the pleasant southern smell of wisteria and lemon leaves." Auden, who had rented a house nearby, extolled its blessings in verse.

> . . . my thanks are for you,
> Ischia, to whom a fair wind has
> brought me rejoicing with dear friends
> from soiled productive cities. How well you correct
> our injured eyes, how gently you train us to see
> things and men in perspective
> underneath your uniform light.

But Auden confined his rejoicing within the boundaries of that poem, and his prickly and tyrannical personality did not win him many dear friends on Ischia. "What a bore Auden was!" complained Truman. "He had not a spark of humor or wit. He was all intellect. I gave a party on the roof of our pension. I decorated it with Japanese lanterns, and about fifty people came, including the most beautiful fishermen on the island. Everybody had a good time. Everybody, that is, except Wystan, who wouldn't dance or talk to anyone and sat all by himself in a corner, looking as glum as he could. That's my image of Auden: sitting all by himself in a corner, looking glum." Auden and his companion, Chester Kallman, were agreeable, after their fashion, to Truman and Jack, but for mysterious and inexplicable reasons, they went out of their way to snub Tennessee and Frankie. "What Wystan saw in Chester, who was one of the meanest men I've ever known, I'll never understand," Truman added. "Auden was already pretty well known as a poet, but the way Chester acted you would have thought that behind the scenes he was the important one. Chester was extremely rude to Tennessee and Frankie, and he made it a point not to invite them to their house. Tennessee was very hurt."

Truman and Jack had come to Ischia to work, not to dance on the roof or feud with their neighbors, and that they did. Although their pension, the Lustro, had no running water, it did provide, for only two hundred dollars a month, two pleasant rooms, breakfast, and two five-course meals a day, along with good Ischian wine with which to wash them down. Truman's routine was a familiar one: work in the morning, usually in bed; lunch and a swim; more work in the afternoon; and an evening of society, if any was to be found.

If not, he read; he was belatedly discovering the sly pleasures of Jane Austen. Most of his working time was occupied by his second novel, *Summer Crossing*, the book about a Manhattan society girl he had put aside to write *Other Voices*. "I have fine hopes for *Summer Crossing*," Truman wrote Linscott on April 1, "and I feel alive and justified in doing it, but it makes me nervous all the time, which is probably a good sign, and I do not feel like talking about it, which is another."

Linscott, who was wise and experienced enough to discern the worry peering through that underbrush of optimism—nervousness is never conducive to good writing—responded with properly soothing and encouraging words. "I am happy that *Summer Crossing* goes so well. I have thought of it again and again since that day in your apartment when you unveiled the story—and each time with contentment for the theme and desire to read it." Perhaps thus encouraged, Truman wrote swiftly, and early in May he was pleased to report that he had finished the first third, "which is making very good time, don't you think? If I can finish a draft of it before going home, then I probably will have it all polished by the first of the year, which means you could publish it the following June—that is, if you have a mind to. But we will see what happens—it is by so far the most difficult thing I have ever tried to do."

"Silly goose that I am, I seem to think myself very happy—so perhaps I am," Truman told Cecil a few days after arriving, and Ischia remained a happy place for him. Its chief enchantment was neither the sun nor the water, Auden, or the Mussolini family; it was Jack. "Truman was wrapped around him like a boa practically every minute," Tennessee tartly told Donald, "except when he was making invisible little pencil scratches in a notebook that was supposed to be his next novel." Truman had known from the start that he loved Jack; now he believed that Jack was also beginning to love him. One of the reasons he had wanted to rush off to Europe with him was his fear that Jack might somehow reconcile with Joan. That now seemed unlikely. Their weeks together in the Pensione di Lustro had pushed her into the background and had made Truman feel that his own position was secure. "I am attending to my work with a fair degree of concentration," he wrote Cecil. "That makes me content, and so does Jack, who has proved to be a really extraordinary person—of a perceptivity too rarely encountered and a strength almost never."

By June the charms of Ischia had begun to fade, for them and many others, and by a peculiar coincidence, half of the island seemed to decamp at the same time. In a letter to Carson, Tennessee described the arrival of the Ischia crowd in Rome. "Truman and Auden and Chester Kallman and various other of the spiteful sisterhood were all clustered on the little island of Ischia for several months, but all at once there was some convulsion among them and they all came off at once. Truman and his paramour passed through town for a few days last week. Auden and Chester also at the same time. There was a great collision in the public rooms of the Hotel Inghilterra, all hissing and flapping like geese, and there are rumors that the island of Ischia has dropped back into the sea."

A curious pair from Tangier, a countess of undetermined nationality and her American boyfriend, had passed through Ischia one day. They traveled in an exuberant and expansive style—along with a Great Dane, an Afghan, two dachshunds, two Chihuahuas, and a tiny mutt called Mr. Brown—and to Truman, who by then was becoming bored with the island's familiar faces, they seemed to carry with them the glamour and mystery of the Casbah. Tangier, which happened to be on the itinerary of several of his friends, including Cecil and Paul and Jane Bowles, suddenly presented itself as an ideal successor to Ischia, an inexpensive place to relax and work through the summer and fall. Thus it was that after a quick visit to Paris and a long, dusty train ride through Spain, he and Jack crossed the Straits of Gibraltar and landed in Tangier on July 2.

Yet even before they set foot there, that "ragamuffin city," as Truman was to call it, was a disappointment. Knowing how galling his own presence would be to Truman, Gore, who was not one of the friends Truman had expected to see, had flown from Paris and prepared a small surprise. "Come to the dock with me," he told Paul Bowles. "Watch his face when he catches sight of me." As the boat from Spain nudged the pier, Truman first spotted Bowles, who was tall and stood out from the crowd. He leaned over the railing, grinning broadly and waving the inevitable Bronzini scarf. Then he saw Gore, who was smugly grinning back at him, and, in a kind of slapstick routine, both he and his smile abruptly vanished. "His face fell like a soufflé placed in the ice compartment," said Bowles, "and he disappeared entirely below the level of the railing for several seconds. When he had assumed a standing position again, he was no longer grinning or waving." His comical expression of dismay was all that Gore could have hoped for, and after staying only long enough to make Truman think that his entire summer would be ruined, Gore triumphantly departed.

A more enduring irritant was the hotel, the El Farhar. "Rhymes with horror," said Tennessee, who had stayed there earlier; "spectacular view: every possible discomfort!" Located on what Tangerines call the Mountain, about twenty minutes away from the center of town, it consisted of a Victorian house and several ramshackle bungalows, one of which Truman and Jack unhappily occupied. Bad as it may have been in January, when Tennessee was there, it was worse in July and far worse in the broil of August: with their corrugated-iron roofs, the bungalows might just as well have been ovens, so efficiently did they retain the heat of the North African sun. "I don't care how hot it's been in New York," Truman complained to Linscott in August, "it's been just twice as hot [here]." To add to their misery, what sounded like a regiment of British soldiers, on holiday from their posts in Gibraltar, had made themselves at home in neighboring quarters, in which they chattered, sang, and caroused from eight in the morning until ten at night. The Farhar, in short, was not a congenial place in which to work or relax. Cecil Beaton, who arrived in August to stay in a rich friend's comfortable house in town, commiserated in his diary: "[The hotel] is hellishly hot and altogether unattractive, but Truman cannot afford to move and he is good at making the best of a bad job."

The only thing that made living there bearable at all was the presence of the Bowleses, who were one of the most interesting couples in American literary history: the fact that their marriage was without sex in no way diminished their obvious devotion. He was both a composer and a writer; she was a writer and playwright, whose hallucinatory, surrealistic style had already won her a small but fanatical following. A leader of her claque was Tennessee, who proclaimed her to be the finest writer of fiction the United States had ever produced. "You will probably think this a wild opinion," he admitted in his memoirs, "but I must stick to it." Truman did not go that far, but he nevertheless placed her near the top of his own list of favorite American women writers, right behind Willa Cather and Edith Wharton. "There was nobody else like Jane

Bowles," he said. "She had an odd turn of mind, both in her writing and her person."

That may have been because she was mad, in the philosophical, if not the clinical, sense, driven by obsessions so ludicrous that even she could find them amusing. Like a demon-possessed character in one of her own books, she had developed a bizarre attachment to an abnormally tall, slightly moustached and altogether unattractive peasant woman who wore blue jeans and brown golf shoes under her Berber robe. Every day that summer Jane would walk to the grain market, where the woman had a stand, to offer gifts and pay obsequious court. She was always back in time for dinner, when she would report, in a torrent of laughter, how her campaign was going. But Truman entertained her as much as she entertained him. "Everything," she wrote a friend, "has changed since Truman Capote arrived."

The best picture of Tangier at that time, the feeling of the place rather than a factual description, can be found not in histories or guidebooks, but in Hollywood films like *Tangier* and *Casablanca*. For foreigners residing there, daily life had the melodramatic quality of a glossy B movie: a highly charged mixture of the romantic, decadent, and dangerous. Smuggling was a major industry, and fortunes were made within hours—and spent almost as quickly. French designers flew mannequins from Paris to show their latest collections, the newest American cars crowded the narrow streets, and almost anything, from drugs to flesh, could be bought or sold in the openair cafés that dotted the Little Market.

Alongside that city of frenzied and sometimes sinister activity existed an older, lazier Tangier, where, as Truman phrased it, the days slid by "less noticed than foam in a waterfall." As before, he and Jack usually worked in the morning, swam in the afternoon, then, after dinner at the El Farhar, attended one of the many parties given that summer in Tangier, which, though no one knew it, had reached the pinnacle of its brief and unnatural prosperity.

The most pleasurable such event was a midnight beach party Cecil gave for Jack's thirty-fifth birthday in the beachfront Caves of Hercules. One of the grottoes was decorated with flowers, lanterns, and colorful hangings; Arab musicians played unseen in another; and champagne, cooled in ocean water, washed down the marshmallows that Cecil's sybaritic Boy Scouts toasted by the fire. The only thing Cecil could not do was banish the scorpions that infested the cliffs above. Protesting terror, Truman refused to walk down, and Moroccan peasants had to be summoned to carry him, like Nero, to the revels below.

Despite that adolescent display, both Cecil and Paul Bowles were impressed by the serious side of his character, the hitherto unsuspected scope and clarity of his ambition. "One day Truman outlined for us his literary plans for the next two decades," said Paul. "It was all in such detail that naturally I discounted it as fantasy. It seemed impossible that anyone could 'know' so far ahead what he was going to write. However, the works he described in 1949 appeared, one after the other, over the years that followed. They were all there in his head, like baby crocodiles, waiting to be hatched."

The crocodile being hatched that summer was still *Summer Crossing*. He worked steadily, and by August 30 Truman was able to inform Linscott that he was two-thirds through the first draft. "Some of it I'm pleased with, some of it not, naturally. I think it will run to about 80,000 words, rather longer than I expected—but then it has turned into quite a different, infinitely more complex novel than I originally proposed, and to pull it into shape will take a monumental effort." Two weeks later he confirmed that "if all goes well, you will have a book to read by the first of the year, or somewhere around there." Thoroughly weary of Tangier by then, he plaintively added: "Is it autumn in New York? I like it best then, and long to be there."

At the end of September, after nearly three months in that ragamuffin city, he and Jack finally did leave, carrying with them a beautiful white Pekingese puppy—Manchester he was called—that Jane Bowles had given them. Accompanied by Cecil, they sailed across the Mediterranean to Marseille. It was not New York, but after Tangier, it looked immensely appealing to Truman nonetheless. "Well, at any rate," he said, "Marseille is a real town, and the shops are real shops."

While Cecil hurried north, Truman and Jack savored Provence, arriving in Paris the first week in October. Their funds were lower than they had been when they were there in March, and after a few days at the Pont Royal, they settled nearby, in the less expensive and more relaxed Hôtel de l'Université. Jane, who had temporarily abandoned her pursuit of the moustached Berber woman, took up residence a few weeks later, and the raffish amiability of the El Farhar was reestablished in Saint-Germain-des-Prés.

Because Frank Price, the Paris editor of Doubleday, had the only private telephone in the hotel, Truman, still in his pajamas or bathrobe, would come padding in every morning to make calls, ask the time—he never wore a watch—and check his appearance in the mirror. He reminded Price's secretary, Judith Jones, of a sleepy little boy, always bubbling with laughter as he described the supposedly wicked events of the night before. Interviewing him then, a French reporter described him thus: "Small, bordering on the fragile, precious, he's a literary seraph with heavy-lidded eyes, decked out for the Rue Jacob: the inevitable blue jeans which are the trademark today of intellectuals from across the Atlantic, a gray tweed raglan covering an argyle sweater, a raspberry scarf which accentuates his pale complexion. Disheveled blond locks cover, or uncover, the forehead of a thinker." The author who had informed American readers that he had danced on a riverboat could not resist giving his biography a still further fictional twist for the French: his ancestors were Spanish, he said, and he had been born into a family of Louisiana weavers.

In March he and Jack had passed through Paris so quickly that he had had little time to renew old acquaintances. Now he made his rounds, taking Jack and Jane Bowles to Natalie Barney's Friday afternoons and paying his respects to Jenny Bradley and Alice B. Toklas, among others. He was also a frequent guest at the house of Marie-Laure de Noailles, one of Paris's most celebrated hostesses and a woman who enjoyed adding talented newcomers like Truman to her circle. "All day Truman would be living in our cheap little hotel," said Price, who watched with near-amazement his comings and goings. "Then in the evening he would come in and say, 'Well, I'm going to have dinner with Marie-Laure. How do I look?' And off he'd go. He knew everyone in Paris! He was a young literary lion, invited everywhere."

Denham Fouts was dead, and gone were Tennessee, Gore, Waldemar Hansen, and most of the other Americans he had spent time with in 1948. But a new group had arrived, including Ned Rorem, who was beginning his career as a composer, and James Baldwin, who was trying to make his way as a writer. Baldwin was working on two novels simultaneously, the autobiographical *Go Tell It on the Mountain* and *Giovanni's Room*. "One thing I want to be sure of is that it is not going to be one of those problem novels," he earnestly said, speaking of the latter. "Jimmy," replied Truman sweetly, "your novel is about a Negro homosexual who is in love with a Jew. Wouldn't you describe that as a problem?" Baldwin was "absolutely flattened," according to Price. "Truman's remark changed the course of Baldwin's life. He went right back to *Go Tell It on the Mountain*, which got magnificent reviews and established his career."

Since he had last seen Truman, John Malcolm Brinnin had become director of the Poetry Center at the Ninety-second Street Y.M.H.A. in Manhattan, where he was responsible for arranging readings by poets and writers. Months before, Truman had agreed to read from his own works, but as the date, December 8, approached, he seemed to have second thoughts. He had not made much progress on *Summer Crossing* in Paris, and, with Jack's customary acquiescence, he was considering postponing their return to America and proceeding directly to Sicily, where he believed he could work undisturbed. Yet he was also bored with traveling, "tired of sparking up the foreign scene," as he jokingly told Brinnin. He procrastinated so long that to make the reading, he finally had to fly, leaving Jack to return with their luggage a week later on the *Queen Mary*. Brinnin met him at the airport in New York and watched as he emerged from the Air France Constellation. "When the ramp was settled into place and the door wrenched open, out he stepped, bareheaded, with a little dog [Manchester] squashed in his left arm. When I waved, he picked me out and waved back, then lifted the dog's paw and waved it in my direction before he disappeared into the customs shed."

The day of the reading found him in poorer spirits, however, racked by nervousness. Brinnin gave him a steadying brandy, helped him on with his black velvet suit, ushered him through the overflow crowd in the lobby of the Y.M.H.A., and led him out onto the stage. As Truman sat on a high stool, waiting to begin and clutching the copy of *A Tree of Night* from which he was to read, Brinnin had a small attack of nerves himself, wondering how the mostly conservative audience would react to that odd-looking little figure and that "baby seal's voice." His question was soon answered. When Truman finished reading, there was a blast of applause and the loud shouts of "Bravo!" and "Encore!" usually heard only in opera houses. "Bowing low," Brinnin wrote, "blowing kisses with both hands, he returned again and again and, with a hop and a skip, left for good only when the stage manager had started the house lights blinking." New York had welcomed him home.

N EW York, Truman had told a French reporter, is "the most stimulating of all the cities in the world. It's like living inside an electric light bulb." And incandescent it was in the weeks following his return. His absence had not dimmed people's memories; it had made him more than ever an object of curiosity. His name was in gossip columns and cartoons—even a crossword puzzle —and no one seemed to tire of Truman tales. In an article on younger artists and writers, *Flair* magazine described, with some amusement, the stir he was creating two years after the publication of *Other Voices*. "The most richly embroidered legend, of course, is that of Mr. Truman Capote. It has been reported that on one of his trips across the Atlantic, Mr. Capote hired the bridal suite on the *Queen Mary*; that in Italy he was taken for the President's son and, stepping into the role of goodwill ambassador, did a power of damage to the Communist party; that after traveling through Spain, he landed in North Africa partially accoutered as a bullfighter (and so on in this vein)."

Without a second's hesitation, Truman picked up where he had left off in February. Two days after his triumph at the Y.M.H.A., he traveled to Northampton to see Newton. "Truman, the little monkey, arrives at the old time in the afternoon," Newton wrote in his diary. "Poor child! There is something intolerably touching about him just now." He returned in January and again in March and sneaked more furtive looks into that blabbermouth diary. "Many thoughts of Morton," Newton had written at the end of one entry, and Truman felt jealousy stab him once again, like an old war

wound. He asked Brinnin if he knew who Morton was—Brinnin
did not—and the phrase became a familiar joke between them. The
embers of his romance with Newton remained warm—on all three
visits he and Newton had sex together—but except for those few
hours, he was content to let the mysterious Morton occupy Newton's bed as well as his thoughts.

Jack, not Newton, was now Truman's concern, and Truman
wanted to make permanent a relationship that, in Jack's mind at
least, had not been formally sealed. The only way to do it was to do
it, and, uninvited, he moved into Jack's tenement walk-up on East
Seventy-sixth Street, a habitation so primitive that it did not have
its own bathroom; the tub was in the kitchen, the toilet in the hall
outside, shared with the neighbor next door. Overlooking those in-
conveniences, Truman carried his own furniture up several flights
of stairs, and invited his friends, including Charlie and Oona Chaplin, to make that arduous journey as well. Manchester, the little
Pekingese, was given to Jack's family—Jack refused to walk a dog
that looked like a powder puff—and gained a devoted protector in
Jack's father. Proudly pointing him out to taxi drivers when he came
home from a night on the town, James Dunphy would say, "See
that dog? It came all the way from Africa." To take its place, Truman gave Jack a Kerry blue, a breed renowned for its pugnacity.

Leo was still holding open house on Sunday nights, and Truman
showed up to see old friends and to try to make a new one: William
Faulkner. Then as now, Faulkner's giant talent loomed over other
Southern writers, all of whom sometimes felt that they were merely
scribbling in his margins. "The presence alone of Faulkner in our
midst makes a great difference in what the [Southern] writer can and
cannot permit himself to do," said one of them, Flannery O'Connor.
"Nobody wants his mule and wagon stalled on the same track the
Dixie Limited is roaring down." Although Truman had already met
him—Faulkner also was a Random House author, as well as a good
friend of Bennett Cerf and Bob Linscott—he was not long in joining
the crowd that hovered around when Faulkner made a surprise visit
to Leo's.

Knowing how such attention alarmed Faulkner, Ruth Ford, who
had brought him, quickly tugged at his sleeve. "We have to go home
now," she declared. "I wanna go! I wanna come along!" said Truman, jumping into a taxi with them. Faulkner was one of the few

who did not succumb to his charms. "Truman never stopped talking and Faulkner never talked at all," Ford recalled. "The more Truman talked, the more nervous Faulkner became—which speeded Truman up all the more." Assuming, probably correctly, that Faulkner did not admire the work of Ernest Hemingway, Truman gleefully recounted the many failings of Hemingway's newest novel, *Across the River and into the Trees*. Not above criticizing Hemingway himself, Faulkner did not grant such rights to Truman, and he finally broke his silence long enough to say: "Young man, I haven't read this new one. And though it may not be the best thing Hemingway ever wrote, I know it will be carefully done and it will have quality." Truman probably still felt the sting of that spanking when he wrote Bill Goyen several months later, following Faulkner's acceptance of the Nobel Prize for Literature in Stockholm: "I am pleased that Faulkner got the Nobel Prize—but am far from pleased with his *Collected Stories*. With three exceptions they seem to me unwritten, unreadable, absolute frauds. Did you read that, when he arrived in Sweden, he listed his profession as farmer? I'm not so sure he was wrong."

Truman had what was probably his last encounter with the Dixie Limited in the mid-fifties, at the end of Faulkner's romance with Jean Stein, who was a daughter of the Hollywood movie tycoon Jules Stein. "I didn't know it, but Faulkner had a Lolita complex— he was a Humbert Humbert. Jean knew it instantaneously, and made herself look like fourteen. Faulkner fell madly in love with her, and he was going to divorce his wife so they could marry. But her parents said they would never speak to her again if she did, and she had to stop seeing him. She told him one day over lunch at the Algonquin. When I stopped in at Random House that evening—I had a key and used to go there sometimes—I heard this terrible sobbing from the little room they gave him. The room was dark, and he was lying on the couch, completely drunk; a bottle of bourbon was sitting on the floor. 'It's all over,' he kept saying. 'It's finished. It's ended.' I sat down beside him and took his hand and said, 'It's just Truman.' I stayed there for a couple of hours, until he fell asleep. He went back to his wife in Mississippi, and Jean married Bill vanden Heuvel. When Faulkner died a few years later, it was really of a broken heart."

. . .

Although he was not able to give Linscott *Summer Crossing*, as he had pledged from Tangier, Truman did give him the makings of a book nonetheless: all the travel articles, nine in all, that he had written since "Notes on N.O." in 1946. Now he busied himself bringing them together for September publication. As a result of working so long with the fashion magazines, where looks are paramount, he was more concerned than most other writers with the physical appearance of his books—such things as the color of dust jackets and the layouts inside. For this, his third book—*Local Color* he titled it—he made all the major decisions, doing everything but don a printer's green eyeshade and set the type. "Maybe it seems strange that anyone should put such stress on the 'physical' appearance of a book," he was later to write Linscott. "But there you are, I can't help it." Far from finding it strange, Linscott was enormously impressed. "You see, Bill, you would never do this," he cheerfully told Goyen, prompted perhaps by a mischievous desire to feed Goyen's obvious envy of Truman. "You would never have enough chutzpah to say what you really wanted with your book. Truman won't listen to anybody but himself, and he knows exactly what he wants. And we do it."

When it came to his own life, Truman did not always know exactly what he wanted, however: in Europe he had longed to be in New York; now, in New York, he longed to be back in Europe. The inside of a light bulb is an exciting place to live, he was discovering, but it is not a tranquil and productive place to work. Manhattan was expensive, moreover; being in the gossip columns nearly every day had not even secured him an apartment with a private toilet. To add to his depression, he contracted a case of viral pneumonia, which sent him to the hospital for several days. Sunny Sicily beckoned once again. In early April, 1950, he and Jack finally heeded its call and boarded a Norwegian freighter bound for Italy.

After three weeks at sea and a long train ride from Palermo, they at last reached their destination, Taormina, a picturesque hill town near Mount Etna that had provided a haven for foreigners since the time of Euclid. One side was dominated by an ancient Greek theater, the other by the ruins of a medieval castle; in between was the piazza, with its baroque church, fountain, and cooling oleander trees. Before World War II, German and English tourists had crowded its bars and cafés; in 1950, currency restrictions kept most of them at home, and besides the natives, there were only a few outsiders around to savor that postcard-pretty scene.

It was in that square that Donald Windham, who had arranged to meet them, heard Truman's familiar shriek on the morning of May 3: Truman, Jack, and Kelly, their Kerry blue terrier, had finally come, days after they were expected. Donald had dinner with them that night, and the next day he helped them find a house. Hung on the side of a hill and approachable only by foot, over a rocky goat path, the Fontana Vecchia, as it was called, seemed to offer everything they wanted at an affordable price. Indeed, it all but carried a guarantee of good writing to come: D. H. Lawrence had lived and enjoyed two of his most creative years there in the twenties. "We have had luck, at least I hope it is luck, in finding a place to live," Truman reported to Linscott. "It is the top two floors of a little villa about twenty minutes walk from Taormina, very isolated, but plenty of room and a wonderful view. It costs $50 a month, which is rather a lot, at least by Italian standards, but I like it tremendously."

The top floor had two bedrooms and a bath; the living room, dining room, and kitchen were on the floor below; a partially detached tower contained a small room for guests; and the ground level was occupied by the owner. Plenty of space it had, but the Fontana Vecchia was far from luxurious. There was no phone or refrigerator; the two-burner stove always seemed to run out of fuel at dinnertime; hot water was dispensed by a wood-burning heater; and the only space heating came from fireplaces. Not much of a drawback in May, that was a considerable hardship during the winter, which was short but so cold that Truman sometimes wore gloves to write. A stone shack was what Cecil, who usually was entertained by grander hosts, was to call the house, and he was not altogether wrong. "With any one else [but Truman] the discomfort would have been unbearable," he would complain. "As it was, the daily trek to buy provisions in town, and lugging the heavy packages back in the heat of the day, was quite an ordeal. My bedroom possessed no furniture except a pallet on which to sleep and it was best never to use the bathroom."

The view from the huge windows and broad terraces was as wonderful as Truman said, however, a more than adequate reward for the hike up that steep and stony path: down below, a valley of olive and almond trees, the blue Ionian Sea beyond, and, in the distance, the miragelike outline of the Italian mainland. "It is very like living in an airplane, or a ship trembling on the peak of a tidal wave," said Truman. "There is a momentous feeling each time one looks from the windows, steps onto the terrace, a feeling of being suspended, like the white reeling doves, between the mountains and above the sea."

A girl in her late teens, Graziella, was paid seven dollars a month to clean and cook lunch, usually minestrone, and the new tenants happily returned to the productive schedule of Ischia and Tangier: work in the morning, lunch and a swim, and often more work in the afternoon. Toward evening, Truman walked into Taormina to buy meat for dinner. The undernourished brats who lived in caves on the outskirts of town invariably screamed at him as he walked by. He learned just enough Italian to reply that he planned to boil them alive if they did not shut up, and the exchange of insults became as much a part of his daily routine as the stops at the post office for mail, the *tabacchi* for newspapers and magazines, and the Americana Bar for a martini.

The new arrivals were quickly introduced to the peculiar Sicilian mentality. Graziella often came to work with loud bruises and once even a split lip, results of beatings by her brother, who objected to her going out by herself. When Truman expressed shock at his brutality, she politely told him to mind his own business. "He is good-looking and has many friends," she said. "Only to me is he *brute*." In late summer there was a werewolf scare. Someone claimed to have been attacked by a human on all fours. "You don't believe in werewolves, do you?" Truman asked the boy who delivered ice. "Oh, yes," the boy gravely replied. "There used to be many werewolves in Taormina. Now there are only two or three." In the fall Etna erupted, an awesome sight, and Truman joined the crowds who packed baskets with food and wine and picnicked as close as they dared to its fiery rivers. Only one group of revelers was hurt, beaten up by peasants whose homes had been swallowed by the lava and who were furious to see their neighbors making holiday out of their tragedy.

A martini was not all Truman wanted at the Americana Bar: it was a meeting place and the center of gossip for Taormina's small foreign colony. André Gide, who was then in the last year of his long life, was in town when Truman and Jack arrived, for instance, basking in the sun and finding pleasure in the company of the compliant boys he paid to visit his hotel room. Eugene O'Neill showed up later ("a nervous little man at loose ends and lonely; but rather likable" was how Truman described the great playwright to a friend), and so did Jean Cocteau, Christian Dior, Emlyn Williams, Orson Welles, Gayelord Hauser, and an M.G.M. film crew that was shooting a B movie, *The Light Touch*, with Stewart Granger and Pier Angeli. At Truman's request, Richard Brooks, the director, placed him in a street scene. "I can just imagine Tennessee's face when he sees this!" Truman rejoiced. But his acting career was soon derailed. Screening the rough cut in Hollywood, the producer spotted his face and demanded its removal. "Isn't that Truman Capote?" he asked Brooks. "You can't use him! Cut him out!"

For months the patrons of the Americana were captivated by the continuing soap opera of Bobby Pratt-Barlow, a moneyed Englishman and a decades-long resident of Taormina who sometimes stopped by to see Truman and Jack on his way to his own house in the hills. "He liked beautiful boys, and he turned them into very good and accomplished servants," said Truman. "When he was ready for a new one, the hill families around Taormina would vie for him to consider their sons for adoption. Then a rich Texan came to town, bought a big house, put in a swimming pool, and drove around in a large car. At the time Bobby had a boy of thirteen, Beppe, who was the greatest love of all the boys he had ever had. The Texan spied him and stole him away—the kid was just undone by the swimming pool and the car. After that, it was open warfare in that town! People were outraged that the boy had gone off and left Bobby, and they tried all kinds of voodoo to kill off the American. But none of it worked. The boy stayed with him and was eventually married in his house."

But the only soap operas that really interested Truman were those involving his friends and enemies in New York. He wrote letters, he pointedly informed one laggard correspondent, only so that he could receive them, and the visit to the post office was the most exciting part of his day. "Such a newsy letter," he purred to Pearl Kazin after receiving one of her fact-filled dispatches. "You are the only person who writes the kind of letter I really enjoy." The Cerfs, on the other hand, received a reprimand for not writing more often. "Many's the night I've trudged down to the post office, then trudged back empty handed," he wailed, "thinking, a fine lot they are, whirling from one gay event to another, never giving a thought to poor Truman: far off there on a windswept hill with nothing but the sound of the sea to cheer him up. Oh chilluns, it do get mighty powerful lonesome here."

Even Pearl's news was stale by the time it reached Taormina, and frustrated by the lack of fresh gossip, Truman resurrected old gossip and used it in a new way, in a parlor game, his own version of Monopoly, which he played with almost anyone who made it up the goat path. "It's *SO* educational," he bragged to the Cerfs, "and you can slander people right and left, all in the interest of le sport. It's called IDC, which stands for International Daisy Chain. You make a chain of names, each one connected by the fact that he or she has had an affair with the person previously mentioned; the point is to go as far and as incongruously as possible. For example: this one is from Peggy Guggenheim to King Farouk. Peggy Guggenheim to Lawrence Vail to Jeanne Connolly to Cyril Connolly to Dorothy Walworth to King Farouk. See how it works? Peggy Guggenheim had an affair with L. Vail who had an affair with J. Connolly etc. Here is another, and much more difficult, not to say raffine, example: from Henry James to Ida Lupino. As follows: Henry James to Hugh Walpole to Harold Nicolson to the Hon. David Herbert to John C. Wilson to Noel Coward to Louis Hayward to Ida Lupino. Perhaps it all sounds rather dreary on paper; but I can *assure* you that, with a few drinks inside you and some suitable folk to play with, you'll be amazed." Later he added: "P.S. forgot to include my most favorite IDC: Cab Calloway to Hitler. Cab Calloway to Marquesa Casamaury to Carol Reed to Vanity Mitford to Hitler. Get Moss and Kitty [Hart] to play this game; I bet they'd be wonderful at it. If you get any good IDC's, *please* send them along."

Seeing his friends was even better than corresponding with them, and he began issuing invitations almost as soon as he had unpacked. "It is terribly quiet and pretty and *cheap* and we want awfully for you to come here. Why don't you, Bill?" he pleaded with Bill Goyen. A like request was directed to Cecil, who, to Truman's consternation, was considering vacationing in France instead of Italy. "But why are you going to Brittany?" he asked. "Absolutely you must take a holiday here." A similar courtship was carried on with Pearl Kazin. "Pearl Lamb," he wrote in June. "La vie Taormina est la vie en Rose—except, of course, that there is no Pearl." And later: "Honey, *why* are you going to the south of France? Why not *Italy!* So much warmer, nicer, cheaper. Or here, Sicily. At least, before settling anything, come down and visit with us."

Goyen ignored his pleas, but Cecil and Pearl succumbed, Cecil staying two weeks in August, Pearl for a full three months during the fall and winter. "Truman was one of the kindest people I've ever known, generous to a fault," she said. "I was running out of money, and he said, 'I'll support you.' And he meant every word of it." Scarcely had she put down her bags, however, when Peggy Guggenheim, the millionaire art collector, descended on them from her palazzo in Venice. "With that incredible generosity of Truman's, he had simply thrown out the suggestion that she come down to Sicily," recalled Pearl. "I moved out of the tower and slept in the living room, but she still found it absolutely impermissible that there should be another woman around. She insisted that we all had to accompany her on her 'giro'—it's what the Sicilians called an automobile trip—around the island. So off we went for five or six days.

"It was a ghastly trip in some ways. Peggy was flirting with Jack, which didn't interest him at all, and, failing that, with the driver of the car, whom she was also trying to cheat on the number of kilometers that she was supposed to pay him for. He was about thirty-five and Peggy herself was fifty-two. I remember her age because Truman sneaked a look at her passport, ran to me, and said, 'Guess how old she is!' At that point fifty-two seemed awfully old to both of us. The journey ended with a violent outburst on Jack's part in the lobby of the hotel in Palermo. Screaming at the top of his lungs, he gave her a dressing-down the likes of which I don't think she had ever had in her life. He was also angry at Truman because he didn't appreciate at all the carte blanche invitations Truman was always giving people. We made the return trip to Taormina in rather stony silence."

One invitation Jack could not object to was that extended to Truman's mother. Touring Europe for the first time since the war, she and Joe showed up at the beginning of September. Although Truman did not know it, Nina had a reason for making a detour to Sicily, and before leaving New York she had told Phoebe Pierce what it was. "She telephoned me and asked me if I could have lunch with her," said Phoebe. "She was completely sober and less 'Southern belley' than I had ever seen her. She said that she had always hated me, but that she was sorry she had been unkind to me. 'I was wrong and I know you loved Truman,' she told me, 'and I don't know why I hated you.' Somehow she made me feel worse after she had apologized than before: that was the ambiguity of Nina. Then she said to me, 'I'm going over to Europe to see Truman. I want to put things right. I don't think I have behaved very well.' "

In Taormina she did behave well—though it was too late, of course, to put things right. She was on the wagon, drinking nothing but endless cups of coffee, as she had for many months, and she treated Jack, whom she detested, with elaborate courtesy. Jack was equally polite to her, though he disliked her with at least equal intensity. "She was nothing but a hillbilly from the South, a pushy climber who only wanted to be in the New York Social Register," he declared. "She hated the fact that she had a talented kid, and she hated Truman all the time, I'm sure. And he hated her. That poor little boy! He came from the mines." If Nina and Jack had remained together much longer, there might have been an explosion—they were both primed bombs with short fuses—and Truman and Joe must have been relieved when after three or four days, the two of them went their separate ways: Jack to visit a friend near Naples, and Nina, along with Truman and Joe, to take in the beauties of Venice.

Local Color was published while Truman was there, and before heading home to America, Nina and Joe gave him a party in the roof garden of the Danieli, which was then, as now, one of the best hotels in the city. A few weeks later, the reviews, which were mostly favorable, reached him in Sicily. "At least the great chest-pounding he-men spit less venom than usual," he wrote Linscott. "God forbid they should ever take me to their hearts; when that time comes, I'd best retire." At the end of the month he also celebrated another birthday: he was now too old ever to be called a kid. "Dear God, I am 26," he lamented, probably only half in jest, to Mary Louise. "I wanted always to be 25."

Another visitor to Taormina was Robert Horan, whom Truman used to see at Capricorn, the Menotti-Barber house in Mount Kisco. Horan's relationship with the two composers was rapidly disintegrating, and Thomas Schippers, a strikingly handsome nineteen-year-old who was to become the golden boy of American composers, was taking his place in Gian-Carlo's affections. Devastated by the downward turn in his life, Horan was, in his own words, "drunk most of the time, in a kind of fog, just falling apart." Finally, in December, he did fall apart. He became seriously ill and sardonically—such was his mood—told the hotel doctor that he had tried to commit suicide. The doctor, along with Truman and most others, believed him. For several days, Truman was nurse, companion and fixer, using all his power of persuasion to summon other doctors, who did not want to become involved in an attempted suicide, and to keep away the police, who did. Unable to work, under attack from Jack, who wanted him to stay away from "that son-of-a-bitch black Irishman," as he called Horan, Truman desperately wired Gian-Carlo, who was in Milan, to come and get his young friend. When Gian-Carlo said that he could not take time from rehearsals at La Scala, Truman packed Horan aboard a train and delivered him to the maestro in person.

"The rest of the story is just too sad and sordid," Truman reported to Bill Goyen several days later. "When we finally got to the hotel in Milan, G-C wasn't there. He was at a rehearsal. I could have killed him. But Bob, for his part, was dramatizing the situation as much as possible. When G-C at last turned up, Bob was incredibly insolent to him—made him out to be a monster of ambition and stupidity. And there was G-C jumping around pretending it was all a joke. Then came the really sickening denouement. G-C came to my room, his face white as cold cream. All in a burst he said: Bob was ruining his life, that he'd spent $2,000 a month since he'd come to Europe and B's extravagance was taking all his money—*but* that none of this mattered so long as he did not have to go to bed with him, that for the last few years B forced him to make love and afterwards he, G-C, had to go and throw up. He also said that he was terribly in love with somebody else—some young American boy—and he was terrified of B's finding out." Disgusted with both of them, Truman returned to Sicily the next morning. "Have been going through a terrible experience," he told Linscott. "As a result am quite, quite exhausted."

Shortly into the New Year, 1951, Jack's father died. Jack decided that it would be too expensive and too complicated to return home for the funeral, but he paid his own kind of homage. His father was such a clean man, he told Truman and Pearl, that the greatest tribute he could pay his memory was to take a bath—it was not bath night. He lit a fire under the water heater, and when he had dried off, Truman and Pearl used the rest of the precious hot water to take their own baths. "Little things keep coming at me, remindful and barbed," Jack wrote his sister Gloria. Chief among them was his regret that his father, with whom he had maintained a kind of truce in recent years, had not seen him write a best-seller, as his father had said he wanted him to do.

ULLING *Summer Crossing* together would take a monumental
effort, Truman had warned Linscott, and in the end it was
either too great an effort or one he was unwilling to make.
Nor did he receive any encouragement from Linscott, who was
unimpressed by what Truman showed him of the first draft. It was
the kind of novel any good writer could have produced, Linscott
said; it did not have Truman's distinctive artistic voice. Jack did not
like it either; he thought that it was "thin"—an adjective that causes
shivers to dance up the spine of any writer. Reluctantly, Truman
came to the same conclusion. "I read it over maybe two or three
times, and one day I just decided: I don't really like it. I think it's
well written and it's got a lot of style, but I don't really like it. And
so I tore it up."

Despite his cool analysis of how he wanted to build his career,
Truman had chosen the wrong subject nonetheless, and it had cost
him at least a year. He had to find another theme, and quickly.
Now, sitting on the terrace of the Fontana Vecchia in Taormina, his
gaze shifted homeward, to Alabama and a subject that had never
failed him: his childhood. If *Other Voices* had been an attempt to
exorcise demons, his new novel, *The Grass Harp*, was an attempt to
raise the bittersweet spirits of remembrance and nostalgia. "Those
were the lovely years," his hero, Collin Fenwick, says of his youth
in a town that sounds very much like Monroeville. If Joel Knox
represents one half of his character, then Collin represents the other
half. *The Grass Harp* is the bright, obverse side of *Other Voices*, and
Collin is the sunny, happy side of Truman Capote.

"It is very real to me, more real than anything I've ever written, probably ever will" was the way he described the new book to Linscott. "Satisfying as, in that sense, it is, it keeps me in a painful emotional state: memories are always breaking my heart, I cry—it is very odd, I seem to have no control over myself or what I am doing. But my vision is clear, and if I can half execute that vision it will be a beautiful book." Indeed, *The Grass Harp* bears much more factual resemblance to his life than does *Other Voices*. Sook is the model for his heroine, Dolly Talbo, who makes and sells a dropsy cure from secret ingredients she collects in the woods. Callie and Jennie are combined in the character of Dolly's sister Verena, the richest, meanest woman in town. Anna Stabler, the black woman who helped Sook with her chores, is Dolly's best friend, Catherine Creek. Truman is of course Collin, the boy who is sent to live with his old-maid cousins after his mother dies.

The action begins when Verena, spying big profits in Dolly's dropsy cure, tries to extract the formula from her so that she can sell it commercially. Dolly refuses and runs away with Catherine and Collin to take up residence in a tree house in the woods. Soon they are joined by two other free spirits, Riley Henderson, an older boy whom Collin idolizes, and Judge Cool, a retired judge, who has eyes for Dolly. Verena calls out the powers of law and authority to shake the rebels from their tree, but the runaways will not budge, and their leafborne raft takes each of them on a voyage of self-discovery. Judge Cool becomes Truman's spokesman, as Randolph was in *Other Voices*, and his message is much the same: no matter how it is expressed, love is always sacred. "A leaf, a handful of seed—begin with these, learn a little what it is to love," says the Judge. "First, a leaf, a fall of rain, then someone to receive what a leaf has taught you, what a fall of rain has ripened. No easy process, understand; it could take a lifetime, it has mine, and still I've never mastered it—I only know how true it is; that love is a chain of love, as nature is a chain of life."

Eventually the "five fools in a tree," as the Judge calls them, return to ground, and having learned who they are, make their compromises with society. Dolly declines the Judge's offer of marriage and goes home to a much-chastened Verena. Collin becomes a lawyer. He does not turn his back on the world, as Joel did; he joins it, as Truman himself had done, albeit in his own way and on his own terms.

. . .

Just as Truman had hoped, Taormina proved to be an ideal spot in which to write. Except for occasional interruptions, such as that caused by his involvement in the Robert Horan melodrama, his days were placid; even when there were visitors, and he had drunk too much or stayed up too late, he doggedly marched up to his room every morning to work. "I hope this book will be half-worth all these sacrifices—like coming home, like being with the people I love," he grumbled to Mary Louise. "When I think back on our years together, I think of that as the heroic time," Jack was to remark of the first years of their relationship. "We lived a straight, almost a hard life. We were miraculously cocooned against the traveling faggots and deep neurotics. It was a soldierly sort of existence, but very, very enjoyable, because neither of us had any fear. That's the whole thing: we did not know fear."

In that soldierly spirit, Truman began *The Grass Harp* about the first of June, 1950, completing it almost exactly a year later, on May 27, 1951. He sent two chapters to Random House in September, 1950, before leaving for Venice with Nina and Joe. While he was there, he received Linscott's first reaction by cable: "WONDERFUL WONDERFUL WONDERFUL." Sweeter music a writer could not have heard, and a few days later Linscott added more such cello notes: "There is a perfection about these two chapters that is simply miraculous. I read and reread and love every word." Linscott could be stern as well as supportive, however. Hearing that Truman was considering returning to New York in the spring, he virtually forbade him to leave Sicily until he had finished his book. "Rumor has it that you plan to return in March," he said in January, 1951. "I hope this means with the completed manuscript, as it would be a pity to leave such ideal working conditions before the job is done."

Truman dutifully stuck it out on his windswept hill—probably he would have done so even without the exhortation—and before April was over, Linscott had all but the last fifteen percent of the book. "I adore every word of the novel that you have written to date," he said. "I read it all through last night from beginning to its present end and had to stop every few paragraphs to hug myself with pleasure. If the last chapter is as good as the preceding ones, this is really going to be a masterpiece."

That closing comment must have caused Truman some pause, for it was precisely that last part that worried him most, causing him even more agony than the final pages of *Other Voices*. His problem was: having placed his five free spirits in the tree, how was he to bring them down without making his ending an anticlimax? how could he let Dolly say no to Judge Cool's offer of marriage and return to Verena, as he felt she must if she was to be psychologically true to her character? Such concerns loomed before him, he said, as daunting as Mount Everest or Kilimanjaro. To Mary Louise he confessed: "A great deal depends on the last chapter—unfortunately I am very tense with it; I feel as though I were holding my nose under water: when I'm finished, I'm going to take a long gulp of air and do a mile of handsprings."

With what he termed a "kind of slave anguish" he did finish, and on June 4, 1951, airmailed that much-anticipated last section to New York. "Oh Bob, I do hope you are pleased with the book," he said. "Let me know at once." But he was in no mood to turn handsprings, or even dance a jig, as he had done when he closed his notebook on *Other Voices*. "I'm relieved that it's over, but sad too," he explained to Donald Windham. "As the tension drains away I feel as though my head were made entirely of biscuit." Jack had finished his novel as well, and on June 10, thirteen months after they first ascended that rocky goat path, they said their farewells to the Fontana Vecchia, where they had worked so well. Their friends saw them off at the train station, and after a four-day stopover in Rome, they proceeded to Venice, where, in the congenial atmosphere of Harry's Bar, Truman anxiously awaited Linscott's verdict.

When Linscott did not reply as quickly as he usually did, Truman nervously prodded him, unable to bear the suspense any longer. "As of this moment I've not heard from you about my chapter etc.—but daresay I will in the next day or so," Truman hopefully wrote on June 19. A week later he learned the cause of the delay, and it was worse than he had feared: Linscott did not like his ending, and neither did anyone else at Random House. "You are no doubt indignant—and justifiably so—at my failure to cable," Linscott belatedly responded. "The reason, as you may have guessed, lies in the fact that I wasn't altogether happy about the last chapter, probably because the first half was so absolutely divine that I had hoped for a continuing miracle. Anyway I wanted to wait until Bennett and Bob Haas had a chance also to read it, hoping—in vain as it turned out —that their great enthusiasm would counter balance my small lack of it. Not, you understand, that it isn't good as a story and superb as a piece of writing. Nor is there any specific criticism to be made; just that we all had a slight feeling of letdown; of the story tapering off a little, with the end coming too soon and lacking the profusion of delight that had so entranced one up to that point."

A similar response, but with more detailed criticism, came from Bennett. "In our opinion, the book is absolutely perfect until Dolly and her party all climb down from the tree house and go back home. From this point forward, I couldn't help feeling that you had gotten a little bit tired of the book and were hurrying to close it in much shorter a space than you originally had intended. Dolly's giving up the Judge so promptly the moment Verena shows signs of wanting her back home may be necessary for your story, but will give a lot of readers, I am sure, a feeling of frustration. After all, we've learned to consider Verena the enemy, and to suddenly feel sorry for her and see her get Dolly back home, even if on altered terms, did not make me happy. The last chapter, when you are wrapping up the story, seemed particularly like a synopsis to me. I do wish this part of the book could be expanded a little bit, especially in light of the fact that the overall length is now little more than a novelette. We'll have trouble selling it as a complete novel." If Truman disagreed and did not want to follow their suggestions, Bennett added, Random House would swallow its doubts and publish the novel just as it was written. "We'll pray the critics won't have the same feeling of vague letdown in the last half that afflicted us."

Though he may have expected some reservations about the ending, Truman had not anticipated such a fusillade. "I cannot endure it that all of you think my book a failure," he wrote Linscott. "I am stricken by such an overpowering trinity of opinion. Perhaps you are right about the last chapter. Yet I don't see what could have been done differently. You describe it as tapering off . . . which is exactly what I intended. When they leave the tree house, that is the climax of the book; but what point would the book have unless the last chapter were written in exactly the mood it is: the destination of each character has been prepared from the beginning. I think the end very moving and right. But of course at the moment I am too near to it really to know."

Unfortunately, his Random House editors were right. The conclusion of *The Grass Harp* is a letdown; it does lack the profusion of delight, as Linscott had so elegantly phrased it, of all that had gone

before. Linscott was also right not to offer any specific criticism, as
Bennett had done. The problem with the ending is not that it is too
short or that Dolly should have set up housekeeping with the Judge
—although either or both of those things may be true. It is rather
that having cast his spell of fantasy, Truman has not dispelled it in
a believable way. "The test of whether or not a writer has divined
the natural shape of his story is just this," Truman was later to say.
"After reading it, can you imagine it differently, or does it silence
your imagination and seem to you absolute and final?" *Other Voices*
passes his test; *The Grass Harp* does not. *Other Voices* seems complete,
final, and, taken on its own terms, real. *The Grass Harp* seems nag-
gingly incomplete, less final and less real.

Flawed though it is, it cannot be regarded as a failure, however.
It contains several scenes of brilliant comedy, an enduring warmth
and charm, and some of Truman's best writing. His prose is under
firmer control than it was in *Other Voices*, yet still so rich and vivid
that Linscott was probably not exaggerating when he said that he
had to keep stopping to hug himself with pleasure as he read it.

"Flaubert's attitude toward writing, his sense of perfectionism, is
what I would like mine to be," Truman said, and his approach to
fiction was, like his French master's, almost teleological: he knew
from the start where his characters were going and what they would
do when they got there. He could not comprehend how some writers he admired—Dickens, for example—could give in to impulse,
letting their pens fly across the page and allowing their characters to
wander down their own, often surprising paths. His own temperament was such that he had to be in control, and Flaubert's dictum
was his as well: "We must be on our guard against that feverish state
called inspiration, which is often a matter of nerves rather than
muscle. Everything should be done coldly, with poise."

His practice was in distinct contrast to the image he conveyed or
the seeming spontaneity of his writing style. When he sat down in
the morning with his pad and pencil, Truman was not the flighty-
looking young man the Sicilians saw rushing toward the Americana
Bar in the late afternoon, trailing an absurdly long scarf and yelling
in a high-pitched voice to his friends across the square. During those
prenoon hours, he was as calculating as an accountant checking
receipts. He endlessly deliberated over such basics as structure and
order; he could spend hours examining a single paragraph, like a

diamond-cutter deciding how to transform a rough and homely stone into a glittering jewel; and, with some exceptions, he constantly and compulsively revised what he had already written. "If only I were a writer that could write, not just rewrite," he lamented to Donald Windham. When he made a mistake, as he did in the ending of *The Grass Harp*, it was an error of judgment, not a casual slip caused by sloppiness or inattention.

So much investment in his work sometimes made him even more thin-skinned than many other authors: his critics seemed to be attacking not just a few pages, but his judgment as well. It also, paradoxically, made him tougher: when he had finished with something, he was convinced that it was as good as it could be, and few could shake his confidence. Thus, after he had read his novel afresh, from beginning to end, he no longer felt stricken by the rebuffs from his friends in Manhattan. He liked it—all of it—and, holding Bennett to his word, he cabled: "HAVE READ PROOFS AND PREFER PUBLISH BOOK AS IS." Bennett gave in with stylish grace. "If it is now in the form that you wish to keep it, it's good enough for me," he replied, and in that form *The Grass Harp* was presented to the public on October 1, 1951.

Bennett's generosity was in a sense rewarded: the reviewers did not agree with him and Linscott, and *The Grass Harp* was generally, sometimes excessively, applauded. Truman's second novel, said the Sunday *New York Herald Tribune*, showed "the maturing and mellowing of one of America's best young writers." Orville Prescott in the daily *New York Times* thought it a "vast improvement" over *Other Voices*. "Within the slim compass of this work, Truman Capote has achieved a masterpiece of passionate simplicity, or direct, intuitive observation," said Richard Hayes in *The Commonweal*. With almost audible relief, several critics praised the absence of the homosexual theme that had bothered them in *Other Voices*. Bennett was also mistaken in suggesting that readers would not buy such a short novel (it came to only 181 pages). Sales totaled 13,500, almost double those of *A Tree of Night* and triple those of *Local Color*. "All books today are far too long," Truman cheerfully informed an interviewer. "My theory is that a book should be like a seed you plant, and that the reader should make his own flower."

"ᴛᴇʟʟ me, darling, do you know anything about a young man called Saint Subber?" Truman had inquired of Cecil in May. "He had something to do with producing Kiss Me Kate etc. What is his reputation—professionally, I mean. Because he has made a crazy proposition: wants to give me option money—*just* in the event I ever *do* write a play. It's rather mad. I'm tempted only because at the moment I do need money. Should I?" In fact, Saint Subber had not just had something to do with *Kiss Me, Kate*, a Cole Porter musical that ran for more than two and a half years on Broadway; he had produced it, and he had come to Taormina to persuade Truman to move his tree house to a stage—to turn *The Grass Harp* into a play.

If he had taken his own lofty advice, Truman would have said no instantly. He had forcibly expressed his opposition to such adaptations just two years before, in a review of a dance interpretation of Faulkner's *As I Lay Dying*. "The transposition of one art form into another seems to me a corrupt, somewhat vulgar enterprise," he had stated sternly. "Nature being what it is, these experimental inbreedings must logically make for Cretin offspring. Why can't a novel be simply a novel, a poem a poem?" But he had been speaking then about an adaptation of another writer's work; now that he had been asked to do one, the concept no longer seemed corrupt or vulgar. He had loved the smell of greasepaint ever since he had played Little Eva in the fourth grade, and, like many other writers, he envied the camaraderie of those who work in the theater. Beyond everything else, he was indeed short of cash—"more broke than Little Orphan

Annie," as he phrased it—and a Broadway hit was a money-making machine that would answer all his financial problems. If Carson could turn her slim novel *The Member of the Wedding* into dollars at the box office, why couldn't he do the same with *The Grass Harp*?

He had ample time to answer that question during the weeks that followed Saint Subber's departure. After their Venetian idyll, at the end of July he and Jack departed for home on another slow Norwegian freighter. In the middle of August, a few days after they docked in New York, he left for Cape Cod to spend the rest of the summer with Newton—old habits die hard. He undoubtedly discussed Saint's suggestion with Newton, and by the time he received a contract, he had made up his mind. He signed it—and then sat down to master the unfamiliar art of creating dialogue for the stage. Thus, less than three months after he thought he had said goodbye forever, he reintroduced himself to his five fools in a tree.

Saint wanted to begin rehearsals as early as February, 1952, which did not give Truman much time to write a two-hour play, even if he did have an outline—the novel itself—already in front of him. As he sat down to write, he realized, moreover, that he had a bigger job than he had thought: substantial changes needed to be made to make *The Grass Harp* work dramatically. He discovered, for example, that he had not defined Collin sharply enough in the book to make a convincing stage character, and he merged him with the colorful and more robust Riley Henderson, eliminating Riley altogether. For the sake of simplicity, he also discarded the wandering evangelist, Sister Ida, and her fifteen children, who provide much of the book's humor. To take their place, he gave a brief spot in the second act to a new comic character, a traveling cosmetics saleswoman he named Miss Baby Love Dallas.

When he had finished, the first act followed the original plot fairly closely, but the second act was greatly different, concluding on a considerably happier and more upbeat note: the criticisms of Bennett and Bob Linscott had produced results they could not have imagined. "I think I do like to work under the pressure of a deadline," he told one interviewer. "There's something exciting about knowing you have to get something done by a certain time. It's not at all like having months to write in." His breathless pace eventually exacted a price, sending him to the hospital in November with a combination of flu and fatigue. But he met his deadline; in early January, 1952, less than five months after he began, he handed Saint two polished acts. "I have been working so hard and under such pressure," he said when he had finished, "that I feel as if I were in a perpetual coma."

His exhaustion was physical, not emotional, as it had been during the last few weeks of writing the book, and busy and harried as he was, Truman was having fun. All the people he knew were talking about him, his name was popping up with gratifying frequency in the papers and magazines, and most of Manhattan seemed to be lining up to buy tickets for the first play of its favorite *Wunderkind*. Sassy was a word he applied to himself, and sassy he was. "Well," he told a reporter who requested a description, "I'm about as tall as a shotgun—and just as noisy." Like a traveler returning from some primitive spot where he had been required to eat tasteless meals out of cans, he greedily feasted on the rich and delicious gossip that, as far as he was concerned, was the native cuisine of that skyscrapered island. "Isn't it extraordinary about George Davis getting married?!!!" he wrote Cecil, joyfully indignant at the latest and perhaps most curious episode in the chronicle of that singular man. "And to *that* Lotte Lenya. I've always thought myself a lad of the world; but this beats all—and is in such bad taste, don't you think?"

He may not have been quite as loud as a shotgun, but Truman did make his voice heard, much more than freshman playwrights usually do, in the maneuvering that precedes any large theatrical enterprise. He stipulated that *The Grass Harp* had to have a "topflight production," and he insisted that topflight people be in charge. Shy and soft-spoken, Saint regarded him with some awe and usually let him have his way, just as Linscott did. Clearly, the director had to have imagination and insight, and Truman wanted Peter Brook, who, though only twenty-six, had already demonstrated the remarkable range of his invention to the British theater and opera world. He also wanted Cecil to design the sets, Virgil Thomson to compose the incidental music, and Alice Pearce, a nightclub comedienne, to play Miss Baby Love Dallas. Saint concurred on all four, and they both agreed that the Gish sisters, Lillian and Dorothy, would be perfect as Dolly and Verena.

Cecil, Thomson, Pearce, and the Gish sisters all said yes, but Brook declined, and his refusal caused a key part of Truman's cherished plan to unravel. His replacement, Robert Lewis, had a long history on Broadway and had recently made a success of another play with a fantastical theme, the Lerner and Loewe musical *Brigadoon*. But Lewis did not want the Gish sisters, and Saint, taking the recommendation of an experienced director over that of an inexperienced playwright, dropped them from the cast list. The central role of Dolly went instead to the accomplished Mildred Natwick, the part of Verena to the less well-known Ruth Nelson.

Hiding his chagrin, Truman tried to convince himself that after Brook, Lewis was the best choice for director. "Between us, he has a certain vulgarity," he wrote Cecil, "but, kept within check, I am perfectly certain he is the right director for us—he does really understand the play, has a very real sensitivity and also a strong realistic sense—which, as you pointed out, is so necessary to a play such as this." A certain vulgarity Lewis did have—he startled Truman by informing him that he knew his play better than Truman did himself—but he also knew how to direct. Invited to the final rehearsal before the play was sent on the road, two hundred guests were enchanted, "crying buckets" at the end, according to Virgil Thomson, just as they were supposed to. Saint was so encouraged that he moved the New York opening up a week to beat the March 31 deadline for Pulitzer Prize consideration.

Few audiences ever cried again. The first indication that something was wrong came during the tryout in Boston, where Cecil's sets—Dolly's kitchen and the tree—were unwrapped. With no regard for budget, Cecil had bought lavishly at Madison Avenue antique shops, packing Dolly's kitchen with everything he thought an old maid might have, including upholstered Victorian furniture and red velvet draperies for the windows; Escoffier could not have been better provided for. "Honey, you know," said Alice Pearce to Andrew Lyndon, whom Truman had got a job as Lewis' assistant. "Is that what a kitchen in the South looked like?" Cecil's tree was even more impressive: twenty-four feet high, thirty-four feet wide at its broadest point, it might have been a soaring sequoia rather than a humble Alabama chinaberry, so completely did it dominate the stage of the old Colonial Theater. By comparison, commented one awed newspaperman, all other stage trees he had seen looked like shrubs. In Lewis' eyes, that was precisely the problem. "Cecil, this is not a play about a tree," he tartly observed, but Cecil gave him only a haughty stare in reply.

Lewis was also displeased with Truman's creation of Miss Baby Love Dallas. Her comic routine, he maintained, interrupted the mood of the play. "Tell y' what," Truman said reassuringly. "It needs an audience. If it doesn't work in Boston, I'll change it. That's why we go on the road, isn't it?"

Unfortunately, the Boston tryout, which began March 13, did not give a clear signal as to what worked and what did not. The local critics were evenly divided. "A moving and tender drama," said one of them; "thin, vague and unconvincing," said another. *Variety*, the show-business weekly, ominously predicted that "without a pretty extensive rewrite, the sound of *The Grass Harp* will probably not be long heard in the land of Broadway." But there was no rewrite. Back in New York before the official opening, Truman ran into his old friend Paul Bigelow. How was his play going? Bigelow asked. Marvelously well, Truman said; nothing had to be changed. "I was astonished," recalled Bigelow, "because I was used to working in the vulgar Broadway theater. And to have a playwright come back into town and say that nothing had to be changed! I remember walking back to my office, thinking: you know, that play is going to fail."

Early on opening night, March 27, 1952, Truman and Andrew sat in a bar near the Martin Beck Theater and leafed through a thick stack of congratulatory telegrams. "All good wishes for tonight from your admirers," said Lynn and Alfred—the Lunts. "Good wishes for your great and glowing success tonight and our love," added Vivien and Larry—the Oliviers. "We are all thinking of you and praying for your success tonight. All love, Daddy"—Arch. Half an hour or so before curtain they walked back to the theater. "My, my, I think something's happening down the street," Truman said in mock surprise when they spied the glittering crowd that was beginning to gather on Forty-fifth Street. "Let's see what the excitement's about." Forbidden by Lewis from going backstage—the presence of the author upsets the actors, he claimed—he then joined Saint across the street, where the two of them watched a regiment of celebrities step out of their limousines. Mingling with that glamorous throng were Jack and Newton, who did not meet, and Joe and Nina, who looked beautiful in a formal gown and mink coat.

When the curtain had descended, Linscott rushed to a pay phone to tell Bill Goyen what all those famous people had thought. "Well, it's not going to work," he declared. "I walked through the lobby and I heard voices saying, 'It's too thin,' and 'The characters are not really believable.' I think Truman's in a lot of trouble." Truman and

Newton nervously waited for the reviews in the Beekman Place apartment where Newton was staying. The *Times* was the first and most important paper to be delivered, and its critic, Brooks Atkinson, contradicting all that Linscott had overheard, quickly decorated the room with smiles. "Out of good impulses and sensitive perceptions Truman Capote has written a beautiful play," he said.

But the other papers, which arrived all too quickly, erased those happy smiles. Several other critics also saw merit in the play—and promise in the playwright—but none shared Atkinson's enthusiasm. "Seeing *The Grass Harp* is like coming across a handful of flowers in an old scrapbook," said Walter Kerr in the *Herald Tribune*. "The flowers have been pressed into attractive patterns, but they are quite dead." The critic of the *Times* can sometimes kill a play, but he cannot save one, and Truman's nostalgic little drama lasted only thirty-six performances.

Every lost battle is refought by the defeated generals in their memoirs, and each of those involved had his own explanation for the failure of *The Grass Harp*. Thomson blamed Cecil's overpowering sets. Lewis faulted both the sets, particularly "the goddamn tree," and what he thought was the disruptive inclusion of Miss Baby Love Dallas. Saint accused Lewis for not having used the Gish sisters and himself for not having demanded them. "I didn't serve Truman well, because I should have insisted on them," he said. "I believe if they had been in it, the play would have been a success." Truman also criticized Lewis, who, he concluded, had never understood his work at all. Most of all he condemned himself. "Frankly, I don't think it was a very good play," he later confessed. But it had ardent fans who did not agree, selling out the Martin Beck on April 26 to yell, scream, and cheer at the final performance.

28

Two weeks before *The Grass Harp* closed, Truman went backstage to say goodbye to the cast. Hours later, he, Jack, and Kelly were aboard ship once more, on their way back to Europe. Stopping first in Paris, where they bought a tiny red Renault, they then drove to Italy and south again to Sicily. "Well, here we are back in Taormina," Truman wrote Pearl Kazin, "and I'm delighted to be here, believe me." Unfortunately, the Fontana Vecchia had been rented, but they became the only tenants of a newly completed hotel that was not otherwise scheduled to open until winter. "There are two long spooky hallways—more than twenty rooms and, as far as I can make out, hundreds & hundreds of doors, all of which *have* to be locked and barred at night," Jack told Mary Louise. "We want you to come—we have a room and bath—lots of them in fact—and we think of them as waiting mostly for you." Truman, characteristically, painted a somewhat grander picture of that ghostly residence. "We could not get Fontana," he reported to Donald Windham, "so have rented an *entire hotel*—22 rooms and six baths, all super moderne."

Graziella came back to work, and they picked up life where they had left it the year before. The hotel, like the Fontana Vecchia, sat high on a hill above the town, but the car made it easier to travel to the beach; hiring a boat for the summer, they learned to swim underwater, with snorkels and masks. Joining Kelly as a dependent was Lola, a black bird—whether a crow or raven, no one could say —that liked to hide small objects, such as keys and fountain pens. "She adores Jack—but is a good deal less fond of me," Truman told

Jack's sister Gloria. "I guess because I try to discipline her. Only *how* do you discipline a bird?" Renewing old friendships, he soon caught up on the latest news of the piazza. "It seems all so much the same," he told Donald, "except there are more cafes, more tourists, and Carlo Panarello has opened a nightclub. The Panther no longer parades the beaches: he got involved in a great scandal by trying to blackmail one of Gaylord Hauser's guests, and the police told him to stay out of Taormina."

When he was asked in New York what he would do next, Truman had said that he planned to write short stories, a new novel, and more plays—just about everything, in short, but nothing in particular. "When one of them seizes me, I'll do that one first," he informed one questioner. In fact, though he may not have known it himself, he had been seized. The actors at the Martin Beck, who recognized all the symptoms, said that he had become completely stagestruck. Despite the failure of *The Grass Harp*, he wanted to write another play. Saint Subber, who had not given up on him, saw the makings of a musical in "House of Flowers," his amusing, touching story about a Haitian bordello, and again approached him about an adaptation. This time Truman did not hesitate. He said yes.

Saint hoped to begin preliminary work on the production in the fall of 1952, but Truman, still panting from his months of exertion on *The Grass Harp*, was not yet willing to enter another round-the-clock writing marathon. Although he worked fairly hard, reaching the halfway point of his first draft in early September, he was in no rush to finish the rest; not willing to give up prose entirely, he found enough spare hours to write a short story and at least forty pages of a novel. By the time he returned home after Christmas, he told Linscott, he expected to have completed not only the play, but a hundred pages of the novel as well. He was overly optimistic. He found it too confusing to try to concentrate on two large projects at once, and the novel was soon put aside. "Sometimes I wish I did not have this urge to write for the theater," he told Jack's sister. "Life was so much simpler when I just wrote stories."

And so much quieter too. Accustomed to the frantic pace of Broadway, "the mad Saint," as Truman nicknamed him, expected a more single-minded dedication and dispatched telegrams inquiring about his progress. To Truman's annoyance, he even threatened to come to Taormina so that they could talk in person. "Had a *two-page* cable from the Saint yesterday," he complained to Cecil in July. "He is very anxious to come over here and seems to feel he needs a visa from me. Christ! But I just don't want to see him until I have done enough work to feel less vulnerable." Worse yet, from Truman's point of view, was the likelihood that Saint would bring along his companion, Robbie Campbell, the young black who had attracted so much attention singing "Nature Boy" at Le Boeuf sur la Toit in 1948. "I rather fear he [Saint] will be headed this way toward the end of the month, and I strongly suggest you put up storm windows at 8 Pelham Place," he advised Cecil in August. "For my own sake, I pray to God he doesn't bring the Tar Baby with him. Because I will *not*, no never again, put up with the boredom of *that*." He did not have to. Saint stayed home and Campbell did not show his handsome face.

In mid-September, Truman and Jack stuffed their belongings into the little Renault. With the pugnacious Kelly barking out the window at goats and donkeys and the regal Lola perched commandingly on one or the other's shoulder, they said farewell for the last time to Taormina, whose appeal had depended, more than they had thought, on the charms of the Fontana Vecchia. Leisurely driving north, they picnicked in the Calabrian mountains, sunbathed on the remote beaches of Cape Palinuro, and slept on the ground amid the surf-soothed ruins of majestic Paestum before settling in Rome, in a three-room penthouse on the Via Margutta.

"We decided to spend the winter here in Rome and have found, I must say, a beautiful apartment, a dream really," Truman wrote Cecil. "We have a first-rate cook! *Everything* is so different from Taormina—I guess this is the first time in my life I've ever lived the way I really want to—such a pity that I can't afford it." Mary Louise, who was still at *Harper's Bazaar*, heard much the same tale of joy mingled with woe. "[Our apartment] is very sunny and charming, and I would be a very happy boy if it weren't so outrageously expensive, and I am next-door to penniless. If you hear of anyone who wants an article about Rome (or horticulture, hair styles, Famous People I Have Known) send them my way." Though he had been in Rome only a few days, already he had managed to snub or be snubbed by several of their mutual friends. In a wickedly amusing, but probably accurate aside, he added: "Heaven knows there are enough old acquaintances about—I am going to buy a heavy veil to wear in the streets. Sister (the famous Carson Mc-

Cullers, you remember *her*?) and Mr. Sister are frequently to be observed *staggering* along the Via Veneto, where they are now established members of the movie crowd (she is writing a movie for David Selznick); but of course Sister and Mr. Sister are too exalted, and usually too drunk, to recognize my poor presence. The Cow (the not so famous Marguerite Young) is still here, but quite easy to avoid if you go nowhere near the lobby of the Inghilterra, where she broods all day with a cup of coffee."

Actually, Truman had been offered Carson's movie job first—or so he informed Cecil in November—but had deliberated so long that Selznick gave up on him. "Now I'm just a little sorry," he confessed, "if only because it would have put an end to my financial straits, which grow increasingly serious. But it would have been dishonest of me to have accepted, for I did not feel at all sympathetic to the story they outlined, and besides I *must, must* get on with my own work." Writers, particularly those with empty bank accounts, should not be bound by such rash promises of artistic purity, however, especially when large sums are offered for little toil. Before the month was over, he had temporarily abandoned his own work and assumed the job from which Carson had just been fired. Again transformed into a frantic scribbler, he was in a constant huddle with the illustrious Selznick, the producer of *King Kong*, *Rebecca*, and the greatest of all Hollywood spectaculars, *Gone with the Wind*. "Capote will be rich someday," Jack jokingly told Mary Louise, "so we must all stay friends with him."

The movie was titled *Stazione Termini*, and it was the result of an unnatural collaboration between Selznick, who wanted his wife, Jennifer Jones, to star in a prestigious European production, and Vittorio De Sica, one of the leaders of Italy's postwar film renaissance. Jones was to play an American housewife on a visit to Rome, Montgomery Clift was to play her Italian lover, and the story of their adultery was to be told with De Sica's characteristic simplicity inside Rome's new railway station—hence the title. But the picture was doomed from the start. As shooting began, it became clear that Selznick had only imagined he wanted the unvarnished quality of Italian neorealism. What he really wanted was the kind of Hollywood polish for which he was famous. He compulsively supervised every detail, as was his habit, and tried several writers besides Carson in his search for what he considered a workable script.

His latest scriptwriter he did not fire—"David absolutely adored him," said Jones—and Truman worked at furious speed, sometimes running into one room of the station to write the lines the actors were waiting to recite in another. In the end his contribution was small, and he could neither claim credit nor receive blame for the picture that rolled across American screens a year later. Both credit and blame belonged to the producer. When he returned home, Selznick added a saccharine love song by Patti Page and cut what De Sica had shot by nearly a third, to an extraordinarily short sixty-three minutes. Even at that abbreviated length, *Indiscretion of an American Wife*, as he retitled it, was a flop. "Lousy" was Truman's one-word judgment, and both the public and the critics concurred. "*Indiscretion* is, for the gifted men who made it, an indiscretion indeed," said one reviewer, reflecting an apparently universal opinion.

Truman had known one of the picture's two stars, Montgomery Clift, in New York, but only in Rome, in the hermetically sealed world of a film set, did they become close. "Monty was really gifted," said Truman. "He was serious about only one thing, and that was acting. He was an exception to my theory that a movie star has to be ignorant to be good. You have to be smart to be on the stage, but a film actor is just a conduit for the writer, the director, and everybody else who puts something into a picture. He has to react to what they do. If he's too smart, he resists them and then he's no good. Brando never really made it as a movie star—he always resisted. Garbo, on the other hand, never had a thought in her head and she was fabulous! She was the perfect instrument for the writer and director. Monty was smart *and* good, but that was because he was also very shrewd: he knew just what he was doing. I once asked him why he wanted to act in movies, why he didn't do something more interesting. He looked at me and said, 'You don't understand. It's my life! This is what I know how to do.' He was an artist, with all of an artist's sensibilities and flaws.

"But the last eight years of his life were a terrible mess, and when he was high on something, he was absolutely impossible. There is one incident that stands out most in my friendship with him. It happened sometime in the fifties, a few days before Christmas. He phoned me in the morning and invited me to lunch. 'I can't,' I said, 'because I haven't done any Christmas shopping.' He said, 'Listen, I haven't bought anything either. If you take me shopping with you,

I'll buy you lunch.' So I met him at his house and we walked to the Colony. He seemed perfectly normal and full of good humor, and we were laughing and having a fine time. No one could have been more charming. Everybody on the street kept stopping and turning —they recognized him, me or both of us. It was a cold, blue day, and the whole thing had a kind of jolly, jingling quality about it.

"When we finished eating, we went shopping at an Italian store that specialized in beautiful, expensive sweaters. At lunch he had had just one drink—one drink! But he must have shot up or taken pills in the men's room, because suddenly he went utterly, completely to pieces, just like an insane person. He pointed to the counter, where all the sweaters were stacked, and counted, 'One, two, three, four, five . . . sixteen. How much are all of those?' The salesman told him, and Monty picked up *all* of the sweaters in one huge bundle—there were so many they were falling out of his arms —and somehow got the door open. It had begun to rain by this time —in fact it was pouring—but he walked out and threw them all in the gutter. When he came back, the salesman just asked, 'And to what address do I send the bill, Mr. Clift?' I've never seen anyone so cool in my life as that salesman. Monty wouldn't speak to him, but I gave his address and made him sign the bill.

" 'Monty, you've got to go home,' I said when we went outside. 'I'm not going anywhere!' he replied, and we began to have a struggle in the street. I shoved him into the back seat of a taxi, but he got out, walked around the back and got into the front seat, where he tried to grab the wheel away from the driver, who told us to get out or he would call the police. 'Oh, please God, do anything except that!' I said. 'This man is very ill. Take us to this address, and I'll give you a big tip. Please!' So he did, through all the Christmas traffic, while I was holding on to Monty, who was screaming and shouting. It was a nightmare. When we got to his house, his colored houseman managed to get him inside and called his doctor, who gave him an injection. After that experience, something went snap in our relationship. I still liked him very much, but I was always wary of him. It just got to the point where one dreaded to see him, no matter how much one liked him.

"In the sixties—it must have been 1964—he was living with a guy who just ripped him off, stole him blind. By that time he was so far gone on drugs and liquor that he didn't know what he was doing, and he was a virtual prisoner in his own house. So I went over there and told him what was happening and that he had to leave. I told him I would do everything, take him away and find him a place to live. He said that it didn't matter because he would be dead in six months anyway. I called up Elizabeth Taylor, who had been in love with him, and she said that she would take care of him in the Regency Hotel, where she was staying. So I went back to his house, packed his bag, and took him to the Regency. He remained there three days and then went home. 'I can't stay in a hotel,' he told me. 'I have to be at home.' He died about two years later."

A few weeks after Truman finished work on the Selznick film, Humphrey Bogart and John Huston, the director of some of Bogart's best movies, including *The Maltese Falcon* and *The African Queen*, were sitting in George's American Bar in Rome, drinking double martinis and gloomily discussing their problems. They had come to Italy to make a picture from a novel titled *Beat the Devil*, a mystery in an offbeat key, somewhat like the famous *Falcon*. They had hired a cast that boasted, besides Bogart, Jennifer Jones, Peter Lorre, Robert Morley, and Gina Lollobrigida, the gorgeous new Italian star. They had found a picturesque location, the village of Ravello, perched high on the Amalfi coast south of Naples, and they had procured financing, much of which Bogart had put up himself. What they did not have was a script: they both disliked the one prepared by two professional screenwriters. "Couldn't read it," said Bogart. "Neither could I," admitted Huston. "Stinker, isn't it?"

Hearing of their dilemma, Selznick said that he knew of just the writer for them—and as luck would have it, the man he had in mind was already in Rome. "I do urge you to consider calling in Capote, even if it is only for two or three weeks," he wrote Huston. "His is, in my opinion, one of the freshest and *most original* and most exciting writing talents of our time—and what he would say through these characters, and how he would have them say it, would be so completely different from anything that has been heard from a motion-picture theater's sound box as to also give you something completely fresh—or so at least I think. Moreover, I know you very well, and I know of very few writers other than Capote whose work is of the sort that I *know* would appeal to you. He can also be quite fast, but *only* if he is whipped every day. In this case, he can turn out *at least* one solid scene a day, and more if necessary, and certainly more in collaboration with you. Also, he is easy to work with, needing only to be stepped on good-naturedly, like the wonderful but bad little boy he is, when he starts to whine."

Out of desperation, probably, more than desire, Huston and Bogart accepted Selznick's advice, and on a chilly day in early February, 1953, wearing an overcoat that fell almost to his ankles and trailing a long lavender scarf, that wonderful, bad little boy arrived in Ravello. "Nobody was prepared for the entrance of this incredible figure," said John Barry Ryan, a rich young New Yorker who was working as one of Huston's assistants. In a letter to his wife, Lauren Bacall, Bogart described his own reaction to that incredible figure: "At first you can't believe him, he's so odd, and then you want to carry him around with you always."

Truman did write at least one solid scene a day—without being whipped or stepped on—but he was never able to keep more than a day or two ahead of filming. Usually he wrote much of the night, testing out lines and ideas on Huston (who was listed as coauthor but almost certainly had little to do with the screenplay itself). Then, just before lunchtime, he sauntered over to the scene of the shooting with the following day's script tucked under his arm. "He wrote it page by page and read it aloud to us all, page by page, every morning," said Robert Morley. "He never seemed to manage to write very much on any one day, but then as we didn't film very much either it didn't matter."

There were only two interruptions in that tight schedule. One occurred when Truman had to return to Rome. "Truman had to go back to his raven," the production manager informed Morley. "The bird simply refused to talk to him on the telephone and may be quite ill. On the other hand, as Truman says, he may be just sulking." In fact, the bird—Lola, of course—had flown off the terrace of the Via Margutta apartment and was never seen again. The other interruption was more serious. One morning Truman awoke with a swollen jaw, the result of a dangerously abscessed wisdom tooth, and he had to be rushed to a hospital in Naples. "I swear his face was twice its size," said Huston. "But that night something like ten or twelve pages of script came back that he had written in the hospital! He was a bulldog."

Something completely fresh Selznick had promised, and something completely fresh Truman delivered. Before anyone else knew what was happening, the offbeat mystery that Bogart and Huston had thought they were making disappeared, and a mystery-comedy of Truman's own devising took its place: a plot of wild skids and hairpin turns, unpredictable characters, and nutty dialogue reminiscent of the screwball comedies of the thirties. Morley is the leader of a quartet of inept cutthroats who are on their way to Africa to steal title to uranium deposits. Bogart is their reluctant confederate, Lollobrigida is his Italian wife, and Jones, playing a character who seems particularly dear to her creator, is a liar of Rabelaisian ingenuity, someone who, in Bogart's words, "uses her imagination rather than her memory." All are stuck in Ravello, waiting for repairs on the freighter that is to take them across the Mediterranean.

"When I started, only John and I knew what the story was, and I have a suspicion that John wasn't too clear about it," Truman said. But it is doubtful that Truman was entirely clear either: though he may have known where he was going, he did not know how he was going to get there. The plot veered this way, then that, and characters grew larger or smaller, or changed their personality, a practice that dismayed a methodical actress like Jones. "I always wanted to know where my character was going, whether she was going to drop dead or jump in the ocean or be knocked over the head. The beginning, the middle and the end was the way I was structured, so it sometimes threw me a little bit not to know from day to day what she was going to do or not do."

Playwriting had not come naturally to Truman. Screenwriting did, giving him the same opportunity as prose to paint visual images without the restrictions of a proscenium stage. He did not have to be taught how to write for the screen: he knew how. Greenwich's Pickwick Theater had been his classroom, several hundred Hollywood movies had been his teachers, and hours of drinking sweet brandy and making up new dialogue with Phoebe Pierce had been his homework. Now, writing a screenplay for real, he packed it with everything he found funny, from Lollobrigida's comic malapropisms to his favorite cinema clichés, which, as one critic was to observe, he put within the faintest of mocking quotation marks. "It was perfectly obvious," said John Barry Ryan, "that he was making a movie for his own amusement. I always meant to sit down with him and ask: 'Truman, were you doing what we all thought you were doing? Was it really all a game to you?' "

By some mysterious alchemy, the mood of a movie set is often reflected on the theater screen. One of the reasons *Beat the Devil* is such a lark to see is that, as Huston recalled, "it was a hell of a lark doing it." For ten weeks Ravello was one giant house party. Huston was the indulgent and genial host; Jones and Bogart were the guests of honor; and Truman, of course, was the entertainer, the Puck. "Things happened that could only have happened on a John Huston set in winter in an Italian town where there was no heat, no electricity, and nothing to eat or drink except what was shipped in," said Ryan. "Every night there was a great poker game, with Huston, Bogart and David Selznick. Jennifer was being pursued by a tall Italian lesbian, who was in turn being pursued by a short, dumpy Italian lesbian. David was trying to fight everyone off, and Truman was encouraging the whole thing, the marvelous turmoil that he loved to create."

Bogart nicknamed him "Caposy" and liked to tease him until one day Truman showed he could dish it out as well as take it. "We were all in the lobby of the Hotel Palumbo," he remembered, "and Bogie was arm-wrestling with the crew. He kept winning over and over. I was just watching, and he called over, 'How would you like to take me on?' I said okay. We used to arm-wrestle all the time in school. We put our arms together, and I immediately pushed his arm down. I've never seen a look of such complete sorrow on anyone's face. 'Would you mind doing that again?' he asked. 'Yes, for fifty dollars,' I said. He put the fifty dollars on the table, and we did it a second time. Bang went his arm again.

" 'I don't get it. How did you do that?' he asked. 'It's just a trick,' I said, and as we stood up, he caught me in a bear hug. He meant it affectionately, but there was also a certain kind of frustration—malice in the way he did it. 'Cut that out, Bogie!' I said. But he kept on squeezing me. 'Cut that out!' I said and hooked my foot behind his leg and pushed. Boom! He fell down and fractured his elbow, which was a big disaster, because it meant two or three days lost in shooting. But I think that that incident, more than anything else, is what made us very good friends. After that he knew better than to fool around with me. I really liked Bogie. He was one of my all-time favorite people."

Hearing of the amusements in Ravello, other movie folk, such as Orson Welles and Ingrid Bergman, stopped in to say hello. But the visitor who occasioned the most affectionate talk had nothing to do with show business. She was Truman's old friend the regal Carmel

Snow, who came for a weekend and had such a good time that she stayed for a week. Mrs. Snow being Mrs. Snow, she did not watch silently. The women's dresses were unacceptable, she proclaimed, and summoned from Paris her new discovery, Hubert de Givenchy, to redesign them. That done, she left, waving a white-gloved hand as she marched through the lobby of the Palumbo.

"Why, honey, what's wrong? Ain't we chic enough for you?" Bogart inquired.

"My dear man, compared to you my life is lived in a salt mine," she said as she got into her car. "No, it's just that now I must straighten my face and stop having fun."

"Well, remember, I like you, honey," he said, leaning in the back window. "You're a very ballsy-type type."

Mrs. Snow, who had been given the Legion of Honor by the President of France, regarded him coolly for a moment. Then, perhaps deciding that she had just received an accolade that was almost as good, she replied: "Am I? Well, so are you. Bye-bye, tough boy."

"Bye-bye, tough gal." And off she went.

In April, the company moved to England to shoot interiors in the Shepperton Studios. This time, Jack, who had never visited the Ravello set, came along, enjoying three or four weeks at Claridge's, all expenses paid by the production. As a demonstration of the company's affection, Jack Clayton, the associate producer, gave Truman a puppy, an English bulldog. To repay so much hospitality, Truman gave a dinner party. "[It] ended with John Huston and Humphrey Bogart fistfighting," Jack wrote his sister Gloria. "But it appears they always act that way. All concerned in the movie were nice to Truman. But I suppose he's nice to work with, if only because he's sane and they aren't."

Huston may well have wondered if the order of that equation should not have been reversed. As he sat down to edit the movie he and Truman had made, it must have looked odder and odder. Instead of giving it the standard praises, he warned the critics not to expect very much from it. "This is such a slight, tiny picture in this age of great ones," he said. "You can't get more trivial."

In fact, many of the critics loved it. *The New Yorker* thought it was "hugely entertaining," and *Time* called it a "screwball classic." The public, however, agreed with Huston, and it never made a profit. "Personally if you don't see this picture you are not missing much," said a theater owner in Michigan, who bought a newspaper ad to apologize to his patrons for showing it. Even those dearest to Truman disliked it. Jack did not understand it, and Newton walked out after half an hour. One Hollywood wit declared that no matter where you came in, you seemed to have come in in the middle.

Yet the film has survived in revival houses and probably will continue to entertain for a long time to come. Writing in 1975, Charles Champlin, the critic of the *Los Angeles Times*, offered the appreciation of an aficionado. "However antic and loopy the circumstances of its making may be, *Beat the Devil* holds up as a fast and disciplined comedy, with a richness of invention which even now, after fifteen or twenty viewings, I find astonishing." Huston may have been more prophetic than he knew when he told Jones, who had won an Oscar for *The Song of Bernadette*, "Honey, this is the picture for which you will be remembered."

FOR both Truman and Jack, summer always meant the sea, and in the spring of 1953 they moved to Portofino, a fishing village south of Genoa that was a magnet for chic tourists. "Fortunately," said Noël Coward, who was one of them, "the Americans don't care for it much because there is no sandy bathing beach and nothing to do." But the two Americans who arrived with a pair of noisy dogs in a red Renault disproved his snobbish theorem; they were as enchanted as he was and found perhaps too much to do. Taking the top floor of a house on the harbor, they sunned themselves, swam, snorkeled, and worked. Jack was revising a novel; Truman was busy finishing the script of *House of Flowers* and attempting, after a long hiatus, to write short stories again.

"I *need* to write short stories now," he explained to Linscott, whose paternal presence had been largely forgotten during the months of movie madness. "Partly because they interest me and, perhaps more importantly, I am entering a new area of style, developing a different cast of characters and themes—and only when this is set in my mind can I really write a novel. I *have* a novel to write—but I want to try, with a short story, trial and error, to set my guns right." A few weeks later he plaintively added: "I wish so much I could talk to you right now, Bob—about my work. I have so many plans, ideas—maybe you could help me sort them out. I do need counsel—no two ways about it. I could *write* it all, I suppose—but it would take 50 pages. However, I am coming to New York the middle of October—then you really must devote some time to me. I'm looking forward to seeing you far, far more than anyone else!"

Never before had he sounded so confused and uncertain about what direction his writing should take. Reading between the lines of those cryptic and intriguing letters, Linscott guessed, probably correctly, that what he was trying to say was that he could not decide whether he should return to his first love, fiction, or continue his romance with stage and screen. He was obviously tempted by the latter, and he had every prospect of a lucrative career writing for the movies; indeed, he already had been asked to do another screenplay, an adaptation of Richard Hughes's novel *A High Wind in Jamaica*. The chance of losing him to Hollywood and Broadway alarmed his old editor, who, without waiting for October, quickly offered his own opinion, summarizing in a few words what he would have said in many over a two-martini, three-course lunch. "Naturally, my advice would be to stick to fiction; prejudiced obviously. Nevertheless, it's my hunch that a talent, delicate and evocative as yours, would illuminate more deeply from the printed page than in the theater, where coarser effects are perhaps essential and where you are at the mercy of the interpreters."

Truman did not reply, but his actions spelled out his ambivalence: he unsuccessfully tried to write his play and fiction too. He was not the kind of writer who could easily switch his attention from one project to another; he was not able to sit down with his play in the morning, for instance, then put it away and concentrate on fiction in the afternoon. When he was engaged in something, it occupied his entire imagination, and *House of Flowers*, for which he had both a contract and a deadline, automatically assumed most of his time and energy. Not until it was completed did he turn seriously to the stories he wanted so much to write. "I've been working with zombie-like concentration the last 2 months (after having squandered most of the summer) and have put everything else out of my mind," he wrote Newton in October. "I finished my 'House of Flowers' play (if indeed a play is ever 'finished') and am working on some new stories—what a pleasure to return to the sanity and 'space' of straight prose."

If he squandered most of the summer, he had a good excuse: a battalion of friends and celebrities converged almost simultaneously on that little fishing village. Some, like Coward and John Gielgud, stayed with Rex Harrison and his wife, Lilli Palmer, who had a house in the hills. Others, like Tennessee Williams, Frankie Merlo, and Paul Bowles, were just passing through. A few, like Cecil, Saint

Subber, and John Malcolm Brinnin, came to visit Truman himself. Whatever their reasons for being there, Truman could not resist the pleasure of their company. He saw them all. He could not complain, as he had in Taormina, that he heard nothing but the sound of the sea. In Portofino there was a gabble of voices, a cascade of laughter, a buzz of gossip. He was in his element.

Jack was not in his element, however, and never before during the nearly five years they had been together had their different attitudes toward the world been so sharply defined. It appeared that two more mismatched souls could not have come together: oil and water, Cavalier and Roundhead, Truman and Jack. The differences between them could have filled a thick catalogue. Truman sought notice; Jack shied away from it. Truman loved to be around people; Jack worshiped solitude. Truman wanted to charm the world; Jack seemed to delight in offending. "You take your life into your hands when you invite Jack to a dinner party," Mary Louise once said, "because you never know at what point he will suddenly turn against someone in the room, give him a dressing-down, and storm out."

Jack's friends traded anecdotes about his turbulent exits. The classic departure occurred in 1949, when he and Truman were overnight guests at a house several miles outside Paris. After breakfast, Jack went out, presumably to take the air. When he failed to come back, Truman and their host became alarmed, afraid that he had fallen down an abandoned well in the garden. The host organized a search, but hunt as they might, Jack could not be found. Not until Truman, sick with anxiety, opened the door to their hotel room in Paris was he located. He had been there for hours: when he had left the house, he had not stopped walking until he was back in the city.

From the start he had made it clear that with a few exceptions like Mary Louise, he did not like or want to meet Truman's friends. They were all babies in his estimation. Few of them ever got close enough to know him. Those who did considered themselves among the elect; those who did not were usually intensely curious about him. "I've always wanted to know him because I thought him attractive and mysterious, but I never got to first base," said Glenway Wescott with a sorry sigh.

Truman had had fair warning, but only with time did he realize just how obstinately antisocial and eremitic Jack was. In Portofino he pouted like a child, for instance, when Truman invited Greta

Garbo to their apartment. Her name was almost a synonym for misanthropy, but compared with him, she was as affable as a Rotarian. "The other night Greta Garbo was eating at a restaurant with some friends," Jack told his sister. "I did not recognize her and was displeased with Truman when he pointed her out to me. She looked too much like her awful newspaper pictures. Truman later invited her to the apartment, but I did not feel like going up then. He tells me she played with the dogs and complained of a pain in the neck."

That incident was symbolic of many others over many years: Truman in their apartment, laughing with one of the most beautiful, sought-after women in the world; Jack sulking down below, walking the waterfront until she had left. Still, for several years, despite many embarrassments and many more such rebuffs, Truman tried to convert him to some semblance of sociability. "I beat my head against that wall for a long time," Truman said. "Finally I just went my own way. The alternative would have been for me to become a kind of recluse. But that was against my nature. I like going out." The pattern of his relationship with Newton was being repeated, and both he and Jack had other, casual sexual partners, Truman occasionally, Jack frequently. So overheated was Jack's libido indeed that, in a scene of pure farce, he once chased the composer Ned Rorem around a table, panting to a stop only when Rorem shamed him by telling him how much Truman adored him.

There was one difference between Truman's relationship with Newton and his relationship with Jack, and it was fundamental. Newton had made it clear that Truman was a visitor in Northampton, and not always a welcome visitor at that. With Jack he had a home, even if it was only a hotel suite in Portofino. Although their paths often diverged, they continued to live together, they still were lovers, and they still had sex together. By their own standards they also remained faithful to each other. "I did not have affairs," Jack maintained. "I just went to bed with people. In those days I thought I should go to bed with everyone. The homosexual world was all new to me."

Life with a famous person, particularly one as hungry for attention as Truman was, can shatter any ordinary ego. Living with Tennessee had already robbed poor Frankie Merlo of his identity, and it was a broken spirit, in Jack's opinion, that caused the cancer that eventually killed him. Jack's own position was even more precarious. Frankie was not a playwright, not someone who could be compared with Tennessee; but Jack was a writer, and, like it or not, he was Truman's rival, as all writers are rivals. His ambition was as large as Truman's, his efforts were as great, his standards were as high, and his confidence in his abilities was as unbounded. It therefore must have been galling that his reputation was immeasurably smaller. The harsh truth was that although he was talented, he was not gifted. His work did not reverberate, as Truman's did, and he did not have Truman's uncanny ear for the music of a sentence. To most people he was known, and always would be known, not as a writer but as Truman Capote's lover.

Keeping his equilibrium in such circumstances would have required a more serene and secure disposition than Jack possessed, and he fought fiercely and sometimes irrationally to proclaim his independence. Frustrating as it was to Truman, Jack's antisocial attitude was more than a flaw in his personality. It was the wall that protected him. It was his crude but effective means of asserting himself, of saying that though he stood in Truman's shadow, spiritually he stood by himself. "I would have debased myself if I had done everything Truman wanted me to do. And Truman would have hated me because I wouldn't have been a person. I would have devirilized myself because I would have had to do everything on his terms. I escaped from all that social life. I never went on anyone's yacht, even though I was invited. I think I would have become a drunk or a terrific pleaser if I had. Frankie Merlo died because he lost himself in Tennessee's glare. He got sick on fame. I've never, never wanted to be famous. I wanted to be a writer."

In every way he could, Jack created his own world, as distant from Truman's as he could make it. He had his own circle of friends, whom Truman saw only occasionally; he retained close ties with his family; and to anyone who would listen he proclaimed a different and, to his mind, purer set of values. He should have become a Jesuit, he later said, and he was not altogether wrong. There were no ambiguities or grays in the world he had constructed for himself; there were only absolutes—blacks and whites. Like his father, who did not have enough money to own a car and who sneered at those who did—"grease monkeys," he called them—he despised the adornments that more successful writers acquire. He kept himself as ignorant as a child of the details of domestic finances, as if by not knowing how much money it cost the two of them to live he could escape the knowledge that it was Truman who paid the bills.

A partnership of such complicated checks and balances was a strain on both of them, and they were frequently at war. Yet as mismatched as they seemed, as much as they argued, some miracle of geometry made them fit together like pieces in a picture puzzle. From the outside, their relationship appeared impossible. But it worked, in its own cranky fashion. "We didn't live the life that most people lived," said Jack, "but, with great leaves of absence, we lived perfectly fine lives and enjoyed and amused each other all the time. That's a very rare thing. Through the years, whatever would happen, Truman would come home and I would be there."

Jack was correct in believing that Truman could not have abided a slave or a toady. Instinctively, Truman had known what he was doing when he rushed to Leo's on that autumn night in 1948. His unerring ability to find the right person at the right time had once again caused him to make the right choice. As irritating and in many ways as selfish and self-absorbed as Jack was, he was nonetheless a man of absolute integrity, a craggy rock in slippery waters. "He is the only person I trust one hundred percent," Truman said. "He is everything to me. He is not my shadow. He is not my alter ego. He is the one person I will love until the day I die."

Jack was his lover, but his best friend in those days, the one who made up for many of Jack's deficiencies, was Cecil Beaton. At first glance, he and Truman also appeared utterly mismatched, as different as two men could possibly be. Twenty years older than Truman, tall, slim, and silver-haired, Cecil was the personification of English high style, London's *arbiter elegantiarum* since the thirties, when he had become the favorite portrait photographer of the rich and social on both sides of the Atlantic. Hidden behind his chill blue eyes was a unique visual imagination, and he was also in demand as a designer of costumes and sets for operas, movies, and plays, including, of course, *The Grass Harp*. Impeccable in dress and manners, he had so snobbish an outlook that it could only have belonged to someone who had climbed up from the middle class. "Cecil's perfect manners become radiant as a saint's gestures in Holy pictures," wrote Jack, who groaned audibly every time Truman invited him to visit. "An extraordinary man, but I am not comfortable avec lui."

Truman was comfortable with him, however, and the things that separated them, such as age and accent, were minor compared with those that united them. They both venerated style, they both had achieved early success, and they both loved to gossip and entertain. "Perhaps the world's second worst crime is boredom; the first is being a bore" was one of Cecil's maxims. They both had wanted to eat at the tables of the rich and sail aboard their yachts, and they often did so. Cecil introduced Truman to the world of international society; Truman introduced Cecil to those few rich Americans Cecil did not already know. "They considered themselves small-town boys," said one mutual friend. "They were outsiders poking fun at the establishment. They loved to peek. They were like naughty little boys peering into their parents' bedroom."

They liked being together so much, indeed, that a few people assumed that they were having an affair, which was not the case. Theirs was a friendship of the spirit, not the flesh. In some sense, Truman looked up to Cecil as a mentor. "I respect and trust you almost more than anyone I know and love you accordingly, which is to say hugely," Truman told him in 1952. "I admire you as a man as much as anyone I've ever known," he added a few years later. Cecil returned his affection. His reserved, almost gelid personality was warmed by Truman's enthusiasm. "We are now each other's best friend," Cecil observed in his diary that August of 1953. "I am always stimulated & happy in his company & wish nothing more than to continue to be with him."

In Portofino they were like two boys on summer vacation. John Gielgud, who was there before Cecil, was appalled by the appearance Truman presented to the world. "He had very long toenails, dirty shorts, two awful dogs, and that ghastly little voice." Gielgud expected Cecil to "clean him up a bit. But he didn't. The next thing I knew I looked out the window and saw them in a boat together. Truman looked just the same, in his dirty little shorts, and Cecil, who had very fair skin, was red as a beet, wearing a great big hat with two ribbons behind it that had been chewed by Truman's dogs." Cecil did not seem to mind. Tom Sawyer and Huckleberry Finn could not have had a better time rafting down the Mississippi than did these two men of style as they splashed around in the cobalt waters off Portofino. While they swam and sunbathed, they talked—and talked and talked. "We discussed our beliefs and doubts, gossiped, argued, talked seriously, frivolously and bawdily," wrote Cecil. "We were vastly entertained by each other's revelations."

Truman had grown up, in Cecil's opinion; he had changed from that "fluttery willowy little wraith" he had met in 1948 into a man of remarkable strength and vitality. "In some ways I feel anxious lest this phenomenon may be too extraordinary to last," he confided in his diary, "and that like Bebe [Berard, a French artist who died in the late forties] he may not survive to old age. There is something almost frighteningly violent about the way he crowds so much into such a short lifetime. He sleeps so soundly, enjoying sleep so sensually; he gets such violent reactions to everything in life when once he has come out of his drowsy, slumbrous wakenings. He is so surprised, so full of wonder. He is so conscious of the deliciousness of rare & expensive things as well as the simple things. I feel slightly scared that someone who lives so intensely, so warmly, so generously, may be packing into a short span more than most people are capable of enjoying or experiencing in a long lifetime."

Toward the end of October, Truman and Jack left Portofino. They spent several days in Switzerland, where they saw Oona and Charlie Chaplin, then proceeded to Paris, their last stop before they were scheduled to sail home on the *Queen Mary* in January, 1954. Those weeks in Paris were unrewarding for both of them. "I am working, but not well," Jack wrote Mary Louise in an uncharacteristic note of near-despair. "Everything seems rather hopeless to me —my own work, that is—and I grow more unpleasant as a person day by day. Two or three drinks and I'm all bitterness and resentment—most of which is directed not half so much against others and their achievements, so much as against myself and my lack." Saint Subber had appeared in Portofino while Cecil was there in August, making Truman feel so guilty for not having worked harder on *House of Flowers* that he sat down immediately after Saint left and did finish it. But now in Paris he reread what he had written and belatedly realized that he would have to rewrite the second half, "stem to stern," as he told Newton. The prospect of long days and nights doing more rewrites in New York filled him with gloom. "Paris is cold and yellow, not very exhilarating," he added. "But I dread the thought of N.Y. so much I'd hawk hot chestnuts in the Tuileries sooner than set sail a moment before necessary." To John Malcolm Brinnin he wrote: "Nothing seems to be going right for me

—I seem to be in a welter of unsolvable problems, literary and otherwise."

He and Jack were not alone in their despondency, and in November Truman received a call from Carson's husband, Reeves McCullers. "This is your friend from across the River Styx," said Reeves—a bit of black humor that Truman did not fully appreciate until a few days later. Carson had angrily left for America, refusing to advance Reeves any more money, and Truman invited him to his hotel for dinner that night. Reeves never appeared, and it was that night, apparently, that he committed suicide, taking an overdose of barbiturates on top of liquor. "Carson treated him very, very badly," said Truman afterward. "There was nothing wrong with Reeves except her. He should have been running a gasoline station in Georgia, and he would have been perfectly happy." At Carson's insistence, Reeves's ashes were buried in France, rather than Georgia, as his family wanted, and Truman, much shaken, was one of only a handful who attended his funeral in early December. "My youth is gone," he lamented to one of the other mourners.

It was a remark more prophetic than he knew. A few days after New Year's, Joe Capote called from Manhattan with more bad news. After a night of heavy drinking, Nina had also swallowed a bottle of barbiturates—Seconals—and was in a coma. A second call quickly followed, telling him she was dead. Leaving Jack to sail home with the dogs, Truman flew to New York.

FOR several years Nina had managed to pull herself together, imbibing nothing stronger than coffee. Then, toward the end of 1952, disaster struck and her life suddenly collapsed beneath her. Joe lost his job and most of their money, and their comfortable way of living ended abruptly. She was back where she had been with Arch, examining every dollar as if it might be the last one she would ever see. With Joe's job went both her self-respect and her hard-won sobriety. She began drinking again, more than ever.

In fact, the clouds had been long gathering. For years she and Joe had been spending more than he made as treasurer of his firm of Wall Street textile brokers, and the luxuries upon which they depended came from the profits of another textile concern he owned secretly with Nina's brother-in-law James Rudisill, the husband of her sister Tiny. Over the years, their enterprise, the Rudisill Textile Company, did more than $550,000 worth of business with Joe's Wall Street employers, Taylor, Pinkham and Company, whose other officers knew nothing of his involvement. That arrangement might have continued undetected had Joe not also begun gambling in the highly volatile textile commodity market. In that endeavor he was not so fortunate. He lost heavily, taking money from Taylor, Pinkham funds to cover his shortfall. When Taylor, Pinkham was purchased by the giant J. P. Stevens Company in 1952, his improprieties were discovered: close to a hundred thousand dollars was found missing from its books. He was dismissed, and the Manhattan district attorney began to investigate.

To escape jail, he needed to repay what he had taken. Using what

little capital he had left, he went into business with a Cuban manu-
facturer of sewing threads. "We'll come back either broke or very
rich," Nina told Andrew shortly before they left for Havana, and
they soon returned to New York, even poorer than when they had
left. The best job Joe could find was an accounting job that paid
only seventy-five dollars a week, and if it had not been for Truman,
who sent them much of the money he had earned working for the
movies, he and Nina would have had to move to a cold-water flat in
the Bronx. "Everything would be fine, except for the terrible and
constant worry about my mother and father—but I will not burden
you with that," Truman wrote Mary Louise in June, 1953. In October he elaborated to Newton: "Odd, I seem to think about money
all the time; I used not to ever. But the whole Nina–Joe situation
has given me such a jolt; and it goes on and on—and I have to pay
straight down the line because I don't know what else to do."

As long as she had had money, Nina was able to maintain the
pretense that she was a Park Avenue society woman. When the
money disappeared, that facade was shattered, and during the weeks
before her death, she avoided most of her old friends, too depressed
and embarrassed to enjoy their company. "Do call her," Joe urged
Andrew. "She always enjoys your conversations." But the last time
Andrew saw her, walking down the street, he received the distinct
impression that she did not want to see him or anyone else. Eleanor
Friede, who had lunch with her at the Plaza, was surprised to find
her acting wild and distracted, as if she were close to a nervous
breakdown. Pretty Nina suddenly looked terrible, Eleanor thought.
She was too thin, and her hair, which had always been so expertly
dyed that Friede had assumed that she was a natural blonde, was
showing both its darker roots and traces of gray—the beauty parlor
was a luxury she could no longer afford.

A few days before New Year's, her brother Seabon, whose wife
was recovering from surgery in a Manhattan hospital, came to stay
the night at 1060 Park. Nina was already drunk when he arrived,
and when Joe went to bed, brother and sister sat drinking for another hour or two, until Seabon also said good night and retired into
Truman's room. In no mood for sleep, Nina then woke Joe, accusing
him once again of infidelity and screaming that she had hired a
private detective to follow him, which, according to Seabon, she in
fact had done. Joe retreated into Truman's room with Seabon, but

her rage followed him there as well. Unable to escape her in the apartment, both men dressed and left about two o'clock. "Get out, both of you!" she yelled. "Get outta here!" Seabon drove Joe to the best hotel poor Joe could afford, the West Side Y.M.C.A, and then proceeded to Queens, where he worked, and bedded down on a couch in his office.

No one can know what went through Nina's alcohol-befuddled mind after they left, but her future could scarcely have appeared bleaker and more hopeless to her. As she had done before, she swallowed a lethal dose of Seconals. She apparently had second thoughts about killing herself, however; when Joe discovered her the next morning, the phone was off the hook, indicating that she had tried to call for help, and the windows were open, as if she had hoped that the cold December air would prevent her from lapsing into oblivion. It did not, and she was lying unconscious on the floor when Joe unlocked the door in the morning. She was taken to Knickerbocker Hospital, where she lingered for several days. She died on the morning of Monday, January 4, 1954, a few weeks before her forty-ninth birthday. That night Joe asked Andrew to join him for dinner in a restaurant near the apartment. "Don't stop talking," Joe commanded. "Talk about anything, any subject in the world. Don't worry about whether it will interest me or not. Just talk so I won't break down."

Truman had telephoned his mother just before Christmas. Then, in quick succession, came the calls from Joe. Truman left Paris for New York the next day. Jack described his sorrowful departure to Gloria: "When the night maid came in to make up the bed, he was in the bedroom and I was out here at my table. She asked him who was going to America—which of the two of us—and he said 'me— I'm going.' He sounded so little—so sad. He seemed to want her to *know* everything just by looking at him. I put him on the bus to the airport—he was the only one—all the other passengers had driven out, presumably in their own cars. The driver said: Look, Mr. C., you have a bus to yourself. Truman was holding his dog. He looked at the driver, then at me, and then, to please the driver, he said something he would never say if he'd not been so desolate: 'That's because all the other passengers are so rich,' he said—making a joke. Then he drove away in that big blue bus. It began to snow. It sounds like a story, but it really did snow—and the wind rose—and it was freezing cold."

Saint Subber met his plane in New York and drove him to 1060, where Truman immediately went back to his room to lie down. "Truman's in the back," Saint said when Andrew arrived a few minutes later. "You're the only person he wants to see. Go on back there." He had been crying, Andrew said, and he was so tired— transatlantic flights took more than fifteen hours in those pre-jet days —that he had not even bothered to take off his overcoat. "She didn't have to do it," he told Andrew. "She didn't have to die. I've got money." Andrew lay down beside him and held him, as he had done so many times before.

The funeral was on Thursday, January 7, at Manhattan's best-known funeral parlor, Frank Campbell's, on Madison Avenue at Eighty-first Street. Two of Nina's sisters, Tiny and Mary Ida, came North for the services, but cousin Jennie, who, at eighty, was the last survivor of the house on Alabama Avenue, stayed in Monroe-ville, angry, it was said, because Nina's body would not be brought home for burial. In fact, there was to be no burial; to the dismay of her Baptist relatives, who did not believe in cremation, her remains were cremated and the ashes were placed in a crypt in a Westchester County crematorium.

Except for Joe, who had been drinking so steadily since her death that he was scarcely able to walk, everyone appeared composed, and the service proceeded so quickly and quietly, without outward signs of grieving, that Leo Lerman was almost shocked. "I'm a Jew," he said to Andrew. "Is that how Christians bury people?" Afterward, some of those in attendance walked back to 1060 for a somber wake. Dorothy Kilgallen, one of the Hearst chain's top gossip columnists, infuriated Mary Ida by immediately asking for a drink. "People don't ask for a drink after a funeral," said Mary Ida. "Even if I come out of the backwoods, I know that that's not good manners. Not to me, it isn't!" Jennifer Jones, on the other hand, won her heart by bringing homemade cookies. "I was so astounded that a movie star would make cookies!" While they were all there, a reporter from *The New York Times* called to ask if it was Truman Capote's mother who had died. "Hang up!" Joe ordered, and the phone was put back on its cradle.

Although most people knew better, ousiders were told that Nina had died of pneumonia. "Well, I'll eventually find out the true story," Harper Lee said to herself, and she did. For years to come, Truman almost never talked about the way his mother had died. He mentioned it just once to Phoebe Pierce, and then only after Phoebe's own mother had killed herself. Yet, as with all children, including Phoebe, who have lost a parent to suicide, the manner of her death never ceased to bother him. "I don't think Truman has ever written a word about Nina," said Phoebe. "I don't see anything of her in any of his characters. But I know that when my mother killed herself, it almost killed me as well. You can bury such a thing miles deep, miles and miles and miles deep, but it must be a central experience in your life." Lyn White, Nina's best friend, was one of those privy from the beginning to the family's secret. "You know, Lyn, my mother loved you more than anybody but Papa and me," Truman told her. "But this is all so sordid." White barely held herself back from making a sharp reply. "I didn't think it was sordid," she said. "I thought it was a tragedy."

Arch appeared several days later, sniffing around, or so it appeared, to determine if there was any estate he could share in. There was none, of course, and Truman angrily told him so. "There's nothing here for you," he said. "You're not my father. Joe's my father. He's taken care of me." It was a brutal but accurate statement of fact, and since Nina had conveyed him North in 1933, Truman had seen very little of Arch, who had remarried, been widowed, then remarried again. In 1941 and 1942, Truman spent parts of two summers with him in Mississippi and Louisiana. They got along well, but, true to his nature, Arch disappointed with a promise he had no intention of keeping. He gave Truman a white Cadillac convertible, then snatched it back a week later. "He was always one with the grand and hollow gesture" was Truman's bitter comment. "He never did anything for me." When he was living in New Orleans two years later, struggling financially while he was working on *Other Voices*, Arch was one person he did not call upon for help.

Whatever Truman thought of him, Arch was his father, his nearest blood relation now that his mother was dead. After those initial harsh words, he relented, took Arch to dinner at the Colony, and—like father, like son—bragged about his conquest of Europe, which must have sounded, by the time the dessert cart was wheeled around, only slightly less impressive than the D-Day invasion. Arch believed every word. Like all inventive liars, he appreciated the tales of other inventive liars. "He told me that he had been going out with Princess Margaret and that he had had dinner with Queen Elizabeth," Arch recalled. "I looked at him and said, 'You mean to tell me that if I were to go to London today and check in at the Dorchester Hotel, you could call Princess Margaret on the telephone?' And he looked at me like he thought I was crazy! 'Hell, I'll get her from here,' he said. 'Do you want to talk to her?' And he meant it, too!" Truman had in fact been introduced to Princess Margaret, but of course they had not gone out, and the dinner with the Queen had taken place entirely in his imagination.

In the weeks following Nina's death, Joe walked around in a drunken daze. Trying to revive his spirits, Truman took him to parties and nightclubs, and for several weeks they were rarely seen apart. His efforts were in vain. Undone by all the calamities that had befallen him, Joe acted more and more erratically, running up big bills on Truman's charge accounts, forging checks in his name, and gambling away the proceeds. "Truman is having a bad time with Joe—who *implies* he's in bad trouble," Jack told Gloria. "I think he spends all his money as soon as he gets it, like a boy. Takes some dame to Atlantic City (Marlborough-Blenheim Hotel, no less), hires cars, etc. During the week he's desperate enough to murder, I think."

The district attorney at last concluded his investigation into Joe's activities at Taylor, Pinkham, and on December 21 he was indicted on several counts of forgery and grand larceny. On January 5, 1955, a year and a day after Nina's death, he pleaded guilty, and on March 30 he entered Sing Sing Prison, from which he was released on May 14, 1956.

Truman visited him several times and gave him money while he was there, and still more money after his release. Joe was his father, in his eyes, and he did his duty as a son, and perhaps a bit more. In the late sixties, however, Truman complained about pesky phone calls from Joe's latest wife, who suffered from paranoid delusions that she was being persecuted by the Mafia and the F.B.I. Joe reacted angrily, and they did not speak again. Joe managed without him, living in near-poverty until his death, at the age of eighty-two, in 1982. "You sometimes have to perform a little lobotomy and cut people out of your mind or they will drag you down," Truman said by way of explanation. "I cut my father out long ago. He never did anything for me and he was not my responsibility. I finally cut Joe out too. I gave him a lot of money and saw him through two marriages after my mother died. But after a year-and-a-half of this current crazy wife, I said, 'Enough!' There have been a lot of people who have tried to take me—and a few have—but I got to the point where if they were found in the East River, with a note tied around their necks saying, 'Truman Capote did this to me,' I could say, 'They were not my responsibility.' "

Nот long after Nina's funeral, Truman turned once again to *House of Flowers*, which now seemed well on its way to Broadway. Harold Arlen, the composer of such popular classics as "Stormy Weather" and "Over the Rainbow," had been hired in November to write the music and collaborate on the lyrics—Truman confessed to knowing nothing about how a song is put together. They began work immediately, exchanging ideas by mail and transatlantic telephone, and by the time Truman returned to New York, they had finished the title song. There was a setback in February, when Arlen was hospitalized with bleeding ulcers. But even before the intravenous tube had been taken out of his arm, he invited Truman up to his room, where he used a spoon to tap out rhythms on a dinner tray. Only when they started singing the chorus together did the nurses call a halt.

Although they were separated by almost twenty years, the two collaborators formed an affectionate bond. Every day when he visited Arlen in the hospital, Truman automatically went through the letters and telegrams that had accumulated on the dresser since the day before. That was a closer collaboration than Arlen had contemplated, and he took to hiding them under books and drawers. It did no good. Not at all embarrassed, Truman searched them out. "Dads, where are they?" he would demand. Once Arlen put a message of his own in the middle of the pile: "Aren't you ashamed of yourself, you little bastard?" The little bastard did not seem to be. Dressed in sneakers and jeans, he was soon making himself equally at home in Arlen's Park Avenue living room, curling up on the couch next to the piano while Arlen tested his newest tunes. "We used to work three hours every day," said Arlen. "He used a little pad and I used a large one. I thought he was a fine versifier, but he needed direction as far as songs go. It's a special art."

Peter Brook had been Truman's first choice to direct *The Grass Harp*, and Truman was convinced that if Brook had only agreed, his play would have been a success. Like many others, he still considered Brook the reigning genius of the stage, and he was determined to do whatever was necessary to induce him to direct *House of Flowers*. By June, Arlen was well enough to fly, and together they flew to London, where they outlined the story and sang their songs for that brash young man, who thereupon consented to take on his first Broadway musical.

Truman's original story came out of a trip he took to Haiti in the winter of 1948. In the absence of other nightlife, he spent many of his evenings sitting on the porches of the whorehouses along the Bizonton Road, buying beer for the girls, who told him the local gossip while they fanned themselves and waited for customers. From those nights emerged one of his finest short stories, "House of Flowers," the tale of Ottilie, a pretty young prostitute from the hills, who forsakes the bright lights and sophisticated men of Port-au-Prince for true love with a country boy, handsome young Royal. Plagued by Royal's evil grandmother, a famous caster of spells, Ottilie proves she is not so innocent as she seems and turns the spells back on the old woman, who is so shocked and chagrined that she obligingly drops dead, leaving the lovers to live happily ever after.

That story was the one Truman had dramatized in Portofino. But a play is not completed until opening night, and when he sat down with Saint, Arlen, and finally Brook, it became apparent that what Truman thought was a finished script was only a first draft. "Brook is a very creative force and he's wonderful at cutting," he told an interviewer a few months later. "And there was plenty of cutting to be done. I don't usually tend to overwrite, but in this case I had written a full-length play plus a full-length musical. If we'd kept all of my original script, we'd have been in the theater from eight o'clock until two in the morning." As the weeks progressed, his plot was revised, his characters were changed, and his script was altered almost beyond recognition.

The romance between the young lovers took second place to a plot line that was not even hinted at in the original story, a rivalry between the madams of two competing brothels. The evil grandmother disappeared altogether, and Ottilie was transformed from a prostitute into a sweet virgin—who just happened to make her home in a whorehouse. Even the house of flowers changed location. In Truman's story it had been Royal's house in the hills, which was covered by wisteria; on Broadway it was to be Madame Fleur's bordello, where Ottilie lived and where each of the girls was named after a flower: Tulip, Gladiola, Pansy, Violet.

Truman once again had demanded a topflight production, and he got one. Pearl Bailey took on the part of Madame Fleur; Juanita Hall, who had played Bloody Mary in *South Pacific*, became Madame Tango, her rival in sin; and Diahann Carroll played Ottilie. The world's greatest choreographer, George Balanchine, was in charge of a cast of dancers that included Alvin Ailey and Geoffrey Holder. Unpaid, but not unseen, was Arlen's lady friend Marlene Dietrich, who bought coffee and pastries, helped with costumes—even rubbed Pearl Bailey's tired feet. On the first day of rehearsals Truman showed up with real blooms for his house of flowers: red roses, which he solemnly distributed to the women in the cast and crew. "Here's a little rose for you, Pearl, honey," he said, "and one for you, Juanita, darling. . . ."

Rarely has a show wasted as much talent as did *House of Flowers*. For two days, for example, Balanchine's dancers watched with respectful awe as the master carefully, lovingly devised what he thought was a new step. "When he was through, it was a mambo!" said Holder, remembering his disappointment. "All he had to do was say 'mambo' at the beginning, and we would have jumped!" Confessing that he had accepted the assignment only because he needed the money, Balanchine realized that he was in the wrong place and gracefully withdrew.

Although he was only twenty-nine when he was hired, Brook understood Shakespeare as well as anyone alive. But a Broadway musical, particularly a black musical, was beyond his comprehension. "Tell me, how do you handle them?" was one of his early questions to Lucia Victor, the stage manager.

"Who do you mean by 'them'?" she asked.

"The blacks," he answered. "I just don't know how to handle them."

Nor did he. He gave no direction, for instance, to Pearl Bailey, who had spent most of her career in nightclubs and who knew that she needed help in this, her first starring role on Broadway. "What am I doing wrong? What is Madame Fleur like?" she kept begging. Brook's answer was always the same: "What you're doing is just perfect. Just be yourself." She made a final appeal to him two days before they finished rehearsals and left for Philadelphia, where they began their out-of-town tryout November 24, 1954. "Peter, I'm desperate, and you haven't helped me," she said. "Tell me what I'm doing wrong. If you don't, I'm not going to make a fool of myself. I'm going to play the only thing I know how to play—and that's Pearl Bailey. And then your show will be down the drain."

Brook may have realized what she meant after one of the first performances before an audience. Calling the cast together afterward, he did not waste time trying to charm or cajole. "Before I left London, somebody told me that all you blacks were a lazy, shiftless lot and that it was going to be a lot of trouble working with you," he said. "If you don't all snap to it, get it together and start giving it your best, I think you should just all be sent back to the islands, or wherever you came from!" A near-mutiny erupted, and not long after that Simon Legree–like speech, Bailey marched out of the theater, pulling her dignity around her like a great fur coat. "When Pearl walked out, Peter became insanely angry," said one production assistant. "He took it out on the girls in the chorus and kept them working for seven hours straight. It was that action that led to the Equity rule that there must be an hour-and-a-half break after five hours of rehearsal."

Pearl demanded—and "not gently," as Arlen phrased it—that Brook not only leave the theater, but leave Philadelphia as well. She was granted her first wish; stage carpenters were ordered to bar the door to him. She could not evict him from the entire city, however, and he watched performances, suggesting changes to Truman, Arlen, or Herb Ross, the young choreographer who replaced Balanchine. "Peter's ego was such that he was sure that he knew how to do everything a little bit better than everybody else," said D. D. Ryan, one of the production's assistants. "He thought he could draw a little better than Oliver Messel, the set designer; he thought he was a better musician than Harold; and he thought he could certainly fix and edit the flaws in Truman's script. Truman let him do it, until all that was left was an incomplete puzzle that could never be put back together again."

Part of Truman's own ego was a naive but indestructible belief that whoever represented him was the best at what he did, whether he was a doctor, dentist, lawyer, or stage director. He had insisted on Brook, and mountains of evidence could not persuade him that he had been wrong. If an editor had tampered with his prose, he would have smacked his hand. He had no similar confidence in his ability as a playwright, and when Brook, the expert, demanded changes, he meekly acquiesced. While they were in Philadelphia, he scarcely ever left his hotel room, writing most of the night, as he had during the filming of *Beat the Devil*, in order that his new version would be ready for rehearsal the next morning. When he did emerge, said Holder, he was white as paper. A strong producer, a Jed Harris or an Irene Selznick, might have put reins on Brook, mollified Bailey, and protected the playwright. But Saint was not a strong producer, and Brook did what he wanted.

Most of those who saw *House of Flowers* in Philadelphia liked it. But instead of getting better, as shows are supposed to do during their out-of-town trials, it got worse: each change weakened it. "The first act was very good," said Arlen, "but we didn't have a second act. We could never make it stronger, no matter how hard we tried." On December 30, opening night in New York, Arlen and Dietrich sat in the audience. Walter Winchell was four rows in front of them, and at the end of the first act he turned around and indicated his approval. "I hope he doesn't come back for the second act," Arlen whispered to Dietrich. Winchell did, and so did the other critics, who, with a few exceptions, praised Arlen's music and Messel's sets and panned Truman's script. "Mr. Capote has run out of inspiration too soon," said Walter Kerr in the *Herald Tribune*. The reviewer for *Variety* wrote perhaps the most fitting epitaph: "It's one of those shows in which everything seems to have gone wrong."

The morning after the opening, Truman, dressed in his habitual sneakers and jeans, showed up at the theater to spread some much-needed cheer. "I don't know what's happening," he complained. "They all got good reviews and I got bad ones, and I'm trying to console everybody." He never understood what had gone wrong and, then and thereafter, blamed poor Pearl, who, as good as her

word, had played Madame Fleur as if she were a nightclub performer. "I begged Saint to fire her," he said. "If he had, that show
would have been one of the most memorable things anybody ever
saw on Broadway. But she single-handedly wrecked it with her
paranoia, egomania, and insane behavior."

Still, *House of Flowers* lasted nearly five months, closing on May
22, 1955, after 165 performances. Like *The Grass Harp*, it had fanatical admirers. The last show was a sellout, which turned into what
the *Daily News* called "a ripsnorter of a wake that kept the capacity
audience in its seats until the early hours." At the end, Pearl and
Juanita Hall sat on the edge of the stage, throwing roses into the
audience. Tears rolling down her cheeks, Hall asked, "Where were
all you people last week?" When the audience finally departed, the
party moved to El Morocco. Then, his bags already packed, Truman went to the airport, on his way to a two-month vacation in
Europe.

THREE

32

ALTHOUGH he was disappointed by his two failures in the theater, Truman seemed otherwise unfazed. He may have been finished as a playwright, but he was still in demand as a writer. Indeed, he had rarely appeared more self-assured, optimistic, and high-spirited than he did in the weeks and months that followed the closing of *House of Flowers*. He had made many new friends from show business and high society—the peacocks, Jack called them—and doors were being unlocked all around him. One by one and with breathless impatience, he was opening them all. His life seemed to be exploding, so swiftly was everything happening, and yet he had never been as firmly, as confidently in control.

Most of his new friends, like so many of his old ones, were women: his rapport with the opposite sex had now flowered into perfect communion. Discovering a marvelously apt entry from the journal of a nineteenth-century romantic, he quoted it in a *Harper's Bazaar* article to express his own rhapsodic admiration of women, beautiful women: "Sat on the stone wall and observed a gathering of swans, an aloof armada, coast around the curves of the canal and merge with the twilight, their feathers floating away over the water like the trailing hems of snowy ball-gowns. I was reminded of beautiful women; I thought of Mlle. de V., and experienced a cold exquisite spasm, a chill, as though I had heard a poem spoken, fine music rendered. A beautiful woman, beautifully elegant, impresses us as art does, changes the weather of our spirit; and that, is that a frivolous matter? I think not."

Truman thought not as well. No Casanova had ever admired

lovely women more fervently or had been so fervently admired himself. He flattered them, consoled them, tried to guide their destinies. When they came to him with their problems, he could be depended on to ask the right questions and give the right answers. "That's just fine," he would say, or, "Oh, that's not good for you, honey. You shouldn't do that." Pygmalion was his favorite role, and any woman who took his advice, whatever her age or position in life, he looked upon as his protégée, a work of art that needed only his word or hand to bring her to perfection. Women delighted him, and he pleasured them in every way but one—the physical act of love.

His ability to mold and influence them was a kind of sexual power, however, and probably not the least potent kind at that. A woman might go to bed with other men, but she listened to Truman. "He would tell me things, what to wear, for instance," said Carol Marcus. "He was very smart about those things, and I don't mean in that supercilious, chic, or homosexual way at all—he really knew what was right. He thought about it and got the sense of what a person wanted to be, or how she wanted to appear, and then he helped her to achieve it. It was his way of getting close to her. He was the best pal ever, someone who would coo at you and tell you that you were wonderful. What's love? It's a mirror saying you're a perfect person."

When all else failed, he employed the most irresistible of the seducer's arts: he humbled himself and begged for love. "We were once in Copenhagen," recalled Slim Keith, one of his new, glamorous friends, who was then married to the Broadway producer Leland Hayward. "When we came back to the hotel one evening, he said, 'Let's talk.' I told him that I was so tired that I was going to get into bed, and I did.

" 'I'm gonna tuck my Big Mama in, I love her so much,' he said.

" 'Well, I love you too, Truman,' I told him.

" 'No, you don't,' he said.

" 'Yes, I do,' I replied.

" 'No. Nobody loves me. Do you have any idea what it is to be me? I'm a dwarf . . . ' And he listed all the things he thought were wrong with him. It was the most heartbreaking little monologue I've ever heard. He was testing me to see if I really cared."

She did care, of course, and her company, and the company of attractive women like her, helped to brighten the weather of his spirit—and that, most certainly, was not a frivolous matter. He sought out and became the loving mirror to a whole new group of such remarkable women. He danced with Marilyn Monroe at El Morocco, he conspired with Elizabeth Taylor to save Montgomery Clift, he talked through long nights with Jacqueline Kennedy, and he became the trusted confidant of the most regal of his armada of swans, the grand and social ladies whose very names prompted floor-sweeping salaams from headwaiters on both sides of the Atlantic.

John Huston introduced him to Marilyn Monroe early in her career, and they formed a close, if brief, bond. "By the time you get this, Marilyn M. will have married Arthur Miller," he reported to Cecil in June, 1956. "Saw them the other night, both looking suffused with a sexual glow; but can't help feeling this little episode is called: 'Death of a Playwright.' " He later picked her to play Holly Golightly in the movie version of *Breakfast at Tiffany's*, but Hollywood, which had different plans for his heroine, chose Audrey Hepburn instead. "Marilyn would have been absolutely marvelous in it," he stubbornly maintained. "She wanted to play it too, to the extent that she worked up two whole scenes all by herself and did them for me. She was terrifically good, but Paramount double-crossed me in every conceivable way and cast Audrey. Audrey is an old friend and one of my favorite people, but she was just wrong for that part."

He last saw Marilyn a few weeks before her death in 1962. "She had never looked better. She had lost a lot of weight for the picture [*Something's Got to Give*] she was going to do with George Cukor, and there was a new maturity about her eyes. She wasn't so giggly anymore. If she had lived and kept her figure, I think she would still look terrific today. The Kennedys didn't kill her, the way some people think. She committed suicide. But they did pay one of her best friends to keep quiet about their relationship with her. The friend knew where all the skeletons were, and after Marilyn died, they sent her on a year-long cruise around the world. For a whole year no one knew where she was."

Elizabeth Taylor he enjoyed for her raucous sense of humor, for what he called her "hectic allure," and for a lively intelligence that surprised him. "She's a very unusual girl, really bright. She was always finding unknown novels by well-known writers, and she would give me rather interesting, curious books. She was the first person who ever gave me a P. G. Wodehouse book to read, for example. I've seen her with three or four husbands, and Mike Todd was the only one who really knew how to handle her. He loved her, but he also knew how to say, 'Screw you!' Not long after they were married, I visited them in Connecticut, where they had a house. It was a beautiful day in early summer, and they were lying on the grass together with about ten Golden Retriever puppies climbing all over them—Elizabeth loves animals. It was my idea of perfect love.

"For some reason Todd liked that dreary little Eddie Fisher, who was like his son or younger brother. When Todd was killed in the plane crash, Fisher and Elizabeth just naturally got together. She never really loved him. I happened to be staying at the Dorchester Hotel in London when she was waiting to make *Cleopatra*, and we used to make bad jokes about him. We called him the Bus Boy. He was so boring! But I felt sorry for him too. He was so much in love with her, and she was so rude to him. I don't think I've ever seen anybody as rude as she was to him.

"That was the time she got so desperately ill that she nearly died. She had a tracheotomy, and they put a cork in her throat to plug up the hole in her windpipe. I used to take her champagne, which she wasn't supposed to have, and we hid it under her hospital bed. One night Fisher and I were leaving her room at the same time and he said, 'I'm afraid we're going to lose our girl.' Little did he know! I asked him if he'd like to have dinner, and the next day she said to me, 'You won't believe it, darling, but the Bus Boy thought you were making a pass at him!' At that moment she played a trick on me and pulled the cork out of her throat, spurting champagne all over the room. ["I thought Truman was going to pass out!" she gleefully recalled. "He turned green and sort of huddled into his sheepskin coat."]

"I spent several days and evenings with her and Richard Burton. That's when they used to sit up all night, drinking champagne. Theirs was an affair based entirely on tension. They would have terrific but at the same time sort of affectionate rows. They really riled each other up, and I always felt that they did it on purpose so that they could have a big makeup in bed. She was faithful to him, but he was never faithful to her. He flirted with everything and made dates with waitresses practically in front of her. She put up with an awful lot from him. He was terribly indiscreet. 'Oh, I'm just getting too old for him,' she would say. 'We could be perfectly happy as long as I didn't mind his running around with all these chicks. But I just can't take it.' He was obsessed with money. I don't remember ever having a conversation with him in which at least half of it was not about money. That was the career he wanted—money, money, money. He married her because he wanted to be a movie star. She loved him, but he didn't love her."

Jacqueline Kennedy he also met in the mid-fifties, when she was the wife of a glamorous but still relatively unknown senator from Massachusetts. "I used to have dinner with her and Jack when they had this awful old apartment on Park Avenue, around Eighty-sixth Street. But mostly Jack was out-of-town, and she and I would have dinner or go to the theater by ourselves. We used to sit talking until four or five o'clock in the morning. She was sweet, eager, intelligent, not quite sure of herself and hurt—hurt because she knew that he was banging all these other broads. She never said that, but I knew about it rather vaguely. What I don't understand is why everybody said the Kennedys were so sexy. I know a lot about cocks—I've seen an awful lot of them—and if you put all the Kennedys together, you wouldn't have one good one. I used to see Jack when I was staying with Loel and Gloria Guinness in Palm Beach. I had a little guest cottage with its own private beach, and he would come down so he could swim in the nude. He had absolutely nuthin'! Bobby was the same way; I don't know how he had all those children. As for Teddy —forget it.

"I liked Jack, and I liked many things about Bobby. But I wouldn't have wanted him to be President. He was too vindictive. Teddy is crazy. He's a menace. He's a wild Irish drunk who goes into terrible rages. I'd want anybody to be President before him."

Truman visited the Kennedy White House on several occasions. Andrew was present when he received his first invitation, a telephone call from Jackie asking him to what she promised would be the best party she had given since Jack was inaugurated. "Madame Queen Kennedy was talking, telling him about the evening and the music they would hear," recalled Andrew, "and suddenly Truman interrupted, 'But, Jackie! Isn't that an opera?' He was just wailing! She had told him that one of the selections would be from *The Magic Flute*. But she quickly assured him that it wouldn't go on too long and that after everyone else had left, they would go up to the private apartment."

Jack Kennedy found Truman almost as entertaining as his wife did, occasionally calling him himself. He liked to show off the detective powers of the White House operators, who were famous for their ability to find anyone anywhere; without giving them his unlisted number, he would put them to the test by asking them to ring Truman. They almost always located him, once tracking him down in Palm Springs, where he was visiting a friend who also had an unlisted number.

When their newborn son Patrick Kennedy died, Truman sent the bereaved parents flowers and a seven-line letter of condolence. "I keep thinking what power a great writer has," Jackie responded. "All the things you write move people. It is a selfish thought—but if all you have written all your life was just training to write those seven lines which were only seen by me—and Jack—I am glad you became a writer." On the first anniversary of the assassination he gave her a porcelain rose. Obviously touched, she wrote, "Dear Truman, thank you for thinking of me always—in times that are difficult for me with such beautiful things." He wrote her another letter after the murder of Bobby Kennedy in June, 1968, and she replied: "All the times of insouciance so long ago, when we all first knew each other—and now these numb, numb letters we write—"

They remained friends a year or two more, until he made the mistake of bragging about their intimacy. They were so close, he said, that she invited him into her bedroom while she was dressing to go out for the evening. That indiscretion was repeated to her, and it was enough to cause her to drop him, as she had many other people in her life. When they saw each other afterward, as they inevitably did, they spoke as if nothing untoward had occurred. But they were no longer friends.

"There is some Myth for every man," said Yeats, "which, if we but knew it, would make us understand all that he did and thought." Truman's myth can be expressed not by words but by an image: the young Nina sweeping into the fusty old house on Alabama Avenue, dazzling him with her sleek silk dresses, making him dizzy with her fragrance, then, after a day or two, driving away again, leaving him choking in a cloud of red dust, lonelier and more forlorn than if she had never come at all. To his child's eyes, she was the embodiment of sophistication, and it did not matter that by the standards of Park Avenue or Lake Shore Drive she was still a country girl, that her clothes were not really smart, or that her perfume was common and inexpensive. She was a symbol of style, and his memories of her visits helped to shape his entire life.

"Style is what you are," he was to conclude. It was not just a glittering, shiny surface; it was a Platonic ideal, a way of looking at the world and a manner of living, and all of the extraordinary women and most of the men he admired had it to one degree or another. Money could not buy it, but real style, the grand style he prized most, was nonetheless impossible unless it was watered daily from a deep well at a prominent bank. "When I was young," he confessed, "I wanted to be rich, terribly, terribly rich. My mother, after divorcing my father, married a rich man, but they were upper-middle-class rich, and that's worse than being poor. There's no taste in middle-class rich. You must be either very rich or very poor. There's *absolutely* no taste in between. I was sent to some good schools, but I hated the rich boys. They had no taste. I've always known rich people, but I was *so* aware of not being rich myself."

In fact, he was obsessed not so much by money as he was by many of those who have it. He was not interested, except in rare cases, in the Old Line rich, the ancestor-worshiping blue-bloods of Boston or Philadelphia. And he was of course bored by the vulgar rich, shopping-center magnates from Ohio and oil barons from Texas or Oklahoma. It was the other rich who fascinated him, New Yorkers mostly, but Europeans too, people of power and achievement who knew, as he himself did, the difference between what was stylish and what was merely expensive.

He looked upon those special few—the stylish rich—the way the Greeks looked upon their gods, with mingled awe and envy. He believed that money not only enlarged their lives; it also excused them from the ordinary rules of behavior—or, indeed, any rules at all. "He explained to me that when you are a very, very rich girl, you don't marry the same way a real girl marries," said Carol Marcus. "You marry the way another person travels in a foreign country. You stay there until you tire of it. Then you go elsewhere."

Like Arch, he regarded the rich as heaven's anointed, the only truly liberated people on earth. "The freedom to pursue an esthetic quality in life is an extra dimension," he explained, "like being able to fly where others walk. It's marvelous to appreciate paintings, but why not *have* them? Why not create a whole esthetic *ambiente*? Be your own living work of art?" Although he never had the cash to buy his own wings—or very many expensive paintings, for that matter—he was resolved that at the very least, he would be granted a guest membership in the celestial society of those who did.

His friend Oliver Smith likened him, not altogether whimsically, to a cat that once lived in Smith's Brooklyn Heights garden. "He was just an alley cat that wandered around the neighborhood eating whenever he could. He was thin—very, very thin—and he would stand on the porch looking wistfully into the kitchen. He was determined to get into the house, but I didn't want him. I had four other cats, which was a big enough feline population. Well, we eventually fed him on the porch, but still didn't allow him in. Finally he got himself into the kitchen, and of course now he just rules the house. He's huge! He can't get enough to eat. Truman's craving for a luxurious environment was something like that cat's."

In all the world there was no more brilliant an assemblage than the regal women Truman now called by their first names. What drew him to these elegant swans was not just their beauty, riches and style—he disliked many women who had all three. What captured his imagination, what made his favorites shine so brightly in his eyes, was a quality that was essentially literary: they all had stories to tell. Few of them had been born to wealth or position; they had not always glided on serene and silvery waters; they had struggled, schemed and fought to be where they were. They had created themselves, as he himself had done. Each was an artist, he said, "whose sole creation was her perishable self."

He installed perhaps a dozen—no more—in his pantheon of class and beauty. There was Gloria Guinness, for example, a Mexican by birth, who after years of poverty and privation had emerged triumphant as the wife of Loel Guinness, a member of one of Britain's great banking families. There was Barbara Paley, in Truman's eyes superb and unsurpassable. Like her two sisters, she had been groomed to marry wealth and had achieved her goal by becoming the wife of the founder of CBS. There was C. Z. Guest, who, rebelling against the Boston society in which she was born, had worked as a showgirl and had posed nude for Diego Rivera—the picture he painted hung for a time above the bar of Mexico City's Reforma hotel. Then, her rebellion over, she married Winston Guest, the beneficiary of ancient trust funds, and settled down to a life of parties and horses.

There was Slim Hayward (later Slim Keith), who had listened to his heartbreaking little monologue in Copenhagen. Slim was born Nancy Gross in Salinas, California. Her slimness—hence her nickname—and distinctly American beauty had so impressed Carmel Snow that during the mid-forties, Mrs. Snow had featured her in almost every issue of *Harper's Bazaar*. Howard Hawks, her first husband, had used her as the model for his screen heroines, including Lauren Bacall, and Leland Hayward was so taken with her wit and high spirits that he had divorced Margaret Sullavan to become her second husband. There was Pamela Churchill, Winston's ex–daughter-in-law, whose magnetic charms eventually lured Hayward away from Slim herself; and there was Marella Agnelli, the wife of Fiat king Gianni Agnelli and "the European swan *numero uno*," in Truman's words.

If their stories had a novelistic quality, so did his own, and the role he reenacted is familiar to readers of classical French fiction: that of the young outsider who, with nothing more than charm and the force of his personality, conquers the most elite society of the great metropolis. It was what Julien Sorel had done in Stendhal's *The Red and the Black*, what Lucien Chardon had done in Balzac's *Lost Illusions*, and what Proust's narrator, Marcel, had done in *Remembrance of Things Past*. And it is what Truman did in his own life. To his mind there could have been no better match between affection, his almost worshipful adoration of the lovely swans in whose aloof armada he now paddled, and profession: he was aware that every one of them could become a memorable character in a great work of fiction.

It was then, most probably, in that period of excited conquest in the mid- and late fifties, that he conceived of himself as the American Proust, a writer who would someday do for the modern American rich what Proust, laboring through the night in his cork-lined room, had done for the French aristocracy of the *belle époque*. In a way, he said, he regarded Proust as his mentor. Proust had not influenced his writing style—Flaubert would always be the master there—but he had set a personal example. "I always felt," Truman confessed, "he was a kind of secret friend."

Fortunately for him, his adored swans enjoyed his company as much as he enjoyed theirs. Their love of gossip was as consuming as his own, and as long as they believed themselves exempt, which they naively did, they laughed when he skewered the others in their group, and they were diverted by his considerable talent for stirring up discord—the other side of his Pygmalion complex.

Quiet bored him; he delighted in turbulence. When none existed, he would stir it up, then stand back and watch the results. "It was almost an intellectual solitaire that he played," said Slim. "He would invent something out of whole cloth, an absolute fabrication, and say, 'Did you know that X is having a walk-out with Y?' I would say, 'Oh, Truman, for God's sake! That's ridiculous!' Then I began to think about it more and wondered: is it that ridiculous? And something usually did come of his invention. Whether he willed it into being or not, I don't know. But he could cause a lot of trouble."

Over the years his tales, true and false, helped to wreck more than a few friendships and marriages, including, as it was to turn out, her own. "I can break up anybody in New York I want to," he bragged to Slim. Some of his old friends, who formerly had found his imitation of Puck endearing, now detected a spitefulness in his gossipy accounts. One of them was Newton, who, after a two-year separation, lunched with him at the Plaza in the spring of 1954. Truman's mood seemed to have soured in the interval, concluded Newton, who was so upset by their meeting that he cancelled the rest of his stay in Manhattan and fled immediately to the safety of Northampton. That night he once again confided his thoughts about Truman to his diary. "A painful time," he wrote, "so filled as it was with gossip, malice, and so much unkindliness."

When he was not busy telling stories about other people, Truman was telling them about himself. He told his new friends about his childhood, about saintly Sook and his eccentric Faulk cousins, even about his sex life. "A friend of mine once went to a dinner at which the host and hostess had just spent a weekend with Truman," said Glenway Wescott. "They were sophisticated people, but they were still talking about it with their jaws down to their chests. They said that they had never had such an experience. They had asked something about how his homosexuality started, and he sat down and told them about his first orgasm, his first childhood experience, his first older friend, and so on. I thought it was irresistibly funny. What he had discovered was that ladies in society want to know about everything."

He had also discovered that, surfeited as they were with all the pleasures that money can buy, ladies in society—and gentlemen too —were desperate for amusement. And who could provide better amusement, who had had more practice at it, than Truman? "He was a constant joy to be around in those days," recalled Eleanor Lambert, a close friend of Gloria Guinness. "Everything was fun about him. He was like a precocious child, so cute and funny; he was able to bring people's childhoods back to them. He and Gloria laughed all the time. The three of us once visited the Hotel Fontainebleau in Miami Beach, which was supposed to be the nadir of taste. Behind the bar was a giant glass wall. It was the wall of the pool, and while you were sitting at the bar, you could see what the swimmers were doing underwater. They would swim by, and though they didn't know it, we could see that they were urinating in the water! It was absolutely awful, and I wanted to leave. But Truman and Gloria thought it was hilarious. I couldn't drag them away."

Where the wives led, the husbands followed. Even those who had not read his books realized that there was more than a jester behind Truman's observant blue eyes. "He was such a mercurial, many-colored, many-sided person, like a big mirrored ball with light hitting it at different angles," said Slim. "But inside that ball was a really extraordinary mind; he was one of the three or four brightest people I've ever known in my life. His head excited me immensely! Going to lunch with him in a good restaurant was the most fun there was! But the most rewarding thing of all was to sit alone with him after dinner and just let him go. He was an adored friend."

It was a small world the stylish rich inhabited in those days. Slim was married to Leland Hayward, for instance, in the garden of the Paley estate on Long Island; the Paleys and the Guinnesses were best friends; and just about everyone had visited one Greek ruin or another on either the Guinness or the Agnelli yacht. Knowing and playing host to Truman became the fashionable thing to do. "Once he got into that part of society, he moved very fast," said Oliver Smith. "The wealthy find objects that amuse them: that's history."

He was a frequent visitor to their houses, he had a private stateroom on their yachts, and he was a privileged passenger in their private planes. He had a reserved seat by the fire, and he was there listening when the brandy was poured after dinner, when voices were lowered, hearts were opened, and secrets were passed. Spread out before him were enough plots for a hundred novels: the case histories of showgirls who became great ladies, of kept boys who inherited ducal mansions in the shadow of Notre Dame, of hushed-up society murders, and of all kinds of couplings within the sumptuous smoothness of Porthault sheets. He saw, he heard, and in the back of his mind he recorded everything. Nothing escaped him.

Yet of all the extraordinary tales that were whispered in his ear, none was more remarkable than that of the absurdly small, baby-voiced writer from Monroeville, Alabama, who, all by himself, had climbed to the very peak of golden Olympus.

Truman admired all of his swans, but the one who captured his head and heart was in some ways the loveliest of all. "The beautiful darling!" her father had called her when she was a child in Boston, and as long as she lived, that was the universal opinion of Barbara Paley—or Babe, as she was usually called. "So great is her beauty that no matter how often I see her, each time is the first time," marveled Billy Baldwin, society's favorite decorator.

Her father was Harvey Cushing, one of the most illustrious American doctors of the century. A man of enormous ambition and energy, he single-handedly transformed brain surgery from a dark and uncertain art into an exact science; in his spare time he wrote a two-volume, Pulitzer Prize–winning biography of another renowned doctor, Sir William Osler. Her mother was no less ambitious, using her own talent and energy to mold her three daughters into the kind of women who would attract the richest and most distinguished men in America.

And that is precisely what "society's three fabulous Cushing sisters," as the gossip columnists dubbed them, did—twice each. Minnie married Vincent Astor, whose family owned much of New York; she then divorced him for James Fosburgh, an artist and a member of an old Manhattan family. Betsey married James Roosevelt, F.D.R.'s son, then settled on John Hay Whitney, who was as handsome and dashing as he was rich. Babe's first marriage was to Stanley Mortimer, Jr., with whom she had two children; a model member of the American aristocracy, he was a graduate of St. Mark's and Harvard, the grandson of one of the founders of Standard Oil, and a descendant of John Jay, the first Chief Justice of the United States. By such standards, her second marriage, to William Paley, with whom she had two more children, was something of a comedown. He was rich, certainly, but he was not an American aristocrat: he was the son of a Jewish immigrant from Russia who had made his fortune manufacturing cigars.

That did not bother Babe, however, whose "immaculate quality and immense serenity"—Billy Baldwin's description again—elevated her above common feelings. All those who knew her considered her character as faultless as her beauty. She had chiseled features, dark hair, exquisitely shaped brown eyes, and a tall, slim figure that made any dress she wore look elegant. Permanently enshrined on the list of the world's best-dressed women, she made fashion news every time she walked out the door. Whatever she wore or did became instantly acceptable. When she began wearing pantsuits, they suddenly became respectable; when, in middle age, she refused to color her graying hair, smart women all over America threw out their bottles of dye.

Her only apparent defect was that she may have been too flawless to be real, more like a goddess than a creature of earth. As Truman observed in one of his notebooks: "Mrs. P. had only one fault: she was perfect; otherwise, she was perfect." Try as she might, she could not help keeping most people, including her own children, at a discreet distance. "She was warm but not tactile," said one of her closest friends. "She was not a toucher. She would never pick up and hold her children, for example, and they suffered from the lack." She was not, in fact, as confident as she appeared, nor quite as saintly. Although she professed to be embarrassed by her reputation as a stylish trendsetter, or to treat it as a joke, it meant more to her than she liked to admit, and she secretly envied Gloria Guinness, her good friend and chief rival as Queen of Chic. Gloria, she more than once pointed out to Truman, had started her career as a shill in a Mexico City nightclub.

Beautiful Babe, he discovered, was human after all, and lonely on the pedestal on which her looks and breeding had placed her. Perhaps more than any of the other swans, she needed a friend like him, someone with whom she could relax and who in turn would tell her, time and again, that she was a perfect person. "She had an icy exterior," he said, "but once you got behind that fine enamel outside, she was very warm and very young."

. . .

He met the Paleys in January, 1955, just after the opening of *House of Flowers*, when the Selznicks, David and Jennifer, were invited for a long weekend at the Paley house in Round Hill, Jamaica. "Do you mind if we bring Truman along?" David asked Bill Paley. "No, of course not," Paley replied. "It would be an honor." And so early one cold morning Truman boarded Paley's private plane and was introduced to that golden couple, Bill and Babe. Although Bill looked startled when he saw him walk into his airplane, the inevitable scarf trailing behind him, he said nothing until they were airborne. He then turned to David. "You know, when you said Truman, I assumed you meant Harry Truman. *Who* is this?"

"This is Truman Capote, our great American writer," responded David.

On such mistakes do fortunes turn. By that time Truman and Babe were already deep in conversation and had begun a friendship that was to last more than two decades, an attachment that had much of the passion but none of the complications of a sexual entanglement. "Babe looked at him and Truman looked at her, and they fell instantly in love," said Jennifer. "I had a few jealous pangs because up until that time I had been his best friend—we really did adore each other. By the time we got to Jamaica not only was Babe absolutely enchanted with him, but so was Bill. Truman was almost adopted by them. The three of them became inseparable."

From then on, wherever the Paleys went, Truman often followed. He was a frequent guest at their house in Jamaica, and then at a later warm-weather house at Lyford Cay in the Bahamas; he spent weekends at Kiluna Farm, their eighty-five-acre estate overlooking the Sound on Long Island; he went with them on other people's yachts, and he vacationed with them in Europe. Indeed, the three of them traveled the world together and, in Truman's words, "did every kind of conceivable thing. I loved them both because they were bright, they were attractive, and they were with it in every sort of way. We were a great little trio. I was really their best friend, the best friend they ever had."

That was undoubtedly the case with Babe, who was more protective of him than she probably was of her own children. "There's great beauty in his face," she said, "especially in his eyes just after he takes his specs off. They look so vulnerable." Bill was less effusive, but obviously enjoyed his company. An exception to Truman's observation that the rich are cheap, Bill was exceedingly generous, paying Truman's way on most of their travels and once even offering to buy him a house, an offer that Truman wisely but gratefully refused. Most of all, Bill was generous in giving him his wife, in allowing Truman to join them on their travels and in their homes. "He handed Babe to Truman on a silver platter," said Jack Dunphy, who knew and liked both Paleys. "It wasn't the Cushing family in Boston that made her. It was Bill. She would have been nothing if she hadn't married him, and Truman wouldn't have had much to do with her either. Whether he admitted it or not, he was attracted to money and power."

If Newton was Truman's Harvard, Babe was his Yale. Along with her sister Minnie Fosburgh, who was also devoted to him, she gave him a graduate degree in the manners and mores of the cultured rich. "He had a passion to identify with quality," said Oliver Smith. "He eagerly wanted to know how you behave in society, and Mrs. Paley and Mrs. Fosburgh educated him. They taught him about decoration, painting, and all the other things that are the intelligent result of great wealth." Truman willingly admitted as much. "Babe taught me a lot of things," he said; "how to look at a room, for instance. She showed me how to decorate by throwing things together, expensive things with cheap things from the dime store. She showed me that a room could be fun and personal, and that's the way I've decorated ever since. I taught her a lot of things too, such as how to read and how to think."

Like many women of her class and generation, Babe had ended her formal training with secondary school, just as he had, and the world of books was, by and large, terra incognita to her. He instructed her in the things in which Newton had instructed him, and in her found an equally avid pupil, who was excited to be introduced to Flaubert, Henry James, Willa Cather, Edith Wharton, and of course Proust. "[Truman's] opened up avenues for me," she said. "He made me read Proust, the whole thing."

To Truman, Babe represented the ultimate in style. She was the genuine article, everything he had once dreamed his mother was. "I was madly in love with her," he said. "I just thought she was absolutely fantastic! She was one of the two or three great obsessions of my life. She was the only person in my whole life that I liked everything about. I consider her one of the three greatest beauties in the world, the other two being Gloria Guinness and Garbo. But Babe, I think, was *the* most beautiful. She was in fact the most beautiful woman of the twentieth century, and with the single exception of Gloria, who was sort of neck-and-neck with her, she was also the most chic woman I've ever known. When I first saw her, I thought that I had never seen anyone more perfect: her posture, the way she held her head, the way she moved.

"She was the most important person in my life, and I was the most important person in hers. I was her one real friend, the one real relationship she ever had. We were like lovers; she loved me and I loved her. The only person I was ever truly in love with was her. She once joked that her analyst said that she loved me more than anyone else, more than Bill or her children, and he thought she should have an affair with me. It was one of those jokes that wasn't actually a joke. He was right; we had perfect rapport. We had an understanding: if I suspected she was feeling bad about something, no matter what time of the year it was, I would send her lilies of the valley, without any note. And she would do the same for me. She once told me that she had bought her funeral plot on Long Island and that there was a place for me, because she wanted me to be buried beside her.

"I was her sounding board and the only one who really knew her. She was the real enigma inside an enigma. She was a wonderful woman, but she also had a cold, cruel streak that nobody but me knew about. After Slim divorced Leland Hayward and married Lord Keith, who was rich—but not very, very rich—Babe said, 'Slim never quite made it, did she?' Even I, who thought I knew all the intricacies of her mind, was surprised, and for two reasons. The first was that it was surprising to hear Babe talk about someone 'making it.' The second was that Slim was one of her very best and most devoted friends. But she was deadly accurate and one hundred percent right. Slim never did quite make it in that small circle of theirs."

In matters of style, Bill Paley was also the genuine article. His taste was as assured as his wife's, and he was even more of a perfectionist. When CBS built its new headquarters on Sixth Avenue, for example, he supervised every aspect of the building's design, right down to the shape of door handles. When he created the little park that bears his name on East Fifty-third Street, he put his stamp on the smallest detail, not excluding the hot dogs that were to be sold at the concession stand. Unsatisfied with the dozens of different kinds of frankfurters he tasted, he ordered one made to his own recipe—then specified how it was to be cooked.

From early manhood, he had been accustomed to being obeyed and to getting precisely what he wanted when he wanted it. He could turn off his charm as quickly as he could turn it on. Associates who assumed they were his friends invariably learned otherwise. "I don't think I am a very easy person to know," he wrote in his memoirs. "It is my impression that although I have had a multitude of acquaintances in my life, many of whom call me friend and whom I call friend, I have had very few intimates. Apart from these few, I think I do not like the idea of depending on others. I don't feel safe."

He did feel safe with Truman, however, on whose bed he sometimes sat for long talks, like those a doting father might have with an overindulged son. "He gave me marvelous advice," said Truman. When the occasion demanded, Bill could also perform the role of the stern father. Once, recalled Christopher Isherwood, Isherwood and his lover, Don Bachardy, were booked with Truman and Bill on a flight from Los Angeles to New York. The night they were to leave, fog enveloped the airport. Looking into the gloom, Truman declared that he had a premonition of disaster, citing several examples of the terrible things that had occurred when he had had similar feelings in the past.

"In spite of all the knowledge he had of Truman and the world, Bill Paley was made just a little bit uncomfortable by all of this talk," said Isherwood. "It was getting to him, and in a tone that was both firm and paternal, the tone a colonel might use in talking to one of his men, he said: 'Truman, if you don't come on this plane tonight and if anything happens to us, you'll never forgive yourself. So you're coming!' Truman did as he was told, and finally, after hours and hours of delays, we tore along the runway and off into the fog. Suddenly, despite the fact that no one was supposed to leave his seat, he came scooting down the aisle from first class, where he and Bill were sitting, jumped into our laps, threw his arms around our necks and said, 'Are my bunnies scared?' It was, I think, the single most lovable thing I've ever seen him do."

Friends Truman and Bill remained; but as the months and years passed, their relationship became decidedly more complicated. Truman admired, liked, and respected Bill, but, given his love for Babe, he could also be jealous and resentful, afflicted by all the emotions associated with the Oedipus complex. For his part, Bill could be generous and indulgent, but Truman thought that he could also be mean and petty. "Everybody who meets Bill thinks he is Mr. Cool and that he never loses his temper about nothin'," said Truman. "That's not the person he really is. The person he really is is a highly disturbed man with a terrific inferiority complex, despite all of his success. He has a terrible temper, which nobody realizes, and Babe was scared of him.

"There was a children's wing to that big house of theirs on Long Island, and every weekend she would bring a rabbi in to see the two Paley children while the two Mortimer children were packed off to an Episcopalian Sunday school. Bill didn't know anything about it. The funny thing about him was that he was the least Jewish Jew I've ever seen. If you didn't know he was a Jew, you would never have guessed it. He usually slept late on weekends, until eleven or so, and the rabbi came at nine and was gone by ten. This went on for maybe three years. Then one day he got up early for a golf date and wandered over to the children's wing while the rabbi was holding services. Bill can walk into any room and size things up immediately, and he didn't let on for a second that he was surprised to see the rabbi there. He even sat down and talked with him for several minutes before walking out. *Then* he rushed over to the other wing. I was sitting at the foot of Babe's bed with a breakfast tray when he stormed up the stairs. I've never seen anyone so mad! 'What the hell do you mean by bringing a rabbi into this house?' he asked her.*

"He's the most jealous person I've ever known in my life—and that's saying a lot. We were in Venice once and went out to dinner with an Italian count and his wife. The count came from one of the oldest Venetian families and was very handsome and very rich. He and his wife had about seven children, but he was totally gay: it's one of those situations that can only happen in Italy. He spent the whole evening dancing with Babe on the terrace, and then she, Bill and I went back to our hotel. I could see that Bill was in an absolute rage, and when we got upstairs he said to Babe, 'That was quite an

---

* Paley denied that the rabbi's visits were arranged behind his back and in fact claimed that he had set them up through the Jewish Theological Seminary.

exhibition you put on tonight. I don't think you stopped dancing for four and a half hours while I was sitting there at the table.'

" 'Oh, Bill, don't be such a bore,' she said. 'I like him. He's sweet, he's charming, and he's a good dancer. I like to dance and you don't. It was fun. I had a good time.'

" 'There's something going on between the two of you,' Bill said.

" 'There's nothing going on between them,' I said—and then he turned on me.

" 'What the fuck would you know about it?' he asked me.

" 'Well, what the fuck I would know about it is that he's gay, and all the affairs he has are with men.'

" 'That's true, Bill,' Babe said. 'What Truman says is absolutely true.'

" 'I know a lot of guys who go around pretending that they're gay,' said Bill, 'and they're fucking everybody's wife from here to Maine. It's just an act. I don't believe he's queer at all.'

" 'Well, I can positively assure you of the fact he is,' I said, 'and I've known him a great deal longer than you have.'

"At that point he began throwing the furniture around the room, and Babe and I locked ourselves in one of the bedrooms. He tried to knock down the door and we put all kinds of furniture against it to keep him out. And he wasn't drunk! He was just in a fantastic rage! He is a very violent man. Babe and I were quite calm. In a way we were amused. We were safe and we knew that nothing too terrible was going to happen. So we just waited in the bedroom until he had exhausted himself. I think we actually fell asleep during that incredible scene.*

"Bill has the best taste of any man I've ever met, and I think he realized that Babe was 'it' so far as women are concerned. He married her because she was so chic. It wasn't because of love and I don't think it was because of her social position—though that certainly helped. To him she was the ideal woman, perfect in every way. But what he wanted was Marilyn Monroe, a sexy broad. I tried to tell her that he did love her, but she never believed me. She thought that love and sex had to go together.

"She had a love-hate relationship with him: she loved, loved, loved him and hated, hated, hated him. I have never met anybody

---

* Paley denied that this episode ever took place.

who was so desperately unhappy as she was. Twice I saved her when she tried to kill herself. One time she took pills and the other time she cut her wrists. Once she was ready to leave him, and I sat her down and said, 'Look, you don't have any money and you've got four children. Think of them. Bill bought you. It's as if he went down to Central Casting. You're a perfect type for him. Look upon being Mrs. William S. Paley as a job, the best job in the world. Accept it and be happy with it.' She cried and said, 'I've got to think it over. Let me take a nap.' She lay down and slept for a couple of hours. When she woke up, she shook herself and said, 'You're right.' And that was the end of it.

"She had one affair with a man, now dead, who had been the American ambassador to an Eastern European country. She invited me over to a restaurant on the West Side for lunch with him. Their romance lasted a few months, but she broke it off because she was afraid that Bill would find out. She had everything: beauty, chic, all the money anyone could want. But she discovered when she got it that it wasn't what she wanted. I regard her life as a great tragedy, though no one else in the world would agree with me."

Yet if Bill behaved badly toward beautiful Babe, so did Truman himself, who betrayed her trust by putting the Paleys' sex life, or, as he said, lack of it, at the top of his list of lunchtime stories. Perhaps—to make the best case for him—he thought that his disclosure would somehow diminish Bill in the eyes of his peers and gain sympathy for Babe. Or perhaps—to make the more probable case —he was such an addicted gossip that he could not resist telling a juicy story, making it clear that he was the only one to whom she had entrusted her embarrassing secret. In either event, he did her an injury, whether she knew it or not.

Whatever his motive, the reputation most tarnished by his breathless report was neither Babe's nor Bill's, but his own. "Babe made a mistake in trusting him," said one of her friends. "My husband and I had lunch with him in the early sixties, just after he had spent some time with her. He told us that Bill would no longer sleep with her and that she was greatly bothered by it. We were both horrified by his indiscretion, and my husband wanted me to tell her. But I just couldn't do that. I couldn't tell her about Truman, and I didn't want to humiliate her by saying that he had spread the intimate facts of her life from coast to coast. He didn't tell just a couple of us who were closest to her. He told everybody."

That is not the last word on Truman and the Paleys, however. Most close relationships between intelligent and strong-minded people suffer changes of temperature, heat and cold, sun and storm. And so did theirs, which was one of the most unusual combinations of all. He was their friend, their confidant, their child. He was also the sharer of all that was good and bad in their marriage. They depended on him; he depended on them. He loved Babe, and he liked Bill more than he disliked him. Through fair weather and foul, their great little trio endured for twenty years, and it was the wonder of all those who witnessed it.

An early photograph, taken beside the Paley pool in Jamaica, gives an indication of the nature of that curious alliance. Bill, the robust tycoon in his middle fifties, is in sport shirt and shorts, beaming as confidently as the sun itself. Babe, no more than forty or forty-one, is smiling radiantly, immaculate and serene. Truman, shirtless, in white trunks and a jaunty striped cap, is holding an apple and grinning impishly, as if the camera had caught him in the midst of some devilment, which he will resume the instant the shutter clicks.

No three people could have looked happier together, and on that cloudless, sun-drenched afternoon Truman might have borrowed a line from Proust himself: "Greedy for happiness, I asked nothing more from life, in such moments, than that it should consist always of a series of joyous afternoons."

34

In the spring of 1955, while *House of Flowers* was still playing, Truman made certain that he and Jack once again would be able to spend the summer by the sea. Hearing about an isolated cottage on Fire Island, he telephoned the owner. "How many of you would be staying there?" asked the man. "There would just be two of us," said Truman. The owner was dubious. "It's kind of lonely for two girls out there," he volunteered, which caused a scream of displeasure on the other end of the line. "This is Truman Capote!" A deal was soon struck, and Truman was able to leave for Europe with some of his new fancy friends. From Venice—which to Truman of course meant Harry's Bar—Angelo, the headwaiter, dispatched a touching note to Jack. "Dear Mr. Jack," he said. "We miss you, and wish you were here with our beloved Mr. Truman."

By July 6, when he joined Mr. Jack and the two dogs on Fire Island, Truman was rested and eager to begin writing once more. At least some good had come from all his wasted efforts in the theater: he now knew what road his career should take. Bob Linscott had been right all along; his talent did shine brightest on the printed page. An apostate no longer, he worshiped once again at the altar of prose. "Now, true to my word, I've settled down to work," he wrote his old editor, "and hope that I will have something interesting to show you come September."

The something interesting was the novella that he had already titled *Breakfast at Tiffany's*. Before he could get very deeply into it, his attention was diverted anew, however, this time not by the theater, but by a form of prose that had long excited him: journalism. For years he had wanted to test his skills at it, and now Harold Arlen suggested an almost irresistible subject. Arlen's friend Robert Breen was the director of a company, the Everyman Opera, that had performed George Gershwin's opera, *Porgy and Bess*, around the world. At Christmastime, Arlen said, Breen's mostly black troupe was going to make its most daring expedition of all. Taking advantage of a thaw in the Cold War, it was going to carry the Stars and Stripes into the center of the enemy camp, becoming the first American company to perform in the Soviet Union since the Bolshevik Revolution. Truman should go along, the composer said, and write an account of the group's adventures. Truman agreed; *Breakfast at Tiffany's* would have to wait.

The New Yorker, which promised to publish the story he brought back, paid his expenses; Babe Paley presented him with cold-weather gear from Abercrombie & Fitch; and to repel the fierce Arctic winds, he bought himself a yellow cashmere scarf, three or four times the ordinary width. All bundled up, "he looked just like a little bunny," said one of Breen's troupe. Thus attired, he crossed from West Berlin to East Berlin on December 19, 1955. There, along with more than ninety other nervous Americans, he boarded the *Blue Express* which was to convey them to the frozen heart of Muscovy: first to Leningrad, where *Porgy* was to open the day after Christmas; then to Moscow itself, where performances were scheduled to begin January 10, 1956.

Breen, his wife, Wilva, and most other members of their hardy band regarded their trip as a historic event that would raise the Iron Curtain for further Soviet-American cultural exchanges. The Russians seemed to share their hopeful opinion. "Your visit is a step forward in the march toward peace," proclaimed their chief host, a representative of the Ministry of Culture. "When the cannons are heard, the muses are silent; when the cannons are silent, the muses are heard."

But Truman was not interested in writing an account of a historic event; indeed, he was probably constitutionally incapable of such a portentous undertaking. Almost immediately, probably before the *Blue Express* had left the East Berlin station, he realized that in Breen's history-making enterprise there was also material ideally suited to his comedic talents. Writing later, he said that he imagined *The Muses Are Heard*, which is what his chronicle was titled, as a brief comic novel. "I wanted it to be very Russian, not in the sense of being reminiscent of Russian writing, but rather of some Czarist *objet*, a Fabergé contrivance, one of his music boxes, say, that trembled with some glittering, precise, mischievous melody."

It was in that spirit of mischief that he observed his fellow travelers, beginning with the performers themselves, who were exuberant, uninhibited and, not unpredictably, more concerned about getting ahead than in improving East–West relations. Truman shared a compartment with two of them, Earl Bruce Jackson and Helen Thigpen, who planned to be married in Moscow. "Bound to be a big story," predicted Jackson, who had purchased a special wedding suit, brown tails with champagne satin lapels, before he left Germany. "The first couple of Negro Americans married in Moscow. That's front page. That's TV."

Next Truman cast his eye on the Breens, who viewed their role as cultural ambassadors with exaggerated gravity, and on Leonard Lyons, the columnist of the *New York Post*, who, in an unconscious parody of the old-fashioned newshound, saw banner headlines everywhere he looked. Despite a serious space squeeze aboard the train, Lyons commandeered an entire compartment for himself, evicting his erstwhile roommates. "I can't write with a lot of characters sitting around," he announced. After Lyons, Truman shifted his gaze to the wife of *Porgy*'s coauthor, Mrs. Ira Gershwin, in whom he saw a flighty *arriviste* who indiscriminately sprinkled her speech with such terms of endearment as "darling" and "love" and who never appeared, even at breakfast, without her diamonds.

Finally, with far more affectionate amusement, he examined Breen's secretary, Nancy Ryan, who also shared his compartment. A tall blonde, three years out of Radcliffe, she was the ideal Capote woman, bright, brash, and somewhat scatty. By curious coincidence she possessed many of the traits of Holly Golightly, the heroine of *Breakfast at Tiffany's*. She was also almost as attractive as her mother, Mrs. William Rhinelander Stewart, one of Manhattan's most famous society beauties. When she had read *Other Voices* as a teenager, Nancy had shown her mother the picture of the author reposing on the dust jacket. "I think he looks capable of deviltry," that formidable woman had said. Watching Truman watching everyone else, a worried Lyons had the same impression. Taking Nancy aside, he asked, "Is Truman planning something really evil?"

Truman is also a protagonist in *The Muses Are Heard*, which he wrote in the first person, as he did all of his comic, sunlit works. He injects himself so far as to note that his presence caused stares on Soviet streets, but he leaves the reader with the impression that any American would have received the same attention. Of all those who reviewed the book, only the English critic Kenneth Tynan, who knew him, guessed that the Russians were not staring at just any American, but at one in particular. "I think it only fair to point out," Tynan wrote in the London *Observer*, "that his somewhat unusual appearance—elfin, diminutive and extravagantly animated—has often created similar commotions in his native land."

If he was not wearing his yellow stole, Truman was trailing the flaming red scarf that Lenore Gershwin had given him, or covering his head with it, as if it were a babushka. On at least one occasion pedestrians tittered when he walked by. "Laugh, you dreary people," he replied. "But what will you do for laughs next week, when I'm gone from here?" One day Breen was talking with his Russian hosts in the lobby of Leningrad's Astoria Hotel, where the company was staying, when Truman appeared at the top of the operatically grand marble staircase. Conversation stopped in mid-sentence. Mesmerized, the Russians followed his stately descent. Without giving any indication that he even knew he was being observed, much less that he was being spotlighted, Truman walked majestically past them and through the revolving door. Then, just when they thought they had seen the last of him, he reappeared, having made a full circle with the door, kicked up his right heel in their direction and disappeared for good. After that eloquent exit, there was a long silence, which was broken at last by the somber man from the Ministry of Culture: "Ve have them like that in the Soviet Union, but ve hide them."

Not everyone laughed or stared at him. Although none of his work had been translated into Russian, his writing had been read surreptitiously by a few people, who greeted him with discreet enthusiasm. His most ardent fan, an English professor at the University of Leningrad—Boris the Bunny, Truman called him—took him drinking. That night Nancy found them sprawled in Truman's hotel room, which was connected to hers by a common bathroom. "Found them totally potted in his room, both of them somewhat disheveled," she wrote in her diary. "Incoherent tales of vodka, caviar, 'the most absolutely *divine* restaurant.' Morning after, T crawled into my bed and was fed Alka-Seltzer. Felt ghastly all day." Describing Boris to Newton, Truman said he was "witty and charming and fun: qualities rarer than platinum in the Soviet."

In Moscow he addressed the Soviet Union of Writers, declaring that his primary concern as a writer was not content but style. In the Soviet Union, replied the head of the union, the order was supposed to be reversed. "We think every poem and song should be a bullet and a banner," he said. "I was *quite* silenced by that," Truman told reporters when he returned to New York.

He was also taken up by the sons and daughters of prominent members of the Soviet hierarchy. "His contact was a young man named Victor," said Nancy. "Truman referred to him, very frivolously, as his Moscow beau. He was a rich, good-looking layabout who came up to him at the theater one night and introduced himself in perfect English. The next afternoon Truman got a mysterious call telling him to be in his room at three thirty. He was then picked up —I was furious with envy because I wasn't asked—and driven to an elegant Southern-style mansion where the Russian jet set was out in force. It turned out that Truman was a great sort of literary figure to these young people, and they took him to their dachas, where he saw that they all subscribed to *The New Yorker* and led a very Westernized life. 'Only in a culture where refinement is valued do trousers narrow,' said Victor, who was trying to look Western, but didn't quite pull it off. One of his friends, referring to ordinary Russians, said, 'The humbles are so dreary.' That was such a wonderful expression! 'The humbles are so dreary.' "

There was also time for Truman to indulge his lifelong passion for what Lyons called "foul-smelling, vile places," and he organized a pub-crawling tour with Lyons, Nancy, and Priscilla Johnson, a Russian-speaking Radcliffe classmate of Nancy's who served as interpreter. "We kept telling her to tell the taxi driver that we wanted a real low dive, not a tourists' nightclub," said Nancy. "Finally we passed a bar and Truman said, 'There's our place.' Just as he said it, the door opened and a huge female bouncer threw a drunk into the street. So that's where we went."

In the career of every writer, even one who complains as often and as vocally as Truman did about the pain of putting words on paper, there is a book that seems to write itself, a magical moment when the ink rolls from his pen as smoothly as Old Man River. For

Truman that book was *The Muses Are Heard*, and that moment began as the *Blue Express* started its slow journey across the plains of Eastern Europe. Looking back, he said, "*The Muses Are Heard* is the one work of mine I can truly claim to have enjoyed writing, an activity I've seldom associated with pleasure."

What made his task so easy, what gave him such pleasure, was the tone of the writing, which mirrored his lunchtime conversation at its best—observant, gossipy, bitchy, and always entertaining. The Breens hoped that he would concentrate only on high matters; he was more interested in the low. He was an eavesdropper, and he recorded the things people actually said, not the things they wanted history to believe they had said. That style of reporting—the New Journalism, as it came to be called a decade later—is common now, but it was fresh and unusual then. Truman was not the first to experiment with it. Indeed, he was encouraged, if not inspired, in his effort by the example of Lillian Ross, who pioneered the technique in two earlier, much-celebrated *New Yorker* pieces, "Portrait of Hemingway" and *Picture*, her narrative of the making of John Huston's film *The Red Badge of Courage*. But Truman went a step further. To her skills as a reporter, he added the craft of the novelist, who gives shape and structure to the facts he has gathered.

Like many later New Journalists, he took substantial liberties for the sake of lively reading, sometimes changing the order of events and occasionally bringing separated episodes together. In one case, he even invented a whole scene—a hilarious encounter in the Brest-Litovsk railroad station—and fabricated, or made composite figures of, some of his characters. "He fiddled with things," said Nancy Ryan. "But he didn't destroy basic truth or genuine spirit at all."

Although several of those who made the journey with him across the steppes were offended by his portrayals, no one offered evidence to dispute Nancy's assertion. Lyons, who felt most wounded, devoted a column to a refutation of some of the silly comments attributed to him; but to judge from the fatuous dispatches Lyons actually did send home, he was probably not misquoted in any substantial way. He retaliated by hitting Truman where he thought it would hurt most, by using his column to shower Gore Vidal with favorable publicity. Truman ignored the columnist's many flattering references to his favorite enemy until one day Lyons said that the remarkable Gore had written sixteen books—"and he's not yet thirty."

Truman instantly phoned to correct him. "He's thirty-TWO!" he shrieked.

The Muses Are Heard, a relatively short work of about 52,000 words, appeared in two issues of *The New Yorker* in October, 1956; Random House published it in hard cover at the end of the year. The critics, for once, were almost unanimous in their praise, regarding it, as Truman did, as an amusing bauble, "wicked, witty and utterly devastating," in the words of one reviewer.

After returning to New York at the end of February, 1956, Truman went back to Europe, where he spent several weeks working on *The Muses Are Heard* in Peggy Guggenheim's Venetian palazzo. "He was very keen on keeping his line and made me diet also," she said. "Every night he took me to Harry's Bar and made me eat fish." He was back in Manhattan in early May, and in mid-June he and Jack set up housekeeping by the ocean again, this time in Stonington, a Connecticut seaport. "You would adore it," he told Cecil. "The most beautiful trees and old houses. We have a huge, rather amusing house with wonderful views."

It did not take long, however, for both him and Jack to discover that they did not in fact adore it. There was no beach for swimming; most of their neighbors were elderly; and pugnacious Kelly was in constant combat with the town's other dogs, one of which locked its teeth so deeply into Truman's hands that they had to be swathed in bandages. In that otherwise placid setting he and Jack also went to war, a half-serious, half-comic battle in which Truman, for a change, was the aggressor.

"It was the greatest quarrel we ever had," he recalled, "and it was over Medaglia d'Oro coffee! Jack had a passion for Medaglia d'Oro coffee, but there was no Medaglia d'Oro coffee in Stonington. One day I was going to do errands in Providence, Rhode Island, which was not far away, and he said, 'Don't come back until you get Medaglia d'Oro coffee!'

" 'Sure,' I replied, thinking, 'My God, of course they're going to have Medaglia d'Oro coffee in Providence.' But I went to seven or eight places there, and not only did they not have Medaglia d'Oro coffee, but they had never heard of Medaglia d'Oro coffee! Of course the first thing Jack said when I came back was 'Where's my Medaglia d'Oro coffee?'

" 'I'm sorry,' I said, 'but they didn't have it. I went to several places.'

" 'You didn't go to a single one,' he said. 'You forgot it! You don't care!' There are certain things that happen in a relationship that lasts a long time, tensions that accumulate. I don't lose my temper very often, but when I do, watch out! When he said that, I became furious. I went through that house systematically, throwing things around. He was in a state of terror because he had never seen me like that." A peace treaty was soon signed, and for the rest of the summer Jack drank ordinary coffee.

One of the paradoxes of Truman's character was that although he was as fond of luxury as a Roman emperor, he usually lived, without quibble or complaint, as simply as a Trappist monk. In the nearly eight years he and Jack had been together, they had moved around like gypsies, without a permanent address in either New York or Europe. Almost all their residences, including the Fontana Vecchia, had been spartan in the extreme; some had been primitive. Their current Manhattan apartment, for instance, two floors in a moldering town house on East Sixty-fifth Street, lacked a component as essential as central heating.

Now, as his thirty-second birthday approached, Truman wanted an apartment that had at least the basic comforts, a place he could call his own and decorate in the way Babe had taught him. He wanted to be able to entertain, as well as to be entertained. It was probably no coincidence that Holly Golightly—*Breakfast at Tiffany's* was still much on his mind—had similar yearnings for permanence and stability. "In some part of his nature he was trying to find a home," said Oliver Smith. "Where I don't know."

The immediate and mundane answer was Oliver's own house in Brooklyn Heights. Built before the Civil War, it contained as much space, nearly twenty rooms, as a small hotel and had a basement that Oliver had already begun turning into an apartment. In mid-May he invited Truman and Jack for dinner and an inspection. They were delighted with what they saw. The basement apartment that he planned to rent had a large living room, a parlor, a small kitchen, and two bedrooms, one of which had windows and a door opening onto the backyard, where a giant purple wisteria was in fragrant bloom. "I'd like to live here if I could have this room," Jack declared, and his wish was granted. "We're very excited," he wrote Mary Louise. "Truman wants to make 'a beautiful home.' "

Overjoyed at the prospect of settling down at last, Truman spent much of the summer searching Connecticut for bric-a-brac and furniture, which he then refinished in their Stonington backyard. "He saw a lamp in an antique shop he wanted," Jack reported to his sister Gloria. "The woman said she couldn't sell it—it didn't even belong to her: she kept it because it made the shop cheery. A big correspondence then began between Truman and the *real* owner. Anyway, Truman got the lamp. He bought me an old brass bed for eleven dollars for my birthday—and is painting and polishing it!"

In time, Oliver's basement did become a beautiful home. Truman asked Billy Baldwin for advice. Taking advantage of its darkness, rather than trying to overcome it with bright colors, Baldwin picked out a dark green wallpaper, which, combined with bright lights and glittering appointments—such as Battersea boxes, a Fabergé pillbox, and a pair of gold mirrors in the shape of butterflies—created an atmosphere of perpetual Christmas, of winter by the fire. Oliver was willing to lend his own dining room for formal entertainment, and Babe and her sister Minnie visited often, as did Jackie Kennedy and her sister, Lee Radziwill. When Oliver said he would like to meet Jackie, Truman arranged a lunch in Oliver's dining room. Only later did Oliver learn that Truman had told her, or at least had strongly implied, that the whole house was his. "She laughed about it," said Oliver, "because suddenly in the middle of lunch she got the idea that it wasn't his. I suppose I acted as if it were mine."

Unlike most of the rest of Brooklyn—or most of Manhattan, for that matter—the Heights still retained the leisurely and capacious feeling of nineteenth-century New York. Truman made friends with the shopkeepers; strolled the nearby Promenade, with its stunning views of Wall Street and the harbor; and snooped around the ships that docked below. As extensively as he had traveled, he still could not untangle the New York subway system; when he crossed the river to Manhattan, it was almost always by taxi. However far he wandered, he was always glad to return to the bright yellow house at 70 Willow Street. "Home! And happy to be," was the way he concluded a description of his life there. "I love Brooklyn Heights," he told a reporter. "It's the only place to live in New York."

——

THE success of *The Muses Are Heard* had made him eager to do more journalism, and a little over a year after he had boarded the *Blue Express*, Truman set off again in hopes of repeating his Russian triumph. Though his destination was the Far East, his subject was similar: another American company trying to open doors to an alien society. Shortly after New Year's, 1957, Warner Brothers was to begin shooting a big-budget movie called *Sayonara* in Japan's ancient imperial capital, Kyoto. Set during the Korean War, the film was to have as its theme the cultural clash between Orient and Occident; playing its lead, an ace American fighter pilot, would be one of the world's biggest stars, Marlon Brando.

As soon as he heard about the Warners' project, Truman realized that the cultural clash depicted in the script could not be half as entertaining as that between Hollywood and Nippon, or between director Joshua Logan and the temperamental and reclusive Brando. A comic novel was again what he had in mind—a Japanese box lacquered in brilliant red, perhaps—and without leaving Willow Street, he could see boundless possibilities for his deadpan brand of satire. Although they were sparing neither time nor money to ensure that *Sayonara* accurately reflected Japan and its people, the filmmakers saw nothing incongruous, for example, in asking Audrey Hepburn to play Brando's Japanese lover or in hiring a Mexican, Ricardo Montalban, to assume the part of a famous Kabuki performer. (Hepburn declined, predicting that audiences would laugh at her, and a Japanese-American was chosen in her stead.) *The New Yorker*, which hoped for a sequel to his Russian adventures, gave its blessing, Cecil

Beaton agreed to keep him company, and on December 27, 1956, Truman and Cecil left for the Land of the Rising Sun.

Almost instantly things began to go wrong. In San Francisco, their first stop, Truman somehow got his head stuck in an elevator door of the St. Francis Hotel. It was extracted undamaged, but when he reached Honolulu, their second stop, he had to wait three days for his baggage to be found. Then, just as they were preparing to depart for Tokyo, he and Cecil both discovered that they had neglected to procure Japanese visas, without which they could remain in the country only three days. To stay longer, they would have to fly to Hong Kong, obtain visas there, and then return. When they reached Tokyo, Truman telephoned Logan in Kyoto and received the worst news yet: Logan did not want him to write about the film at all and planned to bar him from the set. "Of all the hypocrites!" Truman hissed to Cecil as he hung up the phone.

There obviously had been a misunderstanding, but whose fault it was is still not clear. The Logans knew he was coming. Nedda Logan, who had closely followed her husband's production, had even invited him to lunch at the end of November to give him background. But Josh Logan did not want a visitor with such big ears on his set, and he professed to be outraged by *The Muses Are Heard*. "It treated human beings like bugs to be squashed underfoot," he wrote in his memoirs. "And Truman would have even juicier fodder to chew on with us. Boorish Hollywood invades Japan, and with golden ladies' man Marlon Brando. I knew from his conversation at many parties that he had it in for Brando and wanted to shatter his powerful image. Both Bill [producer William Goetz] and I called *The New Yorker* and complained vehemently. We also wrote letters through our lawyers. But with all our protests, I had a sickening feeling that what little Truman wanted, little Truman would get."

Logan did not make his protests until the end of December, however, and it may be that Truman and Cecil were already on their way; or that in the usual holiday confusion, *The New Yorker* had failed to pass on the bad news; or that Truman knew but, given his genial lunch with Nedda, thought that he could change her husband's mind. In any event, having traveled so far and having promised a story to *The New Yorker*, he was more determined than ever to get his story. Impressed as always by his "courage & incredible fighting qualities," Cecil wrote in his diary: "His assurance is deep-seated. His brain is twice life-sized. His memory unfailing. His curiosity boundless. A foreign country in no way inhibits him. Within a few moments of arrival here he had telephone operators buzzing. New friends had become old friends automatically. (The preliminaries of friendship do not exist with him.) Without seeming to see, he finds his way down the labyrinthine corridors of the hotel, knows his way about town & knows where the martinis are best."

In the seventy-two hours between landing and leaving, Truman saw much of Tokyo, got drunk on sake, and met the novelist and playwright Yukio Mishima, who greeted him as a comrade. In fact, he and Truman had much in common. They were almost exactly the same age, they were both homosexual, and they had both achieved early renown. On January 6, 1957, Mishima took him and Cecil to a Kabuki performance, then backstage to meet the leading player. The following night he entertained them at a restaurant and guided them through a red-light district.

What seemed like a natural friendship did not develop much further. Mishima came to the United States in the summer of 1957 and later complained that Truman had not reciprocated his hospitality. Truman denied the charge. "I *was* nice to him," he maintained. "He said he wanted to suck a big white cock. (I don't know why people always think I can fix them up. I'm not really in the pimping business—though actually I do know a lot of people.) I telephoned a friend of mine, and he did go out with Mishima. But Mishima never called to thank me and he never paid the boy."

In the seventies, a few years after Mishima's public act of hara-kiri, Truman was much perturbed by a biography of Mishima in which Mishima confidently predicted Truman's own suicide. "Reading something like that really brings you up short when you're in bed late at night," said Truman. "I don't know why he said that. We never talked about suicide, and I certainly had no idea that *he* would commit suicide. He seemed like the last person who would do such a thing."

The problems with visas caused a reversal of schedule, and instead of returning immediately to Tokyo, Truman and Cecil spent two weeks in Hong Kong, Thailand, and Cambodia, which originally had been the last stops on their itinerary. They did not enjoy themselves. Tokyo had struck Truman as "an ugly Oriental Toledo," while Bangkok staggered him with its heat—even the dogs did not have enough energy to bark, he observed. He and Cecil were cordially received by Bangkok society—rich Thais and Western expatriates—but he was nonetheless delighted to leave. "Bless Jesus I don't live there," he jotted in his journal. At the haunted ruins of Angkor Wat Cecil was annoyed by the presence of a group of American tourists. "Absolute swine," he called them. "How vomitous!" he added when their late-night carousing kept him awake.

Besides Angkor Wat, only Kyoto, which they at last reached on January 23, excited genuine enthusiasm. "A delightful city of wide avenues and narrow alleys, shopping arcades and some 200 (I think more) bars—where there is a girl for every customer," wrote Truman. "Kyoto is nearest to seeming what I thought Japan would be like." Unfortunately, Logan and his *Sayonara* associates continued to rebuff his efforts to write about them. Reluctantly and without telling anyone but Cecil—his revenge was to keep everyone else guessing—he abandoned the project. Articles can be written without help from those involved, but his was not one of them; Truman required a favored position from which he could see and hear what was going on. And that, clearly, he was not going to get.

As he wandered those narrow alleys over the next several days, a new enterprise took hold of his mind. "Am intrigued," he wrote, "with an idea for a thriller-novel." Having seen all the sights he wanted to see, he scarcely moved from his hotel for three days while he jotted down a five-page outline of an East–West spy story. Titled *Monkeys and Old Stone*, it would be set in Kyoto, Hong Kong, and Angkor Wat—almost all the places he had just been, in other words. "It is fascinating to watch his mind at the work of creation," the ever-admiring Cecil observed in his diary. "He has so much knowledge about such a wide number of subjects that his possibilities are tremendous." Truman was so excited, in fact, that he decided to stay an extra week in Kyoto, so that he could saturate himself in the atmosphere of that most Japanese of all Japanese cities.

It was during those days in the first week of February that his luck abruptly changed and his story on *Sayonara* sprang back to life. Logan had stopped him from following the making of the movie, but he could not prevent him from talking to his star, whom Truman knew from New York. "Don't let yourself be left alone with Truman," Logan had warned Brando. "He's after you." But Brando, who loathed interviews and interviewers—"My soul is a private place," he declared—invited Truman to dinner in his hotel suite nonetheless, simply to be polite. "He didn't know that I was going to do a whole piece about him," said Truman. "How could he? I didn't know either."

But like many other normally reticent people, once he started to speak, Brando could not stop. "What an experience," Truman wrote in his diary afterward. "And how he loves to talk—and *such* a vocabulary: he sounds like an 'educated Negro'—very anxious to display all the long words he's learned. He talked, non-stop, from 7:15 until 12:30 in the morning." Truman quickly realized that he had struck oil. Not only did he refrain from capping that gusher, but he did his best to keep him spouting, by trading confidence for confidence, as he had done so often before.

"The secret to the art of interviewing—and it is an art—is to let the other person think he's interviewing you," he later explained. "You tell him about yourself, and slowly you spin your web so that he tells you everything. That's how I trapped Marlon." With rue and regret, Brando later confirmed that that was what had taken place. "The little bastard spent half the night telling me all his problems," he told a friend. "I figured the least I could do was tell him a few of mine."

No subject was spared. One of their mutual friends had bragged that Brando had gone to bed with him. "I asked Marlon and he admitted it. He said he went to bed with lots of other men, too, but that he didn't consider himself a homosexual. He said they were all so attracted to him. 'I just thought that I was doing them a favor,' he said." Knowing that Brando's mother had been an alcoholic, he described his own problems with Nina. That confession induced Brando to describe in detail the torture of watching his own mother break apart in front of his eyes like a piece of porcelain until "one day I could just step right over her, her lying on the floor, and not feel a thing, not give a damn." In his journal, Truman added his own poignant postscript: "How well I understand that."

Brando enjoyed their joint confessional—he told his makeup man so the next day—but he soon learned something most of Truman's friends already knew: Truman could not keep a secret. *Monkeys and Old Stone* was put aside, never again to be picked up, as Truman succumbed to the thrill of a scoop and the delight of thumbing his nose at Josh Logan. "Oh, you were so wrong about Marlon not being gossipy," he gleefully informed him. "He talked his head off." He undoubtedly told others as well of Brando's garrulousness, and word eventually got back to the star, who, belatedly realizing that he had been tricked, responded on May 16.

"Here, of course, is the inevitable communication," Brando began, in a letter that he apparently both wrote and typed himself: it is full of misspellings, curious uses of words, and unique grammatical constructions. It was vanity alone that had deluded him into believing that they were exchanging private confidences in Kyoto, Brando said. But his "unutterable foolishness" was now clear to him. "It is, indeed, discomforting to have the network of one's innards guywired and festooned with harlequin streamers for public musing, but, perhaps, it will entertain . . . In closing let me just say, I am sorry, in a way, that you didn't complete your plans for the full travesty you had planned to do because it has come full upon me that there are few who are as well equipped as yourself to write, indeed, the comedy of manners."

Truman's Brando profile, "The Duke in His Domain," appeared in *The New Yorker* the following November and caused every bit as much comment as Truman had hoped it would. A "vivisection," Dorothy Kilgallen called it; Walter Winchell said it was "the type of confession usually confined to an analyst's couch." They were both right. Word for word, Truman repeated much of what Brando had told him: his inability to love or trust anyone, his contempt for acting, the scars left by his mother's alcoholism. It was the public disclosure of that last memory that apparently upset Brando most. His soul could not have been more public if it had been on exhibition at Madame Tussaud's.

"I'll kill him!" he shouted to Logan.

"It's too late, Marlon," said Logan, who could not resist an I-told-you-so. "You should have killed him before you invited him to dinner."

Despite the unhappiness it caused, "The Duke in His Domain" is a remarkable work of journalism, displaying Truman at his shrewdest. A few days before publication, William Shawn congratulated him: "Thank you for writing this piece—or, to come right out with it, masterpiece."

On February 8, a few days after his night with Brando, Truman and Cecil left Japan for Honolulu, where Cecil overlooked his dislike of most things American long enough to pick up two sailors. It was a mistake, as Truman tried to tell him, and around midnight Cecil phoned Truman's hotel room in great distress: the sailors were trying to rob him. Truman rushed to his rescue, and his arrival frightened them away. "Cecil blew them each twice and then he did something incredibly dumb," he said. "As they were getting ready to leave, one of them said to him, 'Aren't you going to give us something for this?'

" 'So you're those kinds of guys!' Cecil replied, and that got them mad. They started picking up all of his photographic equipment and throwing it into bags. That's when he called me. I ran up the stairs without even thinking, and they ran down, pushing me aside." Though they managed to get away with his watch and a camera, Cecil was unrepentant. "He enjoyed it so much," Truman recalled, "that he said he would do it all over again." The two travelers parted company two days later when Cecil flew back to San Francisco and then New York. Truman remained in Honolulu for a few more days in the sun, then did the same. On his way through San Francisco, he had one more encounter, a bittersweet rendezvous with a voice from the past, from his adolescence and the secret trips he and Phoebe used to take from Greenwich to Manhattan. "Went to a small boite to see Billie Holiday," he wrote in his journal. "She was soaked in gin (or something) and her voice is gone. So sad."

36

IN the summer of 1957 Truman and Jack joined with Oliver Smith to rent a huge Victorian beach house in the Long Island village of Bridgehampton, midway between the more fashionable resorts of Southampton and East Hampton. Built on stilts, the house was named Sailaway, and at high tide, when the waves swirled under it, it did look as if it were about to sail away. They worked hard in that house in the surf: Oliver was busy with various stage designs, Jack, who had caught Truman's theatrical fever, was trying to put together a play, and Truman was returning to *Breakfast at Tiffany's*.

Even as he was concluding the adventures of Holly Golightly, Truman was thinking about a new venture into journalism, however, a profile of the pampered, privileged, and thoroughly Westernized young people he had met in Moscow. No one had ever written about them—few Western reporters probably even knew of their existence—and yet he, who spoke no Russian and knew very little about the Soviet Union, was in a position to do so.

"Everybody in the West seemed to be so fantastically naive about Russia," he said, "as though it were different from any other country. Well, it basically isn't, because human nature is what it is. The people I knew weren't all that much younger than I was. They were very hip, with it; they even had their own club in the Hotel National, which is right on Red Square. I decided I wanted to write a piece on this other Moscow, this whole other country they lived in." It was an opportunity he could not pass up, and once again he approached Mr. Shawn, who gave him the blessing of *The New*

Yorker and a check for expenses. Shortly after the beginning of the new year, 1958, he bundled up and made his second trip to frigid Muscovy.

This time he went in style. Slim was his companion, and joining them on various segments of their journey were Cary Grant, who was shooting a picture in London, and Sam Spiegel, the producer of such movie epics as *Doctor Zhivago* and *The Bridge on the River Kwai*. "As he had been there before, Truman knew the terrain, as well as some people," said Slim. "He was a wonderful eye, like a child lying on the grass and seeing a whole jungle in it." In Moscow he spent much of his time by himself. When he had obtained the information he needed, he and Slim went on to Leningrad and then Denmark, where he introduced her to one of his literary icons, Baroness Karen Blixen, or Isak Dinesen, as she was known to most of the world.

Isak Dinesen had many admirers, but Truman was among the most devoted. *Out of Africa*, her memoir of her life as a coffee planter in the highlands of Kenya, he regarded as one of the finest books of the century. At some point, perhaps on his earlier trip to Russia, he had visited the fragile baroness at Rungstedlund, her house on the Baltic Sea, and they had charmed each other: two exotic creatures from different worlds and generations, both self-made. "I am really three thousand years old, and have dined with Socrates," she once said, probably only half in jest.

When he knew her, she was in her early seventies, but in fact looked much older, emaciated by years of illness. " 'I have such a longing for darkness,' she told me. 'You know, I've only been staying alive for the last two years because I want to get the Nobel Prize.' That took me down quite a lot, because she was such a fabulous, marvelous woman and a great artist, and if ever I have known anyone who was above any kind of nonsense like that it was Isak Dinesen. But she really wanted the prize." When he visited her with Slim, she served a high tea and asked many questions: she was planning her first trip to America and wanted to know everything.

She was the last person he would have wanted to hurt, but, quite inadvertently, he did later that year with the publication of *Observations*, a book of Richard Avedon photographic portraits for which he wrote his own portraits in prose. He meant his short profile of her to be flattering, and to most readers that is how it must have sounded. "Time has reduced her to an essence, as a grape can become a raisin, roses an attar," he wrote. "Quite instantly, even if one were deprived of knowing her dossier, she registers as *la vraie chose*, a true somebody. A face so faceted, its prisms tossing a proud glitter of intelligence and educated compassion, which is to say wisdom, cannot be an accidental occurrence; nor do such eyes, smudges of kohl darkening the lids, deeply set, like velvet animals burrowed into a cave, fall into the possession of ordinary women."

Unfortunately, he proceeded downward from her eyes to her lips, which he described as twisting "in a sideways smile of rather paralytic contour." That description, along with Avedon's photographs, one of which showed only her veined and gnarled hands, wounded her, and she wrote Truman to complain of his unkindness and lack of generosity. She considered reneging on her commitment to write the preface to the Danish edition of *Breakfast at Tiffany's*, deciding in the end that it would be mean and vindictive to break her promise. "But I wrote it with bitterness in my heart because of his ungallant treatment of me," she said.

Yet she was, as he had said, not an ordinary woman, and by the time Cecil made the pilgrimage to Rungstedlund, shortly before her death in 1962, she had forgiven him. "He's a nice chap and a good writer and he's improving all the time," she told Cecil. "His last books are the best. Tell him that I have evaporated my spite and that I wrote a preface for his last book *[Breakfast at Tiffany's]* translated into Danish. He's a friend and I'm fond of him. Give him my love."

Breakfast at Tiffany's had taken longer than Truman had expected, the result mainly of his perennial difficulty in finding a satisfactory ending. "I read several versions and watched him struggle," said Phyllis Cerf, who had witnessed similar struggles with *Other Voices* and *The Grass Harp*. "I think quite often the problem was that he hadn't thought of the ending, though he swore to me that I was wrong, that I didn't know what I was talking about—and in truth, I probably didn't." But end it he did in the spring of 1958. In accordance with a promise he had made to Carmel Snow, *Harper's Bazaar* was to publish it in the summer, before Random House brought it out as a book.

Between his promise and publication, however, Mrs. Snow had been booted out by the Hearst Corporation, and her niece, Nancy White, had taken her place. Mrs. Snow had been the protector of editorial integrity, the abbess of the convent, and while she was there, the men from the publisher's office rarely had the nerve to ask questions about her fiction. Now they did, objecting to Truman's use of a few four-letter words and the relaxed lifestyle of his heroine: Holly Golightly was not exactly a call girl, but she did make her living from sex.

"I used to get these lists of objections from either the publisher's office or the Hearst offices across town," recalled Alice Morris, who had taken Mary Louise Aswell's place as fiction editor. "They all were reading as they had never read before, word for word. I kept saying to Nancy, 'This is a slightly raffish society Truman's talking about. There's nothing ugly or pornographic about it. He's only used words where they would be absolutely natural, never simply for effect. Tiffany's will someday display it in their window.' Finally I got all the objections boiled down and showed the list to Truman.

" 'I'm not going to change a word,' he said. But finally he agreed he would. I think he said yes partly because I showed him the layouts. We had about six pages with beautiful, atmospheric photographs. Then when all the changes had been made and we were just about to send the whole thing to the printer, Nancy called me into her office and said, 'I've just had a call from Dick Deems [a Hearst executive], and we're not going to be able to run *Breakfast at Tiffany's*.' " Without much ado, *Harper's Bazaar* had ended its long and distinguished history of printing quality fiction. Although he subsequently sold his story to *Esquire*, Truman never forgave the new, Snow-less *Bazaar*. "I'm not angry, I'm outraged—that's an entirely different thing," he told a reporter. "Publish with *them* again? Why, I wouldn't spit on their street."

The bad news from *Bazaar* had come as he and Jack were packing for a summer in Greece, but on May 28, 1958, they sailed, as scheduled, on the *Vulcania*. Truman's friend Irving Drutman happened to see their arrival at Athens' Grand Bretagne Hotel a week or so later. "The Grand Bretagne was the Ritz of Athens, very snobbish," Drutman said. "They came in the lobby with something like seventeen pieces of luggage: bags, oddly shaped bundles, things carried in knapsacks, things tied in neckerchiefs. Jack was holding two ferocious-looking dogs. The clerk looked at them and at the dogs and said there was no reservation.

" 'Of course there's a reservation,' said Truman. 'We have it confirmed.'

" 'Sorry, there's no reservation,' repeated the clerk. Truman began arguing and said that he would call the owner of the hotel, whom he knew. The clerk of course had heard that sort of thing before, but in this case I'm sure Truman did know the owner. Truman made a great fuss, and they finally gave them a room, which the dogs proceeded to tear to pieces during the several days they were there."

Truman did not care for Athens—ruins, no matter how important, never appealed to him—but both he and Jack fell instantly in love with Paros, the Aegean island where they spent the next three and a half months. "Have written you from many places," Truman told Newton, "but never before from heaven. Adore this island, prefer it to anywhere I've ever stayed." To Cecil he added: "Absolutely beautiful. Just sun, sea, and serenity. No tourists to speak of. The town is dead-white—with blue courtyards and walls covered with morning-glory vine and terraces roofed with grape-arbor: like a clean, cool Casbah. And it is *cool*, by the way; even sometimes chilly—we sleep under a blanket. The food is fairly good, the wines delicious. We are living in a very clean and delightful hotel. There is a little villa next door that we are trying to acquire. But really I don't care if we do—because we have such a quiet, pleasant apartment with a terrace overhanging the sea and a flight of stairs going down to a nice-enough little beach."

While Jack began another play—his previous one, *Light a Penny Candle*, had closed Off Broadway just before they left—Truman worked on his Moscow piece. He also devoted some thought to the Proustian work he had been contemplating since he was first admitted to the company of the rich and powerful. "A large novel, my magnum opus" was how he described it to Bennett Cerf. "A book about which I must be very silent, so as not to alarm my 'sitters,' and which I think will really arouse you when I outline it (only you must never mention it to a soul). The novel is called 'Answered Prayers'; and, if all goes well, I think it will answer mine." His characters were to be his rich friends, the sitters, as he referred to them. The title was borrowed from a saying that he attributed to Saint Teresa of Avila: more tears are shed over answered prayers than unanswered prayers.* It was a truism that he had already seen confirmed many times: those who achieve their highest goals are rarely happy; something almost always intervenes to turn dreams into nightmares.

" 'Answered Prayers,' a novel," he wrote in his journal in July. "*Anne Woodward*, C-Z, Rosie, the Duchess, Elsa, Elsie Woodward, Thelma (leukemia) and David (leukemia)." From that brief notation, it appears that the main character was to be Ann Woodward, the chief protagonist in what *Life* magazine called "the shooting of the century." A former showgirl and the daughter of a Detroit streetcar conductor, Woodward had shot and killed her rich, blue-blooded husband in the fall of 1955, claiming that she had mistaken him for an intruder. Few believed her, but Elsie Woodward, her mother-in-law and a much-loved figure in New York society, stood by her for the sake of the two grandsons. As a result, the new widow's implausible story was accepted as fact, and she never went to trial. Old Mrs. Woodward was also one of those mentioned in his journal, together with C. Z. Guest; the Duchess of Windsor; Elsa Maxwell; and two New York and Southampton heiresses, Rosie Chisholm and Thelma Foy.

Their sorry fates seemed to bear out his pessimistic thesis. Bill Woodward, who was born with the money and position most people only dream about, had got what he wanted—sexy Ann—and twelve years later she blew his head apart with No. 7 English shot from a double-barreled gun. Ann had got the name and fortune she wanted, but the shooting had made her a pariah, a social outcast. And so on down his list; all had had their prayers answered, and all, for one reason or another, would have been happier if their appeals had been denied. In their unhappy histories Truman discerned a plot on which he could build his own magnum opus.

But great novels require time and concentration, and his always precarious financial situation allowed him neither. "I said I was happy," he wrote Newton. "I am; except about my work. Simply because I'm not able to work at what I want. I'm on some dreadful treadmill of having to do dollar-making articles: because of my internal revenue troubles, the Joe Capote problem (who, aside from *all* else, has now married an invalid who is living in a hospital at *my*

---

* Many aphorisms have been falsely attributed to the Spanish saint, and this is apparently one of them. She did express similar sentiments, however, and Truman probably assumed that a paraphrase was a direct quotation.

expense); and, I suppose, my own past extravagance. Meanwhile, I have a novel, something on a large and serious scale, that pursues me like a crazy wind: *but!* How did I ever work myself into this cul-de-sac?"

Paros at least continued to enchant him, and he even talked to Jack about buying a little farmhouse to which they could come every year. "Now the nights are so moon-bright you can see a ship twenty miles at sea," he wrote Newton, conveying in a sentence much of the wonder of the place. The only fault he could find was with the littlest Greeks, who he thought were among "the world's meanest bunch of brats." In most countries in which he traveled he managed very well with English alone: the word martini sounds the same all over the world. But the brats of Paros, he told a friend, had caused him to enlarge his vocabulary. "Have learned only five Greek words, in order to say: 'Shut up, fat girl' and 'shut up, fat boy.' "

Jack learned to hold those brats in equal disdain. Early one morning in August, he saw two boys playing with a kitten, which one of them suddenly hurled into the sea. Running barefooted over the rocky ground, Jack jumped into the water and swam to the rescue. "When I reached it," Jack told his sister Gloria, "the mute sufferer climbed into the palm of my right hand and raised its voice in a seemingly endless series of wild agonized meows. I swam to shore cursing the boy, furiously now, since I remembered him telling me the cat had gone swimming. I had to splash him with water to get him out of my sight, but his brazen murderer's face, his total inability to understand my concern, remains with me yet—as does the kitten. I wrapped her in my shorts, her bloody face, one leg half chewed away, more fleas than hairs, more scratches, cuts and bruises than a man could take and live, and yet this lived! Suddenly I began to cry for all the world's cruelty, and my own. I have called her Diotima after the woman who taught Socrates all about love."

He and Truman never bought a farmhouse, and it was probably just as well. Much as he liked Paros, Truman was showing some restlessness by the time they left at the beginning of October. He asked Doris Lilly for Manhattan gossip, and he waited eagerly for the weekly boat that brought the latest magazines. In Athens he had picked up a pornographic version of *Robinson Crusoe* in which Crusoe and Friday engaged in practices unrecorded, and perhaps unimagined, by Daniel Defoe. "The whole notion opens vistas of pornographic possibility," he pointed out to Newton, enthusiastically suggesting other revisions of great literary works: such as a *Pride and Prejudice* that paired Mr. Darcy with Mr. Bingley and an *Uncle Tom's Cabin* that made a sexual quartet of Topsy, Little Eva, Simon Legree, and Uncle Tom himself. "And you can't tell *me*," he concluded, "that Tom Sawyer wasn't in bed with Huckleberry!"

A week before leaving Paros, he celebrated his birthday. Peering into the mirror that morning, he sadly observed that there had been a change: he no longer appeared ten years younger than he actually was. "My Birthday," he noted in his diary: "34—and I almost look my age; wrinkles around the eyes."

1948. IRVING PENN

*"Big Mama," Truman called Slim
Hayward (later Slim Keith), who in
1958 went with him on his second visit
to Russia and who regarded him as the
best companion in the world.*

45

46

*In 1957 Truman and Cecil Beaton
journeyed to Japan, where Truman
planned to write the story of the
filming of* Sayonara. *The fearful
producer barred him from the set, but
Truman nonetheless managed to extract
an extraordinarily intimate interview
from Marlon Brando, who, upon
reading it, vowed to kill him.*

47

48

"We were a great little trio," said Truman of his relationship with Babe and Bill Paley. For more than twenty years he traveled the world with them, spent weekends at their estate on Long Island, and amused them at their house in Round Hill, Jamaica. These pictures were shot in the mid-fifties, at the beginning of that long and famous friendship.

50

52

51

In the fifties and sixties Truman was allowed into Olympus itself—the world of the international rich. Marella Agnelli, the wife of one of Italy's great industrialists, begged him to tour the Greek islands aboard her yacht. Gloria Guinness, Babe Paley's rival for the title of Queen of Chic, mothered him. Charlie and Oona Chaplin entertained him and Jack at their chalet in Switzerland.

53

54

"I am always drawn back to places where I have lived," begins Breakfast at Tiffany's, *the first draft of which is shown here. Audrey Hepburn (between Truman and her husband, Mel Ferrer) played his heroine, Holly Golightly, in Hollywood's much-altered version, which Truman disliked intensely.*

In 1961 Truman flew from Switzerland, where he and Jack had bought an apartment, to London to write a movie adaptation of Henry James's story The Turn of the Screw. *He believed that the script for* The Innocents, *as the film was titled, was the best he had written, and the critics agreed.*

58

The murders of four members of the Clutter family drew Truman to Kansas at the end of 1959. The gregarious Harper Lee, his friend from Monroeville days, went along to help with the research, and Alvin Dewey, the detective who led the investigation, provided support and information.

59

60

61

62

They had driven across Kansas to kill the Clutters—in cold blood, as Truman was to say—and then raced away. But a few weeks later Dick Hickock and a smiling Perry Smith (Alvin Dewey is standing behind him) were arrested in Las Vegas and driven back. During their nearly five-and-a-half years in jail, Truman became their main link with what Dick liked to call "the free world." He sent books and magazines to Perry and art supplies to Dick, whose pen-and-ink self-portrait is seen here.

63

64

67

After In Cold Blood, *Truman felt that he had been in solitary confinement himself, and in November, 1966, he gave perhaps the most celebrated party of modern times, his masked ball at Manhattan's Plaza Hotel. The guest book read like "an international list for the guillotine," joked Leo Lerman, and he was not wrong. Truman takes to the floor with his guest of honor, Kay Graham; Bill Paley beams between Gloria Guinness and his wife Babe; Princess Luciana Pignatelli peers out from under a sixty-carat diamond; and Marella Agnelli makes a regal advance into the ballroom.*

66

65

*"Splendor Runs Over at Capote Ball of Decade,"
headlined one newspaper, and no one disagreed. Lauren
Bacall bestows a kiss on Truman's balding head, while an
amused D. D. Ryan stares into the camera. Billy
Baldwin, society's favorite decorator, arrives in a golden
unicorn mask; Frank Sinatra sits with his bride, Mia
Farrow; and Tallulah Bankhead, who had begged for an
invitation, happily preens for photographers.*

*"I love everything about her," Truman said of Lee
Radziwill, who stands between him and Norman Mailer at a
1972 party and who demonstrates her acting skills, or lack
thereof, in a 1967 revival of* The Philadelphia Story.

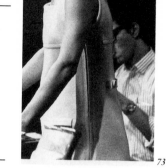

*In Palm Springs Myrtle
Bennett was his housekeeper,
friend and protector.*

*When he was a student at Greenwich High School, his
English teacher, Catherine Wood (left), predicted that
Truman would be famous. They remained friends and in the
mid-sixties he showed her and her friend, Marjorie Pierce, his
new apartment in the United Nations Plaza. (James
Fosburgh's portrait of him hangs behind them.)*

On his first trip to Kansas, few people in Finney County knew who he was. In 1967, when he returned to watch the filming of In Cold Blood, *nearly everyone in America recognized him.* Life *put him on its cover, between Scott Wilson, who was playing Dick Hickock, and Robert Blake, who was playing Perry Smith. He revisited the Clutter house and talked with director Richard Brooks, who finally asked him to leave, so great was the commotion he was causing.*

For several years after the publication of In Cold Blood, *Truman was sought out for his views on prisons, capital punishment and the criminal justice system.*

The sound of the sea could always be heard in Truman's little house in Sagaponack, which was a rural and unspoiled part of eastern Long Island when he moved there in the early sixties.

To play his comic villain in 1975's Murder by Death, *Neil Simon wanted someone like Truman Capote, and finally he chose Truman himself, who is seen here with actors Richard Narita, Peter Sellers and Eileen Brennan.*

Andy Warhol interviewed him
and was also a fellow celebrant in
the rites of Studio 54.

The thin Truman in 1979,
after a diet and a facelift.

The fat Truman in 1975, with Diana Ross at a
Hollywood party.

A bartender by profession, Rick
Brown nonetheless tried to keep
Truman away from the vodka
bottle.

Joseph Petrocik and Myron
Clement helped him through
some bad times in the late
seventies and early eighties.

Cartoonist Edward Sorel summed up the feelings of many of Truman's friends after the publication of "La Côte Basque, 1965."

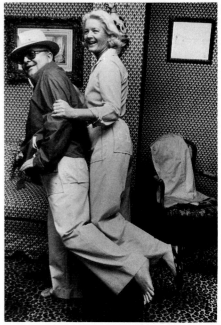

C. Z. Guest was one of his few society friends who stuck by him after the fall.

The Christmas holidays on Long Island, 1975, with John O'Shea and John's pretty daughter Kerry, whom Truman later rechristened Kate Harrington.

90

The last years of Truman's life were punctuated by a series of disasters. In 1977 he became so incoherent at a reading in Maryland that he was led off the stage. In 1981 he was carried, comatose, from his apartment in Manhattan. In 1983 Joanne Carson took him to Palm Springs, where he recuperated from various ailments.

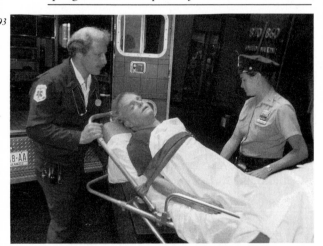

Yet even during those dark days, Puck, the old merrymaker, occasionally reemerged, ready to amuse and be amused.

91

Truman and Jack, shown here peering from the bedroom of Jack's house in Sagaponack in 1981, remained companions, but their relationship became increasingly strained and difficult in the seventies and eighties.

August 23, 1984: The last picture of the most photographed writer of his generation, taken at Joanne Carson's house in Los Angeles, with Joanne's Doberman, Cinnamon.

WHEN he docked in New York, in late October, 1958, *Breakfast at Tiffany's* was in the bookstores, and Holly Golightly had already taken her place in America's fictional Hall of Fame. Of all his characters, Truman later said, Holly was his favorite, and it is easy to see why. She lives the Capote philosophy that Randolph and Judge Cool only talked about in *Other Voices* and *The Grass Harp;* her whole life is an expression of freedom and an acceptance of human irregularities, her own as well as everybody else's. The only sin she recognizes is hypocrisy. In an early version, Truman gave her the curiously inappropriate name of Connie Gustafson; he later thought better and christened her with one, Holiday Golightly, that precisely symbolizes her personality: she is a woman who makes a holiday of life, through which she walks lightly.

Almost all of the scatty young women he had known and admired sat for her portrait: Carol Marcus, Doris Lilly, Phoebe Pierce, Oona Chaplin and Gloria Vanderbilt. In many ways she is also like the young Nina Capote, as seen through the blinders of childhood. Both Nina and Holly grew up in the rural South and longed for the glitter and glamour of New York, and they both changed their hillbilly names, Lillie Mae and Lulamae, to those they considered more sophisticated. But the one Holly most resembles, in spirit if not in body, is her creator. She not only shares his philosophy, but his fears and anxieties as well—"the mean reds" she calls them. "You're afraid and you sweat like hell, but you don't know what you're afraid of," she says by way of explanation. For her the cure is to jump into a taxi and head for Tiffany's; nothing bad could happen, she says, amid "that lovely smell of silver and alligator wallets," and her dream is to have breakfast in that soothing setting. Her wish—the title of his story—is also borrowed. Truman had once heard an anecdote and filed it away, waiting for the time he could use it. During World War II a man of middle age entertained a Marine one Saturday night. The man enjoyed himself so much in the Marine's muscular embrace that he felt he should buy him something to show his gratitude; but since it was Sunday when they woke up, and the stores were closed, the best he could offer was breakfast.

"Where would you like to go?" he asked. "Pick the fanciest, most expensive place in town."

The Marine, who was not a native, had heard of only one fancy and expensive place in New York, and he said: "Let's have breakfast at Tiffany's."

With publication came what Truman called the Holly Golightly Sweepstakes: half the women he knew, and a few he did not, claimed to be the model for his wacky heroine. Shortly after it appeared, Doris Lilly telephoned Andrew. "Have you read Truman's new book?" she asked excitedly.

"Why, yes," said Andrew, who knew what she was really asking, but pretended to be ignorant. "Truman sent me a copy, and I enjoyed it very much."

"It's me! It's me! It's me!" she screamed, unable to play the game any longer. Andrew repeated the conversation to Truman, who said, "Honey, you tell her, her, her for me, me, me that it is her. But it's also Carol Marcus and Oona Chaplin."

Unfortunately, a Manhattan woman who bore the name Golightly also entered the sweepstakes. Charging invasion of privacy as well as libel, Bonnie Golightly sued him for eight hundred thousand dollars. Her case did not go very far. "It's ridiculous for her to claim she is my Holly," said Truman. "I understand she's a large girl nearly forty years old. Why, it's sort of like Joan Crawford saying she's Lolita."

Most of the critics were kind both to his Holly and to *Breakfast at Tiffany's*. The most gratifying praise, however, came from a colleague who was usually as combative as Gore Vidal. "Truman Capote I do not know well, but I like him," wrote Norman Mailer. "He is tart as a grand aunt, but in his way he is a ballsy little guy, and he is the most perfect writer of my generation, he writes the best sentences word for word, rhythm upon rhythm. I would not have changed two words in *Breakfast at Tiffany's*, which will become a small classic."*

In the early spring of 1959, Truman went back to Russia to do more research on his Moscow piece. When he returned, he and Jack went to Clarks Island, a small island just off the coast of Massachusetts, for the summer. Although their house had neither phone nor electricity—light was provided by kerosene lamps—he told Cecil that it was "wonderful, big, clean, light and breezy, surrounded by beautiful tree-filled lawns sloping down to beaches—much the best place we've ever had. Wonderful for work."

He did not do much work, however, and, to judge from his letters, even in that isolated spot he was mesmerized by the biggest society drama since the Woodward killing: Leland Hayward had left Slim for Pamela Churchill. "Your item about Leland and Pam C. *stunned* me," he wrote Cecil, who had informed him of the news. "I'd heard nothing about it! Babe, who is in Biarritz, did not mention it in her last letter, though that reached here several weeks ago. Toward the end of May, just before I came here, I saw Leland and Mrs. C. in tete-a-tete at a restaurant—and I kidded them, and said I was going to write Slim (who had already left for Europe, where Leland was supposed to join in a week—but never did). As a matter of fact, with my usual gaucherie, I *did* write Slim asking if she knew her husband was running around with the notorious Mrs. C. Oh dear! Are you sure it's true? Has he really left Slim? *Please* write me what you know. I am devoted to Slim; I'm amazed she hasn't written me, I must find out where she is at once."

Cecil's news was indeed true. In New York, Bennett Cerf told Truman, people were taking sides—for Slim or Pamela—as if they

---

* Mailer had good reason to call him a ballsy little guy. When he wrote that appraisal, he was still bruised from a television encounter with Truman in the winter of 1959. They had appeared, together with Dorothy Parker, on David Susskind's program *Open End*, to talk about writers and writing. The Beat Generation came under review. Mailer defended it; Truman attacked it. "None of these people have anything interesting to say," Truman declared, "and none of them can write, not even Mr. [Jack] Kerouac . . . [It] isn't writing at all—it's typing." The phrase was to be attached to poor Kerouac for the rest of his life. No one recalled Mailer's response. Instinctively, Truman had realized that what television audiences remember is not an argument, but the amusing and pithy phrase they can repeat to their friends the next morning.

were watching a World Series. In August, Truman visited the Paleys at their retreat in New Hampshire and dispatched a report to Cecil. "There was much talk about what is termed 'Topic A'—the Hayward-Churchill fandango. I had a long letter from Slim, very touching, very regretful, but full of good-sense; it seems that Leland has *never* asked her for a divorce, though Mrs. C. tells everyone she will be Mrs. H. in November. The whole thing has caused a 'situation' among the Cushing girls: Babe and Minnie have vowed undying enmity to 'that bitch,' while sister Betsey is Mrs. C's greatest partisan (so grateful is she that the threat to her own happy home has been removed).

"Tout New York is divided into warring camps—the pro-Slim contingent, led by Mrs. Paley with Jerome Robbins and Mainbocher [America's reigning dress designer of the forties and fifties] as seconds in command, have already sent Mrs. [Arthur] Hornblow to the firing-squad because she gave a dinner for Leland and Mrs. C.—which *was* odd, considering she has always been so close a friend of Slim's. No doubt Mrs. C. will be the winner in the coming contest. Needless to say, I am a Slimite to the death." Mrs. C. was the winner, and she became the new Mrs. Leland Hayward on May 4, 1960. Shortly thereafter, Slim cabled Truman. "I wonder," she said bitterly, "if she tied a ribbon on it."

Truman remained a Slimite. A year or so later he telephoned her, begging for help. "What possible trouble or disaster could befall Pamela?" he inquired.

"I don't know. Why?" demanded Slim, who had probably been asking herself the same question.

"Well, I sent a cable to Gloria Guinness saying, 'Isn't it a shame about Pam?' Now I know I'm going to get a cable back, saying, 'What do you mean?' And I've got to invent something quickly. But what can it be? She can't be pregnant."

"No. She can't be pregnant. We *know* she can't be pregnant. I don't know what it could be, but I'll try to think of something." Slim was as good as her word, and her telegram soon arrived with the answer: "How about clap—as in applause?"

After finishing forty pages of his Moscow article, Truman went to William Shawn with an embarrassing confession: he could not complete it. If he did, he said, and his subjects' pro-Western views were revealed, they might be sent to Siberia, or perhaps even a firing squad. He offered to give back his advance, but Mr. Shawn graciously told him to keep it, to apply it to his next project for *The New Yorker*.

Although he still talked about *Answered Prayers*, Truman's mind was really on nonfiction. "I like the feeling that something is happening beyond and about me and I can do nothing about it," he explained to a reporter. "I like having the truth be the truth so I can't change it." He was too restless to settle down to fiction, he told the now elderly Glenway Wescott. "I couldn't sit there to write," he said. "It was as though there were a box of chocolates in the next room, and I couldn't resist them. The chocolates were that I wanted to write fact instead of fiction. There were so many things that I knew I could investigate, so many things that I knew I could find out about. Suddenly the newspapers all came alive, and I realized that I was in terrible trouble as a fiction writer."

In that mood he opened *The New York Times* on Monday, November 16, 1959. There, all but hidden in the middle of page 39, was a one-column story headlined, "WEALTHY FARMER, 3 OF FAMILY SLAIN." The dateline was Holcomb, Kansas, November 15, and the story began: "A wealthy wheat farmer, his wife and their two young children were found shot to death today in their home. They had been killed by shotgun blasts at close range after being bound and gagged."

In describing the genesis of a successful work, a writer often will say that he stumbled across his idea, giving the impression that it was purely a matter of luck, like finding a hundred-dollar bill on the sidewalk. The truth, as Henry James observed, is usually different: "His discoveries are, like those of the navigator, the chemist, the biologist, scarce more than alert recognitions. He *comes upon* the interesting thing as Columbus came upon the isle of San Salvador, because he had moved in the right direction for it."

So it was that Truman, who had been moving in the right direction for several years, came across his San Salvador, his interesting thing, in that brief account of cruel death in far-off Kansas: he had been looking for it, or something very much like it. For no apparent reason, four people had been slain: Herbert Clutter; his wife, Bonnie; and two of their four children, Nancy, sixteen, and Kenyon, fifteen. As he read and reread those spartan paragraphs, Truman realized that a crime of such horrifying dimensions was a subject that was indeed beyond him, a truth he could not change. Even the location, a part of the country as alien to him as the steppes of Russia, had a perverse appeal. "Everything would seem freshly minted," he later explained, reconstructing his thinking at that time. "The people, their accents and attitude, the landscape, its contours, the weather. All this, it seemed to me, could only sharpen my eye and quicken my ear." Finally he said to himself, "Well, why not *this* crime? The Clutter case. Why not pack up and go to Kansas and see what happens?"

When he appeared at *The New Yorker* to show Mr. Shawn the

clipping, the identity of the killer, or killers, was still unknown, and might never be known. But that, as he made clear to Shawn, was beside the point, or at least the point he wanted to make. What excited his curiosity was not the murders, but their effect on that small and isolated community. "As he originally conceived it, the murders could have remained a mystery," said Shawn, who once again gave his enthusiastic approval. "He was going to do a piece about the town and the family—what their lives had been. I thought that it could make some long and wonderful piece of writing."

Truman asked Andrew Lyndon to go with him, but Andrew was otherwise engaged. Then he turned to Nelle Harper Lee. Nelle, whose own book, *To Kill a Mockingbird*, was finished but not yet published, agreed immediately. "He said it would be a tremendously involved job and would take two people," she said. "The crime intrigued him, and I'm intrigued with crime—and, boy, I wanted to go. It was deep calling to deep." Watching with some amusement as the two amateur sleuths nervously made their plans, Jack wrote his sister: "Did you read about the murder of the Clutter family out in Kansas? Truman's going out there to write a piece on it. The murder is *unsolved!!* He's taking Nelle Harper Lee, an old childhood friend, out with him to play his girl Friday, or his Della Street (Perry Mason's sec't.). I hope he'll be all right. I told him curiosity killed the cat, and he looked scared—till I added that satisfaction brought it back."

He also enlisted the aid of Bennett Cerf, who, he correctly assumed, had well-placed acquaintances in every state of the union. "I don't know a soul in the whole state of Kansas," he told Bennett. "You've got to introduce me to some people out there." By coincidence, Bennett had recently spoken at Kansas State University in Manhattan, Kansas, and had made a friend of its president, James McCain. By further coincidence, McCain had known the murdered Clutter family, as he did nearly everyone else in Finney County. He would give Truman all necessary introductions, he told Bennett, if, in exchange, Truman would stop first at the university to speak to the English faculty. "I accept for Truman right now," Bennett responded. "Great!"

Thus assured, in mid-December Truman boarded a train for the Midwest, with Nelle at his side and a footlocker stuffed with provisions in his luggage. "He was afraid that there wouldn't be anything to eat out there," said Nelle. After a day and a night in Manhattan, where the Kansas State English faculty gave him a party, they rented a Chevrolet and drove the remaining 270 miles to Garden City, the Finney County seat. They arrived at twilight, a month to the day after he had come upon his interesting thing in the back pages of the *Times*. But if he had realized then what the future held, Truman said afterward, he never would have stopped. "I would have driven straight on. Like a bat out of hell."

When people speak of Middle America or the American heartland, they are talking about Garden City, or somewhere very much like it. Located at the western edge of the state, only sixty-six miles from the Colorado line, it sits on the semiarid high plains, at a point where the continent begins to stretch upward before making its great leap to the Rocky Mountains. "Pop. 11,811," read a brochure of the Santa Fe Railroad, whose trains passed through there on their daily runs between Chicago and the West Coast. "Largest irrigation area in midwest with unlimited supply of underground water. World's largest known gas field. Sugar beet factory. Largest zoo in Kansas, largest buffalo herd in midwest." Although the pamphlet did not note it, in December, 1959, Garden City was also prosperous, mostly from wheat and natural gas, and staunchly Republican, a town of teetotalers and devout Christians who filled twenty-two churches every Sunday morning.

There was not much more to say. Unlike Dodge City, forty-six miles to the east, where Bat Masterson and Wyatt Earp had dispatched a platoon of outlaws to Boot Hill—the real Boot Hill— Garden City had led a colorless and relatively placid existence. The terrible events in the outlying village of Holcomb, just six miles west on U.S. Route 50, were thus even more shocking than they might have been in many other places. As Truman had predicted, the murder of the Clutters had started an epidemic of fear. Robbery did not seem to be the motive, and the peculiar brutality of the killings —Herb Clutter's throat had been cut before he was shot—led most people to believe that the killings were the doing of a vengeful psychopath, someone local who might well have other targets in mind. Lights burned all night; doors that had never been locked were bolted; loaded guns were placed next to beds.

It was into that atmosphere, darkened by fear and mistrust, that Truman and Nelle now came. A few people may have recognized his name; the Garden City public library owned two of his books,

Other Voices and *Breakfast at Tiffany's*. But no one in those parts had ever seen anyone remotely like Truman. In their eyes, said Nelle, "he was like someone coming off the moon." Inevitably he was greeted with derision. Asked what he had thought of Truman, one resident was most likely replying for the majority when he later drawled, "Well . . . I'd sure hate to tell you." Jokes were made about his mannerisms and his height. "By God! Don't he look like a little old banty rooster?" observed one farmer to everyone within earshot. At Christmas parties imitations of his voice were heard as often as "Jingle Bells." Some people were openly hostile; a few suspected that someone so strange-looking might be the killer, returning to rejoice in the commotion he had caused. Truman did not look like a reporter, certainly, and it did him no good to say that he was on assignment for *The New Yorker*—the magazine had more readers in Moscow than in Finney County.

His ability to charm, which had overcome many other formidable obstacles, momentarily failed him, moreover. Soon after arriving, he and Nelle walked into the office of Alvin Dewey, who was supervising the investigation for the Kansas Bureau of Investigation. He needed a long interview, Truman told Dewey. Telephones were ringing, other detectives were waiting to make their reports, and Dewey, a tall, good-looking man of forty-seven, was not at all impressed by the names Truman dropped. He refused to grant an interview. Truman would have to get his information from the daily press conferences, he said, just like all the other reporters. "But I'm not a newspaperman," Truman objected. "I need to talk to you in depth. What I'm going to write will take months. What I am here for is to do a very special story on the family, up to and including the murders. It really doesn't make any difference to me if the case is ever solved or not."

"Well, he could have talked all day without saying that," Dewey recalled. "Solving the case made one hell of a difference to me." Truman was lucky, in fact, that the detective, who had lost twenty pounds in an almost round-the-clock search for leads, did not throw him out. Not only was he the agent in charge, but the Clutters had been family friends, fellow parishioners of Garden City's United Methodist Church, people much-admired and much-liked. Time and again Dewey had looked at photographs of their bodies in hopes of discovering some hitherto hidden clue. Time and again he had seen nothing but horror. "Nancy's forehead, where the shotgun blast exited, reminded me of the jagged peaks of a mountain range," he remembered.

Under those circumstances, his reaction to Truman's flippant remark was surprisingly indulgent. "I'd like to see your press card, Mr. Capote" was all he said. Truman meekly admitted that he had none, but offered to display his passport instead. Dewey was not interested and told him once again the time of his press conferences. At last Truman gave up, and the next morning he and Nelle took their places among the other reporters.

James McCain's letters and calls opened a few important doors, but Nelle's help proved more valuable during those difficult first days. Her roots were still in Monroeville, and she knew how farmers and the inhabitants of small towns thought and talked. She was the kind of woman people in Finney County were accustomed to; where he shocked, she soothed. "Nelle walked into the kitchen, and five minutes later I felt I had known her for a long time," said Dolores Hope, a columnist for the *Garden City Telegram*.

Not once was he or Nelle seen taking notes: it was Truman's theory that the sight of a notebook, or worse still, a tape recorder, inhibited candor. People would reveal themselves, he maintained, only in seemingly casual conversations. Unless they saw a pen or pencil flying across a page, they could not believe that their words were being recorded. "It wasn't like he was interviewing you at all," said Wilma Kidwell, the mother of Nancy Clutter's best friend Susan. "He had a way of leading you into things without your knowing it." Only when they had returned to the Warren Hotel did he and Nelle separate and commit to paper what they had learned. Each wrote a separate version of the day's interviews; they then compared notes over drinks and dinner. "Together," declared Nelle, "we would get it right." Their method was time-consuming but productive. When their combined memory failed, as it sometimes did, they went back and asked their questions in a slightly different way. On occasion they talked to the same person three times in one day.

The farmers who plowed that flat and forbidding terrain did not work harder than the two who came to talk to them. "It was always bitter cold, really so incredibly cold on the plains," said Truman. "We would drive out to some lonely ranch or farmhouse to interview the people who lived there, and almost invariably they had a television set on. They seemed to keep it on twenty-four hours a day.

They would sit there talking—and never look at us! They would go on looking straight at the TV screen, even if there was just a station break or an advertisement. If the television wasn't on, if the light wasn't flickering, they began to get the shakes. I guess television has become an extension of people's nervous systems."

Nowhere else had he felt at such a loss. The Kansans spoke the same language, paid their bills in the same currency, and pledged allegiance to the same flag. Yet they seemed utterly different. If they thought that he had dropped from the moon, he may have wondered if that was where he had arrived. A CARE package from Babe Paley, a tin of delicious black caviar, reminded him how far he was from his friends and all the things he loved. At one particularly bleak point, he despaired, telling Nelle that he was thinking of giving up and going home. "I cannot get any rapport with these people," he told her. "I can't get a handle on them." She bucked him up. "Hang on," she said. "You *will* penetrate this place."

So he did, on Christmas Day, appropriately enough. Dolores Hope had told her husband, Clifford, one of the town's leading lawyers, that they ought to share their holiday dinner with someone who had no other place to go. The visitors from New York fitted that description and were invited to partake of the Hopes' dinner of duck and twice-baked potatoes. "Of course, Truman dominated the conversation," recalled Mrs. Hope. "Once you got over the high-pitched voice, why, you didn't think about it, really. It was not your everyday Garden City talk. The things he said were from another world, and they were fascinating for us. It was a right pleasant day. People started calling me. Had I really had him to dinner? I said yes, and then things kind of started for him. Entertaining him became the in-thing to do. He was an attraction and people didn't want to be left out."

The switchboard at the Warren Hotel began buzzing with invitations from the local aristocracy. Instead of imitating his voice, people found themselves listening to the real thing and, for the most part, liking what they were hearing. Even Alvin Dewey, who attended one of those parties, melted when his wife, Marie, who had been born and bred in New Orleans, discovered another native of that city. Within a night or two, Truman and Nelle were at the Dewey house dining on grits, gumbo, and red beans and rice, a menu that few steak-and-potato Midwesterners could properly appreciate. Within a week the Deweys had become such good friends that Truman felt free to give Alvin a nickname, Foxy. "Foxy, you're not telling me everything!" he would say, with an accusing wag of his finger. He and Nelle were at the Deweys' the night of December 30, 1959, when Alvin received the phone call he had been praying for: two suspects in the Clutter murders had been arrested in Las Vegas. Elated, Alvin made plans to go get them. Truman asked if he could go along. "Not this time, partner," Alvin replied.

But Truman and Nelle were part of the crowd shivering outside the Finney County courthouse a week later, when Alvin and his colleagues returned with their handcuffed quarry, Dick Hickock and Perry Smith. All the theories about the murders had been wrong. The two killers—both had confessed—were not local men, but alumni of the Kansas State Penitentiary. Robbery had been their motive after all. They had erroneously heard that Herb Clutter kept large amounts of cash in an office safe, and they had made their plans with meticulous care. Nor had the killings been spontaneous. From the start they had decided to kill all witnesses—in cold blood.

Their arrest fundamentally altered the nature of Truman's project. By the time Alvin heard the good news from Las Vegas, Truman and Nelle had completed most of their reporting for the relatively short piece he had initially conceived: the reaction of a small town to a hideous crime. But now, with the men who had committed the crime behind bars on the fourth floor of the courthouse, his story had expanded far beyond his original conception. He had done only half his reporting; and a worthless half at that unless he could reconstruct the lives of the killers as precisely and minutely as he had those of their victims.

He received his first close look at them only when they were arraigned in Garden City. Hickock was twenty-eight, blond and slightly above average in height, five feet, ten inches. A car collision had disfigured his face. His eyes were at different levels, and his head appeared, as Truman phrased it, to have been "halved like an apple, then put together a fraction off center." Appearances aside, he was in no way unusual or interesting—just a "two-bit crook" in Alvin's words. His parents were poor but honest, and he had grown up on their small farm in eastern Kansas. Instead of going to college, as he had hoped, he had become an auto mechanic, forced to scratch for every dollar. Twice married, he had also been twice divorced. He was a braggart, consumed with envy of all those who had had it easier, and he had a mean spirit: his notion of fun was to run down dogs on the highway. He was easy to talk to, however, and he had an extraordinarily accurate memory, which was to prove invaluable to the biographer of his short and shabby life.

Except for the blood on his hands, Perry Smith was Dick's exact opposite. From his mother, a Cherokee Indian, Perry had inherited his black hair and sad, droopy eyes; his almost pixielike features came from his Irish father. "A changeling's face," Truman called it, which meant that he could alter it at will, making it seem gentle or savage, vulnerable or ferocious. He too had been in a near-fatal accident, a mishap with a skidding motorcycle that had so deformed and shortened his legs that he was only an inch taller than Truman himself.

His parents had been rodeo performers—"Tex & Flo," they had billed their riding act—who fell apart because of hard times and Flo's weakness for alcohol and other men. She became a messy, hopeless drunk, and Tex went off into the Alaskan wilderness to earn a meager living as a trapper and prospector. After Flo died, choking on her own vomit, her four children were sent to various homes and orphanages. Perry fared worst. His habit of wetting his bed made him a target of scorn and abuse. Nuns beat him; an attendant rubbed a burning ointment on his penis; another held him in a tub of ice water until he developed pneumonia. In a recurring dream, a parrot, "taller than Jesus," swooped down to rescue him from his enemies, pecking out their eyes and carrying him to paradise. But no such miraculous bird appeared, and he ran away to live in the wilds with his father until he was old enough to join the Merchant Marine. His life after that had been, as Truman was to observe, "an ugly and lonely progress toward one mirage and then another." Convinced, obviously with good reason, that the world had not given him a fair chance, Perry bathed himself in self-pity. "Oh," he exclaimed, "the man I could have been!"

Yet he never gave up hope of becoming that man, devouring self-help learning books, making lists of vocabulary-broadening words, and nursing adolescent fantasies of finding gold in Mexico; he had sat through *The Treasure of the Sierra Madre* eight times. Unlike Dick, he considered himself to be kind and considerate, and by his own mingle-mangled logic, he was. Worried that Herb Clutter would be uncomfortable on his cold basement floor, for instance, he gently lifted his bound body onto a mattress—and then butchered him with as little emotion as he might have a hog. "I thought he was a very nice gentleman," he said. "Soft-spoken. I thought so right up to the moment I cut his throat."

Such a kaleidoscope of contradictory emotions fascinated Truman and all those who were to read his narrative. Norman Mailer went so far as to call Perry one of the great characters in American literature, and there is a pathetic irony in the fact that the twisted little man who hungered for education, who constantly corrected Dick's grammar and who peppered his speech with large and ungainly words, has achieved a kind of immortality as a literary darkling. But there he stands, alongside such other native Iagos as Roger Chillingworth in Hawthorne's *The Scarlet Letter*, Claggart in Melville's *Billy Budd*, and Flem Snopes in Faulkner's Yoknapatawpha saga.

When Perry sat down in front of the judge to be arraigned, Truman nudged Nelle. "Look, his feet don't touch the floor!" Nelle said nothing, but thought, "Oh, oh! This is the beginning of a great love affair." In fact, their relationship was more complicated than a love affair: each looked at the other and saw, or thought he saw, the man he might have been.

Their shortness was only one of many unsettling similarities. They both had suffered from alcoholic mothers, absent fathers, and foster homes. At the orphanages he had been sent to, Perry had been a target of scorn because he was half-Indian and wet his bed; Truman had been ridiculed because he was effeminate. A psychiatrist could have been speaking about both of them when he said of Perry: "He seems to have grown up without direction, without love." Finally, both had turned to art to compensate for what had been denied them. Perry was convinced that with a little encouragement, he could have made his mark as a painter, a singer, a songwriter.

In Joel Knox, the thirteen-year-old hero of *Other Voices*, Truman had projected his fictional alter ego. In Perry, it is not too much to suggest, he recognized his shadow, his dark side, the embodiment of his own accumulated angers and hurts. When he looked into those unhappy eyes, he was looking into a tormented region of his own unconscious, resurrecting the nightmares and fears that had found form and body in such early stories as "Miriam" and "The Headless Hawk." Reversing the coin, Perry perceived in Truman the successful artist he might have been. "He saw Truman as someone like himself," said Donald Cullivan, an Army buddy who visited him in jail. "He thought Truman also had been kicked around, and he thought Truman had spunk."

Like the good folk of Garden City, Perry had never encountered anyone like Truman. He was fascinated by him and quizzed him endlessly. "After I had known him a couple of years, he wanted to know whether I was homosexual," Truman said, "which seemed to me to be quite ludicrous—it should have been perfectly clear to him by *that* time. He was a very sophisticated boy on that level, and I don't know what he thought. I think somewhere in the back of his mind he thought I was living with Harper Lee. He was one of those people who think if you're living with a girl, you can't be homosexual, and if you're living with a guy, you can't be heterosexual. Everything has to be black and white. He wanted to know who I lived with and whether I was promiscuous, and I was very frank with him."

From the beginning, theirs was a confused, uneasy, but unremittingly intense relationship. Although Truman knew he needed Perry's trust and goodwill, he could not restrain himself from objecting to Perry's ever-moist self-pity. When Perry blamed his unhappy background for all that he had done, Truman indignantly interjected: "I had one of the worst childhoods in the world, and I'm a pretty decent, law-abiding citizen." Perry answered with a shrug.

Perry was in only slightly less need of Truman, who listened to him and gave him books, magazines, and small amounts of money —items worth more than all the treasure of the Sierra Madre to a man behind bars. Nonetheless, Perry was often sulky and quick to take offense. "He was suspicious, like many people in prison, and uncertain as to whether Truman was using him," said Cullivan. "He waffled back and forth." Flexing his weight lifter's muscles during one interview, he pointed out to Truman that he could kill him in a minute, before a guard could come to his rescue. "I've half a mind to do it," he said. "It would give me pleasure. What do I have to lose?"

Perry was deeply offended by Truman's inscription in a gift copy of *Breakfast at Tiffany's*. "For Perry, from Truman who wishes you well," Truman had scrawled in his small and distinctive hand. But in Perry's outraged opinion, those few words were cold and unfeeling. "Is that all!" he had exploded when Truman handed it to him. On the opposite page, in the beautifully formed script he had learned from a book on handwriting, he later wrote: "Capote, you little bastard! I wanted to call you a name at the time, I was getting angered. It's not to [sic] late yet—'You little Piss Pot!' "

By the middle of January, 1960, Truman had spent hours with both Dick and Perry, and he felt that he had done all he could for the moment in Kansas. In a driving snowstorm he and Nelle boarded a Santa Fe sleeper for the trip home. "An extraordinary experience, in many ways the most interesting thing that's ever happened to me," he wrote Cecil a few days later from Brooklyn Heights. How had he been greeted on the lone prairie? asked Glenway Wescott, who met him at a Manhattan party. How had those hardy Kansans reacted to such an exotic species as a Truman Capote? "At first it was hard," said Truman. "But now I'm practically the mayor!"

HE was not exaggerating by much. When Truman and Nelle returned to Garden City for Dick and Perry's trial in March, he was so esteemed that there was a competition for his company at parties and dinners. Indeed, as Dick Avedon, who had come along to take pictures, recalled, his conquest of Kansas had made him more than a little cocky. The farmer who had compared him to a banty rooster was not altogether wrong. Avedon was with him when he swaggered into the sheriff's office one morning and went up to Roy Church, one of the K.B.I. agents waiting to testify. "You don't look so tough to me!" he sneered.

Church replied by stamping over to the wall, pulling his arm back, and smashing his fist into it. "Oh, my God!" Avedon thought. "What can we do? This is it. Truman's gone one step too far." But he had not. Although it had taken him a while, he had learned how to handle those tough Kansans. Putting his hands over his head, he jumped from side to side and, assuming a thick Southern accent, cried: "Well, Ah'm beside mahself! Well, Ah'm beside mahself! Well, Ah'm beside mahself!" Joining in the laughter, Church relaxed his still-clenched fist. "It was one of the most brilliant, physically inventive and courageous things I've ever seen in my life," said Avedon. "Truman would have survived in the jungles of Viet Nam. He won that duel in the same way he had won the town."

The trial began Tuesday morning, March 22, with Judge Roland Tate presiding. There was never any doubt that the defendants were guilty. Besides their confessions, the prosecution had conclusive physical evidence, including their boots, whose heelprints matched those found at the Clutter house; the knife that had cut Herb Clutter's throat; and the shotgun that had actually killed him and his family. The question was not guilt or innocence, but life or death, and on March 29, after deliberating for only forty minutes, the jury answered it. Both were guilty and should be executed. As they were led away, Perry snickered to Dick, "No chicken-hearted jurors, they!" No more so was Judge Tate, who pronounced sentence a few days later. Their execution was set for Friday, May 13, 1960, when they were to be hanged at the Kansas State Penitentiary in Lansing.

That was a scene Truman did not want to witness. Shortly after the trial ended, he and Nelle left for home. He realized that he could not write in New York, however, between lunches with Slim and weekends with the Paleys. "Gregariousness is the enemy of art," he explained to a reporter, "so when I work, I have to forcibly remove myself from other people. I'm like a prizefighter in training: I have to sweep all the elements except work out of my life completely." Two weeks after his return to New York, he and Jack sailed for Europe, where he planned to stay until his book was finished. He estimated that that would take about a year.

Landing in Le Havre in late April, they picked up a car and drove south to Spain, where they had rented a house in the fishing village of Palamós, on the Costa Brava between Barcelona and the French border. Although he had brought with him trunks full of notes, Truman continued his reporting by mail, bombarding his friends in Garden City with more questions and requests for updates on the news. Bulletins were not long in coming. The Kansas Supreme Court granted Perry and Dick a stay of execution while it reviewed their request for a new trial; but Perry, who did not have much hope, decided to beat the hangman by starving himself to death. "You can wait around for the rope, but not me," he informed Dick, who occupied an adjoining cell. After neither eating nor drinking for six weeks, he began hallucinating, believing that he was in constant communication with the Lord. "It is really too awful," Truman wrote Donald Cullivan. "They are only keeping him alive in order to hang him."

Since that November day when he had learned about the Clutter killings, Truman had been moving so fast that he had not had time to sit back and take stock. In Palamós he did have time, and his thoughts were sobering. When he had begun most of his other projects, he had had a fairly good idea of how long they would take and what the result would be. Almost from the start, however, his murder story had taken its own independent and unpredictable course. Now it had veered again. No one could say how long the appeal process would last or what would happen to Perry. There was no end in sight.

As he sat there in his cliffside house, gazing out at the gentle waters of the Mediterranean, he also comprehended, probably for the first time, the full dimensions of what he was seeking to do. *In Cold Blood*, as he had titled his book, was not just the chronicle of a gruesome crime; it was a tale of a good and virtuous family being pursued and destroyed by forces beyond its knowledge or control. It was a theme that reverberated like Greek tragedy, a story that Aeschylus or Sophocles might have turned into a drama of destiny and fate.

That same fate, Truman was convinced, had sent him to Kansas and had given him an opportunity to write a work of singular power and grandeur. He had a sacred responsibility to his subject, to himself, and to the art he worshiped to create a book that was, as he told Cecil, unlike any other that had ever been written. If *Answered Prayers* would someday be his *Remembrance of Things Past*, then *In Cold Blood* would be his *Madame Bovary*. "[It] may take another year or more," he declared to Newton. "I don't care—it has to be perfect, for I am very excited about it, totally dedicated, and believe, if I am very patient, it could be a kind of masterpiece; God knows I have wonderful material, and lots of it—over 4,000 typed pages of notes. Sometimes, when I think how good it *could* be, I can hardly breathe. Well, the whole thing was the most interesting experience of my life, and indeed has changed my life, altered my point of view about almost everything—it is a Big Work, believe me, and if I fail I still will have succeeded."

What was hidden between those lines was the fear that fate might have entrusted him with too big a task. Imagining how good *In Cold Blood* could be made him realize at the same time how high he had to reach—how much higher, in fact, than he had ever reached before. No one valued his rich gifts more than he did himself: there was no other American of his generation, he felt, who had such a clear ear for the music and rhythm of the English language, no one else who wrote with such style and grace. But the truth of the matter was that until now, he had exercised that style only in small spaces.

Other Voices, a short novel by any measure, was his longest piece of writing.

His Kansas book, on the other hand, would be not only long, but complicated; he would have to weave together a bewildering collection of characters, facts, legal explanations and psychological studies. It demanded skills he had never demonstrated and was not certain—could not be certain—he possessed. He was like a composer of string quartets who was nervously wondering if he was capable of a symphony. He was trying to scale Parnassus itself, and he could not help but approach the job ahead with awe and dread.

He plunged quickly ahead, nonetheless. In June he flew to London, where he talked with a psychiatrist who helped him unravel the psychology of his two murderers. He did not linger, returning almost immediately to his pencils and pads in Palamos. By October he was nearly a quarter done. "Whether it is worth doing remains to be seen!" he fretfully told Mary Louise Aswell. "I think it is going to be 'good'—but it will have to be more than that to justify ALL I HAVE GONE THROUGH."

To Donald Windham he expressed the worry that he might be writing too much for *The New Yorker* to digest. "Never thought that I, of all writers, would ever have a length problem," he said, "but actually it is very tightly written, and really can't be cut (I've tried). Well, if I can't come to terms with Shawn (and I can see that they might hesitate to devote 4 full issues to this enterprise—especially since it is not 'pleasant' reading, and not very 'entertaining,' as the word is used) my only regret will be that I have spent over $8,000 on research, which I will not be able to recover. But I shall go right on with the book, regardless. I suppose it sounds pretentious, but I feel a great obligation to write it, even though the material leaves me increasingly limp and numb and, well, horrified—I have such awful dreams every night. I don't know now how I could ever have felt so callous and 'objective' as I did in the beginning."

Those fierce prairie winds had followed him across the Atlantic, and they howled in his ears through the soft Spanish nights. "Alas, I am rather too much involved emotionally with the material," he confessed to Newton. "God, I wish it were over."

There were, of course, a few pleasures on that Mediterranean shore, and in June he and Jack changed addresses, moving down the beach to a grander house, staffed by a cook, two maids, and a gardener. "I'll think 3 times before taking on such a responsibility again," he grumbled to Donald Windham. From time to time a boat dropped anchor offshore, and fancy friends like Noël Coward and Loel and Gloria Guinness paid their respects. "Every once in a while friends of Truman's come in on a yacht," wrote a surprisingly genial Jack, "and so I'm forced to meet people I would not ordinarily even *see*. I really don't mind any more, though, about that sort of thing. Most of the time if I'm asked I go. It's the least I can do. I suppose I used to take it all seriously. I know now that these people are like hummingbirds, feeding here and there off flowers they really don't take in at all. All they ask is that you behave. Then—as far as I'm concerned anyway—it's out of sight, out of mind."

With Truman Jack was not always so mellow. After a visit in May, Cecil, who was always fascinated by their paradoxical relationship, described it in his diary: "It was sometimes embarrassing to hear Jack lambasting T. for his duchesses & his interest in rich people & his being considered a genius by the Mrs. Paleys. Jack lashes out with Irish articulation & American violence. Sometimes it must hurt T. very much. But it teaches him also. He learns when not to argue, when to let Jack have his own way. He knows when Jack is right, & accepts the healthy criticism, but if Jack is unfair then he will fight bitterly & courageously.

"It is interesting that these two should have found one another, that they should recognize the fact that each gives the other an essential that would be otherwise lacking in their lives. This was a true glimpse of both of them, & it was very touching to see, despite the banter & tough onslaughts from Jack, how when anything serious occurred they were together closely knit as one unit. Jack had received a letter of despair from his sister Gloria. She was in hospital suffering from hepatitis (jaundice) & after 2 days her sister had had Gloria's pet, a Pekinese, & another dog destroyed. T. was so upset that he trembled: 'We must send Gloria a ticket to come out & stay with us & we must have Gloria to live with us always.' "

Jack liked to ski, Truman enjoyed cold weather, and at the end of October they traded the seashore for the mountains, driving to Verbier, a Swiss ski resort where Loel Guinness' son Patrick had found them a small apartment. It was cold, dark and raining when they arrived, and their car became mired in the mud. So inauspicious was their first night that Jack was afraid to wake up the next morning, dreading that they might be stuck in a place they despised. But when they woke up, the sun was shining, the thin air tasted delicious, and the apartment was just what they had hoped it would be. "It is rather like living on the side of a moss-green bowl whose rim, zigzagging sharply up and down, is covered with snow," Jack wrote Gloria. "I asked, where do you ski? and was told—everywhere."

The apartment had already been rented for the Christmas holidays, unfortunately, and they spent three weeks in Munich, where, almost without warning, their bulldog Bunky died. Freud, who learned to enjoy canine companionship late in life, declared that an owner's feeling for his dog is the same as a parent's for his children, with one difference—"there is no ambivalence, no element of hostility." Truman and Jack felt that way about Bunky, who had been with them since the making of *Beat the Devil*. "Last week we found out Bunky had leukemia, and yesterday he died in my arms," Truman told Donald Windham. "I know you know how much I loved him; he was like my child. I have wept till I can weep no more."

Back in Verbier, Truman put aside *In Cold Blood* for a few weeks to write a movie adaptation of another dark tale, Henry James's *The Turn of the Screw*. The story was one of Truman's favorites: a psychological thriller about an English governess who believes she is battling two ghosts for the souls of her young charges. When the director, Jack Clayton, who had worked with him on *Beat the Devil*, begged him to do a rewrite of the script, he could not refuse. "He did it in the most unbelievable speed," recalled Clayton, "most of it in eight weeks, with a little bit of touching up afterward."

Titled *The Innocents*, the picture, which starred Deborah Kerr and Michael Redgrave, contained his best film script, Truman thought, better even than that of *Beat the Devil*. "I thought it would be a snap because I loved *The Turn of the Screw* so much," he said. "But when I got into it, I saw how artful James had been. He did everything by allusion and indirection. I made only one mistake. At the very end, when the governess sees the ghost of Miss Jessel sitting at her desk, I had a tear fall on to the desktop. Up until then it wasn't clear whether the ghosts were real or in the governess' mind. But the tear was real, and that spoiled everything." Few of the critics agreed. "A beautifully turned film," said the *New York Herald Tribune* reviewer, "one of the most artful hauntings to come along on film in a long time."

After the cold and drizzle of a London winter, Verbier looked more appealing than ever. "Oh how glorious it seems here," he exclaimed when he returned in February, 1961. "Such *sun*, *skies*, silence, *air*. I really do like it." He liked it so much, in fact, that he used part of the money he had earned from *The Innocents* to buy a two-room condominium. After moving from one rented place to another, he and Jack enjoyed the feeling of permanency. "Today I stood in back of the little church with the men folk—farmers," Jack wrote his sister. "It was a comfort. The strangest people go to church, rich and poor, dumb and bright. The priest was a big man with a long grey beard. I have to walk a mile or so to the church, which has a *rooster* on its steeple. I like that."

The pattern of their lives changed hardly at all during the next two years: spring and summer in Palamós; fall and winter in Verbier. Truman worked on *In Cold Blood*; Jack persisted with his plays. Kelly, the Kerry blue terrier that had been with them since 1950, also died, causing more pain. Although he had vowed that he would never go through the agony of love and loss again, in July, 1961, Truman bought another bulldog. In London for last-minute chores on *The Innocents*, he heard a familiar-sounding bark in Harrods. "Is there a pet shop here?" he asked, and was taken down a corridor to a room that held a macaw, a parrot, an owl, a fox terrier, and, as he told Cecil, "the most adorable, cuddly little bulldog pup you've ever seen." Marching over to the saleswoman, he said, "I've bought that bulldog."

"No, that's a special order," she replied. "That dog's not for sale. We can order you another."

"No," said Truman. "That dog is mine. I wish to buy *that* dog. Here's my checkbook."

"You can't buy that dog," she insisted. "Besides, he costs fifty-five pounds!"

"My dear woman. I've come all the way from Spain and have been directed straight to that dog. It is my destiny to have that dog." After an appeal to higher authority, destiny prevailed. When he returned to Palamós, the puppy—Charlie, he was called—was with him. "Charlie J. Fatburger is (as Diana V. [Vreeland] would *scream*), deevine," he wrote Cecil that fall.

In January, 1962, Truman returned to the United States to interview Perry's sister, whose testimony was crucial to an understanding of her brother's character, and to visit Perry and Dick on Death Row—"an extraordinary and terrible experience," he told Cecil. While he was in New York, Babe Paley gave him a large welcome-home party. But the sight of a hundred famous faces turned in his direction, which would have thrilled him not long before, now left him almost numb. Back in Verbier, he described his feelings to Cecil: "Somehow they, it, the whole thing seemed quite unreal, remote. The only thing that seemed real was Kansas, and the people there—I suppose because of my work. Actually, it is rather upsetting—the degree to which I am obsessed by the book. I scarcely think of anything else. The odd part is, I hate to work on it: I mean, actually *write*. I just want to think about it. Or rather—I don't *want* to; but I can't stop myself. Sometimes I go into sort of trance-like states that last four or five hours. I figure I have another 18 months to go. By which time I should be good and nuts."

After two summers in Spain, he and Jack planned to spend the summer of 1962 in Corsica. Within hours they realized their mistake. The other tourists were loud and pushy, and Jack watched with disgust as one group noisily drove off on a boar hunt. "Of course they all arrived back at the hotel the next morning not speaking to one another," he gleefully recounted, "and without so much as a Boar Turd amongst the lot of them." Describing their stay as a nightmare, Truman added that the Corsicans "combine the worst characteristics of both the wops and the frogs—ugh." Back to Palamós they scurried, to the best house yet, with a private beach, a large garden, and a cottage by the sea. Jackie Kennedy's sister, Lee Radziwill, came in the middle of July; she was followed by the Paleys. When the Paleys left, Gloria Vanderbilt arrived, accompanied, Truman informed Cecil, "by a lady-in-waiting in the form of Tammy Grimes—who wears *mink* eyebrows and a leather bikini."

In the process of changing husbands again, Gloria had warned her future Number Four, a sometime editor and writer named Wyatt Cooper, to be discreet in the letters he addressed to Palamós. Truman, she said, was certain to open and read them before she did. What she apparently did not explain to Wyatt was that she did not want Truman to know of their affair while she was telling him about another romance entirely. "Well, Gloria has come and gone and we had a 'real nice' visit," Truman wrote Marie and Alvin Dewey, adding, with the excitement of a reporter in possession of a hot scoop: "There *is* a new man in her life. It's supposed to be a great secret, but I will tell you because I just must tell somebody, it's so fantastic: Nelson Rockefeller. Heaven knows what will come of it—it would certainly be a strange thing if they got married." Nothing did come of it, and Gloria married Cooper, with whom she had two sons.

Truman and Cooper later became good friends, and in 1972 they collaborated on a television prison drama, *The Glass House*. Truman's friendship with Gloria, on the other hand, which had been tenuous from adolescence, progressively deteriorated. "She was a nasty little girl," he said. "She lied about her mother during her custody trial, and she was terrible to her until shortly before she died. She had a father complex. Her first husband, Pat DiCicco, was a rough-and-ready type who used to really beat her. She finally got rid of him and married Leopold Stokowski, who was more like a grandfather, or a great-grandfather, than a father. I introduced her to Sidney Lumet, and she only married him because she thought he would make her a movie star. But the only part she ever got was as a nurse in some television thing. When she found out he wasn't going to make her a star, she dumped him quick.

"Why she married Wyatt is a mystery. He certainly wasn't like anybody's father, although he did tell me that when they had sex together, she would scream, over and over, 'Daddy! Daddy! Daddy!' He grew to hate her, and he was terrified that she would leave him and take their two boys, to whom he was devoted. He was always calling me, asking me what he should do. I think that that anxiety contributed to his death. In fact, I had lunch with him just before he died [in 1978]. He seemed fine, but he kept talking about those boys. 'If only I can live another ten years,' he said, 'everything will be all right. But Gloria just isn't responsible enough to raise them.' "

In early October, Truman and Jack were back in Verbier, where, Truman said, he was "bedded down with my book—on which am now heading into *fourth* year. Maybe one day it will all seem worth it: I wonder though." In November he interrupted his work long enough for a lunch with royalty in London. The lunch, in honor of the Queen Mother, was given by Cecil, who boasted to his diary that it was "another milestone—the biggest yet perhaps—in my social rise." Besides Truman, just three others had received invitations to his house on Pelham Place: Frederick Ashton, principal choreographer of the Royal Ballet; June Osborn, a comely widow whom Cecil once had hoped to marry; and that poet with the medieval manner, Edith Sitwell, who profusely apologized for not being able to rise from her wheelchair to curtsy to the royal guest. "Oh! Oh! Oh! Ma'am, I'm so ashamed that I can't get up to greet you," she said.

The conversation was lively and energetic. For his part, Truman told the Queen Mother the latest gossip about the Whitney family —Jock Whitney, Babe Paley's brother-in-law, had recently retired as ambassador to Britain—and he talked about the book he was writing. By dessert "restraint was far away," said Cecil. "T was yelping with laughter & gave a great whoop of joy when the summer pudding appeared." Truman had made yet another conquest. After Cecil had escorted the guest of honor to her car, she pulled down the window to say "she thought Mr. Capote quite wonderful, so intelligent, so wise, so funny."

"Yes, he's a genius, Ma'am," Cecil gravely replied.

40

By the beginning of 1963, *In Cold Blood* was three-quarters completed. "I have been rising every morning at 3 or 4 to work —it is now 4," Truman told Cecil in February. "But *yesterday* I *finished* Part Three! I have never worked so hard in my life. But it is done, and I know you will be really thrilled by it. It is all I wanted it to be—which is saying a great deal. But I am exhausted; tense as nine newly tuned pianos."

True to his vow, he had stayed in Europe, away from the distractions of Manhattan, so that he could concentrate on his work. He could not do much more until he had an ending, however, until Perry and Dick had either been hanged or given reduced sentences. Neither of those possibilities appeared imminent; after nearly three years on Death Row, they were still bouncing appeals between the state and federal judicial systems. To the Deweys he confessed, not for the first time, his chagrin and frustration: "Will H & S [Hickock and Smith] live to a ripe and happy old age?—or will they swing, and make a lot of other folks very happy indeed? For the answer to these and other suspenseful questions tune in tomorrow to your favorite radio program, 'Western Justice,' sponsored by the Slow Motion Molasses Company, a Kansas Product."

There was no longer any point in isolating himself. It was time to go home, and in early March, after nearly three years away, he and Jack returned to America and once again took up residence in Oliver Smith's basement apartment in Brooklyn Heights. For Truman, coming back to New York was like coming back to the world. "I lead such a monastery life," he had grumbled in Europe. "No news at all." Now, throwing off his monk's robe—"*I need a rest from my book*," he emphatically explained—he let loose and enjoyed himself, slipping into old routines as easily as he slipped into his old back booth at the Colony. He lunched with his favorite swans, spent weekends at Kiluna Farm with Babe and Bill Paley, and visited the Kennedys in the White House. As an emblem of his liberation, he bought what was to be one of his proudest possessions: a silver-blue Jaguar sports car. "It's like Fabergé on wheels," he bragged. "I sailed into the Jaguar place and said, 'I'll take it.' "

He was home in time to say a few last words to Newton, who died of pancreatic cancer at the end of March. Paradoxically, his arrest and the scandal over the pornographic pictures seemed to have strengthened Newton. Not only had he regained his self-esteem, but he had also acquired a stoical serenity he never before had possessed. From wisdom born of torment he said: "The staple of life is certainly suffering, though surely not its real meaning, and we differ mainly in our capacity to endure it—or be diverted from it."

Some of Truman's other friends could do neither. Montgomery Clift long since had descended into a netherworld of drink and drugs. Now he was joined by Cole Porter, whose buoyant spirit had succumbed at last to age, disillusion and the unrelenting pain caused by a long-ago riding accident. In the fifties, when Truman first knew him, Porter was a symbol of the sophisticated world he venerated. Lovingly decorated by Billy Baldwin, his aerie on the thirty-third floor of the Waldorf Towers was a cloud-capped citadel of elegance and luxury. The incandescent grin that once had illuminated those concinnous quarters disappeared with the decade, however. Guests who had once jumped at an invitation to dinner now came out of loyalty alone.

"Cole had a wonderful secretary who kept a revolving list of guests —he couldn't get that many people to go there," Truman recalled. "I would go about once every six weeks. I looked forward to dinner there like I looked forward to the guillotine. During his later days Cole wasn't exactly *non compos*, but he wasn't all there either. He was always immaculately dressed—I mean immaculately—and the food was superb. He would have one double martini before dinner, and after that he wouldn't say a word for the rest of the night. He just sat there, not talking and not eating, and I would talk to myself. After a while I got used to it and really didn't mind it so much. I would even turn on the television while we were eating. Then exactly at 10:30 his valet would come in and say, 'It's time for you to go to bed, Mr. Porter,' and I would leave.

"Cole wasn't always like that, of course. When I first knew him, he was very funny and witty. He used to describe his sex life in great detail—I think it excited him. I used a story in *Answered Prayers* about a wine steward he tried to get to go to bed with him.* Cole thought it was amusing, and now every time I see the man, who's the maître d' of one of the most expensive restaurants in Manhattan, I just smile. Because I know what his past was. But there was another story Cole told that I didn't use because it sounded rather unpleasant—and I liked Cole. It was about his long affair with that actor, Jack Cassidy. Cassidy would say, 'Do you want this cock? Then come and get it!' Then he would stand away so that Cole, whose legs had been paralyzed in that awful riding accident, would have to crawl toward him. Every time Cole got near, Cassidy would move farther away. This went on for half an hour or forty-five minutes before Cassidy would finally stop and let Cole have it."

Yet while he was dining with Cole, lunching with Babe, or sitting through Jackie Kennedy's Mozart evening at the White House, Truman was thinking about, and usually talking about, his book. "If only I could empty my soul and heart and head of it for a while," he lamented. But that he could not do—nor did he want to do. *In Cold Blood* had become part of his life: he could put it aside, but he could not forget it. "Eventually it began to own him," said Phyllis Cerf. "Emotionally, it became something bigger than he could handle. Those boys began to own him, and the town [Garden City] began to own him."

One night, at a dinner party given by Diana Vreeland, he spoke briefly about what he was writing, then, seeing the fascinated faces around him, continued, describing Holcomb and Garden City, the people who lived there, the Clutters, the killers—everything. "He spoke the way he wrote," recalled D. D. Ryan, his old friend from *House of Flowers* days. "He was writing, but orally. It was all formed

---

* One of Truman's characters relates how the composer lured the steward onto his living-room couch by claiming he needed advice on storing his wine. Every time Porter made an advance, such as squeezing his leg, the steward coolly named his price for allowing such a liberty. As the advances became bolder, so did the bill. When it reached two thousand dollars, Porter angrily wrote out a check and, quoting the lyrics of one of his most famous songs, said: "Miss Otis regrets she's unable to lunch today. Now get out."

in his mind. This went on for two hours, maybe even three or four. Nobody said a word. Nobody moved all that time. It was the greatest tale-telling I've ever witnessed."

The magnetic attraction of Kansas soon pulled him west again. In mid-April he set off in his Fabergé on wheels, detouring first to Monroeville to visit his remaining relatives—Jennie, the last of the Faulk cousins, had died in 1958—and to pick up Nelle Harper Lee, who was joining him again. On their way, they passed through Shreveport, Louisiana, where Arch now lived. "Well, should I?" Truman asked. "Why not?" Nelle answered, and they both giggled. Registering at a motel, he called his father, whom he had not seen since Nina's death, nine years before. "My wife Blanche had never met him," said Arch. "Never, not in eighteen years of marriage; and we had a lovely visit."

It is impossible to know which of those tellers of tall tales, father or son, told more lies during their hours together, but the honor probably belonged to Truman. The Queen Mother's words of praise, which would have turned anyone's head, still rang in his ears like the chimes of Big Ben. In the months since November, Cecil's lunch had been transformed into a royal tribute to Truman himself. As he recounted it, it had taken place not in Cecil's house, but in Buckingham Palace—he even altered Cecil's carefully chosen menu —and the Queen, not her mother, had been the hostess. ("I was in London last week, and the queen asked me to lunch," he had written his grandmother. "She was very bright and charming, and very pretty!") A version of the story found its way back to Cecil, who was understandably annoyed.

Arch had a photograph taken of Truman standing proudly beside his new car in the Persons driveway. Never one to overlook a promotional gimmick, Arch then had it printed on postcards, which he sent to his friends and customers. The caption underneath read: "Truman Capote, beloved only son of Arch Persons, owner of the Dixie Scale Co., on a recent visit to his father at Shreveport, La., in his new 1963 Jaguar Special. Author of 'Breakfast at Tiffany's,' 'Other Voices Other Rooms,' 'The Grass Harp,' 'House of Flowers,' and many other famous books, he is ranked among the first three of his profession throughout the nation. He was recently a guest at both The White House and at Buckingham Palace."

. . .

Truman's most important destination in Kansas was the State Penitentiary, a forty-minute drive from downtown Kansas City. Built in 1864, it resembled a turreted English castle; there was no disguising its grim purpose. Inside its walls, on the second floor of a small two-story structure, was Death Row, twelve cells, each of which measured seven by ten feet and was furnished only with a cot, a toilet and a basin; burning twenty-four hours a day, a bulb of low wattage emitted the glow of a perpetual twilight. The world outside was seen through a sliver of a window, which was barred and covered with black wire mesh. Inmates were let out just once a week for a three-minute shower and a change of clothing; during the summer, when temperatures inside sometimes reached 110 degrees, they were disgusted by their own odor. Although they were allowed newspapers, magazines and books, residents were not permitted radios or television sets. Perry and Dick could talk to each other from their adjoining cells—not that they had much to say to each other—but they had to be cautious in their conversations, which could be overheard by guards and other prisoners.

Truman had visited there twice before. But to finish *In Cold Blood*, the last part of which was mainly a history of their lives in those tiny cells, he needed regular communication with them. Gaining that right was not an easy task. Usually only relatives and lawyers were granted the privilege to come and go and exchange letters with condemned men. Prison authorities refused to cooperate with him, and finally, in desperation, he bribed his way in, he said, paying a powerful political figure to pull the right strings. "If I hadn't got what I wanted, I would have had to abandon everything. I had to have access to those two boys. So I went for broke and asked for an interview with this behind-the-scenes figure, who was a man of great distinction and renown in that state. 'I'll give you ten thousand dollars if you can arrange this,' I said. I didn't know if he was going to accept the money or not. He could have said, 'The hell with you! Now you'll never get inside that penitentiary!' But I guess my offer was very tempting, and he just nodded his head."

However the deal was managed, Truman was allowed to visit Perry and Dick almost at will and, beginning in June, 1963, to correspond with them as well. Their letters to him number in the hundreds—his to them were destroyed, alas—and they document more graphically than could any movie or play the endless tedium of hell, which is what Death Row was. Aside from their never-ending legal battles, Truman became the chief focus of their lives, their main contact with what Dick called "the free world."

His correspondence started first with Perry, who immediately requested *Webster's New World Dictionary*, which, along with the thesaurus that followed, became the source for the high-flown words he loved to use—and often misuse. To Perry a letter was an epistle, good weather was salubrious, and to be fat was to be adipose. He was fascinated by everything about Truman, the master of words. "Amigo mio, I have a multitude of questions I'd like to ask you," he said, "and many diverse subjects I am desirous to discuss." Constantly advising Truman to be careful, he would end his letters with such comments as "If you're driving be extra cautious. Lots of crazy people on roads."

A photograph of Truman with his Harrods bulldog touched him almost to the point of tears. "I have your picture with Charlie before me now. It packs a lot of affection. That half smile is infectious and I can't seem to keep from smiling myself whenever I chance a glance at it. I cannot believe that I have ever seen a more pleasing and contented expression—it appears to have an effect on me similar to an anodyne and it would be useless for you to ask me to return it. (smile). A little poem comes to mind—please allow me to insert it here—it may help you to understand me and I must put it down on paper before it escapes me.

> Far beyond the distant hills,
> The plaintive sounds of whippoorwills,
> Reverberates the rocks and rills,
> 'Tis such a plaintive cry.
> Is the Mockingbird so often heard,
> Intent to make himself absurd,
> Or just a melancholy bird,
> In truth, as sad as I."

His compliments were more effusive than the Queen Mother's. "I like talented personalities very much and I feel that you are a very perspicacious homo sapien." Truman was father, mentor, perhaps even surrogate lover.

Perry scarcely tried to hide his jealousy at the fact that Dick was also receiving epistles from such a perspicacious homo sapien. He liked to point out to Truman that while he was requesting volumes of real literary value—works by Freud, Thoreau and Santayana, among others—Dick was asking for the potboilers of Harold Robbins. "This kind of literature is only degenerating minds that are already degenerated & perverted," Perry angrily asserted. To Dick himself he sneered, "If you had any sense, you would realize that [Truman] thinks twice as much of me as he does you."

His own letters from Truman Perry kept secret, but he expected Dick—"Ricardo," he called him—to share his. When Dick once declined, Perry went into a deep sulk. "P. has another 'madon' at me because I won't let him read your letters!" reported Dick. "Every time he knew I had heard from you, he asked to read it. To keep from hurting his feelings I would let him. Finally I got tired of his crust, and refused. It shows ignorance, ill-manners and no home raising to request the privilege to read someone's mail—especially their personal mail. *I* would never have the gall to request the reading of P's mail. I suppose I should over-look P's faults, because he *is* kind of ignorant and stupid. He has a very low I.Q., and it is difficult for him to understand a lot of things."

Dick's own letters were more in keeping with those that might be expected from someone in his situation. They began in a fairly good humor—he had had a bedmate like Holly Golightly, he joked—and they became progressively darker. "Forty two months without exercise, radio, movies, sunshine, or any physical means of occupation, is a steady strain on a man's nervous system," he said in September, 1963. "Add the mental strain of facing a death sentence, and you have a man—or men—who slowly becomes an animal—or human vegetable." He was, or said he was, sorry that the Clutters had been murdered, though, he claimed, probably accurately in Truman's opinion, that it was Perry who had actually fired the fatal shots. "I doubt if hell will have me," he declared at one point. "I'm feeling lower than whale manure, and *that* is at the bottom of the ocean," he said at another. In April, 1964, he marked the fourth anniversary of his arrival on Death Row: "At times it seems *forty* years instead of four."

After all those months without sun or exercise, prisoners 14746 (Dick) and 14747 (Perry) began to suffer from the illnesses of old age. Perry complained of excruciating pains and occasional paralysis of the shoulders and discussed possible cures with Truman, who was suffering from the similar symptoms of bursitis. In one or another of the many magazines Truman sent him, including *Science Newsletter* and *Nature & Science*, he had discovered a remedy for everything except what ailed him. At the same time, Dick's eyesight began to deteriorate, and he was bothered by fainting spells. What seemed to cause him the most anguish, ironically, was the possibility that he might grow bald. "My hair line, at my forehead, has receded a full inch," he said in September, 1964. "I'm almost frantic with worry about it. I certainly do not wish to be bald headed; I am ugly enough. Also, *no one* in my family was ever bald headed. If you have any suggestions, please state them in your next letter." Truman, who was losing his own hair at an equal rate, was of no help.

Perry and Dick also wondered and worried about how they would appear in Truman's book. One concern was practical. Their appeals rested on their claim that the Clutter murders had not been planned, and they were afraid that Truman would tell a different story—as, indeed, he did. Another was, in a sense, esthetic. They did not want to be remembered as psychopathic killers. "My concern is that the info. you have collected is accurate, correct, and not perverted by the relator to his or her purpose for any ulterior motive," Perry said in one letter. "What is the purpose of the book?" he asked in another. Truman danced around the subject, pretending, until the day they were executed, that he was barely half-done and, in fact, might never finish.

When they discovered his title—which said, in three words, that they had planned the murders—Truman lied and informed them they were wrong. But they knew better, and Perry indignantly told him so: "I've been told that the book is to be coming off the press and to be sold after our executions. And that book *IS* entitled 'IN COLD BLOOD.' Whose fibbing?? Someone is, that's apparent. Frankly, 'In Cold Blood' is shocking to the conscience alone." Truman continued his fibs, and with an unhappy sigh, Perry wrote Donald Cullivan, "Sometimes it's hard to know what to believe." Dick was no less concerned, telling him that any suggestion of premeditation "has me extremely disturbed because, as I have repeatedly informed you, there was *no* discussion at *any* time to harm the Clutters." In a nine-page letter, Dick laid all the blame on Perry.

As 1963 passed, and then 1964, their hopes drained away, slowly at first, then faster and faster, like bathwater swirling down a drain. They watched while another inmate, whose last appeal had been turned down, was taken away for a ride on the "Big Swing." Perry dispassionately described the aftermath. "After we heard the trap door sprung, it was quite awhile there after [eighteen minutes, in fact] that he was lowered to the ground, layed on a stretcher & carried out in a hearse." With his usual thoroughness, he looked up the medical definition of death by hanging and sent it to Truman: "Death by hanging produced by asphyxia suspending respiration by compressing the larynx, by apoplexy pressing upon the veins & preventing return of blood from the head, by fracture of the cervical vertebrae . . . "

Dick began to complain that he could not sleep at night, and Perry wrote less frequently, confessing in February, 1965, that he had been "pretty well depressed & broken in spirit lately." His once precise handwriting had become a scrawl. "My Dear Friend," he said, "what a pair we are? Yes what a pair of poor wretched creatures we are!" Left tantalizingly unclear was who the other half of his pair was, Truman or Dick. On January 27, 1965, came a new execution date, February 18. "Well, the fat's in the fire!" said Dick. He was only slightly premature. They received another stay of execution— their fifth—and then, as Perry wrote Truman, a new date was set: "April 14 you know is the date to drop thru the trap door—in case you haven't been apprised."

For the better part of two years Truman's life was in a state of suspended animation. He could not finish his book until he had an ending, but neither could he put it aside and go on to something else. Although he was no longer consumed with putting words on paper, his work continued in dozens of nagging chores, not least of which was the composition of two letters a week, the maximum permitted, to Perry and Dick. "The writing of the book wasn't as difficult as living with it all the time," he said. "The whole damn thing, day by day by day by day. It was *just* excruciating, so anxiety-making, so wearing, so debilitating, and so . . . sad."

His frustration was made worse by his knowledge that, lying in front of him, missing only thirty or forty pages, was the best-seller that would alter his life irrevocably, that would make him rich and bring him what he coveted above all else: recognition as one of the foremost writers in America—indeed, the world. At that point such a conviction was a matter of fact, not opinion; the success of *In Cold Blood* was as predictable as the future movements of the planets. All those who had read the first three-quarters—and there was a large number of such people—confessed to being mesmerized. Everybody in the publishing world knew about his new work, and so did many others, all across the country. It was mentioned frequently in syndicated columns; in 1962 *Newsweek* had even run a story, complete with a picture of the author, on "the overwhelmingly factual book he has been working on for more than two years."

Such publicity could not have been purchased, particularly for a book that had yet to be completed. *In Cold Blood* had been touched by a magic wand. At both Random House and *The New Yorker*, where all copies were locked in Mr. Shawn's office, there was the thrill of anticipation, the excitement that comes with the possession of a sure thing. But nothing—nothing at all—could happen until the courts had at last decided the fates of the two Clutter killers.

So Truman watched and waited and went on, as best he could, with the normal business of living. Following his return from the Midwest in 1963, he and Jack went out to Long Island, to the same beach house in Bridgehampton they had shared with Oliver Smith six years before. "The house is divine, and I am working on my *endless* task," Truman wrote Cecil in July. "But I am very restless—waiting for final developments in Kansas. It's all so maddening." Two months later he added: "I am in a really appalling state of tension and anxiety. Perry and Dick have an appeal for a *New Trial* pending in Federal Court: if they should get it (a new trial) I will have a complete breakdown of some sort." Although they were not granted a new trial, the appeals continued, and in November, still tense and anxious, Truman made yet another trip to Kansas.

He went first to California to visit Cecil, who was designing the sets and costumes for the movie version of *My Fair Lady*. They met in San Francisco, where Cecil was eager to introduce him to his new, thirty-year-old lover, who was everything that Cecil had ever desired. He was tall, blond and athletic; he had been a member of one of the American teams at the 1956 Melbourne Olympics. An art historian who was studying and lecturing at Berkeley, he was also far better educated than Cecil himself; he had attended both Harvard and Princeton, where his roommate had been his lover and where belly-rubbing was so common that it was named "First Year Princeton." By some miracle, this handsome all-American was as enthralled by Cecil as Cecil was by him. To Cecil's gratification, Truman heartily endorsed their May-December romance, telling him that his athlete was "adorable, intelligent, appreciative, very fond of you, an important addition to your life." Glowing in the reflected praise, Cecil added, "Felt very proud of my choice, who today seemed more delightfully gay & intelligent than ever."

If Truman showed any of the tension he had referred to in his letters, it was not noticed by Cecil, who was caught up not only in his love affair, but also in a running feud with George Cukor, the director of *My Fair Lady*. During the following days in Los Angeles, Cecil was once again impressed by Truman's ability to instantly take command. "He was completely at home on the [studio] lot here," Cecil observed. "He was effusively received by the hypocrite Cukor & confided in by Rex [Harrison], who says that he likes working with Audrey [Hepburn], as she has such discipline, but she possesses no fire. Liz Taylor for all her slatterliness does possess this quality."

After his California holiday, Truman dutifully went to Kansas, where he saw friends in Garden City and spent perhaps an hour and a half each with Perry and Dick in Lansing. "I had so much to say & discuss with you and so little time to say it in," complained Perry a few days later. "It seemed as though we no sooner greeted each other, had a few brief words and here I was, back in my limbo again, feeling as though I was cheated of something and a little confused and disappointed."

Truman associated Verbier with hard work and isolation, and in December, 1963, he let Jack go there by himself while he drove to Florida to stay with rich friends, the Gardner Cowleses in Miami Beach—Cowles owned *Look* magazine—and the Guinnesses in Palm Beach. He took Donald Windham with him to the Cowleses', where he received a phone call telling him that Perry and Dick had won another appeal. Donald was witness to his depression and sudden nervousness, which manifested itself as a twitch in his cheek, a compulsive blink, and a darting, snakelike movement of his tongue. "I really have been feeling very low—almost bitter," Truman confessed to the Deweys. "It's all absolutely beyond belief. My God! Why don't they just turn them loose and be done with it. . . . Well, there's nothing to be done—except try to get through another year of this totally absurd and unnecessary torture."

Jack lent his support from a distance. "Go on with your work, it's a miracle of writing," he said. "That's what you must keep before you, day in, day out, waking and sleeping—your story." But Truman's restlessness sent his imagination off in a dozen different directions. He considered buying a house in Westchester, for example, not far from the Cerfs; but he quickly gave up the notion when Jack wrote back: "No, I want to be at least within bicycling-distance of water. Salt water!" He then said that he would like to spend the summer in Spain again. Jack sent a second veto, advising him to stay in America, close to his story. In the end, they again rented a house on Long Island, where Truman at last bought a piece of American real estate, a small house in Sagaponack, just east of Bridgehampton.

About a hundred yards from the ocean, the house had a high-ceilinged living room and a tiny bedroom downstairs; upstairs, reached by a spiral staircase, were two or three more rabbit-warren bedrooms. Jack hated the place immediately, believing, probably rightly, that they both would go mad in such a small space. He said nothing, but Truman undoubtedly read his face: not long after, he also bought the house next door. He would live in the first house, he said, and Jack would live in the second.

Thus they had found the ideal arrangement: they were within hailing distance, but they could not see each other through the trees and shrubs. Truman's house was just right for him. He removed walls upstairs, giving his little house a more spacious feeling. Jack's house was just right for him, an old-fashioned gingerbread cottage, with one large room downstairs and another one upstairs. He was so pleased, in fact, that, hat in hand—an unusual gesture for him—he asked Truman for title to his own house: he was forty-nine and, standing on his own ground at last, he yearned for the security of actual ownership. "I never asked Truman for anything," he said. "I never asked him for favors. But I did ask him for my house, and he gave me the deeds for both of them in a butterfly box. He said that it was too much trouble to separate titles, so I could have them both in my name. I have never seen anybody else in my life do anything as generous as that."

In October, 1964, Truman went back to Kansas, taking with him Sandy Campbell—Donald Windham's lover—who was a fact checker at *The New Yorker*, assigned, at Truman's request, to check the accuracy of *In Cold Blood*. They first flew to Denver, where Truman had arranged a party for some of his Garden City friends, most notably the Deweys, and Mary Louise Aswell, who had left *Harper's Bazaar* in the fifties for a new life in New Mexico. The Deweys, Sandy noted in his diary, were almost like parents to Truman: he called Alvin Pappy, and Alvin had nicknamed him Coach. They then drove east to Garden City, where Sandy verified such things as dates and distances. Sandy said that he had worked with many *New Yorker* writers, including A. J. Liebling, Richard Rovere and Lillian Ross, but Truman was the most accurate. It was the opinion of Mary Louise that Truman most treasured, however, and he anxiously awaited her verdict on the first three-quarters of his book. He was profoundly pleased by her response. "That you really liked my book was so touching, and such a *reward*. I sort of dreaded your reading it—because I knew that if I was fooling myself, and had made a real mistake (about the artistic possibilities of reportage) you wouldn't have been able to lie (successfully)."

Just before Christmas, Truman spoke, as he had before, at the Poetry Center of Manhattan's Ninety-second Street Y.M.H.A. The program said he would read from *Breakfast at Tiffany's*. But some, suspecting that he would surprise them with *In Cold Blood* instead, arrived with more than the usual eagerness, like movie fans hoping for the sneak preview of a long-anticipated film. They were not disappointed. *Newsweek*, which sent a reporter, said that the effect he created was like that of "a fabulist of the old order, weaving a spell with voice and word, making one hear, see, feel, *sense*. What he shaped was a whole landscape and the fateful people in it."

Perry's and Dick's numerous appeals not only caused him depression and anxiety. They presented him with an insoluble moral dilemma. He desperately wanted his book to be published. But publication almost certainly meant the painful deaths of two men who regarded him as their friend and benefactor, two men whom he had helped, counseled, and, in Perry's case, tutored. "It wasn't a question of my *liking* Dick and Perry," he carefully explained to an interviewer. "That's like saying, 'Do you like yourself?' What mattered was that I *knew* them, as well as I know myself."

His entire future awaited their walk to the Big Swing, and his comments to his friends, which indicated his real feelings, ran like a grim counterpoint to the consoling comments he was making to Perry and Dick. Perry was of course unhappy when the Supreme Court refused in January, 1965, to hear their latest appeal. But where he saw a black cloud, Truman saw a ray of sunshine. "As you may have heard," he told Mary Louise, "the Supreme Court denied the appeals (this for the *third* damn time), so maybe something will soon happen one way or another. I've been disappointed so many times I hardly dare hope. But keep your fingers crossed." To Cecil he added: "I'm finishing the last pages of my book—I *must* be rid of it regardless of what happens. I hardly give a fuck anymore *what* happens. My sanity is at stake—and that is no mere idle phrase. Oh the hell with it. I shouldn't write such gloomy crap—even to someone as close to me as you."

In Verbier, waiting out events, he decided not to go back to America for the execution in February, working out an arrangement by which Sandy Campbell would cable him, word for word, the story in the *Kansas City Star*. "Hope this doesn't sound insane," he wrote Sandy, "but the way I've constructed things, I will be able to complete the entire ms. within hours after receiving [the] cable. Keep *everything* crossed." At the last moment the hangings were postponed once again. Desperate for information, he made a transatlantic call to one of the defense lawyers, who infuriated him by suggesting that Perry and Dick might not only escape the noose, but actually gain their freedom. "And I thought: yes, and I hope you're the first one they bump off, you sonofabitch," he told the Deweys, who shared his frustration. "But what I actually said was: 'Is that really your idea of justice?—that after killing four people, they ought to be let out on the streets?' "

The lawyer's optimism was unfounded, and the hangings were rescheduled for the early hours of April 14. This time Truman could not stay away—Perry and Dick had asked him to be with them—and he returned to America. Accompanied by Joseph Fox, who had replaced Bob Linscott as his editor at Random House, Truman arrived in Kansas City a day or two early. "He was incredibly tense and unable to really talk to anybody for more than two or three minutes at a time," recalled Fox. "Tears rolled down his cheeks at the thought of what was going to happen. Alvin came to call, along with a couple of the other K.B.I. agents, and Truman would pace around our suite at the Muehlebach Hotel. At night we went to the movies or strip shows and transvestite shows—Kansas City is one of the six or seven biggest transvestite centers in the country."

For some reason, Perry and Dick thought that Truman might help them obtain another stay of execution, and they tried desperately to reach him. Perry telephoned the hotel two or three times, and an assistant warden, acting on their behalf, tried seven or eight times more. But another delay was the last thing Truman wanted. Rather than say no, he let Fox answer the phone and make his excuses. Finally Perry telegraphed the Muehlebach. "AM ANTICIPATION AND WAITING YOUR VISIT. HAVE BELONGINGS FOR YOU. PLEASE ACKNOWLEDGE BY RETURN WIRE WHEN YOU EXPECT TO BE HERE." Tru-

man cabled back: "DEAR PERRY. UNABLE TO VISIT YOU TODAY. BECAUSE
NOT PERMITTED. ALWAYS YOUR FRIEND. TRUMAN."

Perry was aware, of course, that he was lying—that he would
have been permitted to visit. At 11:45 that night, one hour and
fifteen minutes before the noose was put around his neck, he sat
down and wrote a joint letter to him and Nelle. "Sorry that Truman
was unable to make it here at the prison for a brief word or two prior
to [the] neck-tie party. Whatever his reason for not showing up, I
want you to know that I cannot condemn you for it & understand.
Not much time left but want you both to know that I've been
sincerely grateful for your friend[ship] through the years and everything else. I'm not very good at these things—I want you both to
know that I have become very affectionate toward you. But harness
time. Adios Amigos. Best of everything, Your friend always,
Perry."

In a heavy rain, Truman and Joe drove to the prison, and Truman
was able to say a few last words to each of them. Dick was hanged
first. "I just want to say I hold no hard feelings," he said. "You
people are sending me to a better world than this ever was." Less
than half an hour later he was dead. Just after 1 A.M. Perry was
brought into the warehouse where the gallows had been set up. "I
think it's a helluva thing to take a life in this manner," he said. "I
don't believe in capital punishment, morally or legally. Maybe I had
something to contribute, something . . ." He stopped, and in a
lower voice, added: "It would be meaningless to apologize for what
I did. Even inappropriate. But I do. I apologize." The rope was
placed around his neck, a black mask was put over his eyes, and at
1:19 A.M. he too was pronounced dead.

Crying, Truman later called Jack to describe the terrible scene
he had witnessed. Jack was unsympathetic. "They're dead, Truman," he said. "You're alive."

42

And so at last the wait was over. Truman flew back to New York, tightly gripping Joe Fox's hand all the way and carrying with him a forty-page essay in which Perry had set down his thoughts on life and death. *"De Rebus Incognitis"* ("Concerning Unknown Things"), Perry had titled it, ending with a sentiment that may or may not have consoled him when the rope was placed around his neck: "Did we not know we were to die, we would be children; by knowing it, we are given our opportunity to mature in spirit. Life is only the father of wisdom; death is the mother."

Reading those unexpected words from the grave only prolonged Truman's distress, and in the next few days he made many more tearful phone calls to friends and relatives. "Perry and Dick were executed last Tuesday," he wrote Donald Cullivan. "I was there. I stayed with Perry to the end. He was calm and very brave. It was a terrible experience and I will never get over it. Someday I will try to tell you about it. But for the moment I am still too shattered. Over the years I'd become very devoted to Perry. And Dick, too." Then, as if to assuage his guilt for refusing to talk to them until the hour before they were hanged, he added: *"Everything possible was done to save them."* Days later, at a cost of seventy dollars and fifty cents each, he ordered simple granite markers for their graves, which were placed side by side in a cemetery near the prison:

RICHARD EUGENE
HICKOCK
June 6, 1931
April 14, 1965

PERRY EDWARD
SMITH
Oct. 27, 1928
April 14, 1965

By the middle of June he had completed the pages describing their last night, when the rain, rapping on the high warehouse roof, sounded "not unlike the rat-a-tat-tat of parade drums." *In Cold Blood* was finished. "Bless Jesus," he exclaimed to Cecil. "But incredible to suddenly be free (comparatively) of all these years and years of tension and aging. At the moment, only feel bereft. But grateful. Never again!"

Everything he had set out to do Truman succeeded in doing. He had gambled and he had won. On a superficial level, *In Cold Blood* is a murder story of riveting vitality and suspense. On a deeper level, it is what he had always known it could be, a Big Work—a master-piece, in fact, that he has infused with the somber energy of Greek tragedy. With stately, even majestic confidence he sets his scene in the first paragraph. "The village of Holcomb stands on the high wheat plains of western Kansas, a lonesome area that other Kansans call 'out there.' Some seventy miles east of the Colorado border, the countryside, with its hard blue skies and desert-clear air, has an atmosphere that is rather more Far West than Middle West. The local accent is barbed with a prairie twang, a ranch-hand nasalness, and the men, many of them, wear narrow frontier trousers, Stet-sons, and high-heeled boots with pointed toes. The land is flat, and the views are awesomely extensive; horses, herds of cattle, a white cluster of grain elevators rising as gracefully as Greek temples are visible long before a traveler reaches them."

Employing the skills he had learned as a screenwriter, he presents his main protagonists in short, cinematic scenes: the Clutters, unsus-pectingly awaiting their fate in the shadows of those dignified grain elevators, and their killers, racing across Kansas to meet them, Nem-esis in a black Chevrolet. Going about its peaceful pursuits in Hol-comb is one America—prosperous, secure, and a little smug. Along with his many good qualities, Herb Clutter is rigid and self-righ-teous; he promises to fire any employee caught "harboring alcohol," and he refuses to let Nancy even consider marrying her boyfriend, whose only offense is that he is Catholic. Speeding across the plains is the other America—poor, rootless and misbegotten. "Transient hearts," Randolph prophetically named such people in *Other Voices;* envy and self-pity are their only legacies, violence their only handi-work. Together, victims and killers are America in microcosm—light and dark, goodness and evil.

Truman had long maintained that nonfiction could be both as

artful and as compelling as fiction. In his opinion the reason it was not—that it was generally considered a lesser class of writing—was that it was most often written by journalists who were not equipped to exploit it. Only a writer "completely in control of fictional techniques" could elevate it to the status of art. "Journalism," he said, "always moves along on a horizontal plane, telling a story, while fiction—good fiction—moves vertically, taking you deeper and deeper into character and events. By treating a real event with fictional techniques (something that cannot be done by a journalist until he *learns* to write good fiction), it's possible to make this kind of synthesis." Because good fiction writers had usually disdained reporting, and most reporters had not learned to write good fiction, the synthesis had not been made, and nonfiction had never realized its potential. It was marble awaiting a sculptor, a palette of paints awaiting an artist. He was the first to show what could be done with that unappreciated material, he insisted, and *In Cold Blood* was a new literary species, the nonfiction novel.

By that he meant that he had written it as he would have a novel, but, instead of pulling characters and situations from his imagination, he had borrowed them from real life. Perry and Dick, Herb Clutter and Alvin Dewey were as much figures in history as George Washington and Abraham Lincoln. He could no more have altered their characters for the sake of his story than he could have affixed a moustache under Washington's nose or shaved off Lincoln's beard. He was fenced in by the barbed wire of fact. Yet within those boundaries, he believed that there was far more latitude than other writers had ever realized, freedom to juxtapose events for dramatic effect, to re-create long conversations, even to peer inside the heads of his characters and tell what they are thinking. "An author in his book must be like God in the universe, present everywhere and visible nowhere," said Flaubert. And so, in the universe of *In Cold Blood*, is Truman's presence felt in every sentence.

One by one, he repeats the themes, images, and leitmotifs that permeate his novels and short stories: loneliness, the death of innocence, and the danger that lurks in every shadow. In an uncanny way, his true-life chronicle is the culmination of his fiction, the logical extension of all that he had written before. From a multitude of facts he presents only those that interest him. Or, in his words: "I built an oak and reduced it to a seed." Another writer might have laid emphasis on Holcomb's small-town closeness and the warmth and good-heartedness of its citizens. Truman chooses instead to pick up a thread from his fiction and to dwell on its isolation. Though one sits on arid plains and the other is surrounded by swamps, his Holcomb sounds very much like the Noon City of *Other Voices*— lonesome is the adjective he applies to both. Finney County becomes Capote country, and the people who move through his pages become Capote characters.

In Cold Blood may have been written like a novel, but it is accurate to the smallest detail—"immaculately factual," Truman publicly boasted. Although it has no footnotes, he could point to an obvious source for every remark uttered and every thought expressed. "One doesn't spend almost six years on a book," he said, "the point of which is factual accuracy, and then give way to minor distortions."

Challenged by such a flag-waving declaration, several out-of-town reporters made trips to Garden City, hunting for mistakes that would force him to eat those words. A man from the *Kansas City Times* assumed he had found one when he talked to Myrtle Clare, one of the book's most colorful bit players. Dressed in a stylish purple suit, she did not at all resemble the dowdy woman Truman had described. But she had looked every bit that bad, she assured the reporter; she had been postmistress when the Clutters were killed, and she had worn old clothes to drag around seventy-pound sacks of mail. If some people objected to Truman's account, she said, it was because he described Holcomb "as a broken-down place with hicks, but that's the way it is and if the shoe fits, wear it, that's what I say." Inevitably, a few slips were uncovered. After the murders, Nancy's horse Babe was sold to a local man, for instance, not to an outside Mennonite farmer, as Truman had said. But in the end, none of those who dogged his tracks unearthed any errors of substance.

Although the newspaper sleuths did not know it—Alvin and Marie Dewey were careful not to contradict him—Truman did give way to a few small inventions and at least one major one, however, and *In Cold Blood* is the poorer for it. Following his usual custom, he had anguished over his ending, suffering so much from indecision that his writing hand froze and he was forced to compose on a typewriter. Should he end with the executions? he wondered. Or should he conclude with a happier scene? He chose the latter scenario. But since events had not provided him with a happy scene, he was forced to make one up: a chance, springtime encounter of Alvin Dewey and Susan Kidwell, Nancy Clutter's best friend, in the tree-shaded Garden City cemetery, an oasis of green in that dry country. The Clutters are buried there, and so is Judge Tate, who sentenced their killers. Susan is now completing the college that she and Nancy had planned to attend together, Nancy's boyfriend has recently married, and Alvin's older son, who was just a boy on that murderous night, is preparing to enter college himself. The message is clear: life continues even amidst death.

It is almost a duplicate of the ending of *The Grass Harp*, which brings together Judge Cool and young Collin Fenwick in a similar reunion in a cemetery. But what works in *The Grass Harp*, which is a kind of fantasy, works less well in a book of uncompromising realism like *In Cold Blood*, and that nostalgic meeting in the graveyard verges on the trite and sentimental, as several otherwise admiring critics obligingly pointed out. "I could probably have done without that last part, which brings everything to rest," Truman admitted. "I was criticized a lot for it. People thought I should have ended with the hangings, that awful last scene. But I felt I had to return to the town, to bring everything back full circle, to end with peace."

In Cold Blood is a remarkable book, but it is not a new art form. Like the picture on the cover of *Other Voices*, Truman's claim that it was obscured rather than spotlighted his achievement. Indeed, the term he coined, nonfiction novel, makes no sense. A novel, according to the dictionary definition, is a fictitious prose narrative of considerable length: if a narrative is nonfiction, it is not a novel; if it is a novel, it is not nonfiction. Nor was he the first to dress up facts in the colors of fiction. Although literary historians could refer to examples as far back as the seventeenth century, there were several of more recent vintage, including John Hersey's *Hiroshima*, Rebecca West's *The Meaning of Treason*, Lillian Ross's pieces for *The New Yorker*, and Cornelius Ryan's *The Longest Day*. The trend in both journalism and history was to tell real stories through detail and anecdote, to relate not only what characters did, but also what they ate for breakfast on the day they did it. "Field Marshal Rommel carefully spread a little honey on a slice of buttered bread," wrote Ryan, for instance, as he described the activities of the German commander just before D-Day.

Yet Truman did have a case, though it might have been better if he had let someone else make it for him. He had written something original, perhaps even unique. *In Cold Blood* was not a new species, but to many readers it seemed like one. Others had used fictional techniques, but no one else had actually written a book of nonfiction that could be read as a novel. He was the first novelist of stature to chance his time, talent and reputation on such a long work of reportage, and to many of his peers, *In Cold Blood* was the pioneer that opened up a new territory. In the years to come there was the literary equivalent of a land rush as they followed his lead, searching for equally engrossing material in the day's news. Many of the titles that have jumped onto the best-seller lists since then, from Norman Mailer's *The Armies of the Night* to Bob Woodward's *Veil*, probably would not have been written, or would not have been written in the same way, if he had not come upon his interesting thing in the fall of 1959.

During its long history *The New Yorker* has printed many important and influential pieces, but never, before or since, has it printed one that has been as eagerly anticipated as *In Cold Blood*. The excitement that had been building for five years was finally to be satisfied. As always, the magazine's cover offered no hint as to what was inside; readers had to know when and where to look. *In Cold Blood* was not even listed in its skimpy table of contents. But people found what they wanted; the four issues broke the magazine's record for newsstand sales. Searching for precedents, some reached back to the time of Dickens, when California gold miners sat around campfires, listening to the latest chapters of *The Old Curiosity Shop*, and crowds waiting at a pier in Manhattan shouted to a ship arriving from England, "Is Little Nell dead?"

Perhaps the hardest place to find the magazine, ironically, was where interest was most intense: Finney County, Kansas. For the first issue, *The New Yorker*'s sleepy circulation department had not considered shipping more than the customary five copies. "They evidently didn't give it a thought back there in the inner sanctum in New York City," said the *Dodge City Globe*, which ran an editorial assailing the condescending ways of city slickers. Worse still, even those few copies were lost in transit. "Drug stores say they are being besieged with customers wanting the magazine," reported the *Garden City Telegram*. "Those who have read Capote's first installment praise it with great enthusiasm. One local reader, who happened to get a copy while in Kansas City on a business trip last week, said he started to read the article and 'couldn't put it down until I finished.' "

"Couldn't put it down until I finished" is beautiful music to any writer, and it was a tune Truman heard endlessly in the weeks to come, from friends and strangers alike, who often added, in some embarrassment, that it was the first time they had ever been moved to write a fan letter. "My wife read each *New Yorker* as it came, tearing it out of the postman's hand," wrote a Lutheran minister from Fresno, California. "Now we will re-read all of them; the first time we gobbled them down, glub-glub!" A woman from Massachusetts said that she was glad when it was all over, "so that ordinarily reasonable people can go to bed at an ordinarily reasonable hour, instead of reading slowly and late on the day *The New Yorker* arrives. I am glad that I was able to resist the temptation to fly to New York to be able to read it two days earlier."

Knowing either the author or the facts did not diminish the suspense. "It's tremendous," said Harold Nye, one of the K.B.I. agents who had worked on the case. "Now I can appreciate the painstaking effort you have given to this little murder scene in Kansas. I found myself caught in the web of the story to the point that I couldn't stop to eat. At the end of part one, I told the wife, 'By God, the old boy has really got something here.' " Leo Lerman grumbled that it was "exhausting to wait a week. I have never before seen people glued to anything—on buses—as they are to *The New Yorker*." In her house, said Truman's Greenwich High School teacher, Catherine Wood, there was a tussle over each copy: "*Who gets it first?* That is the big question as the second installment comes out today. I have made myself stop a few minutes to say a word to you. It seems to me this is a perfect accomplishment. I think I have never read anything so *visual*. I *see* the area, the people and I hear them." A few weeks later, after she had finished Part Four, she added, "I suppose you will have imitators; all I can say is: Let them try! I am immensely proud of you."

The panegyrics went on and on. "I would never have believed such a wild, mongrel subject could be brushed and groomed to give off such beautiful glints and inspire such tenderness," stated the poet James Merrill. Anita Loos adjudged that he had written "a Homeric poem as terrifying as the awful age we live in." Noël Coward, who confessed that he was "in a state of dithering admiration," revealed why at generous length: "Before any of the clever boys have a word to say, *I* should like to say that in my—not particularly humble opinion—you have written a masterpiece. The suspense is almost intolerable & your compassion infinitely moving. There is not one character who does not emerge complete and true. I, who love form and shape in writing, was unable to find one moment of overemphasis or underemphasis. It is a long book without one moment of ennui or one slipshod phrase. I have been haunted by it ever since I put it down so the only thing to do obviously is to take it up again. I will not apologize for the effusiveness of this letter. Praise from fellow writers is always gratifying and this, believe me, comes from the heart."

When the book itself was published in January, 1966, the modern media machine—magazines, newspapers, television and radio—became a giant band that played only one tune: Truman Capote. He was the subject of twelve articles in national magazines, two half-hour television programs, and an unparalleled number of radio shows and newspaper stories. His face looked out from the covers of *Newsweek, Saturday Review, Book Week,* and *The New York Times Book Review,* which gave him the longest interview in its history. *Life* ran eighteen pages, the most space it had ever given a professional writer, and advertised its huge spread by continuously flashing the words *In Cold Blood* on the electronic billboard in Times Square. "Such a deluge of words and pictures has never before been poured out over a book," observed a somewhat dazed-sounding reporter for *The New York Times.* The downpour would have been even greater if he had not refused many interviews, including an offer to become the first writer to appear on television's *Meet the Press,* which usually favored politicians and statesmen.

By a peculiar stroke of luck, even a bloody fight at the "21" Club became part of the campaign. Movie director Otto Preminger accused Irving ("Swifty") Lazar, who was handling the book's film rights, of reneging on a promise to sell it to him as a starring vehicle for Frank Sinatra. (It was never explained what part Sinatra wanted.) Harsh words were exchanged, and Lazar abruptly ended the argument by smashing a water goblet on Preminger's bald head. Until they saw pictures of that battered dome, which required fifty stitches to repair, some were tempted to imagine that "L'Affaire '21,' " as one newspaper dubbed it, had been a clever stunt to grab the headlines.

The *In Cold Blood* Express was thundering down the tracks. Jean Ennis, director of publicity for Random House, happily acknowledged that she was only a passenger on the Capote Special. "I would like to take responsibility for this publicity windfall, but I can't," she said. "What has happened, has happened." How could she say otherwise when one of Random House's fiercest competitors had pitched in to help? "I'm mad about the new Capote," said Kenneth McCormick, the editor-in-chief of Doubleday. "His new book has upgraded the entire publishing industry. He believes that reporting is more interesting than fiction, and he's proven it." Truman did his best to keep the engine fueled. "A boy has to hustle his book," he joked, and the story behind the book became as familiar as the book itself. He told the tale of his nearly six-year ordeal so often that it almost became part of the national lore, like Washington's chopping down the cherry tree.

Americans do not expect serious books to make money. When they do, as *In Cold Blood* did, they become news. Even before it was published, New American Library had bought paperback rights for an unprecedented half-million dollars (of which Random House had taken a third), Columbia Pictures had paid a record half-million more for movie rights, and foreign publishers and other sales had all but guaranteed another million. "A Book in a New Form Earns $2-Million for Truman Capote," declared a headline in *The New York Times*, which reckoned that he would make fourteen dollars and eighty cents a word. Truman's impatient reply caused more head-shaking: "When you average it out over six years, and consider the taxes, any small-time Wall Street operator gets at least that much."

Sometimes, when a book, a play, or a movie is preceded by so much praise and hyperbole, critics become tetchy, making it a point of honor to show their independence by finding fault. That was not the case with *In Cold Blood*, and most reviews were all that Truman could have hoped for. The smart boys—and the smart girls too—were just as excited as everyone else. "*In Cold Blood* is a masterpiece," proclaimed Conrad Knickerbocker in *The New York Times Book Review*, "agonizing, terrible, possessed, proof that the times, so surfeited with disasters, are still capable of tragedy. There are two Truman Capotes. One is the artful charmer, prone to the gossamer and the exquisite, of *The Grass Harp* and Holly Golightly. The other, darker and stronger, is the discoverer of death. He has traveled far from the misty, moss-hung landscapes of his youth. He now broods with the austerity of a Greek or an Elizabethan."

He had recorded "this American tragedy in such depth and detail that one might imagine he had been given access to the books of the Recording Angel," said Maurice Dolbier in the *New York Herald Tribune*. In a critique for *Harper's* magazine, Rebecca West, who had produced some extraordinary nonfiction of her own, described him as "an ant of genius" who had crawled over the Kansas landscape in pursuit of his story. "Nothing but blessing can flow from Mr. Capote's grave and reverent book," she said. Writing in *The New York Review of Books*, F. W. Dupee, like most of his colleagues, genially dismissed the notion of the nonfiction novel—"to this claim the only possible retort is a disbelieving grin"—but went on to say that "whatever its 'genre,' *In Cold Blood* is admirable: as harrowing as it is, ultimately, though implicitly, reflective in temper."

One of those who wanted to derail that speeding train was Stanley Kauffmann, who had not liked what he had read and who was incensed that so many others had. "It is ridiculous in judgment and debasing of all of us to call this book literature," he declared in *The New Republic*. "Are we so bankrupt, so avid for novelty that merely because a famous writer produces an amplified magazine crime-feature, the result is automatically elevated to serious literature just as Andy Warhol, by painting a soup-carton, has allegedly elevated it to art?" But his diatribe was itself assailed by several of his readers, whose letters, mostly in defense of Truman, took up five columns of a succeeding issue. "Stanley Kauffmann has himself created a new genre," complained one correspondent, "the Non-Review of the Non-Fiction Novel."

Most of the critics in England were also warm with praise when the book appeared there in March. For Truman the congenial atmosphere was ruined, however, by a bitter and rather cheap personal attack in *The Observer* from an old friend, Kenneth Tynan, who argued, among other things, that Truman probably could have saved Perry and Dick from the gallows if he had spent the time and money to prove that they were insane. "For the first time," Tynan wrote, "an influential writer of the front rank has been placed in a position of privileged intimacy with criminals about to die and—in my view—done less than he might have to save them. . . . It seems to me that the blood in which his book is written is as cold as any in recent literature."

Tynan's thesis was based on a sloppy reading of the book and false assumptions about Kansas law, which would not have permitted the psychiatric defense he was suggesting. Truman set him straight in a lengthy reply, during the course of which he charged him with possessing "the morals of a baboon and the guts of a butterfly." The victory was Truman's, but Tynan's accusation stung more than it otherwise might have because it hit an exposed nerve. Truman could not have saved Perry and Dick if he had spent one million dollars, or ten million, but Tynan was right when he suggested that Truman did not want to save them.

Yet Tynan's much-quoted assault, followed by Truman's much-quoted counterassault, furnished still more publicity, and the *In Cold Blood* Express kept on rolling. Jimmy Breslin, the street-smart columnist of the *Herald Tribune*, told his own readers to ignore everything that was said about it and buy the book itself. "The important thing is [it] could affect the type of words on pages you could be reading for a while. This Capote steps in with flat, objective, terrible realism. And suddenly there is nothing else you want to read."

NINETEEN sixty-six was his year, and a new, or almost new, Truman greeted it. "I've gotten rid of the boy with the bangs," he said. "He's gone, just gone. I liked that boy. It took an act of will because it was easy to be that person—he was exotic and strange and eccentric. I liked the idea of that person, but he had to go." He was no longer the comparative youth of thirty-five who had first gone to Kansas. He was forty-one, a man of substance and fame, one of the best-known writers in America.

Money had begun coming his way, first in driblets, then in a steady flow, months before *In Cold Blood* was published. During most of the time he was researching and writing, he and Jack had lived decently, but not lavishly, chiefly on the sale of *Breakfast at Tiffany's* to Paramount (sixty-five thousand dollars), his advances from *The New Yorker*, and his fee for writing the screenplay of *The Innocents*. Added together and divided by the more than five years he had labored, it did not make a large annual income. He had had to strain to buy the condominium in Verbier and the houses in Sagaponack. His Jaguar had been his only real luxury—and one he could ill afford, at that.

Now, for the first time in his life, he possessed the options that money alone allows. He was not rich. Some of the two million dollars the newspapers had mentioned was eaten up by fees to agents and lawyers; much also went for taxes. But he had a sizable income nonetheless and began to enjoy some of life's expensive pleasures. He traded in his Jaguar hardtop for a later model, a sporty convertible, and bought a Ford Falcon station wagon for Jack, who needed a roomier car to carry Charlie, the bulldog, and Diotima, the cat.

Brooklyn Heights, he decided, was no longer the only place to live in New York, and he purchased a two-bedroom apartment in what a fashion columnist called "the most important new address" in Manhattan, the United Nations Plaza at First Avenue and Forty-ninth Street, next to the East River and the United Nations. Many of the other tenants were heads of corporations, and the lobby was like that of a luxurious modern hotel, hushed, dignified and a little intimidating. But dignified luxury was exactly what the mature Truman Capote desired, and the sixty-two-thousand-dollar price tag, which was regarded as high in 1965, did not deter him. "He wanted to be in the thick of things," said Oliver Smith. "At the time, the U.N. Plaza was very glamorous, *the* place to live in Manhattan."

His apartment, on the twenty-second floor, was as bright as Oliver's basement had been dark, and it had a panoramic southern view that stretched to the bottom of Manhattan and beyond. With the help of Evie Backer, who had decorated for some of his friends, Truman ransacked Third Avenue antique shops to furnish it. From Brooklyn he brought his collection of paperweights, including the White Rose that Colette had given him in 1948, and his menagerie of ornamental birds, animals and reptiles. His portrait, painted several years earlier by James Fosburgh, Minnie's husband and Babe Paley's brother-in-law, was hung over a sofa in the living room. Every room but one was done with elegant restraint. The exception was the library–dining room, which was a combination of dark reds; walking into it, he wrote in *House Beautiful*, was "rather like sinking into a hot raspberry tart—a sensation *you* may not relish, but I quite enjoy."

Along with his studio in Sagaponack, his aerie at 870 U.N. Plaza was the place he liked most to be, and he never regretted moving there. "I once stayed on the top floor of the Excelsior Hotel in Naples, overlooking the bay," he said. "You could see the shore curving around and the ferries sailing back and forth to Capri. The view from my apartment reminds me of that. I love it at all times. I love it when the sun makes everything sparkle. I love it in the fog when everything looks misty. I love it at dusk and I love it at night, when the green lights on the bridges look like strings of emeralds."

• • •

In February, 1966, shortly after *In Cold Blood* came out, he joined Jack in Verbier. He flew to London in March to help publicize the British edition, and was back in America by April. Followed by a camera crew from NBC News, which was preparing a story, "Capote Returns to Kansas," he gave a reading to an estimated thirty-five hundred students at the University of Kansas in Lawrence. The "Lion of American Literature," the student newspaper called him. He then proceeded to Garden City—his first visit since his book was published—and seemed nervous about what reaction he might expect. He need not have worried. The municipal library placed a framed photograph of him in a prominent position and held a reception to which five hundred fans came, clutching copies for him to autograph. "Garden City Opens Arms to Capote," read the next day's headline in the *Wichita Eagle*.

Manhattan was no less friendly when he gave a reading at Town Hall several days later. His rich friends gave small dinners beforehand, then disembarked at the door from a flotilla of limousines. "His light and somewhat nasal voice held the audience spellbound," said *The New York Times*. "In the eye of the daily beholder," added *Newsday*, "Truman Capote may appear as a slight, balding man. But last night to a rapt audience of New York's most socially prominent readers, he stood 10 feet tall." As usual, "A Christmas Memory" was the favorite, and some still had tears in their eyes when they embraced him afterward. "It was a very moving moment for me," said Babe.

In Cold Blood had established him as an authority on the criminal-justice system, and during the next few years he was often called upon to comment about it. He was opposed to capital punishment —"institutionalized sadism," he termed it—and in favor of prison reforms that would emphasize rehabilitation. His opinions were generally conservative, however, and he did not subscribe to the fashionable view of the sixties that criminals were victims of society. Prosecutors across the country used the examples of Perry and Dick, who had confessed only after some artful prodding by Alvin Dewey and his colleagues, to buttress their opposition to the Supreme Court's *Miranda* ruling, which severely limited the use of confessions in court. Testifying before a Senate subcommittee in July, Truman attacked the ruling, saying that it had all but handcuffed the police. "People simply will not accept the fact that there is such a thing as a homicidal mind," he told the Senators, "that there are people who would kill as easily as they would write a bad check, and that they achieve satisfaction from it as I might from completing a novel or you from seeing a proposal of yours become law."

A week later he was in France, on his way to Portugal with Lee Radziwill, then to Yugoslavia for a cruise down the Dalmatian coast with the Agnellis. "Have not had a genuine holiday in God knows when," he told Cecil, "so am taking off all of August." In Paris he proudly informed a reporter that *In Cold Blood* was not the only Capote book that would be published in 1966. "A Christmas Memory," first published a decade before, would now be brought out in a special boxed edition. "Serious writers aren't supposed to make money, but I say the hell with that. My next book will be called *A Christmas Memory*. It's forty-five pages long, and it's going to cost five dollars and be worth every cent. How do you like that for openers?"

Alexander after the Battle of Issus, Napoleon after Austerlitz could not have been cockier than Truman was after *In Cold Blood*. He had the golden touch, and he was already looking forward to his next triumph, a party that would end the year as it had begun— with all eyes focused on him.

The idea came to him in June, and it immediately captured his imagination. Nothing, he reckoned, could be a better symbol of the new, grown-up Truman. In one evening he could not only repay his peacock friends for all their years of entertaining him, but also satisfy a wish he had nursed most of his life. "I think it was something a little boy from New Orleans had always dreamed of doing," said Slim. "He wanted to give the biggest and best goddamned party that anybody had ever heard of. He wanted to see every notable in the world, people of importance from every walk of life, absolutely dying to attend a party given by a funny-looking, strange little man —himself."

Once he grabbed hold of something, he did not let it go, and until he left for Europe at the end of July, he sat by Eleanor Friede's pool in Bridgehampton nearly every afternoon, jotting down ideas. He was not merely planning a party; he was creating one. It would have his name attached to it, and his presence would be felt in every detail, just as it was in *In Cold Blood* or any of his other books. Bit by bit, his scheme evolved. The date would be Monday, November 28, 1966; the place, the Plaza Hotel, which, in his opinion, had the only beautiful ballroom left in New York. To add a touch of the fantastic, he settled on a *bal masqué*, like those in storybooks. Until the masks came off at midnight, identities would be secret, or so he liked to think, and strangers would meet, dance and perhaps fall in love. And like Prospero, he would be the magician who had arranged those revels.

Unlike fabled gatherings from New York's past, in which champagne spurted from fountains, live swans floated on artificial lakes, or gilded trees were hung with golden fruit, his would be a model of good taste and simplicity. Inspired by the Ascot scene in *My Fair Lady*, which Cecil had costumed in black and white, he decided to call his party the Black and White Ball and require his guests—the characters in his own play—to dress in nothing else. Worried that the multihued sparkle of rubies, sapphires or emeralds might destroy his austere design, he considered adding a stern "Diamonds Only" to the bottom of the invitations, but relented when Eleanor, who was one of his oldest friends, told him that if he did, she could not go. "Truman," she said, "I haven't got any diamonds. My tiaras have all been hocked."

Most hosts who give large balls permit their guests to bring companions of their choosing. Truman would not. His control was to be absolute. No one could walk through the door whom he did not know and like, and when he sent an invitation, it meant the named person or persons, and no one else. If he did not like a friend's wife or husband, he dropped both. Single people were expected to come singly. "You can't bring anybody!" he told Eleanor, who, as a widow, protested vigorously. "There will be a hundred extra men. I'll see to it. They'll all be marvelous."

"Come on!" she replied. "You can keep your hundred extra men! I'm not going to get myself all dolled up and put on a goddamned mask to go to the Plaza by myself. I just won't come. And Truman, dear, it's not just me. I'm sure half the single women on your list won't come either." Afraid that she might be right, he pondered and returned the next afternoon with the solution. He would arrange small dinners beforehand, and the diners would come in groups. No woman would have to endure the humiliation of arriving by herself.

The secret of a successful party is not lavish food, expensive wine or extravagant decorations; it is the right mixture of lively guests. No one else had friendships as diverse as his, and lounging by Eleanor's pool, he matched names as carefully as he usually matched nouns and adjectives. Marianne Moore and Marella Agnelli, Henry Ford and Henry Fonda, Sargent Shriver and John Sargent, Andy Warhol and Mrs. William Rhinelander Stewart, Frank Sinatra and Walter Lippmann, Irving Berlin and Isaiah Berlin. "I don't know whether or not I should invite the Johnsons," he said in a tired voice. "It's such a *bore* when you have to have the Secret Service and all that. No, I don't want the President to come. I think I'll just invite his daughter Lynda Bird." He did, along with the daughters of Teddy Roosevelt (Alice Roosevelt Longworth) and Harry Truman (Margaret Truman Daniel). He also wrote down the names of several princes and princesses, two dukes and a duchess, two marquises, a marchioness and a marquesa, two counts, a countess and a viscomtesse, an earl, a maharajah and a maharani, three barons and two baronesses, and two lords and a lady.

Leo Lerman joked that "the guest book reads like an international list for the guillotine." Thinking along the same line, Jerome Robbins, the choreographer, speculated that perhaps Truman had made up a roster of those who were to be shot first by those fearsome radicals of the sixties, the Red Guards. Oh, no, said John Kenneth Galbraith, not while *he* was on it. Some suggested that maybe Truman was bringing them all together for some momentous announcement, such as the end of the world. But not everyone on his list of more than five hundred was rich and famous. There were many whom celebrity watchers could not begin to identify—farmer friends from Sagaponack, acquaintances from Garden City, and of course Jack and Jack's friends and relatives.

Rarely had Truman enjoyed himself as much as he did during those hours in Bridgehampton. Many of those whose names he was inscribing in his schoolboy notebook could buy and sell great corporations, dictate fashions for millions of women, snap their fingers and cause armies of flunkies to jump up and salute. That was not the kind of power he desired. The power he coveted he held in his hand on those sun-scorched afternoons: he could put their names on his invitation list, and he could just as easily cross them out.

One of his masterstrokes was his choice of Katharine Graham, head of the family that owned both *Newsweek* and *The Washington Post*, as his guest of honor. Babe had introduced them in the early sixties, and she had immediately become one of his favorites. Kay Graham was neither beautiful nor stylish like his swans—in those

days Washington wives took a perverse pride in their dowdiness—
and she was shy and lacking in confidence. The suicide of her dy-
namic but philandering husband in 1963 had forced her to take
command of the family empire, but she was still walking gingerly,
step by step. Though she was in her late forties, she was, in short,
ideal clay for Truman's eager sculptor's hands: rich, powerful and
yet amenable to instruction. When her own lawyer, who also had
an apartment in the U.N. Plaza, suggested that she buy there too,
she said no; when Truman recommended it, she said yes. "Now,
honey," he told her, "I think you ought to have an apartment in
New York, and if you can't run it, I will!"

With considerable reluctance, she had also heeded his command
to join him on the Agnelli yacht in the summer of 1965. With him
at her side, her fear that she would appear dull proved groundless,
and she and Marella became good friends. Sailing off the coast of
Turkey, she also had an opportunity to read *In Cold Blood* in galleys,
before anyone else. "Truman wouldn't give them to me all at once.
He'd just let me read one section at a time, and then we would
discuss it. It was wonderful, like going to school, and he would tell
me what the people in it were like, what Kansas was like, and why
he had done what he had done. Before we finished, I felt I knew all
those characters." In November, not long after their return, she gave
a dance for him and the Deweys at her house in Georgetown.

"Now, don't think you can ever hide something from me!" he told
her. "Because I'll find out about it anyway." She laughed, but he
did see a side of her she showed to few others. "She's a very, very
warm person," he said. "And very down-to-earth. She once said
that seventy percent of the men who came into her office, whether
they were Senators or journalists who worked for her, made it clear
one way or another that they would like to go to bed with her. 'They
just want to say that they've fucked a tycoon,' she told me. But she
said she would never have an affair with anyone who either worked
for her or was somehow influenced by her paper.

" 'Kay,' I said, 'that leaves out everybody in the country, with the
possible exception of some cowboy in Wyoming.'

" 'Well,' she answered, 'maybe someday I'll meet a cowboy in
Wyoming.' "

He liked her and wanted to pay her back for her hospitality to the
Deweys. But he doubtless had other reasons as well for picking her
as his guest of honor. More than Babe, Marella or any of the other

swans, she would attract attention. She was arguably the most powerful woman in the country, but still largely unknown outside Washington. Putting her in the spotlight was also his ultimate act as Pygmalion. It would symbolize her emergence from her dead husband's shadow; she would become her own woman before the entire world.

She was vacationing on Cape Cod when he called her up to tell her his plans. "Honey, I just decided you're depressed and need cheering up, so I'm going to give you a party."

"What do you mean?" she said. "I'm not depressed. I'm all right."

"I'm not so sure about that, honey. Anyway, I'm going to do it very big. I've always wanted to give a party in the Plaza ballroom, and it will be in your honor."

She thanked him but thought little more about it. "But as the thing gathered steam," she said, "I was just incredulous. I was stunned by what was happening."

Invitations, written in longhand, went out in early October.

In honor of Mrs. Katharine Graham
*   Mr. Truman Capote*
Requests the pleasure of your company
*   At a Black and White Dance*
On Monday, the twenty-eighth of November
*   At Ten O'Clock*
Grand Ballroom, The Plaza

RSVP	DRESS
Miss Elizabeth Davis	*Gentlemen: Black Tie; Black Mask*
46 Park Avenue	*Ladies: Black or White Dress*
New York	*White Mask; Fan*

What happened after that can best be described as a chemical reaction. By itself, each of the ingredients Truman had poured into his flask—the select guest list, the strict dress code, the thrill of a masked ball—might have remained inert. Together, they fizzed and gurgled, bubbled and boiled, and all of New York knew that something remarkable was soon to occur. "I've never seen women putting so much serious effort into what they're going to wear," said Halston, who was making many of the masks.

As word spread, the scenario went precisely as Truman had hoped: everyone he had ever cared about or thought to impress, from Fifth Avenue aristocrats to West Side intellectuals, was longing to come. For some reason, he had not included his old friend, the actress Ina Claire, and she telegraphed from San Francisco, asking for an invitation. No, he replied. He said the same to Tallulah Bankhead, but when she continued to beg, telling him how important it was to her, he gave in. One acquaintance told him that his wife cried herself to sleep every night because they were not on the list. His heart touched, Truman lied and told him that their invitations must have been lost and that a new set would be forthcoming. But he did not send one to his aunt Marie (Tiny) Rudisill, who, as a result, nurtured a grudge that was never to die. "I feel like I fell into a whole mess of piranha fish," he moaned, joking that he was making so many enemies that he might as well have called his party *In Bad Blood*.

"People were really carrying on," recalled Diana Trilling. "There was a woman who lived in Europe who was absolutely incensed that she hadn't been asked. Oh, there was a great to-do! I never heard anybody who was so voluble about not having been invited to a party! She was so wildly, ludicrously offended that Leo Lerman tried to intercede. For my own part, my dressmaker, a terribly nice man I'm devoted to, said, 'You couldn't possibly get me an invitation, could you? It's the one thing in this whole world I want to go to.' He was so desperate that I wanted to give him mine." But she could not have surrendered it even if Truman had permitted: her husband, Lionel, the most glittering ornament on Columbia's literary faculty, was also eager to attend.

Hearing the commotion from her house in Nyack, Carson McCullers, who was not among the chosen, became increasingly agitated. She had bitterly resented the success of *In Cold Blood*, and she was so tortured by the prospect of a second Capote triumph that she began talking about giving a party of her own, but bigger and better in every way. "I'll invite Jacqueline Kennedy," she told her cousin Jordan Massee.

"Do you know Jacqueline Kennedy?" Massee inquired.

"No, but she'll come. I'll see to it that she comes. And if she comes, you can be certain everyone else will come." Ill and an invalid—she was to die less than a year later—Carson did not give a ball. But the following March she did have an ambulance deliver her to the Plaza, where she celebrated her fiftieth birthday as a steady stream of admirers came to her suite to pay court.

Truman did not stop at dictating the makeup of his own party; he arranged the preball dinners as well, pairing hosts and guests like a general placing his regiments along the line of battle. "He *ordered* his friends to give preliminary dinner parties," said Glenway Wescott, "and he told me whom I had to have." He changed those guest lists too, juggling names from one group to another. The Haywards were given a show-business contingent that included Claudette Colbert and Frank Sinatra and his new wife Mia Farrow; the Paleys were presented with the Deweys, the Agnellis and Cecil, who had made a special trip from England to see what his *My Fair Lady* design had inspired. Kay and Joe Meehan—he was a leading figure on Wall Street—were assigned some of their society chums, including Elsie Woodward, the mother of poor Bill, whose shotgun death had caused such a scandal in 1955. And Glenway was entrusted with such eminent geriatrics as Thornton Wilder, Katherine Anne Porter, Virgil Thomson, Anita Loos and Janet Flanner, who had been *The New Yorker*'s Paris correspondent since the twenties. In her excitement at being asked, Katherine Anne forgot that she had heartily disliked Truman ever since their summer at Yaddo. "The pimple on the face of American literature," she had called him. Now, cooing to Glenway, she declared, "Oh, I like Truman. I always have."

For a few tense weeks, however, it appeared that Glenway's Rich Amella (minced veal) might never leave the oven. Wilder said he would be in Berlin on November 28, and a variety of ailments finally confined Katherine Anne to her house in Washington. Flanner, who was preparing to fly in from Paris with the first long dress she had purchased in nearly thirty years, was ruffled because Natalia Murray, her best friend and New York hostess, had not received her expected invitation. Flanner asked Glenway to drop Truman "a blackmailing note" saying that unless Murray came, she would not come either. "Without her," said Flanner, "it is inconceivable that I should go and dance with a merry heart—I don't dance at all anymore, actually." Glenway did as he was bidden and was soon pleased to report that she could keep her long dress and plane ticket. "Piping away like Blake's little devil in the cloud," he told her, Truman had sworn that Murray's invitation had merely been misplaced. "He sounded innocent," Glenway said, "and in any event, having had our way, we'll never know. My general principle about him is that it isn't necessary to like him as much as one admires him."

Others of the appointed dinner hosts doubtless witnessed similar scenes of comedy and consternation. "This city's normally blasé social set is flapping like a gaggle of geese over a not-so-private party being thrown by author Truman Capote for 500 guests here Monday night," a reporter for *The Washington Post* wrote a few days before the momentous night. "The magic Capote name—immortalized by his recent blockbuster nonfiction book, *In Cold Blood*—coupled with a guest list that reads like Who's Who of the World, has escalated his party to a social 'happening' of history-making proportions. The New York newspapers are calling it variously the party of the year, the decade or the century."

Indeed, nearly everyone in the five boroughs seemed to be watching the flutter overhead. When Herb Caen, a columnist for the *San Francisco Chronicle*, arrived at Kennedy Airport, a cabdriver noticed his wife's feathered headpiece and said, "Hey, you gonna go to Truman's party, huh?" Guests came from all parts of America—eleven from Kansas alone—as well as from Europe, Asia and South America.

"The ladies have killed me," said Halston, who had been busy for six weeks designing the masks for which he charged as much as six hundred dollars. One woman, he said, had come in eight times, taking an hour each time to have hers fitted. "I think I've lost my mind, and it's just too much," added his rival, Adolfo. By the twenty-eighth, the furor had reached Kenneth's, Manhattan's elite hairdressing salon. Arriving that afternoon, Kay Graham automatically went to the second floor, where ordinary customers were sent, rather than the third, where the smart set went. "But I didn't know Kenneth, didn't know anybody," she said. "I had never really done my hair much. I had never made up my face. I hardly knew how to do it! We didn't *lead* that kind of life in Washington. Then, while I was on the stairs, a wonderfully funny, Cinderella-ish thing happened.

" 'Oh, Mrs. Graham,' one of the hairdressers said. 'We're all so busy with this Black and White Ball! Have you heard about it?'

" 'You won't believe it, but I'm the guest of honor.'

" 'You are? Well, who's doing your hair?'

" 'I don't know. I was just trying to find out.'

" 'Kenneth has to do it,' she said. And so I went to Kenneth himself. But I had to wait while Marisa Berenson had curls placed all over her head. I was the last one in and the last one out."

Many of those expensive coiffures unraveled a few hours later, in a chill, end-of-November rain—Truman had arranged everything but the weather. As the Caens were leaving the Regency Hotel for their dinner, the bell captain whispered, "Boy, is this town full of phonies. Do you know there are people hanging around here in black-and-white clothes who ain't even going to Truman's? Whoo— eeee!" At Eleanor Friede's, where soft background music was playing on the radio, a newscaster interrupted to say that crowds were already beginning to gather outside the Plaza to watch the guests arrive. Eleanor's group, mostly editors and publishers, were amused, but still did not realize how fascinated people were by what seemed, after all, like only a dance. Truman and Kay Graham had drinks at the Paleys', then went to the Plaza for a supper for two, in the suite he had taken for that purpose. But they also were late, not arriving until 9:10, and had time only to enjoy a few bites of caviar before taking up their posts at the ballroom door, alongside a man in white tie and tails, who was to announce each guest to them.

Television cameras had been set up in the lobby, and almost two hundred still photographers and reporters jostled for position, stepping on the delicate toes of every fashion columnist in the city. Security guards had been stationed in the kitchen to keep out gate-crashers, and black-tied and black-masked detectives waited to mingle and watch for jewel thieves. A dozen Secret Service agents came along to look after Lynda Bird Johnson; like it or not, Truman was forced to endure the boredom of Government agents. Four bars had been set up to dispense four hundred and fifty bottles of Taittinger champagne, and chefs were preparing a simple midnight buffet: chicken hash, spaghetti bolognaise, scrambled eggs, sausages, pastries and coffee. (As such things go, Truman spent relatively little on his fete: about sixteen thousand dollars, part of which he was able to deduct from his taxes.)

At 10:15, the ballroom was all but empty. Onlookers began to mutter that there were more reporters and photographers than guests, and it appeared that Pamela Hayward might have been right in fearing "that with all the publicity, the party might flop." But that, of course, was an impossibility. At 10:30 masked faces began emerging from the rain. "Your names, please," intoned the man in the white tie and tails, who then turned to Truman and Kay and announced, "The Maharajah and Maharani of Jaipur."

The masks did not actually hide many faces, but then, despite Truman's fantasy, they were not really supposed to. Many of the women, like Marella Agnelli and Rose Kennedy, attached theirs to elaborate feather headdresses. Others wore fur around their eyes. Candice Bergen's mask was topped by giant rabbit ears; Frank Sinatra's had cat's whiskers. Mrs. John Converse, Gary Cooper's widow, wore black velvet, from which sprouted a gardenia tree bearing live blooms. Breaking Truman's rule that men wear black, Billy Baldwin had engaged a Tiffany craftsman to make him a golden unicorn's head. "Oh, Billy, that's fantastic!" exclaimed Truman. Princess Luciana Pignatelli had also cheated by painting her mask on her face. She made up for it, however, by attaching to her feathered headdress a sixty-carat diamond, which bobbed above her pretty nose like a piece of bait on a fish line.

In a gesture that hinted of reverse snobbery, the host himself proudly announced that he had paid only thirty-nine cents for his simple Halloween mask. Hearing that, Alice Roosevelt Longworth was even prouder to say that she had bought hers for only thirty-five cents. Whatever they cost, most were removed long before midnight. "It itches and I can't see," complained Alfred Gwynne Vanderbilt.

At 11 o'clock, Arthur Schlesinger, Jr., the historian, was asked if it was a good party. "It's too early to tell how it's going," he judiciously answered. "History is made after midnight." So it was, and most of those who were there talked about it afterward the way they might have a cherished childhood Christmas. There were no spectacular scenes, but there were dozens of memorable ones: Lauren Bacall and Jerome Robbins holding the floor to do one of the best dance numbers since *Top Hat*, the daughters of three Presidents exchanging White House anecdotes, Kay Graham dancing with one of the doormen at the U.N. Plaza, who thanked her for the happiest night of his life. "It was always shimmering," said David Merrick, the Broadway producer, who was not usually given to praising other people's productions. "It was never still, nor was there a static moment." Even Jack, who had resisted coming, had a good time. "It was *formidable vraiment*," he told Mary Louise Aswell, who had elected to stay home in New Mexico. "*Extra!*"

Across the country the party made front-page headlines. "Splendor Runs Over at Capote Ball of Decade," said the *Houston Chronicle*. "Capote's Big Bash Was Just That," added the *Fort Lauderdale News*. Some who had not been there grumbled that such frolics had also attended the fall of the Roman Empire. Pete Hamill wrote an outraged column in the *New York Post* that contrasted what Hamill thought were silly comments from the merrymakers with grisly scenes from the Viet Nam War. A soldier in an Army training camp sent a letter to *Time* objecting to being called upon to protect "this fat, lethargic, useless intelligentsia." To which another correspondent, who said he had spent seven years on active duty, responded: "So Truman Capote had a blast. So what? Must we read the trite analogies about the Roman Empire and the U.S. every time somebody has a [party]?"

Truman himself heard few complaints. One came indirectly from Gloria Guinness, who said that she had made a terrible mistake in adorning her elegant neck with not one, but two heavy necklaces, one of rubies, one of diamonds. Their combined weight had exhausted her, she said, and she would have to stay in bed all the next day to regain her strength. Another came from an actress who had taken a handsome stranger home for the night. She had assumed that he was also a guest, but when she woke up in the morning, she discovered, to her vocal dismay, that he was just one of the detectives in black tie.

"So?" Truman inquired. "What's wrong with that? You had a good time with him, didn't you?"

"Yes," she admitted. "I did."

"Well, then, what are you complaining about?"

On the floor of the New York Stock Exchange, Joe Meehan's friends lined up to quiz him about what had happened. A few days later Russell Baker, the resident humorist of *The New York Times*, said that "sociologists are still debating whether it was the most important party of the Twentieth Century." Baker's own thought was that "writers surely will experience an instant inflation of self-esteem from the knowledge that one of their colleagues has seized Mrs. Astor's former role as social arbiter." Diana Trilling, an amateur sociologist herself, declared the party "a very complicated social moment in this country's life."

Those who study such things agreed that something important had occurred—exactly what, no one could say. The Museum of the

City of New York assembled masks and souvenirs, which were placed alongside memorabilia from such other social moments in the city's history as George Washington's first inaugural ball and a gala tribute to General Lafayette in 1824. Also taking her cue from *My Fair Lady*, Suzy Knickerbocker, the gossip columnist, all but burst into song when she told her readers: "He did it. He did it. We always knew he'd do it—and indeed he did."

YOU might say Truman Capote has become omnipotent,"
declared *Women's Wear Daily*, and for several years he
very nearly was. His party did not fade from memory; it
became a legend, magnified by the hyperbolic atmosphere of the
sixties. Every subsequent ball was compared with his, and magazine
or newspaper profiles of famous people often noted if they had been
on the guest list, which was the irrefutable proof of their importance. So great was Truman's reputation—"his name has a magic
ring to people today," Kay Meehan told a reporter—that his mere
presence virtually guaranteed the success of any event he attended.
"Anything he does, everyone sort of gravitates to," said Jan Cowles.
He no longer received invitations; he received beseechments: come
to lunch, dinner, cocktails, anything—but come.

"There's a little secret to charity benefits these days," wrote a
society reporter for *The New York Times*. "It's called Truman Capote.
Mr. Capote is considered by many to be a 64-inch, 136-pound magnet, particularly attractive to the gilded people who count when it
comes to fashionable fund raising. His name on an invitation to just
about anything, even if it costs money, is as potent as a Rockefeller
signature on a check. There is just about no chance that it won't be
honored."

Among ordinary, ungilded folk his name was equally potent. Like
most other things, fame can be measured, and his was now on the
level of a movie idol or a rock star. He was as sought after by the
television talk shows as he was by Manhattan hostesses, and nearly
every public move he made was considered newsworthy by national

magazines. He had not given a ball; he had presided over his own coronation. He was Truman, Rex Bibendi—King of the Revels.

Every monarch needs a consort, and he had his, Jacqueline Kennedy's younger sister, Lee Radziwill. They were together so often that a woman friend wrote to complain: "I don't want to see another picture of you holding Lee Radziwill's hand. I want you to hold my hand." Suzy Knickerbocker jokingly chided him in her column: "Somebody has got to tell Truman that Lee Radziwill can't have him ALL THE TIME. There's only one Truman and we saw him first." Their jealous finger-waving did no good. Truman was besotted, as enamored of "Princess Dear," as he called her—she was married to a former Polish prince—as he was of Babe. "I love her," he gushed. "I love everything about her. I love the way she looks, the way she moves, the way she thinks." Writing in *Vogue*, he said, "Ah, the Princess! Well, she's easily described. She's a beauty. Inside. Outside."

Although she was less effusive, Lee felt much the same about him. "He's my closest friend. More than with anyone else, I can discuss the most serious things about life and emotional questions. I miss him *terribly* when I'm away from him. I trust him implicitly. He's the most loyal friend I've ever had and the best company I've ever known. We've always been so close that it's like an echo. We never have to finish sentences. We just know what the other one means or wants to say. I feel as if he's my brother, except that brothers and sisters are rarely as close as we are."

It was easy to see why he appealed to her; he was the man of the moment. It was harder to understand why she appealed to him, and many searched in vain for the extraordinary qualities that made him prattle like a moonstruck adolescent. She was stylish and undeniably lovely: slim, dark-haired, and favored with eyes that were, to use his words, "gold-brown like a glass of brandy resting on a table in front of firelight." Even so, she did not seem to belong in his pantheon of goddesses: she lacked Babe's stellar presence, Gloria Guinness' transcendental chic, Pamela Hayward's fabled charm. Lee seemed, indeed, to have no clear sense of her identity, possessing nothing like the cast-iron egos of those formidable females. Just the reverse; she appeared to be spoiled—even he admitted that—and rather shallow.

But those who were puzzled by his infatuation did not judge her by his standards. He saw her through the eyes of a novelist; he viewed her, as he did all those he enshrined, as a character in a work of fiction. Seen from his perspective, she was a modern Becky Sharp for whom fate had chosen an exquisitely poignant torture: her childhood rival—her sister, Jackie—had grown up to be the wife of a President and the most celebrated and admired woman in the world.

Lee's father, John Bouvier III, had been a darkly handsome, blue-blooded wastrel—"Black Jack," he had been called—who had squandered his inheritance and cheated on his wife even during their honeymoon. After their divorce, her mother had married Hugh Auchincloss, who was boring but safe, rich enough to provide his wife and two stepdaughters with all the perquisites of the privileged class, including estates in both Newport and Virginia. Having learned her own lesson the hard way, the new Mrs. Auchincloss taught her daughters one simple rule: marry money. And they did, Jackie spectacularly well, Lee a little less so, marrying first Michael Canfield, whose father was a well-known publisher, then Stanislas Radziwill.

Though he was not Kennedy-rich, Stas Radziwill (who, as a naturalized British subject, had no real claim to his Polish title) had made enough money in London real estate to provide her and their two young children with an exceedingly comfortable life: a three-story Georgian town house near Buckingham Palace, staffed by a cook, a butler, two maids, and a nanny; a Queen Anne country house with a huge indoor swimming pool near Henley-on-Thames; a twelve-room duplex on Fifth Avenue; vacations in Portuguese and Italian villas.

She was not happy, however, as Truman quickly discovered. Stas, who was nineteen years her senior, was jealous, moody and unsympathetic to her desire for greater independence. "Understand her marriage is all but finito," Truman wrote Cecil in 1962, following what was probably his first intimate conversation with her. So it seemed to be. A year later she and Stas spent much of the summer on the yacht of Aristotle Onassis, and she appeared to be deeply in love with the golden Greek, who, despite his froglike appearance, was irresistible to many women. The irate husband of his longtime lover, Maria Callas, went so far as to crow to the press that Onassis tossed Maria aside so he could be with Lee. Washington columnist Drew Pearson asked, "Does the ambitious Greek tycoon hope to become the brother-in-law of the American President?"

When the Kennedys' newborn son Patrick died in August, 1963, Lee told Ari how shaken Jackie was. He responded by inviting Jackie to join the cruise as well; the *Christina* would go anywhere she wanted, he said. "Oh, Jackie, it would be such fun," Lee assured her and Jackie was persuaded. But for Lee it was not fun, and if she had dreams of marrying Ari, they were soon forgotten. At the end of the cruise, he bestowed on Jackie a diamond-and-ruby necklace. Lee's reward for bringing them together was only three little bracelets, so "dinky," she complained to Jack Kennedy, that little Caroline Kennedy would have been embarrassed to wear them to her own birthday party. That was not the end of Lee's complaints, and nearly five years later she called Truman to inform him of the final, bitter result of her good deed. "She's crying and weeping and sobbing," he told friends. "I can't tell you what she said, but it's going to be in the news. It's the biggest piece of gossip there is, and she's crying her eyes out because of it." The piece of gossip, which resulted in headlines all over the globe, was that Jackie and Ari were soon to be married. Lee's consolation prize, according to Truman, was a valuable parcel of land on a promontory near Athens, which Ari apparently had given her in hopes that Jackie would build a house there.

Her sister's climb from peak to peak was thus the second and perhaps more enduring cause of Lee's melancholy. When they were growing up, Lee was the center of attention, and Jackie sat off in the corner reading a book. "Lee was the pretty one," sighed Jackie. "So I guess I was supposed to be the intelligent one." From then on, the fickle spotlight turned the other way, and Lee seemed condemned to live in Jackie's shadow forevermore. "Why would anyone care what I do when there are so many more interesting people in the world?" Lee asked not long after Jackie became First Lady. "I haven't done anything at all." Only a few perceived the resentment that lay behind that plaintive comment. "My God, how jealous she is of Jackie: I never knew," wrote Truman in 1962.

Lee was desperate to make a name for herself, but did not know how. Enter Truman, the master of self-promotion. If Lee yearned for recognition, he yearned to give it to her. Never before had he had either the time or the opportunity to play Pygmalion on such a grand scale. Babe and the other swans were several years older than he was; he could give advice here and there, but the plots of their lives had been laid out long since. Lee was nearly nine years younger; her future was still undetermined. It was his dream to shape it, to make of her life a work of art. He saw her not merely as a character in a novel, but as a character in his novel. Molding her into a woman who could rival and perhaps surpass her sister became a cause to which he would devote much of the year following his ball. "She doesn't want to be just somebody's sister," he said. "She wants to have a life and identity of her own. She's a very, very extraordinary girl. She's got a really good, first-class mind. It just has to get released!"

In January, 1967, he joined that extraordinary girl for a leisurely week or so in Morocco, which the international set had turned into its playground. Lee had been there twice the previous year. They traveled south, from Rabat to exotic Marrakesh, to pink-walled Taroudant. She rode horses while he slept and relaxed under the palm trees of their hotel gardens. Parting from her at the end of the month, he flew to Switzerland, going first to St. Moritz, where the Aga Khan was giving a party for the Shah of Iran, then to Verbier, where Jack and the animals—Charlie and Diotima—awaited him. He returned to New York with Charlie in early March, then proceeded to a spa in Miami Beach, where he went on a crash diet and lost, by his own account, eleven pounds.

In April he was back in Kansas, watching the filming of *In Cold Blood*. He had chosen the director, Richard Brooks, over the many others who had wanted to make the picture because he thought that Brooks was especially tough. "I don't know if any other director would have the strength or the stamina to do this movie right," he said. Brooks, who had previously directed such movies as *Cat on a Hot Tin Roof* and *The Blackboard Jungle*, proved that he had both. The studio expected *In Cold Blood* to be filmed in color; he insisted on the stark clarity of black-and-white. The studio wanted Steve McQueen and Paul Newman to play Dick and Perry. "For chrissake," said one executive, "we'll have a big hit!" Brooks demanded two unknowns: Scott Wilson and Robert Blake, who bore an eerie resemblance to Perry. Though Truman promised not to interfere, he did ask to see the script, which the director had written himself. Brooks said no to him, just as he had to everyone else. "Truman, I can't work that way," he said. "Either you trust me to make it or you don't."

Truman did trust him, and Brooks went to uncommon lengths to capture his book on film. Many people in Finney County, including the editor of the newspaper, wanted to hear no more of *In Cold Blood*. "Why in hell they can't let people stay dead—rest in peace—is beyond me," grumbled one of Herb Clutter's neighbors. But Brooks maintained that the movie had to be made there and nowhere else, persisting until he had obtained permission to film not only in the courtroom, but also in the Clutter house itself. He then persuaded seven of the twelve original jurors to sit in the jury box once again, hired the same hangman who had executed Perry and Dick, and brought Nancy Clutter's horse Babe out of retirement. When the young actress who was portraying Nancy sat on her back, faithful Babe instinctively headed toward the Clutter orchard, where Nancy had always guided her.

Shooting was well under way when Truman arrived in his Jaguar, in time to greet the planeload of foreign and American journalists Columbia's publicity department had flown in. An intense director who liked to keep outsiders off his sets, Brooks was visibly irritated by the disruption, and when they were alone, walking in a field of freshly planted winter wheat, Truman asked why. "You're not happy. What's the matter? Am I in the way?"

"You're not in the way, Truman, but your personality is, bringing all these people out here. I can't shoot with them around."

"My personality?"

"Truman, you're a big star."

"When do you want me to take them away?"

"As soon as possible. Tonight would be fine."

"Well, if that's what you want, I'll have them out of here tonight." Truman kept his word, but only after he had been interviewed and photographed. Two weeks later *Life* put him on its cover, standing on a lonely prairie road between the two actors who were portraying the killers he had known so well.

The movie opened at the end of the year to generally excellent reviews. It is as accurate and uncompromising as Truman had hoped, but despite Brooks's efforts, it has little of the book's impact. Paradoxically, it is also less cinematic than the book; its flashbacks are clumsy; its pace, tedious. Worst of all, Brooks added a new character, a tall, lugubrious-looking reporter whose main purpose is to preach against capital punishment. Though he praised the film in public, Truman had private reservations. "The introduction of the reporter, who acted as a kind of Greek chorus, didn't make sense. There also wasn't enough on the Clutter family. The book was about six lives, not two, and it ruined it to concentrate so much on Perry and Dick. On the other hand, I thought that the actors who played the two boys were very well cast, acted well, and were directed well."

Still sunning himself in the glow of the book's renown, Truman embarked on several new projects, the most important of which were for television, a medium in which he already had had one conspicuous success. *A Christmas Memory*, which he had adapted the previous year with the husband-and-wife team of Frank and Eleanor Perry, had won both popular and critical approval, including an Emmy. Thus encouraged, he and the Perrys began dramatizing several of his other stories. Working on a commission from ABC, he was also writing a documentary on capital punishment, which sent him to several Death Rows to interview still more prisoners awaiting execution. But the question of Lee's future was rarely far from his mind: how could he help her make a name for herself? In the end, the answer seemed obvious. He would turn her into an actress—a movie star.

As they discussed it, probably under a palm tree in the Sahara, the idea made eminent sense. Between them, they had everything she required. She had the looks, the desire and some training; he had the brains, the experience and the connections. He persuaded Milton Goldman, who represented Laurence Olivier and John Gielgud, to be her agent, and he and Goldman decided that in her first appearance, she would twinkle brightest away from the lights of New York and Hollywood; a Chicago dinner theater, the Ivanhoe, seemed sufficiently out-of-the-way. Although she preferred to play a Chekhov heroine, they further decreed that she should begin with an easier role; Tracy Lord, the rich, spoiled heroine of Philip Barry's comedy *The Philadelphia Story*, sounded about right. She was understandably annoyed at the inevitable suggestions that she would really be playing herself. "I feel absolutely *nothing* in common with that girl," she said. "She has none of the feelings I understand, of sadness, despair or of knowing loss."

Determined to succeed, she studied the part with a drama coach in London, and in late May she joined the rest of the cast for rehearsals in Chicago. Kenneth flew from New York to do her hair; George Masters, a Hollywood makeup artist, came from California to prepare her face; and Truman and Stas arrived to hold her hand. With such a crowd in attendance, the scenes of pandemonium in her penthouse suite at the Ambassador East Hotel may well have been funnier than those in Barry's comedy. Much of the humor was provided by Masters, who called Stas "Princie" and complained that the colors of her Saint Laurent dresses—shocking pink, purple and chartreuse—were all wrong. One of them, he said, looked like "a dog's lunch—the Supremes wouldn't even *think* of wearing something like that."

But Lee did, and as opening night, June 20, approached, she professed to be philosophical about her reception. "I have a feeling of now or never," she said. "Maybe it will be a flop, but all I can do is hold my nose and take the plunge." After examining her signs, the Cabala Woman, a California astrologer Masters introduced to her by long-distance, pronounced them "very promising for theater work."

Either the signs lied or the Cabala Woman miscalculated, and the career of Lee Bouvier—she used her maiden name—should have received a quick but dignified burial. Searching for something to praise, the reviewer from the *Chicago Sun-Times* settled on her spunk, observing that, given the pressures, it was a triumph that she had remembered all her lines; searching even harder, the critic from the *Daily News* noted that she had "at least laid a golden egg." For all his planning, Truman had neglected to ask a basic question: could she act?

Ignoring the unpleasant truth, he proceeded as if she had heard nothing but cheers in Chicago. And astonishingly enough, he almost convinced other people that she had—or that the boos were irrelevant. When he returned to Manhattan, he asked David Susskind, who was an independent television producer as well as a talk show host, to give her the lead role in a TV special. As an inducement, he said, he would write the script himself. Although Susskind had not been favorably impressed by Lee's acting, he had been impressed by the publicity she had received. He soon announced that ABC had signed Lee Bouvier, at a salary of fifty thousand dollars, to star in Truman's adaptation of John Van Druten's comedy *The Voice of the Turtle*. Truman had performed an act of magic: he had persuaded Susskind and the network to gamble a large budget and two hours of prime time on a pretty amateur with not a hint of talent.

Reflecting on her inability to find the humor in *The Philadelphia Story*, Susskind discarded Van Druten's comedy and chose a drama for her instead, an adaptation, also to be done by Truman, of the 1944 movie *Laura*. She would take Gene Tierney's part and George Sanders would take Clifton Webb's. She did not mind the switch, and in her letters to Truman, sounded uncharacteristically ebullient. "I wish we could begin tomorrow—it's going to be marvelous," she said in August. "My interests have narrowed down in such a violent way that now I'm just possessed. Thank you!" Although she would not have to leave home this time—Susskind had arranged for *Laura* to be shot in London—Stas was not encouraging her new endeavor, which caused her to lean even more heavily on Truman. "When I want advice I feel you're in the room giving it to me," she told him. "When I want to laugh at something I can hear you laughing with me & that makes me so much happier." As taping time approached and Stas became more difficult, she added, "I was *so* happy to get your letter except that it made me weep because I miss you so much & need you to make life worthwhile." As an expression of her gratitude and appreciation, she sent him an elegant gold-lined Schlumberger cigarette box, in which she had had inscribed: "To my Answered Prayer, with love, Lee. July 1967."

Despite the fact that she required direction so extensive that it might more accurately have been called on-the-job training, Susskind insisted that "there *is* something there." Perhaps, but when the show was broadcast in January, 1968, that something eluded most viewers. Indeed, she was as close to being invisible as an actress playing a title character can be. Susskind had done what the director of *The Philadelphia Story* may have wished he could have done: he had left much of her performance on the cutting-room floor. More than one reviewer pointed out that when the camera should have been looking at her, it wandered off in other directions, as if it were too polite to embarrass her. As a result, her Laura "was reduced to a stunning clotheshorse upon whom no discernible thespian demands were made," said Jack Gould, the *New York Times* television critic. When she was glimpsed on screen, she was, said *Time*, "only slightly less animated than the portrait of herself that hung over the mantel."

The negative reaction finally finished Lee's acting career, and Truman was released from his rash promise to write something original for her. It is hard to say who looked sillier at the end of their quixotic adventure. But that unhappy honor probably belonged to Truman, who publicly demonstrated that where Lee was concerned, he had no judgment at all. Trying to be kind, he had succeeded only in being cruel. Instead of making her a star, he had turned her into a figure of fun and ridicule.

Laura had yet to be broadcast and that bad news had yet to be delivered when she returned to America in the late fall of 1967 and joined him in Alabama to watch the filming of "The Thanksgiving Visitor," the story he had dedicated to her. Turning the occasion into a family reunion, he also invited, at his own expense, a dozen or so of his relatives, including Arch and his wife Blanche.

After not having written or talked to him since 1963, Truman had telephoned his father in August, then sent him five hundred dollars for his seventieth birthday. Arch was ecstatic, believing that it was merely the down payment on the rewards due him as the father of a rich man. "When that check fell out of the letter as I opened it, I could not believe my eyes," he exclaimed to Truman. "It was the first gift of any kind you ever sent me in my whole varied, interesting and eventful life." The years had not diminished his cupidity, and the gold mine he had spent most of his life hunting for he now espied in his own son. "He is now the No. 1 writer, and the wealthiest, now ten million, and a *guaranteed* million a year from now on," he bragged to a friend, greatly inflating both Truman's assets and his income. Making up for lost time, within the space of five days Arch wrote Truman three letters and a postcard, alternately flattering him, scolding him for past neglect, and trying to make him feel guilty enough to provide the annuity he wanted so much.

Like all good salesmen, he began with the compliments. "Where I was dumb was not in realizing early that you were a 'genius,' not like other people, and treating you as a genius! That mistake won't occur again! You are not only a genius as a writer, but you are a genius in the manner in which you keep yourself constantly ahead of the public. Just when they begin to think the Truman Capote hubbub is dying down, a new avalanche lies just ahead transcending even the public imagination. In other words, you maintain and even increase the momentum and keep it going to the boiling point. Some of that, if not the writing capacity, you inherited in an elementary way from me."

Then came the reproaches for Truman's having neglected him,

particularly, he said, in the "sunset period" of his life. "Now in my four years of isolation, I told Mama and any others not to intercede for me. I feel that such things have to be spontaneous and come from the heart. I felt we were the same flesh and blood, and somewhere in your innerself, the right elements would assert themselves in due time. I just worried it might be too late for me to enjoy it."

Finally he reached his main point. "You must of course realize that almost everyone thinks that because you have millions with a future earning capacity of even more, that this fact automatically gives your father the position of sharing more or less, when we know that is not the situation at all. I do believe in families sharing their lot in life, both good and bad, but it does not work out that way in many cases." If he were in Truman's financial position, he asserted, he would help a mere friend, and of course do much more for his own father. He made the same argument in several different but similarly graceless ways, then underlined it by adding: "I would like also for you to remember that whereas you are undoubtedly the greatest exponent of the powers of description alive today, I can still clearly and vividly remember when it was the ultimate struggle for you to say just 'Ma-ma and Da-da.' "

All but hidden behind his blatant self-pity, his whining rebukes, and his unguent wheedling was almost certainly a grain of genuine affection; in his own way he loved the son to whom he had given so little and from whom he now expected so much. "It is hardly necessary for me to say HOW PROUD I am," he said, "proud—not that I am your father, BUT PROUD THAT YOU ARE MY SON. There IS a difference!!" What Truman felt about that midsummer downpour of words he did not say. He was not mortally offended, in any event —it was the same old Arch—and three months later came Truman's invitation to see the filming of "The Thanksgiving Visitor."

On Monday, December 4, groups from both sides of Truman's family converged on Montgomery. From Shreveport came Arch and Blanche; from various parts of Alabama and Georgia came representatives of the Persons clan; from Monroeville came his favorite aunt, Mary Ida Carter, her two sons and their wives. And from New York came Truman and Lee, whose superannuated Polish title had caused the staff of their Montgomery motel several days of nervous anticipation. "Should we call her Princess or Your Highness?" the waitresses in the coffee shop had anxiously asked. Truman and Lee were immediately driven to the decrepit farmhouse in the piney woods country south of town where the Perrys were re-creating his childhood. Holding Lee's hand—as if he were still a child, a reporter noted—Truman walked through the old place, which had been decorated to look like Jennie's house in Monroeville. "Marvelous!" he exclaimed. "Absolutely marvelous!"

The following day the entire party assembled there for a picnic under a hot winter sun. Almost as if by prestidigitation, Gene Callahan, the film's inventive art director, had spread two Oriental rugs on the muddy field next to the house and had piled them high with Italian food and wine, which were served from crystal bowls and silver wine coolers. Despite its incongruous splendor, however, the backwoods *fête champêtre* was not a total success. "Truman's relatives just wouldn't integrate," said Eleanor Perry. "They gathered on one rug, and the rest of us on the other rug. I think they felt we were all New York people and too chi-chi for words, even though, except for Truman and Lee, we were all dressed in filthy blue jeans. Truman, who was wearing a Cardin jacket with more zippers than I could count, was nice to them, but his male cousins were very chip-on-the-shoulder with him. 'He's made it,' they seemed to be thinking. 'He's a millionaire, and we're just being tolerated.' I remember especially the sullen face of a young cousin, a sheriff or God knows what, who obviously didn't adore him. It really was a funny scene, like something out of a Fellini movie. There we were, surrounded by mud and cow dung, eating our Italian food and drinking wine that was cooled in silver buckets. At one point I looked up to see a goat and a black sharecropper, who was probably starving to death, watching us over the fence."

From the minute he arrived until the minute he left, Truman never stopped holding Lee's hand. Arch, who all along had refused to believe that a son of his could be truly homosexual—he blamed Jack, whom he called "that bastard," for leading him astray—saw his faith confirmed. "Don't you never think he's homosexual," he later asserted. "He's screwed more women than he has fingers and toes! He's a real stud. I think he just loves it both ways, that's all. He's what you call a bisexual." Watching him mooning over Lee on Callahan's rug amid the cowpats, he was convinced that Truman's preference had swung decisively toward women; above the clatter of plates and crystal he began to hear the stately progress of a wedding march. "I think he's going to marry Lee Radziwill," Arch announced with excitement. "He's going to marry the princess!" Assuming the unaccustomed role of concerned father, he said to the princess herself, "Lee, I hope that you'll work it out so that you and Truman can get married."

No doubt amused by his naïveté, she indicated that she shared his wishes, later repeating his remark to Truman, who did not find it equally funny. "I think you used very poor taste in saying that to Lee!" he yelled over his shoulder as he passed Arch during the evening. When he and Lee left for New York the next morning, December 6, Truman did not bother to say goodbye. By themselves, Arch's misdeeds did not seem serious enough to provoke so much anger: added onto a thousand other grievances, promises broken and hopes smashed, they had been sufficient for Truman at last to cry, Enough, no more.

Truman never saw his father again. Four years later, after losing his job and suffering a serious accident, Arch wrote to ask for an allowance of ten thousand dollars a year. But even in old age the huckster in him could not be stilled; he made a plea for help sound like a once-in-a-lifetime bargain, pointing out that because of inflation, ten thousand dollars in 1971 was equivalent to only two thousand in the distant past. Nor could he resist going perhaps one step too far, suggesting in addition that Truman provide him with a house in Colorado, Arch's favorite state in the Union.

Truman did not jump to grab that bargain. He thanked Arch for his frankness, but replied that at the moment an income-tax problem was tying up all his funds; he would be in touch when it was settled, he said. Ever the optimist, Arch translated that bland and equivocal reply into a promise. He was thus all the more disappointed a few months later when he received an unmistakable no. "He had that Jew lawyer he's got write me a letter of three or four lines saying he couldn't do anything for me. Down in the corner it said, 'Copy to Mr. Capote.' It was just as brutal as hell. It's awful to have one son and have him turn his back on you, especially for no reason at all. It's one of the mysteries of the world and I'm just flabbergasted. It hurts like hell, I'll say that. I never did him anything in my life but good."

So he doubtless believed: Arch's powers of self-deception were infinite. But Truman, who knew the true story behind "The Thanksgiving Visitor"—the mother and father who had abandoned him in a household of old maids while they were off pursuing their own lives elsewhere—was not deceived, and as he himself advanced into a troubled middle age, he was not disposed to forgive either. In 1977, four years before Arch died at the age of eighty-three, Truman entered a clinic for alcoholics and was handed a form that asked whether his parents were alive or dead. "I put down 'mother deceased,' " he said. "Then I thought a minute and put down 'father deceased' too."

FOUR

45

THE day *In Cold Blood* was published, Jack attached a piece of paper to the screen door of Truman's house in Sagaponack. *"Le Beau Jour,"* he had scrawled on it—"The Good Day." But he was only half right; it was a day that was both good and bad. In some lives there are moments which, looked at later, can be seen as the lines that define the beginning of a dramatic rise or decline. It was Truman's misfortune that for him the same day marked both. Even as he was reaching the summit, he was starting his descent. For years he had pondered the aphorism attributed to Saint Teresa —more tears are shed over answered prayers than unanswered prayers—and had collected illustrious examples for his projected novel. Now he too was destined to join that unhappy list. His life began to slip out of control, and slowly at first, then with terrible speed, it careered ever downward.

The proximate cause of his tragic fall—for that is what it was— was *In Cold Blood* itself. "He never really recovered from that book," said Phyllis Cerf. "Until then he had been able to cope with all of his problems extremely well. But it was very destructive for him, especially when those boys wanted him to witness their hanging. I don't know why he put himself through that, but he did. He thought that he was tougher than he was and that he could take it. But he couldn't. That book started the unsettling of his life. He began to live—I don't know—recklessly."

He had mined his subject, but his subject had also mined him, exhausting his nerves, his reservoir of patience, and his powers of concentration; depleting, in short, his capital as both a man and a writer. "No one will ever know what *In Cold Blood* took out of me," he said. "It scraped me right down to the marrow of my bones. It nearly killed me. I think, in a way, it *did* kill me. Before I began it, I was a stable person, comparatively speaking. Afterward, something happened to me. I just can't forget it, particularly the hangings at the end. Horrible!" The memory of all he had gone through continued to reverberate in his head, he said, like the echo in the Marabar Caves in E. M. Forster's *A Passage to India*. And it delivered the same dark message: life is meaningless; or, as Forster phrased it, "everything exists, nothing has value."

Deepening his despair was his doubt that the book had been worth the sacrifice. He had been accorded money and acclaim in abundance, but he had been denied what he perhaps had yearned for most, the respect of the literary establishment—"how he longed for praise from the right people," he had once confessed to Cecil. But that respect and praise were withheld. *In Cold Blood* did not receive either of what he believed, somewhat ingenuously, to be the establishment's official seals of approval, the Pulitzer Prize and the National Book Award, the latter of which Newton had won a quarter of a century before for his Melville biography. Displaying what in retrospect seems like a willful blindness, the judges for both awards passed over the most talked-about book of the year in favor of worthy but less important contenders.*

Truman felt like a war hero who has hobbled home, expecting a parade, only to discover that others, who have never even seen the enemy up close, have picked up all the medals. His triumph was incomplete and therefore not a triumph at all: the right people, the ones who had snubbed him when he was Newton's boyfriend with the blond bangs, were still looking down their snooty noses at him.

His belief that he had been robbed of his just reward was confirmed when a spy informed him that one of the judges for the National Book Awards, *Newsweek*'s Saul Maloff, had persuaded his colleagues that the honor should go to a work less commercial than *In Cold Blood*. Truman never forgave an insult, and his revenge came a year and a half later when *The Washington Post*'s Sunday supplement, *Book World*, asked him what volumes he would like to give for Christmas. Maloff's novel *Happy Families* would be just what Frank

---

* David Brion Davis' *The Problem of Slavery in Western Culture* won the Pulitzer Prize; Justin Kaplan's biography of Mark Twain, *Mr. Clemens and Mark Twain*, won the National Book Award.

Sinatra needed, he said. With a pleasure that can be felt in every word, he explained why: Sinatra suffered from a bad case of insomnia, and "this numbing little novel, an anthology of every chichi literary cliché extant, would tranquilize a kangaroo revved to the rafters on speed."*

Truman's conviction that he was the victim of a conspiracy was reinforced two years later when Norman Mailer was given both the Pulitzer Prize and the National Book Award for *The Armies of the Night*, his story of his participation in protests against the war in Viet Nam. There were significant differences between Mailer's book and *In Cold Blood* (the most important was that Mailer made himself the main protagonist, while Truman never mentioned himself), but there was, as far as Truman was concerned, an even more significant similarity. Mailer also wrote nonfiction as if it were fiction, something he had never done before, and like Truman, he affixed a fancy but nonsensical label to his work: "History as a Novel, the Novel as History." Whatever he called it, Truman was convinced that Mailer would not have thought of doing it but for the example of *In Cold Blood* and that if his old friend and rival had been honest, he would have added: "Variations on a Theme by Capote."

"I do something truly innovative, and who gets the prizes? Norman Mailer, who told me that what I was doing with *In Cold Blood* was stupid and who then sits down and does a complete ripoff. There has never been a greater literary ripoff in the twentieth century. He took everything that I had done, all of my hard work and experimental technique, and ripped it off. But I resent only one thing, and that is that neither Mr. Mailer nor all the others who copied me, like Mr. [Bob] Woodward and Mr. [Carl] Bernstein, ever said, 'We owe Truman Capote something; he really invented this form.' They got all the prizes and I got nothing! And I felt I deserved them. The decisions not to give them to me were truly, totally unjust. So at that point I said: 'Fuck you! All of you! If you

---

* Maloff had good reason to regret the day that he became a literary judge. A few weeks later James Michener, one of Truman's admirers, wrote a letter to *Book World* professing to rebuke Truman for his ill-tempered attack, but in fact taking a second swipe at Maloff: "Granted that Mr. Maloff's novel was one of the most pathetic offerings in recent years, granted that it was a polished up re-working of some deep-think college essays remembered from Freshman English 3, and granted that Mr. Capote was right in describing the novel as a pompous travesty on popular prototypes, there was still no reason to abuse Mr. Maloff personally. He deserves compassion rather than ridicule."

are so unjust and don't know when something is unique and original and great, then fuck you! I don't care about you anymore, or want to have anything to do with you. If you can't appreciate something really extraordinary like *In Cold Blood* and the five-and-a-half years I put into it, and all of the artistry and the style and the skill, then fuck you!' "

Yet it is doubtful that he would have been satisfied even if he had swept the honors. Sooner or later, some professor at Yale or Harvard would have written a disparaging article that would have persuaded him that the right people were still against him. His need for admiration had become insatiable; all the prizes in the world could not have filled it. *In Cold Blood* may have started his slide, but if it had not, something else almost certainly would have. As he entered middle age, the demons he thought he had exorcised long ago, the desperate fears of his lonely childhood, returned to tug at his elbow and whisper in his ear. "No words can express the secret agony of my soul," said Dickens, describing the torments inflicted by the unyielding fears of his own childhood. "Even now, famous and caressed and happy, I often forget in my dreams that I have a dear wife and children; even that I am a man; and wander desolately back to that time in my life." So, in nearly the same words, might Truman have spoken. "Something in my life has done a terrible hurt to me," he did in fact say, "and it seems to be irrevocable."

That hurt—so he believed, and so was probably the case—was caused by his mother's unending rejection, and it was symbolized by the sound of a key turning in a door: the young Lillie Mae locking him in a hotel room as she left for an evening on the town. "I remember it all in such detail," he said, his mind wandering back, as it did, more and more, to that time. "At this very moment I can see those rooms in St. Louis and New Orleans. That's when my claustrophobia and fear of abandonment began. She locked me in and I still can't get out. She was the cause of all my anxiety—'free-floating anxiety' is what all the psychiatrists say I have. If you've never had it, you don't know what it's like. It has the same relationship to ordinary anxiety as a migraine has to an ordinary headache. I live with it constantly. I'm never ever free from it." Holly Golightly had given a name, "the mean reds," to that hyperanxiety. "You're afraid and you sweat like hell" was how she described it.

"But you don't know what you're afraid of. Except something bad is going to happen, only you don't know what it is."

"All our acts are acts of fear," Truman had written in one of his early stories, "Shut a Final Door." For a long time thereafter his own fears had been largely disguised by his high spirits; they may even have contributed to that puckish, clownish side of him. A frightened child has a choice of either hiding in a corner or showing off, demanding the spotlight that will drive away the darkness. Truman instinctively chose the latter course, and for years that immature side of him had served him well. One of the secrets of his appeal was his infectious exuberance and his refusal to be bound by grown-up conventions, his willingness, so rare in adults, to show affection and dislike and to say exactly what he was thinking. He could brag, lie and behave outrageously, but his friends, recognizing the excesses of a child, adored him anyway. Even his anger at Maloff and the National Book Award committee was evidence of a refreshing candor. All good writers want recognition and feel wounded and resentful when their best work is rejected; few are willing to expose and perhaps embarrass themselves by saying so. But the rebellious child within him had usually been kept in check by an adult of exceptionally clear vision and sound judgment. A remarkably sensitive gyroscope had prevented him from leaning too far in one direction or another.

In the years after *In Cold Blood*, that gyroscope became less dependable and at last broke down altogether. "It's as if two different people were inside of me," he said. "One is highly intelligent, imaginative and mature, and the other is a fourteen-year-old. Sometimes one is in control, sometimes the other." Flexing his muscles, the pugnacious adolescent more often pushed aside the increasingly weary adult, and the man in the middle, the Truman Capote the world saw, found it harder and harder to distinguish between the possible and the impossible, between reality and unreality. It is unlikely, for example, that the Truman of a decade before would have embarked on such a feckless enterprise as trying to make Lee Radziwill into a movie star; or that he would have responded with quite such self-lacerating bitterness to the slights by the award givers.

Contributing to the cloudiness of his judgment was an increasing dependence on pills and alcohol. Both had been part of his life since he was a teenager in Greenwich, stealing sleeping pills from his mother's bedroom and sweet fruit brandies from Joe Capote's bar. By the sixties, he had become addicted to tranquilizers and various other mood-altering pills, and alcohol, that old and trusty ally, had turned against him. "When I first knew him, we would have a little wine with lunch, then a martini," said Phyllis Cerf. "But during the writing of *In Cold Blood* his drinking grew, grew, grew, grew. He would start with a double martini, have another with lunch, then a stinger afterward. That kind of heavy drinking was new with him." By the early seventies, it had become obvious to him, as well as to everyone else, that he could no longer exist without the bottles in either his medicine chest or his liquor cabinet.

"This phenomenon" Cecil had once christened him, worrying that someone who lived so intensely might someday burn himself out, might be too astonishingly incandescent to last. For a decade and more Truman had proved him wrong, moving more feverishly than ever. But in the months that followed publication of *In Cold Blood*, Cecil's prediction at last came true: the phenomenon of the forties and fifties was no more. "I secretly feel T. is in a bad state and may not last long," Cecil wrote in the spring of 1966. "He has become a real neurotic case."

From the first, Truman's writing had been tinged with nostalgia, a yearning for a serene and smiling past that he himself had not known, nor given to his fictional characters. "Don't wanna sleep, don't wanna die, Just wanna go a-travelin' through the pastures of the sky" was the song Holly had sung as she sat on her fire escape, plaintively strumming her guitar. But nostalgia did not provide him the bittersweet pleasure it offers many others. It was, rather, the manifestation of a pessimism so profound that it darkened every waking moment. "People think I do frivolous things, and I do," he said, "but it's in defiance of this feeling of mutability and death being the central factor of life."

Since his childhood had not provided him with the parental love that usually brings later contentment, he had manufactured his happiness, conjuring it out of his imagination as he had his fiction. After *In Cold Blood* he was no longer able to summon the energy to perform that magic act. Nostalgia descended into sorrow, and to those who knew him well he seemed to be in perpetual mourning, overwhelmed by a sense of loss that was no less keen because he could not say precisely what it was that had been taken from him.

There were even signs that he was growing disenchanted with the very rich and that, on occasion, he was bored by the swans. He had walked on Olympus and had discovered that those who resided there were not heaven's anointed after all. It was a shock—not to his intellect, which had always known better, but to his emotions, which had not. The myth by which he had lived was starting to crumble. He floundered like a man who has lost his religion, and his confidence ebbed with his faith. The sunshine of prior years shone less and less frequently, the clouds gathering so swiftly that it seemed as if they had come from nowhere. That was not the case: they had been there, circling the horizon, all along.

The theme that ran through his life—a ceaseless but unsuccessful search for love—can be likened to a leitmotif in certain symphonies and operas. Surrounded by strings and trumpets at the beginning, the chord sparkles with optimism and laughter; all is possible, it seems to say. Then the tempo of the music slows, and mellow oboes and deep-voiced horns crowd out the lighter instruments that had danced around that melodic line; the best is over, the chord now seems to say, it is past and done. The same notes that once had sung with the high spirits of spring begin to speak of melancholy autumn and the winter that will come after. To the audience that still hears the exuberant echo of their earlier incarnation, they sound, indeed, heartrendingly sad.

46

"IF an idea is really haunting you, it will stay with you for years and years," Truman had once said. "Drain you like a vampire until you get rid of it by writing it down." So had he been haunted by the idea of *Answered Prayers*. Although he put it aside when he went to Kansas, he never doubted that one day he would return to it. "Oh, how easy it'll be by comparison!" he told a reporter in 1965, a week or so after he had finished *In Cold Blood*. "It's all in my head."

But the day of return was continually postponed as he embarked on one bootless project after another, an increasingly lengthy list that included not only his ill-conceived television adaptations for Lee, but also his documentary on capital punishment, *Death Row, U.S.A.*, and a new second act for *House of Flowers*, which was being produced Off Broadway. Added to all the other diversions that are thrust upon a famous author, those endeavors disguised the fact that except for the few final pages of *In Cold Blood*, he had written scarcely anything of his own since the summer of 1964.

Perhaps, unconsciously, that was his wish, and haunted though he was, he seemed curiously reluctant to begin *Answered Prayers*. What had seemed an easy task in the summer of 1965, when it lay off in a hazy distance, appeared considerably more difficult when the time approached to sharpen his Blackwing pencils. One of the reasons may have been that the subject now repelled as much as it mesmerized him. He had not become fixed on Saint Teresa's aphorism because he saw in it the kernel of a novel. He had fastened on it because it expressed his own bleak vision of life, his belief that fate punishes those it seems to favor by giving them precisely what they desire. It was a variation on an ancient adage: every large gift exacts a large price—"she who lent him sweetness made him blind," said Homer. Again and again he had watched different casts reenacting the same pathetic drama.

In the fifties, when he first conceived the idea of transforming that theme into fiction, he could only have imagined, or have had a presentiment of, finding himself once again an actor in that mournful play. His greatest triumph was still ahead of him; his own prayers were yet to be answered. By the late sixties they had been answered, and he realized that he was paying a price for them. It must have occurred to him that *Answered Prayers* would not only be his most ambitious work; in the loosest sense, it would also be his autobiography. He would be writing about his own disenchantment, as well as that of his characters.

The other reasons for his hesitation were probably more practical. He shuddered at the prospect of another long and lonely labor. And he feared that even if he did make such a commitment, his talent might not match his ambition. Except for two short stories, "Among the Paths to Eden" and "The Thanksgiving Visitor," he had not attempted fiction since *Breakfast at Tiffany's* ten years before. As he thought again about *Answered Prayers* in the late sixties, he must have wondered if he were still in trouble; whether, indeed, he could still write a novel.

Raising the level of his anxiety even higher was an ambition that had grown beyond the bounds of reason. Inspired by the example of Flaubert, he had always set for himself the most elevated standards—"I aspire," he had jotted in a schoolboy notebook—but until *In Cold Blood* he had been a practical perfectionist. He had aimed high, but he had not insisted that he produce a great work every time he picked up his pad. That sensible approach was another victim of his malfunctioning gyroscope: his expectations now exceeded rational limits. *Answered Prayers* had to be a masterpiece. Nothing less would do if he were to be true to his art and, at the same time, thumb his nose at those mocking, smirking faces in the literary establishment. "When I didn't get those prizes, I said to myself: 'I'm going to write a book that will make you all ashamed of yourselves. You're going to find out what a really, really gifted writer with a great determination can do!'"

Setting such an extravagant goal did not send him rushing to put words on paper, however. It did for him what it probably would have done for any other writer: it constructed a writer's block as impenetrable as the Great Pyramid. His approach toward his craft, so admirable in theory, was well-nigh paralyzing in practice. Even the steady and productive hand of Henry James, the Master himself, would have shaken if he had sat down at his desk every morning with such a warlike, uncompromising spirit.

Small wonder that Truman stopped and allowed himself to be continually detoured from his path and purpose. Looking at that most intoxicating but daunting of sights—a blank sheet of paper—he must have wondered: had he taken on more than he could handle? could he create another masterpiece? did he in fact want to live with characters whose unhappy experience mirrored his own? He might have said, as Flaubert did when he prepared to write *Bouvard and Pécuchet:* "How scared I am! I'm on tenterhooks! I feel as if I were setting off on a very long journey into unknown territory, and that I shan't come back."

By the fall of 1967 it was clear that Truman could no longer delay starting his own journey. He had publicly announced his title and theme: a dark comedy about the very rich. He had received a twenty-five-thousand-dollar advance from Random House, and without showing anybody as much as the first line of the first chapter, he had sold movie rights to Twentieth Century–Fox for the staggering sum of three hundred and fifty thousand dollars—a figure one would have to multiply at least three times to find an equivalent in today's dollars. All he had to do for that money was sit down and write the contractually guaranteed minimum of sixty thousand words: a short novel, in other words, of less than two hundred and fifty pages. But where was he to sit and write those pages? New York, with its distractions, was not the place. Nor was Long Island; although it had heat, his cottage in Sagaponack had been built for warm weather, not cold, and the flat potato fields that surrounded it, which were so lovely in other seasons, were unrelievedly dreary in winter. Verbier was the obvious spot, but the tiny apartment there was too confining and contained too many memories of the tortures of *In Cold Blood*.

He settled the question, at last, by renting a house in Palm Springs, Hollywood's favorite retreat. It had an ideal winter climate. It was small, yet, unlike Verbier, had all the sybaritic services he enjoyed and was now able to afford. It was out of the way, yet within convenient reach of his California friends, a number that now included even the Governor. "I have a strange new friend—Ronald Reagan," he informed Cecil, adding, as if he were already hearing snickers from London: "Yes, I *know*. But really he's *very* nice and we get on just fine." Reagan had helped him by pulling strings so that he could visit San Quentin for his TV documentary. Truman in turn had helped Nancy Reagan raise funds for one of her own pet projects, the restoration of the executive mansion in Sacramento, by introducing her to some of his rich friends. "Write when you can," she admonished him in November, 1967. "I don't want to lose touch."

At the end of December, Truman headed west in a Buick station wagon. Donald Windham was in the front seat beside him; Happy, a newly adopted black cat, was in the back; and Charlie was halfway in between, panting in Donald's face as he put his paws over the top of the seat to see where they were headed. Averaging five hundred miles a day, the four of them arrived in Palm Springs shortly after New Year's, 1968, and Truman was pleased to discover that his rental, an ordinary but comfortable house at 853 Paseo El Mirador, had exactly what he needed: absolute privacy. A high wall enclosed the garden and pool, and all that could be seen of the world outside was the tops of nodding palm trees and purple desert mountains. "It was a perfect setup for working," said Donald, "especially as no one Truman knew was there."

Truman did not appear to do much work, however, during the two weeks Donald was with him. Much of his time was spent on the phone to New York, conferring with Harold Arlen, who was trying to put together the new *House of Flowers*, and with the women friends who were arranging dinners before the show and a charity party on stage afterward. Less than three weeks after arriving, he interrupted his stay to fly back to Manhattan for his play's January 28 opening. But the renovated *House of Flowers* fared even less well than the Broadway original. "Whatever changes have been made, it is difficult to imagine that they are improvements," said Clive Barnes, the drama critic of the *Times*. The show closed after only fifty-seven performances, and the usually genial Arlen put much of the blame on Truman. "If he had stayed for rehearsals instead of going off to Palm Springs, I think we would have had a fighting chance," he said.

Truman quickly returned to Palm Springs, where a reporter for *West Magazine*, C. Robert Jennings, described a life that seemed to consist mostly of work, massages at The Spa, and frequent stops for drinks. What came through most clearly in Jennings' piece, if only between the lines, was something Truman doubtless did not mean to disclose: the aimlessness of his life in that plush oasis. Although he had many friends there, he was depressed and lonely. "I don't get bored here at all," he said, but added rather poignantly: "But then I have an infinite capacity for boredom."

In fact, just the opposite was true: Truman had little capacity for boredom, and he could scarcely sit still inside his protective walls. In the middle of March he left for ten days in Europe, half of which he spent in London, probably with Lee Radziwill, who had visited him in California only a few weeks before. Returning in late March, he awaited the arrival of Jack. He did not want to spend his winters in Verbier anymore, and he hoped that Jack would join him in making the descent from the Alps. At first, that seemed possible, and Jack was entranced by the desert's strange beauty. "I'm told not to walk out on the desert because there are snakes," he wrote his sister Gloria, "but it is hard not to, the evenings being so beautiful."

Jack's good opinion quickly changed. "Thirst's End" he called Palm Springs, adding, with his peculiar touch of poetry: "Every time I raised my eyes, they bumped into mountains the color of turds." He also hated Truman's house, which he thought was common, and Truman's life in it, which he thought was insanely frantic. "There was something terribly wrong with his life," Jack said. "The doorbell kept ringing with people asking him to do this and that. He was under terrific stress. He was going crazy. He was like a person who has gone into a dangerous nightclub and can't get out. He had gone too far. I didn't say anything, but I just caved in, I felt so lonely. I've never known such depression. The boredom was almost frightening. Pretty soon I began to reel. I went black.

"One day I ate two fried eggs and then went swimming in the pool. Suddenly I had a funny feeling around my heart. I thought I was having a heart attack and was going to die. Truman called a doctor, a tough little Jew, who actually came to the house and gave me a pill—what I had was a terrific case of indigestion. Truman watched me: he had been trying to get me to do something I could not do, which was to stay in a place I loathed so much I couldn't physically be there. He knew what was happening to me. I think he hated it himself. 'You'll be all right when you get wheels under you,' he said. And he was right. As soon as we drove away, I felt better."

In mid-April, two weeks before the lease on the house expired, they started back to New York. "God, what a big lonely country the USA is, and how beautiful," Jack wrote Gloria from Sagaponack. "But I like Long Island best. My heart's here. Here I feel home." He never returned to Palm Springs. But Truman did, buying that rented house and remodeling it to his liking. At the time it seemed like a logical thing to do. Only later did he realize his mistake. "Buying the house in Palm Springs was the beginning of the end for me."

47

In much of the world, and America in particular, 1968 was a year of riots, protests, and assassinations. Although Truman cared nothing about politics—he and Jack were both proud to say that they had never voted—he did have strong views about crime and criminals. He had, after all, just finished interviewing a large number of convicted murderers for his television documentary. A few days after returning to New York, he made his first appearance on Johnny Carson's *Tonight Show* to declare that the FBI was looking for the wrong person in its search for the man who had killed Martin Luther King, Jr., in early April. He had carefully studied the record of James Earl Ray, the fugitive suspect, Truman said, and had concluded that Ray was "not capable of this particular kind of very calculated, and exact and precise kind of crime." Ray was, in his judgment, a pawn in an elaborate plot and had himself been murdered at least ten days before King.

A week later, having delivered that portentous opinion, he flew with Frank and Eleanor Perry to France, where *Trilogy*, a combination of three of his stories that they had adapted for television, was contending for a prize at the Cannes Film Festival. "The people who ran the thing wanted big stars and big celebrities, and our picture was accepted on condition that we deliver Truman Capote," said Eleanor. "Of course Truman agreed. Everybody's expenses were paid, so what was the pain? We received royal treatment. We were met at the airport, I got flowers, and there were lunches and dinners for Truman. We were big deals."

But that year's unrest had spread to France as well, and shortly after they arrived, the entire country erupted in strikes and protests. "We went into the Great Hall where some Spanish director's film was about to be screened, and it was chaos," recalled Eleanor. "Geraldine Chaplin was holding the curtain shut, people were screaming and punching one another, and Jean-Luc Godard was knocked into some plastic flowers. Everyone was told that this marked the end of dinner jackets, starlets, bikinis and all the other crap that was associated with the festival. From now on Cannes was only going to have real movies for the people, we were told. Our picture was canceled before it was shown. There was nothing else to do, so we beat it." Eager to take part in the developing drama, Eleanor suggested that they go to Paris, to witness the far more serious disruptions that were occurring there. But Truman, who was no more interested in French politics than he was in those of his own country, said no, and they returned to New York by way of Venice.

He was back in Sagaponack, listening to the radio in the early hours of June 5, when he heard that Robert Kennedy had been shot in Los Angeles. They knew each other from dinner parties and had many friends in common, including Lee and Jackie. Truman was convinced that Bobby's influence over Jackie was so great, in fact, that if he had lived, he would have dissuaded her from marrying Aristotle Onassis. Truman had the impression that although he himself made Bobby uncomfortable, Bobby believed that he should like him, in the same way that some people who fail to appreciate opera grit their teeth and go anyway, in hopes that someday they will get the point. "I always felt that he was asking himself, 'Well, what is this all about?' There was something exotic about me that he couldn't entirely accept." Bobby tried nonetheless. Also a resident of the U.N. Plaza, Bobby occasionally called Truman on the house phone to ask if he could stop by for a drink before heading out for the evening, and he had read at least some of Truman's books. His favorite, he said, was not *In Cold Blood*, as might have been expected from a former Attorney General, but *The Muses Are Heard*, which made him laugh, Bobby said, more than any other book he had ever read.

The last time they met was on an early morning in May when they were both walking their dogs. Bobby, characteristically, had stopped to give a spirited lecture to two boys he had caught smoking. "One of the kids looked up at him," Truman recalled, "and said, 'Honestly, honestly, Mr. Kennedy. I swear we'll never do it again.' It was as if he was some sort of avenging angel who had fallen out of heaven upon them." A month later Truman attended Bobby's funeral in St. Patrick's Cathedral. Feverish with the flu, he could not bring himself to ride the special train that carried Bobby's body to Washington for burial, however, watching that long journey on television instead and crying so much that he became even sicker. In response to his letter of condolence, Rose Kennedy thanked him, sadly adding, "I keep thinking of Hecuba's Lament in Euripides' Trojan Women."*

Truman's credentials as an expert on crime were somewhat tarnished when James Earl Ray—far from being dead, as Truman had assured the audience of *The Tonight Show*—was arrested in London. That did not stop Truman from going on the program again on June 13 to expound a second and even more bizarre theory that connected the King assassination to those of both Bobby and John Kennedy. It was possible, he said, that all three murders were part of a giant scheme to destabilize the United States by killing its leaders. He was not the only one to harbor such suspicions during that bloody year, but he went further than most, pointing his finger at a specific group, the theosophists. Such a plan of wholesale murder, he said, had been expounded in the nineteenth century by Helena Blavatsky, the founder of theosophy; he noted darkly that soon after his arrest, the man accused of Bobby's murder, Sirhan Sirhan, had asked for a copy of Madame Blavatsky's *The Secret Doctrine*.

His second theory was as shaky as his first, as the angry theosophists were quick to point out. "Mr. Capote is in complete confusion or abysmally ignorant of the society, its aims and teachings," said Joy Mills, the president of the Theosophical Society. In fact, Madame Blavatsky promoted brotherly love, not murder, and Truman may have confused her with nineteenth-century Russian anarchists like Mikhail Bakunin, who did advocate assassination. Newspaper commentators accused him of irresponsibility, an editorial in the *Christian Science Monitor* adjudging that "the entire discussion was utterly in bad taste."

In July he removed himself from the American tumult to cruise the Mediterranean once again on the Guinness yacht. But he no longer derived pleasure from such luxurious excursions. "It was the

* "Ah woe! . . . For what woe lacketh here? My children lost, my land, my lord."

third time I had done the Turkish coast and I was absolutely frantic! Every day we would drop anchor and get off to look at some ruins, some dumb old rocks in the middle of nowhere. There was even a professor from some university in Italy who would explain what these incredible heaps meant.

"Finally I said, I believe it was to Babe: 'I can't stand it any longer. I want off! I want to go back to New York or Long Island.' And she said to me: 'Don't go with us when we get off. Stay on the ship, swim, play phonograph records, drink, get drunk, have a good time.' So that's precisely what I did. I went swimming, read books and played records—the yacht had a wonderful stereo—and got a terrific tan. Tan is scarcely the word! I looked like a mulatto! I would be relaxing when the others would all come back fatigued and dripping with sweat, just because they had gone to see some big old bunch of fucking rocks someplace in Turkey.

" 'Truman, I really don't understand why you're not coming with us,' Gloria would always say to me. 'We're seeing some quite extraordinary things.'

" 'Gloria,' I said. 'What you're doing is the single most boring thing I can conceive of. I have been on six cruises with you, but never before have I been crucified like this. I don't care anything about these things, and I am not getting off this boat to look at those old dead tombs and rocks!' "

A greater disappointment awaited him in the fall when ABC, employing a logic unique to the entertainment industry, refused to run *Death Row, U.S.A.* The program was too grim, said the network, a remark that prompted Truman to retort: "Well, what were you expecting—*Rebecca of Sunnybrook Farm*?" He was the victim of a not uncommon corporate shuffle. The program had been commissioned by ABC's former president, his friend and Palm Springs neighbor Thomas Moore, but the network's new president, Elton Rule— "that sun-tanned Uriah Heep," Truman derisively labeled him— wanted nothing to do with such a somber subject. Though Truman declared himself "terribly disillusioned" by the outcome, his chief regret was that he had wasted a year and a half of his time. "My primary thing is that I'm a prose writer," he said rather lamely. "I don't think film is the greatest living thing."

He had begun 1968 with a firm resolve to work. He ended it with little to show for his efforts—in either film or prose. "I have been working hard, doing nothing else," he wrote Cecil. "But it all has been so fragmented—writing my book, and doing (all by myself) a very complicated documentary film. That, and all the tragedy in our American lives, has kept one feeling like an insoluble jigsaw puzzle."

Shortly after Christmas he left for Palm Springs again, accompanied this time by C. Z. Guest and his cousin Joey Faulk, one of Seabon's three sons. Joey, a former Army paratrooper, did the driving; C.Z., who was not used to traveling by car, sat beside Joey in the front seat asking questions about the towns they were passing through; and Truman, reading books and magazines, reclined regally in the back seat with Charlie. (Happy, the misnamed cat, had been killed by a car on Long Island.) They reached California at the beginning of January, 1969, and C.Z. stayed with him about two weeks, Joey a little longer. His routine was much like that of the year before, but, no longer pretending to be locked in seclusion with *Answered Prayers*, he became an active member of a winter party circle that included Frank Sinatra, Bob Hope and Walter Annenberg, the owner of *TV Guide*. At Eastertime, Joey returned to drive him back to New York.

He had not completed his book by January, as he had predicted, but in May, Random House gave him a generous new contract nonetheless. As an advance against his next three books, it delivered him title to five blue-chip stocks valued at seven hundred and fifty thousand dollars; the details ran to many pages, but the end result was that his Random House portfolio was supposed to provide him with a safe and substantial yearly income. A new deadline was set for *Answered Prayers:* January 1, 1971.

Back in Manhattan, he resumed his rounds of the TV talk shows. He attacked what he called the "Jewish Mafia," a mutual-admiration society, as he viewed it, of Jewish writers, critics and publishers. He once more denounced liberal Supreme Court decisions on criminal rights, and he began his most amusing literary feud, a fierce but, in the end, harmless scratching match with Jacqueline Susann, the author of history's most popular potboiler, *Valley of the Dolls*.

He struck first, using the familiar forum of *The Tonight Show* to slight her writing abilities. Carson invited her rebuttal, and instead of minimizing his talent, which would have been a losing move, she ridiculed his mannerisms, imitating his baby voice, his rolling eyes and his effeminate hand movements. Gestures are soon forgotten.

Vivid phrases become indelible labels, and when his turn came up again in July, 1969, he was ready to attach a couple to Susann. Making reference to her dark, exaggerated and somewhat masculine features, he said that she looked "like a truck driver in drag."

His remarks were cruel, of course—though no more so than her imitation of him—but they contained enough truth to cause howls of surprised recognition from the studio audience. "Words are like chemicals," wrote her lawyer, Louis Nizer. "Some combinations fizzle. Others explode. The laughter which burst across the nation drove her and Irving Mansfield, her husband and gifted partner in the dissemination of her works, right into my office. They insisted on an immediate suit."

Although he believed she had grounds for a libel suit, Nizer advised against taking legal action. The issue was not worth the trouble and fees, he said; she had not suffered actual damage, and she had offered some provocation. Much as she wanted to see "the little worm squirm under cross examination," she reluctantly let the matter drop. Smelling victory, Truman did not. The reason she had backed down, he boasted to his friends, was that Nizer had informed her that if Truman's lawyer dressed a dozen real truck drivers in women's clothes and paraded them before a jury, she would lose: any jury would instantly agree that she did indeed look like a truck driver in drag. Eventually Truman's wishful misstatement found its way into print, and Susann prodded her counsel again. "Now the little 'capon' has put words in your mouth," she said. "It's really wild. What do you think?"

Nizer thought it was time to ask for a correction. He received it by return mail. "How pleasant to have a letter from the admirable Mr. Nizer—*even* a scolding one," Truman wrote. "It was so well written; if only your client, Miss Susann (sp?) had your sense of style!" Although he apologized for fabricating Nizer's words, he did not apologize for comparing Susann to a truck driver. "That seems to me merely an aesthetic opinion—a spontaneous observation. Bitchy, yes; malicious, no. I feel no malice for your client; on the contrary, I respect her as a very professional person who knows exactly what she's doing and how to do it. On the other hand, I suggest you examine a few of the remarks Miss S. made about me— as recently as an interview 3 weeks ago in the Los Angeles Times. Over and again she has implied that I am a homosexual (big news!)

and a lazybones jealous of her productivity. As far as I am concerned, I couldn't care less if she won the Nobel Prize—so did Pearl Buck, alors."

Susann, who was dying of cancer, did not pursue the issue. But she did manage to get in the last word, even if it was posthumous. In her final novel, *Dolores*, a tedious *roman à clef* about the Bouvier sisters, Jackie and Lee, she parodied the "little capon" in the character of Horatio Capon, the painter friend of the younger sister. "He had become a television personality," she wrote, "looked like a blondish pig, but gushingly told outrageous stories and gossip."

Most of the summer and fall Truman spent on Long Island, where he brought Maggie, a new bulldog, into the Sagaponack household. She was even more dangerous than Susann, however, and at the end of October he was nearly killed trying to stop her from jumping out of his Jaguar convertible. In his panic, he stepped on the accelerator instead of the brake, sending the car smashing into a tree and propelling him through the windshield. Knocked unconscious, he was taken to Southampton Hospital, where he was treated for cuts to the head and face and kept for two days. Maggie, the cause of all the trouble, was unhurt, but his beautiful Jaguar—"Green Girl," he had christened it—was demolished.

In late November he flew to Teheran with Robert O. Anderson, the chairman of the Atlantic Richfield oil company. Anderson had more diverse interests than most other businessmen, and their friendship was not quite as curious as it might have seemed. Anderson entertained Truman at his ranch in New Mexico, and Truman introduced him to the Shah, who was a valuable acquaintance for the head of an oil company to have. "Bob wanted his company to put oil rigs in the Persian Gulf, but he couldn't get anywhere with the Shah," said Truman. "The Shah wouldn't even see him. Well, I happened to know the Shah. I used to go for long walks with his wife, Farah Dibah, in Switzerland. They told me to come visit anytime I wanted, so I wrote her a letter and asked if I could bring a friend. She wrote right back and said they would have cars to meet us. They went with us to their palace in Isfahan, and Bob and the Shah got along famously. Bob got what he wanted in Iran, and his company made several million dollars."

At the end of their trip, Anderson asked him where he would like to have dinner. "Harry's Bar in Venice," Truman immediately answered—and off they flew in Anderson's jet. When they landed in Venice, a waiting speedboat rushed them to Harry's, whose management, flattered that they had come so far for a meal, kept the kitchen open past its usual hours. Truman returned to New York just in time to say goodbye to Jack, who was about to leave for Verbier. He himself went in the opposite direction, back to Palm Springs. "Jack refuses to go to California under any circumstances," he sighed to Cecil. "Same old Jack!"

48

THEY had been together twenty-one years. They had loved and fought and traveled side by side into middle age: at the beginning of 1970, Truman was forty-five, Jack a decade older. But although Jack was indeed the same old Jack, the Truman who saw the sixties out was not the same Truman who had seen them in. Nor was their relationship what it had been in 1960 and the years preceding, when they had spent most of their time together, quietly working. "We were both vocation-driven," said Jack. "We felt that if you stop writing, you die."

The publication of *In Cold Blood* disrupted that pattern, as it did nearly everything else in Truman's life. He could no longer bear being cooped up in Verbier all winter, yet he did not want to be by himself at the U.N. Plaza either. If Jack had stayed with him in New York, he later maintained, he would never have gone to Palm Springs. But Jack would not stay, and every year his departure for Switzerland was a source of anxiety, something that Truman anticipated with dread weeks and months before it actually happened. In his increasingly fragile state of mind, he viewed Jack's yearly leave-taking as a form of rejection and abandonment. Unwilling to remain in Manhattan by himself, Truman began his winter wanderings, first to Morocco with Lee in 1967, then to Palm Springs. Without actually planning it that way, he and Jack had so arranged things that they were apart as much as they were together.

The rules that governed their lives had evolved so slowly that not until the end of the decade was it clear how profound the change had been. On Truman's initiative, they had even ceased being lovers and had become nonsexual companions instead. "Twenty years is a long time to live with someone," said Truman. "Certain things come to an end, and this had come to an end with me. I wasn't having an affair with anyone, and I decided that I didn't want to go to bed for any reason that I can remember now, or could put my finger on then. All I know is that one day I said to myself, 'I like Jack, but I don't love him.' It was as simple as that." It is not too much to speculate, however, that there was an additional reason: he was retaliating, if only subconsciously, for Jack's annual flight to Verbier.

If Truman's decision hurt Jack, as it did, the bruise quickly healed. In fact, as he looked back, Jack concluded that cutting the sexual bonds had probably preserved the other and, to him, more significant ties between them. "The platonic companionship of two men is the highest form of human relationship," Jack declared. "If any homosexual relationship works, it has to mature into something beyond sex. Truman and I were the only ones I know of who managed it. It was unthinkable that we would ever break up. People thought that our relationship was based on sex. It wasn't. It was never important to either of us. Truman wasn't highly sexed, and there is something cold—hyperborean, as Joyce would say—about me. I'd rather talk to people than screw them, much to their annoyance. Truman didn't want to go to bed with me anymore, and I forgot about it. I became pretty celibate. Steady nooky isn't good anyway."

When Truman later changed his mind and wanted to go to bed, Jack was willing, but his body was not; it would not function. He was convinced that Truman had gone to bed with Lee—that "gold digger and out-and-out pirate," as Jack called her—and, rightly or wrongly, he felt betrayed. "We tried, but I couldn't do it," he said. "The same thing happened with Joan McCracken. I can't do it when I feel someone has been with another person. I can't have sex to order." Thus did Truman begin anew his search for sexual love, a pursuit that was to multiply his woes beyond easy reckoning. "It all started—all these affairs—because I didn't want to go to Switzerland," Truman was later to say, as if he were beginning a long, sad story, which of course was precisely what he was doing.

Enter Danny, the first of Truman's "men without faces," as Wyatt Cooper was to characterize them, men "you always have trouble remembering unless they're with Truman."* Those who saw him many times were hard pressed to describe him afterward; photographs display not a single distinguishing feature. He was forty, or close to it, and about five feet nine inches tall; he had brown hair that was starting to gray, and he was neither handsome nor ugly. He came from a small town in Illinois, and living in the sophisticated resort of Palm Springs, as he did, had affected him not at all. "He wore what they wear in small towns in the Middle West," said Charlotte Curtis, the society columnist for *The New York Times*, who was Truman's houseguest for a few days that winter of 1970. "Open shirt, short sleeves, his hair slicked down for a Saturday night in Peoria. There was something of the fifties about him."

His education was limited; a year of vocational training after high school was all. He had served in Korea, worked as a guard at a prison in Illinois, and married and fathered two sons; he had recently separated from his wife. In Palm Springs he made his living repairing air conditioners and, in his off hours, fueling planes at the airport. Confusing planes with cars, Bennett Cerf informed Truman's friends that he was a filling-station attendant. "I'm furious with Bennett for saying that!" Truman told Wyatt. "He is *not* a filling-station attendant. He came to repair my air conditioner."

When Marella Agnelli met him, she shrewdly observed that Truman must have had "a great nostalgia," that Danny must have reminded him of a boy from his adolescence. She was right. That boy, a cadet at St. John's Military Academy, had been the other half of what Truman termed his first affair. "I had had sex before," he said, "but I didn't know what I was doing. That boy was smarter than Danny, but he had the same kind of looks, the same kind of temperament." Danny represented that boy thirty-five years later. But he also represented all those carefree, freckle-faced Alabama country boys Truman had wished he could have been, mocking him, even if they uttered not a word, with the nonchalant assurance of the absolutely average. In every way Danny stood for the common man: that was his allure. If he had been handsome, had boasted a fine physique, or had been out of the ordinary in any other way, Truman would not have given him a second glance.

Puzzled by his choice, Wyatt tried to find out what it was in Danny that appealed to him. "I don't understand what it is you like.

---

* Danny was Truman's private name for him; it was not his real name.

What movie stars, for instance, do you find attractive?" Scorning the names of those stars most of the world found appealing, Truman finally admitted that he always had had "rather a yen" for Lloyd Nolan, a Hollywood character actor whose plain, horsey face had often cast him in the role of the cop on the block. "Now, Mrs. Lloyd Nolan never had a yen for Lloyd Nolan!" said Wyatt, laughing as he recalled their exchange. "But when he mentioned his name, I knew what he meant. The normal, the dull and the average had great glamour for him because they were the opposite of what he was."

Growing up in a town not much different from Monroeville, Danny doubtless had been the image of the normal, uncomplicated son Nina had longed for. When he met Truman, probably in the first weeks of 1970, he was still normal and uncomplicated, "sweet and simple," in Truman's words, "a combination of Tom Sawyer and Huckleberry Finn. He was the type of person I found very attractive. He was like a puppy dog—a very sexy puppy dog. On a sex level, I don't like people that are too smart, and from my point of view he was perfection. I think he must have been just about the stupidest person I've ever known. I cannot imagine anybody being dumber than Danny."

Dumb as he was, it was still a matter of enormous pride to Truman, a testimony to his own appeal, that he was able to seduce someone who appeared to be impregnably heterosexual, who was, if proof were needed, both a husband and a father. "Truman was always nagging on about Danny's heterosexuality, as if he was the only man Danny had ever fancied," said John Richardson, an English art critic who lived in Manhattan and traveled in Truman's circles. "This colossal conquest was a terrific feather in his cap, he thought, though it seemed to me that Danny's sexuality, such as it was, was so precarious and vague that anybody who had the interest or the patience could have, as it were, penetrated it. In fact, I thought Truman could only get heterosexual men because homosexual men would have found him extremely unattractive. I didn't dare put it to him in that light, however."

Nor did anyone else, and Truman's chief attraction for Danny—money—was obvious to everyone, including Truman. "He knew he was deceiving himself," said Saint Subber. "He kept saying to me, 'Tell me he's not doing this for any reason other than love.' I didn't want to hurt my best friend by telling him the truth." Prostitution disgusted him, and Truman never would have purchased the services of a call boy. But he saw nothing wrong in giving Danny an average of two thousand dollars a month, or in promising something like twenty thousand dollars to set him up in a housekeeping business for Palm Springs' itinerant rich.

He had two weapons besides money in his armory, however. The first was his charm, potent still. Under the scrutiny of his intense blue eyes, Danny's sleeping ego awoke, stretched and smiled with pleasure. Never before had he been lavished with so much attention. "Here was a man nobody else would have been interested in," said Wyatt, "and suddenly Truman found him attractive. So Danny said to himself, 'Well, I knew all along that I really was somebody!' The fact that Truman was also unattractive was almost irrelevant, because Danny's narcissism had been awakened." The second weapon was his celebrity. "Fame is the great aphrodisiac," Truman said. As his friend, Danny was no longer a hired man; he sat as an equal beside tycoons and movie stars.

Wherever Truman went, he dragged Danny with him. When they first heard the name of the friend Truman was bringing to dinner, the local grandes dames fluttered with excitement, assuming he was a popular poet and singer who, inconveniently for them, bore the same last name. Their enthusiasm dimmed noticeably when they learned their mistake; it flagged altogether when they discovered that he could talk about little but air conditioners, which, even in the desert, are rarely a topic of conversation. "He was an authentic primitive," said Charlotte Curtis. "He never said a word. He couldn't hold up his end of the conversation, which is a trial socially." But Truman persisted in making it clear that where he was invited, Danny had to be asked too. "Truman knew what people were thinking," said Alan Schwartz, a Manhattan lawyer he had retained some months before. "But it was his way of saying, 'Look, you bring whoever you want to my house, and I can bring whoever I want to yours. It's up to me.' He was also saying, 'I'll show you I'm not your court jester! I'm equal!' "

Yet he was hurt nonetheless by the consternation Danny unwittingly caused. Late one night, a small group ended the evening at a Palm Springs discotheque, and Truman, who had been drinking heavily, pulled Curtis onto the dance floor. Half in tears, he shouted above the crash of the amplifiers: "I suppose you want to know about Danny. I cannot tell you how wonderful he is for me. He's exactly what I need. People make fun of him and they don't like him. But he's important to me. You don't know what it is to have someone there who doesn't put any pressure on me." As he explained it, his obsession made perfect sense to her. "Danny was one of the few people who didn't force him to rise to some brilliant occasion and perform," she said. "He didn't have to do anything when he was with him, whereas the rest of the time he had to go out and be Truman Capote."

In June Danny went with him to New York, where the consternation of Palm Springs was repeated on a larger stage. Trying, like everyone else, to find out what Truman could see in him, Slim cornered him at a party. "Do you know what Truman does?" she demanded. "Do you know what he has done? Do you understand what his work is?" But her questions, she soon realized, were addressed to "an empty suit. He had no idea what I was talking about." In Washington, which was also on Truman's itinerary, Kay Graham was no less aghast. "I was horrified. Ooooh! I didn't want an air-conditioning man for a friend. I said, 'Truman, this is terrible. You shouldn't be doing this. Where is Jack? What's happened here?' "

It was a question all of his friends were asking. "When he was with this man, Truman was just repulsive, a totally different person," said Phyllis Cerf. "He was a terrible show-off and name-dropper. It was pathetic how determined he was to impress him. And you looked at this dunce and wondered what in heaven's name had got into Truman! We couldn't believe it. People were whispering behind their hands at his insistence on taking this man with him. They didn't want him. He didn't have the background, social or otherwise, of the people Truman was foisting him on. He was indeed an air-conditioning man. It was the beginning of the destruction of Truman's friendships."

The Cerfs invited them to Mt. Kisco one weekend nonetheless, along with Frank Sinatra and Kay and Joe Meehan. "As a sweet little gesture to me, the man said that he wanted to show me how to clean my air conditioners," said Phyllis. "I had no desire to learn how to clean my air conditioners, but he insisted, and not wanting to be rude, I went with him into a room where there was a window air conditioner. He started taking it apart to get the filter out—and he broke the front of it!" Later, when they set their luggage down in their bedroom, Danny and Truman broke both of the beds, a coincidence so improbable that Bennett mischievously spread the story that his beds had been sacrificed to their sexual frenzy. A few weeks later, at a party at the Cowleses' house nearby, Phyllis heard Bennett's more entertaining version from Pamela Hayward. "Oh, don't say that!" Phyllis angrily commanded, causing the entire room to snap to attention as she brushed Pamela's shoulder with her hand. Within seconds the Tale of the Broken Beds had become legend, and an equally apocryphal sequel had been added—the Society Slap. According to some accounts, Phyllis had not merely touched Pamela, she had slugged her. So does gossip spread, and it was perhaps only justice that Truman, who was so often the purveyor, was now the subject.

In Europe, where they went next, Truman at last began to share his friends' doubts about Danny. "We went to a grand party in the Agnellis' vast, vast palace in Turin. When I say grand, I really mean it. There was a footman behind every chair. No royalty has ever lived like the Agnellis. Danny was sitting next to the Queen of Denmark, and she asked him if he had ever been to Europe before. 'No,' he said, 'except for that time in Korea.' I was sitting across the table and heard every word, and I laughed until the tears came to my eyes. Marella liked him, but didn't know how dumb he was. To Europeans like that all Americans are the same. We're all niggers. They don't see any difference because they think we're totally unimportant. You can pass anyone off on them."

In some ways, however, Danny may have been smarter than Truman: he realized that he did not belong, and it was cruel of Truman, and selfish as well, to place him in a position where people whispered about him behind their hands. He could help neither his ignorance nor his upbringing. The initial thrill of meeting celebrities had passed, moreover, and he was as wearied by Truman's friends as they were by him. He did not want to sit next to the Queen of Denmark; he may never even have heard of Denmark. He did not even want to see the sights of Europe.

John Richardson, who saw them in Venice toward the end of their tour, recognized in him the same homesickness he had seen in GI's in Britain during World War II. "He seemed like a plant that had been uprooted and was very unhappy out of its element. The one thing he wanted in Venice was a baked Idaho potato. He just longed for one! It was an emblem of American life that he felt starved of. Truman asked me to find him one, so I went to the market, found some large potatoes, and took them back to the chef at the Cipriani Hotel, where we were all staying. 'They must be baked in their skin,' I said, 'not cut up, not sautéed.' Both Danny and Truman were in a state of great excitement. And of course when the waiter arrived with them, they were chopped up and sautéed as they always were in Italy. So Danny's great treat turned into a hideous disappointment, and he looked sadder and glummer than he had done before."

Reaching London the first week in September, they visited Lee. She was no more impressed by Danny than anyone else—"totally nondescript" was her two-word description—and Danny felt the same about her, which Truman took as a personal insult. Deciding finally that he had had enough of disapproving looks, Danny told Truman that he wanted to go home, and on September 7, 1970, four days after they had arrived, they abruptly left for America, Truman stopping in New York while Danny continued by himself to Palm Springs.

After their disastrous weeks in Europe, Truman may have intended to drop him. But Danny, glad to be home, made the first move himself, seeking a reconciliation with his wife. That changed the emotional equation for Truman, who once again experienced the familiar feeling of rejection, disguised this time as jealousy. "My whole life has been dominated by jealousy," he confessed not long after. "It's the one uncontrollable thing with me. It's the key to my character. I'm jealous about everything. If I pass a shop with an antique cup in the window, for instance, and I see someone else looking at it, I'll turn around and go back and buy it." It was not a pleasant sensation. Appearing on Dick Cavett's television talk show in early October, he spoke rather startlingly of "the haze of pain one experiences when there is a separation from a friend, or more so, a loved one." His mind turned to thoughts of retaliation, and in mid-October he made plans to return to California.

His ostensible purpose was to cover the murder trial of Charles Manson and three of his female followers for *The New York Times Magazine*. But almost certainly his real reason for going west was to break with Danny and to hurt him in the only way he knew how, by withdrawing his support for the Palm Springs housekeeping service. He asked Alan Schwartz to go along to give him legal pointers on the trial; but his real motive was almost certainly different. Alan

had been recruited to be the bearer of bad tidings, saving Truman
the awful chore of informing Danny that both their relationship and
the business were finished. Not until a few days before he and Alan
were to leave did Truman mention to Alan that there was yet another problem in California: out there he was considered a fugitive
from justice; he might be arrested when they landed at the Los
Angeles airport.

His criminal status was fallout from his abortive documentary.
The conviction of one of the killers he had interviewed had been
overturned on a technicality, and the prosecutor insisted that Truman testify at the new trial. Believing, like any other honorable
reporter, that interviews are confidential, Truman had ignored the
subpoena and on the appointed date he had fled with Danny to a
seedy motel in the mountains. There he had heard on television that
he had been cited for contempt of court—he was a wanted man.

In his panic, all he could think of was escaping to his safe and
secure aerie on the East River. The following morning Danny
dropped him off at the Los Angeles airport and he raced down its
interminable corridors to catch a noon flight to New York. "But the
police were watching everything going out of Los Angeles," he said,
"and there, standing at the very gate of the very plane that I was
going to take was this big tall policeman I knew. The plane was to
leave in ten minutes, and I ducked into a telephone booth. How was
I going to get past this guy? At this moment who should come sailing
by, wearing a marvelous gray sable coat and surrounded by six or
seven of her musicians, but Pearl Bailey! So I opened the door of
the telephone booth.

" 'Pearl! Pearl! Pearl! It's me! It's Truman!'

" 'Darling, what are you doin' in that telephone booth?' she asked,
and I explained quickly. 'Think real fast,' I said. 'How can I get on
that plane?' So she told her boys to go into the men's room with me,
and they loaned me clothes. Then she sent somebody ahead with
the tickets and wrapped me up in her sable coat. We sailed right
through that gate! The policeman didn't notice anything. He
thought I was just part of this freak brigade."

As Truman had suspected, his testimony had not been necessary
to reconvict the killer he had interviewed, and now, in October,
Alan telephoned Truman's Palm Springs lawyer to learn if the state
of California was still feeling sulky. "The judge says it's okay," the

lawyer assured Alan. "They won't arrest him at the airport, and they'll just fine him a couple of hundred bucks and slap his wrists." When they walked into the courtroom in Santa Ana three days later, however, Alan could see instantly that the Palm Springs lawyer had been misinformed. Things were not at all okay. Furious at what he labeled Truman's "plain old contempt," the judge fined him five hundred dollars and sentenced him to three days in jail.

That was more like a knockout punch than a slap on the wrist, and back in his bungalow at the Hotel Bel-Air, Truman swallowed several pills, crawled shakily into bed and pulled the covers over his head. "Call Ronald Reagan!" he yelled to Alan, who was in the next room, and Reagan, who was still Governor, was more soothing than a Miltown. "No problem," he said. "Just give me the name of the judge and I'll take care of it." But when he heard the name, even Reagan confessed helplessness. "Oh, no," he said. "He's the only Democratic judge in Orange County. He hates me." There was no time for further appeal, and late on the afternoon of the following day, October 21, Orange County's most-wanted fugitive was placed behind bars. "I've been in thirty or forty jails and prisons, but this is the first time I'll ever be in one as a prisoner," Truman jauntily told reporters, successfully masking his real feeling, which was one of stark terror.

Leaving Truman in Santa Ana, Alan drove to Truman's house in Palm Springs to deliver his message to a sad, bewildered and almost catatonic Danny. "I'm here to tell you it's all over," Alan said after a couple of amiable drinks. "You can't be here when Truman comes back from jail." The next morning Alan received a call from the judge's office in Santa Ana. After serving only eighteen hours of his three-day sentence, Truman was to be released at noon; the judge had merely wanted him to realize what a serious offense it was to defy a court order, an assistant said. Racing over the freeways, Alan arrived a minute before Truman emerged from a door in the back of the courthouse. Appearing jaunty no longer, he looked, in Alan's words, "as if he had been raped, rolled and beaten up."

The combination of confinement in a jail cell—even if it was for only eighteen hours—and the end of his romance shattered Truman, and he spent several days in a Manhattan hospital trying to recover from the ensuing nervous breakdown. "He was absolutely flattened," said Slim. "His breakup with Danny rocked him more than the breakup of any marriage I've ever seen. He would shake and cry and say, 'Oh, the hell with it! I'm glad he's out of my life, and I don't ever want to think about him again.' But he was like a dog with a bone. He couldn't let go of it. 'Do you know what he said to me?' he would say. 'Do you know what he did?' He was in real and terrible pain. Babe was marvelous with him. She wanted to take him to Nassau with her. 'One or the other of us should be with him,' she said. 'I think he may try to commit suicide.' " His vanity and self-esteem had been mortally wounded, and Truman could neither forget nor forgive. In the end, it seemed, his achievements, his fame, even his money were not enough: those freckle-faced boys were still mocking him.

In his rage, he plotted schemes of revenge, which, like everything else in the Danny affair, sounded comical to everyone but him. He had paid to have caps put on Danny's teeth, and he toyed with the idea of demanding them back. "They're my teeth and I want them!" he told Johnny Carson's wife Joanne. "I want to string them on a necklace and wear them around my neck." A more practical notion was to repossess the car he had also paid for; but since it was registered under Danny's name, he was frustrated in that too. Finally, in his fury, he dispatched Joanne and Myrtle Bennett, his Palm Springs maid, on a midnight sabotage mission to the parking lot of the Palm Springs post office, where poor Danny, no longer employed as an air-conditioning repairman, had taken a night job. Their weapon: a one-pound box of sugar, which was to be poured into the car's gas tank.

"We were both so terrified that we giggled a lot," said Joanne. " 'Don't worry, honey,' said Myrtle, who was black. 'They ain't gonna spot me. There's no moon out.' " Her hands trembling, Joanne broke a nail opening the box's spout. But that was the raid's only casualty, and after pouring the sugar into the tank, she and Myrtle made a successful getaway. Their mission accomplished, they called him in New York with their report. He could scarcely have been more pleased if they had blown Danny's car into a thousand pieces. He had had his revenge.

Exit Danny; enter Rick Brown, a combination barker and bartender at the Club 45, a rough sailors' bar on West Forty-fifth Street, between Broadway and Sixth Avenue. Rick was standing in the doorway one night early in 1971 when he saw Truman, whom he recognized from television, walking home from the theater with Donald Windham and Sandy Campbell. "How are you, Truman?" he called out.

"Fine, fine," said Truman, who was surprised into stopping. "What kind of place is this?"

"Just a little bar. Come in. I'll buy you a drink." Though they stayed only a few minutes, Truman came back a few nights later with two other friends—he was gathering material on Manhattan's lowlife for *Answered Prayers*, he told them—and invited Rick to lunch at the Oak Room of the Plaza, where he quizzed him about his past and his hopes for the future. "He said I seemed too bright to be in a place like that," recalled Rick. "I wasn't naive, but I had no idea what he was leading up to." What he was leading up to was soon clear: he had found another Tom Sawyer, someone who met his specifications in almost every way.

Rick was five feet eleven inches tall; he had an ordinary build; he wore thick glasses and he had a pleasant but homely face and thinning blond hair. Beyond that, there was not much to tell. Barely twenty-six, Rick was a West Virginia hillbilly who had grown up in a backwoods hollow near where the Hatfields and McCoys had fought and feuded. Except for the introduction of electricity, living conditions had changed little since then, and he had grown up without running water or an indoor toilet. To escape, he quit high school and joined the Navy. When he got out, he married, fathered a son, and then, like Danny, separated from his wife. Although he was poorly educated, he was far from stupid and aspired to be both a writer and an actor.

During the weeks that followed their lunch at the Plaza, Truman returned to the Club 45, took him to celebrity-packed parties, introduced him to tycoons like Robert Anderson, and acquainted him with some of Manhattan's most expensive restaurants. He also gave him a key to his apartment and showed him the drawer in his bedroom in which he kept an envelope stuffed with several thousand dollars, mostly in fifty- and hundred-dollar bills, which were fresh from the bank and still had the bosky smell of uncirculated currency. "If you ever need money, here it is," he said, as casually as someone else might have offered entrée to his liquor cabinet or refrigerator. After his experience with Danny, he apparently planned to make sure that this time he would dangle bait large enough to bag his quarry.

He did not need to worry. Rick was where he had always yearned to be. He was thrilled to meet and talk to stars, he was delighted to hear headwaiters crooning in French as they bowed him to the best table in the room, and he, who had never seen more than two hundred dollars at one time, was pop-eyed at the thought that without so much as saying please, he had access to ten, twenty, thirty times that much. "This is the way for a boy from West Virginia to live," he said to himself. "Well, hell, it's just a matter of time before I'm one of these jet-setters myself." That belief turned into certain conviction after a trip home, where he was reminded of the mean and arid existence that awaited him there. "I didn't want to waste twenty years of my life and be like the people there," he said. "I wanted more. It's not a sin to want more."

Truman, who had always wanted more himself, understood perfectly. But at the moment all he desired was Rick. Proving once again that he was his father's son, he sweetened his other inducements with a pitch that never fails: he told Rick exactly what he longed to hear. After reading his unfinished fiction and screenplays, Truman proclaimed him a writer of unquestionable promise. "A lot of people don't become great writers until they're forty-five or fifty. Very few have hit the mark before they reach their thirties. I feel that you have that gift, if you will just sit down and do it."

Truman also discussed with him, as he had with Danny, a joint business venture, an elegant Manhattan bar that would capitalize on Truman's name and Rick's experience. "TC's" or "Truman's Place," as they thought of naming it, was to have a literary atmosphere, with bookcases and—so ran Truman's macabre fancy—decorative rubbings from the tombstones of the many writers and poets whose remains reside in Paris' Père Lachaise cemetery: sip a brandy next to Proust, raise a glass to Oscar Wilde, carry on a romance beside Colette. "Put me down for five grand," asserted Frank Sinatra, who was impressed by the notion. "No, make it ten!"

With a casual sweep of his hand, Truman thus brushed away the clouds that had always hovered over Rick's head and spread before him a sky of brilliant blue. "All of a sudden all these dreams woke up," said Rick, "and I realized, well, Christ, maybe I can have them. He made me feel like everything was there for me. I didn't want to hit it when I was forty-five, fifty-five, or sixty-five. I wanted it then. He gave me hope, and he actually convinced me that, through him, I was going to get more out of life." All of those who had been gulled by Arch over the years, who had invested in one of his cockamamie schemes or who had quit their jobs to follow him down that dead-end road to riches, might have made the same speech. But none could have stated it with more pathetic eloquence.

Truman invited him to Palm Springs, and when Rick protested that he could not leave his job, Truman offered to find him a better one, one more commensurate with his creative abilities. In the meantime, Truman said, he would take care of him himself. "Truman, I have never lived under those circumstances," Rick grandly replied. "I can't humble myself."

"I promise you you'll never have to. I'll pay your rent and give you whatever you need to live on during the week, a couple of hundred dollars."

"A couple of hundred dollars? Fine."

So it was settled, and as an expression of his good intentions, Truman wrote out a check for seven hundred dollars, the amount Rick needed to pay off a couch he had bought for his apartment. On the plane west, Truman also surprised him with an envelope containing four hundred-dollar bills—"just in case you need anything," he said. Not once had they mentioned sex, and only after they had been in California a few days, sleeping in separate rooms, did Truman spell out the obvious, that he expected something more than companionship for his money. "I don't know," said Rick, who of course knew very well. "Okay, we'll give it a try."

Three or four nights later, after a skinny-dip in the pool, they did give it a try, and Rick, who claimed that he had never had sex with a man before, was relieved to find that it was not objectionable. "It was really nothing difficult, so I felt, There's no sweat, I'll make it."

Sex was not the only reason Truman had pressed him to come to Palm Springs, however; it was not even the most important reason. His real purpose became apparent when Danny was invited to Truman's house for one of Myrtle Bennett's fancy lunches, then asked to come again for dinner with his two sons. The atmosphere was calm and amiable, and not until later did Rick realize that he was there largely for display, that he had been flown from New York to demonstrate to Danny that Truman did not need him, that he had found someone else, somebody who was just as ordinary, just as masculine and just as heterosexual.

Sinatra gave them a ride back to New York in his private plane, and for several months, through the spring and summer of 1971, Truman and Rick adhered to a comfortable routine. With Truman paying the bills, Rick rented a two-room penthouse on East Forty-sixth Street, just south of the U.N. Plaza, so that Rick would have somewhere to retreat when Jack, who remained ignorant of their arrangement, came in from Long Island. "You could stay with him till Jack came to town; then you had to leave," said Rick, a little bitterly. "You were allowed to have no other affairs, whether they were with women or whatever, but yet you had to make the concession to him to have his affair with Jack."

Otherwise Rick had full run of Truman's apartment. Truman, who had a fear of markets crashing and banks closing, placed sufficient confidence in him to show him where he kept his real money, which was several times the piddling amount in the bedroom drawer. Like a boy who was showing his hidden treasures to his best friend, Truman led him to the red-lacquered Chinese secretary in the living room, pushed aside a seemingly immovable panel, and revealed a secret cubbyhole inside which nestled four transparent bank envelopes, one containing ten thousand dollars, the other three containing five thousand dollars apiece.

Despite the disparity in both age and status, in many ways Rick assumed the role of a protective, often hectoring older brother, urging Truman to lose weight and cut down on his drinking. "You look grotesque!" said Rick, employing the direct diplomacy of the Hatfields and McCoys. "You're still a young man. Take care of yourself!" he added, putting him on a diet and signing him up at a gym on Forty-seventh Street. But no amount of insulting speech could persuade Truman to cut down on his consumption of alcohol. "He drank to get drunk," said Rick. "Instead of ordering one screwdriver at a time, for instance, he'd order a double or a triple." When talk failed, Rick sometimes took sterner measures, forbidding Truman anything stronger than a glass of wine at dinner. "If you take one drink—one drink!—I'm getting up and leaving," he would say as they went out for the evening. "But before I do, I'm going to embarrass you by dropping the tablecloth in your lap."

Forceful as they were, such guerrilla tactics were doomed to failure. All they managed to do was to make Truman both more devious and more determined. Like all other alcoholics, he won in the end. Staying home one night, for example, he was suspiciously agreeable when Rick told him that he could drink only 7-Up. In fact, he seemed to have developed a taste for it, sending Rick back to the kitchen for glass after glass. To Rick's bewilderment, he became drunk anyway and grew ever more so as the night progressed. While Truman was out the next day, Rick rummaged through his bedroom and discovered the explanation: miniature vodka bottles hidden under the pillows and blankets of his bed. "Every time he'd send me to the kitchen for a 7-Up, he'd open one up and—phffft—down it would go. He used the 7-Up to wash down the vodka. When he came back later that day, I had eleven empties all lined up. 'How did they get here?' he asked."

During the summer Truman recruited Wyatt Cooper to work with him on a television play, a prison drama titled *The Glass House*. Rick wanted the part of the young lead, a character who was supposed to be so attractive that teenage girls swooned over him, and Truman insisted that Wyatt, who was vacationing in Southampton, drive into Manhattan to meet Rick over lunch. "Here was this boring and totally uninteresting-looking man who sat and told us the plot of a Joan Crawford movie he had watched on television the night before," said Wyatt, who was baffled as to why he had been summoned. "And Truman hung on his conversation as if it were full of gems!" The mystery was dispelled a few days later when Truman called again and announced, as if the idea had just occurred to him, that he had found an ideal candidate for their young protagonist. "You know who could play the part? Who would be kind of marvelous? Rick!"

"Truman, you're kidding. It's got to be somebody who's good-looking and sexy."

"Obviously your idea of good-looking and sexy is very different from mine" was Truman's chilly reply.

He next tried to persuade Wyatt to collaborate with Rick on one of Rick's own screenplays. "*You* collaborate with him!" shot back Wyatt. "You're the one who wants to be around him."

Rick soon had second thoughts about his friendship with Truman. By his reckoning, he had lived up to their unwritten agreement. By his further reckoning, Truman had not; Rick had expected not just a weekly allowance, but a push into the future. That, he could now see, he was unlikely to receive; believing himself wronged, he became more cynical and calculating. "I guess I adopted the attitude I just didn't care," he said. "The relationship turned strictly commercial. I would do my best to spend as much money as I could and to see as little of him as I could."

At the same time, the sexual part of their relationship was becoming increasingly onerous to him. "Physically, Truman did nothing for me, and that's why, sexually, we weren't knocking the fireworks off. Plus, many nights he was drunk. It is very hard trying to be affectionate with someone if they're drunk, excuse themselves to throw up, then come back. How could you kiss someone after that? You can't. It was just hard, hard for me." Making it harder still was the ragging he was taking from many of his old friends, who assumed that he was homosexual; even his estranged wife threw the word "fag" at him. "It hurt my feelings a lot, and I was thinking, 'Jesus, do I look gay? Or am I gay?' " He had never imagined himself in such a predicament. "If a heterosexual who has sex with a man is called homosexual," he plaintively inquired, "why isn't a homosexual who has sex with a woman called heterosexual?"

As Rick was having such doubts, Truman was making matters worse by becoming both less generous and more possessive. He began to watch Rick's expenditures, he kept track of where he spent his time, and he accused him of having a romance with a woman friend. What Rick had feared would happen was happening: he was required to ask every time he needed money, as if he were a sixteen-year-old begging Saturday-night-date money from his father. "I had no identity. There was no way that he was going to let you become your own person because you'd have felt you didn't need him anymore."

In the midst of his agonizing, Truman took Rick to California, where he planned to establish Joanne Carson in Hollywood society. He had met Joanne shortly after the publication of *In Cold Blood*, and had been drawn immediately to someone whose childhood had been as lonely as his. She had been born in California. After spending most of her first eleven years in a convent and moving from relative to relative during her teens, she had survived to become a stewardess for Pan American. Following a plot line too corny not to be true, she had met Howard Hughes on a Pacific flight and had been given a contract with his studio, R.K.O. Though she was pretty, with dark hair and a superb figure, she was not a star. Giving up her modest movie career, she had moved to Manhattan and in 1962 had married Johnny Carson, who was then the host of an afternoon TV game show, *Who Do You Trust?*

His selection to be host of *The Tonight Show* had dramatically changed her life, as well as his. Suddenly she was the wife of one of the most popular and powerful entertainers in America, with servants, a limousine on call, and, by coincidence, a vast duplex at the U.N. Plaza, several times the size of Truman's own apartment. Blinded by the spotlight unexpectedly aimed in her direction, she turned around to find Truman, who was always eager to direct the lives of rich and attractive women. "I was a little mouse," she said. "I didn't know anything. He went through my closets and told me what to wear and what not to wear. I grew up basking in the sunlight of his approval."

Prey to anxiety and depression, she was probably more of a challenge than he had anticipated, however. Nor was she helped by Johnny, who had problems of his own, in Truman's opinion. "Since he lived in my building, he used to call me all the time, and I knew him better than anyone outside of that small circle of people who work with him. People talk about how calm he is. Johnny Carson is consumed by rage! Under that calm surface there are tornadoes! He's not a heavy drinker, but two glasses are enough to set him off. He can be very mean. There's not an ounce of kindness in that man.

"But I know where it comes from. He hates his parents, particularly his mother. He comes from a very rigid, authoritarian family in Nebraska. He had to be home at a certain time, and if he was so much as fifteen minutes late, there would be terrible scenes. Once when he was drunk, he told me that his mother would throw herself on the floor and scream, 'I bore you from these loins, and you do this to me! All that pain and this is what I get in return!' I met his mother once, and she was an absolute bitch. Despite everything he's done, she's never really accepted him, and he constantly wants her approval. I think that that's what keeps him going."

Despite her unhappiness, Truman advised Joanne against a divorce, suggesting to her, as he had to Babe Paley, that she look upon her marriage as a lucrative career. When it broke up anyway, he persuaded her to return to her roots in California. A few months before her fortieth birthday, she bought a house on Sunset Boulevard overlooking the UCLA campus, started her own TV talk show, and waited for calls from the friends she had made with Johnny. None came. The people she had seen when she was married to Johnny ignored her the minute their separation was announced, and for two months she sat alone in her new house.

Feeling at least partly responsible, Truman was determined to remedy that. He and Rick moved in with her in early September, and he set up lunches and dinners with his friends in Hollywood's "Group A," the entertainment industry's social elite. Yet try as he might, pushing and shoving, pleading and wheedling, he could not nudge her into Hollywood's inner circle. To his old friend Carol Marcus, who was now married to Walter Matthau, he confessed that she was not a natural candidate for membership.

"Honey, you've got to meet this girl," he told Carol, as he invited her to lunch with them at the Bistro in Beverly Hills. "You're going to absolutely hate her. She's a bore and a pain in the ass, but I feel sorry for her and I like her. So, as a favor to me, please be nice."

Carol was nice and, for his sake, asked Joanne to a party after he left. But Joanne's first solo flight ended in a crash. When she arrived, she startled the other guests by announcing that she was sick and needed fresh orange juice. She then anxiously followed Carol, who, dropping her other duties as a hostess, rushed into the kitchen to squeeze oranges. They in turn were followed by Audrey Wilder, the wife of movie director Billy Wilder, who delivered what was to be Group A's unyielding verdict on Joanne. "You know, you're a pain in the ass," she said. "If you're really sick, you shouldn't have come." Barred from the inner circle, Joanne eventually made her own way in Los Angeles, achieving some success as a television interviewer.

Although he never admitted Joanne into his pantheon, Truman liked her and grew dependent on her almost idolatrous devotion. "You have to understand that I would walk through fire for Truman," she said. She reserved a small room and bath next to her kitchen for him, and he often stayed in it when he was in California, enjoying her pool, which she heated to ninety-two degrees, and her patient mothering.

During his weeks in California Truman also talked with Paramount executives about their newest version of F. Scott Fitzgerald's *The Great Gatsby*—it had been filmed twice before—and he was commissioned to write the screenplay for a fee of one hundred and thirty-five thousand dollars. In its structure, which is an extended flashback, in its brevity, and, most of all, in its elegiac mood, *Gatsby* has much in common with *The Grass Harp* and *Breakfast at Tiffany's*, and he approached the assignment with some excitement. "Fitzgerald has charm," he said. "It's a silly word, but it's an exact word for me. I love *The Great Gatsby* and its sad, gay nostalgia."

But capturing such elusive qualities in a film script proved a more formidable task than he had anticipated. "When I had the parts disassembled, I saw that there are so many things in that book that are so bad. It was like going into the kitchen and finding the garbage strewn all over. I must say that the same thing happened when I adapted *The Turn of the Screw* for *The Innocents*. It is incredible how James fudged that story." (Ironically, Fitzgerald, who also labored for Hollywood, had similar complaints about adapting the work of other writers. "It's all beautiful when you read it," he said, "but when you write it down plain it's like a week in the nuthouse.")

In early December he and Rick flew to London so that he could discuss his first draft and make revisions with Jack Clayton, who had directed *The Innocents* and who, at Truman's suggestion, had been chosen to direct *Gatsby* as well. He finished his scenario a few weeks later, in January, 1972, and, on the whole, was pleased with it, he told Alan Schwartz. But Paramount was not and rejected it, calling it "unacceptable."

"Well, Truman, this is just like the book," complained a studio executive.

"I was under the impression we were adapting the book," Truman answered. Using the excuse that he had missed his deadline by more than a week, the studio refused to pay him the remainder of his fee, which amounted to a little more than one hundred and one thousand dollars. But Truman, who replied that he had been delayed by an attack of the flu, sued and got what was owed him.

It was in London that Rick, concluding that his dreams were not going to be realized, decided that he had had enough of Truman, who, when he was not working on *Gatsby*, spent most of his time in bed, drinking and watching television. One of the few times he left their suite at the Connaught Hotel was to take Rick to dinner at Lee Radziwill's. But that visit only underlined for Rick his position as a hanger-on. "What a rude bitch!" he exclaimed. "She shook my hand, turned her back, and never looked at me again."

Rick wanted to go home, and just as Danny had done the year before, he made a plane reservation. Reenacting that by-now-familiar scene, Truman abruptly changed his own plans so that he could join him, and on December 14, a week after they had left New York, they flew back. Unchastened, Truman continued to gulp down vodka over the Atlantic, causing Rick at last to turn to him. "Truman, I just don't think it's going to work. Here, I want you to have your keys back because I'm not going to honor our bargain anymore." With those words, he made a symbolic exit, handing him the keys to the U.N. Plaza apartment as he departed for the lavatory.

Rick soon repented. He had become accustomed to the good life. "You get addicted," he explained. "It's murder. It's habit-forming, like heroin." But when he called to make up, Truman's phone did not answer; without saying anything, he had flown off again, to Palm Springs and then to Switzerland. In a panic because his rent was coming due, Rick finally tracked him down in Verbier and dispatched a telegram: "GET IN TOUCH WITH ME." Truman cabled back: "I SUGGEST YOU GET A JOB." Then, in a more mellow mood, Truman wrote a long letter, saying, in essence, that although he cared about him, their relationship had no future. He asked Saint Subber to give him sixteen hundred dollars, money enough to carry him for several months.

Rick returned to the Club 45 to tend bar again, and then, a year later, in 1973, moved to Los Angeles and found a job in a similar establishment, the Pussy Cat Café on Santa Monica Boulevard. Although they kept in close touch, Rick was convinced that his life would have been better if he had turned the other way when he first saw Truman walking along Forty-fifth Street. "Just as quick as the door opened, it closed again," he said. "And, my God, what a disappointment it was! He promised me the world and gave me a pot of beans."

Truman had been fond of Rick, but he had not been in love, and the end of their affair did not send him into a spin, as the breakup with Danny had done. "I'm sinking back into my book," he wrote Alan Schwartz from Verbier, "and every day I feel more removed from the bad vibrations, that incredible syndrome of juvenile nonsense that started some two years ago." It seemed, for a while anyway, that his encounters with Danny and Rick had stopped his roving eye. "It is totally necessary to develop loneliness if you are going to be a writer, if you are really going to give yourself up to it," he later proclaimed to an interviewer. "You can't get around it —you've got to be alone."

HE did not sink very deeply into his book, however, and many were starting to wonder, sometimes publicly, whether they would ever see it. When he missed his January 1, 1971, deadline, Twentieth Century–Fox demanded the return of the down payment it had made on film rights, two hundred thousand dollars, and to his chagrin, Truman had to give it back. To the reporters who asked how much he had actually written, he said that he was two-thirds done, which was the same reply he had been giving for several years.

Even he began to talk as though he might never finish. "Of course I basically don't really want to finish it," he confessed at last. "It's just that it's become a way of life. It's like suddenly taking some beautiful animal, say, or a child, some lovely child and you just took it out in the yard and shot it in the head. I mean, that's what it means to me. The moment I give it up it's just like I took it out in the yard and shot it in the head, because it will never be mine again."

Whatever his reasons, he was in no hurry. During the months that followed his return from Switzerland, he seemed eager to do nearly anything rather than lock himself away and confront the problems inherent in any long and complicated novel. Drinking less than he had in the two preceding years—in that respect the bad vibrations had indeed receded—he jumped from project to project, job to job, taking on almost any assignment, it seemed, that would keep him away from *Answered Prayers*.

His first venture was into journalism. Peter Beard, Lee's boy-friend—she finally had separated from Stas—and Jann Wenner, the editor of *Rolling Stone* magazine, persuaded him to cover what was expected to be one of the media spectaculars of 1972, the North American tour of the Rolling Stones. Beard was to take the pictures that would illustrate his article, and after it appeared in Wenner's magazine, their collaboration was to become a book—*The Muses Are Heard* a generation later, with a hard-rock beat. He was in competition with any number of hungry young writers, all itching to become famous by using the journalistic techniques that he had pioneered. But only he and, for a time, the hip novelist Terry Southern, middle-aged men both, were allowed to travel in the Stones' plane and to observe the private, as well as public, behavior of a group whose appeal rested largely on its reputation for appetitious depravity. He thus had an invitation to do what he did best: to become the fly on the wall that sees all.

With that sweeping charter, the "fantastic T. Capote," as Southern labeled him, joined the Stones in late June, midway through their thirty-one-city, two-month tour. It was an easy mix: the Stones liked him, he liked them, and he was stimulated by their company, the like of which even a planet-wanderer like him had never encountered. After attending their last performance at Madison Square Garden on July 27, he went out to Sagaponack, where he sifted through his notes and started his story. Its title, "It Will Soon Be Here," he borrowed from a nineteenth-century painting of Midwestern farmers rushing to save their hay from an oncoming storm. To his mind, that title had an ironic symbolism: in the twentieth century things had been so turned around that instead of rushing from the storm—the Stones and the chaos they represented— the young descendants of those God-fearing farmers were running toward it, desperate to be engulfed in the maelstrom.

His first deadline passed, and then his second, and although he read part of it to Beard, "It Will Soon Be Here" never reached its destination. He could write no more than a few pages. It may have been that he did not have the energy or power of concentration to devote himself to any significant piece of prose; or it may have been that, on examination, the idea bored him. The tour had been a new experience for him, he said, but in no way surprising; everything that had occurred, including the hysterical outbursts of the fans, had been coolly and efficiently manufactured by the Stones and their managers. "Since there was nothing to 'find out,' " he explained, "I just couldn't be bothered writing it." Later, in a long interview with the magazine, he admitted that if he had been twenty-five years younger—and if he had not already written a history of a musical tour—he just might have been bothered. But why, he asked, "should I do a game that I've already done?"

It was a good question, but it did not stop him from engaging in other games he had already done: a film script, a television play, a documentary, and three crime shows for ABC. The first three he did with Robert MacBride, a free-lance writer he met in the summer of 1972 in a Rockefeller Center bookstore. Theirs was a bond of brothers rather than of lovers, according to MacBride, and Truman may have latched on to Bob MacBride because he could see in him traces of the Jack of earlier years. The physical resemblance was obvious. At forty-six, Bob too was thin and ascetic-looking, with rust-colored hair and pale, bleached skin. "He seemed sort of uncooked, like a blancmange that hadn't been in the oven long enough" was the way Slim Keith described him.

There were also other, equally striking similarities. Bob too had grown up in Philadelphia, and he too was mostly self-educated, with an astonishingly diverse knowledge, ranging from computers and the navies of the Civil War to space and sculpture. Like Jack, he also spoke fluent French. Although the pliable Bob lacked Jack's percussive temperament, he had the same unsettling habit of grabbing a conversation and turning it into a monologue. "When I see Jack is going off on one of his tantrums, I just tune out," said Truman. "I don't hear a thing, and then when he's done, I tune back in. I do the same thing with Bob when he starts talking about space, stars and the universe. I don't understand a word of it."

Bob was married, not happily, to his second wife when he met Truman, and he supported his six children as a commercial artist and as the author of corporate brochures. His labors with Truman promised greater reward, and during the next year, from the summer of 1972 to the summer of 1973, they worked together on their three projects, none of which was ever produced. Working with Bob much as he had with Wyatt on *The Glass House*, Truman sketched out his ideas over lunch or dinner; Bob then sat down by himself and filled in the details, which Truman revised at another lunch or dinner. For Truman at least, it was a pleasant and painless process, as little like work as work could be.

In the fall of 1972 they flew to New Orleans, where they exam-

ined locations for their murder mystery, *Dead Loss*. In the winter
they put together *Second Chance*, a TV documentary about transsex-
uals. Finally, in mid-June, 1973, they drove to Canada, where, during two weeks in a Montreal hotel and a nearly empty, out-of-season
ski lodge, they completed *Uncle Sam's Hard Luck Hotel*, a TV play
about a California halfway house. Their relationship was entirely
amicable, and Bob was therefore puzzled and hurt when, not long
after their return from Canada, he detected a distinctly gelid tone in
Truman's voice over the telephone. "It was obvious that he didn't
want to talk to me," Bob said. Without explanation or apology,
Truman was giving him the brush-off. His wife soon complained of
Truman's "perfidy," and Bob, who had expected much more from
their collaboration, agreed. In October he wrote in his diary:
"Dreamed that Capote returned." But that Truman did not do.

The explanation was simple: Truman was in love again. Not
merely in love, as he had been with Danny, but enraptured and
enthralled. His new lover's name was John O'Shea, and although
Truman thought that he was "one of the best-looking people I've
ever seen in my life," most other people described him as nondescript. He was five feet ten inches tall, and he had the build, neither
fat nor thin, of the average man of forty-four. He had dark brown
hair, pronounced eyebrows, and blue eyes that were magnified by
thick glasses. In every way he looked like what he was, a low-level
bank vice president.

"Charlie Middleclass," John jokingly called himself, and search as
he might, a sociologist could not have found a better representative
of the typical American, circa 1973. He and his devoutly Catholic
family lived in a split-level house in a middle-class development
about forty-five minutes from Manhattan. Both his wife, Peg, and
his son Brian, who was sixteen, were leaders in their parish; his
daughter, Kathy, who was fifteen, was one of the top students in
her class; and his two youngest, Kerry and Chris, twelve and nine,
were training to be runners—in his spare time John was a track
coach, and a very good one at that.

That was only half of the picture, of course, and John too bore
the wounds of a terrible childhood. His parents had come to New
York from Ireland, and when his father, who was a skilled carpenter, could not find work, his mother supported their family with her
job at the telephone company. Disappointed with his life and long-

ing to return to Ireland, his father became an alcoholic who regularly beat his wife and two sons. John grew up, and one day, after his mother had been thus roughed up, he threw his father out of their Bronx apartment. But that solved only half of his parental problem. His mother was perhaps even worse than his father. Her idea of an Irish lullaby was to hear him howl with pain. When he caught poison ivy, she poured ammonia on him in the shower. When she wanted to punish him, she made him sit in the bathtub and whipped him with an electric cord; naked wet flesh is easier to hurt than dry, she had learned.

Like his father, John grew up to become a profoundly disappointed man. After serving in the Navy, he spent a year at a college in upstate New York, then returned to the Bronx to take a job in a bank, marry Peg and start their family. At that point what appeared to be a modest success story took an unexpected turn. Although his banking career slowly advanced, he was dissatisfied; his real ambition, which he nurtured at night and on weekends, was to be a novelist. Nor was he happy with his marriage, and he saw prison walls wherever he looked. "He was just a classic Irish guy," said his son Brian. "He got beaten growing up, he went into the Navy, he came back, and when he woke up, he had a house and a bunch of kids. He never had a life."

Emulating his father again, John became an alcoholic, "an extraordinarily violent man," in Brian's words, who beat Peg and Brian both. But Brian grew up and became something of a martial-arts expert. One Sunday, when his father disrupted a family dinner— John threw vegetables at Peg—Brian angrily rose from his chair, and using a trick he had learned, he stuck a finger up each of John's nostrils, sending him crashing to the floor, and, for a moment, knocking him unconscious. So did hostility and violence descend through three generations. Like his father, John had lost control even in his own house.

Such was his situation when he met Truman, probably in the first week of July, 1973. He had come into Manhattan to be interviewed for a job he had been all but guaranteed; but to his surprise and chagrin, he did not receive it. When two tranquilizers failed to relieve the resulting tension and anger, he decided, as he sometimes did when he was anxious, to pay a call at a gay bathhouse near the Plaza Hotel: he looked upon the sex he had there as a form of masturbation; he did not consider himself homosexual. "An older guy was doing a number on me," he recalled, "and I looked to my right, and there was Truman. I felt compelled to talk to him, thinking he'd be sympathetic to my plight. I wanted to unravel my whole tortured existence, to tell him how I had been impressed into working for a bank when I was really a writer. He would tell me how to write."

In a private room Truman had rented upstairs, John did spill out his woes, and Truman was, or pretended to be, sympathetic. Once again Truman was swimming in the treacherous currents of nostalgia, reaching out for the absolutely average. But there was more to John's appeal than his ordinary condition. Like Danny, he unwittingly pressed a button in Truman's memory. Just as Danny had reminded him of a military-school classmate, so did John remind him of a Monroeville boy, a boy whose personality had stamped itself so indelibly on Truman's memory that he had made him the title character in his story "The Thanksgiving Visitor." Only later did Truman recognize how accurate and prophetic that association was: that boy was the school bully who had made his days miserable and filled his nights with foreboding. Odd Henderson he had called him, "the meanest human creature in my experience."

He did not find John mean on that afternoon in the baths, however. Telephone numbers were exchanged, and they met again, and again after that. By the end of July their affair was on and, in John's words, "flying like a kite." Each saw in the other what he most desired. For Truman, John was the satisfaction of a passion; he was in the grip of an obsession that was sexual, as well as psychological. He never had enjoyed the lurid, promiscuous sex life he sometimes claimed, and like many men his age who feel that the best is behind them, he keenly regretted his omissions. Ever since he had met Danny, he had been trying, albeit with only limited success, to make up for lost time. Now, as he was approaching fifty, Truman had found someone who was all he desired in a lover, who was both exciting in bed—"on a list of my all-time favorites, Johnny was the best, Jack was second and Danny was third"—and a never-ending challenge.

What John saw in Truman was opportunity. Truman did not appeal to him physically; he may even have repelled him. A few years before, recalled Brian, his father had angrily switched channels when Truman walked onto *The Tonight Show*—"damned fag!"

John had muttered. But like Danny and Rick, John believed that that damned fag could make his dreams come true. Scrambling to find a device that would enable him to turn Truman's infatuation to his own advantage, he hit at last upon what seemed to be, in his words, "a wonderful solution." Truman did not know how to manage money; he did. What Truman needed, he concluded, was someone who could take that burden off his shoulders, who could be his factotum, agent and business manager.

Truman agreed, as he probably would have agreed to any proposal that would tie them together, and papers were drawn up. Conveniently enough, Truman already had a paper corporation called Bayouboys, Ltd.—Alan Schwartz had established it as a tax shelter—that could give John a fancy title and a salary. Quitting his bank job, John was appointed executive vice president at an annual salary of fourteen thousand four hundred dollars. He was starting a whole new career; soon, he believed, he would be managing not only Truman's affairs, but those of Truman's rich friends as well. "I'm breaking out!" he told Brian. "I'm getting out of here, out of this middle-class bullshit! I'm going to manage money for writers, movie producers and winners."

His family, who had not believed that he even knew Truman until they heard his baby voice on the telephone, were informed that John's new duties required extensive travel, and in early August the president and executive vice president of Bayouboys were on their way to Los Angeles, and then, on September 3, to Europe. Flying first to Athens, they later were lifted by Aristotle Onassis' helicopter to the island of Spetsai, where Slim Keith was vacationing, along with such other fashionables as Mary Martin and Stavros Niarchos. Renting a house, they remained there for three weeks, sunning and sailing. "They were lazy days and everything was wonderful," said John.

After a trip to Istanbul, which they hated and quickly departed, they rode the Orient Express to Venice, where they commuted between the Gritti Palace Hotel and Harry's Bar, with a few stops at Peggy Guggenheim's palazzo in between. After three weeks, they traveled on to Switzerland, staying in Verbier and making several visits to Charlie and Oona Chaplin in nearby Vevey. Touched by Charlie's husbandly devotion—"so sweet, so endearing," John thought—John began feeling guilty about his own wife and family. He still carried with him the expression on Peg's face as she had said goodbye at Kennedy Airport: it said to him that she did not believe for a second that he was merely Truman's business manager, that she knew exactly what was going on between them. "It must have been a terrible ordeal for her to tell her friends that her husband had flown off with the world's number one queer," he said.

Thus, when Marella Agnelli asked them to prolong their trip and cruise the Greek islands on her yacht, a luxurious excursion John could scarcely have dreamed of when he was sitting behind his desk at the bank, he did not hesitate to say no. "I've just ordered Truman to turn down Marella Agnelli's offer," he proudly wrote Peg. "He agreed but thinks it's a first for them." To Truman he spoke more directly: "Fuck the Greek islands! I'm going to New York!" In late October they flew home. The honeymoon was over.

John may have had second thoughts about their relationship, but Truman had not: he was besotted, and to keep his new companion from returning to banking, he more than doubled his salary, to thirty thousand dollars a year. If John had wanted to, he would have been hard pressed to refuse such generosity. Whatever doubts he had were put aside, and he invited Truman home for dinner: it was time he met the family.

Despite John's guilty conjecture, Peg did not suspect that he was Truman's lover. It was inconceivable to her that her husband could have an affair with another man. Far from being angry or jealous, she was delighted by their family's good fortune. "Truman had doubled the salary he was making at the bank," she said. "I thought he had found a marvelous job. Wouldn't anybody?" Nor, as John had also dourly imagined, had she been humiliated when he flew off with the world's most famous admitted homosexual. Their neighbors were apparently as innocent and trusting as she was. As best anyone in the family could tell, there had been no sly winks around the barbecues that summer, no whispers over backyard fences.

When John told her that his new boss was coming, her only reaction therefore was nervousness. "What should I serve him?" she anxiously inquired. "Lamb chops," replied John, and out she went to buy fourteen lamb chops, an expensive cut unfamiliar to the budget-minded O'Shea household. "I told the kids that instead of saying, 'What's that?' they should say. 'Oh, no, not lamb again!' Knowing that Truman was Southern, I also had a friend bring some black-eyed peas from a black area of the Bronx. But I didn't know how to cook them, and I left them on the stove all day. When it came time to serve them, they were mush. If my husband's job had depended on that dinner—as I thought it did—we would have been lost. Little did I know that Truman would become my best friend. I liked him immediately." Returning a few days after Christmas, Truman gave each of the O'Shea children a hundred-dollar bill, fresh from his cash drawer.

Settling into his job, John actually did begin to manage Truman's career—probably to Truman's surprise, most certainly to his consternation. John's first major act was the negotiation of a lucrative contract, a minimum of ten thousand dollars a week plus expenses, for Truman to write about another murder case—this one involving sex and torture—for *The Washington Post* and its syndicate. The accused was one of two teenage boys who had allegedly helped a Houston electrician sexually abuse, torture and then kill other teenagers before he himself turned around and shot the electrician.

Interest in the case was not so much in the murders—the electrician had killed at least twenty-seven—but in the circumstances that had allowed them to go unnoticed. How could so many boys have vanished so quietly, without arousing the curiosity of the community, the police, or the newspapers? That, at least, was the question Truman planned to ask. "I see the trial as a jumping-off point," he told an interviewer, "to really tell about this whole extraordinary culture—in Texas and the Southwest, all the way to California—of aimless wandering, this mobile, uprooted life: the seven-mile-long trailer parks, the motorcycles, the campers, the people who have no addresses or even last names."

Despite his public enthusiasm, it was not an assignment he cherished. He only accepted it because John had pushed him, and John might not have pushed him if he had been at all familiar with his writing habits. Truman had rarely written on deadline, much less a daily deadline, as the *Post* expected, and the prospect of dictating into a telephone every night, like any other reporter on a fast-breaking story, must have filled him with terror. In any event, the ambitious piece he had outlined could not have been written in small doses; it would have required an effort on the scale of *In Cold Blood*. The project was doomed, and Truman must have known it.

Nonetheless, he and John set out by car for Houston in the first week of January, 1974. Stopping overnight in Washington, they stayed with Kay Graham, who was no more impressed by John than she had been by Danny. "A horrible man! Horrible!" she said. They then proceeded to Monroeville, where Truman's relatives gathered at his aunt Mary Ida Carter's house for the old-fashioned kind of Southern dinner Sook used to make. "I've never enjoyed so much food in my life," said John. In Houston they stayed with Truman's friends Lynn and Oscar Wyatt, who were rich even by Texas standards, and explored the lower-middle-class neighborhood where the electrician had slain his victims.

But Truman's *Houston Diary*, as his account was to have been titled, ended the instant the young defendant was led into the courtroom. "I've seen this before," said Truman, referring to a similar entrance by Perry and Dick fourteen years earlier, and he marched out, with John at his heels.* Packing their bags, they drove on to Palm Springs. Truman's Random House editor, Joe Fox, was assigned the task of breaking the bad news to the editors of *The Washington Post*. Truman, he cabled, was hospitalized at an undisclosed location in the West and would not be reporting on the Houston murders.

Joe Fox was telling the truth. On his arrival in California, Truman entered the Eisenhower Medical Center in Palm Desert, suffering from what the hospital characterized as a respiratory ailment. How sick he was, or whether he was sick at all, is a matter of disagreement. According to John, he was using illness as an excuse to wriggle out of his contract with the *Post*. But Truman wrote Jack, who was in Verbier, that he was very sick, that in fact he had pneumonia. "Most people talk themselves up, Truman talks himself down," Jack told his sister Gloria. "So you never know with him. Much of his trouble has to do with drinking too much. (Says I!) When will it end! He only communicates to me in crises. When it's bad. Otherwise he says nothing."

Though Truman, looking for sympathy, may have exaggerated his illness to Jack, he probably was debilitated by the binge he had been on ever since he had met John, and he may well have had some form of pneumonia. Dispirited he indisputably was. Needing more support than John could give him, he summoned other companions to Palm Springs. His cousin Joe Faulk came from San Diego, and

* Truman's instinct to leave was correct: the proceedings dragged on for six years. The young defendant was twice convicted and twice sentenced to 594 years in prison.

from New York came Saint Subber and John Knowles, a fellow writer and friend from Long Island.

Most of Truman's friends had regarded Danny and Rick as inappropriate but inoffensive. With a few exceptions, John aroused far stronger and far more negative emotions. "When he was cold sober, he was all right, rather mannerly," said Knowles. "But the moment he got a drink in his hand, he thought he could just let it all hang out. He was crude-mouthed beyond belief—'this fucking place, fucking town, fucking restaurant'—and it was unbelievably wearing to have to listen to that barracks talk. He would lurch into Robert and Natalie [Wood] Wagner's house, put his feet up on a table, and start spewing his obscenities. To me, he was a phony in every sense of the word, a fake tough guy with nothing tough about him. 'You're a marshmallow trying to act like a crowbar,' I thought to myself. 'Who do you think you're kidding?' " Kay Graham probably spoke for the majority when she threw up her hands at the mere mention of his name.

Even Truman's amiable cousin Joey Faulk thought that John went out of his way to irritate and embarrass Truman, starting arguments, stalking out of restaurants and slipping away late at night to a popular hangout. "He was always playing some kind of game with Truman and doing mean little things to get him upset," said Joey. "Apparently he was also under the impression that he never paid for anything when he was around Truman. I went out to dinner alone with him once, and he just kept ordering drinks, and then dinner, and never offered to pay. I was living on just the G.I. bill, but I paid for everything."

Yet what most alarmed Truman's friends, then and in the months to come, was John's apparent attempt to become his Svengali. John went so far, according to Knowles, as to have the telephone moved into his Palm Springs bedroom, ostensibly so that he could screen Truman's incoming calls. He seemed to regard himself not only as Truman's business manager, but also as his keeper, and he became furious if Truman refused, as he often did, to accept his instructions. Mixed in with his frustration and anger was an undisguised rage, verging on contempt, toward a man who seemed so incompetent in so many ways, yet who was, in the end, the master of John's own destiny. "I've never seen a situation," John wrote Alan Schwartz, "where there was such ignorance of basic personal business; lack of common sense; and childish impulsiveness as a compulsion. I feel like a trust officer dealing with the senile and the infantile."

To make sure that he held the strings—that all of Truman's business mail and phone calls went through him—he ordered Bayou-boys stationery, listing his address and phone number rather than Truman's, and he wrote a form letter which he sent out, over Truman's signature, to various of Truman's friends and associates: "As many of you are aware, communications with me are often difficult, sometimes impossible, to establish or maintain because of the vast amount of travel I enjoy. To facilitate communications I have asked my associate, John O'Shea, to function as my business manager, agent, secretary and advisor. Mr. O'Shea is completely and constantly attuned to my interest in, and availability for, new projects; and knows the current status of present undertakings. He can and will speak with authority in the functional areas described above. Please communicate with us through the phone and address on this letterhead only for prompt response."

When Kay Graham saw the copy that was sent to *The Washington Post*, she exclaimed to her secretary: "Liz, how ghastly!" So said, in those words or words like them, many of Truman's friends.

BORED and depressed in Palm Springs, in late March, 1974, Truman gathered Joey Faulk, John Knowles and Saint Subber and, leaving John O'Shea behind, drove over the Mexican border to a health spa—a fat farm—in Tecate. They expected to be pampered, to read, relax and sink into soothing whirlpool baths. Instead, on their very first night they were fed nothing but pureed vegetables and scheduled for early-morning exercise classes. They fled back over the border the next morning, Saint and Knowles not stopping until they had reached New York, Truman and Joey continuing up the coast to San Francisco.

There was no happy reunion when they returned to Palm Springs two weeks later, however, and the tension between Truman and John, which had been accumulating over the months, quickly erupted into angry words. When John said that he wanted to attend a track meet in San Diego, Truman assumed the role of tough boss. "You can't take my car!" he declared. But when he and Joey went out to dinner that night, John did take his car, calling from San Diego to say that he was in Phoenix—on his way to New York. Truman knew him well enough to know that he was lying, and when John came through the door twenty-four hours later, he had prepared his own unpleasant surprise. "I have an airline ticket for you to New York," he said coldly as he handed him an envelope with the ticket inside.

After John flew East, Truman stayed only long enough to sell his house, accepting, in his haste to be rid of it, an almost ludicrously low offer of sixty-three thousand dollars. Jack's premonition had proved altogether accurate: the sunny hideaway in which Truman had planned to finish *Answered Prayers* had instead been the scene of some of the worst hours of his life. For him, Palm Springs had indeed been Thirst's End, as Jack had called it, the place in which hope had died and despair had been born. Belatedly realizing what had befallen him in that seemingly peaceful spot, Truman must have felt some bitterness, as well as relief, as he packed up his belongings, said goodbye to Myrtle (who was to succumb to cancer two years later) and joined the exodus back to New York.

"For better or worse," John said, "Truman and I are attached to each other by an invisible umbilical cord for the rest of his existence." So it was to be, and Truman had no sooner landed at Kennedy Airport than they had reconciled. But the confrontation in Palm Springs was only the first of many, and even at its best, their relationship seemed to provide little real enjoyment to either one of them. After spending a weekend in May with them on Fire Island, Donald Windham concluded that John lacked any of the "mental traits" that would have interested the Truman he had known, that the only link between them seemed, in fact, to be pathological. "[Truman] watched Johnny with an obsessed nervousness, but without pleasure, like a man staring at a mirage," wrote Donald. "The effort seemed to drain him." Though Truman allowed John the appearance of power, in most major matters Truman did just what he wanted. "Please be nice to Johnny," he told Alan Schwartz, carefully adding that if Alan should have any problems with John, he should call him privately: he would set things straight. It did not take long for John to catch on to what was going on behind his back and to realize that he was only a make-believe vice president. He was proud enough to resent it and combative enough to keep fighting for what he considered his rightful position.

John's major complaint, however—and the cause of most of his arguments with Truman—was Truman's refusal to break with Jack. It was a source of intense bitterness to him, as it had been to Rick, that he was expected to be constantly on call, whereas Truman, who acknowledged no similar obligation to him, could take off for New Orleans or Mexico with Lee, or bury himself for weeks on end with Jack in Sagaponack. In John's not unnatural view, such an arrangement was distinctly inequitable, and time and again he demanded that Truman leave Jack. At one point Truman appeared ready to do so; but he eventually found a good excuse to change his mind, as he always did. "He couldn't separate from Jack," John reluctantly conceded. "They were too much the same person."

Once he realized that, John could not even look at him without seeing the shadow of Jack in the background. "I could never have committed myself totally to Truman because I suspected his purported love," John said. "I could not understand someone who could say, 'I love you, but I have to go home to Jack.' Or, 'I love you, but I have to go to Mexico with Lee.' Or, 'I love you, but I'm going to be in California for six weeks, and, no, you can't come.' I always had the feeling that I was the tail on the dog, and that when he had used me—when it suited his fancy—he would walk away."

Perhaps to nurse John's bruised ego, Truman took him to Europe again in the middle of July, almost a year to the day after they had met. They stayed with the Wyatts on the Riviera, and, with vivacious Lynn leading the way, attended one gala after another. Twice they lunched at the palace in Monaco, where John, who noticed such things, was surprised that amidst all the informal family photographs, he found not one of Princess Grace's brother, Jack Kelly, whom he had once met at a track meet. "She was a prisoner, absolutely a prisoner," he declared. He later shared his discovery with one of Grace's friends, who agreed, but replied, as if surprised by his innocence: "But she had to make a life."

It was a comment that would have puzzled him twelve months before, but now struck John with the force of revealed truth. If Truman required any more examples for his book, he need not have looked any further than his own lover, whose answered prayers had brought him nothing but unhappiness. John had broken out of his middle-class rut, just as he had promised Brian, but he had only exchanged one jail cell for another: he too was a pampered prisoner. He did not manage money for writers, movie producers and winners, nor did he have any prospect of doing so. Both he and his family were totally dependent on the whims and moods of just one writer, and that knowledge filled him with fear, as well as anger.

Truman and John thus continued to vex each other, each in his customary way. Truman's was the subtle way; he made it clear that he was the one who wrote the checks. John's was the direct way; he seemed to delight in cutting his provider down to size before friends like Kay Graham and Carol Matthau, who was so horrified that she threatened to kill him. "I have a gun in my purse," she warned him, "and I'm a crack shot." John Knowles was with them at a restaurant in Bridgehampton when John threw his drink in Truman's face. "Oh, Johnny, stop that" was Truman's mild reproof. "Sit down and be quiet."

John did not even stop at demeaning Truman in the eyes of his father. Claiming that he was writing Truman's biography, he telephoned Arch for information, taking the opportunity to furnish some of his own. "He didn't try to hide," recalled Arch. "He said he'd been intimate with Truman sexually and he told me all about it." Although Truman's sexual orientation was obvious to most of the world, some ultimate scruple had prevented Truman himself from suggesting it to his father. John had now done it for him.

Unable to stay in one place very long, Truman was on the move throughout the fall and winter of 1974, traveling, sometimes with John, sometimes with Lee, to New Orleans, California and Florida —then back to California, to Mexico and to Florida. Alighting with John in Key West at the end of February, 1975, he finally settled down for several weeks of concentrated writing at the Pier House hotel, rushing to finish a story he had promised *Esquire* two months before. Titled "Mojave," it apparently had been in his mind, and perhaps partly on paper, for some time. Now, with the deadline fast approaching, he sat down to complete it.

By March 12 he was done. But perhaps not since he'd first walked into the offices of *Mademoiselle* had he been so uncertain about the quality of his writing, so eager to be reassured. Not only was he putting on exhibit his first fiction since "The Thanksgiving Visitor," nearly eight years before, but he was also giving the world its first peek at *Answered Prayers*. A bleak tale of disappointed love, "Mojave" was supposed to be a fiction within a fiction, the work of the novel's cynical narrator, P. B. Jones.

He was so nervous that he demanded an immediate reaction, and Don Erickson, *Esquire*'s top editor, obliged by flying down from New York to pick it up himself. When Erickson arrived, Truman ordered him to take a swim in the Pier House pool first, then read it in a deck chair, while he himself anxiously watched from the bar. Erickson's face registered appropriate appreciation—under the circumstances, how could it have been otherwise?—and he soon took "Mojave" back to Manhattan.

"To John, with all my love and gratitude," Truman had written on the manuscript, and for as long as he was writing, he and John enjoyed one of their good periods, ending each night with a tour of Key West's many night spots. Wherever they went, much was made of Truman. One night, in a crowded bar on Duvall Street, a woman asked for his autograph, handing him a felt-tip pen and pulling down her panties to offer him a plump pink pad—her bare buttocks. Not to be outdone, an athletic bartender vaulted the counter and ran over to him, unzipping his pants and hauling out a considerably smaller piece of flesh for a similar inscription. "You won't be able to autograph it," John slyly observed, "but you might be able to initial it." Truman did neither, but, appropriating John's amusing put-down as his own, he repeated the story on several TV talk shows, to giggles and laughter each time.

Harmony expired when Truman grew tired of such late-night revels and John went carousing by himself, sometimes not stopping until the early hours of the morning. Truman was angry, but he did nothing until John brought a young woman back for a skinny-dip in the hotel pool, making so much noise that other guests came out to their balconies to see what was going on. Whether Truman heard about that noisy swim or whether he witnessed it himself from behind a palm tree, John never knew. But find out he did, and early the next morning, March 22, he called John Knowles, who was staying at the Palm-Aire health spa in Pompano Beach, nearly two hundred miles to the north. "Can I come up there?" he whispered into the telephone. "I've got to get out of here." Packing as quietly as he could, he then sneaked out to his car, leaving John a note and a hundred dollars for the flight back to New York.

Truman had meekly accepted almost every humiliation John could contrive, and compared with John's other misdeeds, a romp with a young woman in the Pier House pool seemed almost inno-cent. "I didn't even get into her pants," John regretfully recalled. But Truman saw nothing innocent in it. In preferring her company to his own, John had finally committed the unpardonable offense: he had, so Truman believed, betrayed and rejected him.

Vowing revenge, Truman made two important phone calls from Pompano Beach. One was to inform Alan Schwartz that the presi-dent of Bayouboys had just fired the vice president. "Accordingly," Alan dutifully wrote John a few days later, "you are in no way to consider yourself an employee of Bayouboys Limited nor to hold yourself out as such to anyone." John tartly replied that Truman demanded a twenty-four-hour-a-day attendant, not a business manager. "If Mr. Capote's emotional dysfunction is such to require that he needs a male nurse, then he should have hired one" was his spirited retort.

Truman's second call was to Peg O'Shea, telling her that John's drinking had forced him to flee Key West. For their own safety, Truman advised her, she and her children should vacate their house before he came back. Terrified, Peg began packing. Her signal to leave came when John himself phoned from Florida, asking her to meet him at the airport. Trying not to convey the panic she was feeling, she suggested that he take a cab instead. Then, while he was still airborne, she and her children loaded their belongings into the car and, like refugees escaping an invading army, sought asylum in the home of a friend. A few hours later John entered a silent house.

She had left him before, only to forgive him after a few days; in her world a wife did not abandon her husband simply because he drank too much, or even because he was violent. "He was the father of my children, as well as my husband," she explained. "If you're brought up in my faith, you think you're married for life. He was a very mean person, and I didn't like him. But I loved him." Apparently afraid that such love would prevail once more, Truman returned from Florida and drove out to her hideaway a few days later. He was determined to win, and it was time to call in the artillery.

Standing there in her friend's living room, he told her everything: that he and her husband had been lovers, that their business arrangement had been little more than a front for their affair, that they had met in a bath, and that John had had other homosexual relations before Truman came along. By way of proof, he showed her an affectionate letter he had just received from John, who was eager to make up. As Peg recalled it, it said something like: "Dearest Truman, We've had our ups and downs. Sorry if I've hurt you. I want you to know I really do love you. All my love, Johnny." She read it, and so stunned that her ears rang for hours afterward, she automatically handed it to her friend—an ex-nun, as John's bad luck would have it. "That's grounds for annulment!" declared the friend.

Still, Peg seemed to waver. Who, she asked herself, would take care of her and her family? Despite his drinking, John had always been a good breadwinner; once he found another position, he doubtless would be one again. She, by contrast, had no employment history; at the age of forty-five, she had dim prospects of finding a good job.

"You'll be my personal secretary," said Truman, who had come prepared with an answer for every question. "We'll go on a lot of trips. You need a change. You need to relax."

He thus gave her John's old job, albeit without the title; when John moved out of their house, as he did shortly thereafter, she was even able to use the little office he had set up for his Bayouboys work. Truman had not only taken away John's job; he had also robbed him of his wife, family and home. To John, who was living by himself in a rented room, it seemed as if Truman had planned it that way from the first. "He decided from the beginning that he would make a conquest and that to do that he would have to subvert my relationship with Peg. He had it down to a fine line: how to subvert a married Irish-Catholic life." Truman had had his satisfaction.

Truman now courted Peg as ardently as he had courted John two years before—or Rick and Danny in earlier years. Taking command of her life, he hired a housekeeper to look after her children and in May he flew her to California, where he dazzled her with expensive restaurants and movie-star parties. Carol Matthau, Jack Lemmon and Jennifer Jones (who was now married to the financier Norton Simon) invited them to cocktails or dinners, and Robert Anderson flew them to his New Mexico ranch for the weekend, ferrying them by helicopter from the roof of his headquarters in downtown Los Angeles to a private jet at the airport. Peg was as impressed as Truman had hoped she would be. "Gee, Barbara, how big is your ranch?" she asked Anderson's wife when she saw how far it stretched over the New Mexican landscape. "You don't ever ask!" laughed Barbara.

One long trip with Truman, no matter how glamorous, was enough for her, however, and when it ended three weeks later, she told him so. "It was fun while it lasted," she explained, "but I felt that I was having myself a good time at the expense of the children. All of a sudden they didn't have a father, and now they had a traveling mother. So I stopped." Thenceforth she did her secretarial work from home.

But a secretary, or a business manager, was not what Truman needed. John's angry comments to Alan had not been far off the mark: Truman wanted a full-time companion, if not a nurse. Peg would not provide such company. Her much-chastened husband would, and by the beginning of July, John was prepared to give in. Try as he might, John had still not been able to land another job in a bank, and he was reduced to selling life insurance during the day and working for a collection agency at night. With extreme reluctance—"I fought like a son-of-a-bitch not to get involved with him again"—he called Truman and asked for help in obtaining work in Manhattan.

Grabbing the bait, Truman asked him to join him at a weekend party on Long Island. John accepted, they talked some more then, and he was invited out again to spend the night in Sagaponack. Finally Truman popped the question John was waiting to hear. As a kind of lark, Truman said, he had accepted a part in a Neil Simon mystery-comedy that was to begin filming in the fall. Would John go with him to California? Could they start over? John said yes, and Truman rented him an apartment in the nearby town of Noyac for the month of August, warning his friends not to mention his presence to Jack. So they resumed, as if nothing, including the destruction of John's marriage, had interrupted them. Truman had his revenge and John too.

During the time they had been apart, John had remained sober. But when Truman drank, John drank—and vice versa—and within days they were boozing and fighting again. One typical scene took place at the Mount Kisco estate of Truman's friends Bill and Judy Green. Obviously fishing for an invitation, Truman called Judy one Saturday afternoon.

"What are you doing?" he asked.

"I'm sitting by the pool with Frank and Ava," she injudiciously replied, referring to her houseguests, Frank Sinatra and Ava Gardner.

"If that's true, I'm coming right up."

"Oh, no, please don't! I'm having a dinner party."

"All right," he said grudgingly. "I'll come after dinner."

He and John arrived at 6 or 6:30, before she had even gone upstairs to bathe and dress for the evening. Truman was wearing a Sonny & Cher sweat shirt, khaki pants and sneakers; John was wearing a cotton tweed sports coat and looked, to Judy's sophisticated eyes, like the manager of a grocery store in the Midwest. By

9, when dinner was served, they were both drunk and disrupting a gathering that included several tycoons and the Governor of New York. John accidentally dropped his cigarette, which burned a large hole in an expensive Portuguese rug, and began insulting Sinatra, accusing him of having ties to the Mafia. "Frank took it very well," said Truman, "but I couldn't stand it. I had to get out of there. I went to the car, and Frank said he would drive us to a motel. But John got into the driver's seat and wouldn't move. So the two of us roared off down those narrow paths, hitting fences and trees. Finally I grabbed the wheel and we wound up in a ditch. I jumped out and ran into a field. John called for me, then drove away."

Returning to the house, John said that he had lost his passenger. "That's impossible!" bellowed Ava Gardner. "You can't let somebody jump out of a car! We've got to find him." And she and Judy took another car and went searching for Truman. "Truman!" they shouted across those otherwise peaceful hills and dales. "Truman, where are you?" There was no answer. Giving up at last, they returned for nightcaps in the Greens' pool house. They were still sitting there at 3 A.M. when they heard a tap on the door. Turning, they saw a face pressed against the glass: Truman, looking much refreshed from his long walk in the warm summer air, had come back on his own. "By that time he was completely sober," said Judy, "and I think he was terribly embarrassed by everything that had happened."

Answered Prayers was pursuing him "like a crazy wind," Truman had told Newton in 1958, and for the better part of two decades chase him it had, bawling in his ears like a sirocco. But for a moment at least, the publication of part of it, "Mojave," had stilled that persecuting wind. Calling him "a modern master," *Esquire* had given his story star treatment—the entire cover of its June, 1975, issue—and from those who read it he heard nothing but hosannas. Tennessee Williams, who was not usually an admirer, thought that it even demonstrated a touch of genius. "I've never read anything by him, except possibly 'Miriam,' that was comparable," said Tennessee.

Such an enthusiastic reception erased all Truman's worries and doubts, reducing his writer's block to a small and contemptible pile of dust. At the age of fifty he still had what it took; neither alcohol and pills nor a series of disruptive love affairs had damaged the faculty he prized most: his magician's power over words. Perhaps, he seemed to say to himself, *Answered Prayers* would be the masterpiece he had claimed; perhaps he would be the American Proust after all. Before "Mojave" came out, he had jealously guarded his book's contents; now he could scarcely wait for everyone to applaud his achievement. To the astonishment of the editors of *Esquire*, he promised even more chapters. "We stood back on our heels in amazement that we were able to get from Truman Capote what other people hadn't been able to get in such a very long time," said Gordon Lish, the magazine's fiction editor. "Each time he said yes, that he would go one segment further, we were beside ourselves with delight."

If logic had prevailed, the book's first chapter, "Unspoiled Monsters," would have preceded "Mojave," which was the second chapter. Just as many had suspected, however, he had not written as much of *Answered Prayers* as he had maintained; most of it was still in his head. "Unspoiled Monsters" was only half done, and as he resumed his affair with John and prepared to leave for Hollywood, he realized that he would not have time to finish it before the end of 1975. Rushing to give *Esquire* something new, he again disregarded chronology, plucking from his notebooks what was probably the only other finished chapter, the fifth of a projected eight. "It seemed to be complete in and of itself," he explained. "So without really thinking about it, I sent it on."

That fifth chapter borrowed its title, "La Côte Basque, 1965," from Henri Soulé's renowned restaurant on East Fifty-fifth Street, a popular gathering spot for the swans and one of the few Manhattan restaurants that possessed what Truman regarded as "established chic." The action takes place on an afternoon in 1965 when P. B. Jones encounters his friend Lady Ina Coolbirth on the street nearby, and Lady Coolbirth, who has been stood up by her lunch date, the Duchess of Windsor, drags him along to fill the Duchess' empty seat at one of Monsieur Soulé's choice front tables.

Despite her title, Lady Coolbirth is an American, a "big breezy peppy broad" in her forties, who grew up on a ranch in the West and whose latest husband is a rich English knight. In looks, manners and speech, she resembles another big breezy peppy broad, who in 1965 was also in her forties, who also grew up on a ranch in the West, and whose latest husband was also a rich English knight. She is a photograph, in short, of Truman's old friend Slim Keith. On this afternoon in 1965 the fictional Lady Coolbirth has a lot she wants to talk about, and over many glasses of Roederer Cristal champagne, talk she does. Using her voice as his own, Truman is able to stuff his narrative, like an almost infinitely expandable Louis Vuitton bag, with many of the secrets he had become privy to during his years of hobnobbing with the rich.

As Lady Coolbirth's knowing eyes pass over the other patrons— a singular assembly that includes Babe and her sister Betsey Whitney; Lee and *her* sister, Jacqueline Kennedy; and Gloria Vanderbilt and Carol Matthau—she becomes Truman's mouthpiece. "The truth of the matter is that Lady Ina Coolbirth is me!" he later insisted. "I'm the person who gathered all that information, and her conversation is precisely the kind I might have had with somebody." Lee, for instance, receives the usual valentine. "If I were a man, I'd fall for Lee myself," says Lady Coolbirth. "She's marvelously made, like a Tanagra figurine." Older sister Jackie is given the usual needle. "Very photogenic, of course," Lady Coolbirth reluctantly admits, "but the effect is a little . . . unrefined, exaggerated." But most of Lady Coolbirth's monologue is devoted to two long and scandalous stories: a barely disguised account of the Woodward killing and a tale of a philandering tycoon's comic comeuppance.

The Woodward killing had intrigued the social world since 1955, when Ann Woodward had unloaded a double-barreled Churchill shotgun into the smooth and handsome face of her husband Bill. A sportsman, whose racing colors, red and white, had been worn by the great thoroughbred Nashua, Bill had been a popular figure in New York society; on the day of his funeral, his clubs had lowered their flags to half-mast, and servants all over Manhattan's East Side had demanded time off to pay their respects. A Long Island grand jury had exonerated trigger-happy Ann, who asserted that she had mistaken him for a prowler; but most of Truman's friends, who had heard about her fits of insane rage, believed otherwise. When she pulled the trigger, Bill had just emerged from the shower. How many burglars, they asked themselves, make their rounds in the nude?

When Truman began making notes for *Answered Prayers* in 1958, he apparently had planned to make Ann his central character; in a list of eight names he jotted down in his journal, hers was the only one he had underlined. By 1975 the Woodward affair was largely forgotten, and he had a different heroine. Ann Woodward—Ann Hopkins, he calls her, not even bothering to change her first name —has been reduced to a bit player whose entrance into La Côte Basque induces Lady Coolbirth to lay out the facts of that twenty-year-old case, or the facts as Truman and most of his friends understood them.

His Ann is a West Virginia hillbilly who becomes a Manhattan call girl, then a gangster's moll, and finally, through luck and wile, the wife of one of society's golden boys—Bill Woodward right down to his shirt size. Her career is a smooth glissando until her husband, who is tired of her flamboyant adulteries, learns that she has never dissolved a teenage marriage; in the eyes of the law, she is not his wife at all. Realizing that he is about to send her packing, Ann bangs away with her shotgun. She gets away with it, too, as old Mrs. Hopkins, willing to do anything to avoid ugly publicity, buys off the police and pretends, as Bill's mother, Elsie Woodward, did, that her son has been the victim of a cruel accident. ("My son's death was an unfortunate accident," Elsie had actually insisted. "I have never thought otherwise.") Ending her macabre little history, Lady Coolbirth says that now the old lady never gives a dinner party without inviting her daughter-in-law, the assassin. "The one thing I wonder," adds Lady Coolbirth, "is what everyone wonders—when they're alone, just the two of them, what do they talk about?"

The second of Lady Coolbirth's cautionary tales is prompted by the sight of the wife of a former New York governor, who is also partaking of Monsieur Soulé's expensive hospitality. One night at a dinner party, says Lady Coolbirth, Sidney Dillon—"conglomateur, adviser to Presidents"—found himself sitting next to the lady. He had always hankered after her, and since both their spouses were away, he invited her back to his pied-à-terre in the Pierre hotel, where, without any difficulty at all, he lured her into bed. It proved to be a disappointing conquest: she had neglected to warn him that it was the wrong time of the month, and she was menstruating— nearly hemorrhaging, in Truman's grossly exaggerated account. When she left, the sheets were covered with bloodstains "the size of Brazil."

Expecting his wife to return early the next morning, before the hotel maid came to make up the bed, Dillon struggled frantically to expunge the evidence of his infidelity, scrubbing those crimson sheets in the bathtub with the only soap at hand, a bar of Guerlain's Fleurs des Alpes. "There he was," related Lady Coolbirth, "the powerful Mr. Dillon, down on his knees and flogging away like a Spanish peasant at the side of a stream." The sheets finally came clean, and after baking them in the apartment's tiny oven, he made up the bed and crawled under the covers for a warm but somewhat soggy sleep. He was so exhausted that he did not hear his wife come and go, leaving an affectionate message on the bureau: "Darling, you were sleeping so soundly and sweetly that I just tiptoed in and changed and have gone on to Greenwich. Hurry home."

Of all Truman's writing, "La Côte Basque" is probably the one piece that can be called a tour de force: he has transformed a table in a Manhattan restaurant into a stage on which he has placed his own jet-set Vanity Fair. One by one, he shines a spotlight on his glittering cast, which includes, besides his fictional characters, the very real Carol Matthau, Gloria Vanderbilt and Lee Radziwill. There is no plot—the only unifying element is a tone of profound disenchantment—and he has pulled off one of the most difficult tricks in fiction, which is the fashioning of a seamless narrative out of disparate characters and unrelated deeds. "La Côte Basque" is not great art, but it is superb craftsmanship, storytelling at its most skillful.

But Truman had more than literature in mind when he wrote "La Côte Basque." He also used it to get back at some of his rich friends who, for one reason or another, had offended him over the years. Wrapped inside it is a hit list. Ann Woodward is on that list, of course. Besides being fascinated by her rather compelling biography, he remembered a much-talked-about meeting in St. Moritz in which she had called him a "fag," and he, in return, had nicknamed her "Bang-Bang." Also on his roster are Princess Margaret ("I was about to doze off, she's such a drone," says Lady Coolbirth, who had the misfortune to be stuck with her at a party); J. D. Salinger, who was one of Oona Chaplin's early beaux ("It seemed to me he must be a boy who cries very easily," Carol Matthau thought after reading some of his letters); Gloria Vanderbilt, who is made to appear so vacuous and self-absorbed that she cannot even recognize her first husband when he stops by her table to say hello ("Oh, darling. Let's not brood," says Carol consolingly. "After all, you haven't seen him in almost twenty years"); and Josh and Nedda Logan, whom Truman had not forgiven for sabotaging his *New Yorker* article on the filming of *Sayonara* (How was the Logans' party? Carol asks Gloria. "Marvelous," replies Gloria. "If you've never been to a party before"). All those names might have been anticipated. But one is a startling surprise, and that is Truman's old friend Bill Paley, who is his model for Sidney Dillon, the millionaire turned laundryman.

In an earlier version, Dillon had been based on W. Averell Harriman; the woman he had been in bed with was his mistress, not someone he had lured home for a night; and the bloodstain she had left behind had been a mere spot, not a splotch the size of Brazil. By the time it appeared in "La Côte Basque," the episode had been radically altered. Dillon was no longer, like Harriman, a WASP patrician; he was now a rich and attractive Jew who yearned to be a WASP patrician. He wanted to go to bed with the former governor's wife not because she was appealing—in fact she "looked as if she wore tweed brassieres and played a lot of golf"—but because she was a symbol of what he most desired. "It was simply that for Dill she was the living incorporation of everything denied him, forbidden to him as a Jew, no matter how beguiling and rich he might be," says Lady Coolbirth, "the Racquet Club, Le Jockey, the Links, White's—all those places he would never sit down to a table of backgammon, all those golf courses where he would never sink a putt . . . ." Conversely, the reason she had agreed to go to bed with him was so that she could humiliate him with those bloody sheets; it was her way of putting him in his place. "She had mocked him," concludes Lady Coolbirth, "punished him for his Jewish presumption."

Few readers could have guessed that Dillon was supposed to represent Bill Paley. He did not look or act like Bill, and there were no obvious hints, as there usually are in *romans à clef*. But to some of those who knew Truman and the Paleys well, it was clear that Bill was his target. The first clue was his description of Dillon's deceived wife, Cleo—"the most beautiful creature alive," in Lady Coolbirth's reverential words. Truman employed such extravagant language to describe only one mortal, Babe Paley; even Lee was not accorded such an encomium. The second clue was his emphasis on Dillon's hungering for WASP gentility; Truman was convinced that Bill Paley shared that appetite as well. In any event, he thought that by means of such cryptic signals he was doing to Bill what the former governor's wife had done to Dillon: putting him in his place. Through words, he liked to think that he was hitting perhaps the only vulnerable spot possessed by a man of such monarchical self-confidence: his sensitivity about being a Jew.

"Truman told me that the point of the bloody-sheets story was that Bill Paley was a Jew from the Midwest who was doing a number on a New York WASP," recalled John, who proofread "La Côte Basque" before it was sent off to *Esquire*. Offended by the anecdote —"That's gossip! that's bullshit!" he exclaimed—John tried to shame him into removing it. He pointed out that they had been the Paleys' guests at Kiluna Farm a few weeks before, that over the years the Paleys had laden him with gifts, and finally, that he might hurt Babe, who, as they had had sad occasion to observe, was gravely ill with lung cancer. Take the Dillon section out, John urged him; but Truman could not be persuaded. "It was a vicious story," said John, "and I've never understood, and will never understand, why he put it in. There's something there that defies analysis."

Only someone who had observed that curious trio—Babe, Bill and Truman—in earlier times could have fathomed Truman's tangled reasoning. He liked and admired Bill; some even speculated that he had a crush on Bill as well as Babe. But he was also jealous of him, as he would have been jealous of anyone married to Babe. Yet at the same time, he resented Bill's inexplicable failure to appreciate that glorious woman; he was infuriated by what he saw as Bill's put-downs of her, his insufferable condescensions. Divine Babe! Revered by Truman and so many others, but mocked and belittled by her own husband! Contemplating the unfairness of it all was more than Truman could bear. She was the one person in the world he loved without qualm or reservation, and he alone realized how unhappy she was. Now that she was dying—for that was the case—he was avenging her in the one way he knew how: by holding up to ridicule the man who had caused her so much hurt.

Truman wanted Bill to be aware that he was being ridiculed; otherwise the Sidney Dillon anecdote would have had no purpose. But so confused and contradictory were his thoughts, he also tried to convince himself that neither Bill nor some of the others he had made fun of would recognize themselves. One day in July he took a friend for a swim in Gloria Vanderbilt's pool in Southampton—Gloria and Wyatt were away in Europe—and after the friend had read his manuscript, Truman identified, one by one, the models for his characters. "But Truman, they're not going to like this," protested the friend. Floating on his back and looking up at a sky of cloudless serenity, Truman lazily responded, "Nah, they're too dumb. They won't know who they are."

But they did know, and when "La Côte Basque" reached the stands in mid-October, their wrath shook the ground beneath his feet. The first tremors were felt on October 10, even before it appeared. Learning of her own leading role—someone had smuggled her an advance copy of the November *Esquire*—Ann Woodward swallowed a fatal dose of Seconal, the same drug that had killed Nina Capote. Ann had been deeply depressed anyway, and "La

Côte Basque" may only have been the catalyst that hastened the inevitable. What had bothered Ann most, a weary Elsie Woodward told a friend, was not Truman's dredging up of the sordid past, but his suggestion that her marriage to poor Bill had been bigamous. Few regretted Ann's death, in any event; the general feeling was that justice had been served at last. But many were angered by the embarrassment Truman had caused that beloved icon, ninety-two-year-old Elsie, who had spent twenty years trying to make everyone forget the scandal. Now, in a few paragraphs, he had destroyed all her hard work.

When "La Côte Basque" was available to everyone a week later, the earthquake itself struck, sending shock waves from New York to California, where Truman was beginning rehearsals for his movie. The reaction was most succinctly summed up by a cartoon on the cover of *New York* magazine: a French poodle—Truman, complete with glasses—disrupting a formal party with his sharp and rapacious teeth. "Capote Bites the Hands That Fed Him," read the magazine's headline, which expressed the shocked and outraged feelings of most of his society friends: their favorite household pet, their *ami de la maison*, had turned against them.

Within hours, phones were ringing all over the East Side of Manhattan. One of the first callers was Babe, who asked Slim to identify Sidney Dillon. "Who is that?" Babe inquired suspiciously. "You don't think that it's Bill, do you?"

"No, I don't," answered Slim, who knew very well who Dillon was meant to be—Truman had told her months before. But Babe found out anyway, and instead of accusing Bill of infidelity, she blamed Truman for putting such a distasteful tale into print. Although Truman had studied her with the rapt attention of a lover, he had failed to understand perhaps the most important component of Babe's character: her loyalty to her family. Brought up to honor the stern Roman virtues of Old Boston, she had different values from many of her fashionable friends, including Slim. She believed, as Peg O'Shea did, that whether or not he had strayed, or whether or not he had humiliated her, a wife's duty was to stand beside her husband. She was now standing beside Bill. In attacking him, Truman had also attacked her family and the code by which she lived, and she could not forgive him.

Nor could Slim. "You're in it, Big Mama," he had warned her; but expecting no more than a walk-on part, Slim was totally unprepared to encounter herself as the gabby Lady Coolbirth. "When you read it, there's my voice, my armature, my everything!" she exploded. "She looks like me, she talks like me, she's me! A mirror image of me! I was absolutely undone when I read it, staggered that he could be sitting across from me at a table and then go home and write down everything I had said. I had adored him, and I was so appalled by the use of friendship and my own bad judgment."

Others were equally chagrined. "Never have you heard such gnashing of teeth, such cries for revenge, such shouts of betrayal and screams of outrage," reported Liz Smith, who wrote the article that accompanied the *New York* cartoon. One cry came from the Logans, who were enraged by his witty gibe about their parties; "that dirty little toad is never coming to my parties again," declared Nedda. Another came from Gloria Vanderbilt, who vowed that if she ever saw him again, she would spit at him. "After all," explained her husband Wyatt, "they've known each other a long time. It's not that a secret has been betrayed, it's that a kind of trust has been betrayed."

"It's very hard to be a gentleman and a writer," Somerset Maugham had said, and in the end Truman had elected to be the latter. He had broken the rules of the club, and he had to be punished. Just as it once had been the fashion to take him up, now it became the fashion to put him down, "the chic of the week," as Charlotte Curtis phrased it. Those who were not hurt by "La Côte Basque" were often as angry as those who were. Marella Agnelli, who more than once had begged him to be her guest on one Mediterranean cruise or another, could not even bring herself to mention his first name. "Capote despises the people he talks about," she complained. "Using, using all the time. He builds up his friends privately and knocks them down publicly." Overnight, doors slammed in his face, and except for a few hardy loyalists like Kay Meehan and C. Z. Guest, who had not been made fun of, his society friends refused even to speak to him. Not since Franklin Roosevelt came to power had the rich felt themselves so misused by someone they had considered one of their own. Truman had been accepted, pampered and allowed into the inner recesses of their private lives; in return, he had mocked them and broadcast their secrets. He was, in their opinion, a cad and a traitor.

"In society a great friendship does not amount to much" was Proust's cynical observation, and so it seemed to be, as even Cecil, who was eagerly following events from England, rushed to join the pack of Truman-haters. Forgotten were the unblemished days he and Truman had enjoyed together in Tangier, Portofino and Palamós; disregarded the many words of sticky adulation Cecil had scribbled about him in his diary; banished from mind the time Truman had rescued him from the two sailors in Honolulu. After having dedicated most of his life to protecting his place in the front ranks of fashion, Cecil did not want to be left behind now.

Actually, Cecil, whose chief defect was not snobbery, as many assumed, but a consuming envy, had secretly turned against Truman a decade earlier, after the success of *In Cold Blood*. "The triumph of Truman is salt in one's wound," he had bitterly noted in his diary at the end of 1965. The further triumph of the Black and White Ball had inflamed him still more. For ten years he had waited for the weather to change. To Cecil's envious ears, the howls of indignation he now heard from the other side of the Atlantic were as soothing as a lullaby—Truman's most venomous enemy could not have taken more delight in his downfall. "I hate the idea of Truman," he happily confessed to one correspondent. "How low can he sink?" Even Truman's erstwhile best friend had pronounced his name anathema: there could have been no clearer confirmation that he had been expelled from Olympus.

Naïveté may be a necessary armor for writers who, like Truman, closely pattern their fiction on real people and real incidents. How, after all, could they ever write anything if they could foresee what their words would cost them? Only such protective ingenuousness could explain how Thomas Wolfe, for example, could have imagined that his family and friends would not have been wounded by *Look Homeward, Angel*. Only such deliberate blindness could account for Proust's surprise when some of his titled friends were offended by their portraits in *Remembrance of Things Past*. And only such obstinate self-deception could explain the astonishment and dismay with which Truman now watched the reversal in his fortunes that followed "La Côte Basque."

He had of course hoped to raise the blood pressure of people like the Logans and to cause momentary annoyance to a few more, like Bill Paley and Gloria Vanderbilt. What he had not anticipated was the disaster, complete and absolute, that had now befallen him. Forced to remain in California while he was making his movie, he kept in touch with events from afar. "He was the most surprised and shocked person you can imagine," recalled Liz Smith, "and he would call to ask me—torment me—about what people in New York had said about him. After 'La Côte Basque' he was never happy again." Joanne Carson watched helplessly as he rambled around her house in a near-daze, repeating over and over, "But they know I'm a writer. I don't understand it."

He telephoned Slim to make up. When she refused to take his call, he persuaded John to phone her. Although Lady Coolbirth may have borne a superficial resemblance to her, John was instructed to say, she was really supposed to represent Slim's old enemy Pamela Hayward, the new Mrs. W. Averell Harriman. "Truman's very upset by your reaction," John said. "He thought it would make you laugh."

"I didn't," retorted Slim, who, quite the contrary, had consulted her lawyer about suing him.

"Don't you think it's well written?" John asked.

"No. It's junk," said the implacable Slim, who at that point detected breathing on the other end and hung up, realizing that Truman was listening in on an extension phone. Truman persisted nonetheless, and at the end of the year he sent her a cable in Australia, where she was vacationing. "Merry Christmas, Big Mama," he said. "I've decided to forgive you. Love, Truman."

Bracing himself for more harsh words, Truman also phoned Bill, who did take his call, blandly pretending that nothing untoward had taken place since they had last talked. "I have other ways of torturing the little shit," he later told a friend. Truman asked if he had read his *Esquire* story, and Bill said, "I started, Truman, but I fell asleep. Then a terrible thing happened: the magazine was thrown away." When Truman, with pathetic eagerness, offered to send him another copy, Bill politely declined. "Don't bother, Truman. I'm preoccupied right now. My wife is very ill." My wife! Not Barbara, not Babe, but my wife! As if Truman had hardly known her, had not spent some of the most enchanted hours of his life with her, had not been entrusted with secrets she confided to no one else, including her husband. To be dismissed as a stranger: that was torture indeed.

To Babe herself, Truman wrote two long letters. She did not reply, but in early 1976 chance brought them together in Quo Vadis, a then-fashionable restaurant on East Sixty-third Street—

though ill, she was occasionally still able to go out. He introduced her to his luncheon companions, and like Bill, she was polite but distant, as if he were someone she knew only slightly. Eventually Jack, without prompting, also approached her, phoning her one Saturday afternoon at Kiluna Farm. Forgive him, Jack asked her. "Never! Never! Definitely not!" she declared.

"Babe, what Truman said in that piece is none of your business. Or his business either," replied Jack, in that stern voice Truman himself had so often heard. "He is an artist, and you can't control artists."

"Oh, Jack . . . ," she began, and seemed about to say more; then, after a second's hesitation, she concluded, "Let me talk it over with Bill." Jack knew then that he had lost the argument. He did not make similar entreaties to Slim, which was probably just as well for both of them. "If I ever met Slim on the street, I'd kick her," he promised. "I'd say, 'Jesus Christ, Slim, as nice as that boy was to you!' When Truman and I were living in Spain, Leland Hayward left her. She was in trouble, wandering around, and we took her in."

As consumed with anger as they might have been toward a lover who had deceived them, Babe and Slim were not prepared to make peace. Nothing Truman did, whether it was to write eloquent letters or to send amusing telegrams, could change their minds. All the devices that had worked so well for him in the past were now of no avail. "Babe always spoke of Truman with total loathing, as this snake who had betrayed her," said their mutual friend John Richardson. "Have you heard what Truman's done now?" she would ask her friends, professing to be horrified by each new comment she saw quoted or each new escapade she heard about. When her sister Minnie's husband, Jim Fosburgh, who had once painted Truman's portrait, broke ranks to lunch with him, Babe called to upbraid him that very afternoon. How could he, her own brother-in-law, have been so disloyal? she demanded. Yet carefully hidden beneath her fury lay a great disappointment: like Truman, she too had lost perhaps her best friend. Harper Lee glimpsed that disappointment the few times they met in the ensuing months: seeing her, Babe was reminded of Truman and automatically burst into tears.

For her part, Slim could not stop herself from chewing endlessly on the wrong that had been done her. "If ever there was a woman who was beside herself, it was Slim," said one friend. And it was literally true. When she discussed him, Slim became so agitated that she could not remain seated for more than a moment, moving restlessly from couch to chair, chair to couch. "After 'La Côte Basque' I looked on Truman as a friend who had died," she said, "and we never spoke again. I took the cleaver and chopped him out of my life. And that was it."

In public Truman regretted the loss of Babe, and Slim too, but claimed to be otherwise unaffected by the commotion he had created. Like Jack, he lectured rather loftily on his mission as an artist. "The artist is a dangerous person because he's out of control," he said. "He's controlled only by his art." Defiantly saying that he had done nothing that Proust had not done before him, he tried to wrap his work in the mantle of literature. "Oh, honey! It's Proust! It's beautiful!" he exclaimed to Diana Vreeland.

In a more practical vein, he noted what probably would have been evident all along, if he had not, in Slim's rueful words, been "so wily, so clever and so bright" that even the most suspicious dropped their guard. "All a writer has for material is what he knows," he said. "At least, that's all I've got—what I know." But sometimes in private, late at night and when he had been drinking, he would break into tears. "I didn't mean to hurt anybody," he would cry. "I didn't know the story would cause such a fuss."

53

WHILE the drama of his social demise was being played out in New York, Truman was encountering different kinds of problems in California. One, which might have been anticipated, was his role in Neil Simon's farce *Murder by Death*. Simon had chosen him as the model for his comic villain—a neat turnabout for the author of "La Côte Basque." All Truman was supposed to do was portray someone much like himself: a weird eccentric who gathers the world's greatest detectives to solve a murder he has thoughtfully arranged. It seemed like a not insurmountable assignment, and Truman had expected his debut as a movie star to make him the envy of both his friends and his enemies. "Gore Vidal must be dying," he had gleefully declared. He had looked forward to his weeks in Hollywood as a holiday, a glamorous and well-paid frolic.* The real acting was to be done by a cast of sterling professionals: Alec Guinness, Peter Sellers, David Niven, Maggie Smith, Elsa Lanchester, Peter Falk, James Coco and Nancy Walker.

But standing in front of the cameras was not the romp he had imagined; it was hard and often boring work, as the screenwriter of *Beat the Devil* and *The Innocents* should have remembered. Most days he had to leave for the Burbank studio by 6:30 or 7 A.M. and stay there, either working or on call in his trailer, until late afternoon or evening. At the best of times, such an arduous schedule, coupled with the tension he usually felt before public appearances, would

---

* His salary was ten thousand dollars a week plus expenses; by the time he finished, he had earned nearly seventy-nine thousand dollars.

have filled him with dread. But the days that followed publication of "La Côte Basque" were not the best of times. "Making that film knocked everything out of him," said John. "It was probably the most exhausting thing he ever did psychologically. He used to get up in the morning as if he were going to the gallows, instead of a studio."

If he had been content to play himself, as the producers had hired him to do, he might have shone like the star he longed to be; there have been a few films in which an amateur of a unique stamp has upstaged his experienced colleagues. But such a passive assignment was not enough for Truman. Since boyhood, he had dreamed of being in the movies; now that he was, he was not going to let his chance go to waste: he wanted to act. "The original intent may have been for me to parody myself, but that's not how it's going to work out," he defiantly informed one interviewer. To another he jokingly added: "How am I as an actor? Let's just say, 'What Billie Holiday is to jazz, what Mae West is to tits . . . what Seconal is to sleeping pills, what King Kong is to penises, Truman Capote is to the great god Thespis!' "

The film premiered in the summer of 1976. That he looked the part of a dotty murderer no one disputed. Weighing far more than he ever had before, with cascading jowls and a stomach that threatened to burst the buttons of his gray vest, he appeared funny and sinister at the same time, like a giant frog preparing to pounce on his prey. Looks aside, he was not very good. His characterization was overwrought, a reflection perhaps of his anxiety, and curiously in-authentic—he did not play a convincing Truman Capote. He was the recipient of many harsh words from the critics, as well as a few kind ones, but Guinness' critique—"godawful!"—was the most succinct, as well as the most accurate. That was not the only word, however, and Robert Moore, whose unhappy task it had been to direct him, laid the blame for his performance not on Truman, but on those, including Simon, who had picked him. "To put Capote at a table with international stars was too much of a test for any literary figure to withstand," said Moore. "It's like saying, 'Wouldn't it be great to get [the President of the United States] to play the President of the United States?' The answer is 'No.' "

Truman's second problem, which also might have been anticipated, was his volatile, up-and-down relationship with John. Their journey West had started well enough, with a long and relaxing drive through Canada and the Canadian Rockies, a kind of second honeymoon. That amicable mood had lingered even after Truman began working. Assuming the unaccustomed role of helpmate, John had shared his burden, waking up with him at dawn, driving him to the studio, and staying with him for the rest of the day. Only later, after Truman had become accustomed to the routine—and John had become bored with it—did John arrange for a studio driver to take over his chauffeur's duties.

That congenial spirit soon began to evaporate, however, as the same old difficulties surfaced in the same old ways. Though Truman drank a little less while he was working on the movie, John drank even more. On Thanksgiving he was feeling so low that he poured his first drink at 9 A.M. He and Truman celebrated at Joanne Carson's, and by late afternoon, when the turkey was served, he was so drunk and belligerent that he spat in the face of one of her other guests, then wandered away to pass out on the floor in another room. (Truman had bragged so much about John's sexual equipment that another member of the party surreptitiously followed him and, taking advantage of his stupor, unzipped his trousers to inspect that anatomical wonder. "It's pretty good," he reported to another member of the party. "Truman didn't exaggerate.")

Late one night a week or so later, they had a fight in their own house in Beverly Hills, which Joanne had rented and helped decorate for them. John became so violent, smashing every glass object in sight, that Truman was forced to flee. Dressed in nothing but a T-shirt and Bermuda shorts, he walked barefooted to the Beverly Hills Hotel, where he telephoned Joanne. When she picked him up a few minutes later, he was shaken and white, and his feet were bloody from the broken glass. He and John soon reconciled, but two weeks later they had another fight and Truman again sought refuge at Joanne's.

Destructive as it was, alcohol merely fueled their arguments, which centered, as always, on power: who was to exercise control? John was desperate for that privilege, and once again tried to interpose himself between Truman and the rest of the world. "I've always [concluded] that the best way to handle Truman's affairs was to keep him away from any substantive discussions of money, and to prevent him from making stupid or excessive commitments," he told Alan Schwartz. Not only did he open Truman's mail, but he also gave the studio guards a list of visitors who were to be denied entry into his trailer. Above the name of one man, with whom Truman had enjoyed a brief fling, John wrote the word "*NO*," which he underlined three times.

John's arguments for taking command were familiar; indeed, they had the perfunctory tone that comes from useless repetition. If he shouted louder, if he tried even harder to look important, it was only because he realized that he was being ignored. After two years of fruitless struggle, he knew that Truman would never let him, or anyone else, guide his career. "Truman and I have talked this to death," he wearily confessed to Alan. "Nothing changes."

Although he continued to bluster about the prerogatives that should have been his, John's real demands were now quite modest. In return for his companionship, he asked for only two things from Truman. The first was a place to live. "John was always talking about security," recalled Joanne. "That was his big cry. He said that he had burned his bridges in New York and that he depended on Truman. 'If we have our own house, nobody can bother us,' he said." The second was help in finding employment. He wanted Truman to whisper a good word in the ear of someone—Truman's tycoon friend Bob Anderson was the one he had most in mind—who might give him a job. "It's all very interesting being with you, Truman," he said, "but you have repeatedly done this number where you take off like a big bird and leave me hanging by my thumbs. What I want to do is establish myself in business, and I can't do that if I'm flitting around the country with you. So the first thing I need is a place to live. The second thing I need is to get some kind of career going so that if you take off one time and never come back, I'm not going to be bereft."

The first condition, providing him a place to live, Truman grudgingly agreed to. "I want something dramatic that looks over the ocean down a mountainside," Truman proclaimed, possibly assuming that no such house was on the market at a price he could afford. But something dramatic was precisely what Joanne found in the hills above Malibu: a small, two-bedroom house with a sweeping view of the sea, much like the one Truman had enjoyed from the Fontana Vecchia in Taormina. Nor could he object that Joanne's discovery was too expensive; by local standards it was a bargain, his for just under one hundred and fifty thousand dollars. Even if he had wished to, Truman could not have said no. Taking possession early in 1976, he immediately redecorated, painting the living room a bright salmon and filling it with comfortable white wicker furniture.

Once having committed himself, he even talked about abandoning Manhattan, where so many had already abandoned him, and he ordered an appraisal of his apartment at the U.N. Plaza. In the future, he said, he would divide his time between two oceans, between his house in Malibu and his cottage on Long Island, between John and Jack. In John's eyes, it was an ideal arrangement. "Truman didn't want to spend three hundred and sixty-five days a year with me," he said. "He didn't want to spend three hundred and sixty-five days a year with anybody. And at one time he very frankly acknowledged that."

But to John's dismay, Truman rejected John's second condition point-blank; he adamantly refused to help John find work. "He never helped me—he could not do it—because he was such a possessive fanatic that he didn't want me out of the house," said John. "He knew that if I had a five-day-a-week job and he suddenly got an inspiration to go to Rio, I couldn't go with him." John's analysis was undoubtedly correct. Truman did not want an independent lover; he wanted one who was subservient, in fact if not in manner. But it was probably also true that he perceived that his only hold on John was financial, and that if John ever did find a job, John would be the one who would fly off like a big bird. That was not a chance Truman was willing to take.

At the end of 1975 Truman finished work on *Murder by Death*. He returned briefly to New York, then in the middle of January began a speaking tour that was to take him to thirty colleges and universities. Almost immediately he recognized his mistake. Although he had given readings in the past, they were usually isolated, separated by many months. Never before had he undertaken such a rigorous schedule, which kept him constantly on the road, like a politician running for office.

John Knowles saw him at the University of Florida, where, to accommodate a large and eager crowd, his hosts had arranged for him to speak outdoors. His reading was a singular success, as was the question period that followed. "Are you a homosexual?" asked one truculent young man. With perfect timing, Truman paused, then brought down shouts of laughter on the young man's head with a sly question of his own. "Is that a proposition?" he inquired. But when Knowles visited his hotel room afterward, he discovered that once off stage, Truman had retreated into a numbed daze. "With the jet lag and endless motels, he hardly knew where he was. He had a couple of vodkas to revive himself, and he was on the moon. He just dwindled away. His energy was gone; his coherence was gone."

Some writers thrive on public readings. Others do not. That Truman ever agreed to undertake such a series was yet another sign that he was out of touch, even with his own body and soul. Perhaps he thought, quite erroneously, as his accountant, Arnold Bernstein, could have told him, that he needed the money (fifty thousand dollars, after expenses and agents' fees) to help pay for the house in Malibu. Perhaps he hoped to draw attention to the next chapter of *Answered Prayers*, which was to appear in the May *Esquire*. Perhaps, after all the screaming over "La Côte Basque," he merely needed assurance that he was still loved and admired. Whatever he expected, it was insufficient reward for a tour that he soon confessed was "the stupidest thing I've ever done. It's like going from one torture pit into another."

Adding to his despondency was an unexpected assault from another quarter: Gore Vidal. In a boozy interview he had given some months before, Truman had inadvertently handed Gore the weapon he seemed to have been waiting for. Gore, he had asserted, had once become so inebriated and obnoxious that he had been ejected from a party at the Kennedy White House—literally thrown out, like a drunk at a rowdy bar. "It was the only time he had ever been invited to the White House and he got drunk," Truman had said. "*Annnnnd* . . . he insulted Jackie's mother, whom he had never met before in his *life*! But I mean insulted her. He said something to the effect that he had always hated her. But he'd never even met the woman. And she just went into something like total shock. And Bobby [Kennedy] and Arthur Schlesinger, I believe it was, and one of the guards just picked Gore up and carried him to the door and threw him out into Pennsylvania Avenue."

Not untypically, Truman had embroidered events. Gore had indeed said or done something to alienate the Kennedys during a White House party in November, 1961. He admitted, in fact, to a sharp exchange of words with Bobby Kennedy, in which, sounding more like New York City taxi drivers than the Attorney General of the United States and a writer famous for his wit, they had snarled, one after the other: "Why don't you go fuck yourself!" But Gore had not been thrown bodily out the door, and Truman's comments, which were printed in *Playgirl*, were, at the very least, injudicious. Gore intended not only to brand him a liar—"I'm looking forward to getting that little toad!" he announced—but also to wound him financially. To those ends, he filed suit in a New York State court, charging that Truman had libeled him and caused him "great mental anxiety and suffering" and demanding both an apology and one million dollars in damages. The Capote–Vidal feud, which had seemed to amuse the participants as much as it did most of the rest of the world, had suddenly turned extremely nasty.

The depositions provided the only comedy in an otherwise ugly confrontation. When had he last seen Truman? Gore was asked. At a party in the late sixties, Gore replied.

"Q: What occurred on that occasion?

"A: I sat on him.

"Q: What do you mean?

"A: I didn't have my glasses on and I sat down on what I thought was a stool and it was Capote.

"Q: Where was Capote sitting at the time you sat on him?

"A: On a smaller stool."

For his part, Truman managed to mangle the title of Gore's first novel, *Williwaw*; *Willie Wonka*, Truman called it, thereby indicating how little he had thought of it. He also suggested that in bringing suit, Gore was behaving like a child. Although he considered some of Gore's printed remarks about him to be libelous, he said, he would never lower himself by suing. "I just don't believe in that. I especially don't believe in writers or artists suing each other. I think that is very childish, but that is my own point of view."

Exhausted and suffering from what he termed a "semi–nervous breakdown," Truman concluded his readings at the end of April, 1976, and returned to his new house in California to recover. But recuperation was impossible in John's company, and almost imme-diately they resumed their familiar routine of fights and reconcilia-tions. Truman wanted to stay home. John wanted to go out, and when Truman refused to join his excursions, John went alone. It was as if, in a bizarre reversal of roles, Truman had become Jack, and John had become the Truman of old. "We're on two different wavelengths," grumbled Truman. "Johnny's a very social, gregarious person, and no matter what I once was, I'm not a social person now. He'll come in in the afternoon and say, 'We're having Steve McQueen and Ali McGraw to dinner tonight.' And I'll just want to go into the bedroom and hide. I like Steve McQueen and Ali McGraw, but I don't want to see anybody. Or we'll be invited to a party. If he goes alone, I'll be anxious because I'll know that he'll drink too much. And if I go with him, it will be even worse because there will be fifty people crowding me against the wall. That's what you get for being the freak celebrity of the seventies."

In the middle of May, John threw a huge party. He hired caterers and invited dozens of people to their hilltop hideaway. But at that moment a party was the last thing Truman desired, and he said so. "He made no bones about it, which was kind of unpleasant," John recalled. "It was not his kind of thing, partially because it was what we used to call N.I.H.—Not Invented Here. In other words, if it had been Truman's idea, everything would have been wonderful. But it was my idea."

Three weeks after his homecoming, Truman had had enough. On May 23, taking advantage of one of John's trips to the bars on the Pacific Coast Highway, he packed his bags and left for the airport. Returning later that afternoon, John found a short goodbye note: he was becoming nervous, Truman had said, and he was flying back to New York. In a phone conversation several days later, he added that he had decided to sell the house; John could stay on for several weeks, but then he would have to find a place of his own. That John eventually did. From a house with a view and a heated pool, he moved to a garage without even a toilet. To relieve himself, he either had to make rather primitive use of an adjoining alley or avail himself of the facilities in a nearby restaurant. His worst fears had been realized, and once again he had been left to hang by his thumbs.

Emotionally, Truman did not fare much better. A week after his furtive departure, his car struck an oncoming vehicle, and he was arrested for drunken driving on Long Island. Though no one was injured, the accident was reported across the country, putting his difficulties with alcohol into the public record for the first time. For once he was silent. "Capote Is Mum on Drunk Rap," said the headline on the front page of the New York *Daily News*. Embarrassed and chagrined, he entered Silver Hill, an expensive drying-out clinic in Connecticut. "I've just got to pull myself through the depression

I'm in," he tearfully told a friend the night before he left. His un-
doing, he maintained, was not liquor, but John. "My feelings for
him are more intense than they were for Danny, and I cannot *not*
identify with his problems. At the same time, I can see very clearly
why my relationship with him doesn't work. It's like having double
vision, of being able to see the truth beyond the truth."

T HE Tiny Terror, *Women's Wear Daily* had christened him after "La Côte Basque," and Truman, who had always boasted that he could be a dangerous enemy, rather fancied the title. He also fancied the notion that many of his friends, or former friends, were chewing their nails with worry about what he might say in forthcoming segments of *Answered Prayers*. The ability to make people jump was the kind of power he had always relished, and no one could be quite certain that he was joking when he wagged his finger and cautioned: "You'd better be careful, or you'll be in it!" Capitalizing on his suddenly sinister reputation, in May, 1976, *Esquire* portrayed him as an assassin on the cover of its "Unspoiled Monsters" issue, dressing him all in black and thrusting an ivory-handled stiletto into his hands. "Capote Strikes Again!" declared the headline. "More from *Answered Prayers*: The most talked-about book of the year."

But "Unspoiled Monsters" was not just more from *Answered Prayers*. It was a great deal more, about twenty-four thousand words; it was almost as long, in fact, as *Breakfast at Tiffany's*. It was also the first chapter, the key to everything that was to follow. Combined with the shorter second chapter, "Kate McCloud,"* which *Esquire* published in December, 1976, it set the tone of his novel, which is one of black comedy; it introduced his hero and

---

* He had removed "Mojave," which he had originally projected as the novel's second chapter.

heroine, P. B. Jones and Kate McCloud; and it outlined his basic story line, which seems to be a suspense drama.

"Somewhere in the world," it begins, "there exists an exceptional philosopher named Florie Rotondo.

"The other day I came across one of her ruminations printed in a magazine devoted to the writings of schoolchildren. It said: *If I could do anything, I would go to the middle of our planet, Earth, and seek uranium, rubies, and gold. I'd look for Unspoiled Monsters. Then I'd move to the country. Florie Rotondo, age 8.*

"Florie, honey, I know just what you mean—even if you don't: how could you, age 8?

"Because I have *been* to the middle of our planet; at any rate, have suffered the tribulations such a journey might inflict. I have searched for uranium, rubies, gold, and, en route, have observed others in these pursuits. And listen, Florie—I have met Unspoiled Monsters! Spoiled ones, too. But the *un*spoiled variety is the rara avis: white truffles compared to black; bitter wild asparagus as opposed to garden-grown.

"The one thing I haven't done is move to the country.

"As a matter of fact, I am writing this on Y.M.C.A. stationery in a Manhattan Y.M.C.A., where I have been existing the last month in a viewless second-floor cell. I'd prefer the sixth floor—so if I decided to climb out the window, it would make a vital difference. Perhaps I'll change rooms. Ascend. Probably not. I'm a coward. But not cowardly enough to take the plunge.

"My name is P. B. Jones, and I'm of two minds—whether to tell you something about myself right now, or wait and weave the information into the text of the tale. I could just as well tell you nothing, or very little, for I consider myself a reporter in this matter, not a participant, at least not an important one. But maybe it's easier to start with me."

· And so he does: the narrator and hero of *Answered Prayers* is an orphan who was abandoned in a St. Louis movie theater when he was a baby and who was raised thereafter by nuns. Their goodness did not rub off, however, and P.B. is an opportunist, a heel, a rat, someone who sells anything, including himself, to get what he wants. As a boy, he says, he was "a kind of Hershey Bar whore— there wasn't much I wouldn't do for a nickel's worth of chocolate." At fifteen, he ran away and was picked up by a masseur of a Miami

Beach hotel, who took him home and taught him his trade; in matters of sex, P.B. needed no lessons.

After that, much of P.B.'s biography is borrowed from his creator. Ambitious to be a writer, he heads North, where he sets out
to conquer the New York literary world. He is taken up by a magazine editor, who is a fictional duplicate of George Davis, and he
becomes the lover of Alice Lee Langman, "America's first lady of
letters"—Katherine Anne Porter. (In the latter instance, P.B. is
modeled on Truman's onetime friend Bill Goyen, who used Porter
to boost his mediocre talents much as P.B. uses Miss Langman.)
P.B. then travels to Paris, where he meets Denham Fouts, Natalie
Barney and Colette; Colette gives him the same paperweight, a
white rose, she gave Truman in 1948. Clearly, it is a game with
mirrors Truman is playing. P.B. is even working on a novel titled
Answered Prayers, which he is writing with Truman's favorite
Blackwing pencils.

But P.B., who for a time earns his living as a male prostitute, is
not Truman's self-portrait. He is rather his errant and amoral twin,
a nightmare version of the man Truman thought he might have
become, in spirit if not in fact. "P.B. isn't me, but on the other hand
he isn't *not* me," he said. "His background is totally different from
mine, but I can identify with it psychologically. I'm not P.B., but I
know him very well."

He was also well acquainted with Kate McCloud, who might have
become the most remarkable of his heroines. If Holly Golightly is a
reincarnation of the Little Miss Bobbit of "Children on Their Birthdays," then Kate is a reincarnation of Holly. But she is a beautiful,
rutilant Holly, with hair the pale red of a winter sunset and eyes as
green as emeralds; an older Holly, twenty-seven when P.B. meets
her; and a more sophisticated Holly, the embodiment—indeed, the
apotheosis—of the high style Truman revered. Of all his swans,
fictional and real, Kate was the closest to his heart. As P.B. exclaims:
"Kate! McCloud! My love, my anguish, my Götterdämmerung, my
very own *Death in Venice*: inevitable, perilous as the asp at Cleopatra's
breast."

His heroine underwent several transmogrifications before reaching that glorified, if somewhat forbidding form. After rejecting Ann
Woodward as his model, Truman chose Pamela Churchill, whose

romances, particularly a long fling with Gianni Agnelli, had provided copy for two decades of gossip columnists: the "famous international siren," Cholly Knickerbocker had titled her in the fifties. "We spent a lot of time on yachts together," said Truman. "Anybody becomes a confidant on a yacht cruise, and I think I've lived through every screw she ever had in her life. Believe me, that's an Arabian Nights tale of a thousand and twelve! She's interesting because she has fantastic taste and she knows everything about everything, but she has absolutely no intellectual capacities at all. She's some sort of marvelous primitive. I don't think she's ever read a book, or even a newspaper, except for the gossip column. I guess it's because she comes from one of the oldest families in England, the Digbys, and they figured they didn't have to learn to read or write.

"Pamela's a geisha girl who made every man happy. They just didn't want to marry her. Gianni really did want to, and she even converted to the Catholic faith and learned to speak perfect Italian —everything! But his family were just all going to throw themselves into some Venetian canal and drown if he married her. So at the last minute he married little Marella. Pamela was devastated, but I must say he gave her a very, very handsome settlement, including one of the most beautiful apartments in Paris I've ever seen."

Rose Grantwell was the name of Truman's Pamela-inspired siren, and about her he wrote in one of his early notebooks: "There are certain women, and a few men too, who, though perhaps not born rich, are born to *be* rich. By and large, these persons are artists of an odd variety; money, in astronomical amounts, is their instrument— they require it as a violinist requires a violin, a painter, paint. Without it, they are creatively impotent; with it, they fuse material elements—from food to fine motors—into fantasies that are both visible and tactile. In other words, they know how to spend dough; but in a manner that, while morally arguable, is at least aesthetically valid. The Duchess of Windsor is such a person; and so, to cite other examples from so-called 'real' life, are Mrs. Harrison Williams, Mrs. Paul Mellon, Mrs. Loel Guinness."

By the seventies, the image of Pamela had been largely erased. Truman now borrowed some biographical details for his new heroine from Cappy Badrutt, a charming American gold digger of the sixties and seventies who numbered among her husbands a scion of the Badrutt family that owned the Palace Hotel in St. Moritz. But his chief model for Kate McCloud was the aforementioned Mrs. Harrison Williams. Born shortly before the turn of the century, "Marvelous Mona," as the newspapers had called her, had been a swan of the generation that preceded Babe, Marella and Gloria Guinness. With her perfect posture and vast, exquisitely shaped blue eyes—she was, to Cecil's expert eye, "fascinatingly beautiful, like a rock crystal goddess"—she could stand proudly beside any of them. In the grandeur of her artistic design, her creation being her own incomparable self, she outshone them all.

She came from a modest but genteel Kentucky family, and when she was in her teens, her father was hired to run a Lexington horse farm for Harry Schlesinger, a rich man from Milwaukee. She had not given a second glance to the local swains, but when her father's boss proposed, she said yes immediately. She was too big for Milwaukee as well, and her marriage lasted only long enough to provide her with two hundred thousand dollars, a wealth of social connections, and a son, whom she left with his father after their divorce. She married and divorced again, and then, in 1926, landed the Croesus for whom she had been searching: Harrison Williams, a utilities magnate from Elyria, Ohio, whose fortune was estimated at close to seven hundred million dollars, the equivalent of several billion in today's punier currency.

Furnished at last with an endless supply of greenbacks, Mona sculpted a life of sublime and sumptuous beauty. She had the usual accouterments of the very rich: a yacht, a thirty-room house on Fifth Avenue, a mansion in Palm Beach, a hundred-acre estate on Long Island's Gold Coast, an apartment in Paris, and (not so usual) the Emperor Tiberius' cliff-top villa on the isle of Capri. But she also possessed a subtle taste and imaginative style, in dress, design and gardening, that very few rich people could comprehend, let alone imitate. Her all-white drawing room on Fifth Avenue was celebrated —she went so far as to place only white flowers in her white Chinese vases—and so were her gardens on Long Island, through which coursed rivers of irises, winding floral streams that gradually changed color, from a deep purple to a light violet, as they flowed toward her doorstep.

How well Truman knew her it is hard to say. He had dinner at her Fifth Avenue house at least once in the forties, and he probably saw her on other occasions. Not that it much mattered: what he did not observe for himself he could have read in newspaper or magazine accounts; and what the reporters had not ferreted out he undoubtedly heard from Cecil, who had stayed with her many times. However he learned about it, her history had the storybook quality that excited Truman—she was *his* kind of scheming Cinderella—and with her image before him, along with isolated features of Cappy Badrutt and other women he had known, he constructed Kate McCloud.

He gave his Kate a similar background. Kate's father was the head groom of a horse farm in Virginia, and when she was a child, she was taken up by the owners, the McClouds, who tutored her in the ways of rich folk. Then, when she was only sixteen, they married her to one of their sons, who was, like Mona's first husband, named Harry. But even at sweet sixteen, Kate was thinking far ahead, beyond the McClouds, beyond Virginia, beyond even her native shores. After divorcing Harry, she moved to France and became a decorative fixture of the international set. No one could withstand her charms; at parties in St. Moritz, the Shah of Iran always asked to have her seated at his table. But Truman's Kate was not an angel. "Christ," says P.B., "if Kate had as many pricks sticking out of her as she's had stuck in her, she'd look like a porcupine." When she married again, it was to Axel Jaeger, the richest man in Germany, perhaps in all of Europe.

Something went awry in her second marriage too—Truman does not say what—and less than a year after she gave birth to a son, her new husband booted her out of their Swiss château, keeping their child for himself: her Croesus was not as amiable as Mona's had been. As Truman's plot starts to unravel, she is thinking about kidnaping the boy, Herr Jaeger is planning her murder, and P.B., the Hershey Bar whore, is about to become her paladin. At that pregnant moment, "Kate McCloud" concludes.

The reaction to those first two chapters in no way matched the fire storm that had been ignited by "La Côte Basque," of which, six months after its publication, *Esquire* was still receiving forty requests a day for copies. "Gossip-mongers may be a little disappointed in this latest offering," reported *Women's Wear Daily* after "Unspoiled Monsters" appeared. Most of the talk centered on Kate McCloud: who was Truman's heroine supposed to be? The names thrown out included Lee Radziwill; Babe Paley; Denise Hale; Gloria Guinness; Pamela Harriman; Fiona Thyssen, the New Zealand–born, titian-haired ex-wife of a German steel tycoon; and even Lally Weymouth, Kay Graham's tall and spindly daughter. No one mentioned Mona Williams, who was now the Countess Bismarck and who, at the age of seventy-nine, was happily tending her gardens on Capri; no one talked of Cappy Badrutt, who was still busily collecting diamonds and similar expressions of affection from Continental sugar daddies.

The few critical press comments were divided along surprising lines. In the resolutely radical *Village Voice*, James Wolcott accused Truman of "pornographic obsessiveness"; on the other side, columnist Max Lerner was full of admiration. "The narrative flows like a swift stream after a hurricane and flood," Lerner wrote in the *New York Post*, "and you are swept along with it and with all the detritus of life—the cruel, the funny, the mock tragic, the merely decadent. It is a garish world he displays to us, as if he were the Saint-Simon of our times, writing the annals not of the Court of the Sun God at Versailles, but of New York and Paris, of the salons and hotels and the Left Bank. 'This is how it was,' he seems to be saying to later generations."

Although gossip-mongers may have been disappointed by the absence of society names, the *Esquire* headline for "Unspoiled Monsters" was not wrong: Truman had struck again, albeit at different and, from the viewpoint of *Women's Wear Daily*, less interesting targets, writers and artists like Tennessee Williams, Katherine Anne Porter and Ned Rorem.

Most furious was Tennessee, who was the unmistakable model for the hilarious Mr. Wallace, one of the clients of P.B.'s call-boy service, who is not so much interested in sex as he is in hiring someone to walk his English bulldog; the floor of his Plaza suite is so littered with dog feces that P.B. slips on one deposit and slides, headfirst, into a second. "This thing Capote has written is shockingly repugnant and thoroughly libelous," declared Tennessee. "Capote's a monster of the first order, a cold-blooded murderer at heart. He is a liar and everybody knows he is." Then, with the loony logic that endeared him to so many, Tennessee added the detail which, to his way of thinking, proved that Truman had fabricated the whole episode: "I never had an English bulldog, or any other kind of dog, in the Plaza Hotel."

Porter, who was now in her mid-eighties, was just as displeased at finding herself disguised as Alice Lee Langman, the sex-hungry "grande mademoiselle" of the cultural journals. "I didn't read his piece," she said, "but I read little scraps here and there, and they were all so unspeakably hideous and really low and base! Now he has attacked his artist friends. Apparently his life has turned to a kind of poison that he's spitting out over the world. I don't know why. He's had a pretty lucky time, and I think he's had what he wanted. I don't really like to think about him, or talk about him, because it's as if he belongs to another world, another planet."

Tennessee and Katherine Anne at least had the flimsy protection of pseudonyms. Rorem was pilloried by name. "A Quaker queer," Truman calls him, "which is to say, a queer Quaker—an intolerable combination of brimstone behavior and self-righteous piety." Rorem's response showed a little bit of both. "The more I think about it, the more offended I am," he said. "Truman takes very important people and can only say how ugly they are. All these extraordinary people and all he can talk about is sex! I don't really know what he's aiming at. I'm dismayed for him. He's on a merry-go-round and he can't get off. He's destroying himself. Where can he go from here?"

That no one can ever know: no more of his novel was ever found, and unless unknown manuscripts are one day discovered, all that the world will ever see of Truman's magnum opus is the one hundred and eighty pages that Random House published in 1987 as *Answered Prayers, The Unfinished Novel*. If they do not make up the book he had planned, however, those pages, which contain some of the best writing he ever produced, do at least comprise its foundation and give a few clues to the shape of the rest of the structure. Like other unfinished novels—Dickens' *The Mystery of Edwin Drood*, for example, or Fitzgerald's *The Last Tycoon*—the abbreviated *Answered Prayers* is tantalizingly incomplete. Yet, like them, it is substantial enough to be read, enjoyed and, to a limited degree, judged on its own merits.

Even in its imperfect state—to paraphrase Edmund Wilson's comments about *The Last Tycoon*—it is Truman's most mature piece of fiction. In *Other Voices, The Grass Harp* and *Breakfast at Tiffany's*, he had manipulated small casts on small stages; with few exceptions, his major protagonists were adolescents, either in fact or in spirit. In *Answered Prayers*, by contrast, he was telling a large, sprawling story that spanned thirty years, moved between two continents, and included a vast and influential company of players. He was writing not only about the great world, but also about the people who sat regally atop it. He *was*, in short, attempting to do what Proust had done. "I want to say, 'Here. This is American high society in the second half of the twentieth century. This book is about you, it's about me, it's about them, it's about everybody.'

"I am not Proust. I am not as intelligent or as educated as he was. I am not as sensitive in various ways. But my eye is every bit as good as his. Every bit! I see everything! I don't miss nothin'! What I'm writing is true, it's real and it's done in the very best prose style that I think any American writer could possibly achieve. That's all my claim is, but it's a pretty high claim. If Proust were an American living now in New York, this is what he would be doing."

Such a boast, widely and imprudently broadcast, was widely ridiculed, both by those who had read Proust—a thin minority, it seems safe to suggest—and by those who had not. But his claim had some merit, and what the skeptics overlooked was that his twenty years of hobnobbing with the rich had in fact given him unique credentials. No other major American writer since Edith Wharton had been so well positioned, and he was no more than telling the truth when he asserted: "I am the only person in this country who could write this book—the only person. Nobody else knows the people, nobody else has the experience and the knowledge, and nobody else has the gall. My whole life has been spent developing the technique, the style and the nerve to write this thing. It is the *raison d'être* of my entire life."

That he had done the kind of reporting Proust had done no one can legitimately dispute. Whether he could have turned that knowledge into a novel of comparable stature is the question. The likely, though not final, answer is that of course he could not have—no one could have. Proust was a genius, and *Remembrance of Things Past* is the twentieth century's supreme work of fiction (and probably its longest as well: 1,240,000 words and seven fat volumes in the English translation). It is and doubtless will remain an unscalable monument. The more appropriate answer is that it was a ridiculous contest to enter and that it had been foolish of him to so much as whisper Proust's name. He had gifts and skills of his own, and even if he failed to write a novel of Proustian dimensions, he nonetheless could have written a book of great power and vitality: that much was within his grasp. But he wrote neither, and *Answered Prayers*, his *Remembrance*, can never be more than a fascinating fragment of real but uncertain promise.

If their achievements were not equal, their attitude toward their privileged subjects was, and it is easy to understand why Truman considered Proust to be his secret friend. Both had started out with their noses pressed against the glass, watching with lovesick wonder the radiant creatures who paraded through the golden rooms within. Overcoming severe handicaps, both had been welcomed inside. And like all those who cherish impossible illusions, both had become disillusioned; they felt that they had been robbed of their dreams. Proust's titled aristocrats and Truman's swans and peacocks were, on close examination, no better than their servants. To the contrary, they were often far worse; bound by neither ordinary financial nor moral restraints, they were denied no sin. Theirs was the "kingdom of nothingness," Proust eventually decided, and in the final volume of *Remembrance of Things Past* he conducted what one scholar terms a "ruthless judicial inquiry," convicting them all for being mean, base and boring.

Answered Prayers is a similar inquest, which would have resulted —so much seems apparent—in similar indictments. With one eye Truman had worshiped his rich friends; with the other, the eye of P. B. Jones, he had coolly recorded their shortcomings. Long before they rejected him, he, or at least one part of him, had rejected most of them. As early as 1965, after spending a few days in St. Moritz with the Agnellis and their friends, he had written Cecil, "It was kinda fun. But what a silly lot they are really." Those who believed themselves betrayed by "La Côte Basque" had not been wrong: he had been a fifth columnist. "They assumed that I was living by their values. Which I never was. It's as though, by writing that, I was saying to them: 'Everything you lived for, everything you did, is a lot of shit!' Which is true! I *was* saying that!"

What the completed *Answered Prayers* would have been like can only be surmised. Still, the first two chapters, combined with his own comments, give some indication of what he wanted to do and where he wanted to go. His narrative structure was to be cinematic, shifting back and forth between present and past, with many digressions. "It doesn't occur to you until halfway through where the book is really going," he said. "The second half just goes z-o-o-o-m, which may be a fault: the acceleration is almost too severe. That's why I'm doing all of these little diversionary things."

"Mojave" turned out to be too much of a diversion, and he removed it, as, in the end, he probably would have dropped "La Côte Basque." Some of the chapters that were to be added included "A Severe Insult to the Brain," "And Audrey Wilder Sang," and "Yachts and Things." Comparing the key chapters to a gun, he wrote, in a note to himself, that "Unspoiled Monsters" was to be the handle that held his plot, "A Severe Insult to the Brain" was to be the trigger that set it off, "Yachts and Things" was to be the barrel through which the bullet traveled, and "The Nigger Queen Kosher Café"—the final chapter—was to be the bullet itself.

Denham Fouts tells P.B. about the Nigger Queen Kosher Café in "Unspoiled Monsters." It is, in Denny's dope-induced reverie, a kind of Shangri-la for those who, like him, have lost all hope. "There it is," he tells P.B., "right where they throw you off at the end of the line. Just beyond the garbage dump . . . The Nigger Queen Kosher Café! The cool green, restful as the grave, rock bottom!" Consciously or not, Truman was returning to the site of *Other Voices* and the molding, swamp-enclosed Cloud Hotel, the "place folks came when they went off the face of the earth, when they died but were not dead." *Answered Prayers* was to conclude and P.B. was to find his own cool green in Azurest, a real black beach community not far from Truman's own house in Sagaponack. Alone among his books, he promised, *Answered Prayers* would have a happy ending.

He planned to pattern that ending after the final paragraph of Lytton Strachey's biography of Queen Victoria, in which Strachey imagines the dying queen unconsciously calling up visions from her past: a wood full of primroses, her long-dead husband standing before her in his blue-and-silver uniform, rooks cawing a raucous lullaby in the elm trees at Windsor. "Strachey's ending is the most beautiful I've ever read," explained Truman, "and I said that I would use it someday. Mine is just as good. It's like leaves falling gently from a tree. I could probably do without it, but I feel that I have to end the book with peace, to bring everything to rest, as I did with *In Cold Blood*."

Those were his plans, and he talked as though the projected chapters were inscribed so vividly in his mind that putting them on paper was only a minor matter, like dusting off a car as it rolls off the assembly line. "I have it written in my head to such a degree that I could finish it tonight," he impatiently exclaimed after the appearance of "Kate McCloud." In June, 1977, he said that he had just completed "A Severe Insult to the Brain." Nearly a year after that he confided that he was still polishing it. "I think there's something wrong with a paragraph and go over it again and again, word by word. But even the most sensitive reader wouldn't be able to tell that there's anything wrong. I have an obsession, like those people who are always washing their hands or cleaning their houses." But neither "A Severe Insult" nor any other unpublished chapter was found among his papers after his death. Had he destroyed, lost, or hidden them? Or had he never written them at all?

The answer is unclear, but if he did write more than was printed in *Esquire*, he almost certainly did not write much more. Indeed, his own contradictory comments confirmed that he had lost his way. He could not even make up his mind whether he was writing a long or a short book. Each year he gave a wildly different estimate of its length: eight hundred pages, then six hundred, then three hundred; later still, two volumes of four hundred pages each. "I see it much more clearly now," he said in 1979, in a tired and unpersuasive voice. "I didn't know it, but it was a little fuzzy about the edges before."

He had given up on *Answered Prayers*, but he was too proud to admit it, even to himself. One summer afternoon in 1983, over drinks in Bridgehampton, he came close to confessing his failure. "Writing this book is like climbing up to the top of a very high diving platform and seeing this little, tiny, postage-stamp-size pool below. To climb back down the ladder would be suicide. The only thing to do is to dive in with style."

THEY both knew that their relationship had no future, yet Truman and John could not stay apart for long. After Truman fled the Malibu house at the end of May, 1976, the date of their next rendezvous could have been predicted almost as precisely as the first day of autumn, and in late September Truman anxiously headed West again, right on schedule. This time his destination was not California, but New Mexico. John had suggested that their hopes of starting afresh would have a better chance if they met in a quiet spot, far away from Truman's celebrated friends, and Truman had chosen Santa Fe, where his old friend Mary Louise Aswell had found peace and contentment—her own Azurest.

They rented a house outside of town, Mary Louise gave them a welcoming party, and they attended a meeting of Alcoholics Anonymous, vowing their continuing sobriety alongside a grizzled old miner and three Indians. But John, who had been as eager for a reconciliation as Truman, had come under false pretenses. During the months they had been apart, he had found not only a new job, but also a new love, Joanne Biel, a female graduate student in philosophy at the University of Southern California. Every chance he saw, he sneaked away to cuddle with her on the telephone. It did not take long for Truman to realize that something was wrong, and finally, a week or so into their stay, John told him what was going on.

"Truman, I'm in love with this girl in California and it just isn't working for us," he said.

"But I came here in the expectation that we were going to make a life together," replied Truman.

"Truman, we've done that dance so many times we've worn it out."

"Yes, but now I'm going to be sober and everything is going to be straight."

"I have a feeling that once you do become sober, Truman, you won't even call me." Within hours they had again parted, Truman flying home to New York, John driving back to Los Angeles.

It was one thing for Truman to reject John, as he had done three times already; it was another thing for John to reject Truman. When he had recovered from his shock, Truman was swept up by the same cyclone of anger and resentment that had engulfed him after Danny had left him and after John had gone swimming with his playmate in Key West. He wanted revenge, but as he had already deprived John of his family, his house, his job—even his dreams—what more could he do to him? Rick Brown, who was once again tending bar at the Club 45, had the answer: a muscular friend who, for a fee of ten thousand dollars, promised to break John's arms, legs, or any other bones Truman wanted fractured.

Truman was enthusiastic, but Rick soon had second thoughts. "If you do this, it's going to be like a disease," he warned. "If you do it once, you're going to do it again. Why don't you just save the money and drop the whole thing? Say: 'All right, I got beat and that's it.' We've all been beaten. It happens to everyone. So forget about it! Go out and find yourself another man-friend! Write this one off to experience." Fortunately for John, the bone-crusher became convinced that Truman was too unstable to keep their arrangement secret, and he backed out before Truman could make up his mind. If he could not have the satisfaction of hearing John's bones cracking, however, Truman at least wanted to hear howls of anger, and after several days of nagging, he finally persuaded Rick himself to go to California. "I want you to find this guy and punch him in the nose, break his glasses, destroy his car—whatever" were his instructions as he sent Rick off.

"I found the building," Rick soon reported.

"Oh, thank God!" said Truman, who had been waiting nervously by the telephone.

"And I know which is his window."

"Ohhhh," sighed Truman, who seemed to regard that as a discovery worthy of Sherlock Holmes.

But Rick would not punch John in the nose or break his glasses, and after three days he returned to Manhattan. If Truman really wanted him to do John some serious damage, Rick said, he would have to give something in return: his help and name as the coauthor of a horror movie Rick had been working on. "Fine, fine," said Truman, and after recruiting a giant-sized Navy buddy, Rick headed west again. "We're going to find a guy and beat him up with a baseball bat," he told his friend. But even with that intimidating hulk at his side, Rick's heart was not in the maiming business, and he and his companion were no more of a threat to John than Joanne Carson and Myrtle Bennett had been to Danny. Following Truman's directions, they did nothing more destructive than pour sugar into the gas tank of his car, then, like those earlier saboteurs, beat a quick retreat. It was not much of a revenge, but for the moment it seemed enough to satisfy Truman.

It was not enough, however, to stop him from sinking into perhaps the darkest depression he had ever known. "Johnny was the great love affair of my life," he lamented. "I keep saying he's out of my system, but he's not. I know the best thing would be for me to forget him. But I can't do that." Forgetting the lessons of the Connecticut clinic and the pledge he had made at the Alcoholics Anonymous meeting in Santa Fe, he drank more than ever. A fall during one drunken spell resulted in a bloody head and cracked teeth, and Rick was pressed into service once again to drive him to Miami for several weeks of rest and repairs.

Jack was usually not around on such occasions, escaping, as much as he could, to Sagaponack or Verbier. It would be unfair to blame him—living with an alcoholic requires more-than-human patience —and it is possible that his absence may have helped more than it hurt. When Jack was around, he tended to nag and lecture and hector, which only added to Truman's guilt and anxiety; and Jack sneered at clinics and Alcoholics Anonymous. Instead of relying on such aids, he maintained, alcoholics would do better to study the spiritual exercises of Saint Ignatius Loyola. Yet if it would be unfair to blame him, it would be fair to say that Jack did not offer Truman much emotional support during his alcoholic years, most often leaving it to others, Rick among them, to put him into hospitals and to look after him when he came out.

On his return from Florida in November, Truman sought the aid of two psychoanalysts, one male, one female. But neither did much good. Ten days before Christmas, 1976, he invited a friend to lunch at Quo Vadis. He wanted to talk, and through lunch, drinks and dinner, he kept his guest a virtual prisoner at their prized banquette near the entrance; then, as the restaurant emptied for the night, he dragged him to a bar across from the U.N. Plaza for still more drinks. For twelve hours Truman's monologue continued, as he spoke of his apparently unquenchable despair and explained why, at the age of fifty-two, he was contemplating suicide.

"Every morning I wake up and in about two minutes I'm weeping," he said. "I just cry and cry. And every night the same thing happens. I take a pill, go to bed and start to write or reread something I've written, and suddenly I start to cry. There's just so much pain somebody can endure. How can I carry it around all the time? The pain is not about any one thing: it's about a lot of things. I'm *so* unhappy. I just have to come to terms with something. There is something wrong. I don't know what it is, and I don't think any of these jerky analysts know either.

"Because of my childhood, because I always had the sense of being abandoned, certain things have fantastic effects on me, beyond what someone else might feel. That's why people who I know love me, like Slim Keith, like Babe, like Marella Agnelli, are being stupid. They have a total misunderstanding of what it is I'm doing with *Answered Prayers* and why I'm doing it, and they're being very cruel. They don't know that what they're doing is cruel because they don't know that I spent three or four years of my childhood locked up in hotel rooms. I can name the people on one hand who really care about me and want me to see my way through my troubles. And though they're friends, even they have some vested interest in me.

"I can go three or four months without having a drink. And then suddenly I'm walking down the street and I feel that I'm going to die, that I can't put one foot in front of the other unless I have a drink. So I step into a bar. Someone who's not an alcoholic couldn't understand. But suddenly I feel so tired. I've had this problem with alcoholism for about fifteen years. I've gone into hospitals, I've tried Antabuse, I've done everything. But nothing seems to work. I keep thinking things will be right when I finish the book, when I dump Johnny O'Shea, or when I look beautiful. Well, the book is okay now—I can see the end. I finished with Johnny, and I dropped forty pounds. And things are *not* all right. I don't know what to do next.

"I've asked myself a thousand times: why did this happen to me? what did I do wrong? And I think the reason is that I was famous too young. I pushed too hard too soon. I wish somebody would write what it's really like to be a celebrity. People come up and ask me for autographs in airports, and I give them 'cause otherwise I think they'll hit me over the head. On Long Island they drove right into the driveway last summer—the gate didn't stop them—and some car broke Maggie's jaw and ripped her stomach open. Celebrity! All it means is that you can cash a small check in a small town. Famous people sometimes become like turtles turned over on their backs. Everybody is picking at the turtle—the media, would-be lovers, everybody—and he can't defend himself. It takes an enormous effort for him to turn over.

"I feel that I should make this great effort with Dr. Kleinschmidt [his male analyst]. But I don't have a lot of confidence in analysis. Kleinschmidt is so serious. I sometimes sit there for ten minutes and I don't say a word to him and he doesn't say a word to me. He did say one thing to me and that was: 'I don't think that this guy O'Shea is responsible for your problems. You're using him as a red herring because you don't want to finish your book.' But I had known that all along. I don't want to finish because finishing is like dying. I would have to start my life over again. He also said, 'I think that you are going to kill yourself. It's the number one thing on your mind.' I never heard of an analyst saying that to a person, but the awful part about it was that it was true! I hadn't realized how often I had talked to him about pistols. I have a .38-caliber pistol in a drawer, and it's fully loaded. I also got prescriptions for Tuinal from him and from four or five other doctors, and I've saved them. I now have enough Tuinals to kill fifteen people!"

So it continued, his catalogue of despair, through that December afternoon and night. Finally, around midnight, Jack, who had been searching the First Avenue bars, burst in to escort him home. "It's time to go, Truman," he commanded, so impatient that he prevented him from signing an autograph for a waiting prostitute. Insulted, she seemed prepared to give battle; Jack took no notice. "Come on!" he barked. *"Tout de suite! Tout de suite!"* Truman meekly obeyed, looking like a guilty boy who had been discovered in some forbidden pleasure. A week or so later he spent a few days in the detoxification unit of Manhattan's Roosevelt Hospital. But, as he had wearily observed, nothing worked, and almost immediately— on New Year's Eve, in fact—he suffered an alcoholic blackout and disappeared on his way home from a party. When he returned to his apartment the next day, he was unable to say where he had been or what he had done.

At the end of January, 1977, he followed Jack to Switzerland and entered another clinic, where Jack visited him twice a day. In a letter to a friend, Jack contrasted the melancholy mood of those days to that of their first night in Verbier: "No! It was not sixteen yrs ago, but six hundred yrs ago. Indeed, it wasn't at all. It was another world, another life, and we were all brave and warriors in it, and we were assuredly going to live forever—forever young!"

His energies partly revived by his weeks in Switzerland, on February 21 Truman returned to Manhattan and the question that still dominated his thoughts: how could he get back at John? The answer soon presented itself. Since he had already separated John from his family, why not go one step further and take John's place as head of the O'Shea household? He would become like a husband to Peg and like a father to the youngest children, Chris and Kerry. (Brian and Kathy, the two oldest, had already left home.) It may well be that he never consciously spelled out such a devious plot; and it is true that he was also motivated by affection and a sense of responsibility to the O'Sheas. Whatever the reasons for his actions, the result was the same. He was the man to whom John's wife and children turned thenceforth when they wanted advice or help; John himself they dismissed with a derisive nickname—Mr. Wonderful. Could Truman have had any sweeter revenge?

He put Peg on the Bayouboys payroll again, at a salary of seven hundred and fifty dollars a month, and he began acting like a father to her children. When Chris, who was thirteen, was having problems in school, for instance, he invited him to La Côte Basque for a stern man-to-man talk. Worried that Chris was not being taught proper standards, he also sent him to an expensive summer camp in Colorado, where he bunked with the sons of millionaires. "It will let him know that there's a world outside of that awful suburb," Truman said. He cherished Chris's letter of thanks, and cherished it even more when he mentioned it to John, whom he could hear almost sniffling with jealousy over the telephone. Truman was enjoying the role of daddy.

But most of his attention was focused on Kerry, who, at sixteen, was blossoming into an attractive woman, tall and slim, with dark hair and lovely blue eyes—more clay for Pygmalion. "I've always wanted to be able to mold somebody like this, but the right person never came along," he said, thrilled by his unexpected good fortune. "Kerry is just right, so pretty, so natural, so intelligent."

Once again he concentrated on creating the woman of his dreams, and he planned Kerry's career as carefully as he had planned his own: first he would make her a model, then a movie star. But Kerry O'Shea was not the name for the goddess he was creating, and waving his hand as if he were Louis B. Mayer or Jack Warner, he gave her a new one. Kate Harrington he called her, borrowing the first name from Katharine Hepburn and the last one from Peg—Harrington had been her maiden name. Kerry liked her new name's elegant sound, and she was known as Kate Harrington from then on. Truman had not only assumed John's place; he had also erased John's name from his favorite child: he might just as well have rechristened her Kate Capote.

The first part of Truman's scheme to make Kate a star had met with some success. He had persuaded Dick Avedon to photograph her and one of Manhattan's top modeling agencies to represent her. At the end of April he began the second phase of his campaign and took the new Kate Harrington to California. Though he kept their presence a secret from John, he trumpeted it to everyone else. In his *Hollywood Reporter* column, George Christy reported that at one fancy gathering "there was news of Truman Capote arriving in town, with 17-year-old [sic] Kate Harrington who he believes will be a smash in films (Kate's the daughter of Truman's great friend, John O'Shea)." Helping him out, Carol Matthau gave a party at which he showed Kate off to thirty or so of his California friends, a group that included Johnny Carson, Robert Wagner, Cybill Shepherd and Irving and Mary Lazar. It appeared as if all of Hollywood had turned out to see her, and Truman could not restrain himself from bragging: "Kate does have a quality, but if it wasn't for me getting all these people together and pushing her, she would be just another girl out of a doughnut factory."

He spoke too soon. As his disasters with Lee should have taught him, even he, huff and puff as he might, could not make a Hollywood star. In fact, he could not induce Sue Mengers, the agent who handled some of the biggest—Barbra Streisand, Ryan O'Neal and Mick Jagger—to take Kate on as a client; Mengers relented only enough to invite the two of them to a celebrity-packed dinner at her house in Bel Air. Truman had neither the will nor the strength to do much more, and he spent much of his stay in his bed at the Beverly Wilshire Hotel. Propped up on several pillows and with a bottle of vodka by his side, he said: "I'm a compulsive, and compulsives have enormous amounts of energy for several days at a time. Then they collapse. I'm also an alcoholic. I've tried to say I'm not, but I am, I am—I am because I'm so unhappy. I'm going insane and nobody can bear to watch somebody going insane. Jack can't. Even I can't."

Even during their worst days, Truman and John had remained in touch: they were compelled to talk to each other, if only to trade insults. At the end of May, just three weeks after his return from California, Truman received a five-page letter in which a dispirited John described the downturn in his fortunes since Santa Fe. Without a job again, he was living on unemployment benefits, in a shabby apartment filled with shabby furniture; as a fitting emblem of his misery, he noted that his color television set displayed only a black-and-white picture. His message was crude but clear: he was broke and needed money.

Turning those pages over and over, Truman nonetheless searched for other meanings; "he was talking about that letter last night as if it were something from Saint Paul," grumbled Jack. At the beginning of July, apparently having convinced himself that those mercenary words constituted a love letter, he traveled West, and he and John set up housekeeping in an apartment in Santa Monica. Truman later set down his version of what happened in the painful months that followed.

"When Mr. O'Shea came to see me at the [Hotel] Bel-Air in early July, he used all his wiles, con-trick gifts to convince me that he was now a changed person and had only my welfare at heart and deeply regretted that he had ever caused me so much distress. I should mention that at this time I wasn't truly in control of my emotions or mental processes; I was not functioning in my normal manner due to an overuse of alcohol and sedatives."

Unlike previous reunions, there was not a hint of a honeymoon this time. As Truman should have realized from John's letter, John's first concern was money: he needed cash not only to live, but also to pay his tuition at UCLA, where, his ambition leaping over his ability, he was studying to become an English professor. John's request for dollars was disconcerting enough; far more distressing was Truman's discovery that he was still secretly involved with Joanne Biel, frequently sneaking away to talk to her on the telephone or to visit her apartment. Bitter arguments ensued, and as so often before, more than once Truman sought refuge with Joanne Carson.

In August Truman interrupted their stormy summer with a trip to New York, returning to California in early September with twenty thousand dollars in cash. Their bickering resumed almost the minute John picked him up at the Los Angeles airport. "When we reached the apartment, I felt so weak and nauseated I fell on the bed and almost went to sleep. Almost, but not quite. I watched him expertly ruffle through my luggage. When he found the manila envelope containing the $20,000 he glanced at me sharply; I pretended to be asleep. He looked at his wristwatch; it was about 1:00 pm. He tucked the envelope with the money under his arm and on his way out of the room he stopped at the closet where I had hung the suit that I was wearing on the plane. He took my wallet out of the pocket; there was a little more than $500 in it. He took $300. He also tore several checks out of my check book. Then he left the apartment. I was not surprised. He had done things like this before. He knew that I was ill and helpless. I knew it, too; and also that I had become in some mysterious, psychological way, dependent on him. But what I felt most was: I felt I was in very great danger."

John was usually away from 8 A.M. until late at night, ostensibly pursuing his studies. Sometimes he would also tiptoe out of the apartment at 2 or 3 o'clock in the morning, drive away and return ten minutes later. "At last I figured it out," Truman said. "He took these quick night drives to check on Miss Biel, see if her windows were lighted or if any strange cars were around. He was insanely jealous—and I mean that literally. The few times we went to a movie or restaurant, he would disappear for half an hour. I never bothered to ask where he had been. I knew he had been talking on the telephone, arranging some assignation.

"I felt I was losing my mind. I knew something was being planned, but I didn't know what. Gradually, I began to feel like the blind man in Vladamir Nabakov's [sic] novel 'Laughter in the Dark' —the blind man who is being tormented by a silent boy and girl: he knows they are in his house playing wicked pranks on him, but he cannot see them." On October 5, Truman packed and left for the last time, taking a taxi to Joanne's, where he drank himself into senselessness.

John's own account of those dark days was different—but with the exception of the disposition of the twenty thousand dollars, not necessarily contradictory. What should be said, to balance Truman's version, was that even while they were fighting, John was doing his best to wean him from liquor, taking him to AA meetings and introducing him to a helpful doctor, a member of AA himself. His efforts may have had some influence, because when he emerged from his blackout in October, Truman decided to kick, once and for all, his dependence on drugs and alcohol.

To do that, he made arrangements to spend a month at the Smithers clinic in Manhattan, an institution so tough and uncompromising that some of its successful graduates, like John Cheever, looked back on their stays there with profound dislike. The Devil's Island of alcoholism clinics, Truman termed it, and he seemed genuinely afraid that he might not survive the course. "He feels as if he's died already, and he wonders what he'll be like when he comes out," said Jack, who talked to him by phone. "He was so sad, so elegiac the other night. 'When we sat in Harry's Bar, it all seemed so innocent,' he said."

He was resolved despite his fears, and on October 12, the day before he was to leave Los Angeles, he asked Jack, who was on Long Island, to meet him in New York; he did not want to be alone on his last night as a free man. But Jack was not sympathetic, making it clear that he did not want to rush into town on a fool's errand. It was not a proud moment for either one of them, and Truman's half of their conversation, which Joanne recorded, sounds as poignant today as it must have sounded then: Truman believed that Smithers was his last chance, and he was begging for assistance. "It's always been my nightmare that I would go there," he said. "It's a real charnel house. I talked to John Cheever on the phone yesterday. He said, 'Listen, Truman, it's the most terrible, glum place you can conceivably imagine. It's really, really, really grim. But I did come out of there sober, and I have been sober for two and a half years.'

I've tried everything else," Truman added, his voice breaking into sobs. "I am really frightened about it. I feel that it's the end of everything. I've got to get all of this out of my system, because if I don't, nothing is ever going to work." Jack could not resist such a plea and he did drive into Manhattan.

Smithers was as tough as Truman had feared. "I hate this place," he said shortly after his arrival. "They wouldn't give you an aspirin if you had pneumonia." But he soon had to admit that the Smithers regime was working; for the first time in many years he found that he could get through the day without pills or alcohol. Overlooking their just-concluded battles, he and John planned yet another reconciliation after his release—a sober Christmas in Palm Springs.

That happy moment never arrived, and as the day of Truman's release approached, John grew more and more apprehensive, afraid that the cure had not taken and that Truman's drinking would threaten his own fragile sobriety. Finally, in his own words, he "freaked out" and ran away. When Truman called their Santa Monica apartment, he heard only a recorded announcement saying that the phone had been disconnected. A second call, to their landlady, informed him that John had vacated, taking everything with him. Still a third call, to his lawyer, Alan Schwartz, brought news of a farewell letter. Truman would be happier without him, John said— he was going off to live in the wilderness.

As if that were not enough, John himself phoned the U.N. Plaza the night of Truman's discharge, blaming him, as Truman told Joanne, for ruining his life. After they had hung up, Truman went out and bought a bottle of vodka, which he drank to the last drop. His month in Devil's Island had been wasted, and his post-Smithers abstinence could be measured not in weeks, or days, but in hours. In the game of revenge, John was now the winner.

Truman enacted most of the dramas of his life in public, and taking Peg and young Chris O'Shea along with him, he foolishly kept an engagement to speak the following day, November 13, at Towson State University, just outside Baltimore. Only after they had arrived at their hotel did Peg realize that the bottle he had hugged so tightly in the limousine had been filled not with Tab, as he had claimed, but with vodka. "I am an alcoholic, a genuine alcoholic," he announced to a local reporter, "not just a fake, phony alcoholic, a real alcoholic." As if to prove it, he tripped as he approached the podium; once there, he rambled aimlessly. "I'm not going to let this go on," said the man in charge, and Peg sent Chris to lead him from the stage. The next morning's headline in the New York *Daily News* read: "Is Truman's Song: 'How Dry Am I?' "

However much he had hurt John, John had always hurt him more, or so it seemed to Truman, and as if by reflex, once again he called on Rick Brown to come to his aid. Not only had John taken the twenty thousand dollars he had brought from New York, he told Rick, but he had also filched an unpublished chapter of *Answered Prayers*—the only copy in existence. The first complaint had some truth, although John contended that Truman had in fact given him the twenty thousand dollars as a kind of security deposit, to protect him in the event of another breakup. The second complaint was almost certainly untrue. Truman could not even remember what had been stolen, whether it was two hundred pages, as he originally asserted, or three hundred and twenty pages, as he claimed later.

Rick, in any case, was unmoved. "You deserve it!" he retorted when Truman had finished his list of charges. "After all that man put you through and you still moved in with him! You deserve everything that happened to you for being that stupid!"

"You never change," replied Truman. "You always put me down. You never build me up. Why are you so cruel?"

Rick nonetheless agreed to help. He located John's new apartment house, in the Westwood section of Los Angeles, and, climbing a tree across the street, peered into his second-floor window through binoculars. "I zoomed in and there he was, with his drapes open, walking around naked. He must have been impressed with himself." That description was all Truman needed to hear, and he briskly issued his orders: "Here's what I want done. I want his legs broken. I want his arms broken. Kick him in the back. Do whatever you think."

"How can you be talkin' like this, Truman? Let's be civilized. Why don't I just go up and say to him, 'Mr. O'Shea, I want to talk to you. You have Truman's things. I think it's best that you give them back.' "

"No!" said Truman. "I want to let him know that he's not fooling around with punks."

Again Rick agreed, deciding that a sound whack across the knees with a baseball bat might convey Truman's message. Twice he and a friend pursued John by car, but each time John eluded them with a series of U-turns worthy of a Hollywood stunt driver. Once, on Truman's instructions, they also heaved a brick onto his terrace, with a bullet and the name "The Avenger" (or some such) taped to it—"kid-shit stuff," as Rick admitted. When he heard the thud, John rose from his chair "like a bat out of hell," recalled Rick, and turned off the lights and closed the drapes.

Believing that Truman had persuaded a famous West Coast mobster to kill or maim him, John was terrified by such threats, juvenile or not. When Rick and his friend at last rang his bell, John was not inclined to let them in. "Mr. O'Shea," Rick said through the closed door, "I'd like to talk to you concerning a mutual friend of ours."

"About what?"

"It's a little difficult to talk here in the hall. Could you open your door? Or could you step out?"

"No. Is this about Truman?"

"Can we speak face to face?"

"No. I don't wish to discuss this anymore."

"You know, you son-of-a-bitch, you're going to be sorry you said that," yelled Rick, who, true to his word, went down with his friend into the building's underground garage. Jimmying open the door of John's 1974 Mercury, he doused some rags with lighter fluid, threw them onto the cluttered back seat, and lit them with a match. By the time Rick and his friend reached the exit, John's car was in flames. As he sat in his own car across the street, watching oily black smoke pouring from the garage and frightened tenants running through the lobby, Rick said to himself, "Oh, God, what the hell have I done?"

Afraid that Truman's hit men would get him, a panic-stricken John took flight, fleeing first to Las Vegas, where he bought another car, then to a beach community south of Los Angeles, and finally back to Santa Monica. Acting like a hunted man, he assumed an alias (Timothy O'Brian and Roger Sanderson Christie were among the names he used), kept his whereabouts secret, and had his mail delivered to a post-office box. They were all wise precautions. Prodded by Truman, Rick remained on the case and several times spotted him and gave chase, losing him in crowds or traffic each time.

But the explosion that had so thoroughly terrified John had had a marvelously soothing effect on Truman, who at last felt that he had given measure for measure. John now knew who was boss, and for the first time Truman was able to ignore his emotional plea, conveyed by a mutual friend, for still another reconciliation. "It's as if a boil had been lanced," Truman explained. "I feel very serene. I don't have any of that hysterical anxiety anymore. Everything is going okay." Then, his spirits restored, his hopes revived, he added: "I'm beginning my third act now. My first act ended with *Breakfast at Tiffany's*. My second act was *In Cold Blood*, which was a total switch for me. My third act will go on for the rest of my life."

Indeed, it did seem, during the winter and spring of 1978, as if a curtain were going up on a new, happier phase of his life. John's humiliation was the catalyst, but part of the credit for his resurrection must also go to the fortuitous reappearance of Bob MacBride, whom he had so callously dumped when he met John in 1973. Bob called him on some matter or other, they arranged a meeting, and Truman invited him on a vacation to Martinique. They got along better than ever, and from then on, wherever he went, Truman expected Bob to go as well. "Can't you find somebody younger for Truman?" Andy Warhol finally asked a public relations consultant, Joseph Petrocik, who, together with his companion Myron Clement, became one of Truman's closest friends during the seventies and eighties. "Truman is always getting himself involved with these old guys! They're not very attractive, and they're *so* dull!" But Bob's steady, sober, unexciting company was exactly what Truman required, a safe port after four and a half years of rough and perilous waters.

Although his days were not quite as sunny as he pretended, things were brighter than they had been, and for the first time in years Truman was able to speak with convincing optimism about the future. Trying to rejuvenate his much-put-upon body, he returned to the gym to which Rick had introduced him in the early seventies. Renewing his surroundings, he redecorated his apartment, giving away—in effect banishing—the portrait painted of him when he was in his thirties by Jim Fosburgh. A new purchase, a Texas rattlesnake stuffed with Styrofoam, expressed the sentiments of the older and presumably tougher Truman. Rising to an attack position in the center of his coffee table, it seemed to say, "Don't tread on me!" And like that angry rattler, he felt strong enough to strike at those who had snubbed him after "La Côte Basque," delivering, for example, a public and much-publicized scolding to one minor society figure, Nan Kempner, who dared to advise him about *Answered Prayers*.

For all the others who had lined up against him, he plotted a subtler revenge: he would deny them invitations to the wonderful parties he was already busy planning. First would come a series of small and elegant lunches in his dining room overlooking the East River. "My little raspberry room will become the most exclusive club in New York," he predicted. "If you get invited to Truman's, you will be really and truly, totally, utterly in!" Then, when the outs were beginning to regret having crossed him, he would cause mass hara-kiri, as he had in 1966, by giving what he called his "get-even party," a gathering grander than the Black and White Ball. March 21, 1979, the first day of spring, was to be the day of retribution. The place of honor was to be an indoor tennis court, which was to be decorated like a palace out of *The Arabian Nights*. The host himself was to be disguised in the humble robe of a poor peasant, revealing his true identity only by the huge emerald that would sparkle from his forehead, dazzling all those who approached his royal presence. "I will be the prince of all Araby," he said, "and you will all kiss my hand when you come in."

In the final years of the decade, that lovingly detailed but rather pathetic fantasy faded away, and most of his social energies were focused on a nondescript-looking former theater on West Fifty-fourth Street, inside which was what *The New York Times* called the "Oz of discos"—Studio 54. Discotheques had come and gone in New York since the sixties, but none was as popular as that palace of decadent pleasures, whose real progenitor was not its immediate predecessors, but the gaslit Moulin Rouge of the 1890s, the home of the cancan, Toulouse-Lautrec, and dozens of plump, pretty and available girls.

A birthday party for Bianca Jagger had set the tone: riding a white horse, she had been led around the dance floor by a huge black man, who was naked except for a covering of gold glitter. After that, anything went, so long as it was done with a similarly outrageous mixture of style and fantasy. Among the regulars were Disco Sally, a grandmother who loved to dance; Rollerena, a transvestite who endlessly circled the floor on roller skates; and two young men who showed up in different costumes each night—as cowboys one night, baseball players the next, and so on. "*Le freak, c'est chic*," said the words of a popular song, and in the late seventies and early eighties it was. When any sophisticated tourist returned home, whether home was Paris or Peoria, the first question put to him was: had he been to Studio 54?

"*Rendez-vous du High-Life*," the advertisements for the Moulin Rouge had read. "*Attractions Diverses*." And so, in the same words, might the ads have read for Studio 54, which glorified drugs—its symbol, emblazoned on a curtain behind the stage, was the man in the moon sniffing cocaine from a spoon—and which celebrated sex. The handsome young waiters, who wore nothing but silk basketball shorts, were frequently lured away by the customers, and almost every night at least a few people could be observed engaging in some form of sex in the marijuana-scented balcony.

"I've been to an awful lot of nightclubs, and this is the best I've ever seen," said Truman, who was so smitten with the place that he dragged Bob MacBride there two or three nights a week. "This is the nightclub of the future. It's very democratic. Boys with boys, girls with girls, girls with boys, blacks and whites, capitalists and Marxists, Chinese and everything else—all one big mix!" But Bob, who hated it, usually disappeared into the balcony, where, making a bed of his overcoat, he would fall asleep, blind and deaf to the frenzied cavorting around him. "When I was in the Navy, I used to sleep on the steel deck of a destroyer, with five-inch guns going off over my head," he explained. "So I can sleep anywhere." And there he would remain until Truman sent someone to fetch him.

Truman preferred the deejay's booth above the dance floor, a crow's nest from which he could see without being seen. "Isn't it too bad that Proust didn't have something like this?" he said. "Sometimes, when I'm sitting up [there], I think about all the dead people who would have loved 54. It's a shame they're not around—people like Ronald Firbank or Toulouse-Lautrec or Baudelaire or Oscar Wilde or Carl Van Vechten. Cole Porter would have loved it." Occasionally, he also joined others among the elite in the sanctum sanctorum, a fence-enclosed area in the basement, adjoining the boiler. "It was almost as if we were in jail, but at that time it was the most desirable spot in New York," recalled Bob Colacello, the editor of Andy Warhol's magazine *Interview*. "Now it seems sick, but it all seemed so glamorous then. Truman enjoyed it, but I think he wished that he could have gone to lunch with Babe the next day and have told her about what had gone on."

That was never to be, and as spring turned to summer, Babe's long battle with cancer approached its conclusion. When she did go out, it was most often to visit her sister and brother-in-law, Minnie and Jim Fosburgh, who, by a grotesque coincidence, were also—both of them—victims of cancer.* Babe had not forgiven Truman for "La Côte Basque," in any event. Chance once brought them together on a sick call to the Fosburghs, and for sweet Minnie's sake, they acted as if nothing had happened; but every so often Babe's eyes would meet his and tell him how things stood between them. "When she and Bill left, I pretended I had to make a phone call in the next room," said Truman. "I was afraid that if I went down in

* Jim Fosburgh died in April, 1978. Minnie followed in November, leaving Truman some mementos, a painting of a cat and a pair of pottery rabbits, which seemed to indicate that at least one of the three Cushing sisters had forgiven him.

the elevator with them, I would break down and begin crying. I do that sort of thing. Babe never did."

Yet Babe may not have been as implacable as she seemed; though he was never to know it, Truman may have achieved his goal of turning her against Bill after all. "My own feeling is that there was this weird undercurrent, which she couldn't admit to, of gratitude and a kind of perverse loyalty to Truman," said the art critic John Richardson, who saw her frequently in her last months. "She became very anti-Bill. She would always refer to him as Paley, seldom as Bill, and only in the most cruel terms. It may have been partly the outcome of the cancer—I believe that people who have it tend to take it out on the person closest to them—but I think it was also a consequence of 'La Côte Basque.' People used to talk about Bill as a philanderer, but his affairs weren't the talk of the town until Truman's story came out."

Bill was later to lament that "you understand much more about the value of a marriage when you've lost it," and only when she was dying did he seem to appreciate the remarkable character that lay beneath Babe's beautiful facade; only when it was too late did he appear to see what Truman had seen from the first. As she turned away from him, he turned toward her, making it not just his goal, but his mission to save her life. "I was determined to be the most knowledgeable man in the world about cancer, and I think I was," he said. Yet in the end, all his determination, his money and his power could do nothing but make her more comfortable than she might otherwise have been. "But it will take millions to take care of her at home," her doctors told him when she said that she wanted to leave the hospital. "That's all right," he answered, "I've got millions"—and he brought her home to their apartment on Fifth Avenue.

She died on July 6, 1978, having planned her own funeral, as she had planned everything else. Truman was not among those notified. "She always said to me, 'There's only one person in the world who could hurt me, really hurt me, and that's you,' " he recalled. " 'Bill can't hurt me. Betsey'—that was the sister she was slightly frightened of—'can't really hurt me. But you could really hurt me. You could do something. I don't know what it would be. But I know that you're the one person in the world that could ever really, really hurt me.' And apparently I did hurt her, bizarre and ridiculous as it seems. But because I loved her, she was able to hurt me too—out of loyalty to a man who was so disloyal to her. The tragedy is that we never made up before she died. And I never even went to her funeral . . . I never even went to her funeral."

Her death, combined with a long and unflattering profile of him in *The New York Times Magazine*, was enough to destroy the serenity he had boasted of at the start of the year. Ten days after her funeral he once again mortified himself in public, rambling incoherently on one of New York's morning TV talk shows. "What's going to happen unless you lick this problem of drugs and alcohol?" the host, Stanley Siegel, finally inquired. "What is going to happen to Truman? I'm sure you've thought about it." Truman certainly had, and to that question, at least, his reply was chillingly clear: "The obvious answer is that eventually I'll kill myself."

In New York, and much of the rest of the country as well, his appearance made headlines. "Drunk & Doped, Capote Visits TV Talk Show," reported that afternoon's *New York Post*, which followed up the next day with a savage cartoon: it depicted him as a sleepy-eyed bum, surrounded by hypodermic needles, piles of empty liquor bottles, and a book titled *Breakfast at the Bowery*. Television critics debated whether Siegel should have let him go on the air in his dismal condition. But no one disputed that the show had been riveting. "A talented man of considerable literary stature was making a fool of himself in front of 250,000 viewers," wrote *Newsday*'s John Cashman. "But, strangely enough, it was drama."

Truman himself could remember nothing of what had happened, and he was dismayed to hear about it when he returned to his apartment. "I can't even talk, I'm so upset," he said. "Ohhh, I feel so awful!" Trying to forget, he spent most of the night at a gay disco in SoHo with Liza Minnelli and Steve Rubell, one of the owners of Studio 54. The next day, July 19, he was in such bad shape that Bob MacBride checked him into a hospital. Afraid that he might return to his apartment and try to kill himself, Bob then went back and removed the gun Al Dewey had given him when he was researching *In Cold Blood*; dropping it into a paper bag, Bob carried it to Alan Schwartz' office. Informed that Truman was deeply depressed and suicidal, Jack, who was in Sagaponack, asked a friend to sit with him—he did not want to be alone. "I'm just shaking," he said. "I guess I wanted someone to do my job for me, and I had great hopes that MacBride would take care of him. I thought MacBride was a staff Truman could lean on. Instead, he's a wet towel."

In this instance, however, Jack was the wet towel, Bob the staff on whom Truman could lean. "I saw what that man is about under stress," said Joe Petrocik, admiringly. While Jack nursed his own anxieties on Long Island, Bob took charge in Manhattan, searching for a solution to what seemed to be a desperate situation. Finally, with the help of Winston Guest, C.Z.'s husband and also an alcoholic, he prevailed on Truman to enter Hazelden, an addiction-rehabilitation clinic fifty miles north of Minneapolis. When Truman seemed to waver—if Smithers had been Devil's Island, he moaned, then Hazelden was Alcatraz—Bob and Winston bundled him into Winston's car, virtually abducting him, Bob confessed, and drove him to the Guest estate on Long Island. Afraid that he still might back out, a few days later Winston and C.Z. drove him to the airport and flew with him to Minnesota.

To his surprise, Truman almost enjoyed his month at Hazelden, which was surrounded by woods and water and which, unlike Smithers, gave him a private room and freedom to wander around. "It's highly disciplined—they don't fool around—but it's not unpleasant at all," he admitted. "I've got my nerves back together and I've got a good attitude. Getting better is all in the attitude, actually. My head wasn't in a place to really work things out at Smithers; there were too many things hanging over me. Now I feel as if a hurricane had gone out to sea and that I'm on a kind of fresh beach." But the Hazelden treatment worked no better than the Smithers treatment. By the end of September, just a few weeks after his discharge, he was drinking so heavily again that Rick Brown, who accompanied him on a speaking tour of Western colleges, had a hard time keeping him on schedule.

"At Bozeman, Montana, he was so drunk that they had to drag him out of the plane," said Rick. "I hired a car to drive to the next stop—I didn't want him drinking on an airplane—but after a while he said, 'Rick, you'll have to stop so that I can get a drink.' Finally I pulled into a cowboy hangout. He went up to the bar and asked for a vodka and orange juice. When the bartender said they didn't carry hard liquor—they only had beer and wine—Truman pounded his fist on the bar and yelled: 'Beer and wine! I thought this was a tough place! And you call yourselves men!' I was afraid that those cowboys would kill him. But they just looked at him. I don't think they had ever seen anything like him before. When we got to Denver, he was so bored that on our first day he took me to five porno flicks, straight and gay both. We saw so many that I finally recognized a girl I knew."

Returning to Long Island in October, Truman once again was paralyzed by anxiety. "I'm followed by fear and terror, which hits my chest and then goes up to my throat," he said. "I think a lot—not just a little, but a lot—about killing myself. I'm obsessed with the idea of dying, and I wake up hoping that I will die. But what scares me is the fear that I might injure but not kill myself, that I might do terrible things to my brain with Tuinal, yet not die." Jack believed that he also saw death's approaching shadow. "You're looking at a dying man, you know" were his gloomy words to a friend. "I watch him when he's sleeping, and he looks tired, very, very tired. It's as if he is at a long party and wants to say goodbye—but he can't."

During the summer crisis Jack had also said: "Truman has surprised me before, and he may surprise others too. The tree may seem to have no more leaves on it, but who can say? There may be another spring." And so, miraculously, there was. At the beginning of 1979, in an almost exact reprise of the year before, Truman tried to break the destructive patterns of the recent past, to give himself a fresh start—indeed, a fresh face before the world. Within the space of a few months, he had a face lift, hair transplants and major work done on his teeth. "Why, Truman," exclaimed Andy Warhol, "it's a new same old you!"

This time his efforts seemed to succeed. Though he continued to pop pills and snort cocaine, a drug to which his friends at Studio 54 had introduced him, he was nonetheless able to stop the heavy drinking and reassert control over his life. "My recovery wasn't spontaneous," he said. "It was hard work. I had to go through hell to get there. It was all a question of being ready. I was ready—I always knew I would be—and things that had been impossible for me suddenly became very easy." One of those easy things was writing, and 1979 became perhaps the most productive year of his career. Nearly every day he descended fifteen floors to a maid's studio apartment he had rented in the U.N. Plaza, and there, safe from importuning visitors and the telephone, he scribbled in his notebooks and on his yellow pads. "I've never worked in such a concentrated way as I'm working right now," he said. "I write all the time, and I'm oblivious to everything else. I don't like to talk about it because it destroys the concentration, but bits of it will begin appearing very soon."

He had always been happiest writing short pieces, fiction and nonfiction alike, and some of the bits that followed were among the best works he was ever to produce: the years of self-abuse had not dulled his musician's ear for the rhythms and intonations of the English language. Most of the pieces were later collected in *Music for Chameleons*. They included the title story, which he published in *The New Yorker*; "Dazzle," a confessional story about his childhood yearning to be a girl, which he sold to *Esquire*; and ten pieces he wrote for *Interview*. Among the latter were a profile of Marilyn Monroe ("A Beautiful Child"), an anecdote about his chance encounters with a Soviet spy ("Mr. Jones"), an account of a day with an itinerant cleaning woman ("A Day's Work"), and *Handcarved Coffins*, which was a superbly executed novella-length thriller—his last major work.

The idea for *Handcarved Coffins* had come from Al Dewey, who several years before had told him about a series of bizarre murders in Nebraska—in one instance the inventive killer had used rattlesnakes to dispatch his victims. Truman followed the case by telephone and he may also have conducted interviews. But this "Nonfiction Account of an American Crime," as he subtitled it, was, nonetheless, mostly fictional. His homespun detective was not a real person, but a composite of several lawmen he had known—not the least of whom was Al Dewey—and Truman did not, as he indicated in the manuscript, play Dr. Watson to the detective's Sherlock Holmes.

Handcarved Coffins, like his other contributions to *Interview*, resembled a movie script, with long stretches of dialogue occasionally interrupted by passages of descriptive prose. In his hands such a structure was remarkably pliable and plastic, and he was so happy with the results—"there's not an ounce of fat on these stories," he boasted—that once again he claimed to have discovered a new art form: one that combined the techniques of film, fiction and nonfiction. It was such a radical advance, he said, that it made traditional storytelling obsolete. "It's a distillation of all I know about writing: short-story writing, screenwriting, journalism—everything. There is no future in the novel, so far as I can see. I'm trying to show where writing is going to be. I may not get there, but I will point the way."

In fact, he had discovered nothing but a renewed sense of self-confidence, and when *Music for Chameleons* was published in 1980, some reviewers said as much, dismissing his claim even while praising his achievement. It was not a glorious future he was pointing to, contended the British novelist John Fowles, but a glorious past, namely, the spare, tightly controlled stories of Flaubert and Maupassant. "I take it *Music for Chameleons* is a foretaste of what we can expect when *Answered Prayers* is finally rewritten and published, and I now look forward to it immensely," wrote Fowles in *Saturday Review*. "So also, I suspect, somewhere under a café awning on Parnassus, do Mr. Capote's three masters: Flaubert, Maupassant, and Marcel Proust (who must all have had a dry time of it recently). If I'm not quite sure yet that he will one day join them there, I think he begins, behind the froth and the brouhaha, the name-dropping and the backstabbing, the wicked penchant for recording how real people spoke and behaved, to make a serious bid for their company. And of one thing I am certain: Contemporary literature would be much, much duller and poorer without him."

Froth and brouhaha were as necessary to Truman as his art, however, and it was only to be expected that after several months of hard and steady work he began looking for some mischievous diversion. He found it, all too easily, in a collision with a once-treasured friend, Lee Radziwill.

Gore's libel suit against him (the result of the *Playgirl* interview in which he had alleged that Gore had been kicked out of the Kennedy White House) had been dragging on for more than three years, and there was no end in sight. From the outset Truman had expected Lee to come to his rescue and say that she had been the source for his story. But now, in the spring of 1979, he was startled to learn that without giving him so much as a hint, Lee—his love, his Galatea!—had done just the opposite. She had become a witness for the prosecution. "I do not recall ever discussing with Truman Capote the incident or the evening which I understand is the subject of this lawsuit," she had told Gore's lawyer.

Stunned, Truman indulged himself in another of his retaliation fantasies. Convinced that if the facts were ever made public, Gore would be so embarrassed that he would immediately raise the white flag of surrender, he secretly gave his copies of their depositions to

New York magazine, which in early June obediently printed long excerpts.

"It's all I can do to contain myself," Truman said, so excited that his words tumbled over one another into a long and almost manic monologue. "Until the magazine was actually on the press I could hardly breathe, but right now it is rolling down the chutes along with Gore's career. All along I knew that if people read these depositions, they would know that he was like Captain Queeg in *The Caine Mutiny*. Now they are about to explode and destroy his career. I will have the greatest single revenge in literary history. Nothing equals it. For the rest of his life he'll wake up in the morning and be happy for ten minutes—and then he'll remember what happened on that day in June. The humiliation for him! I love it! I love it! I love it! When he dies, they'll write on his tombstone, 'Here Lies Gore Vidal: He Messed Around with T.C.' "

Why had Lee turned against him? he wondered. Why had she testified in behalf of Gore, whom she disliked? "Why she betrayed me is one of the world's great mysteries, like those statues on Easter Island," he said. When his own call to her was not returned, he nagged Liz Smith into calling her and requesting an explanation. Liz did as she was bidden, and she gave him Lee's answer. "I'm tired of Truman riding on my coattails to fame," Lee had told her. "And Liz, what difference does it make? They're just a couple of fags."

If lightning had struck him, Truman could not have been more shocked. Through sleepless nights he had brooded, asking himself what he had done to offend her, but that was the one reply, probably the only reply, he had not imagined. Just a fag! He who had sacrificed months of his own work to help her become an actress; he who had foolishly gushed over her in countless articles and interviews. "I saved that girl's life, for Christ's sake," he asserted. But now, when he needed her, she ignored him: he was just a fag and therefore someone who, when he was no longer useful, could be discarded like a paper napkin.* No one could offer a credible explanation for her conduct—others were as puzzled as Truman was—

---

* Truman was not the only man Lee discarded that spring. In early May she had left her fiancé, San Francisco hotelier Newton Cope, standing—quite literally—at the altar, even as the wedding guests were assembling and the champagne was cooling in the ice buckets. Speaking of Cope and another ex-boyfriend, Peter Tufo, she said: "Why, no one would have ever heard of either of them if it hadn't been for me."

but a friend of Babe's, still angry about "La Côte Basque," thought that quite unwittingly, Lee had nevertheless served the cause of justice. "Truman did everything for Lee and got nothing," the friend said bitterly. "Babe did everything for him and got nothing."

Lee's "fag" remark changed hurt to rage, and Truman mapped out an attack on the "principessa," as he now derisively labeled her, slowly rolling that flavorful Italian word around in his mouth before spitting it out like a bad piece of candy. "If the lovely, divine and sensitive Princess Radziwill has such a low opinion of homosexuals, then why did she have me for a confidant for the last twenty years?" he demanded.

Throughout the first weekend in June he hatched his revenge, and on Monday, June 4, his plan ready, he arranged to appear on Stanley Siegel's TV show the following morning. If Lee thought he was just a fag, he said, he would do what fags are supposed to do: he would tell all, all of the stories she had told him over the course of those many years, all of her secrets, all of her love affairs, all of her feelings of resentment toward her sister Jackie. "When I finish with her tomorrow, the average rider of the New York subway system will see what a little cunt she is," he proclaimed. "She and her beloved sister had better have ambulances waiting and rooms reserved at Payne Whitney, because they'll be there for a long time. Believe me, you will never have seen anything like this."

Until late Monday night he rehearsed what he called his "crazy queen" act, so that when he went before the cameras, he would be, as he phrased it, "as calm as a *bombe glacée*." Then, early Tuesday morning, *The Washington Post*'s Sally Quinn met him in his apartment and rode with him to the television studio so that she could report the historic event. "A cassette of this show is going to be one of the great comic classics of all time," he assured her.

And in truth, the first half of his performance, which he gave in a thick Southern accent, did have a certain lunatic brilliance. "I'll tell you something about fags, especially Southern fags," he said. "We is mean. A Southern fag is meaner than the meanest rattler you ever met . . . I know that Lee wouldn't want me to be tellin' none of this. But you know us Southern fags—we just can't keep our mouths shut." Opening his own mouth very wide, he began revealing the secrets he claimed Lee had confided to him: how envious she was of Jackie ("The princess kind of had it in mind that she was going to marry Mr. Onassis herself"), how she had once tried to steal William F. Buckley, Jr., away from his wife, and how deeply she had been wounded by the breakup of her romance with Peter Beard ("He met this chick with a little less mileage on her"). He was just hitting his stride when Siegel, who was becoming increasingly nervous at the direction his monologue was taking, interrupted, destroying the mood he had so carefully created and causing his speech to sputter to a depressing conclusion.

Brought suddenly down to earth, he invited Quinn back to his apartment and repeated for her, without the histrionics, the rest of his diatribe, which she duly reported in her newspaper: how Jackie had supposedly told Lee that Lee owed everything to her, for example, and how Lee had had a crush on both Jack Kennedy and Rudolf Nureyev—although she had been taken slightly aback when she saw pictures of nude men in Nureyev's guest room. But most of all he confessed how hurt he was, and how keenly he felt the loss of one of his greatest friends. "Love is blind," he said with a shrug. "I've been in love before with people who were just ghastly. I was in love with her like I would have been in love with anybody." Why had she betrayed him? He believed he had belatedly deduced the answer: she was afraid of Gore, but she had thought that poor drunken Truman was going to die and that she could therefore disregard his feelings. "Unfortunately for Princess Radziwill," he said, "this fag happens to be alive and well and in New York City."

Having spoken so unwisely before, Lee now remained silent. Gore, always combative, did not. "This is pathology," he said. "Real nut-house stuff." If he had been devastated by publication of the depositions, Gore did not let on. Nor did he drop his suit, pursuing his complaint for four more years. It was finally settled out of court in the fall of 1983, when Truman wrote a letter of apology. "Dear Gore: I apologize for any distress, inconvenience or expense which may have been caused you as a result of the interview with me published in the September 1975 issue of Playgirl. As you know, I was not present at the event about which I am quoted in that interview, and I understand from your representatives that what I am reported as saying does not accurately set forth what occurred. I can assure you that the article was not an accurate transcription of what I said, especially with regard to any remarks which might cast aspersions upon your character or behavior, and that I will avoid discussing the subject in the future. Best, Truman Capote."

His furies exorcised, Truman retreated to Long Island after the

Quinn interview, and he returned to work, apparently unfazed by his week of melodramas. A little more than a week after the Siegel show, in fact, he was able to finish one of the best short pieces he was ever to write, his profile of Marilyn Monroe. So his days continued, productively and reasonably happily, during the months that followed, and he ended 1979—and the most troubled decade of his life—on a hopeful note of optimism. "*Music for Chameleons* will be just as good as *Answered Prayers*," he said. "It has in it everything I know about writing. It's the best I can do, and I want everyone to see that it's the work of a great writer. When it comes out next year, my friends are going to be very proud. I think we're going to win. In fact I know we're going to win."

Music for Chameleons had been the product of a supreme, almost heroic feat of concentration: he had wanted to make one last effort to show what he could do when he put his mind to it. Having done that, at the beginning of 1980 Truman surrendered to what he called "my demons." Unable to sit still, he darted nervously from place to place—to California, then Switzerland, New York and back to California. "I'm like a shark," he said. "The shark is the only animal that never sleeps. It keeps moving through the water, forever and ever."

He tossed off ideas for new projects with an energy no less scattered and feverish. One was a novella-length profile of Babe Paley, called *Heliotrope*, after the purple-flowered plant she so much admired. Another was an account of his friendship with Cecil Beaton, who died in January; *The Siamese Twins Visit Siam* Truman titled it, a reference to their 1958 trip to the Orient. For a time he also contemplated writing an autobiographical work about his alcoholic years with John, deciding in the end that their relationship defied his comprehension. "I don't think I'll ever write about what happened to me with John," he sorrowfully concluded. "I don't think I see the truth. What happened between us was too complicated, too idiotic. I could write it as a comedy, but it wouldn't be true, because there was nothing funny about it. But if I wrote it as something serious, it would be ridiculous. People would say that if this person O'Shea is really as dreadful as all that, then Capote must be a complete moron for having become involved with him."

For a year it had seemed that he had managed to escape that

complicated, idiotic relationship. But as the new decade began, it was clear that he had not: he was lost in a maze of multiple obsessions, a sunless labyrinth from which were excluded reason, understanding, sanity itself. Once more that most improbable of figures —an overweight, bombastic, and sometimes violent fifty-one-year-old alcoholic—occupied his dreams and dominated both his heart and his mind. "I told everybody I had forgotten about him, and I thought that I had," he said. "But I hadn't."

His excuse for starting up again was John's request for permission to sell his television script of "Children on Their Birthdays," a favorite story of Truman's youth which Truman, in happier days, had encouraged him to adapt. When Truman now refused to grant him rights, claiming that he too had written a scenario, John irately demanded that Truman send it to him—he would judge its worth. "If Truman feels that some of the material in his lately-written script has enough merit to be included in my script," he wrote Alan Schwartz on March 4, "I have no objection to appraising his version with the proviso that I will detail, in writing, precisely what items in his version which differ from my version, I might be interested in adding to my version."

Instead of laughing at such comical chutzpah, Truman was incensed. But what stuck in his eye was John's further statement that his greatest desire was to forget "the strange interlude of our former relationship." A hundred heartfelt pledges of love and devotion could not have reignited Truman's ardor more successfully than those few contemptuous words. Forget! Truman would tell him when he could forget! And so resumed his never-ending struggle to humble Charlie Middleclass. "My big mistake was in not following through after his car was destroyed," he said. "That really scared him. I should have had some guys take him out into the desert and beat him up. That would have fixed him."

Belatedly attempting to correct that oversight, he resurrected the hoary claim that John had stolen the "Severe Insult to the Brain" chapter of *Answered Prayers*. "I need those pages," he avowed. "I can't do without them. Every word was perfect. That chapter has the climax of the book, a real surprise that no one could guess, and I've always been afraid that John would show it to somebody who would give the secret away. It's a terrible thing he did, but then he's a terrible man. You think of the worst thing anybody could do—the absolute worst—and Johnny will do something three times as bad."

As John still kept his address secret, picking up his mail at a post-office box, Truman hired a Beverly Hills private detective, Joel Michael, to track him down and retrieve those precious pages. "Truman wanted to kill him, and I think he was deadly serious about it," said Michael. "His suggestion was 'Let's find him and do something.'" But John, who had played this game of hide-and-seek before, was not easy to find. Learning that he was once more being sought, he moved around so quickly that even a professional like Michael was hard pressed to locate him. The one time the detective did spot him, walking along Santa Monica Boulevard, John managed to lose him.

Eagerly following the hunt from New York and Long Island, Truman telephoned Michael late every night, Saturdays and Sundays included, to discuss possible leads. "After a time the manuscript became secondary to him," said Michael. "It was the chase rather than the catch that interested him. He loved the idea that O'Shea was running and hiding and that we had scared the hell out of him. What really excited him—you could hear it in his voice—was the thought that O'Shea was literally falling apart." That was not far from the actual fact, and on May 12, 1980, hoping to end the pursuit, John wrote Joe Fox at Random House to formally deny that he possessed anything "remotely connected" to *Answered Prayers*. If Truman claimed otherwise, John tartly advised, Random House should "consider the source, and refer to the expertise of Gore Vidal concerning T.C.'s veracity."

To refute that scornful indictment, Truman wrote a nineteen-page history of the events leading up to the theft nearly three years before: his weeks with John in Santa Monica, John's secret romance with Joanne Biel, and finally, Truman's horrified discovery that when he flew to New York to enter Smithers, he had left behind, hidden under the bed in their apartment, the manuscript John now denied any knowledge of. He ended his chronicle with an eloquent passage that might stand as the coda of his life. "I have been a writer and published a number of successful books during the last thirty-five years," he wrote, "but this book in question, 'Answered Prayers,' is my final contribution for having served fifty years as a supplier at the altar of art. Of art; but especially literature. This has been my life. I am a childless man and my works are my children."

Translating his emotional narrative into the arid wherefores and therefores of a legal brief, his lawyers filed suit in California Superior Court on July 8. They asked for the return of "A Severe Insult" and two hardbound ledgers containing his notes for the last half of *Answered Prayers*, and they demanded that John and Joanne Biel also pay him damages of four and a half million dollars apiece. Michael served Biel with a summons the next day. "She went into total hysteria, completely flipped out and denounced Johnny," chortled Truman, with considerable exaggeration. "It was like Humphrey Bogart and Mary Astor in *The Maltese Falcon*." But Michael was not able to give the elusive John his notice until July 16, when, staking out John's post office, he saw him open his mailbox. John too reacted hysterically when Michael approached him, bolting out the door and running into an alleyway down the block.

Though they did not know it, the detective and the lawyers had been working toward but one end: to force John back into Truman's arms. In that they were totally successful, and after his panic-stricken dash from the post office, John phoned Truman several times, trying to work things out. But that was not the end of Truman's triumph. During the course of his investigation, Michael had alerted California authorities to the false identity John had used on his driver's license, and John, foreseeing more trouble, prudently decided to seek his sunshine in Florida. Thus, almost inadvertently, Truman had turned John's life upside down again, compelling him to desert California and Joanne Biel as well.

Truman's lawsuit had served its purpose—and its only purpose at that. Soothed by their friendly chats and by John's pledge to meet with him, he agreed to drop his complaint (it was formally dismissed on January 14, 1981). "I don't think the manuscript exists anymore," he said. Then, all but admitting that in fact it never had existed, he added: "But now I don't think I want it. It would confuse me. I don't feel the same way about *Answered Prayers* as I once did. It doesn't matter so much now."

He had obtained what he wanted, but the long obtaining of it had driven him back to the bottle, and on the night of July 29, Jack woke to hear his thin cries floating across the lawn that separated their two houses in Sagaponack. "He had fallen on the steps of his studio—in his own pee, of course, with broken glass around him—and he couldn't get up," said Jack. "So I took him to Southampton Hospital, and he did say something honest. 'I drink,' he said, 'because it's the only time I can stand it.' "

· · ·

In accordance with the terms of their truce, Truman and John met in New Orleans on August 11. But the outcome was predictable. Truman was drunk—"gaga," to use John's word—as he stepped off the plane, and John, who had arrived a day earlier, was probably not much better. Believing, quite correctly, that he had been coerced into coming, John was even more belligerent than usual. In fact, they had not been together more than an hour in their suite in the Pontchartrain Hotel when, objecting to Truman's remarks about Joanne Biel, John grabbed him by his shirt and ordered him to shut up. It was Truman's turn to be frightened. After calling a doctor, he took to his bed and remained there almost to the day they parted, August 17. He was probably not much more sober when he left New Orleans than when he had arrived, and he ended the month, as he had begun it, in a bed in Southampton Hospital.

In September he flew to Los Angeles, ostensibly to monitor preparations for Hollywood's adaptation of *Handcarved Coffins*, the rights to which he had sold for three hundred thousand dollars* to his friend Lester Persky, producer of such hits as *Taxi Driver* and *Shampoo*. Once in his suite at the Beverly Wilshire, however, he rarely ventured out. Responding to a drunken, incoherent call, Rick Brown rushed over to find him in bed, lying naked in his own wastes, his legs caked with dried excrement. Rick gave him a bath, fed him— he had apparently not eaten for a couple of days—and made arrangements to move him to Persky's house in Bel Air. "Lester, this guy can't stay alone," he told Persky.

Setting up an informal rehabilitation clinic in Lester's guest bedroom, Rick worked out an elaborate schedule, which he posted on a chart, to slowly wean Truman away from both alcohol and pills. "I can't stop cold turkey," Truman had warned him. But after a week or so of Rick's increasingly spartan regimen, he rebelled, jumping on Lester's bed and shrilly screaming, "This is too much! You can't do this to me!" Lester, who suffered from angina, screamed right back—"get out of my room, both of you! I'm a sick man too!"—and ran into his bathroom to gulp down his heart medicine. "It was really very funny, like something out of the Marx Brothers," said Rick. "Even Truman started laughing."

Rick did not give in to his tantrums, and eventually Truman,

---

* He was to receive another fifty thousand dollars when filming began, together with a percentage of possible profits at the box office.

sober and pill-free, prepared to leave California. But a few days
before his departure he became so agitated that he begged Rick to at
least return his tranquilizers. "I'll give them to you, Truman," Rick
responded. "But first tell me what's bothering you." What was bothering him, Truman confessed, was that he was not planning to fly
to New York, as he had said, but to Jackson, Mississippi, where
John, making another detour on his journey to Florida, was temporarily living with his son Brian. Furious because all his hard work
seemed likely to go to waste, Rick immediately canceled the plane
reservation, and Truman meekly flew home to New York.

Back on Long Island in October, Truman was able to examine his
situation more clearly. "John's poison for me," he said. "I wish I
hadn't seen him in New Orleans. He always disturbs me." But that
moment of insight was fleeting, and without Rick to say no, he was
soon on the phone to John. In November they came together in
Miami, where Truman rented a luxurious apartment, twenty-six
stories above the sparkling waters of Biscayne Bay. "Am I right to
come into Truman's life again?" John asked Joe Petrocik, who came
to visit with his companion, Myron Clement. "What can I say?"
replied Joe, who, in truth, was appalled at the prospect. "I haven't
laid eyes on you in four or five years."

The answer to John's question was postponed until the new year,
and Truman quickly returned to Manhattan, where he had scheduled two weeks of readings over the Christmas holidays. Although
he had given readings in dozens of towns and cities, including New
York, he had never appeared where the stars shine brightest, on
Broadway itself. While *Music for Chameleons* was still fresh in people's
minds—still on the best-seller list, in fact*—he wanted to give a
series of readings on the Great White Way. "I don't want anything
that even looks like Off-Broadway," he loftily declared. After
months of talking with producers and looking for the right house,
small but prestigious, he chose Lincoln Center's elegant Mitzi E.
Newhouse Theater, and it was there that he read during the last
two weeks of 1980, from December 13 through December 28.

The appropriate pills could see him through anything, Truman

* Though collections of stories rarely do well, *Music for Chameleons* was a happy
exception; it surprised Random House by selling 84,471 copies and remaining on
the *New York Times* nonfiction best-seller list for sixteen weeks, from August 31
through December 21, 1980.

believed, and on December 1, two weeks before his readings were to begin, he moved out of his apartment and checked into Regent Hospital for the month, putting himself under the full-time care of one of the country's most prominent pill-pushers, Dr. Nathan Kline. A pioneer in the use of tranquilizers and antidepressants, especially lithium, Kline heartily shared Truman's devout faith in the powers of mood-altering drugs. What poor Truman did not know was that just days before he entered Regent, the Food and Drug Administration had all but defrocked his white-whiskered Dr. Feelgood, charging him with a "lack of regard for the safety of human subjects."

Truman was soon to make much the same complaint—Kline's drugs had nearly killed him, he would assert—but he was able to get through his two weeks of readings nonetheless. Dressed by Halston to look like the author in his library—he wore gray slacks, a gray cardigan, a gray silk shirt and black velvet slippers—he drew enthusiastic audiences. Mitzi E. Newhouse herself flew up from Palm Beach for the opening. "Tonight was one of the great things in my theater," she said proudly.

John flew up from Florida too, still wondering if he was wise to start up with Truman again. "It's very hard to explain, but Truman was a man who had difficulty making his life," he said. "I constantly told my hurt intellect, 'Don't get involved anymore.' " It was good advice, and they began bickering as soon as Truman came home from Regent. Within days Truman was seeking refuge with Joe Petrocik and Myron Clement. When John returned to Miami at the end of the first week in January, 1981, Truman spent a few days in a Manhattan hospital, then followed him South on January 14. "Remember, if something should happen to me," he reminded Joe and Myron, "you promised you'd get even with that Irish bog rat."

He was not joking. April Johnson, a journalist who had seen him in any number of emotional states, was surprised by a new one—he was afraid, obviously terrified of John. One night at dinner in her Coconut Grove house, he tagged along behind her like a clinging child; only when he joined her in the kitchen as she was cleaning up did she realize that he had been desperately trying to talk to her alone. "You've got to call me a cab!" Truman whispered. "I've got to get away from this man. He's going to kill me." While she phoned for a taxi, Truman slipped out the back door, sneaked around the side of the house, and met the cabdriver on the street. Soon noticing that he was missing—"I think he's outside," April vaguely said— John searched the yard. Coming back alone, John did not try to hide his chagrin at being so publicly embarrassed. "Drunken fool!" he bitterly exclaimed.

From April's, Truman went to a motel, where he hid for two or three days. Apparently he phoned John to come and get him, and it was probably then, on Saturday night, March 7, that John, to use his own words, "beat the shit out of him. I was in a titanic rage because he was leaving again—I'd had enough of that—and I just blew my cork. I'm always sorry when something like that happens; it hadn't happened in many, many, many years." Truman had even more cause for regret: he suffered a broken nose, a fractured rib, a cracked finger, and abrasions and bruises of the face, hands, chest and thigh.

Alarmed at the extent of his injuries, John made an urgent call to Dr. Harold Deutsch, Truman's doctor in Miami, who rushed from a formal party with his wife and another couple. When they arrived at the motel, they found Truman with John and John's son Brian, who was visiting from Jackson. Truman told Deutsch that he had been beaten by both father and son. (Brian later denied that he had been involved.) After setting his broken nose in his office, Deutsch, a plastic surgeon, put Truman into Miami's Larkin General Hospital for treatment of his other injuries.

Truman spent twelve days at Larkin, then returned to New York to report, unsurprisingly, that he and John had been fighting. Even so, he said, he planned to go ahead with the purchase of a new house they had agreed to buy on the peninsula's west coast, on Marco Island—"Florida's Fantasy Island," as its ads boasted. "In a way it's my revenge," said Truman. "It's the paradise Johnny's always wanted, and now he can sit down there and rot!" Providing his lover with a place in paradise was a curious definition of revenge, and such a transparent rationalization served only to underline the flat, desolate but invincible truth: no matter what John did to him, no matter how many wounds, physical or emotional, John inflicted upon him, Truman would cling to him as fast as to life itself. Indeed, his bruises had hardly healed before he invited John to spend Easter with him in New York.

A new factor, however, now intruded to further complicate their tangled relationship: Truman was beginning to suffer from paranoid hallucinations, the result, almost certainly, of too many doses of various prescription drugs. As they sat down on that Easter Sunday of 1981 for their holiday dinner at La Petite Marmite, a high-toned restaurant across the street from the U.N. Plaza, Truman squeezed John's hand affectionately. Then, his mood altering so swiftly that for a moment John thought he was joking, he said, "You have behaved unbehavedly." Repeating that odd and ungrammatical remark, Truman stood up, nearly knocking over a neighboring table. "You may finish your meal and I will pay for it," he said before stumbling back to his building.. "Then I never want to see you again."

Stunned, John followed ten minutes later, only to receive another shock when he entered the U.N. Plaza. Truman ordered the desk captain to evict him from his apartment. "Your trick didn't work!" he cryptically shouted in John's direction. Truman was still in the lobby, staring vacantly at the ceiling, when John angrily walked out with his bags and hailed a cab. By the time John phoned from the airport, Truman was back in his apartment. Remembering nothing of what had happened, he was dismayed to learn that John was terminating their happy holiday and flying back to Florida. "But what did I do?" Truman plaintively inquired. "What did I do?"

After John's return to Miami, Truman's hallucinations worsened. At 6:30 on the morning of April 24 he woke up the elderly couple who lived next door, begging for asylum from assassins who he said had invaded his apartment. Using their phone, he called Bob MacBride, who arrived on a scene of pathetic comedy. Wearing only a filthy bathrobe, which hung open to reveal his nakedness, Truman was drinking a large glass of his host's vodka and frantically trying to call Liz Smith at the *Daily News*. If she reported in her column the danger he was in, he said, the invading hit men would be forced to leave him alone—so powerful was his trust in the magic of publicity. Gently taking the phone away from him, Bob led him home and put him to bed.

When he awoke in the afternoon, calm and clearheaded, Truman startled Bob by remembering everything that had occurred and by agreeing that he had been the victim of a psychotic attack—in fact, he had been aware of it at the time. Even as he was describing the hit men, part of his mind had been aware that they were imaginary; but like someone who has been bound and gagged and helplessly watches while thieves ransack his house, that rational part had been unable to intervene. Though he had been afraid to tell anyone, he confessed to Bob, he had suffered similar attacks in previous days and weeks.

Before Bob's arrival that morning, Truman had also phoned Joe and Myron. Call Jack in Paris, he had beseeched them, and beg him to hurry home—he needed him. But Jack, who was planning to come home in three days anyway, refused, making no secret of his irritation at being bothered. His return did not help, in any event. Almost immediately Truman was on the phone to Bob again, pleading to be rescued from Jack himself, who he said was holding him prisoner and plotting to kill him. Increasingly disturbed, Bob confronted Jack a few days later in what was to be their first and last encounter. Truman's condition was so serious that he should go into a psychiatric hospital, Bob insisted, and all his friends, and Jack most especially, should join in pressuring him to do so. But Jack was offended by what he regarded as Bob's presumption and said he would do no such thing. "Where do you pick your friends?" Jack disdainfully asked Truman afterward. "Bellevue?"

Bob might have asked the same question. "I had always heard from Truman what a prince Jack was," he said, "and what did I find but this rather helpless, querulous old woman who had no idea what to do except fulminate against the evils of drink. Within five minutes he was even getting on me for drinking a cup of coffee and smoking a cigarette. All he did was complain about his own problems, that he had things to do, but that he couldn't leave Truman alone. 'Look, go ahead and do what you have to do,' I said. 'I'll watch Truman while you're gone.' As soon as he left, Truman, who had ostensibly been asleep, came tiptoeing out of his room and begged me to buy him a bottle of vodka. When I said no, he put on his clothes to go out and get it himself. At which point I stood in front of the door and said, 'Truman, you're not going anywhere. Get back into bed.' "

Frustrated by his failure to get anywhere with Jack, Bob wrote Alan Schwartz the next day and repeated his appeal for common action by Truman's friends. "It is my opinion that if T.C. does *not* get to a good doctor and a good psychiatric facility—not another drunk farm—he will shortly die, either by an overdose like his mother did, or by something more drastic. (The roof of UN Plaza is just a short elevator ride.) He is fully aware of this, and he is very worried about it." Bob had not exaggerated Truman's anxiety. On

May 14, Truman voluntarily checked into a rehabilitation center on the Hudson River north of Manhattan; in early June, he entered another clinic on Long Island.

Neither was the kind of psychiatric hospital Bob had recommended, and his hallucinations resumed when John accepted his invitation to come North again in mid-June. John had not been staying with him long before Truman again mistook him for an intruder. But this time, instead of calling Bob or the building's desk captain to help him, Truman phoned the police. The entire force, it seemed, was curious to see the inside of Truman Capote's apartment, and a squad big enough to subdue an army of terrorists was obligingly dispatched from the nearby headquarters of the Seventeenth Precinct. Only when John was surrounded by a wall of men in blue did Truman snap out of his delirium and admit that he had been confused. When the same thing happened several nights later, John decided that it was time to look for quieter accommodations. "Oh, fuck this! Let me out of here!" he shouted as he packed his bags and prepared to leave for the airport.

Being subjected to Truman's hallucinations was, quite literally, a sobering experience for John, and the next day, June 21, he went back into AA, pledging never to take another drink. "I will do *anything* to stay sober," he wrote Truman, who, he belatedly realized, had not been responsible for his actions. With the enthusiasm of a fresh convert, John suggested that they start a new life together, sober and drug-free. He was willing to do anything, John said, including spending four months with him at Hazelden, to help Truman gain the sobriety he was now enjoying. "Truman, let's live!" he pleaded. "We have a chance to live! What we've been doing isn't living."

—

B<small>UT</small> Truman did not want to live without alcohol and drugs. Life with them was intolerable, but life without them was unthinkable. They had become his constant companions, his most dependable chums. Sometimes, late at night, he would take his pills and capsules out of his bag—the yellows and reds, the whites and blues, the browns and blacks—count them five or six times to reassure himself that they were all there, and fondle them, as a person of a different piety might caress the beads of his rosary. Merely touching them gave him comfort. "Isn't it beautiful!" he exclaimed one day at lunch, holding up a newly acquired and especially powerful sedative—Lotusate it was poetically named—and turning it round and round, as if it were a sapphire in whose frozen heart he could see the light dancing. "It's the only beautiful drug I've ever seen, a lovely lavender. Because my system isn't used to it yet, it puts me to sleep immediately. I can sleep for five hours; then I wake up and take another one."

Cocaine received a similar encomium—"so incredibly subtle," he called it—and he publicly bragged about how much he consumed. Oblivious to the harsh penalties of the law, he partook of it with blissful indiscretion, interrupting a dinner at La Petite Marmite, for example, for a quick snort in the glass telephone booth near the entrance. Unperturbed, the headwaiter politely suggested that his dinner guest stand in front and block him from view. For a time there was a rumor that he had given up cocaine, and his suppliers, unhappy at the prospect of losing such a good customer, sent him envelopes containing free samples. But the rumors were false. Leaf-

ing through a magazine in the U.N. Plaza apartment, Joe Petrocik
discovered three coke-filled packets that Truman had hidden between the pages, then inconveniently forgotten. "That's just what I
need!" screeched Truman, who instantly grabbed them and ran into
the next room to inhale their contents.

Yet just as some part of his mind remained rational while the rest
of it was conjuring up a roomful of assassins, so did some part of
him stand coolly aside and declare that coke and pills were not what
he needed, that in fact they might someday destroy him. A depressed glance around his apartment, littered with pills and the
containers they had come in, one night caused him to issue another
of his ominous predictions. "First there was Marilyn, then Monty,"
he said. "I'm going to be the next one. You're going to read about
me on the front page of the *Daily News* one of these days. It's a sure
sign when you start seeing pills and pill bottles in corners."

Before the summer of 1981 ended, his prophecy seemed close to
fulfillment. On the morning of August 1 he suffered a convulsive
seizure, something like an epileptic attack, in front of the Sagaponack General Store and was taken to Southampton Hospital in an
ambulance, convinced that he was on the verge of dying. "I was
dead for thirty seconds, alive for four hours, then dead for thirty-
five seconds," he said, repeating what he had been told by hospital
attendants. "If I had been dead for two more seconds, I would have
been dead for good. Little children are brought up to believe that
death is awful. But this was quite, quite pleasant."

After nearly a month in the hospital, he traveled into Manhattan,
only to suffer a second attack in the hallway outside his apartment
shortly after noon on September 15. "Truman Capote Rushed to
Hospital," blazoned the headline on the front page of that afternoon's *New York Post*, which also displayed a picture of him strapped
to a stretcher, unconscious, with his eyes closed and his mouth
agape. His condition was not so grave as the photograph suggested,
and after six days in New York Hospital he returned to Long Island,
pointedly disregarding the admonitions of his doctors, who blamed
the attacks on alcohol, by stopping off for a couple of drinks at a
friend's house on the way home. In the weeks that followed, he
continued to drink as if nothing had happened, as if his weeks in the
hospitals had been erased from his memory.

By so casually ignoring the dramatic—indeed, providential—
warnings of his seizures, he all but announced what had long been

evident: he had lost his will to survive. "Everything is difficult, painfully hard for him now," said Jack. "All the energy he has goes into keeping up a front, into putting up scrims that make people think he's all right." Many days that autumn he could not do even that, lacking sufficient vigor to wash, shave and put on clean clothes. Sometimes he could not even make the effort to walk to the toilet, causing the back steps of his studio, which he often used instead, to stink of urine. "Go some place where they teach people to piss in a bowl!" was Jack's sarcastic advice.

Seeing how helpless he was, well-meaning friends wanted to hire someone to look after him, a combination nurse and companion. His Long Island doctor, William Diefenbach, even volunteered to take a year's leave from his practice to look after him—if only he would spend his time writing. Every possibility was considered, but Truman rejected them all, and Jack, who should have welcomed assistance, was predictably scornful. "What would Truman do with a male nurse?" he asked. "He'd probably teach the nurse to take heroin; or the nurse would introduce him to another drug."

Through some particularly melancholy irony, Truman had become like that wraith of his youth, Denham Fouts, who during the last months of his life had rarely left his gloom-shrouded, opium-scented apartment on the Rue du Bac. Truman had been so disturbed and frightened by Denny's withdrawal into the netherworld of drugs that he had soon fled his company. In fact, he had seen in Denny the ghost of things to come, and more than thirty years later, he had become what he had then feared, a semi-invalid who often could not manage the simplest tasks on his own and who relied on a dwindling circle of friends to take care of him. On his good days he could still charm, amuse and even write; on his bad days he was a burden that many found exceedingly heavy to bear.

The one who found the burden most onerous was Jack, who looked forward to his departure for Verbier each year as a convict might look forward to the day of his release from prison. As the drama of Truman's decline entered its last act, Jack seemed to regard himself as a spectator, not as a leading character, and certainly not as the one who should have led the rescue efforts, however doomed they might have been. It never seemed to have occurred to him that thirty-three years of companionship carried a special obligation. What hitherto had been obscured by the choler and fury of his personality, the eruptions of anger and outrage, was now obvious: it was Truman who had dominated their relationship, Truman who had decided where they would travel and where they would live, and Truman who had been the one who had loved, Jack the one who had been loved. Jack's affection for him had been real, but for the most part he had been remarkably passive and removed—cold and hyperborean, as he himself had observed. He had demanded only one thing and that was that he not be bothered.

Now, at the age of sixty-seven, Jack remained as self-absorbed as he had always been. He still did not want to be bothered, and he responded to the burden that Truman had become by escaping to Switzerland; or, even when he was home, by shifting responsibility onto other shoulders. In January, 1983, at one of the lowest of Truman's many low points, Joe Petrocik thought of cabling Jack in Verbier and asking him to return to New York; then, imagining his response, Joe threw up his hands. "What would he say? 'I'll be there when the ski season is over.' "

It was Truman's fate, and the most melancholy irony of all, that at the end of his life, as at the beginning, he was rejected by the one who was closest to him. Like Nina, Jack was ambivalent about him during his final years, expressing love and contempt almost in the same breath. And like Nina, Jack could be counted on only when it suited him, only when he was not otherwise engaged. "Truman's beyond help," he declared. "What am I supposed to do? I think I'm terrible for him. I'm always lecturing him. I'm not able to handle him any more than I can carry a handful of water from here [Saga-ponack] to East Hampton. How can you live with a thing when you're watching it burn down before your eyes? Truman's dying. He's a dying man. But I can't die with him."

Lonely and frightened by his seizures, Truman clung to Jack nevertheless, and at the end of 1981 he battled bitterly to prevent him from leaving for Switzerland. "He holds on to me like I'm a raft," said Jack. Jack's refusal to stay with him ushered in some of the worst weeks in their relationship. When pleas and persuasion failed, Truman used economic blackmail for the first time, threat-ening to sell the apartment in Verbier. When that did no good either, he angrily struck out, accusing Jack of having put the ailing Maggie to sleep—her hind legs had become paralyzed—simply so that he would be free to travel.

That charge wounded Jack most of all. "Oh, God!" he groaned.

"How I fought for that little dog's life! Truman's vindictiveness is fantastic. He's taken the whole fabric of our life together and ripped it up. The love of his life left him, and Truman thought he was going to come back to paradise with Jack. But he can't. He's changed. But maybe somebody will come along for him. After all, more than half the world still believes in the Messiah. I dread weekends and holidays with him now. For the first time in years I feel I can't get out of bed, I'm so depressed. Everybody who lives with an alcoholic gets to hate him. We're like soldiers after the battle. There's nothing to say."

There was more to say, of course, and Truman had said it not long before: "I can't break the connection with Johnny, but somehow I always know that I will die living with Jack." A thaw came with Jack's return from Switzerland in the spring of 1982, and for a few weeks the clock seemed to have been turned back to a more congenial time. Truman sneaked peeks at Jack's newest book—"I love it," he reported, midway through—and interjected himself into one of the decade's most celebrated court cases, the trial of Claus von Bülow for the attempted murder of his wife Sunny. Siding with the defense, which maintained that Sunny's addiction to drugs and alcohol had caused the coma in which she lay, Truman stated that he had known her and that, contrary to prosecution claims, she was both an alcoholic and a drug abuser: she had even shown him how to give himself injections.

Playing the busybody was about all he was able to do, and even the few words he managed to produce, a story titled "One Christmas" and a column of reminiscences, had a tired quality, reflecting his own unshakable fatigue. For most of the year he was even too weary to give much thought to John, who sent him at least two provocative letters. The first, in April, 1982, asked for money, which Truman apparently gave him. The second, a few months later, revealed that John no longer hated him. His sponsor in AA had convinced him that he could not find peace unless he expunged such negative emotions from his soul, John said, and that was his reason for writing. "So. Consider yourself forgiven and unhated by me . . . If my, selfishly, doing this gives you any peace and happiness I am glad; and I hope that you will consider the efficacy of acting likewise towards whomever you hate. Let it seep away, Truman, it is poison."

In prior years such a condescending letter would have evoked screams of outrage from Truman. But John was now too great a challenge to his depleted strength. Even with all of his nagging, Jack was the one he wanted to be with, and as fall of 1982 merged into winter, Truman made the same old plea: forget Switzerland. And he received the same old answer: no. But in truth, Jack was no longer much company even when he was in New York. On Christmas Eve, a night when, according to all the songs and carols, loved ones gather by the tree, Jack marched off to the opera, to the blood and betrayal of Verdi's *Macbeth*, leaving Truman to fend for himself. A few days later, as Jack packed for Verbier, Truman checked into Southampton Hospital, where, alone again, he saw in the new year, 1983.

Truman's descent now accelerated at an alarming speed, and he was scarcely out of one hospital before entering another. An exact count of his stays is hard to come by; during the first few years of the eighties he was hospitalized in half a dozen states and Switzerland too. But the tally from Southampton Hospital, his favorite, gives an indication of the quickening pace of his decline: he registered there four times in 1981, seven times in 1982, and sixteen times in 1983. "It used to be that he would have a few good months between crises," said Joe Petrocik. "Then it would be a few good weeks. Finally it was a few good days. Now it's a few good hours."

In the first two months of 1983 he ricocheted from hospital to hospital: from Southampton Hospital to New York Hospital, from a clinic in Switzerland to Larkin General Hospital in Miami—then back to Manhattan and Mount Sinai Hospital. "If he straightens out, he has many, many years left," said Bertram Newman, his doctor at Mount Sinai. "But if he keeps going the way he is now, he might just as well put a gun to his mouth. It would save everyone a lot of trouble. I feel so impotent because I know that he knows that this can all stop."

On March 1, 1983, the day he left Mount Sinai, Lester Persky and Alan Schwartz gave him an unwontedly stiff lecture at La Petite Marmite. Alan was moved to tears—"I recognized finally that he really *was* killing himself," Alan said—but Truman was more irritated than touched. "I had an incredibly grim lunch with my lawyer and Lester Ever-Present Persky," he said later that afternoon. "They told me I'd be dead in six months if I didn't stop drinking. I wanted to say, 'So what? It's me, not you. Why do you care?' They all act as if I've made no effort, but I've made a tremendous effort over the last five years. It's almost as if they all have crossed eyes and can't see."

Like Jack—indeed, like Truman himself—his friends began to speak as if he had a fatal disease, as if his death were an impending event whose date had not yet been determined. Some of his friends were reluctant to open the door to him, worried lest he fall asleep on their couch or in their guest bedroom and never wake up. Foreseeing that he would not live long enough to enjoy his money, Alan and Arnold Bernstein, his accountant, took the practical step of persuading Random House to immediately release sums scheduled for payment in future years. "I wanted him to have it right away, even if it meant he had to pay a little more in taxes," said Arnold.

And so the downward spiral continued, hastened by a series of small shocks, including a rejection slip from *Vanity Fair* for his column and a gratuitous assault by his aunt Tiny Rudisill, who, in March, 1983, published *Truman Capote*, a singularly silly account of his childhood. Although her portrait of him was unflattering, what disturbed him more was her malicious depiction of his mother—Tiny's sister—as a slut whose "only enduring passion" was not for Arch, or Joe Capote, but for Teshu, a Creek Indian with a voluptuous mouth and a habit of speaking in romance-novel dialogue. "I have never seen so many misstatements of fact per sentence as in that book," said Harper Lee, who was one of its chief characters. Mary Ida Carter, one of Tiny's other sisters, was so disgusted that she dumped it in the privy behind her house—the "outdoor convenience," as she called it—and pushed it out of sight with a long pole. Yet ludicrous as it was, Tiny's book did have a modest sale and was, unfortunately, accepted by many as factual.* It even reached the hands of Slim Keith, who, in her sleepless rage, sent Truman a brief but uncommonly venomous letter. "So amusing," she said, "to read of your pathetic antecedents & childhood."

Wounded by such an unkind blow from a blood relation, in April

---

* After Truman died, Tiny offered for sale an awkward and lumpish story, "I Remember Grandpa," that she said he had written in 1947, the year he was completing *Other Voices*. She submitted no evidence to support her claim that he was the author, however—the manuscript was typed without any notations in his handwriting—and he obviously was not. *Redbook* printed it nonetheless, an Atlanta publisher brought it out as a book, complete with illustrations, and many readers undoubtedly assumed that it was genuine.

Truman flew to Alabama and the comforting arms of Mary Ida, the only one left on his mother's side of the family whom he liked and trusted. But he never reached Monroeville, and after an overdose, wound up in Montgomery's Baptist Medical Center instead. "I put a knapsack on my shoulder and some old shoes and went to home-land, where decent people are," he joked. "But on the way I had an accident." Returning North, he suffered another sort of accident: on July 1 he was arrested for drunken driving in Bridgehampton and was forced to spend a night in the Southampton Town jail. "Capote Mixes Drinking and Driving Again," said the headline in the *New York Post*.

A longer jail sentence seemed possible—there was a rumor that the Suffolk County District Attorney's office planned to make an example of him—and Truman did not do his case much good by showing up for his hearing in dark glasses, a summer jacket and walking shorts. "People don't come to court dressed like that," an-grily declared the judge, who, after allowing Truman to stew for several months, let him off with nothing more serious than a five-hundred-dollar fine and a three-year probation. "I'm not going to Sing Sing after all!" exclaimed Truman.

For much of 1983 he might just as well have been in Sing Sing, however, so little was he aware of where he was or what he was doing. He was so incoherent at a party for Liza Minnelli in Decem-ber, for instance, that the other guests ignored him, surrounding him with a *cordon sanitaire* of politely averted eyes and blank smiles. Dismayed to see him sitting alone, the gossip columnist Liz Smith organized a relay team, people who agreed, as an act of charity, to stay with him in shifts of half an hour apiece. "It made me so sad," said Liz, who could recall other nights, not so very long before, when they all would have formed a circle around him, eager to hear the latest witticism from the mouth of Truman Capote.

"He could rarely remember the earlier days," Truman had writ-ten in his notes for *Answered Prayers*. "Happiness leaves such slender records; it is the dark days [that] are so voluminously documented." And so, once again, he had unwittingly predicted his own future. The triumphs of the past now seemed to echo from an immeasurable distance, while the dark days of the present stretched to the horizon and beyond. Many of those who had given him pleasure were dead:

Bennett Cerf, Babe Paley, Cecil Beaton and Gloria Guinness; even
Tennessee Williams, to whom, after a belated reconciliation, he had
dedicated *Music for Chameleons*. Many others would no longer speak
to him: Marella Agnelli, Lee Radziwill, Pamela Harriman and of
course the vengeful Slim. The years, more destructive than a hurricane, had dispersed his armada of swans, and perhaps only he, who
had admired them most, could recall how sublimely satisfying it had
been to watch their serene progress through a room, and the smiles
of awe and wonder they left in their wake.

Their passing might have been expected: beautiful women age,
die and make way for other beautiful women. Before Babe there had
been Mona Williams, and before Mona there had been Consuelo
Vanderbilt—the list was long and illustrious. But sometime between the fifties, when Truman had scaled the heights of golden
Olympus, and the eighties, the chain had been broken. There was a
new generation of beautiful women, of course, but none who possessed the style of a Babe or a Gloria or the matchless Mona. The
spirit those three represented had gone out of fashion, and a new
kind of glamour, based solely on publicity, had taken its place. The
rich had multiplied beyond all reckoning, but partly as a result,
Olympus itself, that preserve of the stylish few, had disappeared.
To those who came afterward it doubtless sounded more like a
poetic invention—like Xanadu or Camelot or the lost city of Atlantis
—than the land of sunshine and laughter Truman had known. As
he talked about it on still summer afternoons, he might have been
the lone survivor of some great catastrophe, the last one on earth
who still remembered how things had been.

To his tired eyes, everything now looked stale. He had, as he
often said, used up the world: there was no place that could provide
him contentment, no place for him at all. Manhattan, which had
excited him since he was a teenager, presented no delights, not even
wicked ones like Studio 54, which had closed after two of its owners
had been jailed for tax evasion. The one place he still loved, that flat
stretch of Long Island between Southampton and East Hampton—
it measured a mere eleven miles—had been disfigured by devel-
opers, and around his studio had risen costly houses of bizarre and
almost uniformly hideous design. Forbidden to drive by the State of
New York, he was unable to enjoy his stays there, in any event. No
longer was he seen tooling through the countryside in Jack's red

Mustang, all but hidden behind the wheel as, drunk or sober, he terrified other motorists by his nearly total disregard of the rules of the road.

In the first six weeks of 1984, he had two bad falls, one of which resulted in a mild cerebral concussion, and after three more trips to Southampton Hospital, he flew to Los Angeles to be nursed by Joanne Carson. A week later, on February 27, her doctor sent him back to the hospital, to Los Angeles' Cedars-Sinai Medical Center for treatment of a new and potentially fatal illness: phlebitis, a swelling of the veins that had painfully enlarged his left leg. He was well enough to return to Manhattan on March 11, but the phlebitis quickly flared up again and five days later he was in New York Hospital. Blood clots had formed in his lungs; until they were dissolved by a blood-thinning drug, he was in constant danger. Jack was concerned enough to come back early from Switzerland.

For several weeks after he got out, Truman followed his doctor's orders, which forbade alcohol. "They were sitting around at Alcoholics Anonymous in heaven and asked what they could do to make me stop drinking," he said. "This disease was it." But as soon as the phlebitis had been brought under control, he ran to the bottle. When Jack threw out his vodka, he turned to the alcoholic's last resort, NyQuil, a cold medicine that is twenty-five percent alcohol. A new doctor, George McCormack, Jr., gave him the usual lecture: "I think it's criminal what you're doing to the talent you've got." Instead of pouting, as he usually did, Truman listened and in June agreed to try a rehabilitation clinic near Philadelphia, Chit Chat Carom Hospital. "I'll do as you suggested, provided you take me," he informed McCormack. The prospect filled him with dread, nonetheless, and as the day for checking in—Saturday, June 23—approached, he became more and more anxious, drinking measurably more each day. "I think I've made a mistake to say I'll go there," he fretted. "The minute I get out I'll go back to my old ways. I know me. I'm just the person I am and I'm not going to be any different. I'm always going to drink. Undoubtedly it will kill me in the end."

Equally dubious about his prognosis, Jack was not only unsympathetic to the Chit Chat venture, but almost gratuitously mean— there is no other word to describe his behavior—to Truman. He would not help him pack for the trip, and on Truman's last night in Sagaponack Jack locked himself in his darkened house, not allowing

Truman to stay with him, to visit him, or even to speak to him, except for a shouted exchange through his bedroom window. "For thirty-five years he's had to pay nothing," said Truman, so hurt and angry that his voice quavered as he talked. "And now he says, 'I'm not going to let you into the house.' I haven't done anything to him to make him act that way. He's a monster! A monster!"

Jack did drive him into Manhattan, and Truman was dutifully waiting in the lobby of the U.N. Plaza when Dr. McCormack picked him up Saturday morning for the journey to Pennsylvania. He began shaking so badly, however, that halfway there, McCormack had to stop at a liquor store to buy him a pint of vodka, afraid that without it, he might go into convulsions. By the time they reached the clinic, Truman was so drunk that he needed aid to get out of the car and undress for bed. "This is not my *tasse de thé*," he mournfully observed when McCormack said goodbye. Nor was it. A few days later McCormack received a call from Chit Chat's director, who reported that Truman was preparing to flee. "Not only is he leaving, but he's induced two other people to go with him!" said the director.

Back into his life for a brief moment came John, who had visited him in the hospital in Los Angeles, their first face-to-face meeting in more than two and a half years. John had suffered a heart attack the summer before, and in contrast to Jack, he seemed sympathetic to Truman's emotional and physical ailments, as if his own flirtation with death had purged him of his old anger and resentment. They talked on the phone after the hospital visit and made plans for a later reunion in Florida, where John was working as a salesman in a furniture store. "Truman is just exactly the way he was four years ago—all fucked up," said John. "He doesn't want to get sober, but I want him to come here so that I can have a last crack at him. I just want to set him down and say, 'Truman, what can I do to get you out of this?'"

John was not to have that last crack. On August 2 Truman was taken by ambulance to Southampton Hospital, suffering from his worst overdose yet. The pupils of his eyes were fixed and dilated, and he needed a machine to help him breathe, the first time such assistance had been necessary. "I think he came pretty close to death this time," said Dr. Diefenbach. "It's just in the lap of the gods whether you can sleep such a thing off without your breathing stopping." On his occasional trips into Manhattan, Truman was prey again to hallucinations. One night he saw ghosts, Joe Capote's among them, and was so scared that he banged on the doors of his neighbors, begging to be let in. Afraid to stay by himself in New York and unhappy in Sagaponack, he made plans to spend a few weeks in California with Joanne, even though it meant missing Jack's seventieth birthday. "I'd like to get away from Jack and his harassments," he said. "Every other sentence he's nagging me." The tension between them continued until the day he left, and when he arrived in Los Angeles, he told Joanne, "It's all over with Jack. *Fini*."

But that was a word that might have been applied to everything Truman had known and loved, including his writing. It was all over and done with—*fini*. Not long before, a friend had asked how *Answered Prayers* was progressing. "Let's not talk about *that*," he petulantly replied. Then, his expression softening into a look of both puzzlement and sadness, he added: "I dream about it and my dream is as real as stubbing your toe. All the characters I've lived with are in it, so brilliant, so real. Part of my brain says, 'The book's so beautiful, so well constructed—there's never been such a beautiful book.' Then a second part of my brain says, 'Nobody can write that well.'"

59

T RUMAN was still a month away from his sixtieth birthday when he reached Los Angeles on the afternoon of Thursday, August 23, 1984. But a Polaroid picture Joanne took that evening shows the face of an older man, so tired that his features are almost indistinct, as if they were made of melting wax. He seemed to revive the next day, but his weariness returned on Saturday. When Joanne went to wake him early in the morning, he said he was still tired and wanted to sleep. When she tried to rouse him at noon, he was dead.

That, in any event, was the story Joanne told the police and reporters. But that, as she later confided, was not what happened.

What happened was that when she came to wake him that Saturday morning, probably around 7:30, he looked so pale and exhausted that she felt his pulse, which was fluttery. She thought that breakfast might pick him up, but he prevented her from leaving, grabbing her hand and pulling her down beside him on his bed. "No," he said, "stay here."

"Are you all right?" she asked.

"No, I'm not," he answered. "But I soon will be."

"Truman, I think I want to call the paramedics," she said, starting to rise. Once again he held her down, and for the next three and possibly four hours he talked and talked, until he could talk no longer.

The autopsy, which was performed by the Los Angeles County coroner, could find no "clear mechanism of death," as doctors like to phrase it. "It has been determined that he died as the result of liver disease which was complicated by phlebitis and multiple drug intoxication" was all the coroner's office could say. But in fact he had shown no symptoms of serious liver disease. His liver had been tested by Southampton Hospital just a few weeks earlier, and the worst that could be said about it was that it was precirrhotic—that it showed signs, in other words, of the cirrhosis that might come. The doctors at the coroner's office seemed puzzled.

What, then, killed him? Since there was no alcohol in his blood—for once, he had not been drinking—the most likely culprit was those beautiful little pills he loved to cuddle. In the hours and days before his death he had consumed great quantities of drugs: Valium, Dilantin, codeine, Tylenol and two or three different barbiturates. The Valium alone, about forty milligrams, was enough to put a person who was not accustomed to it, as Truman was, into such a stupor that a shout in the ear would not have awakened him. A healthy person might have survived such an assault on the system. An unhealthy person, particularly one with the slight liver problem Truman had, might not have, and there is every possibility that he took a fatal overdose. The only outstanding question can never be answered. Was it a deliberate or an accidental overdose?

What probably happened, in any event, was that, as a result of a drug overload, he suffered a cardiac-rhythm disorder, a disruption of the normal electrical signals to the heart. Joanne's readings of his pulse support such a conclusion. A disorder of that kind, which is common in alcoholics, would not show up in an autopsy. It can last for hours, during which time the victim can talk, and talk lucidly, as Joanne said that Truman did. It can also be interrupted if the victim receives medical attention. If the paramedics had been called, Truman's life probably could have been saved. But that, clearly, he did not want, and perhaps it is not important to ask whether he had tried to commit suicide: even if he had, he had been given a reprieve, a second chance. But given a choice between life and death, he chose death.

When Truman was a child of five or six in Monroeville, someone gave him a miniature airplane that he could pedal around the yard like a tricycle. It was a vivid green, with a bright red propeller, and one day Truman told his envious friends that he was going to fly, that he was going to take off down that dusty street in front of

Jennie's house, rise above the trees beyond, and soar across the oceans to China, that serene and mysterious land that he often dreamed about. He had convinced everyone, including himself, and furiously he pedaled, faster and faster . . . But he went nowhere at all. Now, sitting in his bedroom in Joanne's house, knowing that something was terribly wrong with him, he was to have his wish.

"Truman, I think you're in a little trouble," Joanne said once more. "Let me call the doctor. We can get you to the hospital."

"No," he replied. "I don't want to go through that again. No more hospitals. My dear, I'm so very tired. If you care about me, don't do anything. Just let me go. I know exactly what I'm doing. I've decided to go to China, where there are no phones and there is no mail service." He continued to talk, about his mother mostly, but also about his writing and *Answered Prayers*. Like leaves falling gently from a tree, he had promised its ending would be, and that is how his own last hours ended, as his life slowly drifted away. As his pulse grew weaker, his conversation was reduced to phrases. "Beautiful Babe" was one. "Mama, Mama" was another. Finally: "It's me, it's Buddy"—Buddy was Sook's nickname for him. "I'm cold," he said at last. Sometime before noon his breathing stopped, and Joanne called the paramedics, who pronounced him dead at 12:21 P.M.

And so, moment by moment, he had returned to the beginning.

Acknowledgments

A writer likes to think that a book is all his own. But that is clearly not the case with a biography, and I am indebted to hundreds of people, not all of whom I have been able to mention in my source notes. Foremost among them, of course, is Truman Capote himself, who for more than nine years allowed me to observe and, indeed, to take part in his life. That is a debt I can never repay, alas, and I confess that I find myself missing his company, good and bad, more than I would have thought possible. Jack Dunphy, Truman's companion for thirty-eight years, gave me the same high privilege, with no strings or conditions. My book would have been greatly diminished without his help. Rick Brown and John O'Shea, who shared Truman's life for lesser periods, were equally forthright, and my final chapters would have been incomplete without their cooperation. Alan U. Schwartz, Truman's executor, very generously permitted me access to Truman's papers and other invaluable information. Arnold Bernstein, Truman's accountant, steered me through the mysterious jungle of financial figures. Joe Fox, Truman's editor at Random House, provided help, as well as wise counsel, in more ways than I can readily enumerate.

At Simon and Schuster I was guided and protected by what I believe to be one of the most talented teams in publishing: my editor Bob Bender, whose steady voice helped me through many trying moments and whose keen eye caught my mistakes; his assistant, Betsy Lerner, whose efficiency and good humor never wavered; my former editors, Diane Cleaver and Joni Evans, whose enthusiasm was constantly invigorating; Vincent Virga, who discovered photographs in the most unlikely spots and, sometimes through charm alone, secured permission rights; Eric Rayman, who gave my manuscript a shrewd but sensitive legal reading; and Richard Snyder, chairman of Simon and Schuster, Charles Hayward, publisher of Simon and Schuster's trade division, and Michael Korda, Simon and Schuster's editor-in-chief, who offered encouraging words at the right times. With almost saintly patience, Barbara Shalvey typed transcripts of hundreds of hours of tape-recorded interviews and showed great ingenuity in collecting odd facts in odd places. I have been singularly lucky in the choice of my two agents. Gloria Safier saw me safely through ten years of frustration and occasional heartache; my greatest regret is that she could not have lived to read this book. Taking her place, Helen Brann has offered me comforting words, as well as her own good judgment, and she has seen me to the finish line.

I regret that I can offer no more than a mention to many of those who follow, some of whom have given me hours and hours of their time: Daniel Aaron; Edward Albee; Robert O. Anderson; Harold Arlen; Mary Louise Aswell; Richard Avedon; Julian Bach; Don Bachardy; Pierre Barillet; Peter Beard; Sybille Bedford; Lucia Jaeger Behling; Pearl Kazin Bell; Andrew Bella; Brigid Berlin; Paul Bigelow; Janice Biggers; Karl Bissinger; Naomi Bliven; Paul Bowles; Jenny Bradley; Susan Braudy; Wilva Breen; Gerald Brenan; Nancy Ryan Brien; John Malcolm Brinnin; John Broderick (chief of Manuscript Division, Library of Congress); Richard Brooks; Stella Brooks; Andreas Brown; Joy Brown; Michael Brown; Rick Brown; C. Bruner-Smith; Patricia Burstein; Paul Cadmus; Maria Theresa Caen; Robin Caldwell; Robbie Campbell; Sandy Campbell; Joe Capote; Marjorie Capote; William F. Carroll; Joanne Carson; Marco Carson; Jennings Carter; John Byron Carter; Mary Ida Carter; Bill Caskey; Lord (David) Cecil; Vincent Cerow; Herbert Chaice; George Christy; Ina Claire; Patsy Streckfus Clark; Jack Clayton; Myron Clement; Walter Clemons; Bob Colacello; Meghan Robbins Collins; Mary Ellen Connolly; Wyatt Cooper; Donald Cullivan; Charlotte Curtis; Joe Curtis; Mina Curtiss; Thomas Quinn Curtiss; Olive Daley; Jimmy Daniels; Matthew Dann; Buster Davis; Susan Davis, curator of manuscripts, New York Public Library; Agnes de Mille; Alice Denham; Harold Deutsch, M.D.; Alvin Dewey; Marie Dewey; William Diefenbach, M.D.; William E. Dorion; Frances Doughty; Irving Drutman; Dominick Dunne; Gloria Dunphy; Robert Ellsworth; Lin Emery; Don Erickson; Joe Faulk; Seabon Faulk; Dorothy Finnie; M. F. K. Fisher; Thomas Flanagan; Ruth Ford; Frederick Fouts; Eleanor Friede; Otto Friedrich, John Galliher; Mrs. Ira Gershwin; John Gielgud; Brendan Gill; Milton Goldman; John B. L. Goodwin; William Goyen; Katharine Graham; Mary Garrison Grand; Judith Green; Graham Greene; Frank Grisaitis; C. Z. Guest; Alec Guinness; Loel Guinness; Brion Gysin; James Hagerman; Ronald Hallett; Waldemar Hansen; Curtis Harnack (executive director, Yaddo); Mrs. Lester Harp; Kate Harrington; Bill Harris; Mercia Harrison; Rex Harrison; Crawford Hart, Jr.; Lillian Hellman; Audrey Hepburn; Shirley Herz; Themistocles Hoetis; Kinmont Hoitsma; Geoffrey Holder; Dolores Hope; Robert Horan; Leonora Hornblow; Eileen Hose; Albert Hubbell; John Huston; Christopher Isherwood; Carl Jaeger; Jo James; Marion Javits; April Johnson; Jennifer Jones; Judith Jones; Ebba

Jonsson; Pauline Kael; E. J. Kahn, Jr.; Father Kieran Kavanaugh, O.C.D.; Donald Keene; Robert Keene; Lady (Nancy) Keith; William Kessler; Wilma Kidwell; Eugene Kinkeid; Carol Knauss (secretary, Bread Loaf Writers' Conference); John Knowles; Ronald Kornblum, M.D.; Louis Kronenberger; Eleanor Lambert; John Lasher; Rupert Latture; Barbara Lawrence; Alice Lee; Harper Lee; John Lehmann; Leo Lerman; Lyle Leverich; Doris Lilly; Elizabeth Linscott; Gordon Lish; Carl Little, M.D.; Andy Logan; Kennth A. Lohf (librarian for Rare Books and Manuscripts, Columbia); Andrew Lyndon; Robert MacBride; Jordan Massee; Carol Matthau; George H. McCormack, M.D.; Frances McFadden; Landis McMillon; Kay Meehan; Gian-Carlo Menotti; Oliver Messell; Joel Michael; Thomas Moore; Truman Moore; Robert Morley; Alice Morris; Ruth Mortimer (curator, Smith College Rare Book Room); Howard Moss; John Moxey; John Bernard Myers; Bertram J. Newman, M.D.; John Nicholson; Scott Nixon; Louis Nizer; Marion Jaeger O'Niel; Brian O'Shea; Chris O'Shea; John O'Shea; Margaret O'Shea; Bernard Perlin; Eleanor Perry; Frank Perry; Lester Persky; Arch Persons; John Knox Persons; Joseph Petrocik; Robert Phelps; Edward Pierce; Arthur Pinkham; Ron Portante; Katherine Anne Porter; Frank Price; Marilyn Putnam; Dotson Rader; Lee Radziwill; Marcus Reidenberg, M.D.; John Richardson; Nathan Rogers; Ned Rorem; Katherine Rowley; Marie Rudisill; D. D. Ryan; John Barry Ryan; William Shawn; Neil Simon; Jeannie Sims; Harrison Smith; Liz Smith; Oliver Smith; Steve Sondheim; M. C. Spahn; Francis Steegmuller; Jean Stein; Verne Streckfus; Saint Subber; Georges Tardy; Mrs. Roland Tate; Virgil Thomson; Diana Trilling; Hugo Vickers; Lucia Victor; Gore Vidal; Robin von Joachim; Diana Vreeland; Phoebe Pierce Vreeland; Phyllis Cerf Wagner; Theodore Walworth, Jr.; Howard Weber, Jr.; Kay Wells; Jann Wenner; Glenway Wescott; Lyn White; Tennessee Williams; Donald Windham; Catherine Wood; Lynn Wyatt; Marguerite Young; Hortense Zera (librarian, American Academy and Institute of Arts and Letters).

Source Notes

Much of this book is based on interviews, chiefly with Truman Capote himself, but also with several hundred others who either knew him or provided information on him or on other subjects I discuss. In the notes below I have indicated my sources for key facts and quotations. I have cited all the important quotations from Truman that I obtained from published stories and interviews. The reader can assume that almost all other quotations from Truman and from his companion, Jack Dunphy, come from my interviews with them. Because I interviewed them so frequently, over so long a period of time, I have not attempted to date each quotation. With only a few exceptions, all other interviews are dated. For reasons that are obvious in the text, a very few people requested anonymity, which I granted.

The book is also based on written material, most of it unpublished: Truman's books and articles; his letters, which are scattered over two continents; the letters of his friends, particularly his first lover, Newton Arvin; and the memoirs and diaries of those who knew him. Truman often claimed that he kept extensive diaries of his own. If so—and I doubt that he did—I know of only two. One is in the Library of Congress; the other he gave to me.

The two main repositories of Capote material are the New York Public Library and the Library of Congress. Columbia University's Random House collection has the letters Truman exchanged with his editors, and the Smith College Library has many of the letters Newton Arvin wrote to him. Truman also gave me some important material, including the aforementioned diary and his letters from Perry Smith and Richard Hickock, the two killers he wrote about in *In Cold Blood*. I was also able to purchase an extraordinarily useful collection of several hundred of Truman's family letters, which were of immense help in providing background and documenting dates.

In quoting from letters, I have, in a very few places, dropped irrelevant passages without noting the omission with an ellipsis, overuse of which I believe often slows down a narrative. For the most part, Truman and his correspondents were excellent spellers, and I have silently corrected minor misspellings, unless, as in a childhood letter, they make a point. When I have given the exact date of a letter within the text, I have not felt it necessary to repeat the citation in the source notes.

CHAPTER 1

page 3 " 'She like to have knocked me dead . . .' ": Arch Persons to GC, September 9, 1976.

page 4 "Her widowed mother had died . . .": Arch Persons (September 9, 1976), Mary Ida Carter (September 7, 1976) and Seabon Faulk (March 8, 1978) to GC.

page 5 " 'Get out and don't ever darken . . .' ": Mary Ida Carter to GC, September 7, 1976.

page 5 "He was obviously not the man he had led . . .": Seabon Faulk to GC, March 8, 1978.

page 6 " 'People in Monroeville thought that Arch . . .' ": *Ibid.*

CHAPTER 2

page 8 "At the beginning, anyway, Lillie Mae put aside . . .": Mary Ida Carter (September 7, 1976), Seabon Faulk (March 8, 1978) and John Knox Persons (September 9, 1978) to GC.

page 8 " 'If you could be sold, Arch . . .' ": Captain Verne Streckfus to GC, April 19, 1979.

page 10 " 'Money is the sixth sense, without which . . .' ": Arch Persons to John Knox Persons, July 30, 1933.

CHAPTER 3

page 11 " 'She thought that she had been hooked . . .' ": Seabon Faulk to GC, March 8, 1978.

page 11 " 'She'd take a notion to a fellow . . .' ": Arch Persons to GC, September 9, 1976.

page 11 "In the seven years they were man and wife . . .": Arch Persons to Mabel Purcell (his mother), January 5, 1933.

page 12 " 'Invariably, ' he complained in one letter . . .": John Knox Persons to Sam Persons, July 12, 1931.

page 12 "The first on the list may have been . . .": Arch Persons (September 9, 1976) and Joe Capote (May 7, 1977) to GC.

page 14 "In the winter of 1929 she even took him . . .": Nancy H. Carwell, assistant to the registrar, Western Kentucky University, in a letter to GC, July 18, 1978.

CHAPTER 4

page 15 " 'She was the strongest woman . . .' ": Seabon Faulk to GC, March 8, 1978.

page 16 " 'Oh, Jennie that's so sinful!' ": Mary Ida Carter to GC, September 7, 1976.

page 18 "In 1930, when Truman went there to live . . .": For my description on Monroeville in the thirties, I relied on the centennial edition (1966) of the *Monroe Journal* and Harper Lee's novel, *To Kill a Mockingbird*, as well as information derived from interviews.

CHAPTER 5

page 21 "All that summer of 1930 he swam . . .": Arch Persons to John Knox Persons, July 24, 1930.

page 22 " 'He wore blue linen shorts that . . .' ": Lee, *To Kill a Mockingbird*, page 13.

page 23 " 'I fear if there is such a thing . . .' ": Callie Faulk to Mabel Purcell, September 28, 1931.

page 23 " 'We give him every pleasure . . .' ": Callie Faulk to Mabel Purcell, August 3, 1932.

page 24 "One night at eleven o'clock, long after . . .": Mabel Purcell to John Knox Persons, June 22, 1931.

CHAPTER 6

page 27 " 'Seems to me she is always studying something . . .' ": Sam Persons to John Knox Persons, January 15, 1931.

page 27 " 'Arch is headed for immediate serious trouble' ": John Knox Persons to Lillie Mae Faulk, March 11, 1931.

page 27 " 'Please excuse this paper . . .' ": Lillie Mae Faulk to John Knox Persons, March, 1931

page 28 " 'When he gets in trouble . . .' ": John Knox Persons to Lillie Mae Faulk, March 17, 1931.

page 29 "Captivated by her vivacity and beauty . . .": Joe Capote to GC, May 7, 1977.

page 29 " 'I never saw a man who was any cleaner . . .' ": Seabon Faulk to GC, March 8, 1978.

page 30 " 'His mental state concerning her . . .' ": John Knox Persons to Sam Persons, July 2, 1931.

page 30 " 'The enclosed wire came last night . . .' ": Sam Persons to John Knox Persons, July 6, 1931.

page 31 " 'I am the deserted boy . . .' ": Arch Persons to Mabel Purcell, July 18, 1931.

page 32 "Lillie Mae, he reported, had phoned to tell him 'that she . . .' ": Arch Persons to John Knox Persons, August 27, 1931.

CHAPTER 7

page 34 "This time John put up bail, wryly remarking . . .": John Knox Persons to Mabel Purcell, August 14, 1931.

page 34 " 'I am as innocent of wrongdoing . . .' ": Arch Persons to Mabel Purcell, August 30, 1932.

page 34 " 'Today is Truman's birthday. . . .' ": Arch Persons to John Knox Persons, September 30, 1932.

page 35 "The car was new, and Lillie Mae was 'dressed to kill . . .' ": Sam Persons to John Knox Persons, October 25, 1932.

page 35 ". . . Alabama's Angola State Prison—the toughest in the world . . .": Arch Persons to Mabel Purcell, November 29, 1932.

page 35 ". . . that was enough to break even Sam's heart . . .": Sam Persons to Arch Persons, December 22, 1932.

page 35 ". . . to save Truman from that 'she-devil' ": Arch Persons to John Knox Persons, August 6, 1933.

page 36 " 'I have never appreciated any home as much . . .' ": Certified copy of testimony of "J. Archie Persons" in the Circuit Court of Monroe County, Alabama, August 24, 1933.

page 36 " 'I think it would be a calamity for the child . . .' ": F. W. Hare, Judge of the Circuit Court of Monroe County, August 28, 1933.

page 37 " 'I didn't know a man could be robbed . . .' ": Arch Persons to John Knox Persons, September 2, 1933.

page 37 "Yet even Arch's mother . . .": Mabel Purcell to John Knox Persons, September 10, 1933.

page 37 " 'We have the goods on her . . .' ": Arch Persons to John Knox Persons, April 29, 1934.

page 38 " 'Can you imagine anything so terrible . . .' ": Arch Persons to John Knox Persons, July 24, 1934.

page 38 " 'As you know my name was changed . . .' ": TC to Arch Persons, undated, probably September, 1936.

CHAPTER 8

page 40 " 'They were madly in love . . .' ": Lyn White to GC, October 16, 1975.

page 41 " 'I will not have another child . . .' ": Marjorie Capote (Joe Capote's widow) to GC, January 7, 1983.

page 41 "Something went wrong on the operating table . . .": Joe Capote to GC, May 7, 1977.

page 42 "She often accused him of lying . . .": *Ibid.*

page 42 "According to his Aunt Tiny, Nina's sisters . . .": Marie (Tiny) Rudisill to GC, June 27, 1982.

pages 42–3 " 'His voice today is identical to . . .' ": C. Bruner-Smith to GC, November 19, 1982.

page 44 " 'I always felt sorry for Truman . . .' ": *Ibid.*

page 45 " 'How could she have been so insane . . .' ": *Ibid.*

CHAPTER 9

page 47 " 'It was fascinating to watch him . . .' ": Howard Weber, Jr., to GC, June 3, 1980.

page 50 "His ninth-grade English teacher . . .": John Lasher to GC, January 19, 1983.

page 50 " 'It was a rather lengthy manuscript . . .' ": C. Bruner-Smith to GC, November 19, 1982.

page 51 " 'Those who knew him accepted him . . .' ": Crawford Hart, Jr., to GC, January 20, 1983.

page 51 " 'Truman was vividly . . .' ": Thomas Flanagan to GC.

page 52 " 'His attendance was very irregular . . .' ": Andrew Bella to GC, July 19, 1983.

page 53 "He came to her attention as aggressively . . .": Catherine Wood to GC, December 19, 1975.

CHAPTER 10

page 55 " 'He had a great, and immense, capacity . . .' ": Phoebe Pierce Vreeland to GC, April 20, 1976.

page 55 " 'Truman brought happiness into . . .' ": Marion Jaeger O'Niel to GC, April 2, 1983.

page 56 "All that day he walked the halls . . .": Marion Jaeger O'Niel and Lucia Jaeger Behling to GC, April 2, 1983.

page 61 " 'a shot here, a shot there,' as he later said": Joe Capote to GC, May 7, 1977.

page 61 "Occasionally he would spend a Saturday . . .": Carl Jaeger to GC, April 2, 1983.

page 62 " 'You're a pansy!' Nina would . . .": Phoebe Pierce Vreeland to GC, April 20, 1976.

page 63 " 'Well, my boy's a fairy . . .' ": *Ibid*.

page 63 " 'How can you let your son . . .' ": Meghan Robbins Collins to GC, January 31, 1983.

page 64 " 'As much as Truman could be in love . . .' ": *Ibid*.

CHAPTER 11

page 67 " 'Goodbye, girls, I'm going back to the city . . .' ": Lucia Jaeger Behling to GC, April 2, 1983.

page 68 " 'In New York,' said Phoebe . . .": Phoebe Pierce Vreeland to GC, April 20, 1976.

page 68 " 'this island, floating in river water like a diamond iceberg . . .' ": TC, *The Dogs Bark*, page 30.

page 68 " 'We thought we were being terrific . . .' ": Carol Marcus Matthau to GC, May 31, 1977.

page 69 " . . . in a poem, 'Sand for the Hour Glass,'. . .": Franklin School magazine, *The Red and Blue*, Winter, 1943, pages 23–24.

page 70 " '*The New Yorker* is a worse madhouse . . .' ": White, *Letters of E. B. White*, page 250.

page 71 " 'like a small boy, almost a child.' ": William Shawn to GC, May 31, 1976.

page 71 " 'You're going to lose your money . . .' ": Ebba Jonnson to GC, January 24, 1977.

page 72 " 'She was a wicked, wicked woman . . .' ": Andy Logan to GC, June 7, 1976.

page 72 " 'It's in his stars, or his destiny . . .' ": Selma Robinson, "The Legend of 'Little T,' " *P.M.*, Sunday Magazine, March 14, 1948, page 8.

page 73 " 'baying the moon of despair . . .' ": Thurber, *The Years with Ross*, page 176.

page 73 " 'The copyboy's job was to clean the place . . .' ": Albert Hubbell to GC, August 12, 1983.

page 74 " 'He used to stand behind my desk . . .' ": Barbara Lawrence to GC, August, 1976.

page 75 " 'There was a tendency—*New Yorker* snobbery . . .' ": E. J. Kahn, Jr., to GC, September 7, 1983.

page 75 " 'Even though we thought that he could probably do it . . .' ": William Shawn to GC, May 31, 1976.

page 75 " 'It is a scandal that we didn't publish any of Truman's short stories . . .' ": Brendan Gill to GC, August 8, 1983.

page 76 " 'It just so happened,' Truman said, 'that I was recovering from the flu . . .' ": Elliot Norton, "Fable Drawn from Life," *New York Times*, March 23, 1952, Arts section, page 3.

page 77 " 'Truman came home crying . . .' ": Joseph Capote to GC, May 7, 1977.

CHAPTER 12

page 79 " 'It was early winter when I arrived there . . .' ": TC, *The Dogs Bark*, page 6.

page 79 " 'He seemed happy-happy . . .' ": Mary Ida Carter to GC, September 7, 1976.

page 79 " 'More and more,' he wrote, '*Summer Crossing* seemed to me thin . . .' ": *Ibid.*, page 6.

page 80 " 'noisy as a steel mill . . .' ": *Ibid.*, page 8.

page 81 " 'He couldn't paint worth a damn . . .' ": Patsy Streckfus Clark to GC, November, 1977.

page 81 " 'the freest time of my life . . .' ": Andrea Chambers, "Going Home," *People*, January 26, 1981, page 56.

page 82 " 'There were extraordinary people . . .' ": Richard Avedon to GC, August 7, 1976.

page 83 " 'That's fine, little boy . . .' ": Andrew Lyndon to GC, April 23, 1977.

page 85 " 'I saw "Miriam" in *Mademoiselle* . . .' ": Mary Louise Aswell to GC, December 17, 1975.

page 86 " '*Harper's* and *Mademoiselle* turned into temples . . .' ": Alfred Chester, "American Gothic: A Powerful, Enigmatic and Troubling Account of Murder in the Nth Degree," *New York Herald Tribune Book Week*, January 16, 1966, page 2.

page 86 " 'The most remarkable new talent of the year was . . .' ": Brickell, *O. Henry Memorial Award Prize Stories of 1946*, page xiv.

CHAPTER 13

page 88 " 'George had pipit monstrosities in his head . . .' ": Leo Lerman to GC, May 5, 1976.

page 88 " 'George had the nastiest tongue . . .' ": Pearl Kazin Bell to GC, August 10, 1976.

page 88 " . . . his friend W. H. Auden called him . . .": Irving Drutman to GC, February 8, 1978.

pages 88–9 " 'Knowing George was a career in itself . . .' ": Phoebe Pierce Vreeland to GC, April 20, 1976.

page 89 " 'George brought out the worst in Truman . . .' ": Pearl Kazin Bell to GC, August 10, 1976.

page 90 " 'The people George knew were a legion . . .' ": Howard Moss to GC, December 18, 1976.

page 90 "he even declared that Truman's 'slender talent' . . .": Letter from Paul Bigelow to Jordan Massee, March 25, 1947.

page 90 "A decade later . . .": Drutman, *Good Company*, pages 113–14.

page 90 " 'It was spectacular in a truly Truman way . . .' ": Leo Lerman to GC, May 5, 1976.

page 91 " 'Nina sometimes became rather violent . . .' ": *Ibid.*

page 91 " 'He knew without a doubt the precise moment . . .' ": Pearl Kazin Bell, "The Jester," *Botteghe Oscure*, Volume 9, 1952, page 282.

page 92 " 'You knew exactly what you were going to get there . . .' ": Mary Louise Aswell to GC, May 7, 1977.

page 92 " 'Little T can be absolutely adorable . . .' ": Selma Robinson, *op. cit.*, pages 6–8.

page 93 " 'Carmel and Diana Vreeland were both fascinated . . .' ": Mary Louise Aswell to GC, May 7, 1977.

page 94 " 'Oh, those were funny days!' ": Mary Louise Aswell to GC, December 17, 1975.

page 94 " 'She was in a very shaky state . . .' ": Pearl Kazin Bell to GC, August 10, 1976.

page 95 " 'As an editor it seems to me as though . . .' ": TC to Mary Louise Aswell, July 12, 1946.

page 95 " 'Who thought about those things?' ": Doris Lilly to GC, October 25, 1975.

page 96 " 'Do you know anything about a writer named Waugh?' ": Andrew Lyndon to GC, April 23, 1977.

page 96 " 'Write about what you know,' he told her . . .": Doris Lilly to GC, October 25, 1975.

page 96 " 'The first time I saw her . . .' ": TC eulogy of Carson McCullers, on file, American Institute of Arts and Letters, New York.

page 97 " 'she was enchanted with him . . .' ": Jordan Massee to GC, February 16, 1977.

page 97 " 'An hour with a dentist . . .' ": Stanton and Vidal, *Views from a Window*, page 180.

page 97 " 'Carson's family was wildly Southern . . .' ": Phoebe Pierce Vreeland to GC, April 20, 1976.

page 98 "she helped no other young writer as enthusiastically as she did Truman": Carr, *The Lonely Hunter*, page 261.

page 98 "signed Truman to a contract . . .": Selma Robinson, *op. cit.*, pages 6–8.

page 98 " 'Now you're going to be a writer . . .' ": Jerry Tallmer, *New York Post*, December 16, 1967, page 26.

page 98 " 'Well, *that* was a day . . .' ": Cerf, *At Random*, page 223.

CHAPTER 14

page 99 " 'Night after night I would see him . . .' ": Joe Capote to GC, May 7, 1977.

page 100 " . . . on May 1, 1946, he . . .": Curtis Harnack, Yaddo executive director, in a letter to GC, March 25, 1977.

page 100 "Surrounded by gentle hills . . .": "LIFE Visits Yaddo," *Life*, July 15, 1946.

page 101 "With the tail of his shirt flapping . . .": Marguerite Young to GC, January 22, 1976.

page 101 " 'Spontaneous when others are cautious . . .' ": Brinnin, *Sextet*, page 9.

page 101 " 'You just go right ahead, honey chile . . .' ": Marguerite Young to GC, January 22, 1976.

page 102 " 'From where did he come . . .' ": Leo Lerman to GC, May 5, 1976.

page 102 " 'She must be about sixty,' he said . . .": TC to Mary Louise Aswell, May, 1946.

page 102 "Sending a dispatch from the front . . .": TC to Mary Louise Aswell, May 18, 1946.

page 102 "In another letter to Mary Louise . . .": TC to Mary Louise Aswell, spring, 1946.

page 103 " 'the strangest thing is going on . . .' ": *Ibid.*

page 103 " 'The little one has been . . .' ": John Malcolm Brinnin to GC, October 18–19, 1981.

page 103 " 'He had a marvelous voice . . .' ": *Ibid.*

page 103 " 'Howard was prone to very . . .' ": Frances Doughty to GC, September 10, 1983.

page 104 " . . . encircled by what he called the 'magic ring' . . .": Newton Arvin to Howard Doughty, June 17, 1946.

page 104 " 'I can't down the desire . . .' ": Newton Arvin to Howard Doughty, June 20, 1946.

page 105 " 'But you know, dearest T.C. . . .' ": Newton Arvin to TC, summer, 1946.

page 106 " 'I have read three of your stories . . .' ": *Ibid*.

page 107 " 'You dope—how can you think . . .' ": Howard Doughty to Newton Arvin, June 19, 1946.

page 107 " 'You are very understanding . . .' ": Newton Arvin to Howard Doughty, June 20, 1946.

page 108 "He looked like 'a million dollars,' Newton . . .": Newton Arvin to Granville Hicks, July 17, 1946.

page 109 " 'Suddenly the tower room was . . .' ": Brinnin, *Sextet*, page 11.

CHAPTER 15

page 110 "Was Newton an important . . .": Brinnin, *Sextet*, page 6.

page 110 "Alfred Kazin, also a critic . . .": Alfred Kazin, "The Burning Human Values in Melville," *New York Times Book Review*, May 7, 1950, page 6.

page 110 "Wilson himself praised him for . . .": Edmund Wilson, "Arvin's Longfellow and New York State's Geology," *The New Yorker*, March 23, 1963.

page 111 "Born in Valparaiso, Indiana . . .": Newton's early life is detailed in an unfinished, unpublished memoir titled *The Past Recaptured*, which is in the Smith College Library. Much of his history is also recorded in various alumni reports from the Harvard class of 1921; these are on deposit in Harvard's Pusey Library. Also of great interest is the introduction to *American Pantheon* by his friend and colleague Daniel Aaron.

page 111 " 'He was a fearful, timorous . . .' ": Daniel Aaron to GC, April 21, 1983.

page 111 "She was outgoing where he was shy . . .": Mary Garrison Grand to GC, April 8, 1975.

page 112 " 'He was extremely generous . . .' ": *Ibid*.

page 112 " 'There is such a thing as . . .' ": Newton Arvin to Howard Doughty, October 30, 1945.

page 113 "One of those attempts was stamped . . .": Andrew Lyndon to GC, April 23, 1977.

page 114 "feeling of 'psychological euphoria . . .' ": Newton Arvin to Granville Hicks, late July, 1946.

page 114 " 'All would be fair indeed . . .' ": Newton Arvin to Howard Doughty, July 25, 1946.

page 114 " 'Look where I am!' ": TC to Howard Doughty, July 29, 1946.

page 115 " 'I had a wonderful time . . .' ": TC to Mary Louise Aswell, August 4, 1946.

page 115 " 'Your letters make a music . . .' ": Newton Arvin to TC, September 11, 1946.

page 116 " 'I am still looking . . .' ": Newton Arvin to TC, August 6, 1946.

page 116 " 'I woke up in the night . . .' ": Newton Arvin to TC, September 11, 1946.

page 116 "Carson, who only a few months before . . .": Carr, *The Lonely Hunter*, page 267.

page 117 " 'I hear all sorts of interesting rumors . . .' ": Howard Doughty to Newton Arvin, September 20, 1946.

page 117 " 'What interesting rumors . . .' ": Newton Arvin to Howard Doughty, September 23, 1946.

page 117 " 'LOST Probably in Manhattan . . .' ": Newton Arvin to TC, February 12, 1946.

page 118 " 'No third meal at all . . .' ": Newton Arvin diaries, September 7, 1946.

page 118 " 'I miss [Newton] most dreadfully . . .' ": TC to Howard Doughty, August, 1946.

page 118 " 'Truman was still writing *Other Voices* . . .' ": Andrew Lyndon to GC, April 23, 1977.

page 119 " 'Newton was only interested . . .' ": Daniel Aaron to GC, April 21, 1983.

page 120 " 'I wish I knew . . .' ": Newton Arvin to Mary Louise Aswell, August 11, 1946.

page 120 " 'They looked like a father . . .' ": Mary Louise Aswell to GC, May 7, 1977.

CHAPTER 16

page 121 " 'It is beautiful here, the weather . . .' ": TC to Mary Louise Aswell, October 12 (or possibly 13), 1946.

page 121 "To Howard he wistfully observed . . .": TC to Howard Doughty, late October 1946.

page 121 " 'He's so stupid, Lyn . . .' ": Lyn White to GC, October 15, 1975.

page 122 " 'I thought that they had a wild . . .' ": Eleanor Friede to GC, October 1, 1975.

page 122 "She slapped his face during . . .": Lyn White to GC, October 15, 1975.

page 122 " . . . and she engaged in affairs of her own . . .": Seabon Faulk to GC, March 8, 1978.

page 122 " 'There was a tragic aura about Nina . . .' ": Michael Brown to GC, February 16, 1976.

page 122 " 'A day or so after she did it . . .' ": Andrew Lyndon to GC, April 23, 1977.

page 123 " 'She was the most uptight person I've . . .' ": Harper Lee to GC, August 10, 1977.

page 123 " 'Nina, would you rather have a football player . . .' ": Lyn White to GC, October 15, 1975.

page 124 " . . . and prompted a delivery boy to scrawl . . .": Andrew Lyndon to GC, April 23, 1977.

page 124 " 'T.C.—pale and tired-looking . . .' ": Newton Arvin's diaries, September 6, 1946.

page 125 " 'Two calls from T.C.—one from 1060 . . .' ": Newton Arvin's diaries, October 27, 1946.

page 125 " 'I have changed addresses, have moved . . .' ": TC to John Malcolm Brinnin, early November 1946.

page 125 " 'Under no circumstances are you . . .' ": *Ibid.*

page 126 " 'Truman regards the trip to Brooklyn . . .' ": Paul Bigelow to Jordan Massee, November 5, 1946.

page 126 " 'It was a bizarre outfit then . . .' ": Eleanor Friede to GC, October 1, 1975.

page 126 " 'As Thoreau would say . . .' ": Newton Arvin to TC, October 15, 1946.

page 126 " 'Wonderful to see him . . .' ": Newton Arvin's diaries, December 7, 1946

page 128 " 'It distresses me unspeakably that things . . .' ": Newton Arvin to TC, October 26, 1946.

page 128 " 'I feel as if I were, indeed I am . . .' ": Newton Arvin to TC, August 22, 1946.

page 129 " 'When I first met him, Truman kissed me!' ": Daniel Aaron to GC, April 21, 1983

page 129 " 'When I want anybody to come to my . . .' ": Diana Trilling to GC.

CHAPTER 17

page 130 " 'After the war . . .' ": Gore Vidal to GC, November 30, 1975.

page 130 " 'The hunt for young authors . . .' ": Connolly, *Ideas and Places*, page 172.

page 131 *"Life,* which could bestow . . .": "Young U.S. Writers," *Life,* June 2, 1947.

page 131 "The day the issue appeared . . .": Cerf, *At Random,* pages 224–25. (Cerf said that this incident occurred in 1948; as there was no such *Life* article in 1948, he must have meant 1947.)

page 131 " . . . they had printed two pictures . . .": *"LIFE* Visits Yaddo," *Life, op. cit.,* page 111.

page 132 " 'the supreme metropolis of the present' ": Connolly, *Ideas and Places,* page 170.

page 132 " 'when the city of New York was still filled with a river light' ": Quoted by Jesse Kornbluth in *The New York Times Sunday Magazine,* October 21, 1979, page 104.

page 133 " 'an unforgettable picture of what a city ought to be . . .' ": Connolly, *Ideas and Places,* page 176.

page 133 "In a scene that was repeated . . .": Phyllis Cerf Wagner to GC, January 17, 1978.

page 135 " 'I do things for Truman . . .' ": Barbara Long, "In Cold Comfort," *Esquire,* June, 1966, page 126.

page 135 "William Goyen, a novelist . . .": William Goyen to GC, December 13, 1976.

page 136 " 'Bob believed Truman led a madly . . .' ": Naomi Bliven to GC, December 14, 1976.

page 136 " 'As an artist . . .' ": Selma Robinson, *op. cit.*, page 8.

CHAPTER 18

page 137 " 'Truman had really begun to move in New York . . .' ": Phyllis Cerf Wagner to GC, January 17, 1978.

page 138 " 'We all went to meet his train . . .' ": William Goyen to GC, December 13, 1976.

page 138 "Wilted by the heat . . .": Robert Horan to GC, April 24, 1977.

page 139 "In his fondest fantasy . . .": TC, *The Dogs Bark*, preface, page x.

page 139 " 'When the bell rang . . .' ": Nin, *The Diary of Anaïs Nin, 1944–1947*, page 111.

page 139 " 'Well, how does it feel to be an *enfant terrible?*' ": Gore Vidal to GC, November 30, 1975.

page 140 "Gore later declared that he wanted . . .": Stanton and Vidal, *Views from a Window*, page 53.

page 140 "Gore took Truman to the Everard Baths . . .": *Ibid.*, page 180.

page 140 " 'It was deadly to get caught . . .' ": "Gore Vidal: Laughing Cassandra," *Time*, March 1, 1976, page 62.

page 141 " 'They began to criticize each other's . . .' ": GC, "Checking In with Truman Capote," *Esquire*, November, 1972, page 188.

page 141 " 'The first time I ever saw Gore . . .' ": Glenway Wescott to GC, January 30, 1976.

page 141 " 'Have you heard what . . .' ": Phoebe Pierce Vreeland to GC, April 20, 1976.

page 141 "Williams privately complained . . .": Tennessee Williams to Carson McCullers, March 1, 1948. Unpublished collection of Jordan Massee.

page 141 " . . .Anaïs Nin, to whom Gore was closely attached, found . . .": Nin, *The Diary of Anaïs Nin, 1944–1947*, page 106.

page 142 "Truman's stories, on the other hand . . .": *Ibid.*, page 111.

page 142 " 'He's infected with that awful competitive spirit . . .' ": Tennessee Williams to Carson McCullers, undated, 1948. Unpublished collection of Carson McCullers.

CHAPTER 19

page 143 " 'Well, is he taking . . .' ": Andrew Lyndon to GC, April 23, 1977.

page 143 " 'It sounds charming . . .' ": Newton Arvin to TC, March 4, 1947.

page 144 "Mornings they all worked . . .": Andrew Lyndon to GC, October 31, 1984.

page 144 ". . . light hammock reading . . .": Newton Arvin's diaries, July, 1947.

page 144 " 'We are keeping a regular schedule . . .' ": TC to Mary Louise Aswell, July, 1947.

page 144 "On Nantucket he wrote in bed . . .": Andrew Lyndon to GC, October 31, 1984.

page 145 " 'These last few pages!' ": TC to Robert Linscott, summer, 1947.

page 145 "He made 'some small corrections . . .' ": Newton Arvin's diaries, July 10, 1947.

page 145 " 'Truman's little voice . . .' ": Mary Louise Aswell to GC, May 7, 1977.

page 145 " 'A difficult day . . .' ": Newton Arvin's diaries, July 15, 1947.

page 146 "Isherwood was visiting . . .": Christopher Isherwood to GC, November 21, 1975.

page 146 ". . . the storyteller who, in Somerset Maugham's . . .": Woolf, *The Diary of Virginia Woolf, Volume Five, 1936–1941*, page 185.

page 146 ". . . who breathlessly quizzed him . . .": Bill Caskey, letter to GC, June 27, 1976.

page 146 ". . . still the 'appreciative merry little bird . . .' ": Woolf, *The Diary of Virginia Woolf*, page 59.

page 147 ". . . remained 'very much in . . .' ": Bill Caskey, letter to GC, June 27, 1976.

page 147 " 'I am uncontrollably eager . . .' ": Newton Arvin to Mary Louise Aswell, July 17, 1947.

page 147 " 'Very happy owing . . .' ": Newton Arvin's diaries, August 23, 1947.

page 148 " 'Oh, my reputation . . .' ": Phoebe Pierce Vreeland to GC, April 20, 1976.

page 148 " 'To Blackie's . . .' ": Newton Arvin's diaries, November 23, 1947.

page 148 " 'I'm the only person of any sex . . .' ": Andrew Lyndon to GC, April 23, 1977.

page 148 " 'the fabled Miss C' ": TC, *The Dogs Bark*, page 52.

page 149 " 'Still on the prowl for celebrities . . .' ": Lopez, *Conversations with Katherine Anne Porter*, page 251.

page 149 " '[Truman's] novel comes out . . .' ": Newton Arvin to Granville Hicks, December 20, 1947.

CHAPTER 20

I consulted and gained insight from several books and articles on Capote, his works, and *Other Voices, Other Rooms* in partiuclar during the writing of this critical section on Capote's first novel. Those most helpful to me were: Hassan, *Radical Innocence*; Goad, *Daylight and Darkness, Dream and Delusion*; Robert K. Morris, *"Capote's Imagery,"* and Paul Levine, "Truman Capote: The Revelation of the Broken Image," in Malin, *Truman Capote's* In Cold Blood; Nance, *The Worlds of Truman Capote*; Schorer, *The World We Imagine*.

page 150 "*Other Voices, Other Rooms* was an attempt to exorcise demons . . .": TC, *The Dogs Bark*, page 3.

page 153 "Noon City, for example, was called Cherryseed City . . .": Original manuscript in Capote collection, Library of Congress.

page 153 " 'That is why the romance . . .' ": Quoted in Goad, *Daylight and Darkness, Dream and Delusion*, page 11.

page 154 "He was 'bounding along like . . .' ": Doris Lilly, unpublished manuscript given to GC.

page 154 " 'There is a look . . .' ": Newton Arvin to TC, February 1, 1946.

page 155 "Booksellers reported . . .": Selma Robinson; *op. cit.*

page 155 "Random House had scheduled . . .": *Ibid.*

page 155 "and unsolicited bids . . .": Roger Bourne Linscott, "On the Books," *New York Herald Tribune*, January 11, 1948.

page 155 " 'Much lush writing . . .' ": Quoted by Dianne B. Trimmier in "The Critical Reception of Capote's *Other Voices, Other Rooms*," *Philological Papers*, West Virginia University Bulletin, Morgantown, West Virginia, June, 1970, page 95.

page 155 " 'The story of Joel Knox . . .' ": Carlos Baker, "Deep-South Guignol," *New York Times Book Review*, January 18, 1948, page 5.

page 155 " 'Mr. Capote has concocted . . .' ": Richard McLaughlin, *The Saturday Review of Literature*, February 14, 1948, pages 12–13.

page 155 " '[The book] is immature . . .' ":"Spare the Laurels," *Time*, January 26, 1948, page 102.

page 155 " 'a deep, murky well . . .' ": "Other Books: 'Other Voices, Other Rooms,' " *Newsweek*, January 26, 1948, page 91.

page 155 " 'A minor imitation . . .' ": *Partisan Review*, March 15, 1948, pages 374–77.

page 156 " '*Other Voices, Other Rooms* abundantly . . .' ": Lloyd Morris, "A Vivid, Inner, Secret World," *New York Herald Tribune Book Review*, January 18, 1948, page 2.

page 156 " 'It is impossible not to . . .' ": Orville Prescott, "Books of the Times," *New York Times*, January 21, 1948, page 23.

page 156 " 'A short novel which is . . .' ": Kelsey Guilfoil, "Exotic Tale of Youth in Odd Setting," *Chicago Sunday Tribune*, January 18, 1948, page 5.

page 156 " 'The clashing of characters . . .' ": Lon Tinkle, "New Young Novelist Makes Brilliant Debut," *Dallas News*, January 18, 1948.

page 156 " 'a book of extraordinary literary . . .' ": Henry Butler, " 'Other Voices, Other Rooms' Expected to Win High Praise of Critics," *Indianapolis Times*, January 17, 1948.

page 156 "He 'is gifted, dangerously gifted . . .' ": Prescott wrote this in the *Yale Review*, spring, 1948. Quoted in Stanton, *Truman Capote*, page 35.

page 156 "James Gray, a syndicated critic . . .": James Gray, "Louisiana Swamps Setting for Capote's Fanciful 'Other Voices,' " *St. Paul Dispatch*, January 16, 1948.

page 157 "One came from Newton . . .": Newton Arvin to Granville Hicks, March 8, 1948, Granville Hicks Collection, University of Rochester.

page 157 "The second such comment came from Truman's onetime mentor . . .": Andrew Lyndon to GC, April 23, 1977.

page 158 "*Other Voices* almost immediately jumped . . .": It first appeared on the best-seller list on February 15, 1948.

page 158 "It sold more than 26,000 copies . . .": Random House records.

page 158 "One night while Truman . . .": Andrew Lyndon to GC, April 23, 1977.

page 158 "Merle Miller, whose own novel . . .": "People," *Time*, March 15, 1948.

page 158 "Someone who signed himself . . .": Selma Robinson, *op. cit.*

page 159 "columnist William Targ . . .": William Targ, "Manhattan Letter," *Cleveland News*, January 28, 1948.

page 159 "humorist Max Shulman . . .": "Other Voices, Other Authors," *Time*, May 3, 1948.

page 160 " 'Truman Capote has the critics . . .' ": *Beaumont* (Texas) *Journal*, February 1, 1948.

page 160 " 'You can't go to any party . . .' ": Selma Robinson, *op. cit.*

page 160 " 'I couldn't go to a . . .' ": Marguerite Young to GC, January 22, 1976.

page 160 " 'In 1948, cruising the . . .' ": Ozick, *Art and Ardor*, pages 85–86.

page 161 " 'I was so shocked and hurt . . .' ": TC in Newquist, *Counterpoint*, page 77.

page 161 "Interviewing him in late January . . .' ": Selma Robinson, *op. cit.*

CHAPTER 21

page 163 "If anyone pressed him . . .": Selma Robinson, *op. cit.*

page 164 " . . . thousands of them—perhaps as many as 100,000 . . .": Flanner, *Paris Journal, 1944–1965*, page 86.

page 164 " 'You take good care . . .' ": Andrew Lyndon to GC, April 23, 1977.

page 164 " 'Truman Capote is all the rage here . . .' ": Waldemar Hansen to John Bernard Myers, May 6, 1948.

page 165 " 'He looked like a child . . .' ": Lord (David) Cecil to GC, letter of October 22, 1976.

page 165 " 'He said that Evelyn Waugh's *The Loved One* . . .' ": Nicolson, *Harold Nicolson, The Later Years, 1945–1962*, page 140.

page 165 " 'I had it fixed in my head . . .' ": "Capote in the Lyons Den," *New York Post*, early July, 1952.

page 166 " 'I was very impressed . . .' ": Waldemar Hansen to GC, September 7, 1983.

page 167 " 'Changing voices, changing rooms. Two dancing . . .' ": Waldemar Hansen to John Bernard Myers, June 13, 1948.

page 167 " 'The French loved the world . . .' ": Robbie Campbell to GC, April 24, 1977.

page 167 " 'It's very hard to describe what Paris . . .' ": Gore Vidal to GC, May 3, 1972.

page 168 " 'Truman gave me very good advice . . .' ": Waldemar Hansen to GC, September 7, 1983.

page 168 "The tabloid *France-Dimanche* . . .": Letter from Lin Emery to GC, September 18, 1977, and letter from Georges Tardy to GC, November 7, 1977.

page 168 " 'You don't haul your friends . . .' ": Karl Bissinger to GC, May 4, 1976.

page 169 " 'The other day at Natalie Barney's . . .' ": Toklas, *Staying On Alone: Letters of Alice B. Toklas*, page 128.

page 169 "An elderly Frenchwoman of formidable presence . . .": Francis Steegmuller, "Meet Jenny Bradley, a Literary Force Extraordinary," *New York Times Book Review*, December 11, 1960, page 5.

page 169 (" 'Ah, poor Marcel . . .' "): Jenny Bradley to GC, November 19, 1978.

page 169 " 'I can see Truman now . . .' ": *Ibid.*

page 169 "Miss Barney also had . . .": See Wickes, *The Amazon of Letters*; Herbert R. Lottman, "In Search of Miss Barney," *New York Times Book Review*, September 18, 1969, page 2; Meryle Secrest, "Writer Natalie Barney Dies," *Washington Post*, February 7, 1972; Secrest, *Between Me and Life*.

page 171 "When he was growing up, Jacksonville . . .": Frederick Fouts to GC, January 19, 1985.

page 171 " ' . . . about the most beautiful boy anybody had ever seen . . .' ": Jimmy Daniels to GC, 1976.

page 172 "Adding his own distinctive colors . . .": Glenway Wescott to GC, January 31, 1976.

page 172 " 'He invented himself . . .' ": John B. L. Goodwin to GC, August 20, 1976.

page 172 " 'His handsome profile was . . .' ": Isherwood, *Down There on a Visit*, pages 193–94.

page 173 " 'He thought that the world . . .' ": Bill Harris to GC, May 19, 1976.

page 174 " 'Our disturbing friend just called . . .' ": TC to Waldemar Hansen, mid-June, 1948.

CHAPTER 22

page 175 "He arrived from Paris . . .": Windham, *Footnote to a Friendship*, page 15.

page 175 " 'For him Venice was Harry's Bar . . .' ": Windham, *Footnote to a Friendship*, pages 18–19.

page 176 " 'An enchanted, infinitesimal village . . .' ": TC, *The Dogs Bark*, page 71.

page 176 "He and Donald chose . . .": Windham, *Footnote to a Friendship*, page 23.

page 176 " 'Peaches precious . . .' ": TC to Donald Windham, August 3, 1948.

page 177 " 'It was right that I had gone to Europe . . .' ": TC, *The Dogs Bark*, page 71.

page 177 "Truman had met Tennessee . . .": Andrew Lyndon to GC, April 23, 1977.

page 178 " 'Aren't you allowing yourself . . .' ": Tennessee Williams to Carson McCullers, July 5, 1948.

page 178 "Truman and Tennessee were together . . .": Williams, *Memoirs*, pages 150–51.

page 178 " . . . that night's television news . . .": Windham, *Footnote to a Friendship*, pages 25–26.

page 179 " . . . he was, as Newton phrased it in his diary, 'much distressed' ": Newton Arvin's diaries, August 12, 1948.

page 179 "Four days later he added . . .": Newton Arvin to Howard Doughty, August 6, 1948.

page 180 " . . . Truman was subdued and sober": Newton Arvin's diaries, August 18, 1948.

page 180 " 'You and your Andrew' ": Howard Doughty to Newton Arvin, July 23, 1948.

page 180 " 'My very dearest Newton' ": Andrew Lyndon to Newton Arvin, undated, spring or summer, 1948.

page 181 " 'Come over, Andrew' ": Andrew Lyndon to GC, April 23, 1977.

page 182 "Holding his three-hundred-dollar prize money . . .": TC to Donald Windham, undated, August, 1948.

page 183 " 'Honey, these cuff buttons . . .' ": Phoebe Pierce Vreeland to GC, April 20, 1976.

page 184 "Two weeks later he recorded . . .": Newton Arvin's diaries, November 7, 1948.

page 184 " 'Sad but also tender . . .' ": Newton Arvin's diaries, February 6, 1949.

page 185 " . . . charged with being 'a lewd . . .' ": Edward Kosner, *New York Post*, September 4, 1960, page 5.

page 186 " 'Day of the Avalanche' ": Newton Arvin's diaries, September 2, 1960.

page 186 " 'All your friends are . . .' ": TC to Newton Arvin, September 6, 1960.

page 186 " . . . delicately, and rather disarmingly . . .": TC to Newton Arvin, October 2, 1960.

page 186 " 'He panicked and ratted . . .' ": Lillian Hellman to GC, April 1, 1981.

page 186 "Writing to his friend Daniel Aaron . . .": Quoted in Arvin, *American Pantheon*, page xvii.

CHAPTER 23

page 188 "Jack happened to be at Leo's . . .": Leo Lerman to GC, May 5, 1976.

page 189 " 'Good Lord! Who wasn't there?' ": Andrew Lyndon to GC, April 23, 1977.

page 189 " 'Truman told me he wanted me . . .' ": Mary Louise Aswell to GC, May 7, 1977.

page 190 " 'My God! You'd think I sold . . .' ": Jack Dunphy to Gloria Dunphy, September 15, 1954.

page 190 " 'He had a terrible temper . . .' ": Olive Daley to GC, August 13, 1979.

page 190 "When his favorite son . . .": Olive Daley and Gloria Dunphy to GC, August 13, 1979.

page 191 " 'All the little good in me . . .' ": Jack Dunphy to Gloria Dunphy, October 10, 1959.

page 191 " 'Poverty is much more than a . . .' ": from *The Schoolteacher*, an unpublished novel by Jack Dunphy.

page 192 " 'When she came to the audition . . .' ": Agnes de Mille to GC, March 14, 1985.

page 193 " 'Hollywood was screaming for her . . .' ": *Ibid.*

CHAPTER 24

page 195 "He was, in his own words, almost hysterical . . .": Williams, *Tennessee Williams' Letters to Donald Windham*, page 237.

page 196 " 'I think you judge Truman a bit . . .' ": *Ibid.*

page 196 "When Jack Warner, who was . . .": Williams, *Memoirs*, page 168.

page 196 " 'What a strange, and strangely . . .' ": TC to Robert Linscott, April 1, 1949.

page 196 "To Cecil Beaton, with whom, during . . .": TC to Cecil Beaton, March 25, 1949.

page 197 "Auden, who had rented a house nearby, extolled . . .": Auden, Collected Poems, page 416.

page 198 " 'I am happy that *Summer Crossing* . . .' ": Robert Linscott to TC, April 6, 1949.

page 198 " . . . early in May he was pleased to report . . .": TC to Robert Linscott, May 6, 1949.

page 198 " 'Silly goose that I am . . .' ": TC to Cecil Beaton, March 25, 1949.

page 198 " 'Truman was wrapped around him . . .' ": Williams, *Tennessee Williams' Letters to Donald Windham*, page 237.

page 198 " 'I am attending to my work . . .' ": TC to Cecil Beaton, May 1, 1949.

page 199 "In a letter to Carson, Tennessee described the arrival . . .": Tennessee Williams to Carson McCullers, June 18, 1949.

page 199 "They traveled in an exuberant . . .": Jack Dunphy to Gloria Dunphy, June 7, 1949.

page 199 "that 'ragamuffin city . . .' ": TC to Donald Windham, August 30, 1949.

page 199 " 'Come to the dock with me . . .' ": Bowles, *Without Stopping*, page 291.

page 200 " 'Rhymes with horror . . .' ": Williams, *Tennessee Williams' Letters to Donald Windham*, page 228.

page 200 " 'I don't care how hot . . .' ": TC to Robert Linscott, August 30, 1949.

page 200 "Cecil Beaton, who arrived in August . . .": Beaton, *The Strenuous Years*, page 49.

page 200 "A leader of her claque was Tennessee . . .": Williams, *Memoirs*, page 159.

page 201 " . . . who wore blue jeans and brown golf shoes . . .": Herbert, *Second Son*, page 124.

page 201 " 'Everything,' she wrote a friend . . .": Dillon, *A Little Original Sin*, page 182.

page 201 "The best picture of Tangier . . .": William Bird, "Eight Powers and a Casbah," *New York Herald Tribune*, June 12, 1949, page 58; Joachim Joesten, "Cinderella City," *The Wall Street Journal*, December 24, 1951, page 1; "Boom Town," *Fortune*, April, 1948.

page 201 " . . . the days slid by . . .": TC, *The Dogs Bark*, page 88.

page 202 "Despite that adolescent display . . .": Beaton, *The Strenuous Years*, pages 49–50.

page 202 " 'One day Truman outlined for us . . .' ": Paul Bowles, letter to GC, March 1, 1976.

page 202 "Two weeks later he confirmed . . .": TC to Robert Linscott, September 12, 1949.

page 202 " 'Well, at any rate,' he said . . .": Beaton, *The Strenuous Years*, page 55.

page 203 "He reminded Price's secretary . . .": Judith Jones to GC, March 2, 1976.

page 203 "Interviewing him then . . .": René Brest, "Avec Truman Capote à Saint-Germain-des-Prés," newspaper unknown.

page 204 " 'One thing I want to be sure of . . .' ": Frank Price to GC, February 20, 1976.

page 204 "Yet he was also bored with traveling . . .": TC to John Malcolm Brinnin, November 6, 1949.

page 204 "Brinnin met him at the airport . . .": Brinnin, *Sextet*, pages 46-49.

CHAPTER 25

page 206 "New York, Truman had told . . .": René Brest, *op. cit.*

page 206 " 'The most richly embroidered legend . . .' ": Charles J. Rolo, "The New Bohemia," *Flair*, February, 1950, page 118.

page 206 " 'Truman, the little monkey . . .' ": Newton Arvin's diaries, December 10, 1947.

page 207 "Knowing how such attention . . .": Ruth Ford to GC, September 1, 1976.

page 208 " 'I am pleased that Faulkner . . .' ": TC to William Goyen, December 16, 1950.

page 209 " 'Maybe it seems strange . . .' ": TC to Robert Linscott, March 20, 1951.

page 209 ". . . Linscott was enormously . . .": William Goyen to GC, December 13, 1976.

page 210 "It was in that square . . .": Donald Windham to GC, March 10, 1977.

page 210 "D. H. Lawrence had lived and enjoyed . . .": Aldington, *Portrait of a Genius, but* . . . , page 223.

page 210 " 'We have had luck, at least . . .' ": TC to Robert Linscott, May 7, 1950.

page 210 "A stone shack was what . . .": Beaton, *The Strenuous Years*, pages 159–60.

page 211 " 'It is very like living . . .' ": TC, *The Dogs Bark*, pages 105–6.

page 211 "A girl in her late teens . . .": Jack Dunphy to Gloria Dunphy, July 8, 1950.

page 211 " 'He is good-looking . . .' ": TC, *The Dogs Bark*, page 115.

page 211 " 'You don't believe in . . .' ": *Ibid*.

page 212 "Eugene O'Neill showed up . . .": TC to Donald Windham, April 18, 1951.

page 212 "At Truman's request, Richard Brooks . . .": Richard Brooks to GC, April 30, 1977, Los Angeles.

page 212 " 'Such a newsy letter . . .' ": TC to Pearl Kazin, May 5, 1951.

page 212 "The Cerfs, on the other hand . . .": TC to Phyllis and Bennett Cerf, April 10, 1951.

page 213 " 'It's *SO* educational . . .' ": *Ibid*.

page 213 " 'It is terribly quiet . . .' ": TC to William Goyen, April 15, 1950.

page 213 " 'But why are you going . . .' ": TC to Cecil Beaton, May 20, 1950.

page 213 " 'Pearl lamb,' he wrote . . .": TC to Pearl Kazin, June 21, 1950.

page 214 " 'Honey, *why* are you . . .' ": TC to Pearl Kazin, October 8, 1950.

page 214 " 'Truman was one of the kindest . . .' ": Pearl Kazin to GC, August 10, 1976.

page 214 " 'She telephoned me and . . .' ": Phoebe Pierce Vreeland to GC, April 20, 1976.

page 215 " 'At least the great chest-pounding . . .' ": TC to Robert Linscott, October, 1950.

page 215 " 'Dear God, I am 26' ": TC to Mary Louise Aswell, October 30, 1950.

page 215 "Horan's relationship with the two composers . . .": Gruen, *Menotti*, pages 51–59.

page 216 "Devastated by the downward turn . . .": Robert Horan to GC, April 24, 1977.

page 216 " 'The rest of the story is just too . . .' ": TC to William Goyen, January 19, 1951.

page 216 " 'Have been going through a terrible . . .' ": TC to Robert Linscott, December 26, 1950.

page 217 " 'Little things keep coming at me . . .' ": Jack Dunphy to Gloria Dunphy, January 10, 1951.

CHAPTER 26

page 219 " 'It is very real to me . . .' ": TC to Robert Linscott, October, 1950.

page 220 " 'I hope this book will be half-worth . . .' ": TC to Mary Louise Aswell, October 30, 1950.

page 220 " 'WONDERFUL WONDERFUL . . .' ": Robert Linscott to TC, September 15, 1950.

page 220 " 'There is a perfection . . .' ": Robert Linscott to TC, September 18, 1950.

page 220 " 'Rumor has it that you . . .' ": Robert Linscott to TC, January 16, 1951.

page 220 " 'I adore every word of the novel . . .' ": Robert Linscott to TC, April 17, 1951.

page 221 ". . . as daunting as Mount Everest or Kilimanjaro": TC to Pearl Kazin, April 1, 1951.

page 221 " 'A great deal depends on . . .' ": TC to Mary Louise Aswell, April 24, 1951.

page 221 ". . . .a 'kind of slave anguish' ": TC to Robert Linscott, May 3, 1951.

page 221 " 'Oh Bob, I do hope . . .' ": TC to Robert Linscott, June 4, 1951.

page 221 " 'I'm relieved that it's . . .' ": TC to Donald Windham, June 4, 1951.

page 221 " 'You are no doubt indignant . . .' ": Robert Linscott to TC, June 22, 1951.

page 222 " 'In our opinion, the book . . .' ": Bennett Cerf to TC, June 22, 1951.

page 222 " 'I cannot endure it that . . .' ": TC to Robert Linscott, June 27, 1951.

page 223 " 'The test of whether or not . . .' ": TC, quoted in Cowley, *Writers at Work*, page 187.

page 223 " 'We must be on our guard . . .' ": Flaubert, *The Letters of Gustave Flaubert*, page 180. (I have joined two sentences from the same letter without using an ellipsis.)

page 224 " 'If only I were a writer . . .' ": TC to Donald Windham, September 8, 1959.

page 224 " 'HAVE READ PROOFS . . .' ": TC to Bennett Cerf, July 9, 1951.

page 224 " 'If it is now in the form . . .' ": Bennett Cerf to TC, July 10, 1951.

page 224 "Truman's second novel, said the Sunday *New York Herald Tribune* . . .": Gene Baro, "Truman Capote Matures and Mellows," *New York Herald Tribune Book Review*, September 30, 1951, page 4.

page 224 "Orville Prescott in the daily . . .": Orville Prescott, "Books of the Times," *New York Times*, October 2, 1951, page 25.

page 224 " 'Within the slim compass . . .' ": Richard Hayes, review of *The Grass Harp*, *The Commonweal*, October 26, 1951, pages 73–74.

page 224 " 'All books today are far . . .' ": Rochelle Girson, "This Week's Personality," *Roanoke* (Virginia) *Times*, September 30, 1951. (Probably syndicated.)

CHAPTER 27

page 225 " 'Tell me, darling, do you . . .' ": TC to Cecil Beaton, May 8, 1951.

page 225 " 'The transposition of one art form . . .' ": TC, "Faulkner Dances," *Theatre Arts*, April, 1949, page 49.

page 225 " 'more broke than Little Orphan Annie' ": TC to Mary Louise Aswell, February 29, 1952.

page 226 " 'I think I do like to work . . .' ": Cyrus Durgin, "Truman Capote Talks of His First Play, 'The Grass Harp,' " *Boston Sunday Globe*, March 2, 1952.

page 227 " 'I have been working so hard . . .' ": TC to Gloria Dunphy, January 6, 1952.

page 227 " 'Well,' he told a reporter who . . .": Harvey Breit, "Talk with Truman Capote," *New York Times*, February 4, 1952.

page 227 " 'Isn't it extraordinary about George Davis . . .' ": TC to Cecil Beaton, August 26, 1951.

page 227 ". . . a 'topflight production . . .' ": TC to Cecil Beaton, December 4, 1951.

page 228 "Saint, taking the recommendation of an experienced . . .": Saint Subber to GC, August 12, 1975.

page 228 " 'Between us, he has a certain vulgarity . . .' ": TC to Cecil Beaton, January 5, 1952.

page 228 "Invited to the final rehearsal . . .": Virgil Thomson to GC, October, 1975.

page 228 "Cecil's tree was even more impressive . . .": "Record-Sized Tree 'Grows' at Martin Beck," *Brooklyn Eagle*, March 23, 1952, page 29.

page 228 "By comparison, commented . . .": *Ibid*.

page 228 "In Lewis' eyes, that was . . .": Lewis, *Slings and Arrows*, page 224.

page 229 " 'Tell y'what,' Truman said . . .": *Ibid*., page 223.

page 229 "Back in New York before . . .": Paul Bigelow to GC, April 23, 1977.

page 229 "Early on opening night . . .": Andrew Lyndon to GC, April 23, 1977.

page 229 "When the curtain had descended . . .": William Goyen to GC, December 13, 1976.

page 230 " 'Out of good impulses . . .' ": Brooks Atkinson, "First Night at the Theatre," *New York Times*, March 28, 1952, page 26.

page 230 " 'Seeing *The Grass Harp* is like . . .' ": Walter F. Kerr, "The Theaters," *New York Herald Tribune*, March 28, 1952, page 12.

page 230 "Thomson blamed . . .": Virgil Thomson to GC, October 27, 1976.

page 230 "Lewis faulted . . .": Lewis, *Slings and Arrows*, pages 222–25.

page 230 "Saint accused . . .": Saint Subber to GC, August 12, 1975: *Ibid*.

CHAPTER 28

page 231 " 'Well, here we are back in Taormina . . .' ": TC to Pearl Kazin, June 9, 1952.

page 231 " 'There are two long . . .' ": Jack Dunphy to Mary Louise Aswell, May 21, 1952.

page 231 " 'We could not get Fontana . . .' ": TC to Donald Windham, May 29, 1952.

page 231 " 'She adores Jack—but is . . .' ": TC to Gloria Dunphy, December 25, 1952.

page 232 " 'It seems all so much . . .' ": TC to Donald Windham, August 4, 1952.

page 232 " 'When one of them seizes me . . .' ": *Show of the Month News*, March or April 1952, page 3.

page 232 "The actors at the Martin Beck . . .": Associated Press report of April 26, 1952; carried in the *Kansas City Star*, April 27, 1952, under headline, "Gals in for the Colors."

page 232 "By the time he returned home after Christmas . . .": TC to Robert Linscott, September 7, 1952.

page 232 " 'Sometimes I wish . . .' ": TC to Gloria Dunphy, December 25, 1952.

page 232 " 'Had a *two-page* cable . . .' ": TC to Cecil Beaton, July 12, 1952.

page 233 " 'I rather fear he . . .' ": TC to Cecil Beaton, August, 1952.

page 233 " 'We decided to spend the winter . . .' ": TC to Cecil Beaton, October 5, 1952.

page 233 "Mary Louise, who was still . . .": TC to Mary Louise Aswell, October 14, 1952.

page 234 "Actually, Truman had been offered . . .": TC to Cecil Beaton, November 8, 1952.

page 234 " 'Capote will be rich . . .' ": Jack Dunphy to Mary Louise Aswell, November, 1952.

page 235 " 'David absolutely adored him . . .' ": Jennifer Jones to GC, November 22, 1975.

page 235 " '*Indiscretion* is, for the . . .' ": "Cinema," *Time*, April 26, 1954, page 11a.

page 237 "A few weeks after Truman finished . . .": M. A. Schmidt, "Battling Bogart's Saga," *New York Times*, September 6, 1953.

page 237 "Hearing of their dilemma, Selznick . . .": Selznick, *Memo from David O. Selznick*, page 462.

page 238 " 'Nobody was prepared for the entrance . . .' ": John Barry Ryan to GC, January 31, 1976.

page 238 " 'He wrote it page by page . . .' ": Morley and Stokes, *Robert Morley*, page 231.

page 238 " 'Truman had to go back to . . .' ": *Ibid*.

page 238 " 'I swear his face was twice . . .' ": John Huston to GC, December 18, 1975.

page 239 " 'When I started, only John and I . . .' ": Otis L. Guernsey, Jr., "Movies: Unusual Collaboration," *New York Herald Tribune*, February 7, 1954.

page 239 " 'I always wanted to know where . . .' ": Jennifer Jones to GC, November 22, 1975.

page 240 " 'it was a hell of a lark . . .' ": Paul V. Beckley, "Nothing, Says Huston, Can Be 'More Trivial,' " *New York Herald Tribune*, August 30, 1953.

page 241 " 'Why, honey, what's wrong . . .' ": Snow with Aswell, *The World of Carmel Snow*, page 183.

page 241 "As a demonstration of the company's . . .": Jack Clayton to GC, August 30, 1976.

page 241 " '[It] ended with John Huston and Humphrey Bogart . . .' ": Jack Dunphy to Gloria Dunphy, May 14, 1953.

page 241 " 'This is such a slight, tiny picture . . .' ": Archer Winsten, "John Huston in Slippers," *New York Post*, September 4, 1953.

page 241 " 'Personally if you don't see this picture . . .' ": Hyams, *Bogie*, page 135.

page 242 " . . . Newton walked out . . .": Newton Arvin's diaries, April 5, 1954.

page 242 " 'However antic and loopy the circumstances . . .' ": Charles Champlin, "Look Back," *Millimeter*, December, 1975, page 56.

CHAPTER 29

page 243 " 'Fortunately,' said Noël Coward . . .": Coward, *The Noël Coward Diaries*, page 218.

page 243 " 'I *need* to write short stories . . .' ": TC to Robert Linscott, May 20, 1953.

page 243 " 'I wish so much I could talk . . .' ": TC to Robert Linscott, August 3, 1953.

page 244 " 'Naturally, my advice would be to . . .' ": Robert Linscott to TC, August 10, 1953.

page 244 " 'I've been working with zombie-like . . .' ": TC to Newton Arvin, October 16, 1953.

page 245 " 'You take your life into your hands . . .' ": Mary Louise Aswell to GC, May 7, 1977.

page 245 " 'I've always wanted to know him . . .' ": Glenway Wescott to GC, January 30, 1976.

page 246 " 'The other night Greta Garbo . . .' ": Jack Dunphy to Gloria Dunphy, August, 1953.

page 248 " 'Cecil's perfect manners become . . .' ": Jack Dunphy to Paul Cadmus, September 14, 1962.

page 249 " 'Perhaps the world's second worst . . .' ": Albin Krebs, "To Bore Was a Crime," *New York Times*, January 19, 1980, page 28.

page 249 " 'They considered themselves small-town boys . . .' ": a nonattributed source to GC, May 2, 1983.

page 249 " 'I respect and trust you . . .' ": TC to Cecil Beaton, November 8, 1952.

page 249 " 'I admire you as a man . . .' ": TC to Cecil Beaton, May 15, 1956.

page 249 " 'We are now each other's best friend . . .' ": This is from an August, 1953, entry in Cecil Beaton's unpublished diaries, which his biographer, Hugo Vickers, was kind enough to show me. In most cases I have relied on Beaton's unpublished diaries rather than those that appeared in print after much polishing and cutting. In a few instances, however, Beaton's handwriting defied me, and I was forced to turn to the published volumes.

page 249 " 'He had very long toenails . . .' ": Sir John Gielgud to GC, June 23, 1983.

page 249 " 'We discussed our beliefs . . .' ": Beaton, *The Strenuous Years*, page 162.

page 250 " 'I am working, but not well . . .' ": Jack Dunphy to Mary Louise Aswell, November, 1953.

page 250 " 'stem to stern,' as he told . . .": TC to Newton Arvin, November 20, 1953.

page 251 " 'This is your friend from across . . .' ": TC to GC.

page 251 "At Carson's insistence . . .": Carr, *The Lonely Hunter*, page 412.

page 251 " 'My youth is gone . . .' ": *Ibid.*, page 413.

CHAPTER 30

page 252 "In fact, the clouds had been long . . .": For the background on Joe Capote's legal problems I am indebted to his lawyer Nathan Rogers, whom I interviewed on June 21, 1978. I also relied on various New York State court documents, including Indictment No. 4195-54, December 21, 1954; Joe Capote's plea before Judge Jacob Gould Schurman, Jr. (Court of General Sessions of the County of New York), January 5, 1955; the statement of Nathan Rogers to the Probation Office, January 27, 1955; and the record of sentencing, March 28, 1955.

page 253 " 'We'll come back either broke . . .' ": Andrew Lyndon to GC, April 23, 1977.

page 253 " 'Everything would be fine . . .' ": TC to Mary Louise Aswell, June 19, 1953.

page 253 " 'Odd, I seem to think about money . . .' ": TC to Newton Arvin, October 16, 1953.

page 253 " 'Do call her . . .' ": Andrew Lyndon to GC, April 23, 1977.

page 253 "Eleanor Friede, who had lunch . . .": Eleanor Friede to GC, October 1, 1975.

page 253 "A few days before New Year's . . .": Seabon Faulk to GC, March 8, 1978.

page 254 " 'When the night maid came . . .' ": Jack Dunphy to Gloria Dunphy, January 6, 1954.

page 255 " 'Truman's in the back . . .' ": Andrew Lyndon to GC, April 23, 1977.

page 255 " 'I'm a Jew . . .' ": *Ibid.*

page 255 " 'People don't ask for a drink . . .' ": Mary Ida Carter to GC, September 7, 1976.

page 256 " 'Well, I'll eventually find out . . .' ": Harper Lee to GC, August 10, 1977.

page 256 " 'I don't think Truman has ever written . . .' ": Phoebe Pierce Vreeland to GC, April 20, 1976.

page 256 " 'You know, Lyn, my mother loved . . .' ": Lyn White to GC, October 16, 1975.

page 256 " 'You're not my father . . .' ": Andrew Lyndon to GC, April 23, 1977.

page 257 " 'He told me that he had been . . .' ": Arch Persons to GC, September 9, 1976.

page 257 " 'Truman is having a bad time . . .' ": Jack Dunphy to Gloria Dunphy, June 16, 1954.

page 257 " . . . on March 30 he entered Sing Sing . . .": A letter of August 29, 1985 to GC from James E. Sullivan, Superintendent, and George McGrath, Program Coordinator, Sing Sing Correctional Facility, Ossining, New York.

CHAPTER 31

page 259 "There was a setback in February . . .": Jablonski, *Harold Arlen*, page 184.

page 259 "Every day when he visited Arlen . . .": *Ibid.*

page 260 " 'We used to work three hours . . .' ": Harold Arlen to GC.

page 260 " 'Brook is a very creative force . . .' ": Nance, *The Worlds of Truman Capote*, page 129.

page 261 " 'When he was through, it was a mambo!' ": Geoffrey Holder to GC, September 5, 1985.

page 261 " 'Tell me, how do you handle . . .' ": Lucia Victor to GC, September 5, 1985.

page 262 " 'What am I doing wrong? . . .' ": *Ibid.*

page 262 " 'Before I left London, somebody . . .' ": John Barry Ryan to GC, January 31, 1976.

page 262 " 'When Pearl walked out, Peter . . .' ": Lucia Victor to GC, September 5, 1985.

page 262 " 'Peter's ego was such that . . .' ": D. D. Ryan to GC, January 31, 1976.

page 263 " 'The first act was very good . . .' ": Harold Arlen to GC.

page 263 " 'Mr. Capote has run out of . . . ,' ": Walter F. Kerr, "House of Flowers," *New York Herald Tribune*, December 31, 1954.

page 263 " 'It's one of those shows in which . . .' ": Hobe, "House of Flowers," *Variety*, January 12, 1955.

page 263 " 'I don't know what's happening . . .' ": Shirley Herz to GC, September 4, 1985.

page 264 "The last show was a sellout . . .": Jablonski, *Harold Arlen*, page 195.

CHAPTER 32

page 267 " 'Sat on the stone wall and . . .' ": TC, "A Gathering of Swans," *Harper's Bazaar*, September, 1959, pages 122–25.

page 268 " 'He would tell me things . . .' ": Carol Marcus Matthau to GC, August 15, 1985.

page 268 " 'We were once in Copenhagen . . .' ": Lady (Nancy) Keith to GC, March 21, 1985.

page 269 " 'By the time you get this . . .' ": TC to Cecil Beaton, June 21, 1956.

page 271 "Andrew was present when he received his first . . .": Andrew Lyndon to GC, April 23, 1977.

page 272 "He liked to show off the detective . . .": Bradlee, *Conversations with Kennedy*, page 106.

page 272 " 'I keep thinking what power . . .' ": Jacqueline Kennedy to TC, August 26, 1963.

page 272 " 'Dear Truman, thank you for thinking . . .' ": Jacqueline Kennedy to TC, December 12, 1964.

page 272 " 'All the times of insouciance . . .' ": Jacqueline Kennedy to TC, June 22, 1968.

CHAPTER 33

page 279 " 'The beautiful darling!' her father . . .": Thomson, *Harvey Cushing*, page 227.

page 279 " 'So great is her beauty that . . .' ": Baldwin, *Billy Baldwin Remembers*, page 142.

page 279 "Her mother was no less ambitious . . .": "The Cushing Sisters," *Life*, August 11, 1947, pages 41–44; Graham, *How to Marry Super Rich*, pages 224–33.

page 279 " 'society's three fabulous Cushing sisters . . .' ": Nancy Randolph, "It's a CBS Heir at Bill Paley's," New York *Daily News*, March 31, 1948.

page 280 " 'immaculate quality and immense serenity' ": Enid Nemy, "Barbara Cushing Paley Dies at 63, Style Pace-Setter in Three Decades," *New York Times*, July 7, 1978.

page 281 "He met the Paleys . . .": Jennifer Jones to GC, November 22, 1975.

page 281 " 'There's great beauty in his face . . .' ": " 'In Cold Blood' . . . An American Tragedy," *Newsweek*, January 24, 1966, page 63.

page 282 " 'He had a passion to identify . . .' ": Oliver Smith to GC, December 18, 1985.

page 282 " '[Truman's] opened up avenues . . .' ": " 'In Cold Blood' . . . ," *Newsweek, op. cit.*

page 283 "When he created the little park . . .": Tony Schwartz, "An Intimate Talk with William Paley," *New York Times*, December 18, 1980, page 14.

page 284 "From early manhood . . .": Halberstam, *The Powers That Be*, page 421.

page 284 " 'I don't think I am a very easy . . .' ": Paley, *As It Happened: A Memoir*, page 2.

page 284 "Once, recalled Christopher Isherwood . . .": Christopher Isherwood to GC, November 21, 1975.

page 287 " 'Babe made a mistake . . .' ": Interview with a friend of the Paleys.

page 288 " 'Greedy for happiness, I asked nothing . . .' ": Proust, *Remembrance of Things Past*, Volume I, *Swann's Way*, page 140.

CHAPTER 34

page 289 " 'How many of you would be . . .' ": Irving Drutman to GC, February 8, 1978.

page 289 " 'Dear Mr. Jack,' he said . . .": Jack Dunphy to Gloria Dunphy, June, 1955.

page 289 " 'Now, true to my word . . .' ": TC to Robert Linscott, July 10, 1955.

page 290 "All bundled up, 'he looked . . .' ": Marilyn Putnam to GC, January 8, 1986.

page 290 "Writing later, he said that he imagined . . .": TC, *The Dogs Bark*, preface, page xvii.

page 291 "When she had read *Other Voices* . . .": Nancy Ryan Brien to GC, September 8, 1977.

page 292 " 'I think it only fair to point out . . .' ": Kenneth Tynan, "Elfin Eavesdropper," *The Observer* (London), June 23, 1957.

page 292 " 'Laugh, you dreary people . . .' ": Leonard Lyons, "The Lyons Den," *New York Post*, July 16, 1966.

page 292 "One day Breen was talking . . .": Wilva Breen to GC, January 3, 1986.

page 292 "That night Nancy found them sprawled . . .": Nancy Ryan Brien to GC, September 8, 1977.

page 293 "Describing Boris to Newton . . .": TC to Newton Arvin, August 14, 1958.

page 293 "In Moscow he addressed the Soviet . . .": Bernard D. Nossiter, "Author Capote Finds Russia . . . , " *New York Herald Tribune*, February 26, 1956.

page 294 "Looking back, he said, '*The Muses Are Heard* . . .' ": TC, *The Dogs Bark*.

page 294 "In one case, he even invented . . .": Nancy Ryan Brien to GC, September 8, 1977.

page 294 "Lyons, who felt most wounded . . .": Leonard Lyons, *op. cit.*

page 295 " 'wicked, witty and utterly devastating' ": "Sterling North Reviews —Truman Capote in Darkest Russia," *New York World-Telegram and The Sun*, November 9, 1956.

page 295 " 'He was very keen on keeping his line . . .' ": Guggenheim, *Out of This Century*, page 348.

page 295 " 'You would adore it . . .' ": TC to Cecil Beaton, June 21, 1956.

page 296 " 'In some part of his nature he was . . .' ": Oliver Smith to GC, December 18, 1985.

page 297 " 'We're very excited,' he wrote Mary Louise . . .": Jack Dunphy to Mary Louise Aswell, May 28, 1956.

page 297 " 'Home! And happy to be . . .' ": TC, *The Dogs Bark*, page 149.

page 297 " 'I love Brooklyn Heights,' he told . . .": Wriston Locklair, "Writer Truman Capote Likes, Adds to Heights 'Local Color,' " *Brooklyn Heights Press*, October 17, 1957, page 1.

CHAPTER 35

page 298 "Shortly after New Year's, 1957, Warner Brothers . . .": The background on the filming of *Sayonara* and the various disputes between Truman and the moviemakers I found in Joshua Logan's *Movie Stars, Real People, and*

Me, pages 93–121; Truman's diaries of his Asia journey, which are in the Library of Congress; and Cecil Beaton's unpublished diaries.

page 299 " 'It treated human beings like bugs . . .' ": Logan, *Movie Stars, Real People, and Me*, page 101.

page 299 " 'His assurance is deep-seated . . .' ": Cecil Beaton's diaries, undated, January, 1957.

page 301 " 'Bless Jesus I don't live there . . .' ": TC's diaries, January 20, 1957.

page 301 " 'A delightful city of wide avenues . . .' ": TC's diaries, January 21–28, 1957.

page 301 " 'Am intrigued,' he wrote . . .": *Ibid*.

page 301 " 'Don't let yourself be left alone with Truman . . .' ": Logan, *Movie Stars, Real People, and Me*, page 106.

page 302 " 'What an experience,' Truman wrote . . .": TC's diaries, undated, early February, 1957.

page 302 "In his journal, Truman added his own poignant . . .": *Ibid*.

page 302 " 'Oh, you were so wrong . . .' ": Logan, *Movie Stars, Real People, and Me*.

page 303 " 'Here, of course, is the inevitable communication . . .' ": Marlon Brando to TC, May 16, 1957.

page 303 "Walter Winchell said it was . . .": "Walter Winchell of New York," *New York Daily Mirror*, November 24, 1957.

page 303 " 'I'll kill him!' ": Logan, *Movie Stars, Real People, and Me*, page 120.

page 303 " 'Thank you for writing this piece . . .' ": William Shawn to TC, October 31, 1957.

page 304 " 'Went to a small boite to see . . .' ": TC's diaries, February 12–15, 1957.

CHAPTER 36

page 306 " 'As he had been there before, Truman . . .' ": Lady (Nancy) Keith to GC, September 24, 1975.

page 306 " 'I am really three thousand years . . .' ": Curtis Cate, "Isak Dinesen," *The Atlantic*, December, 1959, page 152.

page 307 " 'Time has reduced her to . . .' ": TC with Avedon, *Observations*, page 142.

page 307 " 'He's a nice chap and . . .' ": Vickers, *Cecil Beaton*, page 456.

page 307 " 'I read several versions . . .' ": Phyllis Cerf Wagner to GC, January 17, 1978.

page 308 " 'I used to get these lists . . .' ": Alice Morris to GC, January 3, 1976.

page 308 " ' "I'm not going to change . . ." ' ": *Ibid*.

page 308 " 'I'm not angry, I'm outraged . . .' ": "Newsmakers," *Newsweek*, June 2, 1958, page 44.

page 308 "Truman's friend Irving Drutman . . .": Irving Drutman to GC, February 8, 1978.

page 309 " 'Have written you from many places . . .' ": TC to Newton Arvin, undated, summer, 1958.

page 309 "To Cecil he added . . .": TC to Cecil Beaton, June 18, 1958.

page 309 " 'A large novel, my magnum opus' ": TC to Bennett Cerf, September 29, 1958.

page 310 "Many aphorisms have been falsely attributed . . .": For guidance on the works of Saint Teresa of Avila, I am indebted to a noted Saint Teresa scholar and translator of her works, Father Kieran Kavanaugh, O.C.D., of the Discalced Carmelite Monastery in Brookline, Massachusetts.

page 310 "A former showgirl and the daughter of . . .": *Life* provided a long account of the Woodward killing in its issue of November 14, 1955, beginning page 35. In addition I consulted numerous newspaper stories from the time.

page 310 " 'I said I was happy . . .' ": TC to Newton Arvin, July 16, 1958.

page 311 " 'Have learned only five Greek words . . .' ": TC to Donald Windham, August 18, 1958.

page 311 " 'When I reached it,' Jack told . . .": Jack Dunphy to Gloria Dunphy, undated, September, 1958.

page 311 " 'The whole notion opens vistas . . .' ": TC to Newton Arvin, July 16, 1958.

page 312 " 'My Birthday,' he noted . . .": TC's diaries, September 30, 1958.

CHAPTER 37

page 313 "In an early version, Truman . . .": The early versions of *Breakfast at Tiffany's* are in the Capote collection of the Library of Congress.

page 314 "Shortly after it appeared, Doris Lilly . . .": Andrew Lyndon to GC, January 7, 1984.

page 314 "Unfortunately, a Manhattan woman . . .": Paul Berg, "$800,000 Suit Over a Best Seller," *Saint Louis Post-Dispatch*, March 1, 1959, "Pictures," page 3.

page 314 " 'It's riduculous for her to claim . . .' ": "Golightly at Law," *Time*, February 9, 1959, page 90.

page 314 " 'Truman Capote I do not know well . . .' ": Mailer, *Advertisements for Myself*, page 465.

page 315 "Mailer had good reason to call him . . .": Janet Winn, "Capote, Mailer and Miss Parker," *The New Republic*, February 9, 1959, pages 27–28.

page 315 " . . . he told Cecil that it was 'wonderful, big . . .' ": TC to Cecil Beaton, June 12, 1959.

page 315 " 'Your item about Leland and Pam . . .' ": TC to Cecil Beaton, July 15, 1959.

page 315 "In New York, Bennett Cerf told Truman . . .": Bennett Cerf to TC, August 3, 1959.

page 316 " 'There was much talk about what is . . .' ": TC to Cecil Beaton, August 24, 1959.

page 316 " 'What possible trouble or disaster . . .' ": Lady (Nancy) Keith to GC, September 24, 1975.

page 316 "After finishing forty pages of his Moscow . . .": William Shawn to GC, May 31, 1976.

page 317 " 'I like the feeling that something is happening . . .' ": Phyllis Meras, "Writing Isn't Therapeutic for Capote," *Providence Sunday Journal*, July 19, 1959, page W–14.

page 317 "He was too restless to settle down to fiction . . .": Glenway Wescott to GC, January 31, 1976, and February 9, 1976.

CHAPTER 38

Much of the background for the *In Cold Blood* chapters was provided by *In Cold Blood* itself.

page 318 "The truth, as Henry James . . .": James, *The Art of the Novel*, page 159.

page 318 " 'Everything would seem freshly minted . . .' ": George Plimpton, "The Story Behind a Nonfiction Novel," *New York Times Book Review*, January 16, 1966.

page 319 " 'As he originally conceived it . . .' ": William Shawn to GC, May 31, 1976.

page 319 " 'He said it would be a tremendously . . .' ": " 'In Cold Blood' . . . An American Tragedy," *Newsweek*, January 24, 1966, page 60.

page 319 " 'Did you read about the murder . . .' ": Jack Dunphy to Gloria Dunphy, December 3, 1959.

page 319 " 'I don't know a soul . . .' ": Cerf, *At Random*, page 192.

page 319 " 'He was afraid that there wouldn't be . . .' ": Harper Lee to GC, March 2, 1986.

page 321 " 'he was like someone coming off the . . .' ": *Ibid*.

page 321 " 'Well . . . I'd sure hate to tell . . .' ": Robert Pearman, "Reaction to Capote Book Varies at Scene," *Kansas City Times*, January 27, 1966.

page 321 "Soon after arriving, he and Nelle walked into the office . . .": Alvin Dewey to GC, October 25–26, 1976.

page 321 " 'Well he could have talked all day . . .' ": *Ibid*.

page 322 " 'Nelle walked into the kitchen . . .' ": Dolores Hope to GC, October 28, 1976.

page 322 " 'It wasn't like he was interviewing you . . .' ": Wilma Kidwell to GC, October 26, 1976.

page 323 "At one particularly bleak point, he despaired . . .": Harper Lee to GC, March 2, 1986.

page 323 " 'Of course Truman dominated the . . .' ": Dolores Hope to GC, October 28, 1976.

page 323 ". . . when his wife, Marie, who had been born . . .": Marie and Alvin Dewey, October 25–26, 1976.

page 326 " 'He saw Truman as someone like himself . . .' ": Donald Cullivan to GC, February 27, 1986.

page 327 " 'I had one of the worst childhoods . . .' ": Harper Lee to GC, August 10, 1977.

page 327 " 'He was suspicious, like many people . . .' ": Donald Cullivan to GC, February 27, 1986.

page 327 "Perry was deeply offended by . . .": *Ibid.*

page 328 " 'An extradordinary experience, in many ways the most . . .' ": TC to Cecil Beaton, January 21, 1960.

page 328 "How had he been greeted . . .": Glenway Wescott to GC, January 31, 1976.

CHAPTER 39

page 329 "Indeed, as Dick Avedon . . .": Richard Avedon to GC, August 7, 1976.

page 330 " 'It is really too awful . . .' ": TC to Donald Cullivan, July 15, 1960.

page 331 " '[It] may take another year or more . . .' ": TC to Newton Arvin, undated, probably July, 1960.

page 332 " 'Whether it is worth doing . . .' ": TC to Mary Louise Aswell, October 3, 1960.

page 332 " 'Never thought that I, of all writers . . .' ": TC to Donald Windham, October 17, 1960.

page 332 " 'Alas, I am rather too much involved . . .' ": TC to Newton Arvin, November 9, 1960.

page 333 " 'I'll think 3 times before . . .' ": TC to Donald Windham, August 12, 1960.

page 333 " 'Every once in a while friends of Truman's . . .' ": Jack Dunphy to Gloria Dunphy, undated, August, 1960.

page 333 " 'It was sometimes embarrassing to hear . . .' ": Cecil Beaton's unpublished diary, May, 1960.

page 333 "It was cold, dark and raining . . .": Jack Dunphy to Gloria Dunphy, Novembr 4, 1960.

page 334 "Freud, who learned to enjoy canine . . .": Clark, *Freud, The Man and the Cause*, pages 483–84.

page 334 " 'Last week we found out Bunky . . .' ": TC to Donald Windham, undated, early January, 1961.

page 334 " 'He did it in the most unbelievable . . .' ": Jack Clayton to GC, August 30, 1976.

page 334 " 'A beautifully turned film . . .' ": Paul V. Beckley, "The Innocents," *New York Herald Tribune*, December 26, 1961, page 9.

page 334 " 'Oh how glorious it seems . . .' ": TC to Cecil Beaton, February 10, 1961.

page 335 " 'Today I stood in back of . . .' ": Jack Dunphy to Gloria Dunphy, January 22, 1961.

page 335 " 'Is there a pet shop here? . . .' ": Beaton, *The Restless Years*, pages 127–28.

page 335 " 'an extraordinary and terrible experience . . .' ": TC to Cecil Beaton, February 8, 1962.

page 336 " 'Somehow they, it, the whole thing . . .' ": TC to Cecil Beaton, February 25, 1962.

page 336 " 'Of course they all arrived back . . .' ": Jack Dunphy to Paul Cadmus, May, 1962.

page 336 "Truman added that the Corsicans . . .": TC to Donald Windham, June 3, 1962.

page 336 " 'by a lady-in-waiting in the form of . . .' ": TC to Cecil Beaton, July 26, 1962.

page 336 "Gloria had warned her future Number Four . . .": Wyatt Cooper to GC, January 6, 1976.

page 336 " 'Well, Gloria has come and gone . . .' ": TC to Marie and Alvin Dewey, August 3, 1962.

page 337 " 'bedded down with my book . . .' ": TC to Mary Louise Aswell, October 15, 1962.

page 337 "The lunch, in honor of the Queen Mother . . .": Cecil Beaton's unpublished diary, November, 1962.

CHAPTER 40

page 339 " 'I have been rising every morning . . .' ": TC to Cecil Beaton, February 4, 1963.

page 340 " '*I need a rest from my book* . . .' ": TC to Cecil Beaton, February 28, 1963.

page 340 " 'The staple of life is certainly . . .' ": Daniel Aaron, introduction to Arvin, *American Pantheon*, intro. page xvii.

page 341 " 'If only I could empty my soul . . .' ": TC to Cecil Beaton, February 4, 1963.

page 342 " 'Eventually it began to own him . . .' ": Phyllis Cerf Wagner to GC, January 17, 1978.

page 341 " 'He spoke the way he wrote . . .' ": D. D. Ryan to GC, February 23, 1976.

page 342 " 'Well, should I?' ": Harper Lee to GC, August 10, 1977.

page 342 " 'My wife Blanche . . .' ": Arch Persons to GC, September 9, 1976.

page 342 " 'I was in London last week . . .' ": TC to Mabel Purcell, December 14, 1962.

page 344 " 'Amigo mio, I have . . .' ": Perry Smith to TC, June 26, 1963.

page 344 " 'I have your picture with Charlie . . .' ": Perry Smith to TC, June 30, 1963.

page 344 " 'I like talented personalities . . .' ": Perry Smith to TC, January 19, 1964.

page 345 " 'This kind of literature is only degenerating . . .' ": Perry Smith to TC, October 6, 1963.

page 345 " 'P. has another "madon" at me . . .' ": Richard Hickock to TC, January 1, 1964.

page 345 " 'Forty two months without exercise . . .' ": Richard Hickock to TC, September 15, 1963.

page 345 " 'I doubt if hell will have me . . .' ": Richard Hickock to TC, September 8, 1963.

page 345 " 'At times it seems *forty* years . . .' ": Richard Hickock to TC, April 5, 1964.

page 346 " 'My hair line, at my forehead . . .' ": Richard Hickock to TC, September 20, 1964.

page 346 " 'My concern is that the info. you have . . .' ": Perry Smith to TC, January 29, 1964.

page 346 " 'What is the purpose of the book?' ": Perry Smith to TC, April 12, 1964.

page 346 "In a nine-page letter, Dick . . .' ": Richard Hickock to TC, January 25, 1964.

page 347 "With his usual thoroughness, he looked up . . .": Perry Smith to TC, June 4, 1964.

page 347 " 'My Dear Friend,' he said . . .": Perry Smith to TC, November 24, 1964.

page 347 " 'Well, the fat's in . . .' ": Richard Hickock to TC, January 28, 1965.

page 347 " 'April 14 you know is the date . . .' ": Perry Smith to TC, March 18, 1965.

CHAPTER 41

page 348 ". . . in 1962 *Newseek* had even run a . . .": "Romance with Reality," *Newsweek*, February 5, 1962, page 85.

page 349 " 'The house is divine . . .' ": TC to Cecil Beaton, undated, probably July, 1963.

page 349 " 'I am in a really appalling state . . .' ": TC to Cecil Beaton, September 17, 1963.

page 349 "To Cecil's gratification, Truman heartily endorsed . . .": Cecil Beaton's unpublished diaries, November, 1963.

page 350 " 'I had so much to say & discuss . . .' ": Perry Smith to TC, November 24, 1963.

page 350 "He took Donald Windham . . .": Windham, *Footnote to a Friendship*, pages 71–72.

page 350 " 'I really have been feeling very low . . .' ": TC to Marie and Alvin Dewey, January 18, 1964.

page 350 " 'Go on with your work . . .' ": Jack Dunphy to TC, January 20, 1964.

page 350 " 'No, I want to be at least . . .' ": Jack Dunphy to TC, January 25, 1964.

page 351 "The Deweys, Sandy noted in his diary . . .": These references are from Sandy Campbell's unpublished diaries, which he very kindly allowed me to see.

page 352 " 'That you really liked my book . . .' ": TC to Mary Louise Aswell, November 22, 1964.

page 352 "*Newsweek*, which sent a reporter . . .": "The Fabulist," *Newsweek*, December 28, 1964, pages 54–55.

page 352 " 'It wasn't a question of my *liking* . . .' ": Jane Howard, "How the 'Smart Rascal' Brought It Off," *Life*, January 7, 1966, page 72.

page 352 " 'As you may have heard . . .' ": TC to Mary Louise Aswell, January 21, 1965.

page 352 " 'I'm finishing the last pages . . .' ": TC to Cecil Beaton, January 27, 1965.

page 353 " 'Hope this doesn't sound insane . . .' ": TC to Sandy Campbell, February 2, 1965.

page 353 " 'And I thought: yes, and I hope . . .' ": TC to Marie and Alvin Dewey, February 9, 1965.

page 353 " 'He was incredibly tense and unable to really talk . . .' ": Joe Fox to GC, January 20, 1976.

CHAPTER 42

page 355 " 'Perry and Dick were executed . . .' ": TC to Donald Cullivan, April 17, 1965.

page 355 " 'Bless Jesus,' he exclaimed . . .": TC to Cecil Beaton, June 16, 1965.

page 357 "Only a writer 'completely in control . . .' ": George Plimpton, "The Story Behind a Nonfiction Novel," *New York Times Book Review*, January 16, 1966, page 2.

page 357 " 'Journalism,' he said, 'always moves along on a . . .' ": Gloria Steinem, "A Visit with Truman Capote," *Glamour*, April, 1966.

page 357 " 'An author in his book . . .' ": Flaubert, *The Letters of Gustave Flaubert*, page 173.

page 357 " 'I built an oak and . . .' ": Granville Hicks, "The Story of an American Tragedy," *Saturday Review*, January 22, 1966, page 37.

page 358 " 'immaculately factual,' Truman publicly boasted . . .": George Plimpton, *op. cit.*

page 358 " 'One doesn't spend . . .' ": *Ibid.*

page 358 "A man from the *Kansas City Times* . . .": Robert Pearman, "Reaction to Capote Book Varies at Scene," *op. cit.*

page 358 ". . . he described Holcomb 'as a broken-down place . . .' ": " 'In Cold Blood' . . .": *Newsweek, op cit.*, page 61.

page 358 ". . . Truman did give way to a few small . . .": Alvin Dewey and Wilma Kidwell to GC, October 26, 1976.

page 360 ". . . the four issues broke the magazine's record . . .": "The Country Below the Surface," *Time*, January 21, 1966, page 83.

page 360 ". . . and crowds waiting at a pier . . .": Johnson, *Charles Dickens*, page 304.

page 360 " 'They evidently didn't . . .' ": *Dodge City Globe;* quoted in *Books*, November, 1965, page 12.

page 360 " 'Drug stores say . . .' ": "New Yorker Demand Hits City; Magazine Doesn't." *Garden City Telegram*, September 29, 1965.

page 361 " 'It's tremendous,' said Harold Nye . . .": Harold Nye to TC, September 29, 1965.

page 361 "Leo Lerman grumbled . . .": Leo Lerman to TC, October 10, 1965.

page 361 ". . . Truman's Greenwich High School . . .": Catherine Wood to TC, September 30, 1965.

page 361 " 'I suppose you will have imitators . . .' ": Catherine Wood to TC, October 19, 1965.

page 361 " 'I would never have believed . . .' ": James Merrill to TC, November 10, 1965.

page 361 "Anita Loos adjudged . . .": Anita Loos to TC, November 16, 1965.

page 361 "Noël Coward, who confessed . . .": Noël Coward to TC, December 21, 1965.

page 362 " 'Such a deluge of words . . .' ": William D. Smith, "Advertising: A Success Money Didn't Buy," *New York Times,* February 20, 1966.

page 362 "By a peculiar stroke of luck . . .": Louis Sobel and Jack O'Brian, "Otto Preminger Bopped: O'Brian-Sobel Are There," *New York Journal-American,* January 8, 1966.

page 362 " 'L'Affaire "21," ' as one newspaper . . .": *New York Journal-American,* January 9, 1966.

page 363 " 'I would like to take . . .' ": William D. Smith, *op. cit.*

page 363 " 'I'm mad about the new Capote . . .' ": "Capote Story of Kansas Murders 'Upgrades' Publishing Industry," *Books,* November, 1965, page 1.

page 363 " 'A boy has to hustle his book . . .' ": " 'In Cold Blood' . . .": *Newsweek, op. cit.,* page 63.

page 363 " 'A Book in a New Form . . .' ": Harry Gilroy, "A Book in a New Form Earns $2-Million for Truman Capote," *New York Times,* December 31, 1965.

page 363 " 'When you average it out . . .' ": *Ibid.*

page 363 " '*In Cold Blood* is a masterpiece . . .' ": Conrad Knickerbocker, "One Night on a Kansas Farm," *New York Times Book Review,* January 16, 1966.

page 364 "He had recorded 'this American tragedy . . .' ": Maurice Dolbier, "In-Depth Report on Brutal Crime in Rural Setting," *New York Herald Tribune,* January 14, 1966.

page 364 "Rebecca West, who had produced . . .": Rebecca West, "A Grave and Reverend Book," *Harper's,* February, 1966, page 108.

page 364 "Writing in *The New York Review* . . .": F. W. Dupee, "Truman Capote's Score," *The New York Review of Books,* February 3, 1966, page 3.

page 364 " 'It is ridiculous in judgment . . .' ": Stanley Kauffmann, "Capote in Kansas," *The New Republic,* January 22, 1966, page 19.

page 364 "But his diatribe was itself . . .": "In Hot Blood, Kauffmann-Capote Reaction," *The New Republic,* February 5, 1966, pages 36–37.

page 364 "For Truman the congenial atmosphere was ruined . . .": Articles reprinted in Tynan, *Tynan Right and Left.*

page 365 "Jimmy Breslin, the street-smart columnist . . .": "Jimmy Breslin, In Cold Blood," *New York Herald Tribune,* January 19, 1966, page 21.

CHAPTER 43

page 366 " 'I've gotten rid of the boy . . .' ": " 'In Cold Blood' . . . An American Tragedy," *Newsweek, op. cit.,* pages 62–63.

page 367 ". . . in what a fashion columnist called 'the most . . .' ": Eugenia Sheppard's column, *New York Herald Tribune*, October 2, 1965.

page 367 " 'He wanted to be in the thick . . .' ": Oliver Smith to GC, December 18, 1985.

page 367 ". . . walking into it, he wrote in . . .": "Truman Capote Describes His . . . ," *House Beautiful*, April, 1969, page 94.

page 368 " 'Garden City Opens Arms . . .' ": Elvira Valenzuela, "Garden City Opens Arms to Capote," *Wichita Eagle*, April 23, 1966.

page 368 " 'His light and somewhat nasal . . .' ": Harry Gilroy, "Truman Capote Wins Applause as Reader in Town Hall Session," *New York Times*, May 6, 1966, page 53.

page 368 " 'In the eye of the daily . . .' ": Virginia Sheward, "Capote Reading Capote: Poignant Evening," *Newsday*, May 6, 1966.

page 368 " 'It was a very moving moment . . .' ": *Ibid.*

page 369 " 'Have not had a genuine holiday . . .' ": TC to Cecil Beaton, June 20, 1966.

page 369 " 'Serious writers aren't supposed to make . . .' ": "People," *Time*, August 5, 1966, page 34.

page 369 " 'I think it was something a little boy . . .' ": Lady (Nancy) Keith to GC, September 24, 1975.

page 370 " 'Truman,' she said, 'I haven't . . .' ": Eleanor Friede to GC, October 1, 1975.

page 371 " 'I don't know whether or not I should invite . . .' ": *Ibid.*

page 371 "Leo Lerman joked that 'the guest book reads . . .' ": "Modern Living," *Time*, December 9, 1966, page 88.

page 371 "Jerome Robbins, the choreographer . . .": Gloria Steinem, "The Party," *Vogue*, January, 1967, page 50.

page 372 " 'Now, honey,' he told her . . .": Katharine Graham to GC, October 30, 1985.

page 372 " 'Truman wouldn't give them to me all . . .' ": *Ibid.*

page 373 "She was vacationing on Cape Cod . . .": *Ibid.*

page 373 " 'I've never seen women putting . . .' ": Eugenia Sheppard, "Capote Has a Hot Idea," *New York World-Telegram*, October 18, 1966.

page 374 "But he did not send one to his aunt . . .": Marie Rudisill to GC, June 27, 1982.

page 374 " 'I feel like I fell into . . .' ": "Modern Living," *Time*, December 9, 1966, page 88.

page 374 " 'People were really carrying on . . .' ": Diana Trilling to GC.

page 374 "Hearing the commotion from her house in Nyack . . .": Jordan Massee to GC, February 16, 1977.

page 375 " 'He *ordered* his friends . . .' ": Glenway Wescott to GC, February 9, 1976.

page 375 " 'Oh, I like Truman . . .' ": Glenway Wescott to TC, October 8, 1966.

page 375 "Flanner asked Glenway to drop Truman . . .": Janet Flanner to Glenway Wescott, October 14, 1966.

page 375 " 'Piping away like Blake's little . . .' ": Glenway Wescott to Janet Flanner, October 20, 1966.

page 376 " 'This city's normally . . .' ": Leroy Aarons, "Capote Is Cold Blooded to the Uninvited Masses," *Washington Post*, November 25, 1966.

page 376 "When Herb Caen . . .": Herb Caen, "A Supertruman Effort," *San Francisco Chronicle*, December 2, 1966.

page 376 " 'The ladies have killed me . . .' ": Enid Nemy, ". . . And Before It All Started," *New York Times*, November 29, 1966.

page 376 " 'I think I've lost my mind . . .' ": *Ibid.*

page 376 "Arriving that afternoon, Kay Graham . . .": Katharine Graham to GC, October 30, 1985.

page 377 "As the Caens were leaving . . .": Herb Caen, "A Supertruman Effort," *op. cit.*

page 377 ". . . it appeared that Pamela Hayward might have been right . . .": "Modern Living," *Time*, December 9, 1966, page 88.

page 378 " 'It's too early to tell how . . .' ": Charlotte Curtis, "Capote's Black and White Ball: The Most Exquisite of Spectator Sports," *New York Times*, November 29, 1966, page 53.

page 378 " 'It was *formidable vraiment* . . .' ": Jack Dunphy to Mary Louise Aswell, February 9, 1967.

page 379 "Pete Hamill wrote an outraged column . . .": Pete Hamill, "The Party," *New York Post*, November 29, 1966.

page 379 "A soldier in an Army training camp . . .": Private Charles Rosner, "Viewed from the Barracks," *Time*, December 23, 1966, page 12.

page 379 " 'So Truman Capote had a blast . . .' ": Richard Waterman, "His Turn in the Barrel," *Time*, January 6, 1967.

page 379 "A few days later Russell Baker . . .": Russell Baker, "Observer: Truman Capote's Gift to Literature," *New York Times*, December 8, 1966, page 46.

page 380 " 'He did it. He did it . . .' ": Suzy Knickerbocker's column, *New York World-Journal-Telegram*, November 29, 1966.

CHAPTER 44

page 381 " 'You might say Truman Capote . . .' ": Toni Kosover and Ki Hackney, "Capote Does It Again," *Women's Wear Daily*, May 7, 1968.

page 381 " 'his name has a magic ring . . .' ": Enid Nemy, "Capote Magnetism Fills New 'House,' " *New York Times*, January 24, 1968.

page 381 " 'Anything he does . . .' ": *Ibid.*

page 381 " 'There's a little secret to charity . . .' ": *Ibid.*

page 382 " 'Somebody has got to tell Truman . . .' ": Suzy Knickerbocker, "A Grand Party for a Wonderful Cause," *New York Journal-Telegram*, April 26, 1967.

page 382 "Writing in *Vogue*, he said, 'Ah, the Princess!' ": TC, "Lee, A Fan Letter from Truman Capote," *Vogue*, June, 1976, page 113.

page 382 " 'He's my closest friend . . .' ": Lee Radziwill to GC, February 6, 1976.

page 382 " 'gold-brown like a glass . . .' ": TC, "Lee, A Fan Letter," *op. cit.*

page 383 ". . . an exceedingly comfortable life . . .": Christine Kirk, "Starring Lee Bouvier," New York *Sunday News*, June 18, 1967.

page 383 " 'Understand her marriage is all but finito . . .' ": TC to Cecil Beaton, February 9, 1962.

page 383 "The irate husband of his longtime lover . . .": Stassinopoulos, *Maria Callas*, page 252.

page 383 " 'Does the ambitious Greek tycoon . . .' ": *Ibid.*

page 384 " 'Oh, Jackie, it would be such fun . . .' ": *Ibid.*

page 384 "Lee's reward for bringing them together . . .": Martin, *A Hero for Our Times*, page 533.

page 385 "Many people in Finney County, including the editor . . .": Editorials: "Not for the Community," *Garden City Telegram*, May 26, 1986.

page 386 " 'When the young actress who was portraying Nancy . . .' ": "A Nightmare Lived Again," *Life*, May 12, 1967, page 104B.

page 386 " 'You're not happy.' ": Richard Brooks to GC, April 30, 1977.

page 386 "Two weeks later *Life* . . .": "A Nightmare Lived Again," *Life, op. cit.*

page 387 "He persuaded Milton Goldman . . .": Milton Goldman to GC, June 12, 1986.

page 387 " 'I feel absolutely *nothing* in common . . .' ": Jane Howard, "Girls Who Have Everything Are Not Supposed to Do Anything," *Life*, July 14, 1967, page 56.

page 388 ". . . looked like 'a dog's lunch . . .' ": *Ibid.*

page 388 " 'I have a feeling of now or never . . .' ": *Ibid.*

page 388 ". . . pronounced them 'very promising . . .' ": *Ibid.*

page 388 "When he returned to Manhattan . . .": Mark Shivas, " 'Laura'—In Blue Blood," *New York Times*, January 14, 1968, page D17.

page 389 ". . . Susskind discarded Van Druten's comedy . . .": Matt Messina, "News Around the Dials," New York *Daily News*, August 18, 1967, page 64.

page 389 " 'I wish we could begin tomorrow . . .' ": Lee Radziwill to TC, August 19, 1967.

page 389 " 'When I want advice . . .' ": *Ibid.*

page 389 " 'I was *so* happy to get . . .' ": Lee Radziwill to TC, September 19, 1967.

page 389 ". . . Susskind insisted that 'there *is* something . . .' ": Mark Shivas, *op. cit.*

page 389 ". . . her Laura 'was reduced to a stunning . . .' ": Jack Gould, "Cashing In on Crashing Bores," *New York Times*, February 4, 1968.

page 389 " 'only slightly less animated . . .' ": "Specials," *Time*, February 2, 1968, page 57.

page 390 " 'When that check fell out . . .' ": Arch Persons to TC, August 22, 1967.

page 390 " 'He is now the No. 1 writer . . .' ": Arch Persons to Truman Moore, August 16, 1967.

page 390 " 'Where I was dumb . . .' ": Arch Persons to TC, August 21, 1967.

page 391 " 'Now in my four years of isolation . . .' ": *Ibid.*

page 391 " 'You must of course realize . . .' ": Arch Persons to TC, August 22, 1967.

page 391 " 'I would like also for you . . .' ": *Ibid*.

page 391 " 'It is hardly necessary for me . . .' ": Arch Persons to TC, August 21, 1967.

page 391 " 'Should we call her Princess . . .' ": Frank Perry to GC, January 5, 1976.

page 392 "Holding Lee's hand—as if he were still a child . . .": Edith Efron, "When Truman Capote Came Home Again," *TV Guide*, November 23, 1968, page 22.

page 392 " 'Marvelous!' " he exclaimed": *Ibid*.

page 392 " 'Truman's relatives just wouldn't integrate . . .' ": Eleanor Perry to GC, January 29, 1976.

page 392 ". . . whom he called 'that bastard . . .' ": Arch Persons to GC, September 9, 1976.

page 392 " 'Don't you never think . . .' ": *Ibid*.

page 392 " 'I think he's going to marry . . .' ": Eleanor Perry to GC, January 29, 1976.

page 393 " 'Lee, I hope that you'll work it out . . .' ": Arch Persons to GC, September 9, 1976.

page 393 " 'I think you used very poor taste . . .' ": *Ibid*.

page 393 "Four years later, after losing . . .": *Ibid*.

page 393 " 'He had that Jew lawyer . . .' ": *Ibid*.

CHAPTER 45

page 397 " 'He never really recovered . . .' ": Phyllis Cerf Wagner to GC, January 17, 1978.

page 398 ". . . or, as Forster phrased it . . .": Forster, *A Passage to India*, page 149.

page 398 " '. . . how he longed for praise . . .' ": Cecil Beaton's unpublished diaries, May, 1960.

page 398 "Truman never forgave an insult . . .": "Holly and Hemlock: Truman Capote Lists the Books He Will Give His Friends for Christmas," *Washington Post Book World*, December 1, 1968, page 2.

page 399 "Maloff had good reason to regret the day . . .": "Letters," *Washington Post Book World*, January 19, 1969.

page 400 " 'No words can express the secret agony . . .' ": Priestley, *Charles Dickens*, page 12.

page 402 " 'When I first knew him . . .' ": Phyllis Cerf Wagner to GC, January 17, 1978.

page 402 " 'This phenomenon' Cecil had once . . .": Cecil Beaton's unpublished diaries, summer, 1953.

page 402 " 'I secretly feel T. is in a bad state . . .' ": Cecil Beaton's unpublished diaries, April, 1966.

CHAPTER 46

page 404 " 'If an idea is really haunting you . . .' ": *Show of the Month News*, March or April, 1952, page 3.

page 405 " 'I aspire,' he had jotted in a . . .": TC, *Music for Chameleons*, page 250.

page 406 "He might have said, as Flaubert did . . .": " 'Thank You for Making Me Read Tolstoy's Novel'—The Letters of Flaubert and Turgenev," *New York Times Book Review*, October 27, 1985, page 51.

page 406 ". . . he had sold movie rights . . .": A. H. Weiler, "Capote's 'Prayers' Are Answered," *New York Times*, February 18, 1968.

page 407 " 'I have a strange new friend . . .' ": TC to Cecil Beaton, fall, 1967.

page 407 " 'Write when you can . . .' ": Nancy Reagan to TC, mid-November, 1967.

page 407 "At the end of December . . .": Windham, *Footnote to a Friendship*, pages 86–94.

page 407 " 'Whatever changes have been made . . .' ": Clive Barnes, "Theater: 'House of Flowers' Rebuilt," *New York Times*, January 29, 1966.

page 407 "The show closed after only fifty-seven . . .": " 'House of Flowers' Closing; 'Private Lives' to Be Given," *New York Times*, March 14, 1968.

page 407 ". . . the usually genial Arlen . . .": Harold Arlen to GC.

page 408 ". . . a reporter for *West Magazine* . . .": C. Robert Jennings, "Truman Capote: Hot Shorty with Tall Cool," *Los Angeles Times West Magazine*, April 28, 1968, page 10.

page 408 " 'I'm told not to walk . . .' ": Jack Dunphy to Gloria Dunphy, April 11, 1968.

page 409 " 'God, what a big lonely country . . .' ": Jack Dunphy to Gloria Dunphy, April 24, 1968.

CHAPTER 47

page 410 "He had carefully studied the record . . .": "Opinion, The Assassination According to Capote," *Time*, May 10, 1968, page 65.

page 410 " 'The people who ran the thing . . .' ": Eleanor Perry to GC, January 29, 1976.

page 411 " 'I always felt that he was asking himself . . .' ": Stein and Plimpton, *American Journey*, page 199.

page 411 "The last time they met was . . .": *Ibid.*, page 168.

page 412 "That did not stop Truman from going . . .": Jack Gould, "TV: Truman Capote Defines His Concept of Justice," *New York Times*, June 15, 1968.

page 412 "Such a plan of wholesale murder . . .": "Theosophy, Cult of the Occult," *Time*, June 19, 1968, page 61.

page 412 " 'Mr. Capote is in complete confusion . . .' ": *Ibid.*

page 412 " . . an editorial in the *Christian Science Monitor* . . .": "Vigilante Juries," *Christian Science Monitor*, June 20, 1968.

page 413 "The program was too grim . . .": "ABC, Truman Capote Fall Out Over Special," *Broadcasting*, November 4, 1968, page 63.

page 413 " 'Well, what were you expecting . . .' ": "Truman and TV," *Time*, November 29, 1968, page 73.

page 413 ". . . Elton Rule—'that sun-tanned Uriah Heep . . .' ": Dwight Whitney, "I Want It on the Air!" *TV Guide*, July 4, 1970, page 7.

page 413 " 'My primary thing is that . . .' ": "Truman and TV," *Time, op. cit.*, page 74.

page 413 " 'I have been working hard . . .' ": TC to Cecil Beaton, undated, second half of 1968.

page 414 "Shortly after Christmas he left for Palm Springs again . . .": Joe Faulk to GC, March 9, 1978.

page 414 "He attacked what he called the 'Jewish Mafia . . .' ": Jack O'Brian, "Broadway," New York *Daily Column*, April 20, 1969.

page 414 "He once more denounced liberal Supreme Court . . .": "TV: Dick Cavett Gets Talk Show in Prime Time," *New York Times*, May 27, 1969.

page 414 "He struck first, using . . .": Earl Wilson, "The Lady Protests," *New York Post*, July 24, 1969.

page 415 " 'Words are like chemicals . . .' ": Nizer, *Reflections Without Mirrors*; full discussion of Capote–Susann dispute, pages 101–6.

page 415 " 'How pleasant to have a letter . . .' ": TC to Louis Nizer, May 16, 1973.

page 416 " 'He had become a television personality . . .' ": Susann, *Dolores*, page 68.

page 416 "Knocked unconscious, he was . . .": William Diefenbach, M.D., to GC, June 19, 1985.

page 417 " 'Jack refuses to go to California . . .' ": TC to Cecil Beaton, undated, end of 1969.

CHAPTER 48

page 419 ". . . the first of Truman's 'men without faces,' as Wyatt Cooper . . .": Wyatt Cooper to GC, January 6, 1976.

page 420 " 'He wore what they wear . . .' ": Charlotte Curtis to GC, April 12, 1976.

page 421 " 'Truman was always nagging on . . .' ": John Richardson to GC, March 7, 1985.

page 421 " 'He knew he was deceiving himself . . .' ": Saint Subber to GC, August 18, 1986.

page 422 " 'Here was a man . . .' ": Wyatt Cooper to GC, January 6, 1976.

page 422 " 'He was an authentic primitive . . .' ": Charlotte Curtis to GC, April 12, 1976.

page 422 " 'Truman knew what people . . .' ": Alan Schwartz to GC, March 17, 1983.

page 422 "Half in tears, he shouted . . .": Charlotte Curtis to GC, April 12, 1976.

page 423 "Trying, like everyone else . . .": Lady (Nancy) Keith to GC, September 24, 1975.

page 423 "Kay Graham was no less aghast": Katharine Graham to GC, October 30, 1985.

page 423 " 'When he was with this man . . .' ": Phyllis Cerf Wagner to GC, January 17, 1978.

page 425 "She was no more impressed . . .": Lee Radziwill To GC, February 6, 1976.

page 425 "His ostensible purpose . . .": Alan Schwartz, August 18, 1986.

page 426 "Alan telephoned Truman's Palm Springs lawyer . . .": *Ibid.*

page 427 "Furious at what he labeled . . .": "People," *Time,* November 2, 1970.

page 427 ". . . of the following day, October 21 . . .": "Capote Jailed on Coast," *New York Times,* October 22, 1970, page 31.

page 427 " 'I've been in thirty or forty jails . . .' ": "People" *Time, op. cit.*

page 427 "Leaving Truman in Santa Ana . . .": Alan Schwartz, August 18, 1986.

page 427 " 'He was absolutely flattened . . .' ": Lady (Nancy) Keith, September 24, 1975.

page 428 "In his rage, he plotted schemes . . .": Joanne Carson to GC, August 2, 1986.

CHAPTER 49

Rick Brown is the chief source for much of the information in this chapter, although Truman and others corroborated most of his facts. I do not think it necessary to cite each instance in which Brown has provided me with a conversation or background.

page 433 " 'Here was this boring and totally . . .' ": Wyatt Cooper to GC, January 6, 1976.

page 435 "He had met Joanne shortly after the . . .": Joanne Carson to GC, November 21, 1975.

page 435 "She had been born in California . . .": Joanne Carson, M.A., Ph.D., "The Search for the 'Magic Pill,' " book proposal, 1980.

page 436 "To his old friend Carol Marcus . . .": Carol Marcus Matthau to GC, September 21, 1986.

page 437 ("Ironically, Fitzgerald, who also labored . . ."): "Ready or Not, Here Comes *Gatsby,*" *Time,* March 18, 1974, page 71.

page 438 ". . . and, on the whole, was pleased with it, he told Alan Schwartz": TC to Alan Schwartz, February 9, 1972.

page 438 "But Paramount was not . . .": "Ready or Not," *Time, op. cit.*

page 438 " 'Well, Truman, this is just . . .' ": Rick Brown to GC, April 8, 1978.

page 438 "Using the excuse . . .": *New York Times,* March 31, 1972.

page 439 " 'I'm sinking back into my book . . .' ": TC to Alan Schwartz, February 9, 1972.

page 439 " 'It is totally necessary to develop . . .' ": Rosemary Kent, "Tru Confessions," *Women's Wear Daily,* May 30, 1972.

CHAPTER 50

page 440 " 'Of course I basically don't really want . . .' ": Andy Warhol, "Sunday with Mr. C.," *Rolling Stone*, April 12, 1973, page 36.

page 441 "Beard was to take the pictures . . .": Peter Beard to GC, November 13, 1975.

page 441 ". . . the 'fantastic T. Capote,' as Southern labeled him . . .": Terry Southern, "The Rolling Stones' U.S. Tour: Riding the Lapping Tongue," *Saturday Review of the Arts*, August 12, 1972, page 26.

page 441 "Its title, 'It Will Soon Be Here,' he . . .": Andy Warhol, *op. cit.*, page 40.

page 441 " 'Since there was nothing to "find out," ' he explained . . .": *Ibid.*, page 36.

page 442 ". . . he admitted that if he had been twenty-five years younger . . .": *Ibid.*, page 40.

page 442 "But why, he asked, 'should I do . . .' ": *Ibid.*, page 37.

page 442 "Theirs was a bond of brothers . . .": Robert MacBride to GC, August 31, 1986.

page 442 " 'He seemed sort of uncooked . . .' ": Lady (Nancy) Keith to GC, September 24, 1975.

CHAPTER 51

page 452 " 'You can't take my car!' ": John O'Shea to GC, November 2, 1986.

page 453 " 'For better or worse . . .' ": Joseph Petrocik to GC, April 13, 1981.

page 453 "After spending a weekend in May with them . . .": Windham, *Footnote to a Friendship*, page 101.

page 453 " 'Please be nice to Johnny . . .' ": Alan Schwartz to GC, February 12, 1976.

page 454 "They stayed with the Wyatts . . .": Lynn Wyatt to GC, October 7, 1986.

page 454 " 'I have a gun in my purse . . .' ": Carol Marcus Matthau to GC, August 28, 1984.

page 455 " 'Oh, Johnny, stop that' . . .": John Knowles to GC, October 13, 1976.

page 455 " 'He didn't try to hide . . .' ": Arch Persons to GC, September 9, 1976.

page 455 "Truman ordered him to take . . .": Don Erickson to GC, March 10, 1987.

page 456 " 'Can I come up there?' ": John Knowles to GC, October 13, 1976.

page 456 " 'Accordingly,' Alan dutifully wrote John . . .": Alan Schwartz to John O'Shea, April 12, 1975.

page 457 " 'If Mr. Capote's emotional dysfunction is such . . .' ": John O'Shea to Alan Schwartz, April 15, 1975.

page 457 "Truman's second call was to Peg O'Shea . . .": Peg O'Shea to GC, December 10, 1986.

page 457 " 'He was the father of my children . . .' ": *Ibid.*

page 459 " 'What are you doing?' he asked. . .": Judith Green to GC, November 19, 1986.

page 460 " 'That's impossible!' bellowed Ava . . .": *Ibid.*

CHAPTER 52

page 461 "Tennessee Williams, who was not . . .": Tennessee Williams to GC, April 30, 1976.

page 461 " 'We stood back on our heels . . .' ": Gordon Lish to GC, December 5, 1986.

page 462 " 'La Côte Basque, 1965' ": *Esquire*, November, 1975, pages 110–18, 158.

page 466 " 'Truman told me that the point . . .' ": John O'Shea to GC, October 1, 1986.

page 467 "One day in July he took a friend . . .": the friend was GC.

page 468 "What had bothered Ann most, a weary Elsie Woodward . . .": Robert Ellsworth to GC, December 25, 1984.

page 468 "The reaction was most succinctly summed up by a cartoon . . .": Edward Sorel, cover cartoon, *New York*, February 9, 1976.

page 468 " 'Who is that?' Babe inquired . . .": Lady (Nancy) Keith to GC, January 29, 1986.

page 469 " 'Never have you heard such gnashing of teeth . . .' ": Liz Smith, "Truman Capote in Hot Water," *New York*, February 9, 1976, page 44.

page 469 " 'that dirty little toad . . .' ": *Ibid.*, page 50.

page 469 " 'After all,' explained her husband Wyatt . . .": Wyatt Cooper to GC, January 6, 1976.

page 469 " 'It's very hard to be a gentleman . . .' ": Morgan, *Maugham*, page 344.

page 469 " 'the chic of the week . . .' ": Charlotte Curtis to GC, April 12, 1976.

page 469 "Marella Agnelli, who more than once . . .": "Marella Agnelli: Life Is to Be Involved," *Women's Wear Daily*, November 30, 1976, page 7.

page 470 " 'I hate the idea of Truman . . .' ": Cecil Beaton to Patrick O'Higgins, undated.

page 471 " 'He was the most surprised and shocked person . . .' ": Liz Smith to GC, March 6, 1985.

page 471 "Joanne Carson watched helplessly . . .": Joanne Carson to GC, January 14, 1982.

page 471 "He telephoned Slim . . .": Lady (Nancy) Keith to GC, January 29, 1986.

page 471 " 'I have other ways of torturing . . .' ": Interview with a friend of William Paley.

page 472 "He introduced her to his . . .": Joseph Petrocik to GC, June 4, 1978.

page 472 " 'Babe always spoke of Truman . . .' ": John Richardson to GC, March 7, 1985.

page 472 "Harper Lee glimpsed that disappointment . . .": Harper Lee to GC, March 2, 1986.

page 472 " 'If ever there was a woman . . .' ": Interview with a friend of Lady (Nancy) Keith.

page 473 " 'Oh, honey! It's Proust!' ": Diana Vreeland to GC, March 1, 1976.

CHAPTER 53

page 474 "Simon had chosen him as the model . . .": Neil Simon to GC, November, 1975.

page 474 " 'Gore Vidal must be dying . . .' ": Josh Greenfeld, "Truman Capote, the Movie Star?" *New York Times*, December 28, 1975.

page 475 " 'Making that film knocked . . .' ": John O'Shea to GC, October 1, 1986.

page 475 " 'The original intent may have . . .' ": Josh Greenfeld, *op. cit.*

page 475 " 'How am I as an actor? . . .' ": Liz Smith, "Truman Capote in Hot Water," *op. cit.*, page 56.

page 475 " . . . but Guinness' critique . . .": Alec Guinness to GC, February 28, 1986.

page 475 " 'To put Capote at a table . . .' ": Ernest Leogrande, "Moore Doing Nicely in 'Out-of-Work' Role," New York *Daily News*, July 6, 1978, page 73.

page 476 " 'It's pretty good,' he reported . . .": Joseph Petrocik to GC, June 4, 1978.

page 476 "When she picked him up . . .": Joanne Carson to GC, September 16, 1986.

page 476 " 'I've always [concluded] . . .' ": John O'Shea to Alan Schwartz, February 29, 1976.

page 477 " 'Truman and I have talked this . . .' ": *Ibid.*

page 477 " 'John was always talking . . .' ": Joanne Carson to GC, January 14, 1987.

page 477 " 'It's all very interesting being with you . . .' ": John O'Shea to GC, March 7, 1987.

page 477 " 'I want something dramatic . . .' ": *Ibid.*

page 478 " 'Truman didn't want to . . .' ": *Ibid.*

page 478 "John Knowles saw him . . .": John Knowles to GC, October 13, 1976.

page 479 " 'It was the only time he had ever been invited . . .' ": Richard Zoerink, "Truman Capote Talks About His Crowd," *Playgirl*, September, 1975, page 54.

page 479 "He admitted, in fact, to a sharp . . .": Deposition of Gore Vidal, September 16, 1976, pages 31–34.

page 480 " 'I'm looking forward to getting that little toad! . . .' ": Liz Smith's column, New York *Daily News*, February 16, 1976, page 22.

page 480 "When had he last seen Truman?" Deposition of Gore Vidal, *op. cit.*, page 164.

page 480 "For his part, Truman managed to mangle . . .": Anthony Haden-Guest, "The Vidal–Capote Papers: A Tempest in Camelot," *New York*, June 11, 1979, page 54.

page 480 "He also suggested that in bringing . . .": *Ibid.*, pages 60–61.

page 481 "In the middle of May, John . . .": John O'Shea to GC, October 1, 1986.

page 481 "A week after his furtive departure, his car struck . . .": "Capote Is Mum on Drunk Driving Charge," New York *Daily News*, June 1, 1976, front page and page 3.

CHAPTER 54

page 483 "Capitalizing on his suddenly sinister reputation . . .": *Esquire*, May, 1976, pages 55–68, 122–24, 126, 128, 130, 132, 134–35.

page 484 " 'Somewhere in the world . . .' ": *Ibid.*, page 55.

page 485 "After rejecting Ann Woodward as his model, Truman chose Pamela Churchill, whose romances . . .": For background I relied, in part, on the following: "Smart Set," *New York Journal-American*, December 15, 1954, page 18; "Cholly Knickerbocker Observes," *New York Journal-American*, August 30, 1949; Leslie Gordon, "Triumphs of a Churchill," *New York Sunday Mirror Magazine*, May 13, 1956, page 2; Nancy Randolph, "Chit-Chat," New York *Daily News*, July 29, 1959, page 8.

page 486 ". . . 'famous international siren,' Cholly Knickerbocker had titled her . . .": "Cholly Knickerbocker," *New York Journal-American*, June 1, 1959.

page 486–487 "But his chief model for Kate McCloud was the aforementioned Mrs. Harrison Williams": For background on Mona Williams I found the following articles particularly useful: "Harrison Williams, No. 1 Utilities Magnate, a Serene, Vibrant Figure," *St. Louis Post-Dispatch*, August 12, 1937; Morris Gilbert, "Bicycle Craze of 90's Started Williams Toward Utility Coup," *New York World-Telegram*, May 4, 1937; Bettye Lee Mastin, "Lexington's 'International Beauty' Has Led Colorful, Checkered Life," *Lexington* (Ky.) *Herald*, September 15, 1981; Alice Delman, "Louisville's Cinderella Countess," *The* (Louisville) *Courier-Journal Magazine*, February 10, 1963; Helen Worden, "First Ladies of the '400,' " *New York World-Telegram*, January 11, 1938.

page 488 ". . . *Esquire* was still receiving forty requests a day . . .": Arthur Bell, "Bell Tells," *The Village Voice*, April 5, 1976.

page 488 " 'Gossip-mongers may be . . .' ": Nancy Collins, "The Capote Caper, Chapter II," *Women's Wear Daily*, April 5, 1976, page 4.

page 488 "Most of the talk centered on Kate McCloud . . .": *Ibid.*; Liz Smith's column, New York *Daily News*, October 20, 1976.

page 489 "In the resolutely radical *Village Voice*, James Wolcott . . .": James Wolcott, "Truman Capote Sups on the Flesh of the Famous," *The Village Voice*, September 6, 1976, page 65.

page 489 ". . . on the other side, columnist Max Lerner . . .": Max Lerner, "Capote's World," *New York Post*, April 28, 1976.

page 489 "Most furious was Tennessee . . .": Tennessee Williams to GC, April 30, 1976.

page 489 "Porter, who was now in her mid-eighties, was just as displeased . . .": Katherine Anne Porter to GC, April 8, 1976.

page 490 "Rorem's response showed . . .": Ned Rorem to GC, September 8, 1978.

page 490 "Even in its imperfect state—to paraphrase Edmund Wilson's . . .": Fitzgerald, *The Last Tycoon*, introduction by Edmund Wilson, page 6.

page 492 ". . . he conducted what one scholar terms a 'ruthless judicial inquiry . . .' ": Quennell, *Marcel Proust, 1871–1922, A Centennial Volume*, page 44.

page 492 " 'It was kinda fun . . .' ": TC to Cecil Beaton, March 20, 1965.

page 493 ". . . in which Strachey imagines the dying queen . . .": Strachey, *Queen Victoria*, pages 297–98.

CHAPTER 55

page 495 " 'Truman, I'm in love . . .' ": John O'Shea to GC, March 7, 1987.

page 496 "Rick Brown, who was once again tending bar . . .": Rick Brown to GC, May 10, 1987.

page 498 "Ten days before Christmas, 1976, he invited a friend . . .": The friend was GC.

page 500 " 'No! It was not sixteen yrs ago . . .' ": Jack Dunphy to Paul Cadmus, March 13, 1977.

page 501 "In his *Hollywood Reporter* column, George Christy . . .": George Christy, "The Great Life," *The Hollywood Reporter*, April 26, 1977, page 10.

page 501 "Helping him out, Carol Matthau . . .": Carol Marcus Matthau to GC, September 1, 1986.

page 502 " 'When Mr. O'Shea came to see me at the [Hotel] Bel-Air . . .' ": unpublished nineteen-page manuscript by TC, June 12, 1980.

page 504 "John's own account of those dark days . . .": John O'Shea to GC, October 1, 1986.

page 505 "As if that were not enough, John himself phoned . . .": Joanne Carson to GC, June 10, 1987.

page 505 "Only after they had arrived . . .": Peg O'Shea to GC, December 10, 1986.

page 505 " 'I am an alcoholic, a genuine alcoholic . . .' ": "Is Truman's Song: 'How Dry Am I?' " New York *Daily News*, November 14, 1977.

page 505 " 'I'm not going to let this . . .' ": Peg O'Shea to GC, December 10, 1986.

page 506 "The next morning's headline . . .": "Is Truman's Song 'How Dry Am I?' " *op. cit.*

page 506 "Rick, in any case, was unmoved": Rick Brown to GC, May 10, 1987.

CHAPTER 56

page 509 " 'Can't you find somebody younger . . .' ": Joseph Petrocik to GC, November 25, 1980.

page 510 " 'I will be the prince . . .' ": Anne Taylor Fleming, "Truman Capote's World, Part 2: The Descent from the Heights," *New York Times Magazine*, July 16, 1978, page 44.

page 510 " *'Rendez-vous du High-Life* . . .' ": Mack, *Toulouse-Lautrec*, page 130.

page 510 " 'I've been to an awful lot of . . .' ": Leslie Bennetts, "An 'In' Crowd and Outside Mob Show Up for Studio 54's Birthday," *New York Times*, April 28, 1978.

page 511 " 'Sometimes, when I'm sitting up . . .' ": "Steve Rubell, in the Heat of the Night," *Interview*, February, 1979, page 33.

page 511 " 'It was almost as if we were in jail . . .' ": Bob Colacello to GC, September 16, 1986.

page 512 " 'My own feeling is that . . .' ": John Richardson to GC, March 7, 1985.

page 512 "Bill was later to lament . . .": Tony Schwartz, "An Intimate Talk with William Paley," *New York Times Magazine*, December 28, 1980, page 16.

page 512 " 'But it will take millions . . .' ": Interview with a friend of William Paley.

page 513 " 'What's going to happen unless . . .' ": Transcript of *Stanley Siegel Show*, July 18, 1978, prepared by Radio TV Reports, Inc., New York.

page 513 " 'Drunk & Doped . . .' ": Georgiana Pine, "Drunk & Doped Capote Visits TV Talk Show," *New York Post*, July 18, 1978.

page 513 " 'A talented man of considerable literary stature . . .' ": John Cashman, "Capote's On; It's Live TV," *Newsday*, July 19, 1978, page 3A.

page 514 " 'I saw what that man is about . . .' ": Joseph Petrocik to GC, July 20, 1978.

page 514 " 'At Bozeman, Montana . . .' ": Rick Brown to GC, November 7, 1978.

page 517 "It was not a glorious future he was . . .": John Fowles, "Capote as Maupassant," *Saturday Review*, July, 1980, pages 52–53.

page 517 " 'I do not recall ever discussing . . .' ": Anthony Haden-Guest, "The Vidal–Capote Papers: A Tempest in Camelot," *New York*, June 11, 1979, page 56.

page 518 ". . . which in early June obediently printed . . .": *Ibid*.

page 518 " 'I'm tired of Truman riding on my coattails . . .' ": Liz Smith, "Sunday's People: Truman's True Love," New York *Daily News*, September 23, 1984, page 3.

page 518 " 'Why, no one would have ever heard . . .' ": Liz Smith, New York *Daily News*, June 18, 1979.

page 519 " 'If the lovely, divine and sensitive . . .' ": Sally Quinn, "In Hot Blood," *Washington Post*, June 6, 1979, page E1.

page 519 " 'A cassette of this show . . .' ": *Ibid*., page E3.

page 519 " 'I'll tell you something about fags . . .' ": *Ibid*., page E7.

page 520 " 'Love is blind . . .' ": *Ibid*., page E3.

page 520 " 'This is pathology . . .' ": Sally Quinn, "Hot Blood—and Gore, Chapter Two," *Washington Post*, June 7, 1979, page C7.

CHAPTER 57

page 524 " 'Truman wanted to kill him, and I think . . .' ": Joel Michael to GC, August 8, 1987.

page 526 "Truman was drunk—'gaga,' to use John's word . . .": John O'Shea to GC, October 1, 1986.

page 526 "Responding to a drunken, incoherent call, Rick Brown . . .": Rick Brown to GC, November 1, 1982, and August 9, 1987.

page 527 " 'Am I right to come into Truman's life again? . . .' ": Joseph Petrocik to GC, November 25, 1980.

page 528 "What poor Truman did not know was that . . .": Helen Dudar, "The Shrinking World of Doctor Nathan Kline," Manhattan section of New York *Daily News*, June 19, 1981, pages 1–3.

page 528 " 'Tonight was one of the great things . . .' ": Judy Klemesrud, "The Evening Hours," *New York Times*, December 19, 1980, page B8.

page 528 "April Johnson, a journalist who had seen him . . .": April Johnson to GC, May 9, 1987.

page 529 ". . . John, to use his own words, 'beat the shit . . .' ": John O'Shea to GC, October 1, 1986.

page 529 ". . . he suffered a broken nose, a fractured rib, a cracked . . .": Hospital records of Larkin General Hospital, Miami.

page 529 ". . . John made an urgent call to Dr. Harold Deutsch . . .": Harold Deutsch, M.D., to GC, August 20, 1987.

page 529 "(Brian later denied that he had been involved . . .)": Brian O'Shea to GC, September 1, 1987.

page 530 "As they sat down on that Easter Sunday . . .": John O'Shea to TC, April 22, 1981.

page 530 "At 6:30 on the morning of April 24 . . .": Bob MacBride to Alan Schwartz, May 2, 1981.

page 531 "Before Bob's arrival that morning, Truman had also . . .": Joseph Petrocik and Myron Clement to GC, May 5, 1981.

page 531 "Increasingly disturbed, Bob confronted Jack . . .": Bob MacBride to GC, August 22, 1987.

page 531 " 'I had always heard from Truman what a prince . . .' ": *Ibid.*

page 531 ". . . Bob wrote Alan Schwartz the next day . . .": Bob MacBride to Alan Schwartz, May 2, 1981.

page 532 "John had not been staying with him long . . .": John O'Shea to GC, October 1, 1986.

CHAPTER 58

page 534 " 'That's just what I need! . . .' ": Joseph Petrocik to GC, July 12, 1981.

page 534 " 'First there was Marilyn . . .' ": Robert MacBride to GC, August 22, 1987.

page 536 " 'What would he say? "I'll be there . . ." ' ": Joseph Petrocik to GC, February 2, 1983.

page 537 "The first, in April, 1982, asked for money . . .": John O'Shea to TC, April 19, 1982.

page 537 "The second, a few months later, revealed . . .": John O'Shea to TC, August 9, 1982.

page 538 " 'It used to be that he...' " Joseph Petrocik to GC, February 2, 1983 page 538 " 'I recognized finally that . . .' ": Alan Schwartz to GC, March 17, 1983.

page 539 " 'I wanted him to have it . . .' ": Arnold Bernstein to GC, September 29, 1987.

page 539 ". . . as a slut whose 'only enduring passion' . . .": Rudisill with Simmons, *Truman Capote*, page 63.

page 539 " 'I have never seen so many misstatements of fact . . .' ": Harper Lee to GC, March 2, 1986.

page 539 "Mary Ida Carter, one of Tiny's other sisters, was so disgusted . . .": Mary Ida Carter to GC, January 7, 1984.

page 539 " 'So amusing,' she said, 'to read . . .' ": Lady (Nancy) Keith to TC, May 2, 1983.

page 540 " 'Capote Mixes Drinking and Driving Again . . .' ": *New York Post*, July 4, 1983, page 9.

page 540 " 'People don't come to court dressed like that . . .' ": Laura Durkin, "No License to Do *That*, Judge Says," *Newsday*, August 27, 1983.

page 540 "Dismayed to see him sitting alone . . .": Liz Smith to GC, March 6, 1985.

page 542 " 'I think it's criminal what you're doing . . .' ": George McCormack, Jr., M.D, to GC, September 1, 1987.

page 543 " 'Not only is he leaving . . .' ": *Ibid.*

page 543 " 'Truman is just exactly the way he was . . .' ": John O'Shea to GC, August 22, 1984.

page 543 " 'I think he came pretty close . . .' ": William Diefenbach, M.D. to GC, June 19, 1985.

page 544 " 'It's all over with Jack.' ": Joanne Carson to GC, October 11, 1987.

CHAPTER 59

Details on the exact circumstances of Truman's death were provided by Joanne Carson.

For background on Truman's health and help in interpreting his autopsy report, I am indebted to several doctors who treated him: Harold Deutsch; William Diefenbach; George McCormack, Jr.; Bertram Newman.

For further help in interpreting the autopsy, I am indebted to Dr. Marcus Reidenberg, professor of pharmacology and medicine at Manhattan's Cornell University Medical College, and Dr. Ronald N. Kornblum, Chief Medical Examiner–Coroner of Los Angeles County, who was in charge of the autopsy.

page 546 " 'It has been determined that he died . . .' ": Press release from the Department of Chief Medical Examiner–Coroner, County of Los Angeles, September 13, 1984.

Books by Truman Capote

All books published by Random House, New York, unless otherwise indicated.

Other Voices, Other Rooms. 1948.
A Tree of Night and Other Stories. 1949.
Local Color. 1950.
The Grass Harp. 1951.
The Muses Are Heard. 1956.
Breakfast at Tiffany's. 1958.
Observations (with Richard Avedon). New York: Simon and Schuster, 1959.
Selected Writings of Truman Capote. 1963.
In Cold Blood. 1966.
A Christmas Memory. 1966.
House of Flowers. 1968.
The Thanksgiving Visitor. 1968.
The Dogs Bark: Public People and Private Places. 1973.
Music for Chameleons. 1980.
One Christmas. 1983.
Three by Truman Capote. 1985.
Answered Prayers: The Unfinished Novel. 1987.
A Capote Reader. 1987.

Bibliography

Aldington, Richard. *Portrait of a Genius, but . . . : The Life of D. H. Lawrence.* London: Heinemann, 1950.

Alsop, Susan Mary. *To Marietta from Paris: 1945–1960.* New York: Doubleday, 1975.

Arvin, Newton. *Hawthorne.* New York: Russell & Russell, 1961.

——. *American Pantheon.* Edited by Daniel Aaron and Sylvan Schendler. New York: Delacorte, 1966.

Auden, W. H. *Collected Poems.* Edited by Edward Mendelson. New York: Random House, 1976.

Bacall, Lauren. *Lauren Bacall by Myself.* New York: Knopf, 1979.

Baldwin, Billy. *Billy Baldwin Decorates.* New York: Holt, Rinehart and Winston, 1972.

——. *Billy Baldwin Remembers.* New York: Harcourt Brace Jovanovich, 1974.

—— with Michael Gardine. *Billy Baldwin: An Autobiography.* Boston: Little, Brown, 1985.

Barker, Richard H. *Marcel Proust.* New York: Criterion Books, 1958.

Beach, Sylvia. *Shakespeare and Company.* New York: Harcourt, Brace, 1959.

Beaton, Cecil. *The Wandering Years, Diaries 1922–39.* Boston: Little, Brown, 1961.

——. *The Years Between, Diaries 1939–44.* New York: Holt, Rinehart and Winston, 1965.

——. *The Best of Beaton.* Introduction by Truman Capote. New York: Macmillan, 1968.

——. *Cecil Beaton: Memoirs of the 40's.* New York: McGraw-Hill, 1972.

——. *The Strenuous Years, Diaries 1948–55.* London: Weidenfeld and Nicolson, 1973.

——. *The Restless Years.* London: Weidenfeld and Nicolson, 1976.

——. *The Parting Years, Diaries 1963–74.* London: Weidenfeld and Nicolson, 1978.

—— and Gail Buckland. *The Magic Image.* Boston: Little, Brown, 1975.

Benchley, Nathaniel. *Humphrey Bogart.* Boston: Little, Brown, 1975.

Bernstein, Burton. *Thurber*. New York: Dodd, Mead, 1975.

Birmingham, Stephen. *The Right People: A Portrait of the American Social Establishment*. Boston: Little, Brown, 1968.

Bosworth, Partricia. *Montgomery Clift: A Biography*. New York: Harcourt Brace Jovanovich, 1978.

Bowles, Paul. *Without Stopping: An Autobiography*. New York: Putnam, 1972.

Bradlee, Benjamin C. *Conversations with Kennedy*. New York: Norton, 1975.

Brian, Denis. *Murderers and Other Friendly People*. New York: McGraw-Hill, 1973.

Brickell, Herschel, ed. *O. Henry Memorial Award Prize Stories of 1946*. New York: Doubleday, 1946.

——, ed. *Prize Stories of 1948*. New York: Doubleday, 1948.

Brinnin, John Malcolm. *Sextet*. New York: Delacorte, 1981.

Brown, Frederick. *An Impersonation of Angels: A Biography of Jean Cocteau*. New York: Viking, 1968.

Buckley, William F., Jr. *The Jeweler's Eye*. New York: Putnam, 1968.

——. *A Hymnal: The Controversial Arts*. New York: Putnam, 1978.

Carpenter, Humphrey. *W. H. Auden*. Boston: Houghton Mifflin, 1981.

Carr, Virginia Spencer. *The Lonely Hunter, A Biography of Carson McCullers*. New York: Doubleday, 1975.

Cerf, Bennett. *At Random: The Reminiscences of Bennett Cerf*. New York: Random House, 1977.

Clark, Ronald W. *Freud, The Man and the Cause*. New York: Random House, 1980.

Cocteau, Jean. *Professional Secrets: An Autobiography of Jean Cocteau*. Edited by Robert Phelps, translated by Richard Howard. New York: Farrar Straus Giroux, 1970.

Connolly, Cyril. *Ideas and Places*. New York: Harper & Brothers, 1953.

Coward, Noël. *The Noël Coward Diaries*. Edited by Graham Payn and Sheridan Morley. Boston: Little, Brown, 1982.

Cowles, Virginia. *The Astors*. New York: Knopf, 1979.

Cowley, Malcom, ed. *Writers at Work, The* Paris Review *Interviews*. New York: Viking, 1959.

Creeger, George R. *Animals in Exile: Imagery and Theme in Capote's* In Cold Blood. Middletown, Connecticut: Center for Advanced Studies, Wesleyan University, 1967.

Curtis, Charlotte. *The Rich and Other Atrocities*. New York: Harper & Row, 1976.

Curtiss, Mina. *Other People's Letters*. Boston: Houghton Mifflin, 1978.

Davis, John H. *The Guggenheims*. New York: Morrow, 1978.

——. *The Kennedys: Dynasty and Disaster, 1848–1983*. New York: McGraw-Hill, 1984.

Dillon, Millicent. *A Little Original Sin, The Life and Work of Jane Bowles*. New York: Holt, Rinehart and Winston, 1981.

Donald, David Herbert. *Look Homeward: A Life of Thomas Wolfe*. Boston: Little, Brown, 1987.

Doughty, Howard. *Francis Parkman*. New York: Macmillan, 1962.

Drutman, Irving. *Good Company*. Boston: Little, Brown, 1976.

Dunphy, Jack. *John Fury*. New York: Harper & Brothers, 1946.

———. *"Dear Genius . . . ": A Memoir of My Life with Truman Capote*. New York: McGraw-Hill, 1987.

Eells, George. *The Life That Late He Led, A Biography of Cole Porter*. New York: Putnam, 1967.

Ewen, David. *The Story of America's Musical Theater*. Philadelphia: Chilton, 1968.

———. *New Complete Book of the American Musical Theater*. New York: Holt, Rinehart and Winston, 1970.

Eyles, Allen. *Bogart*. New York: Doubleday, 1975.

Fiedler, Leslie A. *Love and Death in the American Novel*. New York: Criterion Books, 1960.

Finney, Brian. *Christopher Isherwood*. New York: Oxford University Press, 1979.

Fitzgerald, F. Scott. *The Last Tycoon*. Foreword by Edmund Wilson. New York: Scribner's, 1969.

Flanner, Janet. *Paris Journal, 1944–1965*. Edited by William Shawn. New York: Atheneum, 1965.

Flaubert, Gustave. *The Letters of Gustave Flaubert, 1830–1857*. Selected, edited and translated by Francis Steegmuller. Cambridge, Massachusetts: The Belknap Press of Harvard University Press, 1980.

Forster, E. M. *A Passage to India*. New York: Harcourt, Brace, 1924.

Fryer, Jonathan. *Isherwood*. New York: Doubleday, 1978.

Fulton, John F. *Harvey Cushing: A Biography*. Springfield, Illinois: Charles C. Thomas, 1946.

Garson, Helen S. *Truman Capote*. New York: Frederick Ungar, 1980.

Gill, Brendan. *Here at The New Yorker*. New York: Random House, 1975.

Goad, Craig M. *Daylight and Darkness, Dream and Delusion: The Works of Truman Capote*. Emporia, Kansas: Emporia State Research Studies, 1967.

Graham, Sheilah. *How to Marry Super Rich: Or Love, Money and the Morning After*. New York: Grosset & Dunlap, 1974.

Grant, Jane. *Ross, The New Yorker and Me*. New York: Reynal and Company, 1968.

Green, Martin. *Children of the Sun*. New York: Basic, 1976.

Green, Stanley. *The World of Musical Comedy*. New York: Grosset & Dunlap, 1962.

Greene, Graham. *Ways of Escape*. New York: Penguin, 1981.

Grobel, Lawrence. *Conversations with Capote*. New York: New American Library, 1985.

Gruen, John. *Menotti, A Biography*. New York: Macmillan, 1978.

Guggenheim, Peggy. *Out of This Century: Confessions of an Art Addict*. New York: Universe Books, 1979.

Halberstam, David. *The Powers That Be*. New York: Knopf, 1979.

Hanna, David. *Bogart*. New York: Leisure Books, 1976.

Hassan, Ihab. *Radical Innocence: Studies in the Contemporary American Novel*. Princeton, New Jersey: Princeton University Press, 1961.

Herbert, David. *Second Son: An Autobiography*. London: Peter Owen, 1972.

Higham, Charles. *Brando: The Unauthorized Biography*. New York: New American Library, 1987.

Holroyd, Michael. *Lytton Strachey: A Critical Biography, Volume II*. New York: Holt, Rinehart and Winston, 1968.

Hoover, Kathleen, and John Cage. *Virgil Thomson: His Life and Music*. New York: Thomes Yoseloff, Sagamore Press, 1959.

Huisman, P., and M. G. Dortu. *Lautrec by Lautrec*. New York: Viking, 1964.

Hyams, Joe. *Bogie*. New York: New American Library, 1966.

Isherwood, Christopher. *Down There on a Visit*. New York: Simon and Schuster, 1962.

Jablonski, Edward. *Harold Arlen*. New York: Doubleday, 1961.

James, Henry. *The Art of the Novel*. New York: Scribner's, 1934.

Johnson, Edgar. *Charles Dickens: His Tragedy and Triumph*, Volume One. New York: Simon and Schuster, 1952.

Jullian, Philippe, and John Phillips. *Violet Trefusis: Life and Letters*. London: Hamish Hamilton, 1976.

Kahn, E. J., Jr. *Jock: The Life and Times of John Hay Whitney*. New York: Doubleday, 1981.

La Guardia, Robert. *Monty: A Biography of Montgomery Clift*. New York: Arbor House, 1977.

Lawrence, D. H. *The Letters of D. H. Lawrence*. Edited and with an introduction by Aldous Huxley. New York: Viking, 1932.

Leavitt, Richard F., ed. *The World of Tennessee Williams*. New York: Putnam, 1978.

Lee, Harper. *To Kill a Mockingbird*. Philadelphia and New York: Lippincott, 1960.

Lewis, Robert. *Slings and Arrows: Theatre in My Life*. New York: Stein and Day, 1984.

Lilienthal, David E. *The Journals of David E. Lilienthal, Volume II: The Atomic Energy Years, 1945–1950*. New York: Harper & Row, 1964.

———. *The Journals of David E. Lilienthal, Volume III, The Venturesome Years, 1950–1955*. New York: Harper & Row, 1966.

———. *The Journals of David E. Lilienthal, Volume V, The Harvest Years, 1959–1963*. New York: Harper & Row, 1971.

Logan, Joshua. *Movie Stars, Real People, and Me*. New York: Delacorte, 1978.

Lopez, Enrique Hank. *Conversations with Katherine Anne Porter*. Boston: Little, Brown, 1981.

Mack, Gerstle. *Toulouse-Lautrec*. New York: Knopf, 1949.

Mailer, Norman. *Advertisements for Myself*. New York: Putnam, 1959.

———. *The Armies of the Night*. New York: New American Library, 1968.

Malin, Irving, ed. *Truman Capote's In Cold Blood: A Critical Handbook*. Belmont, California: Wadsworth, 1968.

Martin, Ralph G. *A Hero for Our Times: An Intimate Story of the Kennedy Years*. New York: Macmillan, 1983.

Menen, Aubrey. *The Duke of Gallodoro*. New York: Scribner's, 1952.

Metz, Robert. *CBS: Reflections in a Bloodshot Eye*. Chicago: Playboy Press, 1975.

Moore, Harry T. *The Priest of Love: A Life of D. H. Lawrence*. Revised edition. New York: Farrar Straus Giroux, 1974.

Morgan, Ted. *Maugham*. New York: Simon and Schuster, 1980.

Morley, Robert, and Sewell Stokes. *Robert Morley*. New York: Simon and Schuster, 1966.

Nance, William L. *The Worlds of Truman Capote*. New York: Stein and Day, 1970.

Newquist, Roy. *Counterpoint*. Chicago: Rand McNally, 1964.

Nicolson, Nigel, ed. *Harold Nicolson, The Later Years, 1945–1962*. New York: Atheneum, 1968.

Nin, Anaïs. *The Diary of Anaïs Nin*. Edited by Gunther Stuhlmann. New York: Harcourt Brace Jovanovich, 1971.

Nizer, Louis. *Reflections without Mirrors*. New York: Doubleday, 1978.

Nolan, William F. *John Huston, King Rebel*. Los Angeles: Sherbourne Press, 1965.

O'Higgins, Patrick. *Madame*. New York: Viking, 1971.

Ozick, Cynthia. *Art and Ardor*. New York: Knopf, 1983.

Painter, George D. *Proust, The Later Years*. Boston: Little, Brown, 1965.

Paley, William S. *As It Happened: A Memoir*. New York: Doubleday, 1979.

Paper, Lewis Jo. *Empire: William S. Paley and the Making of CBS*. New York: St. Martin's, 1987.

Pope-Hennessy, Una. *Charles Dickens*. New York: Howell, Soskin, Publishers, 1946.

Priestley, J. B. *Charles Dickens*. New York: Viking, 1962.

Quennell, Peter, ed. *Marcel Proust, 1871–1922, A Centennial Volume*. New York: Simon and Schuster, 1971.

Rader, Dotson. *Tennessee: Cry of the Heart*. New York: Doubleday, 1985.

Reed, Kenneth T. *Truman Capote*. Boston: Twayne, 1981.

Rorem, Ned. *The Paris and New York Diaries of Ned Rorem, 1951–1961*. San Francisco: North Point Press, 1983.

Ross, Lillian. *Reporting*. New York: Simon and Schuster, 1964.

Rudisill, Marie, with James C. Simmons. *Truman Capote: The Story of His Bizarre and Exotic Boyhood by an Aunt Who Helped Raise Him*. New York: Morrow, 1983.

Ryan, Cornelius. *The Longest Day*. New York: Simon and Schuster, 1959.

Sagar, Keith. *The Life of D. H. Lawrence*. New York: Pantheon, 1980.

Saroyan, Aram. *Trio*. New York: Linden Press/Simon and Schuster, 1985.

Schorer, Mark. *The World We Imagine*. New York: Farrar Straus Giroux, 1968.

Schwartz, Charles. *Cole Porter, A Biography*. New York: Dial, 1977.

Seaman, Barbara. *Lovely Me: The Life of Jacqueline Susann*. New York: Morrow, 1987.

Secrest, Meryle. *Between Me and Life*. New York: Doubleday, 1964.

Selznick, David O. *Memo from David O. Selznick*. Edited by Rudy Behlmer. New York: Viking, 1972.

Snow, Carmel, with Mary Louise Aswell. *The World of Carmel Snow*. New York: McGraw-Hill, 1962.

Stanton, Robert J. *Truman Capote, A Primary and Secondary Bibliography*. Boston: G. K. Hall, 1980.

———— and Gore Vidal, eds. *Views from a Window: Conversations with Gore Vidal*. Secaucus, New Jersey: Lyle Stuart, 1980.

Stassinopoulos, Arianna. *Maria Callas: The Woman Behind the Legend*. New York: Simon and Schuster, 1981.

Steegmuller, Francis. *Cocteau: A Biography*. Boston: Little, Brown, 1970.

Stein, Jean, interviewer, George Plimpton, ed. *American Journey: The Times of Robert Kennedy*. New York: Harcourt Brace Jovanovich, 1970.

Strachey, Lytton. *Queen Victoria*. New York: Harcourt, Brace and World, 1949.

Susann, Jacqueline. *Dolores*. New York: Bantam, 1977.

Thomas, Bob. *Selznick*. New York: Doubleday, 1970.

Thomson, Elizabeth H. *Harvey Cushing: Surgeon, Author, Artist*. New York: Henry Schuman, 1950.

Thomson, Virgil. *Virgil Thomson*. New York: Knopf, 1967.

Thurber, James. *The Years with Ross*. Boston: Little, Brown, 1959.

Thurman, Judith. *Isak Dinesen, The Life of a Storyteller*. New York: St. Martin's Press, 1982.

Toklas, Alice B. *What Is Remembered*. New York: Holt, Rinehart and Winston, 1963.

————. *Staying On Alone: Letters of Alice B. Toklas*. Edited by Edward Burns. New York: Liveright, 1973.

Trewin, J. C. *Peter Brook, A Biography*. London: Macdonald, 1971.

Tynan, Kenneth. *Tynan Right and Left*. New York: Atheneum, 1967.

Vickers, Hugo. *Cecil Beaton, The Authorized Biography*. London: Weidenfeld and Nicolson, 1985.

Vidal, Gore. *The City and the Pillar*. New York: Dutton, 1948.

Viertel, Salka. *The Kindness of Strangers*. New York: Holt, Rinehart and Winston, 1963.

Vreeland, Diana. *D. V.* Edited by George Plimpton and Christopher Hemphill. New York: Knopf, 1984.

West, Ray B., Jr. *The Short Story in America: 1900–1950*. Chicago: Henry Regnery, 1952.

White, E. B. *Letters of E. B. White*. Collected and edited by Dorothy Lobrano Guth. New York: Harper & Row, 1976.

Wickes, George. *The Amazon of Letters: The Life and Loves of Natalie Barney*. New York: Putnam, 1976.

Williams, Tennessee. *Memoirs*. New York: Doubleday, 1975.

————. *Tennessee Williams' Letters to Donald Windham, 1940–1965*. Edited by Donald Windham. New York: Holt, Rinehart and Winston, 1977.

Windham, Donald. *Lost Friendships, A Memoir of Truman Capote, Tennessee Williams, and Others*. New York: Morrow, 1987.

————. *Footnote to a Friendship*. Privately printed, 1983.

Wishart, Michael. *High Diver*. London: Quartet, 1977.

Woolf, Virginia. *The Diary of Virginia Woolf, Volume Five, 1936–1941*. New York: Harcourt Brace Jovanovich, 1984.

Index

PICTURE CREDITS

1–6. no credit
7. Franklyn School
8. Phoebe Pierce Vreeland
9. G. Mallard Kesslere
10–11. no credit
12. Barbara Lawrence
13. Bill Cutler
14. Cartier-Bresson/Magnum
15. no credit
16. Mrs. Howard Doughty
17–19. Lisa Larsen/*Life Magazine* © 1946 Time Inc.
20. Lisa Larsen/*Life Magazine* © 1947 Time Inc.
21. Culver Pictures
22. Jerry Cooke/*Life Magazine* © 1947 Time Inc.
23. Culver Pictures
24. no credit
25. Andrew Lyndon
26. no credit
27. Random House © 1948 Harold Halma
28. Cecil Beaton/Sotheby's
29. Cecil Beaton/Sotheby's
30. Cartier-Bresson/Magnum
31. Karl Bissinger
32. Jared French
33. Cecil Beaton/Sotheby's
34. Paul Bowles
35. Eleanor Friede

36. Cecil Beaton/Sotheby's
37. no credit
38. Neal Peters
39. Pictorial Parade
40. UPI
41. no credit
42. Lester Glassner Collection
43. UPI
44. Courtesy *Vogue*. Copyright © 1983 by Irving Penn.
45–46. no credit
47. Neal Peters
48. no credit
49. John Rawlings, courtesy The Edward C. Blum Design Laboratory at F.I.T.
50–51. no credit
52. John Rawlings, courtesy The Edward C. Blum Design Laboratory at F.I.T.
53–54. no credit
55. Library of Congress
56. Picture People
57. no credit
58. Curtis Studio
59. no credit
60. Curtis Studio
61–62. UPI
63. no credit
64. Henry Grossman/*Life Magazine* © 1966 Time Inc.
65. Laurence Fried
66. WWD

67. WWD
68. Henry Grossman/*Life Magazine* © 1966 Time Inc.
69. WWD
70. Laurence Fried
71. Henry Grossman/*Life Magazine* © 1966 Time Inc.
72–73. UPI
74. St. Louis Post Dispatch/Black Star
75. no credit
76. Steve Schapiro/*Life Magazine* © 1967 Time Inc.
77. Phil Stern
78. Steve Schapiro/*Life Magazine* © 1967 Time Inc.
79. Phil Stern
80. no credit
81. Jamie Ardiles-Arce/*Architectural Digest*
82. UPI
83. James Hamilton
84. no credit
85. Joseph Petrocik and Myron Clement
86. WWD
87. Edward Sorel/*New York Magazine*
88. no credit
89. Joseph Petrocik and Myron Clement
90. Wide World
91. Carol Nash
92. Joanne Carson
93. Arty Pomerantz/*New York Post*
94. Gerald Clarke
95. Joanne Carson